Feasting on the Gospels
Luke, Volume 1

Editorial Board

A Feasting on the Word® Commentary

Feasting on the Gospels

Luke, Volume 1
Chapters 1–11

CYNTHIA A. JARVIS and **E. ELIZABETH JOHNSON**

General Editors

WESTMINSTER
JOHN KNOX PRESS
LOUISVILLE • KENTUCKY

© 2014 Westminster John Knox Press

First edition
Published by Westminster John Knox Press
Louisville, Kentucky

14 15 16 17 18 19 20 21 22 23—10 9 8 7 6 5 4 3 2 1

Book design by Drew Stevens
Cover design by Lisa Buckley and Dilu Nicholas

Library of Congress Cataloging-in-Publication Data

Feasting on the gospels : a feasting on the WordTM commentary / Cynthia A. Jarvis and E. Elizabeth Johnson, general editors.
     volumes cm
  Includes index.
  Contents: Volume 1. Luke, Volume 1, chapters 1–11.
  ISBN 978-0-664-23551-2 (v. 1 : alk. paper)   1. Bible. Gospels—Commentaries.   I. Jarvis, Cynthia A., editor.
  BS2555.53.F43   2014
  226'.077—dc23

2014001710

PRINTED IN THE UNITED STATES OF AMERICA

♾ The paper used in this publication meets the minimum requirements of the American National Standard for Information Sciences—Permanence of Paper for Printed Library Materials, ANSI Z39.48-1992

Contents

Publisher's Note

Feasting on the Gospels is a seven-volume series that follows in the proud tradition of *Feasting on the Word: Preaching the Revised Common Lectionary*. Whereas *Feasting on the Word* provided commentary on only the texts in the lectionary, *Feasting on the Gospels* will cover every passage of the four Gospels. *Feasting on the Gospels* retains the popular approach of *Feasting on the Word* by providing four perspectives on each passage—theological, pastoral, exegetical, and homiletical—to stimulate and inspire preaching, teaching, and discipleship.

Westminster John Knox Press is grateful to the members of the large *Feasting* family who have given so much of themselves to bring this new series to life. General editors Cynthia A. Jarvis and E. Elizabeth Johnson stepped from their service on the editorial board of *Feasting on the Word* to the editorship of *Feasting on the Gospels* without missing a beat. Their commitment, energy, and unflagging enthusiasm made this work possible. The project manager, Joan Murchison, and project compiler, Mary Lynn Darden, continued their remarkable work, bringing thousands of pieces and hundreds of authors together seamlessly.

The editorial board did enormous work under grueling deadlines and did it with excellence and good humor. The hundreds of writers who participated—scholars, preachers, and teachers—gave much of themselves to help create this bountiful feast. David Bartlett and Barbara Brown Taylor took the time and care to help conceive this new project even as they were finishing their excellent work as general editors of *Feasting on the Word*.

Finally, we are again indebted to Columbia Theological Seminary for their partnership. As they did with *Feasting on the Word*, they provided many resources and personnel to help make this series possible. We are grateful in particular to seminary President Stephen Hayner and Dean of Faculty and Executive Vice President Deborah Mullen.

It is with joy that we welcome you to this feast, in hopes that it will nourish you as you proclaim the Word to all of God's people.

Westminster John Knox Press

Series Introduction

At their best, people who write about Scripture are conversation partners. They enter the dialogue between the biblical text and the preacher or teacher or interested Christian and add perspectives gained from experience and disciplined attention. They contribute literary, historical, linguistic, and theological insights gathered over the millennia to the reader's first impressions of what is going on in a text. This conversation is essential if the reading of Scripture is to be fruitful in the church. It keeps reading the Bible from being an exercise in individual projection or uncritical assumption. That said, people who comment on the Bible should never become authorities. While a writer may indeed know more about the text than the reader does, he or she nevertheless writes from a particular perspective shaped by culture, ethnicity, gender, education, and theological tradition. In this regard, the writer of a commentary is no different from the writers and readers of Scripture.

The model for this series on the Gospels is the lectionary-based resource *Feasting on the Word* (Westminster John Knox Press, 2008–2011), now widely used by ministers as they prepare to preach. As central as the task of preaching is to the health of congregations, Scripture is the Word that calls the whole community of faith into being and sends those addressed out as witnesses to the Word in the world. Whether read devotionally by those gathered to pray or critically by others gathered to study, the Bible functions in a myriad of ways to undergird, support, and nurture the Christian life of individuals and communities. Those are the reasons that Westminster John Knox Press has taken the next step in the *Feasting* project to offer *Feasting on the Gospels*, a series in the style of *Feasting on the Word* with two major differences. First, all four Gospels are considered in their entirety, a *lectio continua* of sorts that leaves nothing out. Second, while *Feasting on the Word* is addressed specifically to preachers, *Feasting on the Gospels* is addressed to all who want to deepen their understanding of the Gospels—Bible study leaders and class members, seasoned preachers and seminarians, believers and skeptics.

The advantage of *Feasting on the Gospels* is that the reader encounters multiple perspectives on each text—not only the theological, exegetical, pastoral, and homiletical emphases that shape the essays, but also the ecumenical, social, ethnic, and cultural perspectives of the authors. Unlike a single-author commentary, which sustains a particular view of a given interpreter throughout, *Feasting on the Gospels* offers readers a broad conversation that engages the text from many angles. In a church as diverse as the twenty-first-century church is, such deliberate engagement with many voices is imperative and, we hope, provocative.

A few observations about the particular challenges posed by the Gospels are in order here. The Gospels were written in a time when fledgling Christian communities—probably in their second generation—were just beginning to negotiate their relationships with Judaism (within which they were conceived and born), a community that was itself in the process of redefinition after the destruction of the Second Temple in 70 CE. Some of that negotiation was marked by great tension and sometimes outright hostility. The temptation for Christian readers to read anti-Semitism into texts that portray intra-Jewish conflict has beset the church almost from its beginnings. Our editors have been particularly mindful of this when dealing with essays on texts where the temptation to speak contemptuously of Jews and Judaism might threaten faithful interpretation.

A second observation involves the New Testament manuscript tradition. In *Feasting on the Gospels* we identify and comment on significant manuscript variants such as Mark 16:9–20 and John 7:53–8:11, something we did not have to contend with in *Feasting on the Word*. We identify those variant readings the way the NRSV does, except that we talk about "other ancient manuscripts" rather than the "other ancient authorities" of the NRSV notes.

The twelve members of our editorial board come from a broad swath of American Christianity: they are members or ministers of Presbyterian, Baptist, United Church of Christ, Roman Catholic, and Disciples of Christ churches. Some of them are academics who serve on the faculties of theological schools; others are clergy serving congregations. All of them are extraordinarily hardworking, thoughtful, and perceptive readers of Scripture, of the church, and of the world. The writers whose work comprises these volumes represent an even wider cross-section of the church, most of them from North America, but a significant number from around the world, particularly the global South.

We could not have undertaken this work without the imagination, advice, and support of David Dobson, Editorial Director at Westminster John Knox Press, and his colleagues Don McKim, Marianne Blickenstaff, Michele Blum, and Julie Tonini. We are deeply grateful to David L. Bartlett and Barbara Brown Taylor, our mentors in the *Feasting on the Word* project, who continued to offer hands-on assistance with *Feasting on the Gospels*. We thank President Stephen A. Hayner

and Dean Deborah F. Mullen of Columbia Theological Seminary and the congregation of The Presbyterian Church of Chestnut Hill in Philadelphia, Pennsylvania, who made possible our participation in the project. Joan Murchison, who as Project Manager kept all of us and our thousands of essays in order and enforced deadlines with great good humor, is once again the beloved Hammer. Mary Lynn Darden, our compiler, who corralled not only the essays but also information about their authors and editors, brought all the bits and pieces together into the books you see now.

To the preachers, teachers, Bible study leaders, and church members who will read the Gospels with us, we wish you happy feasting.

Cynthia A. Jarvis
E. Elizabeth Johnson

Feasting on the Gospels
Luke, Volume 1

Luke 1:1–4

¹Since many have undertaken to set down an orderly account of the events that have been fulfilled among us, ²just as they were handed on to us by those who from the beginning were eyewitnesses and servants of the word, ³I too decided, after investigating everything carefully from the very first, to write an orderly account for you, most excellent Theophilus, ⁴so that you may know the truth concerning the things about which you have been instructed.

Theological Perspective

It is a commonplace among Christians to regard the ancient texts of the New Testament as a transcendent source of revelation, a promise of salvation given under divine inspiration or intentionality, addressed to all human beings to reveal the faith. Yet even if we take the inspired character of the Gospels on faith, we do not forget that its texts—transcendent to a community of believers—are also historical documents, inscribed by human beings in the earliest moments of Christianity to deal with the tangled and conflictual tasks of church building, in lieu of well-settled doctrine, liturgy, or traditions. Considering this historicity, we must wonder at the opening of the Gospel of Luke with its dedication to a single person—a certain *Theophilus*. Brief reflection on the four-verse frame of this opening pericope—built around Luke's address to Theophilus—tells us something about Luke's skeletal theological method.

Who was *Theophilus?* His name appears at the opening of Luke, as well as that of its sequel, the Acts of the Apostles. However, we get precious little information on him. He might have been a real person, though centuries of exegesis, historical research, and archaeology have not revealed the identity of a historical Theophilus, any more than of a historical Luke. The alternative is that Theophilus is *a figure of speech*—a fictive character whose Greek name means

Pastoral Perspective

"It was a dark and stormy night . . ." "Call me Ishmael . . ." "A long time ago in a galaxy far, far away . . ." "In the beginning was the Word . . ."

It is worth remembering that as Christians our faith is not simply a collection of ideas or propositions or, for that matter, even a set of creeds or catechisms. Rather, we are inheritors of a story. In these opening verses of Luke's Gospel the author tells Theophilus that he has decided to write an orderly report through which the truth may be known. How does Luke, who is neither an eyewitness nor an apostle, convey such truth? He tells a story: Once upon a time in a faraway land called Judea when Herod was king, there lived a man named Zechariah.

While our knowledge about Theophilus is limited, we know something about the diversity of the Greco-Roman world in which he lived. Even the Judaism of his day could hardly be called a monolithic entity. In a pentecostal world of varying beliefs, languages, and competing narratives that were held together by the metanarrative of the *Pax Romana*, Luke says to Theophilus, "Let me tell you my story, our story, and the lens through which we may make sense of the chaos of this world."

In many ways our world is not that different from the world of Theophilus. There is no such thing today as "the" Christian experience, even if

Feasting on the Gospels

Exegetical Perspective

Luke begins his Gospel (ca. 80–90 CE) with a formal prologue, a literary convention common among historians and other writers of his time. He is the only New Testament evangelist to do so. Matthew commences his narrative with a genealogy that stakes a claim for Jesus as the royal Davidic Messiah, Mark with a one-line heading that launches an apocalyptic tale told with thunder, John with a hymn that celebrates the dazzling glory of the man sent from heaven. The opening in each instance sets down markers of substance and style that inform the whole. Luke mentions his predecessors, alludes to his sources, touts his credentials as a longtime observer of events, acknowledges Theophilus, his patron, and states his basic purpose in writing. The style is elevated, the tone measured and self-assured. We are in the hands of a confident author who invites us, gently, into his narrative world.

Details and Puzzles. For a passage so brief, the prologue is surprisingly full of ambiguities that give rise to interpretive options and questions incapable of being resolved. Luke, for example, informs us that "many" prior to him had written about Jesus. How many we do not know, mainly because there is no way of telling how many writings failed to survive, but also because this sort of statement was

Homiletical Perspective

Following the movement of Luke 1:1–4, two homiletical trajectories may be traced: (1) Luke's evident intention to render Christ as Living Word, not dead letter, and (2) his attempt to speak of Christ in a way coherent with previous gospel testimony. Luke does this to avoid the appearance of idiosyncrasy or mere subjective conjuring. At the same time, he proffers a gospel account at once uniquely personal (addressed as it is to a specific individual of prominence, i.e., Theophilus) and yet universal in its clear concern for a glad and faithful hearing by all persons everywhere of whatever socioeconomic condition, gender, or ethnic identity.

To speak of Christ as a Living Word and not a dead letter, Luke plainly sees himself—as doubtless we preachers should see ourselves—joining a continuing effort to bear witness to a God who, in Christ Jesus, is not captive to the past, but is always and ever entering this life of ours to bear the weight of it himself. The substance of the truth that Luke will set down is the manifestation of God in one who is forever merciful in judgment and just in all his compassion.[1] Luke sees God's salvific, justifying, sanctifying, and reconciling work as already and everlastingly accomplished in Christ.

1. Paraphrase of a prayer by Paul E. Scherer in *Worship Resources for the Christian Year* (Nashville: Abingdon Press, 1959), 169.

Luke 1:1–4

Theological Perspective

"lover of God," perhaps in the double-genitive sense of one who both loves God and is beloved of God.

To which reading do we incline? The Lukan author tells us only that Theophilus is a "most excellent" disciple, presumably in Luke's circle, who has "been instructed" in the matters of his nascent faith, and that this Gospel was written so that Theophilus "may know the truth" more thoroughly than even his prior catechism (*katēchēsis*) had allowed. If Theophilus is a figural addressee, it follows that Luke—poetically, playfully—is pitching his opener to *you*: *You, dear reader, are Theophilus,* the "most excellent," beloved-lover of God who is instructed, but yet incompletely. *You* are the Theophilus who needs to read this Gospel. Whether "Theophilus" was a budding early Christian, or a literary artifice to make us identify with the turns of his Gospel, Luke promises "him" nothing less than a true history of the Christian movement. In the long, solitary sentence spanning this short pericope, Luke gives us a taste of the dynamics of revelation, testimony, and theological traditioning that assured the place of this third of the four canonical Gospels in the history of Christianity.

Addressing Theophilus, Luke seems almost to be apologizing for throwing his lot into what has apparently become a cluttered field of early Jesus-movement histories. Yet his apology is necessary, for evidently early Christian teaching is still quite shaky in Luke's view, and needs "an orderly account of the events that have been fulfilled among us" (v. 1). The rhetoric of the English/NRSV translation understates the more phenomenologically charged Greek language. The operative Greek verb in this verse (*peplērophorēmenōn*) is usually translated as "accomplished," "fulfilled," or "believed." However, the compounding of *plēro* ("utterly, superlatively") with *phorēmenōn* ("luminous or manifest event") suggests that the events (*pragmatōn*) in question are not everyday sorts of happenings, but divine *practices*, originating in a transcendent source, and becoming realized in the phenomenal world. This is not the highly incarnate Gospel of John—with its lyrical declaration (John 1:1) that "in the beginning was the Word, and the Word was with God, and the Word was God." Nevertheless, Luke's first verses do likewise state that the theme of his Gospel is the spectacular revelation of God's incarnation.

Nowhere does Luke imagine that the mere declaration of these great events could suffice to build up the new faith. Instead, he demonstrates the rudiments of a theological method that will become well entrenched in Christian communities over the next

Pastoral Perspective

many wish it were so. We too live in a pentecostal world where other languages are spoken and other religions embraced. From capitalism to nationalism, competing stories and gods vie for our allegiance. In our postmodern world, what is "the" truth? Is there truth per se, or simply perspectives?

Undoubtedly congregations and their leaders will approach these questions in differing ways, but regardless of our differing perspectives, what we can do is tell our peculiar and particular story. We can borrow a page from Luke and say, "Yes, there are other accounts and other interpretations of that which has unfolded, but let me tell you our story as I have come to understand it after investigating everything carefully from the first."

Whether we are pastors or teachers or congregational lay leaders, we are storytellers who invite others to participate in a drama that matters. During our "productions," some of the chapters of the story are read aloud as we listen for the Word. At other times, we sing "the old, old story of Jesus and his love." In the proclamation of the Word, the story is expounded upon and reexamined yet again for hints as to the living of our personal narratives. Holy Communion opens in the liturgical traditions with a Great Thanksgiving or a *grand récit*. It is our big story. It begins with creation and continues with the saints singing forever and ever amen. We remember the story of how our Lord took bread and broke it, and then we reembody that story so that we might become bread broken for the world and redeemed by his blood. Even in the rites of baptism, whether young or old, whether sprinkled or immersed, we are doing nothing less than weaving the story of an individual into the fabric of all those who have gone before us. It is a story of adoption and naming and grace and love.

This is our story. Our responsibility as congregational leaders is as simple as it is daunting: we are to help others live into our Christian stories, so that they might become part of the story; so that they might become a living, breathing sacrament of God's grace.

Yet it is not just our faith communities who need to hear our foundational stories. Many Gen Xers and millennials believe the story of the church is one of hypocrisy, judgment, and irrelevancy. When asked about their religious affiliation, a growing number of young people respond by saying "none." Their doubts about the institutional church notwithstanding, "nones" still hunger to be part of something larger. They still want to find their place in a story that

Feasting on the Gospels

common enough that it too may have been a literary convention.

However many prior authors there were and whatever the scope of their work, they depended on traditions handed on (orally) by eyewitnesses of Jesus' career (v. 2). The authors were apparently not eyewitnesses, nor were the eyewitnesses authors, given that Luke seems to draw a distinction between those cited in verse 1 and those in verse 2. In any case, Luke himself is not an eyewitness but a third-generation Christian, as this passage and others indicate. As for the "eyewitnesses" and "servants of the word" who kept the Jesus tradition alive early on, it is unclear whether there was one group or two. Even if two, there is nothing to indicate, as some scholars have maintained, that the "servants" were charged with monitoring the accuracy of the tradition. They were involved in apostolic proclamation (Acts 13:5).

The most intriguing ambiguity in our text is Luke's attitude toward his predecessors. He tells us they "have undertaken to set down an orderly account of the events that have been fulfilled among us" (v. 1). Does this imply Luke thought they failed? The very fact Luke felt compelled to compile an account of his own (v. 3) suggests that indeed he did, that at the very least he found the work of his predecessors inadequate and somewhat disordered. There is a bit of irony here. The one writing we are virtually certain Luke employed was the Gospel of Mark, and he followed its sequence closely, deviating from it only four times prior to the passion narrative. Luke made his major alterations in other ways: refining the prose, adding birth and infancy narratives, incorporating huge amounts of "new" teaching under the rubric of Jesus' journey to Jerusalem, providing a distinctive passion narrative, enlarging the resurrection narrative, and, above all, writing a sequel of almost equal length, the Acts of the Apostles. If Luke imposes a new order on it all, a new pattern, it is not chronological but geographic. In the Gospel everything funnels into Jerusalem (9:51); in its sequel everything funnels out, "to the ends of the earth" (Acts 1:8).

Purpose. Luke's stated purpose in composing his two-volume work is to provide Theophilus with a firm foundation for such instruction in the faith as he has already received (v. 4). (The NRSV renders *asphaleia* blandly as "the truth" [v. 4], but its fundamental meaning is "firmness, security.") This raises tantalizing questions: (a) Why is it that Theophilus (about whom we know virtually nothing) and presumably others need to be reassured? (b) How is it

Luke 1:1–4 is also an introduction to Acts, and Acts demonstrates that what was definitively accomplished in Christ continues to be accomplished by him through his Spirit in those communities and in those persons who trust in him and who receive from him his accomplished work as their very own gift and task. Following Luke's lead, preachers today are called upon to state what God in Christ is up to on the contemporary scene. Humility is required, for there is danger in doing this—danger, for instance, of claiming divine sanction for partisan political opinions.

However, the greater danger is of disobedience in not attempting to speak the truth concerning the things that Luke has written to the powers and principalities of our day. In order to read this "orderly account" of Luke into our present situation, we must ask, where and how today do we see false pride and brutal power brought to naught? Where and how do we see the "put down" raised up, and the hungry fed, and the careless and sated rich called to account? Where and how, in Pauline terms, can we affirm that "there is no longer Jew or Greek, there is no longer slave or free, there is no longer male and female; for all . . . are one in Christ Jesus. And if [any] belong to Christ, then [they] are Abraham's offspring, heirs according to the promise" (Gal. 3:28–29)?

Luke's Gospel narrative is an account of the gospel deeply influenced by Pauline thought. Therefore the sort of interrogation of our world just commended is not unwarranted. Not least, we recall from the last verses of Acts how Paul, under house arrest in Rome, managed to preach openly and unhindered to Jew and Gentile alike. We recall as well how Dr. Martin Luther King Jr. preached the gospel in his "Letter from a Birmingham Jail," a word that echoes Luke's Gospel and still finds resonance among varied religious and ethnic constituencies with ears to hear it.

One further matter regarding the Living Word of God in Christ and so the recontextualizing of the gospel clearly evident in Luke: Acts needs contemporary homiletic reflection. In Luke's narration of the ongoing word and work of Christ, an apologetic agenda may be discerned. The agenda indicates that Christ's word and work need not be construed as necessarily subversive of reigning temporal political and cultural prerogatives and values (notably, in Luke's time, those of Rome). In Acts Paul's Roman citizenship secures his safety from the perils of religious and political opposition more than once, yet Rome likely executes him in the end. Perhaps it is because the gospel's ongoing witness and sharp

Luke 1:1–4

two thousand years. He immediately acknowledges that he is less the source of this testimony than a link in a *traditioning* of faith that has been "handed on to us." The authenticity of this fledgling tradition is vouchsafed for Luke by two values: (1) the value of *testimony from the original apostolic sources,* "those who from the beginning were eyewitnesses and servants of the word" (v. 2); and (2) the value of *careful historical research*—"investigating everything carefully from the very first"—to vouch for the authenticity of the earliest witnesses, including sources with whom Luke undoubtedly had not spoken.

The idea of producing "an orderly account . . . so that you may know the truth" (vv. 3b–4a) could be advanced as the maxim that will guide theological reflection over the Christian centuries to come. In valuing "the truth," Luke anticipates Anselm's *fides quaerens intellectum*—the "faith seeking understanding"—that becomes a foundation for medieval theology. Moreover, in the value of an "orderly account" we see in embryonic form the Christian impulse to coherence and comprehensiveness that will gird the systematic theologies of the twenty-first century.

In a single sentence, Luke's author presents the basic gestures of a foundational Christian theological method. Careful witness to the Word of God becomes a fundamental faith practice, ensconced as the essential, collective work of a Christian community. That practice promises to perpetuate the community by regularly rehearsing and remanifesting the revelatory truth that Luke will narrate in the chapters and verses to follow. Whether or not Luke is writing to a real-life Theophilus of his own times, or to us latter-day readers, it is clear that he is inviting us to become Theophili—beloved-lovers of God. He calls on us to respect the careful witness he has tried to array in his narrative of a revealed salvation history, and thus join in the unending project of those theologians who comprised the apostolic circle around Christ.

JORGE A. AQUINO

matters. They still need to be reassured. Luke's story is one where the poor, women, lepers, Samaritans, and other toys from the Island of Misfit Toys come to know that they too belong to the kingdom of God. There is not only room but a need for such a gospel of mercy in our world.

We live in a time when many of our congregations are hurting. Many of us are leaching members, some generations have all but disappeared from our pews, and we are unsure about how to fund our ministries. There is a yearning for the glory days of yesterday that are no more. In the midst of such change, our congregations need reassuring. So what will happen? How can the tide be turned? The answers are not clear. Perhaps we need to spend less time talking about doctrinal differences and more time sharing stories. Tell Luke's story; tell our story; tell your story: tell the story of God's redeeming love through which we make sense of the chaos of the world. After all, there was a time when Christianity was spread, not through force or coercion, but through the fascination and awe of a story. Whether we can rediscover and foster again such wonder may say much about the chapters that we have yet to write.

When we share our stories with others, we become part of their stories, and they become part of ours. Once Theophilus heard Luke's story, he became part of that same story. What are the stories of and in your community? What stories have been forgotten or suppressed? What stories need to be sung aloud? As a congregational leader, how can you help others tell their individual stories, even as you ground them in that *grand récit* of grace in which we all participate? What stories of reassurance do they need to hear? What stories of challenge need to be uttered? *Once upon a time there was a man named Luke . . .*

JAMES R. LUCK JR.

that this immense two-volume undertaking is an appropriate vehicle for meeting that need?

An initial clue is tucked into the prologue, where Luke speaks of "the events that have been fulfilled among us" (v. 1). This turn of phrase is heavily freighted (cf. 1:20, 57; 2:6, 21, 22; 4:21; 9:31; 21:22, 24; 24:22, 44). It suggests that Luke views what transpired with Jesus, and what transpired with his followers right up through the mission to the Gentiles in Luke's own day, as the fulfillment of God's promises to Israel. Thus it seems Luke understands these events, and is about to narrate them, in the biblical mode.

That is just what he does. He writes a continuation of the biblical narrative, held together by a progression of prophecies and fulfillments. He reveres Jewish Scripture, makes use of quotations from it, and often adopts the style of the Septuagint. Not content with pericope or anecdote alone, he operates with a grand design. Reports, legends, sayings, itineraries, and fragmentary information in various forms are woven into a story of impressive continuity anchored in Israel's past.

It is then the continuity of salvation history that Luke presents as the firm foundation of the faith. That Theophilus and his community need assurance precisely on this score suggests they may have been troubled by the claim that Judaism, and not Christianity, was the ancient and authentic form of biblical religion.[1] The Jesus movement in this view was a mere novelty. Luke for his part does not shy away from the magnitude of change that the movement represents, especially the inclusion of Gentiles in the people of God under the explosive impact of the Spirit. The new is new, but it is also old—and therefore, Luke insists, authentic.

Luke does not make the case for authenticity in the abstract; he dramatizes. Through his story he makes Jesus, Peter, Stephen, Paul, and a host of others forcefully present to the imagination, so that long after they are gone their exploits impinge on his readers. His is a narrative of roots. It shapes and confirms their communal identity, giving them a foundation for the future by providing a vision of the past.

DAVID R. ADAMS

critique of those prerogatives and values (especially as they may be considered by their adherents to be eternally inviolate) resist every effort to soften them that an apologetic effort was thought necessary.

Yet, as Luke attempted in his time, so preachers in our own time may attempt to indicate how an ongoing gospel critique of presumed eternal indicatives is not subversive of human flourishing, but, instead, is conducive to the flourishing God intends for human existence. It is not, then, finally to the detriment of principalities and powers that they are perpetually under review according to the Word of God that stands forever (Isa. 40:8). It is to their benefit, to their prospering in a way compatible with divine purposes.

Regarding the second homiletical trajectory named at the outset of this essay, we may be brief. In his imaginative grasp of Christ's accomplished and continuing work in the church and in the world, Luke was no religious innovator, inventing stories at will and saying anything to suit his purpose. To the contrary, he avowedly attempted to speak in a way coherent with previous gospel testimony. Preachers today may be encouraged to do the same. For example, Luke's Gospel was addressed to Theophilus ("beloved" or "friend" of God) so that Theophilus might have confidence in the truth concerning the things about which he had been instructed. That Theophilus was a person of considerable stature in the Roman world of Luke's time is suggested by the fact that he was called "most excellent" (v. 3), the same term applied to the Roman governor, Felix, in Acts 23:26.

Yet a case can be made for Theophilus to be a name that includes us all as beloved lovers of God. Luke's Gospel, and our contemporary preaching of it, clearly must be meant for all persons everywhere—ecclesially identified or not—regardless of social position. Preaching the gospel from Luke entails proclamation that is at once personal and corporate, local and yet global in pertinence, for the gospel must never be regarded as the pious, private possession of any of us. It is God's public—at times even disturbing—claim on *all* of us and all of *us*.

CHARLES L. BARTOW

1. Cf. Nils Dahl, *Jesus in the Memory of the Early Church* (Minneapolis: Augsburg, 1976), 96.

Luke 1:5–25

⁵In the days of King Herod of Judea, there was a priest named Zechariah, who belonged to the priestly order of Abijah. His wife was a descendant of Aaron, and her name was Elizabeth. ⁶Both of them were righteous before God, living blamelessly according to all the commandments and regulations of the Lord. ⁷But they had no children, because Elizabeth was barren, and both were getting on in years.

⁸Once when he was serving as priest before God and his section was on duty, ⁹he was chosen by lot, according to the custom of the priesthood, to enter the sanctuary of the Lord and offer incense. ¹⁰Now at the time of the incense offering, the whole assembly of the people was praying outside. ¹¹Then there appeared to him an angel of the Lord, standing at the right side of the altar of incense. ¹²When Zechariah saw him, he was terrified; and fear overwhelmed him. ¹³But the angel said to him, "Do not be afraid, Zechariah, for your prayer has been heard. Your wife Elizabeth will bear you a son, and you will name him John. ¹⁴You will have joy and gladness, and many will rejoice at his birth, ¹⁵for he will be great in the sight of the Lord. He must never drink wine or strong drink; even before his birth he will be filled with the Holy Spirit. ¹⁶He will turn

Theological Perspective

If Luke's opening pericope (1:1–4) introduces his embryonic theological method—by way of introducing us to a mystery man named *Theophilus*—the following passages present the prophetic motif of his Gospel: the annunciation that God is overturning Jerusalem's colonized and reified order, and replacing it with a populist movement of charismatic reformers. Few protagonists were better suited to play the foil for such a narrative than a righteous priest named Zechariah. He has obediently tended his duty as a member of the Davidic priesthood (the order of Abijah) for a life that now has grown long in years. The ritual duties of the priesthood are deeply ingrained in him and his brethren, as they have been for many generations, even down to the banal ritual of drawing lots to determine who will enter the sanctuary for an incense offering. Luke tells us that Zechariah and his wife, Elizabeth, "were righteous before God, living blamelessly according to all the commandments and regulations of the Lord" (v. 6). However, we are also told that, despite their blamelessness, "they had no children, because Elizabeth was barren, and both were getting on in years" (v. 7).

What is wrong with this picture? Why the apparent contradiction between the righteousness of Zechariah and his wife, and their childlessness, which Elizabeth and her people regard as a

Pastoral Perspective

How many people in your faith community are expecting to meet God in worship this week? Yes, many of them, like Zechariah, will be present, honoring their commitments and offering their prayers. They may even long for an opportunity to be emotionally moved, to be challenged from the pulpit to live in the way of the Lord, or to receive from the Table. That is as it should be. Having said that, how many are actually expecting to experience the holy or to have their prayers answered? How many are expecting God to do something new? For that matter, how many of us—clergy and congregational leaders—are expecting such an encounter or experience?

There certainly is no evidence in this pericope that Zechariah was expecting to come into the presence of the holy while fulfilling his duties, and perhaps that is good news in and of itself. If God will remember a faithful but otherwise forgettable priest easily lost in a crowd of hundreds of other priests, then perhaps God will remember us. If God will answer the prayer of a righteous, patient, and barren woman named Elizabeth, then perhaps God will answer our prayers.

Indeed, in this gospel of assurance that Luke has set out to tell, his opening characters reveal much about the promise of grace for those who are

many of the people of Israel to the Lord their God. [17]With the spirit and power of Elijah he will go before him, to turn the hearts of parents to their children, and the disobedient to the wisdom of the righteous, to make ready a people prepared for the Lord." [18]Zechariah said to the angel, "How will I know that this is so? For I am an old man, and my wife is getting on in years." [19]The angel replied, "I am Gabriel. I stand in the presence of God, and I have been sent to speak to you and to bring you this good news. [20]But now, because you did not believe my words, which will be fulfilled in their time, you will become mute, unable to speak, until the day these things occur."

[21]Meanwhile the people were waiting for Zechariah, and wondered at his delay in the sanctuary. [22]When he did come out, he could not speak to them, and they realized that he had seen a vision in the sanctuary. He kept motioning to them and remained unable to speak. [23]When his time of service was ended, he went to his home.

[24]After those days his wife Elizabeth conceived, and for five months she remained in seclusion. She said, [25]"This is what the Lord has done for me when he looked favorably on me and took away the disgrace I have endured among my people."

Exegetical Perspective

With Luke's birth and infancy narratives we enter an enchanted world. It is replete with angels, heavenly signs, startling prophecies, unlikely pregnancies, improbable births, temple rituals, religious function-aries, pious laypeople, isolated shepherds, a child prodigy, and with it all an abundance of echoes from Israel's Holy Writ. This is the religious imagination at its most fertile, an outpouring of legend and imagery fitting for a turning point in human history no less momentous than the coming of "a Savior, who is Christ the Lord" (2:11).

The Birth of John the Baptist Foretold: Literary Features. Our entry into this world is through John the Baptist and his parents. In the announcement of John's impending birth Luke plays the narrative line out slowly, as he does throughout his two-chapter introduction, inviting us to linger over the details and savor their import. The opening episode is a miniseries in three parts.

Verses 5–7. Luke introduces Zechariah and Eliza-beth, and the issue around which the story revolves: the inability of Elizabeth to bear children. Her infer-tility is more than a medical problem compounded by old age (vv. 7 and 18); it is a "disgrace" (v. 25), a harsh judgment backed by centuries of social

Homiletical Perspective

Preaching possibilities in Luke 1:5–25 abound in this story of provocative and improbable characters. The blessed improbability of it all strikes us first. Herod's reign was hardly a historically propitious moment for religious and moral revival. Zechariah and Elizabeth, in their older years, seemed unlikely to have a child at all, let alone a child who would come to play a dis-tinctive role in heralding the approach of God's jus-tice and mercy. Both were of priestly lineage in Israel, but neither was otherwise prominent. Zechariah was dutiful in his role as intercessor on behalf of God's people. Nothing about his being chosen by lot to offer incense in the temple was unusual. Nor was there anything in the present moment that hinted at the awe-full encounter that was immediately to ensue.

The first provocation from God's messenger therefore took Zechariah by surprise. Perhaps he had forgotten that to enter the sanctuary of the Lord and the place of incense offering was to stand in the place of meeting between Israel's covenant God and God's people as represented by priestly orders (Exod. 30:1–12). According to the prophets (e.g., Isa. 1:13), incense offering in Israel had degenerated into a practice divorced from repentance, amend-ment of life, and concern for justice. In the context of Luke's story, Zechariah's encounter with the angel of the Lord was the beginning of God's returning

Luke 1:5–25

Theological Perspective

"disgrace"? There can be no modern explanation for a contradiction so resonant with ontological moralism. The idea that one's fortunes—or misfortunes—manifested divine judgments on one's morality was well worn in Hebrew biblical tradition, long before Zechariah would ever set foot in the sanctuary. The patriarch Abraham is the founding prophet of what might be called an Israelite theology of retribution, which abounds—but is also debated—throughout the Hebrew Bible. As Abraham took up his covenant with the Lord, he was blessed with offspring and wealth. Similar blessings seemed likewise to vouch the righteousness of the subsequent patriarchs. This idea of the blessedness of the righteous takes its place as one of the grounding myths of collective Israelite identity, a cornerstone of the Davidic ideology of an elect people playing a critical role in God's history of salvation. In this theology, God rewards the good in their lifetimes; but the unrighteous are marked by irredeemable failure, because their immorality has brought divine judgment down on them.

Of course, such a theology is mined with the snares of theodicy. The literatures of the Babylonian exile showed that the theology of retribution provoked a crisis of national identity, calling into question either Israel's elect vocation or the credibility of its theology of God. The book of Job presents the challenge of the theology of retribution in its most elemental terms, as Job, a man of vertical righteousness, is caught in a deadly wager between God and Satan. Stricken with disease and the spectacular mass death of his family members, he suffers complete dispossession. Rending his clothes and seated in a sandpit, he laments his unmerited misfortune, wondering at a God who permits the suffering of the good. In the long, poetic polemic between Job and three rather unhelpful friends, Job exercises—and perhaps exorcises—the theodicy that had distorted the Israelites' prophetic vocation, leading them off the track of their true national mission.

The Joban resolution—which reimposes divine authority in place of human self-righteousness (Job 38–42)—may not finally reconcile the underlying theological tensions, but it does interrupt the predominance of a form of religious reflection that had displaced a divine agenda in favor of a human-centered one. We can likewise read reform movements mentioned in the Christian Gospels—especially the Zealots, as represented by Judas, or the party of John the Baptist—in terms of the way Roman domination called into question either Israel's election or its national morality. There is the constant suggestion

Pastoral Perspective

to come. Yes, the powerful Herod is mentioned in the opening scene, but he mainly functions to set the story in the context of real human history. The main actors in this drama will not be the rich and the powerful but, rather, those overlooked by the world. The principalities and powers do not concern themselves with barren older couples, unwed teenage mothers, and those relegated to caring for animals. The good news is that even they play a part in this drama of salvation. The terrifying news, however, is that even *we* may play a part in this drama of hope.

To be given a part in salvation history is terrifying news and understandably so. A messenger of the holy has spoken. Why would Zechariah not ask, "How can I be sure of this?" or Mary question, "How can this be?" (1:18, 34)? Even the patriarch Abraham asks how he is to know that he shall possess the land and thus God's promises (Gen. 15:8). While many interpreters of this material share the opinion that Zechariah's speechlessness was punishment for his lack of belief, might there be other possibilities? After all, Zechariah was hardly the first to be struck mute in the presence of the holy. There are a great many affinities in this pericope with the book of Daniel, especially chapter 10, where Daniel is struck mute. When the holy crashes into our world, and our assumptions are confronted with new realities, a response of fear, shock, and even speechlessness would seem to be reasonable.

Was Zechariah's speechlessness a punishment or a natural response to the presence of the holy? Was it perhaps a sign that God was at work? After all, Zechariah did inquire of the angel how he was to know that this good news was true. Lacking the ability to bless, explain, rationalize, or fill empty space with words might certainly constitute such a sign. In addition, if we take a less literal and more poetic approach to the material, might it also suggest that human speechlessness helps God to be heard, especially when God's word falls so far beyond the scope of our experiences or expectations? In other words, is the problem that God is *not* speaking or that we *are*?

Perhaps part of our struggle is that too many churches are filling the air with the noise of platitudes and judgment. Perhaps we are spending too much time looking for *the* answers when silence would make room for questions and a journey of discovery. Perhaps what God asks of us and offers to us is so beyond the scope of our expectations that we settle for a set of talking points.

Regardless of the whys, Zechariah in his silence and Elizabeth in her solitude find themselves in

convention (Gen. 16:4, 11; 29:32; 30:1; Lev. 20:20–21; 1 Sam. 1:5–6; 2 Sam. 6:23). Not even Elizabeth's blameless life (v. 6) or the fact she and her husband are of priestly stock (v. 5) has spared her the opprobrium of her people (v. 25).

Verses 8–20. At the heart of the story is the promise of John's birth and the dialogue it prompts between Zechariah and the angel Gabriel. Zechariah is on priestly duty at the temple. Note we are not informed that it is from his home in the Judean hill country (1:39) that he has traveled to Jerusalem, nor that as a priest he would have served at the temple for a week at a time once or twice a year. Rather, the focus is immediately on the liturgical routine (vv. 8–10) and the disruption of it by the appearance of "an angel of the Lord" (v. 11). The appearance strikes Zechariah with terror (v. 12), as biblical angelophanies are wont to do, and it is in the context of reassuring Zechariah that Gabriel announces Elizabeth will bear him a son—something, we learn only now, Zechariah has been praying for (v. 13). That takes care of the medical problem and the social disgrace, and would seem to wrap things up, except for one small detail: the child's name is not left to the discretion of the parents; it is divinely mandated (see 1:59–64).

With that the story shifts into a new gear (vv. 14–17). It is no longer simply a domestic tale; it is the prelude to a national epic with universal ramifications. "Many" will rejoice at John's birth, Gabriel proclaims, for it signals the coming of a great reforming prophet, like Elijah, who even in his mother's womb will be endowed with the Holy Spirit. He will create a "people prepared" for the Lord, that is, prepared for the terrible day of judgment, by summoning them to repentance (see Mal. 3:1; 4:5–6; Luke 3:3, 7–18).

Zechariah is incredulous, not at the "good news" of John's prophetic vocation, which he ignores for the moment, but at the promise that he and Elizabeth will conceive a son (vv. 18–19; cf. Sarah in Gen. 18:12–14). Bristling at Zechariah's incredulity, Gabriel produces his credentials as a reliable heavenly messenger and strikes Zechariah mute until the time of John's birth (1:64), either as punishment for Zechariah's doubt or as a sign of the promise of this child, or both (vv. 19–20).

Verses 21–25. The story ends with two vignettes that serve to confirm Gabriel's words. Zechariah is indeed unable to speak, from which the people at

God's people to all three practices. "Do not be afraid, Zechariah," said God's messenger, Gabriel, "for your prayer has been heard. Your wife Elizabeth will bear you a son, and you will name him John" (v. 13). Zechariah had his doubts. Who can blame him?

Further provocation: Zechariah said to the angel who instanced Zechariah's apprehension of God's presence, "How will I know that this is so? For I am an old man, and my wife is getting on in years" (v. 18). In saying this, Zechariah confronted God's messenger not only with his need for a sign but with the fact of his wife's "disgrace." Among the ancients, as is generally known, infertility was considered a female problem and a sign of God's displeasure. Further, it brought on family strife as well as personal despair. This was so with Sarah (Gen. 11:30; 16:1ff.) and with Hannah (1 Sam. 1:1–20), and now with Elizabeth. Zechariah did get from God's messenger, Gabriel, a sign. However, Gabriel's sign was not only a sign of promise; it was also a sign of rebuke. Zechariah was literally dumbstruck.

Then there is the improbability of God's presence. In the totality of his Gospel narrative, Luke makes it clear that signs of God's nearness and caring and attentiveness to prayer can be variously received. People's thoughts may gladly have been turned toward God in light of what came of the sign given to Zechariah, that is, John the Baptist and his ministry (vv. 13–18). Other's thoughts, however, apparently were turned toward rebellion against what came to be understood as the fulfillment of a divine promise (3:7–20).

We may consider, as well, the improbability of answered prayer. Preachers should note that because Zechariah was struck dumb, he was unable to give the blessing from God to the people waiting to receive it outside the temple sanctuary. Preaching signs of God's affirmative answers to desperate prayers and felt needs must suggest the *burden* or *weight* of glory and not only the happy prospect of yearnings fulfilled.

Finally, while the names of the principal characters in Luke 1:5–25 do not necessarily play a significant part in the story as told, they are provocative in that they suggest something of the character and action of God. Zechariah's name can be taken to mean, "YHWH has remembered." Elizabeth's name carries the connotation "God is an oath," or "God is the absolutely faithful one," or "God is the covenant maker." With Gabriel we are given to understand that "God has shown himself mighty" (Dan. 8:16; 9:21). The son promised to Elizabeth and Zechariah

Theological Perspective

from such figures that Roman domination is the bitter fruit of God's dismay with the peoples' self-interestedness, corruption, and collaborationism. In Luke's Gospel, we would do well to read the problem of Elizabeth's barrenness in terms of this history.

Zechariah has no reason to anticipate anything unusual as he enters the sanctuary to perform the privileged, but familiar duty of lighting an incense offering to God. Nevertheless, when he encounters an enormous angel standing to the right of the sanctuary, he trembles in terror—even as the angel, who calls himself Gabriel, begins unfolding good news to him. Despite their advanced years, Zechariah and his wife will be blessed with a son, whom they are to name John. He will be no ordinary child. This prophetic forerunner, who will pave a straight road for the coming of the Messiah, will be remembered by Christians as John the Baptist. "He will turn many of the people of Israel to the Lord their God . . . to make ready a people prepared for the Lord."

Reading this narrative allegorically, the story proposes a powerful prophetic inversion: an emissary of God addresses the pinnacle of temple officialdom, interrupting its compromised tradition, to announce the advent of divine intervention and a new course for the religious life of the nation. This is all too much for Zechariah, who cannot believe his eyes: "How will I know that this is so? For I am an old man, and my wife is getting on in years." The angel invokes his authority as divine emissary: "I stand in the presence of God, and I have been sent to speak to you and to bring you this good news." Because Zechariah has doubted, the angel says, he will be struck dumb, "unable to speak, until the day these things occur" (vv. 18–20).

This pericope is the first of a two-step passage that marks Luke's Gospel as a liberationist text—prophesying the reform of an exhausted, colonized religious order, and the exaltation of those made lowly in its system. The second step arrives in the following pericope (1:26–38), in which a young, just-betrothed virgin named Mary is also visited by the angel Gabriel, who likewise promises her a miraculous child of her own.

JORGE A. AQUINO

Pastoral Perspective

a time of gestation and incubation. It is a time of waiting during which they cannot fill the space with noise and busyness; it is a time of passive watching and discernment. There will be times to act and speak (and in Luke there will be times to sing!), but this is not such a time.

While the people in our faith communities do not need more shame or guilt, they do need help learning to incubate their faith in a time of much noise and little clarity. Some of them have waited for years for their prayers to be answered, even while they struggle with despair and broken dreams. Others long for a birth announcement, for a promise and a sign that new life will spring up in their lives or perhaps in the life of their struggling congregation. Some have come to believe that they are unimportant in the grand scheme of life, that they have been forgotten.

What can we do as congregational leaders? For starters, we can provide opportunities for vital worship experiences led by worship leaders who anticipate a still-speaking God. We can be leaders who manage our own anxiety and seek out opportunities for silence and solitude. We can be pastors and spiritual friends who remember those who believe they have been forgotten, even as God remembered Zechariah and Elizabeth. We can reassure our fellow pilgrims that their lives are not destined to be barren and that they too have a role in preparing a way for the kingdom of God. When they question and doubt, we can let them know that they are in good company.

The days of Herod were not easy days for God's people; yet in the midst of such times, God spoke to and through a faithful couple. These days of postmodernity are also not easy for God's people. Yet even today the world is pregnant with divine possibilities. Perhaps those who can be still and nonanxious enough to watch and wait may again hear the glad tidings of the angels.

JAMES R. LUCK JR.

the temple conclude he has in fact seen a vision, and Elizabeth conceives.

Historical and Theological Considerations. The career of John the Baptist caused problems for the early church. He was an apocalyptic prophet in his own right, founder of a Palestinian reform movement that would eventually count adherents as far away as modern Turkey (Acts 19:1–7). The inconvenient truth is that for a time one of those drawn to this movement was Jesus of Nazareth, who underwent John's baptism of repentance for the forgiveness of sins. In a variety of ways both subtle and overt, Luke, like Matthew and John the evangelist, refutes the implications (a) that John, as Jesus' predecessor, was superior to him, and (b) that Jesus had anything of which he actually needed to repent. Luke gets to that soon enough, especially in chapters 3 and 7. For now, though, in the opening episode of his Gospel he celebrates, and wants us to appreciate, John for the "great" person he was (1:15; 7:28) and the extraordinary mission laid upon him by God.

Scholars have speculated that the legends of John's birth, recounted by Luke in chapter 1, originated in the circles of believers John attracted to himself. Whatever the origin of the material, Luke incorporates it seamlessly into his narrative. The promise of John's birth anticipates and sets in motion a series of momentous events, woven together through prophecy and fulfillment, that radically alter the course of salvation history and the makeup of God's people. Yet those changes take place gradually and never simply obliterate Israel's past. Luke's Gospel begins in the temple with Zechariah faithfully performing his duties, and ends in the temple with the disciples of Jesus "continually blessing God" (Luke 24:53).

In this first story Luke funds the imagination. He paints a picture of a world of religious devotion about to be disrupted and enriched in ways no one could have foreseen. He invites us to make it our own.

DAVID R. ADAMS

is, by Gabriel's insistence, to be called John, an indication that "YHWH has been gracious."

What contemporary preachers decide to make of this story's improbabilities and provocations, and of the indications of God's character and action suggested by the characters' names, will play a role in shaping their sermons on Luke 1:5–25. Those decisions also will play a role in selecting other passages to be incorporated into the liturgy (e.g., 1 Sam. 1:1–18; Mal. 4:1–6, esp. vv. 5–6; and, as pertaining to incense and prayer, Ps. 141, esp. v. 2; and Rev. 8:1–5, esp. v. 3). Finally, those decisions will bear upon the wording of prayers of adoration, confession, thanksgiving, supplication, and intercession.

A final provocation of Luke 1:5–25, especially bearing upon the text's perceived relevance for contemporary preachers and congregations, has to do with the passage's character as literature. It is poetic. It is musical. It sings of visions, and of signs (miraculous at that), and of angels, namely, Gabriel. Verses 14–17 appear to be a canticle in honor of John, Zechariah and Elizabeth's promised son. In fact, the whole pericope has the feel of an evocative literary manuscript in Luke's possession, inserted with only minimal editorial change into his Gospel narrative. It is, then, in some sense a construct of the early church's imagination. How can it be received today as an authoritative witness to an event of revelatory significance in the saga of Jesus Christ? The answer lies in observing that poetry is not always pure fantasy. The truth, the significance of an event for faith, may be *given* to the imagination, not invented by it.[1]

Just so, the virtual may be pressed into the service of the actual. Therefore, preachers might do well to imagine how Gabriel brings the witness of Luke 1:5–25 to bear upon contemporary congregants' hopeful, doubt-filled prayers, that our congregants— and we ourselves—might acquire "the wisdom of the righteous" and become "a people prepared for the Lord" (v. 17).

CHARLES L. BARTOW

1. Garrett Green, *Imagining God: Theology and the Religious Imagination* (San Francisco: Harper & Row, 1989), 28–40; also "The Gender of God and the Theology of Metaphor," in Alvin F. Kimel Jr., *Speaking the Christian God: The Holy Trinity and the Challenge of Feminism* (Grand Rapids: Eerdmans, 1992), 71.

Luke 1:26–38

²⁶In the sixth month the angel Gabriel was sent by God to a town in Galilee called Nazareth, ²⁷to a virgin engaged to a man whose name was Joseph, of the house of David. The virgin's name was Mary. ²⁸And he came to her and said, "Greetings, favored one! The Lord is with you." ²⁹But she was much perplexed by his words and pondered what sort of greeting this might be. ³⁰The angel said to her, "Do not be afraid, Mary, for you have found favor with God. ³¹And now, you will conceive in your womb and bear a son, and you will name him Jesus. ³²He will be great, and will be called the Son of the Most High, and the Lord God will give to him the throne of his ancestor David. ³³He will reign over the

Theological Perspective

Election is a powerful thing, a humbling, supernatural force. When God calls you to a prophetic destiny, your world shakes. An angel appears and throws you to the ground, pinning you down until his weight has pushed the wind out of you. An anonymous bush catches fire and begins to speak to you. The stones at your feet begin to tremble and prophesy in loud cries and strange tongues.

Maybe you are like Zechariah, trudging through your dull, accustomed rite, when an angel suddenly appears. God tends not to call the paragons of virtue and righteousness. His heroes are almost always flawed. The patriarch Jacob was muddy, bloody, and bruised out of joint as the sun came up on the Jabbok, after he had wrestled with the angel who would turn him toward his fate (Gen. 32). Moses regularly angered God with his hemming and hawing. Ordered to liberate the Israelites from Pharaoh, Moses cringed, begging, "Please send someone else" (Exod. 3–4). Zechariah had his tongue stilled because he doubted; the repeated rote rite of his faith had made him forget that *there is a God—one who might actually appear right there in the sanctuary!*

Moral of the story: If you are called to become one of the elect, then shut up, listen up, and get ready to serve.

Pastoral Perspective

Mary has become something of a Rorschach blot test: everyone sees her differently and as they need to see her. Antifeminists hold her up as a model of the obedient woman who embraces her "rightful" place in the family. Feminists champion this strong woman who needed not a man in her life. Greek and Russian Orthodox believers adore her as the *theotokos*, the God-bearer. Secularists mock her as a symbol of the irrationality and antiquity of Christian thinking. Catholics exalt her as the Queen of heaven, while Hallmark romanticizes her and the U.S. Postal Service puts her on Christmas stamps. Then there are the Protestants who argue about whether she is a heavenly intercessor, whether such an intercessor is needed, whether she remained a virgin, and whether she was immaculately conceived and therefore born without sin. Too frequently we ignore or minimize her, making her a porcelain figurine in our crèche: fragile, breakable, and boxed away for most of the year. When we pull her out, we do not actually interact with her. Yes, she helps us feel nostalgic, but in the end she changes nothing.

Although there is a renewed interest among Protestants in the biblical Mary, many faith communities are reluctant to invite their constituents to wrestle with her. After all, were we to truly interact with her, we would have no choice but to change how we live

house of Jacob forever, and of his kingdom there will be no end." [34]Mary said to the angel, "How can this be, since I am a virgin?" [35]The angel said to her, "The Holy Spirit will come upon you, and the power of the Most High will overshadow you; therefore the child to be born will be holy; he will be called Son of God. [36]And now, your relative Elizabeth in her old age has also conceived a son; and this is the sixth month for her who was said to be barren. [37]For nothing will be impossible with God." [38]Then Mary said, "Here am I, the servant of the Lord; let it be with me according to your word." Then the angel departed from her.

Exegetical Perspective

Few scenes in the Gospels rival the annunciation to Mary for its capacity to fire the imagination. Over the centuries theologians, laypeople, painters, and others have been drawn again and again to the prophecy of Jesus' virginal conception and birth. It has immeasurably enriched christological reflection, Marian piety, and the artistic patrimony produced by Christianity, especially in the West. Much of the annunciation's appropriation, however, has occurred with little regard for its literary and cultural context. Our task is to place it firmly in its setting, and in so doing to reclaim the full force of Luke's takeaway line, "Nothing is impossible with God" (v. 37; cf. 18:27; also Gen. 18:14).

The annunciation follows directly upon the prophecy of the birth of John the Baptist and is linked to that prophecy in two ways: (1) it is dated to the sixth month of Elizabeth's pregnancy (vv. 26, 36); and (2) it is constructed out of similar components: the appearance of the angel Gabriel, the perplexity he causes and the assurance not to fear, the announcement of an unlikely pregnancy, the divine mandating of the child's name, and the reference to a legitimating sign.

Given the parallels and the fact that Luke later explicitly subordinates John to Jesus, it is tempting to emphasize the contrasting terms in which their

Homiletical Perspective

In Luke 1:11–20, Zechariah had a vision, and only after seeing Gabriel did he hear the angel speak. Mary, on the other hand, apparently saw no one, but she heard astounding news heaven sent. The news she heard was to become a gestational and lifelong burden. Through her the humanly impossible would be accomplished, a pregnancy more remarkable than that of Elizabeth, who was beyond childbearing years. Despite her virginity, Mary would bear a son who was to be named Jesus. He was to be great, greater than Elizabeth's son John, for he himself was to be the Lord for whom John was "to make ready a people prepared" (1:17). Jesus was to be called "the Son of the Most High" (v. 32a) to whom would be given "the throne of his ancestor David" (v. 32b). Gabriel concluded, "He will reign over the house of Jacob forever, and of his kingdom there will be no end" (v. 33).

As the rest of Luke's Gospel (and Acts also) makes clear, Jesus, at a brutal cost to himself—and to his mother's alarm and grief—would redefine reality as it is commonly ordered under the influence of the principalities and powers with which human beings ordinarily align themselves. His "most high" status would be manifest in humility; his royal power would be exercised through weakness. Finally, in the scandal of the cross, and in the lives of his followers

Luke 1:26–38

Theological Perspective

In this third pericope of Luke 1, we meet the greatest of the elect in the history of the Christian faith—Mary, the mother of Jesus—although she is hardly exalted yet. Betrothed to Joseph, but still a virgin, Mary must have been quite young—fifteen years old, maybe even younger. She is a little girl in what was surely a man's world, an impoverished nobody with nothing of importance to say. Like Zechariah in the prior scene, the last thing she expects to receive is a visitation from an angel, particularly one greeting her as though she were a princess. Christians today pray, "Hail! Mary," after this angel's greeting. Mary—naïf that she was—"was much perplexed by his words and pondered what sort of greeting this might be" (v. 29). The angel explains that Mary is to bear a son and name him Jesus. He "will be called the Son of the Most High, and the Lord God will give to him the throne of his ancestor David. He will reign over the house of Jacob forever, and of his kingdom there will be no end" (vv. 32–33).

What happens next is itself perplexing. Mary asks how she can bear this Messiah if she is still a virgin—a question very much like the one that Zechariah raises when told his barren wife will bear a son in her old age. That parallel marks these stories as the beating wings of a single, symmetrical narrative. The angel answers that "the power of the Most High will overshadow you," and Mary will conceive. In the previous pericope, God strikes Zechariah dumb for doubting the angel's message. Mary suffers no such sanction—and nothing in the text tells us why. Perhaps Mary's youth and inexperience exonerate her, while hardened doubts in a mature holy man such as Zechariah are not so easily excused. Maybe the angel's forgiveness is a foregone conclusion because, as he tells her, she has "found favor with God" (v. 30).

Besides their supernatural surprises, biblical texts of election are also rife with risk. There are the risks internal to the stories themselves. Saying yes to a call of election puts one at risk of death by stoning or crucifixion—or the risk of social death: marginality, ridicule, poverty, maybe prison. Then there is also the collateral risk of the texts themselves, as they provide orientations for identity and action for the faith communities that invoke them. What do these texts of election prescribe to such communities? To what uses is the discourse of election put?

Mary is one of the most famous figures ever to answer the call to bear God's will and witness into history. Later, as we hear her chant her famous

Pastoral Perspective

and how we understand our faith. Better to limit her to a crèche than to acknowledge her central part in the story of our salvation. Better to mock Catholics than to ask whether God might be asking us to give birth to Christ and his kingdom.

When we intentionally consider the biblical Mary, our excuses will not work. If God used Mary, then we are not too young; if God used Elizabeth, then we are not too old. Being from a cultural capital or academic center is not a prerequisite in God's calculus either. If God brought something good out of Nazareth, then God's word can be born anew in the least likely places still. Have you ever been to Nazareth? God has always chosen the most humble of vessels from the most humble of places to give birth to his word. Mary had no rights; no power, and yet . . . No, our excuses will not work here.

Legend has it that Mary was not the first person asked to be the God-bearer, but rather she was the first person to say yes. Ask your community to consider how many others Gabriel approached before Mary said yes. How many others said, "You are out of your mind!" Only Mary said yes. She said yes to the incarnation. She said yes, yes to a God who desired to dwell within and through her. That is incarnational theology. God is not just with us, but can be within us, distinct yet inseparable. This is what Mary's yes was about. She would participate in the divine and the holy, even as the holy and divine chose to participate in and through her. The same is true of Moses and Deborah and Elijah and Esther. A messenger of the Lord comes and says, "Hail, O favored one, you have been called by God to serve the Almighty." You have been called to undertake a journey, and in the process your life will be changed forever.

The gospel is that this message has been extended not just to Mary but to all of us. Every single one of us has received an invitation to help give birth to the kingdom of God. Indeed, as Meister Eckhart believed, we are all meant to be mothers of God. "What good is it to me if this eternal birth of the divine son takes place unceasingly but does not take place within me? And what good is it to me if Mary is full of grace, if I am not also full of grace?"[1] The truth of the gospel is that we human beings are tabernacles, containers of the holy. God wants nothing less than for us to become pregnant with divine possibilities and then to give birth to the holy and precious in our time.

1. Barbara Brown Taylor, *Gospel Medicine* (Cambridge, MA: Cowley Publications, 1995), 168.

identities and missions are cast. For example, John will be great before the Lord (1:15), Jesus too will be great but also Son of the Most High (v. 32); John's ministry is time specific (1:17), Jesus' kingdom is never ending (v. 33); John is to prepare the people (1:17), Jesus to rule over them (v. 33). These contrasts and others are undeniable but subtle, indeed so subtle that they often elude casual readers in our time and probably eluded readers/hearers in Luke's time who lacked the luxury of flipping back and forth between pericopes. Indeed, the overwhelming first impression of the paired annunciations is that John and Jesus are to embark on distinctive yet coordinated prophetic careers that will lead to the radical reconstituting of God's people.

The main burden of our passage is christological, to introduce Jesus as Davidic Messiah and Son of God (vv. 32–35). Each concept has its own history in pre-Christian Jewish literature and its own set of nuances. To be sure, Israel's kings could be regarded as adoptive sons of God. Yet nowhere, with the possible exception of the Qumran text 4QFlor 10–13, is the long-awaited Messiah explicitly called God's Son. To bring the two together in the way that Luke does here is a bit like peering into a kaleidoscope. As the images shift—from Son to Messiah and back to Son again—the total effect is enhanced. It is as though neither image by itself is fully adequate to Luke's purpose at this point, but in concert they serve to convey an initial sense of Jesus' exceptional status and the implicit promise that the ensuing narrative will further disclose and define his identity. The apostle Paul had made use in Romans 1:3–4 of an early kerygmatic formula that proclaimed Jesus as Son of David by virtue of his lineage and Son of God by virtue of his resurrection. Now Luke, a generation later, relates both claims to the moment of Jesus' conception.

As heir to the "throne" of David, Jesus "will reign over the house of Jacob forever, and of his kingdom there will be no end" (v. 33). This prophecy harks back to the oracle of Nathan in 2 Samuel 7, a prime example of royal Davidic theology. Your offspring (Solomon) "shall build a house [temple] for my name, and I will establish the throne of his kingdom forever. . . . Your house [dynasty] and your kingdom shall be made sure forever before me; your throne shall be established forever" (2 Sam. 7: 13, 16). By the first century CE the terms of the oracle, the prospect of a never-ending Davidic dynasty, had long since been empirically disconfirmed. Still, it fed messianic expectations, as we know from

who labored in its shadow, a heroic victory—God's own victory over human sin, and error, and false pride—would be won. Yet the victory would be hidden within the appearance of defeat.

The child Mary was to bear, whose triumph she would soon sing (1:46–55), would not only end up contradicting the world's expectations concerning what the drawing near of God entails. Mary's own soul would be pierced by the sword of this terrible contradiction (v. 35). Mary herself would be confronted with the blunt outrage and unyielding claim of the gospel on the lips of him who "was incarnate" and "was made man" (the Nicene Creed) of her own flesh and blood: "My mother and my brothers are those who hear the word of God and do it" (8:21).

Speaking this blunt outrage and unyielding claim will be the first task of those who preach the gospel from Luke 1:26–38: They will need to hear and to speak the thought-to-be-impossible word/thing (*rhēma*) God has accomplished—and continues to accomplish—under the most adverse conditions and in ways seemingly unimaginable. "For nothing [no word/thing] will be impossible with God" (v. 37).

In her calling to bear the child, Jesus, Mary stands in a unique position within the prophetic tradition. The announcement to her echoes announcement stories from ancient times (Gen. 16:7–13, Ishmael; Gen. 17:1–21 and 18:1–15, Isaac; Judg. 13:2–25, Samson; and, of course, contemporaneously, Luke 1:5–25, the announcement to Zechariah and Elizabeth concerning John.[1]) Preachers can note comparisons and contrasts. Mary's response to Gabriel's announcement concerning Jesus, "Here am I . . . ," (v. 38a), especially calls to mind Isaiah 6:1–13. The Isaiah text surely is worth consideration as a reading prior to the reading and preaching of Luke 1:26–38.

Mary's response to her calling, although expressing astonished incomprehension, has none of the disbelief apparent in Zechariah's response to Gabriel's tidings. It has, instead, the feel of awe-inspired humility, astonishment, and, lastly and most significantly, confident and unhesitating assumption of duty. "Let it be with me according to your word" (v. 38b) is no mere acquiescence to fate or obsequious giving in to a demeaning imposition from on high. To the contrary, in a time when most of the world was enslaved to tyrannical powers, "Let it be with me according to your word" has the ring of glad response to a grand, although admittedly daunting, calling.

1. Brent A. Strawn, exegesis of Luke 1:26–38, in Roger E. Van Harn, ed., *The Lectionary Commentary: The Third Readings, The Gospels* (Grand Rapids: Eerdmans, 2001), 286–90.

Luke 1:26–38

Theological Perspective

refrain of humility, her Magnificat, we recognize in Mary's election the first sign of a new covenant: with the exaltation of the lowly, the prophetic imperative of justice is fulfilled and the promise of liberation confirmed. Mary will be recognized throughout Christian confessions for her selfless humility and faithfulness, becoming likewise the paradigm and archetype of womanly virtue. In Latin America, Mary is the mother of purity, consolation, succor, and protection. Many see her as a divine woman, raised to the heavens in an apotheosis—*mother of God*, the *theotokos*—holding a central place in the cosmic economy of salvation.

Mary has also undergone a different sort of apotheosis, one showing her in a most unbiblical and warlike mien. To the Creole priests who would establish the cult of the Virgin of Guadalupe in Mexico, Mary was a sword-wielding "assistant conqueror," the "first Creole." By her hand Spain had defeated the Aztecs and was ridding the continent of indigenous pagan idolatry and human sacrifice. For the Oratorian Miguel Sánchez, one of two sources of the modern Guadalupan tradition, Mary was the mediatrix of a divine Providence who would raze the pre-Colombian order, making way for insemination of the gospel among the "barbarous Indians." While the Bible depicts the election of a lowly and very uncertain human being in Mary, Mexico's Guadalupe was imagined as a general at the head of an army.

Of course, there are other visions of Mary, more humble and consoling. It is strange that a single text, depicting a poor, naive girl's election, should beget such an incommensurable range of expressions. Then again, this same mother was the begetter of all begetting. If we follow the Christian creed's sometime affirmation of Mary as *theotokos*, as *mother of God*, then she is the calm, consoling *alpha before the Alpha*. Mother of all, she should have many guises, a young, inexperienced, marginal girl from the Palestinian countryside being perhaps just one of those guises.

JORGE A. AQUINO

Pastoral Perspective

In light of such a message many, like Mary, will be perplexed, asking, "How can this be?" Nonetheless, a powerless teenage girl said yes and gave birth to a child destined to transform all of creation. That is Mary's story. What about yours? How is God asking your faith community to give birth to the holy? Do they say yes to God's intrusive invitations? Do they say yes to the new horizons, new possibilities, and new lives? Do they say with Isaiah, "Here am I"? Do they say yes to questions that really question the way things are? Then, if they do say yes, are you willing to be their Elizabeth? Are you willing to bless their pregnancy? Will your congregational leaders midwife the birthing process?

The Angelus is a traditional prayer offered most frequently at the close of evening prayer:

> The angel of the Lord declared unto Mary.
> And she conceived by the power of Holy Spirit.
> Hail Mary, full of grace, the Lord is with you. Blessed are you among women, and blessed is the fruit of your womb, Jesus. Holy Mary, Mother of God, pray for us sinners, now and at the hour of our death. Amen.
> Behold the handmaid of the Lord.
> Be it done unto me according to your Word.
> Hail Mary, full of grace, the Lord is with you.

By placing the prayer at the end of the day, a basic question is posed to those participating: How did we respond this very day to God's call? We know how Mary responded: "Let it be with me according to your word" (v. 38). What about us? What about our people? How have we responded? That is the role of the Angelus. What is your community doing to give birth to our Lord, here and now? Mary, the first disciple, has led the way. She said yes. She gave voice to Christ's vision. She followed. Now it is our turn. Do we have enough courage, enough gumption, to do likewise?

JAMES R. LUCK JR.

Qumran—expectations that from the perspective of Luke and the early church had been fulfilled in Jesus.

The other major element of the annunciation is Jesus' virginal conception. That Mary is a virgin is noted twice, at the outset (v. 27) and again in verse 34, where her amazement at Gabriel's message provides the dynamic for the rest of the pericope and its affirmation that Jesus is to be conceived through the intervention of God: "The Holy Spirit will come upon you, and the power of the Most High will overshadow you" (v. 35). In the end, Mary accepts the angel's message and her role in the divine plan as servant/handmaiden of the Lord (v. 38; cf. Hannah in 1 Sam. 1:11).

Two things of note. First, the language of "overshadowing" is used elsewhere in Luke (9:34) and elsewhere in the Bible (Exod. 16:10; 24:15–18; 40:34–35) to indicate God's presence. The language is figurative, not scientific. It is a way of valuing Jesus, a way of affirming his uniqueness, not a way of explaining the mechanism by which he came into being. The story is a confessional narrative, not a report of a gynecological exam; for that, see the *Protevangelium of James*, chapter 20, where the rationalistic interpretation of the virgin birth is already in evidence. Second, although the message of Gabriel is directed to Mary, it is primarily about her son, his extraordinary identity, his unprecedented mission. Thus, when Mary asks, "How can this be?" and Gabriel responds, "Nothing is impossible with God," it is not just the virginal conception that is in view but the whole sweep of Jesus' saving work as Son of God and Messiah. It is all miraculous.

The annunciation, despite its brevity, is a complex and sophisticated story. To help parishioners and others appropriate it in a manner that does justice to its character, clergy may need to challenge a prevailing assumption in our culture, namely, that the *only* vehicle of truth is fact. This reductive, rationalistic assumption underlies many things, including Christian fundamentalism. If the gospel is to make its way in our world, there must be room for metaphor, myth, legend, and the imagination.

DAVID R. ADAMS

Preachers, therefore, may wish to show how Mary's yes to God is a yes worthy of emulation. The church that says yes to God, despite the inevitable cost in cash and comfort, may find that it too, with Mary, can come to know the intimate indwelling of "the power of the Most High." Just so, such a church may, with prophetic urgency, bear into the world that holy Word that fundamentally contradicts and undermines all enslavement, the impossibly possible word of "the Son of God" (v. 35b).

A final consideration: The doctrine of the virgin birth signaled in this Lukan text (only here and in Matt. 1:18) has been much contested in the church. Tracing the "ins" and "outs" of that controversy should not be the point of preaching on this text. Whatever the preacher's opinion on this matter, it will be good to remember that the sign—that is, the doctrine of the virgin birth—is not greater than the thing signified. The thing signified is nothing less than the incarnation, which attests the true humanity and true divinity of Jesus, son of Mary and Son of God.

However, the sign should not be casually dismissed. It still may speak of mysteries the church has yet to consider fully. To that point, we remember from Genesis 2:18–23 (esp. v. 23b) that "woman" was taken "out of man." Luke's distinctive genealogy for Jesus (3:23–38) traces Jesus' lineage back from Joseph—Jesus' father "*as was thought*" (3:23b)—through Adam to God himself (3:38). May we not, then, regard Jesus, born of Mary, as the "new Adam" so compellingly spoken of by the apostle Paul (Rom. 5:12–21)? In other words, "out of woman," *the Man*, the last Adam, who has become "a life-giving spirit" (1 Cor. 15:45)!

CHARLES L. BARTOW

³⁹In those days Mary set out and went with haste to a Judean town in the hill country, ⁴⁰where she entered the house of Zechariah and greeted Elizabeth. ⁴¹When Elizabeth heard Mary's greeting, the child leaped in her womb. And Elizabeth was filled with the Holy Spirit ⁴²and exclaimed with a loud cry, "Blessed are you among women, and blessed is the fruit of your womb. ⁴³And why has this happened to me, that the mother of my Lord comes to me? ⁴⁴For as soon as I heard the sound of your greeting, the child in my womb leaped for joy. ⁴⁵And blessed is she who believed that there would be a fulfillment of what was spoken to her by the Lord."

⁴⁶And Mary said,

"My soul magnifies the Lord,
⁴⁷   and my spirit rejoices in God my Savior,
⁴⁸ for he has looked with favor on the lowliness of his servant.
          Surely, from now on all generations will call me blessed;

Theological Perspective

After a dense preface that promises "an orderly account of the events that have been fulfilled among us," Luke proceeds to embed Jesus' coming in Zechariah's fulfillment of his priestly office in the temple, a prelude to Jesus' cousin John's untimely conception in Elizabeth, Zechariah's wife, a childless woman well beyond menopause. Moreover, this family drama is framed "in the days of King Herod of Judea" (1:5), while all that follows is composed "that you may know the truth concerning the things about which you have been instructed" (1:4). We shall see that it took centuries for that "truth" to be articulated, although from the outset "Mary [had] treasured all these words and pondered them in her heart" (2:19). First, however, we turn to this text and ponder for ourselves the meaning of Mary's dramatic New Testament entrance.

Following her deferential yet courageous yes to the angel's prophetic rhetoric about the one who will be conceived in her "by the power of the Most High" (1:35), "Mary set out and went with haste to a Judean town in the hill country" (v. 39) to greet Elizabeth, her relative who "in her old age has also conceived a son" (1:36). Art and literature have found a fertile field in this story of a younger woman trekking more than a hundred kilometers to assist her older relative, while Luke exploits the encounter to showcase

Pastoral Perspective

Luke makes clear, from the outset of his narrative, that his research and reflection have led him to present an "orderly account" of the story of Jesus (1:1–3). His birth narrative, therefore, explores time and again the continuities and the discontinuities between what God has done in Jesus Christ and the history of God with the people of Israel. Luke wishes to place the story of Jesus in the continual story of God's faithfulness to Israel, while opening his audience to the expansive love of God that reaches even to the Gentiles. In Mary's visit to Elizabeth and in her song, we see two unique women representing God's covenant faithfulness to Israel and God's new thing being born in Jesus Christ. As a church there is much we can learn by standing in the tension of Elizabeth and Mary, learning from God's covenant faithfulness and using that to welcome the new thing God does among us.

The very description of Elizabeth and Mary displays the continuities and discontinuities between the two characters. In Elizabeth we have heard echoes of Sarai (Gen. 21:1–7). We are told that Elizabeth is descended from Aaron and is married to a priest (1:5–7). She is even promised a son who will carry the "spirit and power of Elijah," Israel's celebrated prophet (1:17). Elizabeth embodies God's covenant promises to Israel. Mary, by contrast, is a

⁴⁹ for the Mighty One has done great things for me,
　　and holy is his name.
⁵⁰ His mercy is for those who fear him
　　from generation to generation.
⁵¹ He has shown strength with his arm;
　　he has scattered the proud in the thoughts of their hearts.
⁵² He has brought down the powerful from their thrones,
　　and lifted up the lowly;
⁵³ he has filled the hungry with good things,
　　and sent the rich away empty.
⁵⁴ He has helped his servant Israel,
　　in remembrance of his mercy,
⁵⁵ according to the promise he made to our ancestors,
　　to Abraham and to his descendants forever."
⁵⁶And Mary remained with her about three months and then returned to her home.

Exegetical Perspective

The two sections of this reading are traditionally referred to as the visitation (vv. 39–45, 56) and the Magnificat (vv. 46–55). Only Luke includes these scenes, as is the case with the rest of the material comprising the first two chapters of his Gospel. Announcements of two extraordinary pregnancies have gone before—Luke has been "investigating carefully from the very first" (1:3)—and narratives of the respective births will follow. Here the story lines of Elizabeth and Mary intersect for the first and last time.

The Visitation. An otherwise unremarkable meeting of relatives takes a dramatic turn when the child in Elizabeth's womb leaps at the sound of Mary's voice. To paraphrase Freud, sometimes a baby kicking is just a baby kicking. Prenatal gymnastics, however, frequently carry deep meaning in the Bible (e.g., Jacob and Esau in Gen. 25:22–23; cf. Gen. 38:27–30). That this jump for joy (v. 44) is no coincidence is confirmed when the narrator ascribes the event to the agency of the Holy Spirit, which imbues not only the two expectant mothers but John the Baptist's father as well (1:15, 35, 41, 67). The Holy Spirit appears more than fifty times in Luke–Acts, more than triple the number of occurrences in the other three Gospels combined.

Homiletical Perspective

"My soul magnifies, proclaims the greatness of, the Lord," Mary replies to the blessing of her pregnant older cousin, Elizabeth. Then she is off and running in an exultation, a lyric of abundance, praising God her Savior. We are off with her as we hear her words sung again in yet another Advent in our lives. Our hearts soar with wonder as we listen to the many musical settings of the Lukan canticle named the Magnificat. Our imaginations are enlarged as we hear the divinely pregnant peasant girl from Nazareth, a poor backwater town in the shadow of the thriving Roman town of Sepphoris, proclaim the mighty work of God in turning the established order on its head in favor of the poor and marginalized. The last shall be first now, because God has looked upon the lowliest of servants with extravagant blessings of love. In fulfillment of God's promises and in response to the people's hopes and dreams, all generations will be blessed as well!

The *lyric of abundance* is a phrase borrowed from scholar Walter Brueggemann. In contrast to God's promises, the *myth of scarcity* is elemental throughout Scripture and has been pervasive in human society since ancient times. "[A] myth of scarcity will never generate 'bread for the world' but only bread for us and ours," writes Brueggemann. "The lyric of

Luke 1:39–56

Theological Perspective

the vibrant faith of these first-time mothers as each celebrates an utterly unanticipated conception: "as soon as I heard the sound of your greeting, the child in my womb leaped for joy" (v. 44). Indeed, nothing can register the signal *truth* of this account better than anticipating how God's fresh revelation will come to us in Mary's child: a person rather than a message, text, or recitation, thereby enfleshing the theological term of art, "incarnation."

Luke has Elizabeth introduce her young cousin with the honorific: "blessed is she who believed that there would be a fulfillment of what was spoken to her by the Lord" (v. 45): in a child, fulfilling a woman as little else can! The peroration Luke puts into Mary's mouth mirrors that of Hannah (1 Sam. 2:1–10), whose prayer to God "out of great anxiety and vexation" (1 Sam. 1:16) had resulted in the unanticipated conception of Samuel. In this way, Luke's "orderly account" anchors Jesus' coming in the canonical story of God's saving history of Israel, as well as in the secular chronology of Roman occupation.

Therefore this miraculous birth can hardly be relegated to mythic status, even while its resonances transcend family stories. Perhaps most telling is that Luke is careful to have it sounded by three woman—Elizabeth, Mary, and their progenitor, Hannah. For if prophets divinely sent to transform the contours of human history needed to be "born of women," they would usually burst on the scene in more spectacular masculine array. So here both Hannah and Mary speak in the forceful unrelenting language of prophecy: "My heart exults in the Lord, my strength is exalted in the Lord. My mouth derides my enemies, because I rejoice in thy salvation. . . . let not arrogance come from your mouth; for the Lord is a God of knowledge" (1 Sam. 2:1, 3 RSV). "My soul magnifies the Lord, and my spirit rejoices in God my Savior, . . . for the Mighty One has done great things for me, and holy is his name. . . . He has brought down the powerful from their thrones, and lifted up the lowly" (vv. 46, 49, 52).

All this had to be too much for two modest women, each nurturing a precious gift of life, so Luke crowns their encounter with the down-to-earth reminder: "Mary remained with her about three months and then returned to her home" (v. 56). She returned to be mother, of course, although it took the ensuing community of believers three centuries to elaborate the words Mary had pondered in her heart into an arresting "divine motherhood," in the Third Ecumenical Council of the early Christian

Pastoral Perspective

young girl. She is not even married, yet the angel Gabriel promises her that she will birth the incarnate Son of God into the world (1:27, 31–33). There remains the continuity of God bringing about life in impossible circumstances. In Mary's story, life comes through a young, virgin girl; in Elizabeth's story, new life comes through an older, barren woman. While consistent with God's work in the past, we experience God's new work.

The encounter of Mary and Elizabeth brings together the past and future of God and points the church to a faithful way of relating across generational divides. First, Mary goes to visit Elizabeth after learning about her pregnancy. We are not told the reasons for Mary's visit, but we know she goes with haste (v. 39). Luke then lets us in on the exchange between the older matriarch and the young faithful girl. We might expect Elizabeth to see herself as a mentor to the young girl, possibly offering her words of advice or encouragement. Instead, we have a declaration of blessing. Elizabeth is filled with the Holy Spirit and cries out in celebration of God's new creation, which Mary will bring into the world.

Immediately after Elizabeth finishes her declaration, it is as though Mary's lips are unlocked and she bursts into song, celebrating God's new work by singing a remix of the classic Song of Hannah (1 Sam. 2:1–10). Mary begins to prophesy a new world shaped by the faith she has known in her tradition. She begins in praise of God's faithfulness to her (vv. 47–50) and then speaks of a world shaped after God's intentions (vv. 51–53). To us, this looks like a world turned upside down, but Mary has the eyes of faith to see that this great reversal is actually the power of God to turn the world right side up.[1] This right-side-up world, however, remains continuous with the faithfulness of God to Abraham and his descendants (vv. 54–55).

This shared celebration between Elizabeth and Mary can show those of us who struggle in communities of faith each day how to learn to celebrate the continuities and discontinuities of our experience, and to learn from, equip, and inspire each other. Generational theorists Neil Howe and William Strauss have suggested in their studies of American society that how one generation relates to the subsequent generation often dictates the prosperity or demise of the people as a whole.[2] A generation that clings to power and seeks to preserve its own

---

1. William H. Willimon, *Why Jesus?* (Nashville: Abingdon Press, 2010), 61.
2. William Strauss and Neil Howe, *Generations: The History of America's Future, 1584–2069* (Minneapolis: Quill House Publishers, 1992).

Elizabeth greets Mary in terms that echo the praises given to women of heroic faith and courage in the Hebrew Bible, such as Jael and Judith (Judg. 5:24–27; Jdt. 13:18–20). Unlike these earlier Jewish heroines, however, Mary neither uses sex appeal to overcome Israel's enemies nor inflicts gruesome bodily harm on them. Her exclamation (KJV "Blessed art thou among women, and blessed is the fruit of thy womb") will in later centuries constitute part of the Ave Maria prayer, which also draws language from the annunciation (1:28: "Hail [Mary], full of grace, the Lord is with thee"). Elizabeth becomes the first of many generations of believers to call her "blessed" (see 1:48). Even more auspicious is her address to Mary as "mother of my Lord." Christian readers are so accustomed to calling Jesus "Lord" that the audacity of this statement may at first elude them. Among first-century Jews generally, as well as in Luke's Gospel, God is "Lord" (1:6, 9, 11, 15–17, 25, 28, 32, 38, 46, 58, 68). Luke may not have Elizabeth articulate the doctrine of the Trinity, but the use of a divine title for Jesus under the influence of the Holy Spirit is striking, to say the least. He gestures in the same direction by having Mary and other characters refer to God as well as Jesus as "Savior" (1:47; 2:11, 30; Acts 5:31; 13:23).

The Magnificat. Of the four Gospels, Luke is certainly the most musical. In addition to Mary's canticle in verses 46–55, the Benedictus (1:67–79), the Gloria in Excelsis (2:13–14), and the Nunc Dimittis (2:28–32) are usually regarded as hymns. The Magnificat has had a place in the liturgy of the Western church since the sixth century. Monteverdi, Bach, Purcell, Vivaldi, Telemann, Mozart, and Schubert have set the text to music, to name only a few. Its traditional title comes from the first word of the Vulgate translation (*Magnificat anima mea Dominum,* "My soul magnifies the Lord"). In terms of its content and its poetic structure, including synonymous and antithetical parallelism, it resembles many of the psalms of praise attributed to David (e.g., Pss. 33, 104, 113, 117, 136).

Although a few Latin manuscripts attribute the song to Elizabeth, most scholars believe that Luke intends to portray Mary as the speaker. The first half of the hymn (vv. 46–50) focuses on the marvelous work God has done for Mary, and the second half (vv. 51–55) broadens the horizon across time and space. Following the conventions of Greek and Roman historians, Luke uses speeches to summarize events, foreshadow plot developments, round out

abundance asserts that in the hand of the generative, generous God, scarcity is not true."[1]

Mary's Magnificat bears witness to the *lyric of abundance* that is prevalent throughout the Hebrew Scriptures. The Israelites experience it in their wilderness journey to the promised land. It is proclaimed in the voices of prophets and psalmists. The people of God are tempted time and again to live by *the myth of scarcity* and must hear anew God's *lyric of abundance.*

New Testament scholar Raymond Brown hypothesized that all the Lukan canticles had their genesis in the songs and hymns of a first-century Jewish Christian community that staked its life on God's lyric of abundance. Its members were known as the Anawim or "the Poor Ones." While this group may have been physically poor, the name came to be associated with "those who could not trust their own strength, but had to rely in utter confidence upon God."[2] Living in stark contrast to the Anawim were not merely the rich but those who showed no need for God through pride and self-sufficiency. In postexilic times, the Anawim thought of themselves as a pure remnant of Israel that held true to God through prayer and sacrifice.

Brown speculates that Luke might have seen Mary as "the idealized representative of the Anawim who constituted the remnant of Israel."[2] Mary proclaims in the annunciation (1:38) that she is willing to rely utterly on God. Elizabeth blesses her for her faithfulness, saying, "And blessed is she who believed that there would be a fulfillment of what was spoken to her by the Lord" (v. 45). Mary's faithful trust in God alone brings her to sing the lyric of God's abundant justice and the fulfillment of God's promises. As so many have noted, Mary is the first disciple of the gospel Jesus will proclaim through his life, death, and resurrection. (Like mother, like son?) Her discipleship empowers her to magnify the good news, the gospel, of God's abundance.

Each Advent we hear the story of these willing women, for Elizabeth too follows her own call to live in utter reliance on God. We sing their stories in carol and anthem and portray them in pageant. They are so lovingly familiar that their power can be missed if we expect them merely to serve our nostalgic grasping for "the meaning of Christmas."

1. Walter Brueggemann, *The Covenanted Self: Exploration of Law and Covenant* (Minneapolis: Fortress Press, 1999), Kindle Edition, Loc. 1776.
2. Raymond E. Brown, *The Birth of the Messiah: A Commentary on the Infancy Narratives in the Gospels of Matthew and Luke,* Anchor Bible Reference Library (New York: Doubleday, 1993), 351.
3. Brown, *Birth,* 353n45.

Luke 1:39–56

Theological Perspective

Church that was held in 431 CE at the Church of Mary in Ephesus in Asia Minor. Called amid a dispute over the teachings of Nestorius, patriarch of Constantinople, which emphasized the disunity between Christ's human and divine natures, the council effectively condemned his teachings when it declared Mary to be "Mother of God" (*Theotokos* [God-bearer]). By conferring so arresting a title on Mary, Ephesus anticipated Chalcedon's articulation of Jesus as the *person* of the very Word of God, albeit "in two natures," twenty years later in 451 CE.

All of this gives us something to ponder: how various and sometimes conflicting assertions of the Christian Scriptures can leave the community of believers with both assurance and queries, not to say dilemmas of interpretation. Yet interpretation demands reflection, often requiring recourse to skills even beyond the language of Luke's "orderly account," in order that we "may know the truth concerning the things about which [we] have been instructed" (1:4).

Interpretation of Scripture requires the guidance of a community as it attempts to be faithful to that same Scripture, using the resources of human reflection and prayer to unravel what had been conveyed by a narrative that turns out to have been more subtle than we first thought. If we do not allow ourselves to be baffled by a sometimes dramatic shift in genre—from story to an array of technical terms—we will find Nestorius and others to have been vitally engaged in trying to confront the very person of Jesus, and so probe the distinctive revelation of the God of Israel in this human/divine person. Yet as we have seen, those unfathomable depths had already been anticipated in the language of Luke 1:39–56, although the prophetic language of this initial chapter can at best intimate the way God will now carry out the promised redeeming action.

DAVID B. BURRELL

Pastoral Perspective

well-being at the cost of the young creates a crisis for the future. The young who refuse to listen to those who have walked before them can become isolated and reactive wanderers with no center point to their lives because of their mistrust and rejection of traditions and institutions.

In Elizabeth's praise of Mary, the church can see a new way to cross generational boundaries. Elizabeth, the representative of all that should be celebrated about the tradition of God in the community, sings praises to the young girl who is bearing God's purposes into the world. This song of praise appears to open the mouth of the young girl to proclaim prophetically and with confidence this new world God is bringing about. Without her encounter and encouragement from Elizabeth, Mary might not have possessed the confidence to envision God's new creation. Mary does not, however, describe a future totally foreign to Elizabeth's understanding of God's will, but a world formed by the revelation of God to that faith community.

Elizabeth has something to teach those in the church who have lived out the tradition faithfully, who would say they have encountered the living Lord in it. She shows us that those in positions of elder wisdom can celebrate the gifts of the young and encourage their prophetic witness to God's work in the world, instead of recoiling in fear and defensiveness when a new generation sees God's will at work in new ways. Mary has something to teach the young in the church: that they are inheritors of a story that they should learn to love and value, rather than reject and abandon. When they see God working in a new and expansive way, they should seek to proclaim that message in continuity with the faithfulness God has shown to the church throughout its history. It is only together, Elizabeth with Mary, that the past and the future come together in the present as prophetic witness. May this be so in each of our communities of faith, by the presence and power of the Holy Spirit.

ANDREW CLARK WHALEY

Exegetical Perspective

major characters in the narrative, reiterate important themes, and interpret key episodes. Mary's ebullient praise contrasts with the initial lack of belief on the part of Zechariah (1:18–20), and in the process she becomes Jesus' first disciple. (Luke, tellingly, does not record Jesus' hard saying relativizing the importance of family ties found in Mark 3:31–35. See the softer version in Luke 8:19–21.)

The final lines feature a motif that recurs throughout Luke–Acts: God's help for "his servant Israel . . . according to the promise he made to our ancestors, to Abraham and to his descendants forever" (vv. 54–55). Mary recognizes that she has entered the unfolding story of God's fidelity to Abraham and his seed (1:72–73; 3:8; 19:9; Acts 3:25; 7:2). In Luke's narrative, the covenant promises made to Abraham (Gen. 12:1–3; 17:7; 22:17) are kept in unanticipated—indeed, unprecedented—ways. It was hardly self-evident that the death and resurrection of Jesus, along with the gift of the Holy Spirit, might represent the means by which God would fulfill the ancient pledge to Israel. Yet that is precisely what Luke emphasizes through his characters' speeches (Luke 24:49; Acts 1:4; 2:33, 39; 7:17; 13:23, 32; 26:6).

Notwithstanding the surprising nature of God's dealings with Israel as they are characterized in the Magnificat, Mary's hymn contains elements of continuity with the Hebrew Scriptures. Similarities to Hannah's prayer of thanksgiving in 1 Samuel 2:1–10, after the birth of her son Samuel, are especially noteworthy. Both women speak of great reversals brought about by God: the proud will be humbled; the lowly will be lifted up; the hungry will be filled; the rich will be sent away empty. (Perhaps the inspiration for the "woes" proclaimed by Jesus in Luke 6:24–26 came from his mother.) Both women celebrate God's holiness, strength, and mercy.

Finally, Hannah's song concludes with an allusion to the Messiah ("the LORD will . . . exalt the power of his anointed," 1 Sam. 2:10). Although explicitly messianic language is absent from the Magnificat, Gabriel has just informed Mary that her son will inherit "the throne of his ancestor David" (1:32) and the Holy Spirit will move Zechariah to praise God for raising up a savior "in the house of his servant David" (1:69). The scene is thus set for the angel to identify Jesus as the Messiah when he is born in Bethlehem, the city of David (2:4–5, 11).

PATRICK GRAY

Homiletical Perspective

How might we hear their story and experience the familiar strains of the Magnificat through the lyric of abundance? How might the testimony of the Anawim open our hearts in surprising ways when our twenty-first-century congregations are consumed more than ever in the myth of scarcity?

The *lyric of abundance* that Mary sings and that her son will bring in story, healing, and love is not just pious, religious sentiment. It is a message encompassing politics, ethics, social structures, and economics. The majority of first-world people need to be compassionately reminded of the effect of their affluence on the Anawim of the world. They need the liberation of the Anawim celebrated in Mary's song, a liberation that frees them from their reliance on money and possessions and for a life of complete trust in God. Likewise, the witness of the poor in developing nations and in the first world to God's wide abundance needs to be compassionately affirmed, for they have a witness to offer to the world of liberation and justice.

The question for all is "Can God be enough? Be the Source of Being?" Can utter reliance on God empower the rich to relax their death grip on goods long enough to see what *is* enough? Can utter reliance teach a lyric of abundance that leads the rich to listen with compassion rather than with pity to the poor, and so respond with generosity? Can utter reliance on God empower the poor and marginalized to speak the truth of God's abundance with compassion, dignity, and strength? Their testimony is imperative to the spiritual liberation of all who seek to be disciples of Jesus. As followers who anticipate and celebrate his birth each year, we have a mandate to listen for the *lyric of abundance* in Mary's song and to put all of our trust in God. How else can our souls magnify the Lord? For God has done, is doing, and will continue to do great things—with and without our help. Why miss out on the joy of trusting God's abundance for all?

JANE ANNE FERGUSON

Luke 1:57–80

⁵⁷Now the time came for Elizabeth to give birth, and she bore a son. ⁵⁸Her neighbors and relatives heard that the Lord had shown his great mercy to her, and they rejoiced with her.

⁵⁹On the eighth day they came to circumcise the child, and they were going to name him Zechariah after his father. ⁶⁰But his mother said, "No; he is to be called John." ⁶¹They said to her, "None of your relatives has this name." ⁶²Then they began motioning to his father to find out what name he wanted to give him. ⁶³He asked for a writing tablet and wrote, "His name is John." And all of them were amazed. ⁶⁴Immediately his mouth was opened and his tongue freed, and he began to speak, praising God. ⁶⁵Fear came over all their neighbors, and all these things were talked about throughout the entire hill country of Judea. ⁶⁶All who heard them pondered them and said, "What then will this child become?" For, indeed, the hand of the Lord was with him.

⁶⁷Then his father Zechariah was filled with the Holy Spirit and spoke this prophecy:

⁶⁸ "Blessed be the Lord God of Israel,
   for he has looked favorably on his people and redeemed them.
⁶⁹ He has raised up a mighty savior for us
   in the house of his servant David,

Theological Perspective

Concerned that his "orderly account of the events that have been fulfilled among us" lead us to "know the truth concerning the things about which [we] have been instructed" (1:4), Luke returns to Zechariah as "the time came for Elizabeth to give birth, and she bore a son" (v. 57). Surrounded by family who "rejoiced with her," realizing "the Lord had shown his great mercy to her," the time came for their son to be circumcised. While "they were going to name him Zechariah after his father, his mother said, 'No, he is to be called John.'"

In Luke's story, women keep taking the initiative from the outset! Indeed, it was not until his mute father confirmed Elizabeth's choice by writing "his name is John" that "his mouth was opened and his tongue freed, and he began to speak, praising God" (v. 64). Luke fills the atmosphere with awe in the face of the efficacious divine presence and in "all these things [that] were talked about throughout the entire hill country of Judea" (v. 65). So far beyond the extended family, everyone who heard these things "pondered them and said: 'What then will this child become?' For, indeed, the hand of the Lord was with him" (v. 66).

Luke then fills Zechariah's praise of God with prophetic content, beginning in a canonical mode: "Blessed be the Lord God of Israel, for he has looked

Pastoral Perspective

John the Baptist is the ultimate preacher's kid. His father is a priest, and his mother is the daughter of a priest. They are an older, barren couple who conceive a child in their old age, causing all the neighbors to jokingly refer to them as Abraham and Sarah. Even his name displays his chosenness: John, meaning "YHWH has given grace."[1] The reader wonders if Zechariah, the aging father whose lips were opened upon the naming of his son, committed his song of praise to heart, often rocking his son to sleep with the song, "And you, child, will be called the prophet of the Most High" (v. 76a). There is much in this passage for the people of God to consider when it comes to divine appointment, parental expectations, and individuals working out their own identity and vocation.

"God has big plans for you," we say to the high school senior on Graduate Sunday. Without being a reflection on any angelic proclamations regarding our young people, our remarks seek to affirm that God is going to honor the life of this adolescent who is moving on into young adulthood. Frequently we use this cliché because a young person bears particular gifts, and we wish the best for their educational, marital, and economic success. These "big plans" we

1. Raymond Brown, *The Birth of the Messiah* (New York: Doubleday, 1993), 261.

^{70} as he spoke through the mouth of his holy prophets from of old,
^{71} that we would be saved from our enemies and from the hand of all who
hate us.
^{72} Thus he has shown the mercy promised to our ancestors,
and has remembered his holy covenant,
^{73} the oath that he swore to our ancestor Abraham,
to grant us ^{74}that we, being rescued from the hands of our enemies,
might serve him without fear, ^{75}in holiness and righteousness
before him all our days.
^{76} And you, child, will be called the prophet of the Most High;
for you will go before the Lord to prepare his ways,
^{77} to give knowledge of salvation to his people
by the forgiveness of their sins.
^{78} By the tender mercy of our God,
the dawn from on high will break upon us,
^{79} to give light to those who sit in darkness and in the shadow of death,
to guide our feet into the way of peace."
^{80}The child grew and became strong in spirit, and he was in the wilderness until the day he appeared publicly to Israel.

Exegetical Perspective

Their paths briefly cross *in utero* when Mary visits Elizabeth (1:39–45), and now the stories of Jesus and John the Baptist resume their separate but parallel courses. In the first half of this text, Luke relates the events surrounding the birth, circumcision, and naming of John (vv. 57–67). The second half consists of Zechariah's canticle of thanksgiving (vv. 68–79), the Benedictus, which takes its traditional title from the first word of the Latin translation.

The Birth of John the Baptist. As will be the case with his cousin's birth in a manger, little fanfare accompanies the actual birth of John the Baptist; only now do Elizabeth's relatives even learn that she was pregnant (vv. 57–58). She had remained in seclusion for five months (v. 24), and Zechariah was presumably in no position to share the happy news, having been rendered mute as a result of his disbelief when informed by an angel that his aged wife would bear a child (vv. 18–20). Luke is the only evangelist to include this story, but the Qur'an (suras 3 and 19) includes a version in which Zechariah prays for a son. All trace of doubt is conspicuously absent in the Muslim retelling, where Zechariah's status as a prophet (cf. Luke 1:67) is more heavily emphasized than his priestly office.

Homiletical Perspective

Through the corridors of the hospital, day or night, little chimes ring out, the first lilting, gentle phrase of the Brahms *Lullaby*: *Lullaby and good night . . .* A baby is born. Staff and patients take note, even if subconsciously. New life happens in the midst of a place where life struggles with death and is not always triumphant. A baby is born. Chimes ring out. A sign to patients and staff alike that there is always hope for transformation and new life, even in the midst of the darkest struggles.

After years of barrenness, Elizabeth is surprisingly pregnant. In her old age she gives birth to a son. This miraculous birth evokes memories of the birth of Isaac to the patriarch and matriarch of God's people, Abraham and Sarah, a birth promised by God. God is at work in history, bringing salvation to God's people. An angel announces the pregnancy to her husband, Zechariah, proclaiming that the child will be the prophet of the Messiah, the one who "will go before the Lord to prepare God's ways" (v. 76). The pregnancy, its announcement, and the baby's birth are signs to the Judean people that God's transforming power is working to transform the world. The story is a sign to those who read it centuries later, prompting us to ponder signs of God's transforming power in our times.

Zechariah's song of praise and blessing, the Benedictus, extols the salvation of God. Although

Theological Perspective

favorably on his people and redeemed them" (v. 68). The themes orchestrated are unsurprising: Israel will be "saved from our enemies and . . . all who hate us," as God remembers "his holy covenant, the oath that he swore to our ancestor Abraham," that we "might serve him without fear, in holiness and righteousness . . . all our days" (vv. 71, 72b, 73a, 74b, 75). What is fresh in this paean of praise, however, is the way it picks up the awe-laden atmosphere of this circumcision celebration: "He has raised up a mighty savior for us in the house of his servant David. . . . You, child, will be called the prophet of the Most High; for you will go before the Lord to prepare his ways" (vv. 69, 76). God's saving action will take place in and through the actions of this child, as the Scriptures have announced before at crucial turning points in the course of Israel's history with God. Yet God acts not in feats of victory, after the manner of the child's ancestor David, but this time by giving "knowledge of salvation to his people by the forgiveness of their sins" (v. 77).

Moreover, the implication grows that the sinfulness peculiar to Israel lies in their attachment to victory over others by power and might, whereas this child's legacy portends something starkly different: "By the tender mercy of our God, the dawn from on high will break upon us, to give light to those who sit in darkness and in the shadow of death, to guide our feet into the way of peace" (vv. 78–79). This radical shift in prophetic tone turns on the point of "being rescued from the hands of our enemies [to] serve [God] without fear, in holiness and righteousness" (vv. 74–75). The messianic time has truly come upon us, for nothing short of fear of the Lord ever succeeded in weaning Israel from idolatry to serve their God. Should such a radical change occur, the people will not be able to claim it for themselves, sitting as they do "in darkness and in the shadow of death." Everything will turn, it seems, on this child whom Luke tells us "grew and became strong in spirit, and was in the wilderness until the day he appeared publicly to Israel" (v. 80).

At this point the narrative shifts to world history by way of a decree issued by "the emperor Augustus," preparing us to recognize how Zechariah's prophecy, though focusing on his son John, immediately points beyond him to another. This might well be Luke's structural way of insinuating how John's announcing "knowledge of salvation" by forgiveness of sins will allow him to "go before the Lord to prepare his ways" (vv. 77a, 76b). Not that the narrative will directly identify the one immediately to be introduced with

Pastoral Perspective

hope God has are often equated with going to a top college, or landing the top job, or finding the right spouse.

For John, however, when his parents declare that "God has big plans for you," this does not mean that he will graduate first in his class from medical school or one day become the president of a bank. The call of John is to be a prophetic witness to the coming Messiah. What if our well-wishes to our adolescents shared that same perspective? Then our act of well-wishing would affirm God's continued involvement in the young person's life after he or she no longer lives under a parents' roof and is no longer a weekly participant in our community of faith. This is an affirmation that this person should continue to remain a witness to the Lord, regardless of educational attainment, relational status, or economic success. As we will see with John in a haunting fashion later in the Gospel, the "big plans" God has do not always lead to worldly success (9:7–9). They do, however, move us toward bearing witness to the kingdom of God that is breaking into the world.

Within that divine plan for the creation we have parental expectations. Did John ever toy with following in his father's and grandfather's footsteps? Obviously the priesthood was held in high esteem in his home. There must have been great holy day celebrations and weekly Sabbath observance. Maybe the story of John's miraculous birth would be told each year before he could blow out the candles on his cake, Dad's eyes tearing up as he rose and warbled through his song again. John does not end up a third-generation priest. With that kind of piety and prophetic pressure all around, it does not seem surprising that John would rebel, leaving for the wilderness, growing out his hair, and eating locusts and wild honey.

Just as there is divine involvement in all of life, we are each challenged to wrestle with parental pressures and expectations. Even if we have not studied family-systems theory and outlined our genograms, we can see patterns in our family lives, remember voices of praise and criticism, and feel the pressure to fulfill the unfulfilled expectations of our parents. Some people accept the mantle laid on them unquestioningly. Others run as far in the other direction as possible. Interestingly, John fulfills the song of his father, but he may not live it out in the way his family has intended. John indeed "will go before the Lord to prepare his ways" (v. 76).

There is something here, then, for those who struggle with family expectations. How do we hear

Gabriel's prediction in Luke 1:14 proves true when the friends and family rejoice at the birth. They celebrate the "great mercy" shown to Elizabeth in her barren state, thereby confirming Mary's declaration about those who fear the Lord (1:50). Because they are righteous, law-abiding Jews, the elderly couple bring the child to be circumcised. This minor detail serves an important function in Luke–Acts. According to Genesis 17:9–14, circumcision was instituted as a sign of the eternal covenant between God and Abraham. Even as virtually every other identity marker came to be debated among the Jews of antiquity, circumcision remained nonnegotiable.

The requirement of circumcision becomes a point of contention in Acts as Peter, Paul, and other missionaries spread the Christian message among the Gentiles, eventually leading to a pivotal meeting in Jerusalem devoted to the subject. Because it is one of Luke's objectives to demonstrate that the messianic faith is in continuity with Israelite tradition and not a radical departure, it is important to show that it begins with pious Jews.

Circumcision on the eighth day was the standard practice in ancient Israel (Lev. 12:3). Normally the child would have already been named by this time. Elizabeth gives no reason for choosing the name John, leaving the reader to wonder whether the subsequent agreement with Zechariah is presented by Luke as a miraculous sign or as an indication of some prior communication between husband and wife. The amazement of the bystanders suggests the former. Yet another of Gabriel's prophecies (1:20) thus comes to fulfillment with the loosing of Zechariah's tongue. "John" is a diminutive of a common male name among Jews of the Second Temple period, meaning "God has been gracious" (1 Chr. 26:3; Ezra 10:6).

No special meaning is attached to the name here, unlike the comment at Matthew 1:23 on the significance of Jesus' name. (The narrative does not call attention to it, but Elizabeth means "oath of God" and Zechariah means "the Lord remembers," echoing themes that appear in Zechariah's canticle in Luke 1:73–74.)

The Benedictus. Nine months of silence have made no small impact on Zechariah. His hymn provides an answer to the question posed in 1:66 by those who hear about the events surrounding the birth and naming: "What then will this child become?" Prompted by the Holy Spirit—as is Elizabeth before him (1:41–42), Simeon after (2:27–32), and so many

written in Greek, the song echoes themes of Hebrew salvation history that are in keeping with the song's possible origin in a first-century Jewish Christian community. As with Mary's Magnificat, Zechariah's song was quite likely a pre-Lukan text written in a community of Jewish Christian Anawim. The Anawim or "Poor Ones" practiced complete reliance upon God, no matter their economic status.[1]

Both songs can stand on their own, independent of the characters who sing them in Luke. However, Luke chose to put these texts in the mouths of characters who are literary signposts, pointing readers of the text to what utter reliance on God looks like. Mary becomes God's handmaid, willing to serve God with her whole being. Zechariah learns through his trial by silence to rely on God's surprising ways. What if twenty-first-century people of faith began to practice complete reliance on God? Not reliance on the "right" stock market figures, or on the "right" governmental policies, or even on the "right" faith community, but on God. Moreover, what does a life lived in complete reliance on God have to do with salvation?

The Hebrew word for salvation had roots in the Hebrew words for "broadening" and "expanding." Salvation was deliverance from an oppressed place, regime, or state of being into the broad safety net of freedom and right relationship, particularly with God. Salvation reordered the political, physical, and spiritual dimensions of Hebrew theology and culture. The Hebrew people remembered God's liberating salvation each year at Passover. During political exile, the prophets continually proclaimed God's salvation. Under Rome's oppression, psalms of salvation were sung in weekly synagogue services as sustenance.

Salvation in our times can easily be relegated to personal piety and purity. It is good to be in right relationship with God, to be saved from the numerous ways we separate ourselves from God's love. However, is personal salvation what Zechariah proclaims? He sings of God's salvation moving through community, transforming its very being in the world into a broad safety net of freedom. In Zechariah's song, salvation is a personal call to individuals only as they are involved in the transformation of God's community. The call is to follow as God "guides our feet into the way of peace," making us vessels of "light to those who sit in darkness and in the shadow

1. Raymond E. Brown, *The Birth of the Messiah: A Commentary on the Infancy Narratives in the Gospels of Matthew and Luke,* Anchor Bible Reference Library (New York: Doubleday, 1993), 351.

Luke 1:57–80

Theological Perspective

"the Lord," the God of Israel; yet Luke's Gospel will culminate in affirming something very close to that, confirming it with the following book of Acts. This early chapter, however, remains prophetic in tone, heightening the suspense and expectation that introduced it.

The most promising clue to the meaning of this singular prophet lies in the concluding words: he will "guide our feet into the way of peace," preparing to do so by a prolonged sojourn in "the wilderness," where Israel wandered for forty years under the guidance of Moses. That clue can only heighten the suspense, suggesting the promise of Deuteronomy 18:15: "The LORD your God will raise up for you a prophet like me from among your own people." Luke masterfully suspends us on words spoken to the people Israel on the cusp of the "coming of the Lord," words heard by us who have the benefit of his extended narrative, to identify what is really taking place.

All of this is structured as carefully as it is so that we might be brought to "know the truth concerning the things about which [we] have been instructed" (1:4). Unfortunately, over the course of human history, our knowing of that truth seems hardly to have been sufficient to "guide our feet into the way of peace." Hence, the promise remains promise, falsifying any triumphal reading of these prophetic statements. That sober reflection reminds us of a dimension of evangelical revelation often eclipsed in the West: how revelation points ineluctably and inescapably toward a fulfillment beyond our accomplishments. For like Israel, we remain "in darkness and in the shadow of death" (v. 79a), despite the fact that, as children of God nourished by the body and blood of Christ, we have been rescued from the hand of our enemy that is death, that we might serve him without fear, in holiness and righteousness all our days.

DAVID B. BURRELL

Pastoral Perspective

the expectations of loved ones for our lives not as manipulation but as a deep longing that we might discover our truest selves? At the same time, how do we step back to differentiate our own identity? How do we remain connected without being enmeshed?

Finally, there is great rejoicing over the birth of John. We hear of amazement; news of the naming spreads throughout Judea; and the question is raised, "What then will this child become?" Immediately we are told that John ventures into the wilderness. When we meet him again, he is a grizzled ascetic preaching of the wrath of God to come. What happens to John out there? We cannot know. We can only know that John accepts, in his unique way, the "plans" God has for him. In this sense, he fulfills the expectations his parents lay on him, even as he continues to wrestle with the particularity of his own vocation.

When we consider our vocation in the church, we can learn from the family ties of Elizabeth, Zechariah, and John. We see that "God has big plans for us," but this may not relate directly to what kind of house we buy or what kind of job we work in day to day. It may instead have to do with a deeper message our lives are called to proclaim, a message that some will embrace and others will oppose. Our vocation is also necessarily wrapped up in the relationships of the people who have nurtured and cared for us. Even with the baggage they pass on, there can be wisdom mined from a shared love and affection. Finally, each of us is to work out our unique vocation, wrestling with God for a blessing. We may end up living out the expectations placed upon us, but not in the manner expected of us. Our vocation as followers of the Lord will not be a path of success and luxury, but one of continual crying out in the wildernesses, a life given to guide others into the way of peace.

ANDREW CLARK WHALEY

other figures in Luke–Acts—Zechariah praises God for the marvelous deeds he is about to perform for Israel (vv. 68–75) before addressing his newborn son (vv. 76–79).

The first eight verses of the hymn comprise a single sentence in the Greek, replete with scriptural language and imagery. God has raised up a Savior (literally, "horn of salvation") from the line of David "as he spoke through the mouth of his holy prophets from of old" (v. 70). After the resurrection, Jesus will have to make these connections clear for the disciples (24:27, 44–47). Although the specter of Roman domination hangs over the narrative, it is not clear that God's redemption of Israel from her "enemies" (vv. 71, 74) is envisioned in purely political terms. The prophetess Anna in the temple will likewise speak of the redemption these events anticipate (2:38).

The text does not specify precisely what form this redemption will take, but Zechariah is emphatic that God "has remembered his holy covenant, the oath sworn to our ancestor Abraham" (vv. 72b, 73a), referring to the promises made to the patriarchs in the law and the prophets (Gen. 22:16–17; Jer. 11:5; Mic. 7:20). John, as the last in the long line of prophets preparing for the coming of the Messiah (16:16), is also the subject of Old Testament prophecies that he will apply to himself in Luke 3:4 (Isa. 40:1–3; Mal. 3:1). Whereas he is "prophet of the Most High" (v. 76), Jesus will be called "Son of the Most High" (1:32). He will announce the salvation made possible by the Messiah "by the forgiveness of sins," which is the very purpose of the repentance he demands of those who come to hear him preach in the wilderness.

Luke shifts the spotlight back to Zechariah's son at the conclusion of his song, if only briefly, before turning his attention to Jesus in chapter 2. According to a legend related in the second-century *Protevangelium of James*, Zechariah dies a martyr when he resists the efforts of Herod to find his son and preempt the advent of the prophesied Messiah. Medieval devotional works known as the Pseudo-Bonaventura include stories of the cousins meeting as infants after Joseph, Mary, and Jesus return from Egypt. No such meeting occurs in the Gospel for about thirty years—the amount of time that transpires in 1:80—when Jesus comes to be baptized by John in the Jordan (3:21).

PATRICK GRAY

of death" (v. 79). This challenges contemporary notions of personal salvation. God calls us to salvation as we physically, politically, and economically show forth God's justice and love in our relationships with family, society, and the natural world.

Zechariah's song reinforces God's historic salvation story, revealing salvation to ordinary, faithful, and in many cases poor, people and calling them to prophesy. It foreshadows the call of the shepherds to proclaim and witness to the Messiah's birth. Utterly relying on God, Elizabeth and Zechariah proclaimed that God was on the move. No longer would the future be hopeless and barren for God's people.

Where do we see God on the move in our times, calling us out of hopeless, barren futures and into the proclamation of God's salvation? What surprising sign of deliverance from an oppressed place or regime or state of being do we see in the world today? Who are the ordinary and faithful people being transformed and called to prophesy? What will happen in the world when these ordinary people in their utter reliance on God begin to prophesy about God's works of salvation? Could we *all* be called to prophesy, once we follow the surprising signs of God's movement in our midst?

In the fourth century a Syrian deacon named Ephrem wrote, "Though the Lord has established the signs of coming, the time of their fulfillment has not been plainly revealed. These signs have come and gone with a multiplicity of change; more than that, they are still present. The final coming is like the first."[2] The signs of God's salvation are as extraordinary and ordinary as the birth of a baby to grateful parents. The miracle is that God never gives up sending salvation's signs because God never gives up on us. The signs of God's salvation come again and again, like chimes that ring out the proclamation of new life amid the death in hospital corridors. Ordinary people still hear surprising songs of God's transforming work of salvation. They still sing, shout, and whisper prophetically of God's guidance to ways of peace. The question is, "Are we listening?"

JANE ANNE FERGUSON

2. Thomas J. O'Gorman, ed., *An Advent Sourcebook* (Chicago: Archdiocese of Chicago, Liturgy Training Publications, 1988), 24.

Luke 2:1–7

¹In those days a decree went out from Emperor Augustus that all the world should be registered. ²This was the first registration and was taken while Quirinius was governor of Syria. ³All went to their own towns to be registered. ⁴Joseph also went from the town of Nazareth in Galilee to Judea, to the city of David called Bethlehem, because he was descended from the house and family of David. ⁵He went to be registered with Mary, to whom he was engaged and who was expecting a child. ⁶While they were there, the time came for her to deliver her child. ⁷And she gave birth to her firstborn son and wrapped him in bands of cloth, and laid him in a manger, because there was no place for them in the inn.

Theological Perspective

John's coming was set "in the days of King Herod of Judea," with Mary trekking from Nazareth to be with her cousin for the unexpected event, while Jesus would arrive in the wake of "a decree [that] went out from Emperor Augustus that all the world should be registered" (v. 1). So "Joseph also went from the town of Nazareth in Galilee to Judea, to the city of David called Bethlehem, because he was descended from the house and family of David. He went to be registered with Mary, to whom he was engaged and who was expecting a child" (vv. 4–5). The domestic scene was at once upset and framed by imperial decree, which must have seemed to them so utterly irrelevant to the impending event.

Yet what is or is not relevant in such cases? Who is to know? Luke seems to be playing on this fact, indeed accentuating it by minimal identifying clues. Moreover, given the apparent press of people displaced by so high-handed an imperial decree, "there was no place for them in the inn" (v. 7). Therefore, when "the time came, . . . she gave birth to her first-born son and wrapped him in bands of cloth, and laid him in a manger" (2:6–7). Was this Luke's way of portraying what Jesus would insist (in Matthew), that the Son of Man would have no place to lay his head (Matt. 8:20)?

Pastoral Perspective

On its own, this birth narrative of Jesus appears incredibly ordinary. After the angelic appearances and prophetic singing that guide the story to this point, the climactic moment of the narrative occurs without trumpet fanfare, additional musical numbers, or heavenly choirs. Luke presents the story in a matter-of-fact way, each line moving the story along to the birth of the child. In a time when we are encouraged to promote our own cause, make a name for ourselves, and push our personal agendas into the public spotlight, Luke's story of Jesus' birth reminds us that there are times when the quiet, faithful action that occurs outside the spotlight is the most faithful way to bring about the kingdom of God.

We live in a society dominated by those who seek our attention. Advertisers work constantly to entice us with new cars, new retirement plans, new energy drinks, and new pills that can solve all our medical problems. Sports events intended to bring communities together and showcase athletic talent are presented to us as issues of life and death, and we base our joy on the success of our teams. In the twenty-four-hour news culture striving for our viewership, how often do we hear anchors declaring that this election or congressional vote is "the most important decision of our times"?

Feasting on the Gospels

Exegetical Perspective

The nativity of Jesus is recounted by Luke with striking simplicity: "And she gave birth to her firstborn son and wrapped him in bands of cloth, and laid him in a manger, because there was no place for them in the inn" (v. 7). No mention of labor pains, no details of the delivery, and no record here of the emotions experienced by Joseph or Mary. Angels and shepherds come and go before his mother's response appears. The particulars of the event receive somewhat less emphasis than the significance various characters see in it both before and after the fact. Its significance is couched in terms of history and prophecy.

Luke takes great pains to situate the story of Jesus in the context of world history. His is not a tale from long, long ago, that takes place in a land far, far away. He includes specific, identifiable names and places (3:1–2). Two elements in this passage merit special attention. First, Rome conducted periodic censuses during its occupation of Judea. Historians have been unable to confirm the administration of a census under Quirinius that corresponds to the timeline suggested in Luke 2. We know just enough about regional variations in imperial policy, loopholes and local customs, and gaps in bureaucratic recordkeeping, however, to reserve judgment on the reliability of Luke's cursory description. Of more immediate

Homiletical Perspective

How in the world does one preach this passage— perhaps one of the most celebrated sacred stories in print, song, and film—with fresh perspectives? What can one do with a passage that is so familiar and beloved that it seems every possible nook and cranny of it has been explored many times over? How does one preach or retell a story that is so often over-sentimentalized? A story layered with the personal memories of family Christmases gone by or gone awry? *Can* this passage be preached again? Is it best for it to remain the subject of children's Christmas pageants and choir cantatas?

Marcus Borg and John Dominic Crossan write that the infancy narratives of Matthew and Luke are best seen as parabolic overtures for the Gospels they introduce. They present the overarching truths of the Gospel's narrative in parable. "Parable is a form of language about meaning, not factuality. . . . [It] is a narrative metaphor, a metaphorical narrative, whose truth lies in its meaning."[1] Jesus told parables that hold the great truths of his teachings. Matthew and Luke used the telling of Jesus' birth as parable to give their respective first-century communities glimpses of the great truth and good news of Jesus as

1. Marcus Borg and John Dominic Crossan, *The First Christmas: What the Gospels Really Teach about Jesus' Birth* (New York: Harper One, 2007), 33–34.

Luke 2:1–7

Theological Perspective

To grasp the distinctive way Luke expresses the distinctiveness of Jesus, it will help to compare this opening with those of the other Gospels. Mark begins his "good news of Jesus Christ, the Son of God," with Isaiah's prophetic announcement: "See, I am sending my messenger ahead of you, who will prepare your way" (Mark 1:2). Jesus arrives "from Nazareth of Galilee [to be] baptized by John" and is confirmed by a "voice from heaven" (*bat kol*): "just as he was coming up out of the water, he saw the heavens torn apart and the Spirit descending like a dove on him. And a voice came from heaven, 'You are my Son, the Beloved; with you I am well pleased'" (Mark 1:9–11). Jesus' temptation in the desert follows, then the announcement of the advent of the "kingdom of God" immediately after John's arrest.

Matthew opens with a fulsome genealogy tracing "Jesus the Messiah, the son of David, the son of Abraham" back to the father of faith, before describing how "the birth of Jesus the Messiah took place in this way" (Matt. 1:18).

John offers a cosmic introduction: "In the beginning was the Word, and the Word was with God, and the Word was God. . . . All things came into being through him" (John 1:1, 3a). Yet "the world did not know him. He came to what was his own, and his own people did not accept him. But to all who received him, who believed in his name, he gave power to become children of God" (John 1:10b–12). "From his fullness we have all received, grace upon grace. The law indeed was given through Moses; grace and truth came through Jesus Christ" (John 1:16–17), who "became flesh and lived among us" (John 1:14). This "Messiah" had been variously figured in the Scriptures, to be sure, but never identified with the creator of heaven and earth, the very God of Israel! So it was doubly arresting for that One to live among us as one of us.

Yet, for all the titles, what makes this One distinctive can best be gleaned from Luke's homegrown account: that the revelation of God is to be found *in Jesus*: not from his teaching or articulated in a text or recitation, but embodied in his very person. Jesus may indeed speak the words of God, but even more centrally, he *is* God's creating Word. Notice that in chapter 6 of John's Gospel, John could hardly have Peter affirm what the Gospel itself had announced at the outset: when Jesus' followers were put off by his referring to his own person as food and drink, Jesus asked the Twelve, "Do you also wish to go away?" Simon Peter answered him, "Lord, to whom can we go? You have the words of eternal life" (John 6:67–68).

Pastoral Perspective

The church falls victim to this cultural phenomenon of seeking attention. We hear the call and respond with attention-grabbing action, whether forming a coalition to influence electoral politics or large public displays against injustice, to draw attention to the concerns we care for most. Change, we often believe, comes through making our voice rise above the rest.

Luke may offer us a different way to think about how we live our faith. He carefully places the birth of Jesus in the midst of a particular political moment. He proclaims the power of Rome in the description of the census, that "*all the world* should be registered" (v. 1, emphasis added). This opens our vision to the vast size of Rome and its conquered lands. It is time to count the people, to work out the tax rates, to remind the citizens and residents of Rome that the empire has the power to exact from the citizens what the empire needs. It is also a reminder to the people of who provides for their well-being and protection. It is the empire that provides the military and the infrastructure these people need to live out each day in peace. Therefore, when the empire comes to take what it needs, it is best to give it.

In the middle of the census are Mary and Joseph, the betrothed couple, who obediently follow the command of the empire, leaving their home in Nazareth to venture to Joseph's ancestral home in Bethlehem. It is an interruption of their ordinary routine and very likely an unwelcome command in the face of the pregnancy, but Mary and Joseph obey. Once in Bethlehem, the time comes for Mary to give birth. Again there is no declaration that the child is the new and superior king to Caesar; he is simply born, swaddled, and laid in a manger.

If this story had been carried out in front of a live audience, I imagine there might have been some whispers, "That is it? That is the fulfillment of all those angels and songs and visits?" In the subsequent scene, those songs and angelic announcements will resume in declarations made by Anna and Simeon (2:25–38). John the Baptizer will declare the Messiah's arrival (3:1–6), and eventually the child born in obscurity and odd normality will proclaim a message that will threaten the political powers. In this moment in Bethlehem, however, there are two ordinary Jewish people following the edict of the emperor, who birth God's Son into the world and lay him in a feeding trough, because there was no place for them to stay. Luke presents this birth as the plan of God and presumes that the actions of Mary and Joseph were an appropriate form of obedience to God's will.

interest is the function of the census. Ruling authorities in the ancient world do not undertake censuses for the purpose of ensuring fair and equitable participation in legislative assemblies. It is about taxation, not representation, and the point would not have been lost on the original audience. (That God does not consider a census a boon to the people is abundantly clear from 2 Samuel 24 and 1 Chronicles 21, where it is Satan's idea to count the Israelites.) Resentment at such times could thus erupt into outright rebellion, as in the case of Judas the Galilean (Acts 5:37).

However, Rome was not simply an agent of oppression. When Augustus became emperor in 27 BCE, he ended a century of intermittent civil war, ushering in the *Pax Romana* that would last for nearly two hundred years. Early in the eighth century, the Venerable Bede remarks on the happy coincidence of the Prince of Peace being born in such a time of relative tranquility (*Homilies on the Gospels* 1.6). This is the second aspect of the text that the historical context illuminates. Roman rule placed any number of burdens on the people, to be sure, but it also came with certain benefits—and many Jews considered the imperfect peace of Rome to be a perfectly acceptable trade-off.

A journey of eighty or so miles from Nazareth in the north to Bethlehem in the south was an arduous one, all the more so for a pregnant woman. Without the extensive system of good roads and the safe travel made possible by the ever-present legions, Jesus might have been born somewhere other than the city of his ancestor David. In this way, even the imperial authorities who will eventually execute Jesus during the reign of Augustus's successor unwittingly further the divine plan. The "events that have been fulfilled among us," according to Luke (1:1), do not happen outside of human history but through it.

The motif of fulfillment in the Lukan prologue implies that the author sees the events at the beginning of Jesus' life, and even earlier, as prophetic in nature. Each of the evangelists regards various events in Jesus' life as fulfillments of prophetic texts from the Old Testament. Matthew (2:3–6) has Herod consult the chief priests and scribes, who connect the advent of the Messiah with the birthplace of Jesus by quoting Micah (5:2): "But you, O Bethlehem of Ephrathah, who are one of the little clans of Judah, from you shall come forth for me one who is to rule in Israel."

While Matthew draws explicit attention to the texts he has in mind, Luke's narrative technique

the Messiah and Savior. Luke's parabolic overture, as well as his Gospel, emphasizes women, the marginalized, and the Holy Spirit in its telling.[2] How can the glimpses of these three themes renew the preaching of Luke 2:1–7?

In Luke 1 there is extensive emphasis on women and the Holy Spirit. The characters of Mary and Elizabeth are painted as faithful believers who rely with utter confidence on the astonishing and good news they receive from God through the Holy Spirit. In contrast, the priest, Zechariah, learns the hard way to trust God's message. The reader knows Mary as a strong woman in willing service to God and attuned to the Spirit before we hear of her late-term pregnancy trip to Bethlehem with her husband Joseph, in chapter 2. Strong women listening to God's Spirit are part of the parabolic backdrop that helps us imagine the young woman far from home giving birth for the first time in a stable with a manger cradle.

Also part of the backdrop is Luke's emphasis on the marginalized, including women. However, Luke's emphasis extends further than gender, to the last and least of society. Mary and Joseph are not prominent, elite people from Jerusalem; they are peasant people from the hill country of Galilee. Joseph is of David's lineage; but this only supports the emphasis on the marginalized, since David was the shepherd raised up by God to become the great king. Likewise, shepherds are the first to pay homage to the newborn king.

Continuing the emphasis on the marginalized, Luke contrasts the power of the emperor Augustus to the "power" of the child born with only a manger for a bed, behind an out-of-the-way inn in Bethlehem. The emperor has ordered a census for the whole world. By implication in this metaphorical narrative, the emperor has power over the whole world. Yet immediately the angels sing the birth announcement of the peasant baby in the manger as Savior, Messiah or Anointed One, Lord—all names that were also attributed to the emperor in the first century. Luke presents this child as a rival power to Augustus.

The Roman Empire promised peace through power, made violently manifest at any cost. The figure of the emperor was "power over" personified. The baby whom angels praised grew into the storytelling teacher and healer who proclaimed the power of God made manifest as peace achieved nonviolently through compassion and the love of God, neighbor, and self. This peace is also personified in this same innocent teacher and healer who

2. Borg and Crossan, *First Christmas*, 46–52.

Luke 2:1–7

Theological Perspective

No first-century Jew would have been able to bring himself to announce: "You *are* the Word of eternal life." Not until the community shaped by the risen Lord had gained the courage and enough insight to pry into the reality of this unique and unparalleled One could John's prelude find proper expression in Nicaea: "of one substance with the Father" (325 CE).

Given the chronology of the two phases of God's covenant, it became commonplace to insist that what was new superseded what went before it. Even more, "what is obsolete and growing old will soon disappear" (Heb. 8:13). Various clichés soon enshrined the inevitable supersession: reality illuminating shadows (Heb. 10:1), grace and truth in Jesus eclipsing law (John 1:17), all bolstered by the apparently inescapable conviction that later supersedes earlier. When the advent of Qur'anic revelation in the seventh century made itself *last,* identifying its revelation with that of Abraham, it effectively eclipsed them all!

The manifestly derogatory assertion of Hebrews 8:13 was itself authoritatively eclipsed when the Second Vatican Council's *Nostra Aetate* explicitly privileged the irenic assertion of Paul in Romans that "the gifts and the calling of God are irrevocable" (Rom. 11:29). God's original people remain God's people, whether or not they can bring themselves individually to acknowledge the revelation of God in Jesus. Ironically enough, the principal obstacle to a Jew granting Jesus that recognition lies in the fact that his followers persistently denied Jews the ancestral right that Vatican II affirmed!

How, then, can a Christian best assert the distinctive reality of God's fresh revelation in Jesus without denigrating the initial covenant with Israel? Quite simply, by following the contours of Luke: Jesus' distinctiveness need not be found in a novel set of words he spoke, but in the simple fact that this unique person, born to Mary, *is* the person of the Word of God made human and living among us, to make us children of God, without needing to deny that Jesus' own people are God's children as well.

DAVID B. BURRELL

Pastoral Perspective

How often those of us who want to be faithful, like Mary and Joseph, feel that faithfulness requires making deep and lasting changes in our society, large public displays of the coming kingdom of God. This may involve ballot measures to protect certain moral stances or protests against unjust laws and business practices. Certainly there are times when we are called to work in these attention-grabbing ways. There may also be a time, however, when faithfulness does not mean shaking our fist at the empire or proclaiming the radical kingdom of God in a way that dares the authorities to chop off our heads.

There may be a time, and there may be a hunger in the world, for a community of disciples who quietly go about being faithful. These are the communities who show up with casseroles when a loved one dies. These are the communities where children are raised to know the stories of Jesus, lead God's people in worship, and go into the world to look for God's mission. These are communities who show acts of mercy each day without recognition on the nightly news or in the local paper. These are communities where people call each other brother and sister, not because it is a religious title, but because they have become a family of faith who struggle and study and worship and grieve and rejoice together.

There is a place for these ordinary communities that quietly birth God's will into the world each day, communities made up of Marys and Josephs who obediently and without fanfare enact the world-changing will of God. These are women and men whose love for God shapes their lives in the empire, the ones whose humble obedience might just show the world that "still more excellent way" (1 Cor. 12:31).

ANDREW CLARK WHALEY

is subtler. The note that Joseph is descended from David (v. 4) hints at Jesus' messianic identity, which is confirmed by the angel a few verses later (v. 11). The birth itself also constitutes the fulfillment of the extraordinary promise made to Mary by Gabriel in the annunciation (1:30–33). It also confirms the words of Zechariah, spoken under the influence of the Holy Spirit, that God "has raised up a mighty savior for us in the house of his servant David, as he spoke through the mouth of his holy prophets from of old" (1:69–70). This sequence, then, contributes to Luke's stated purpose of providing "assurance" (1:4, a better translation than NRSV's "truth") for his readers by depicting God's word, whether ancient or more recent, as completely reliable.

No doubt this was one of the Jewish elements that Marcion excised when in the second century he produced his own version of the Gospel. Marcion rejected anything associated with the Old Testament as the product of a depraved deity who was distinct from the true God, whose Son was Jesus. Mundane details in the narrative furnish material later church fathers such as Irenaeus and Tertullian could use to counter the claims of gnostic Christians that Jesus only appeared to become a man and that his was not a real, fleshly body: Mary gives birth in a humble dwelling instead of in a spacious palace (the *kataluma* may be a small guest room in the home of a relative and not an "inn," *pandocheion*, as one finds at 10:34 in the parable of the Good Samaritan; the "innkeeper" who turns them away in popular retellings of the story is not actually present in Luke). The newborn is placed in a manger, perhaps to keep any animals from trampling him in such tight quarters. Finally, Jesus' body is carefully wrapped in cloth, just as it will be upon his death (23:53).

PATRICK GRAY

was crucified by the violent power of the empire. The baby who becomes the man on the cross is God *with* the people rather than God *over* people, God who lifts up the oppressed and fills those hungry in body, mind, and soul with God's blessings. In Jesus, God turns the tables on the powers of the world.

Luke 2:1–5 succinctly bridges the joyful prophecy of God's topsy-turvy, "last shall be first" salvation of the world in Luke 1 with the deceptively quiet fulfillment of God's promises in the brief birth announcement in Luke 2:6–7. God's power comes into the world born of poor folk oppressed by mighty Rome, who are willing to live in extraordinary reliance on God's promises. The child born to be Savior and Lord is a flesh-and-blood, helpless, crying, hungry baby. "Because of his boundless love, Jesus became what we are that he might make us to be what he is," wrote Irenaeus in the second century.[3]

What is it he would make us into? What is it to be made into the likeness of the babe in the manger, hailed Lord of All and in contrast to the likeness of the mighty emperor of the world, also hailed Lord of All? Who will we be? This question bears repeating time and again.

The hope of this dearly familiar story is to see our true selves in the babe born in the manger. Whether in sermon, pageant, or cantata, the gospel is that we were made in his image. In his weakness and vulnerability, our utter confidence in God is strengthened; by his mercy and grace, we are called to follow God, no matter how poor in body, mind, or spirit we may be. He is the peace of God's power made manifest as "power with" through love and compassion, rather than "power over" through violence.

It seems we can never be too familiar after all with the powerful promise of this all-too-familiar story.

JANE ANNE FERGUSON

3. Mary Ann Simcoe, ed., *A Christmas Sourcebook* (Chicago: Archdiocese of Chicago, Liturgy Training Publications, 1984), 60.

⁸In that region there were shepherds living in the fields, keeping watch over their flock by night. ⁹Then an angel of the Lord stood before them, and the glory of the Lord shone around them, and they were terrified. ¹⁰But the angel said to them, "Do not be afraid; for see—I am bringing you good news of great joy for all the people: ¹¹to you is born this day in the city of David a Savior, who is the Messiah, the Lord. ¹²This will be a sign for you: you will find a child wrapped in bands of cloth and lying in a manger." ¹³And suddenly there was with the angel a multitude of the heavenly host, praising God and saying,

¹⁴ "Glory to God in the highest heaven,
   and on earth peace among those whom he favors!"

¹⁵When the angels had left them and gone into heaven, the shepherds said to one another, "Let us go now to Bethlehem and see this thing that has taken place, which the Lord has made known to us." ¹⁶So they went with haste and found Mary and Joseph, and the child lying in the manger. ¹⁷When they saw this, they made known what had been told them about this child; ¹⁸and all who heard it were amazed at what the shepherds told them. ¹⁹But Mary treasured all these words and pondered them in her heart. ²⁰The shepherds returned, glorifying and praising God for all they had heard and seen, as it had been told them.

Theological Perspective

In Luke's narrative of the birth of Jesus, one finds one of the most stunning ideas and most powerful signs in all history. The idea is this: the essential power of almighty God is utterly different in kind from power in the standard, oppositional, me/us-against-you/them sense. The sign is this: God-a-babe-in-a-marginal-manger.

Luke's story of the birth of Jesus begins with a display of raw power. A poor young couple, the girl pregnant, is forced to travel. Their nation has long been occupied by a foreign power, and their hand has been forced, together with the whole population, by an emperor, Caesar Augustus, who wants to inventory his resources.

Notably, Augustus was famous not for oppression but for peace. Augustus is the famed Caesar of the *Pax Romana*, whose birth was celebrated as a gift from the gods. Luke is counterpoising the plight of Mary and Joseph with the idealized peace of the *Pax Romana*, and also setting up a contrast between the salvation of Augustus and that of Jesus. Insofar as we are moved by the plight of Mary and Joseph, Luke has unveiled the limits of any *Pax Romana*, of any peace dependent upon force, of any peace purchased with injustice. The relationship among "peace," power, and *shalom* is straightforward: the

Pastoral Perspective

Act in haste; repent at leisure. On the other hand, do not lollygag: the early bird gets the worm. Sometimes we do act too hastily. Sometimes we hang back—thinking and thinking and not acting at all. We may learn over time that there is a time to act—quickly!—and there is a time to stop and consider, to reflect.

The shepherds in this familiar story do act in haste. It is not, of course, that they do not have cause to hurry. They are visited by an angel, the night shines with a terrifying glory, the angel speaks. "Do not be afraid!" The news is good—it is of a great joy. It concerns the birth of a Savior in nearby Bethlehem. The angel issues an indirect invitation: "you will find a child wrapped in bands of cloth and lying in a manger" (v. 12). Then, as if one angel were not enough, a multitude appears, praising God and singing.

The shepherds respond to the invitation. They do not stop to consider. No one says even, "What about the sheep?" Instead each says to the other, "We need to see this." Therefore they go at once, and they go in haste. They leave off "keeping watch over their flock by night" (v. 8); they leave behind their task, their job, their responsibilities, *their livelihood* to see this child wrapped in bands of cloth and lying in a feed

Exegetical Perspective

Few biblical passages strike such familiar chords as does Luke's account of the birth of Jesus and few are so packed with emotion, ranging from intense fear to robust joy. How will preachers and teachers speak a fresh word, helping congregants to glimpse the glory and—again or for the first time—hear the good news in the "Christmas story"?

Narrative beginnings are revealing. The preceding verses have painted the birth of Jesus onto a grand backdrop, on which the power of the Roman emperor looms large. Yet the powerful do not fill this stage; instead, the action places us beyond the margins of society among persons low in status and honor. Befitting a story featuring Mary, a young woman lacking pedigree (and pregnant before marriage), and her newborn son lying in a feeding-trough crib, it is not wealthy magi bearing extravagant treasures (as in Matt. 2) but common shepherds who are the first to acclaim the one born to be king. The gifts they bear are simply their words: they disclose what God has revealed to them through angelic messengers, and their praise of God invites other observers, including Luke's readers, to join the chorus. Whatever else is made of this account, a retelling of the story that draws contemporary listeners into joyful praise of a trustworthy God, who fulfills

Homiletical Perspective

Looking at the Lukan themes introduced or developed in this passage can offer the preacher new vistas from which to preach a familiar story. Here are a few possible themes.

Good News . . . for All. Interrupting the shepherds' night watch, God intervenes in the events of human history. Note that the movement in verses 8–14 is in one direction: from heaven (God) to earth (humanity). It is a story of grace that God always initiates. In the beginning, God creates; after the fall, God calls Abraham, Moses, Isaiah, Jeremiah, and so on; now he calls these shepherds with the best news of all.

In a world where the Greek word for "good news" (*euangelion*) was used by the Roman propaganda ministry to herald the "good news" of Caesar Augustus, any so-called "good news" applied to only 7 percent who were the privileged few in the population. There was certainly no "good news" for the shepherds or any of the other 93 percent of the people. Caesar's good news offered little hope. Yet the angel announces "good news" for "*all* the people"—insiders and outsiders, rich and poor, even shepherds! Contrasting the "good news" of Caesar (aka the social, cultural, political, and economic kingdoms in which we live) and the "good news" of Jesus is always timely.

Luke 2:8–20

Theological Perspective

more "peace" depends upon oppositional power, the less it is *shalom*.

Luke knows his readers know that this is all about the baby in that manger, about Jesus the Messiah who does *not* become the next David, who does *not* become the next king of Israel: this is about a Messiah whose reign on earth was and remains anything but predominant among earth's principalities and powers. Nevertheless, Luke still tempts us to think of the opposition between Jesus and Augustus in terms of power in the oppositional sense. When the angel appears, night itself is overcome with shining glory, and the angel speaks of Israel's fabled king David, piling up messianic titles with marked intensity ("Savior," "Christ," "Lord," and "David" are four of twelve words in the sentence).

Moreover, the angel proclaims that the messianic moment Israel has awaited for centuries has come *today*. "Messiah" was commonly interpreted in accord with power in the oppositional sense. In accord with this understanding, toward which Luke knowingly tempts us, we are led to expect this angelic display of power to be only a harbinger; that the titanic power of Caesar is about to be trumped by the power of the next David; that the power of the gods of Rome is about to be surpassed by the power of the God of Israel; that Israel is about to be restored to her former glory.

Now, insofar as we understand the relationship among oppositional power, "peace," and *shalom*, we realize that in this primarily political sense the true Messiah will never arrive; for, again, to the degree peace is established via this sort of power, it is not *shalom*, but only a pause in overt hostilities in an ongoing "war of all against all." The temptation to think of power in this fashion is ancient and enduring. Today many intellectuals think power can be understood only in an oppositional sense. So Luke wisely tempts us to think of power in this me/us-against-you/them sense, the better to cleanse our understanding.

"And this will be a sign for you . . ."

A sign? A sign of the arrival of the Messiah, of the next David, of one whose power will dwarf the power of Caesar? What mighty portent of power will signal this momentous happening?

". . . you will find a babe wrapped in swaddling clothes and lying in a manger."

It is hard to imagine a more jarring juxtaposition. Not only is it contrary to every expectation of a mighty sign. It is God, the Creator of all, *as* a baby in a marginal manger. That baby in the manger, *that* is

Pastoral Perspective

trough. Again, their haste is not without cause: the child, the angel has said, is the Savior, the Messiah.

Here indeed is something more important than anything they could be doing, more wondrously important than their sheep, their watching over their sheep, their everyday responsibilities, their livelihood. There are things more important than these. There is seeing the child lying in his makeshift bed; *then* there is going around telling anyone who will listen; *then* there is singing a song of their own.

There are times to act in haste—quickly: when God calls. There may not be an angel, less likely a whole host of them. Nevertheless, we will recognize somehow that *now* is the time to extricate ourselves from everything that keeps us from running to see. To act in that kind of haste, however, requires that we realize that there are things more important than the kinds of things the shepherds leave behind. There is the birth of a child; there is glad news to share; there is a song to sing in thanksgiving to God for the grace we have been shown.

In contrast to the shepherds' haste, Luke next turns our attention to Mary's heart. I often read Romans 8 at funeral services from the Phillips translation. The section in which Paul declares that nothing can separate us from God's love in Christ Jesus begins, "In the face of all this, what is there left to say?" (Rom. 8:31). In Mary's case, what does "all this" mean? What are "all these words" that Mary is pondering in her heart (v. 19)? What does she consider, worry about? What is filling and both calming and concerning her soul?

There is much. There has been the announcement of the angel—she will bear God's Son; there has been the journey to Bethlehem for the census; there has been the birth of the child; now come these crazy shepherds. What next?

Next is exciting and frightening: it is full of hope and trepidation. We all wonder about *what is next*? We wonder about the future. Sometimes we wish we could see into it, just a little way (and a little way more); sometimes we are glad we cannot.

In the passage that follows this one, we will be given such a glimpse by the ancient Simeon, who has been promised that he will not die before he has seen the Messiah. Taking the baby in his arms, he praises God for the salvation he has seen, a light to the world, but also a light that will bring judgment, division: for the "child is destined for the falling and the rising of many in Israel" (2:34). Moreover, in their response to him, "the inner thoughts of many will be revealed." Then he adds to Mary: "A sword

ancient promises and offers hope to all peoples, will not be far from the mark.

As signaled by Mary's Song in 1:46–55, Luke's Gospel presents good news for the marginalized, for the poor, for those low in status, for those who stand outside. Yet the joyful celebration that has drawn low-status shepherds into the story binds their voices to a heavenly chorus that announces the arrival of a Savior—one who brings rescue and release not to Israel alone but to *all* nations. The upside-down, inside-out reversals that mark God's activity bringing salvation to God's people, to all people, are much in evidence already as the story of Jesus' life begins.

Verse 8 sets the stage, a dark night in the hilly countryside near Bethlehem, and introduces the characters who—socially marginal shepherds that they are—will unexpectedly receive a message dispatched straight from heaven. In verse 9 God's messengers interrupt the shepherds' ordinary night routine, and this theophany (divine appearance) understandably evokes a reaction of fear (the shepherds were "terrified"). Verses 10–11 give the angelic response, first redirecting the shepherds' "great fear" to "great joy" (v. 10), then explaining why this is indeed good news for all people. Multiplying titles of honor in celebration of a baby whose inauspicious arrival has seemed so lacking in honor, the angel announces the fulfillment of divine promise in the birth of a Savior, who is the Christ (i.e., the Messiah, God's anointed ruler and deliverer) and Lord.

In this seemingly inconspicuous birth "today," the first of a series of meaningful "todays" that even now open up access to the bright future God has in store for God's people (see 4:21; 19:5, 9; 23:43), God acts to reconfigure the theo/geopolitical landscape. In one eventful declaration, the status, power, and benefactions of the Roman emperor have been reassigned to a newborn lying in a feeding trough. Good news, to be sure, but also very surprising. A more radically countercultural image of power and honor could scarcely be imagined. Nevertheless, the joyful declaration by the angel intimates that God's people Israel will soon fulfill their divinely given vocation to carry light to all peoples (e.g., Isa. 42:6–7; 49:6, 8–9; 51:4–5; a hint picked up by Simeon in Luke 2:31–32). God's gift of salvation—its character as forgiveness, healing, liberation, and restoration still to be filled out as the narrative proceeds—is about to remake the world Caesar rules.

The angel offers a validating sign that will confirm the announcement as eventful divine word that can be trusted: the shepherds will find in Bethlehem "a

Good News . . . of Great Joy. "Joy to the World," one of the most beloved Christmas carols, highlights a major Lukan theme. In a world where joy is an endangered species, the angelic announcement heralds that there is "Good news . . . of great joy . . . for all," even the shepherds, among the lowest and the least of the day. Luke does not leave this theme of joy in the first chapter. In fact, as Luke begins with "great joy," so he ends with "great joy" (24:52). In the middle of his Gospel (chap. 15), Luke places three parables of joy, parables that tell us more about that joy. Beginning, middle, and end: the Gospel is framed with joy! In a world where joy is an endangered species, we must not just sing about this joy. We must preach it!

Luke's Christology. The angelic announcement in verse 11 offers a concise summary of Luke's Christology. This birth is the birth of a "savior," a uniquely Lukan appellation (cf. Acts 13:23) with both christological and anthropological significance. The need for a savior bespeaks humanity's need to be saved, and the "good news" is that a savior has come. This "savior" is both "Christ" (or "Messiah") and "Lord" (these two titles should be seen in apposition). This savior is the long-awaited, prophet-promised deliverer or Messiah/Christ. He is also "the Lord." In the ten previous appearances in Luke, "Lord" seems to be synonymous with God. This, then, is Luke's version of Matthew's "Emmanuel" (Matt. 1:23), and John's "Word made flesh" to dwell among us (John 1:14).

Reversing Expectations. Luke's Jesus comes to reverse our expectations, and we see these reversals everywhere. Set in the context of the might of the Roman Empire, Mary and Joseph have come to Bethlehem in response to a decree from Caesar Augustus (2:1–7), a decree that will be overshadowed by the angelic announcement in verses 8–14. The destiny of history will not be determined in Caesar's Rome but in the little town of Bethlehem.

The theme is continued in the fields surrounding Bethlehem, where we meet a group of homeless shepherds ("living in the field") on the graveyard shift. Outcast by the religious purists of the day, considered ruffians and riffraff by society in general, they are God's choice to receive the angelic proclamation. No high priest, no chief priest, no member of the Sanhedrin was there; just the least and the lowest are privy to this revelation. Reversal strikes again!

Luke 2:8–20

Theological Perspective

where and how God meets us, *that* is where and how God ever and essentially comes to us.

This is not a vision of God without power. This is a vision of the true power of God—not the power of Caesar, not the power of the sword, not power powerless to bring *shalom*.

What kind of power is this? We can think very literally here. Philosopher Emmanuel Levinas speaks of *agape* in terms of the way we are seized in and by love for the Faces of others. The Face of another is not his or her physical face, not anything in or about that other that we desire for ourselves. The Face is that through which we are seized *for* others. Because of his or her innocence and absolute vulnerability, it is difficult *not* to be seized by the Face of a baby. This is not power in the oppositional sense, but it is real power.

Even people who love life dearly will risk and intentionally sacrifice their lives for a baby. Power in the oppositional sense does not instill such willingness unto death. Only this power, the power of having-been-seized in and by love for the Faces of others, the power of *agape*, the power so perfectly manifest through the Face of a babe, only this power is so potent that it can hold one true unto death (even unto death on a cross).

The power of the call of the Face of a baby is the power of *agape*, the only power capable of *shalom*. This sign—God-a-babe-in-a-marginal-manger—is a clear and poignant sign of the eternal primacy of *agape*. Another sign—God-persecuted-peasant/ prophet-on-the-cross—signifies the same power, the same love in its encounter with a fallen world. However, the sign of the cross is far more complex, and thereby far more susceptible to abuse, sometimes even appropriated for campaigns of power in Caesar's sense.

Living in the light of having-been-seized in and by love, living in the light of the love of God for one's own and for every other Face, living in the favor of God: this is life in the divine power that is greater even than our fear of death, the power that creates *koinonia*, the communion of *shalom*. Let heavenly hosts sing glory to God in the highest.

WILLIAM GREENWAY

Pastoral Perspective

will pierce your own soul too" (2:35–36). The future of Mary's child—and of Mary herself—is both wonderful and frightening. It will bring salvation, that is, healing and wholeness; and it will tear things apart.

Is this what Mary is pondering in her heart? We cannot know. What we can know is that she does ponder; she stops to wonder about what God has done for her and what God has in store for her.

There are occasions for acting in haste, and there are occasions for stopping to ponder things in our hearts. Both may be occasions for wonder. Robert Fuller in his book called *Wonder* notes how the *Oxford English Dictionary*'s definition of the word associates it with curiosity. The shepherds' wonder at the message of the angel makes them curious; they want to understand what they have heard, because they know it to be of greatest importance; then they want others to understand as well. Mary's wonder is more contemplative. Rather than running with haste, she reflects. Both the shepherds and Mary are trying "to discern what is of intrinsic value or meaning (as opposed to what is of utilitarian value or meaning)."[1]

Both kinds of wonder, Fuller believes, help one find "a middle course between a purely secular life and a narrowly religious life."[2] If we can discover our capacity to wonder, it may lead us to ways of being faithful without becoming pharisaical. We may find ourselves both contemplating the God of all, and at work in the real world. We will also know which is more important, when to act in haste and when to pause to reflect.

RICHARD S. DIETRICH

---

1. Robert C. Fuller, *Wonder: From Emotion to Spirituality* (Chapel Hill: University of North Carolina Press, 2006), 9.
2. Fuller, *Wonder*, 2.

child wrapped in bands of cloth and lying in a manger" (v. 12). After mention of the confirming sign, verses 13–14 sound heaven's joyful response to the good news: praise of God, soon to be echoed by the shepherds (v. 20), and assurance of the gift on earth of "peace among those whom God favors" (v. 14; similar phrasing in Dead Sea Scroll texts confirms this translation).[1] Peace that derives from gracious divine gift, however, must take root, must spring to life interpersonally and politically, in the lives of the people to whom it comes. This peace will prove elusive within the confines of Luke's story, as the Messiah's climactic parade into Jerusalem will receive a mixed reception and the city will eventually rebuff the divine offer of peace (see 19:38, 42).

Verses 15–16 narrate the shepherds' response to revelation and their discovery of the promised sign's fulfillment. The message they relay (mediating the divine message they had received, v. 17) evokes a threefold response: while all are amazed at this new information (v. 18), Jesus' mother digs deeper, relentlessly pondering and puzzling over it, to discern what it all means (v. 19), and the shepherds returning to their flocks in the fields model apt response to God's saving work, "glorifying and praising God" (v. 20). They may return to their ordinary life and to business as usual (just as congregants will after Christmas Eve and Day services); but even though their circumstance may not have changed, the world is not the same: a Savior has entered the human story.

As Luke's narrative unfolds, this ruler-Savior will preside over a topsy-turvy, upside-down, inside-out reign, with no home himself after he launches his ministry—just as no guestroom accommodates the expectant parents here. No wonder Mary must ponder. So must we all. What does such a countercultural vision of power say to our own world? The Christmas story is as familiar as any in the Bible, but it speaks a stirring, hopeful, and at the same time world-challenging message that never grows old. It continues to speak of a faithful God who keeps promises, but sometimes in the most unexpected ways.

JOHN T. CARROLL

The "terrified" shepherds find that they/we need not stand before deity with fear; for once again Luke reverses our expectations. "Do not be afraid." The angelic message is "good news of *great joy* for *all* the people," shepherds included! It happens in, of all places, "the city of David"—not Rome, not Jerusalem, but Bethlehem—which according to Micah 5:2 was "one of the little clans" of Judah. Reversal strikes again! The truth of this message will be established by a "sign": This "Savior," this "Christ," this "Lord" will be found not in a royal palace, not in the high priest's home, but as a "babe wrapped in bands of cloth" lying in a manger. If they are to believe the angel's message, the Messiah they have waited for has come, not as David *redivivus*, but as a helpless baby born to a couple of homeless refugees!

Peace. The "heavenly host" provide the exclamation point to the angelic message in a hymn of praise glorifying God and announcing that this birth means "peace" toward humanity upon whom God's "favor" rests. This "peace" (2:14) is not the peace of the *Pax Romana*, a cessation of violence achieved by violence. In the Jewish mind, "peace" (*shalom*) means "wholeness," a "peace" in which our relationship with God, others, the natural world, and ourselves is what God intended, and which alone brings well-being. This peace is no longer just an eschatological hope (Zech. 9:9–10) but a present reality, as a result of the arrival of the prince of peace (Isa. 9:6). This is, indeed, "good news of great joy!"

Obedience. Framed in verses 8 and 20 by references to the shepherds, the text falls naturally into two parts: verses 8–14 focus on the shepherds as receivers of the angelic revelation, while verses 15–20 focus on their subsequent response. The very structure of the text itself suggests a sermon on whether we are receivers only or doers who respond faithfully. Obedient to the heavenly vision, the shepherds go, see for themselves, and tell others (carrying on what the angels have done). In yet another example of Luke's promise-fulfillment motif, they discover the angelic promise (v. 15) to be fulfilled. They tell Mary and Joseph what they have seen and heard. In continuing their mission "glorifying and praising God" (v. 20), the shepherds become the paradigm of discipleship. They hear the good news, in their obedience they discover its truth, and they share the news of what they have seen and heard with others (cf. Acts 4:20).

W. HULITT GLOER

1. See John T. Carroll, *Luke: A Commentary*, New Testament Library (Louisville, KY: Westminster John Knox Press, 2012), 68.

Luke 2:21–24

²¹After eight days had passed, it was time to circumcise the child; and he was called Jesus, the name given by the angel before he was conceived in the womb.
²²When the time came for their purification according to the law of Moses, they brought him up to Jerusalem to present him to the Lord ²³(as it is written in the law of the Lord, "Every firstborn male shall be designated as holy to the Lord"), ²⁴and they offered a sacrifice according to what is stated in the law of the Lord, "a pair of turtledoves or two young pigeons."

Theological Perspective

In the first century Messiah was predominantly understood to accord with power in the sociopolitical, oppositional sense. Luke presents a very different Messiah, for Luke's Messiah is God-a-babe-in-a-marginal-manger and God-persecuted-peasant/prophet-on-the-cross. A question raised by Luke's sign of the manger, then, concerns the relation between Jesus' teachings and Judaism.

With this passage Luke moves immediately to answer this question. First, he makes it clear that, in accord with Torah, Jesus was circumcised. Then he quickly and overtly affirms, reaffirms, and then reaffirms again the fidelity of Mary and Joseph to the "law of Moses" or the "law of the Lord." In short, Luke, a Gentile, moves immediately to affirm that Jesus understands his interpretation of "Messiah" and his gospel of *agape* to be Jewish.

Notably, in Luke the parable of the Good Samaritan, a parable of *agape* offered in response to a question about salvation from an expert in the Law, is positively presented as an interpretation of the standard Jewish summary of the Law: Love the Lord your God with all your heart, soul, strength, and mind, and love your neighbor as yourself (Luke 10:27; Deut. 6:5; Lev. 19:18). Here too, then, Luke affirms that the gospel of Jesus is not outside or superseding the Law, but rightly represents the Law.

Pastoral Perspective

What does it mean to be reverent? In *Reverence: Renewing a Forgotten Virtue,* Paul Woodruff writes that "reverence compels me to confess that I do not know exactly what reverence is." That said, he offers a tentative description: "Reverence is the well-developed capacity to have feelings of awe [even fear], respect, and shame when these are the right feelings to have."[1] Moreover, reverence is an acknowledgment that we are not alone in the universe, there are others; we are not the center of the universe or its governor, there is an Other.

We are seldom "Snowbound" as completely (*or* as contentedly) as the characters in the poem by John Greenleaf Whittier. Still, the winter weather in the northern states can stop us for more than a few moments. The snow blowing off Lake Michigan into northern Michigan, filling the air and coating not only the ground but the roads, creates conditions that people must adjust to, *humbly.* There is something wondrous in the weight of northern winters, something that reminds those that live in colder climates that their lives (their plans!) are not entirely their own, something that induces feelings of respect and can help us begin to understand what reverence means.

1. Paul Woodruff, *Reverence: Renewing a Forgotten Virtue* (Oxford: Oxford University Press, 2001), 8–9.

Exegetical Perspective

This passage comes on the heels of the stirring account of Jesus' birth (2:8–20), with its spectacular host-of-heaven-praise-band choir. Now Luke brings us jarringly back down to earth with a scene that centers on the rite of circumcision, the restoration of ritual purity to a new mother, and the sacrificial offering of two birds. No suitable actions or memorable lines here for a Christmas season pageant!

This compact four-verse unit features three distinct actions, each expressing fidelity to God and to the Torah—covenant-keeping obedience to the instruction from God encoded in the "Law of Moses" in the first five books of the OT. First, as directed by Genesis 17:9–14, which prescribes the covenant-keeping act of *circumcision* (removal of the foreskin of the male's penis) for eight-day-old boys, the newborn Jesus is circumcised (v. 21: the only mention of this event in the canonical Gospels). Actually, the language of the text calls attention to the filling up of a time span (eight days) leading to this event, but rather than narrate it Luke reports the second act, the *naming* of the child. Just as in the longer account of the circumcision and naming of Elizabeth and Zechariah's son and prophet-to-be John (1:57–64), so in 2:21 the accent falls not on circumcision but on the giving of a name to Jesus.

Homiletical Perspective

The Continuity of Redemptive History. This brief section and the one following (vv. 25–40) place Jesus squarely in the flow of redemptive history, a theme of great importance to Luke. Most likely a Gentile himself and writing to a largely Gentile audience (Theophilus et al.), Luke is conscious of the need to emphasize the importance of Christianity's Jewish roots. Jesus is brought to Jerusalem and the temple. Since the rise of David (to whose throne Jesus will ascend, 1:32), Jerusalem has played a central role in redemptive history. Jerusalem receives special attention in Luke, where it is named thirty times (compared to twelve in Matthew, eleven in Mark, and thirteen in John). In Jerusalem, Jesus is taken to the temple, which symbolizes for Luke the continuity between Israel and the new Israel, that is, the church.

The importance of Jerusalem for Luke is also evident in its place in Luke's structure: the Gospel (1:5–25/24:53), the birth narratives (1:5/2:51), and Jesus' teaching ministry all begin and end in the temple (2:41–49/21:38). The early Jerusalem church met daily in the temple (Acts 2:46), the apostles observed the temple hours of prayer (Acts 3:1), and Paul's last act of public ministry in Palestine was in the temple (Acts 21:27–22:22). The importance of this emphasis on continuity with Judaism is as important now as it was when Luke wrote. The failure to remember this

Luke 2:21–24

Theological Perspective

This Lukan interpretation of the relation between *agape*, salvation, and the ultimate character of divine power is in accord with a major stream of modern Jewish thought. Emmanuel Levinas, a preeminent twentieth-century Jewish philosopher, argues that the revelatory heart of the Law lies in the dynamic of obedience, where "obedience" is understood in terms of submission to *agapeic* power: "This obedience . . . derives . . . from the love of one's neighbor, a love without *eros*, lacking self-indulgence, which is, in this sense, a love that is obeyed."[1]

On the other hand, in popular Christianity the salvation and favor of God has often been identified with material riches and political triumph. Luke's understanding of *agape*, salvation, and divine power, then, is shared by Jews and Christians. At the same time, the all-too-human potential to misinterpret divine power in primarily sociopolitical, oppositional terms is an ever-present threat within Judaism and Christianity.

Setting aside obvious factors like greed and selfishness, what might fuel this misunderstanding? Christians see liberating people from poverty, sickness, hunger, and rejection as an essential dimension of love of neighbor (parable of the Good Samaritan) and of God ("just as you did it to one of the least of these . . . , you did it to me," Matt. 25:40). This call for sociopolitical liberation is also a core concern of the Jewish prophets.

Now the struggle to liberate people from sociopolitical oppression will necessarily involve attention to and use of power in the oppositional sense. Thus it is easy to see how one could come to see salvation primarily in terms of sociopolitical liberation, and even begin to see acquisition of material riches, power, and security as a sign of divine favor. Of course, this vision of "salvation" is inconsistent with the prophets, with the twofold summary of the Law, and with the sign of God-a-babe-in-a-marginal-manger and the sign of God-persecuted-peasant/prophet-on-the-cross.

Luke is vitally concerned with *both* sociopolitical liberation and spiritual salvation. He distinguishes these concerns, however, for they involve two very different kinds of power. At the same time, Luke makes clear how the two concerns are intimately related; insofar as one is seized in and by the power of *agape*, that is, insofar as one is seized in and by love for every living creature (including oneself), one is immediately and intimately driven to struggle to liberate all who are oppressed. Again, engaging

1. "Revelation in the Jewish Tradition," in *The Levinas Reader*, ed. Sean Hand (Oxford: Basil Blackwell, 1989), 206.

Pastoral Perspective

How do we express reverence? We create communal responses in order to offer our awe: we invent festivals, ceremonies—around the weather, or at least the seasons of the year. Inhabitants of the Northern Hemisphere celebrate Christmas at the winter solstice: the light of the world comes into the darkest time of the year. Consider also May Day as a celebration of spring, the joyous Midsummer Night in Norway, when bonfires burn to match and maybe capture the sun that does not set, Thanksgiving and Harvest Home.

We create rituals around the seasons of the year and around the seasons of life: birth, coming of age, giving birth, growing old, dying. We create these rituals; then we are loyal to them. They become a way of expressing reverence, of acknowledging an Other who calls forth awe and respect; we are reverent in keeping the festivals, observing the rites and rituals, being faithful to them.

So it is in this little "story" (more a collection of anecdotes) of Jesus' circumcision and his dedication in the temple and of the sacrifice of the doves that are offered for Mary's purification (Lev. 12:2–8) that an Other is acknowledged and reverence expressed. The circumcision acknowledges that Jesus belongs to the people of Abraham; he belongs to "Abraham, Isaac, and Jacob," a people the Lord God formed; from his earliest infancy he belongs to the people of Moses that the Lord God freed from bondage, guided through the wilderness, and brought home; he belongs to the people of David that await a new Messiah. He belongs to a history that tells the story of Something Other at work in the world through a people that apart from that Presence is insignificant, a people that finds its meaning in its relationship with God.

The firstborn is dedicated in the temple. This people dedicates to their God, the God of all, their firstfruits, the firstlings of their flocks, their firstborn sons. These gifts of new life—where do they come from? Not from us, the people acknowledge. The harvest may be plentiful, or there may be no harvest at all. The sheep may lamb one year, and the next year may become barren. We may have children, or we may remain childless. These matters, like the winter weather, are beyond our control or even planning; they are mysterious—even frightening.

The purification is also an act of reverence before a mystery. The messy miracle of birth has placed the woman outside what is normal, everyday (Lev. 12:2–8). It is shameful in the sense that involves those "less honorable parts" of the body that we

Feasting on the Gospels

Exegetical Perspective

So what is in a name? In Luke's rendition, the point is the name itself, not any explanation of its functional significance ("YHWH [God] saves," as Matt. 1:21 elucidates). What matters is that Jesus is given the name the angel Gabriel had directed Mary to call him (1:31). The name and therefore the identity and function of the child originate in God. The spotlight in this passage thus falls on faithful, obedient human response to the divine initiative and command. The narrative priority of name over circumcision, therefore, does not imply any distancing of Jesus from the community of Torah-keeping Jews. Luke takes great pains in his two opening chapters to root Jesus, and John before and alongside him, in the commitments and practices, the ways and hopes, of the Jewish people.

Indeed, the ministry that ensues never loses touch with the Jewish Scriptures or with fidelity to the purposes of God articulated within them—"the law of Moses, the prophets, and the psalms," as Jesus puts it in Luke 24:44. Luke's two-volume narrative (with the Acts of the Apostles) tells of the inclusion of all peoples in the saving work of God, to be sure, but this expansive vision presents the fulfillment of Israel's hopes and vocation and depicts Jesus and the community of his followers after him as faithful to Torah and its claim upon human obedience to God. So the baby boy undergoes circumcision and receives a name.

The third act, also expressing fidelity to Jewish law and custom, brings the young Jesus to Jerusalem and to the temple for the first time (2:22–24)—once again when the time has been "filled-up" (v. 22). Luke's narrative aligns events and calendars with the purposes of God. The general concern with faithful performance of expectations laid down in the Torah is clear in Luke's account: Jesus' parents act "as it is written in the law of the Lord" (v. 23) and "according to what is stated in the law of the Lord" (v. 24; see 2:27, 39). However, the devil is in the details, and in this case the details complicate the picture. Luke has conflated two distinct rituals associated in the Torah with the birth of a child: (1) the mother (not, as in Luke 2, both parents) undergoes a rite of *purification* after giving birth (Lev. 12:2–8), and (2) the parents present a *sacrificial offering* in lieu of a firstborn child who belongs "to the Lord" (Exod. 13:2, 11–16). Luke's account connects both ritual acts to the presentation of Jesus, set apart for God as "holy." His parents thus catch up with God's initiative, and with what readers already know, for from the very beginning the presence of the Holy Spirit in this life has marked Jesus as holy (1:35).

Homiletical Perspective

has led to horrific persecution of the Jews, pogroms, and even the Holocaust. Careful reading and preaching of Luke can deliver us from temptation to forget the root that supports us (Rom. 11:18).

Jesus' circumcision on the eighth day (in keeping with Lev. 12:3) begins a section that emphasizes that Jesus' parents represent the best of Jewish piety. Indeed, all is being done "according to the scriptures." A reminder of this continuity of redemptive history is just as important now as it was in Luke's time.

Prophecy/Fulfillment. Luke 2:21 looks back to the annunciation, when the angel Gabriel informs Mary that her child is to be named Jesus (1:31), a prophecy fulfilled at the circumcision. Here we see once again that all these events are happening as a result of divine superintendence. This theme has already played a large role in this narrative with the prophecies to Zechariah of John's birth (1:13–18), to Mary of Jesus' birth (1:28–37), Mary's song (1:46–55), Zechariah's song (1:67–79), and the immediately preceding story of the shepherds (2:12–20). For Luke it is clear that these stories all demonstrate that God is working out God's purposes and that history itself revolves around the birth of Jesus.

Obedience. Several features of this passage emphasize the importance, yea, the necessity of obedience. Verse 21 highlights Mary's obedience to God's purposes. In 1:31 she is told to name the child Jesus, and she does. When approached by the angel Gabriel with the outlandish notion that she, a virgin, would give birth to a baby who would be called "Son of God" and "the Son of the Most High," who would "reign over the house of Jacob forever," and of whose kingdom "there will be no end" (1:32–35), her response is simple and clear: "Let it be with me according to your word" (1:38). Verses 22–24 continue the theme of obedience with particular emphasis on the law. In this case, two regulations are involved. The first is purification of a mother, which was to take place thirty-three days after the circumcision of the child (Lev. 12:1–8). The law required that a woman bring a lamb for a burnt offering and a pigeon or a turtledove for a sin offering. The poor could take two turtledoves or pigeons instead (Lev. 12:6, 8). The second is to dedicate the firstborn to God (Exod. 13:1–2): "The LORD said to Moses: Consecrate to me all of the firstborn; whatever is the first to open the womb among the Israelites, of human beings and animals, is mine" (cf. Exod. 13:12–16). Numbers 3:47–48 indicates the redemption required

Luke 2:21–24

Theological Perspective

in that struggle will involve attending to and using power in the oppositional sense.

If "we live and move and have our being" (Acts 17:28) in the power of *agape*, that is, in the light of having been seized in and by love, we will be intensely concerned and politically active with regard to social injustice and material suffering, even as first and last we find our salvation not in sociopolitical liberation but in life lived in the light of the love of God. Luke, then, affirms sociopolitical concern, that is, he affirms the concerns of first-century Jews who find themselves occupied and oppressed and who dream of a Messiah who will bring sociopolitical freedom.

Yet Luke discerns a deeper, framing kind of power and salvation in Jesus' interpretation of "Messiah," and he realizes that the right ordering of these distinct powers is critical. If our lives are grounded and guided by power in the oppositional sense, we will remain cut off from the power of *agape* and, thereby, from *shalom* and *koinonia*. Indeed, worldly success may ensure spiritual failure, for the more worldly power one attains, the more tempted one may be to rely on one's own power, thereby falling ever more deeply into the grip of power in the oppositional sense. This explains the hermeneutical/spiritual advantage of those who lack sociopolitical power ("whenever I am weak, then I am strong," 2 Cor. 12:10).

Luke includes and orders a vital concern over sociopolitical liberation and spiritual salvation. *Agapeic* power will make us engage with sociopolitical power, for our love for every living creature will motivate struggle for liberation and justice. Above and beyond all else, however, *agapeic* power delivers spiritual salvation—life in God, life in Christ, *koinonia*, *shalom*—a salvation oppositional power cannot deliver, and a salvation sociopolitical oppression cannot defeat, not even with death on a cross.

The parallels to Levinas's understanding are remarkable. For in Levinas too, the Law, a political instrument meant to prevent sociopolitical oppression and to foster justice in society, is the product of and an always-imperfect means toward reaching the transcending goals of *agape*.

We should not look to deny irreducibly distinct and important aspects of the Jewish and Christian confessions. However, as Luke makes clear, with regard to these vital points about the relations among sociopolitical power, *agapeic* power, the Law/political structure, sociopolitical liberation, and salvation, the Jewish and Christian proclamations are as one.

WILLIAM GREENWAY

Pastoral Perspective

therefore treat with greater honor or respect (1 Cor. 12:23); *and* it is frightening—childbirth is dangerous—and the fear must be acknowledged. All these things are acknowledged in this ceremony, and the woman returns to the community—Mary is brought back into the people—with the sacrifice of two turtledoves. This is not just a sacrifice; it is a ritual offering; it is itself a ritual (an invented ceremony) that acknowledges that the miracle of birth, however well we may understand it now—medically, scientifically—is still ultimately beyond our comprehension. (No more, far less, will we comprehend the offering, the sacrifice that Mary's son will make on our behalf, yet we will celebrate it, reverently.)

The offering here, however, is also a sacrifice on the part of Joseph and Mary. The doves may well be more than they can afford; but they find a way to purchase them and offer them in the temple, God's footstool. Rome may be the political center of this universe—it is Rome that has brought them to nearby Bethlehem—but Jerusalem is its spiritual center. For Joseph and Mary and for many others, wondrous, marvelous, incomprehensible things have happened (and will yet happen) there.

The sacrament of the Lord's Supper is one of the rituals of the church, an occasion for reverence for those who partake in it. We come to the table of our Lord, set before us. We have brought offerings in the bread and the cup, symbols of life, of what nourishes and sustains us. We dedicate these gifts of God to the God who has formed us, who has led us out of bondage; we remember the Messiah who has sacrificed himself for our sin, but who has been raised and will come again—who comes again now to greet us here.

So, we stop. We put aside *our* cares, *our* woes, even *our* joys. In reverence, we put aside ourselves. We remember that we are not our own, that there is Something Else to whom we owe that reverence. In reverence we worship and bow down before the God of Abraham, Isaac, and Jacob, the God of Moses, the Father of Jesus Christ our Lord, who came to save us from our sin and release us to life abundant.

RICHARD S. DIETRICH

Feasting on the Gospels

The fact that Jesus' parents offer two birds (whether pigeons or turtledoves) places them in the ranks of the poor; otherwise a lamb would have been one of the animals slaughtered (Lev. 12:2–8). Thus the story confirms Mary's earlier declaration of her solidarity with the poor whom God honors (1:46–55).

If the reading stops at verse 24, the scene is suspended mid-action. The observance of purification rites and the firstborn Jesus' presentation in the temple provide the occasion for another Spirit-inspired prophetic declaration of his vocation and significance (2:25–35). (He will make his own self-presentation as Son of God in the same temple setting at the age of twelve [2:41–52].) Rituals prescribed by the Torah and the leading of the Holy Spirit converge as a faithful worshiper of God is about to encounter the Savior whose advent he has been assured he will see before death.

Although some details in the account depart from the biblical pattern, readers learn two important things about Jesus. First, even as Savior of all humankind and universal Lord, he is also Jewish Messiah, born to a Torah-observant Jewish family devoted to the worship of the Lord God. Second, he is born into a household with limited economic resources. As Mary his mother has said, God's action in the world turns the tables on the powerful and the wealthy (recall in Mary's Song the images of deposed rulers and honored persons of meager status, of the hungry fed and the rich turned away [1:51–53]). Jesus later brings good news to the poor— embrace, healing, and hope for the socially marginalized and the economically vulnerable—as the core activity of his mission (e.g., 4:18–19; 6:20–26; 7:18–23). He does so, it seems, as one who knows that world intimately. Preachers and teachers do well to keep both of these concrete realities of Jesus' life—his nurture in a devout Jewish family and his acquaintance with poverty—before contemporary communities of faith that may be familiar with neither.

JOHN T. CARROLL

five shekels. Interestingly, while mentioning the offering for Mary's purification, Luke makes no mention of any redemption offering. Jesus is already the "Son of God" (1:35).

Clearly, Luke's strong emphasis on the faithful obedience of Jesus' family suggests an emphasis on the need for faithful obedience in our own families. This faithful obedience placed the child Jesus within a context of the knowledge of and obedience to the purposes of God. The importance of faithfulness to religious practices and genuine piety is nowhere better illustrated than in Luke's infancy narrative. Both John the Baptist (1:5–7) and Jesus are raised in faithful and obedient families. Although our traditions and practices may differ, the importance of faithful practice remains the same.

Kingdom Economy. Luke's interest in economic matters is well known. This text yields important insights. As noted earlier, the poor could substitute two turtledoves or pigeons instead of a lamb and a turtledove or pigeon. The nature of Mary's offering suggests that Jesus' family was of a lower socioeconomic stratum of society and even turtledoves or pigeons might have required a great sacrifice. Luke was keenly aware that obedience can be costly! His portrayal of Jesus' family as homeless refugees (2:1–7) who can afford only the offering of the poor suggests that Jesus experienced life among the disadvantaged. He clearly comes from the "underside" of the society in which he lived.

Perhaps this helps us understand Luke's emphasis on Jesus' teaching about social and economic matters, for example, his blessing of the "poor" and woes to the "rich" and many of his parables, for example, the Rich Fool (12:13–21), the Rich Man and Lazarus (16:19–31). Then there are the stories of the rich ruler (18:18–25) and Zacchaeus (19:1–10). In a society caught in the grips of consumer frenzy and the crass commercialization of Christmas, this would be as good a time as any for a sermon on the economy of the kingdom.

W. HULITT GLOER

25Now there was a man in Jerusalem whose name was Simeon; this man was righteous and devout, looking forward to the consolation of Israel, and the Holy Spirit rested on him. 26It had been revealed to him by the Holy Spirit that he would not see death before he had seen the Lord's Messiah. 27Guided by the Spirit, Simeon came into the temple; and when the parents brought in the child Jesus, to do for him what was customary under the law, 28Simeon took him in his arms and praised God, saying,

29 "Master, now you are dismissing your servant in peace,
        according to your word;
30 for my eyes have seen your salvation,
31   which you have prepared in the presence of all peoples,
32 a light for revelation to the Gentiles
        and for glory to your people Israel."

Theological Perspective

At the very beginning of his Gospel, Luke explains that he began by reading all he could about Jesus and by interviewing eyewitnesses. There was a felt need for the writing of Gospels concerning the life and teachings of Jesus, because eyewitnesses and the first generation of disciples were beginning to die. Furthermore, the early community had widely expected Jesus' return to take place soon, and in part Luke wrote to address theological confusion as it became clear there would be no imminent return.

This expectation is continuous with messianic expectation involving power in the oppositional sense, for both expectations have to do with the reign of God over powers and principalities on earth. Historically, this expectation has repeatedly reemerged (typically in sociopolitically marginal Christian communities).

Luke addressed this confusion when he both affirmed sociopolitical concern for liberation and also contextualized sociopolitical liberation within the parameters of spiritual salvation (power in the *agapeic* sense), thereby distinguishing spiritual salvation as a reality that can be wholly realized even though oppression continues. So the sign of the marginal manger did and should serve as an important corrective for Christians who embrace a neomessianic expectation of imminent return.

Pastoral Perspective

"Patience is a virtue," the old saying goes, meaning the kind of patience that produces endurance, which produces hope (Rom. 5:4). We may be more patient, however, if we know that we are enduring a comedy, not a tragedy; if the drama in which we play our parts ends not in tears but in laughter, by God's grace.

Luke's story of the birth of Jesus is a glorious comedy from beginning to end, full of "low" characters and odd coincidences, not to mention God's continuing intervention (*deus ex machina*). It begins with Zechariah and Elizabeth; they are old and she is barren. When they discover that they will have a much desired child, he is struck dumb and she hides herself. It continues with Mary, a maid from a small town engaged to a carpenter. She will also have a child, though how can this be, as she is a virgin? She will not give birth, however, until she walks from her small town to her husband's hometown, because some far-off bureaucrat has decided that the world needs to be counted. Then she will deliver the child in a barn, attended not by physician or midwife but by shepherds.

Dutifully Mary and Joseph will take their child to Jerusalem that she may be purified and he may be dedicated in the temple. There they will meet more old people, one 112 years old according to legend, the other a widow for 84 years. Old people and more

³³And the child's father and mother were amazed at what was being said about him. ³⁴Then Simeon blessed them and said to his mother Mary, "This child is destined for the falling and the rising of many in Israel, and to be a sign that will be opposed ³⁵so that the inner thoughts of many will be revealed— and a sword will pierce your own soul too."

³⁶There was also a prophet, Anna the daughter of Phanuel, of the tribe of Asher. She was of a great age, having lived with her husband seven years after her marriage, ³⁷then as a widow to the age of eighty-four. She never left the temple but worshiped there with fasting and prayer night and day. ³⁸At that moment she came, and began to praise God and to speak about the child to all who were looking for the redemption of Jerusalem.

³⁹When they had finished everything required by the law of the Lord, they returned to Galilee, to their own town of Nazareth. ⁴⁰The child grew and became strong, filled with wisdom; and the favor of God was upon him.

Exegetical Perspective

In the sacred space of the Jerusalem temple, a man and a woman step forward to aid Luke's readers in making sense of the remarkable events that are unfolding in the narrative of Jesus' early childhood. First, faithful Simeon brings into sharp focus the character of Israel's hopes now rushing to fulfillment, yet cautions that not all will embrace the good news or the one who embodies it (vv. 25–35). Then Anna, equally devout and sporting the label "prophet," connects hope for Jerusalem's liberation to this child in whom God is fulfilling ancient promises (vv. 36–38). Verses 39–40, compressing many years into a brief summary, locate the home of Jesus' family in the Galilean town of Nazareth and chronicle Jesus' growth as a child specially favored by God. Thus Luke prepares for the story of Jesus' return to the temple as a young man on the threshold of adulthood, a scene in which he will first find voice as Son of God (2:41–52).

Simeon: A Promise Fulfilled and a Mission Previewed. Jerusalem, a city whose history is laden with promise and also suffering, the site in Jesus' (and Luke's) time of domination by occupying Roman power, remains the location for the action in verses 25–38, a two-part passage that rekindles hopes for the city's—and the people's—future as

Homiletical Perspective

This section contains three vignettes: Simeon (vv. 25–35), Anna (vv. 36–38), and the return to Nazareth (vv. 39–40), highlighting Lukan themes that lend themselves to homiletical development.

The Universal Nature of the Gospel. God's "salvation" (v. 30) is "prepared in the presence of *all peoples*" (v. 31; see Isa. 40:5), both Jew *and* Gentile. As the angel has declared, "To you is born . . . a Savior, who is the Messiah, the Lord" (2:11; see 2:26). This salvation will bring "a light for revelation to the Gentiles" and "glory" for Israel (2:32, see Isa. 9:2 and 60:1). Verse 32 is classic Hebrew poetic parallelism. Understood this way, "light of revelation" and "glory" are parallel, and "Israel" and "Gentiles" are parallel. Thus, "light of revelation" and "glory" represent "salvation" (2:30), while "Israel" and "Gentiles" represent "all peoples." This salvation found in Jesus is for all people—bar none! The universal nature of the gospel is nonnegotiable for Luke (Acts 1:8). Luke–Acts is about abolishing all the barriers: ethnic, racial, social, political, economic, and/or religious. Simeon's song must still be sung!

The Importance of Faithful Obedience. Simeon and Anna are paradigmatic examples of true "righteousness." Unmatched in devotion and obedience,

Luke 2:25–40

Theological Perspective

With the death of the first generation of followers, there arose a second expectation, also continuous with messianic expectation involving power in the oppositional sense. With a shift from national to personal vision, salvation could be understood primarily or even wholly in terms of the ultimate defeat of death in the physical sense. On this understanding, my greatest need is for freedom from mortality, and my greatest fear is death. What Jesus defeats is death, and the glory of salvation rests in the fact that as a Christian I can be confident that I will be resurrected from the dead.

At worst, this focus upon physical death can turn "salvation" into a wholly individualistic and selfish concern, powerfully inhibiting the spiritual power of *agape*, and so cutting us off from both the love that motivates concern for sociopolitical liberation for all peoples, and also from spiritual salvation, from *shalom* that transcends understanding, from the communion of *koinonia*.

Luke definitively addresses this confusion when he has Simeon declare that he can now die in peace, for he has seen God's salvation. Significantly, Simeon is not dying in peace because he believes that he will live again after death, nor is he dying in peace because he is sure that Jesus will bring about a sociopolitical revolution. What is the character of the salvation, the peace, by which Simeon, inspired by the Holy Spirit, is *wholly and right then* seized? Luke has already told us. It is living in the light of having-been-seized in and by love, living in the light of the love of God for one's own and for every other Face, living in the light of a power greater even than our fear of death, living in *koinonia*, living in the communion of *shalom*.

Luke's handling of hope concerning the defeat of death in relation to spiritual salvation, then, exactly parallels his handling of hope for sociopolitical liberation in relation to spiritual salvation. For just as Luke does not reject hope for sociopolitical liberation, he does not reject hope in resurrection. Death, like sociopolitical oppression, is something we struggle against (though sometimes it may be the best among bad options), and so we understandably hope in a "Day of the Lord" when perfect justice, resurrection, and the end of death will be realized for "all people" (the now all-inclusive proclamation of Simeon, who had waited for the consolation of Israel).

Yet just as Luke enfolds hope for liberation within wholly realized spiritual salvation, he enfolds hope for resurrection within wholly realized spiritual salvation.

Pastoral Perspective

old people, a virgin and a carpenter, shepherds, and people hanging about the courtyard of the temple, a "low" and incongruous lot—these are the court of Christ the King?

Whoever the players, when the curtain falls on Luke's nativity play, all will be well and every manner of things well, for all *is* well that ends well. That is another mark of comedy, if we do not define "well" too narrowly, and we should not. The stories of Simeon and Anna also leave us wondering what will happen next.

As Simeon takes the Christ child into his aging arms, as Anna witnesses the scene, they believe that they are involved in a consummation. Simeon, who has been watching for the consolation of Israel, can now say, "Master, now you are dismissing your servant in peace, . . . for my eyes *have seen* your salvation" (vv. 29–30). Anna, after giving thanks, can run off to tell all who are looking for "the redemption of Jerusalem" that it *is here*. Yet the consummation in this case is a beginning as much as an end. The real world of what is going to happen next is not going to go away in the presence of any child. We see this in Simeon's oracle: "This child is destined for the falling and the rising of many in Israel" (v. 34). With this consummation comes not end but beginning, falling and rising.

This is the case for Mary. "And a sword will pierce your own soul too" (v. 35b), Simeon tells her; and the sword he speaks of is a sword of judgment that will separate families, "father against son and son against father, mother against daughter and daughter against mother, mother-in-law against her daughter-in-law and daughter-in-law against mother-in-law" (12:53). The Christ child's own mother cannot be immune, as Raymond Brown points out. "If his sword of discrimination is to divide families, that is possible even of his own family." Mary may "stand with the . . . number who rise . . . but only because . . . [she will recognize] that the claims of Jesus' heavenly Father far outrank any human attachments between him and his mother, a lesson that she will begin to learn already in the next scene" of the drama, the family trip to Jerusalem at Passover.[1]

What counts as a consummation for Simeon and Anna is only the beginning for all the other players in the drama, including us, whoever we are. Shall we be patient and endure? We shall, if we recognize that

---

1. Raymond Brown, *The Birth of the Messiah* (New York: Doubleday, 1991), 465.

place and people of God. Simeon, epitomizing faithful devotion to God, steps onto the stage with a hybrid prayer-prophetic oracle that celebrates the fulfillment of God's promises to Israel. The imagery of the passage—notably salvation, consolation (comfort) and glory (honor) for God's people Israel, and illumination for the nations (or Gentiles; the word *ethnē* can carry either meaning)—draws generously from the prophecy of Isaiah-of-exile (i.e., Second Isaiah; see Isa 40:1–2; 42:6; 46:13; 49:6, 13; 51:4–5; 52:9–10). As Simeon embraces this infant, hope finds new life as ancient promises of God are fulfilled.

The entire scene bears the stamp of the Holy Spirit, God's guiding and prophecy-prompting presence (threefold mention in 2:25, 26, 27). In the role of mission director who guides the action (a role prominent in the book of Acts), the Spirit prods Simeon to come to the temple courtyard at the very moment Jesus' parents are there to perform their Torah-prescribed duties. The Spirit also informs the message Simeon delivers to Mary and Joseph, as he holds their baby in his arms in a gesture of deep intimacy, tangible evidence of a promise (salvation) kept (by God). Simeon's prayer-oracle blends grateful praise and bold prophecy. He affirms the fulfillment of Israel's long-deferred hopes of divine deliverance; this is the reason for a people's consolation, as well as for his personal sense of "release" to a death in peace. He also expands the scope of blessing to encompass all nations, in the spirit of the message of Second Isaiah: Israel's vocation to bring blessing to the nations is being realized.

When Jesus' parents express astonishment at these words (v. 33), however, Simeon forecasts the mixed reception that will greet God's work of salvation through the Messiah Jesus (vv. 34–35). This "sign" pointing to God's commitments and ways will be resisted. The coming of the Savior is indeed good news to celebrate, but some will turn away from the gracious gift and, Simeon declares, will fall. Even Jesus' family, including his mother, will have their trust and obedience put to the test, as the image of a soul-piercing sword indicates (v. 35; see 8:19–21).

Anna: Liberation Hope. Attention now turns to another exemplar of tenacious religious commitment. Even at the age of eighty-four, the widow Anna (her name and her trust in God reminiscent of Hannah in 1 Sam. 1–2) engages 24/7 in prayerful worship in the temple. Now she transposes praise of God into a new, hope-engendering key, gladly telling about Jesus

constantly in prayer, Spirit-led, and at home in the temple, they are longing for "the consolation of Israel" (v. 25), "the redemption of Jerusalem" (v. 38), and/or "salvation" (v. 30), that is, the coming of the Messiah and the messianic kingdom. Led by the Spirit, Simeon identifies Jesus as God's "salvation" and breaks out into rapturous praise at the fulfillment of God's promises (vv. 29–32). A widow for eighty-four years, Anna's commitment to worship, prayer, and fasting made the temple the center of her life. She is Psalm 130:5–8 and Luke 1:53 in flesh and blood.

In both cases, faithful obedience prepares them to recognize "the Lord's Christ" though he is still an infant. For Luke, such faithful obedience enables one to recognize where God is working, even when it is not obvious to others. Simeon and Anna are among the "pure in heart" (Matt. 5:8), whose obedience to God's purposes enables them to "see God" when those around them do not. Here is a theme that offers significant preaching possibilities!

The Work of the Holy Spirit. Luke's emphasis on the activity of the Holy Spirit is also prominent, being mentioned three times in relation to Simeon. Because of his righteousness and devotion, the Holy Spirit "rests" on him, that is, is free to work in his life. That work is described as "revealing" (v. 26) and "guiding" (v. 27). This Spirit promised that he would not "see death" until he had seen "the Lord's Messiah [Christ]," and this Spirit kept that promise by leading him to the temple that day. While not as explicit, Anna's witness about this child must also stem from the Spirit's leadership. These two exemplify what happens when people are open to the work of the Spirit.

Men and Women. Simeon and Anna also highlight Luke's penchant for demonstrating the significance of *both men and women* in the Jesus story. Already we have had Zechariah and Elizabeth and Mary and Joseph. The infancy narrative is from Mary's perspective, and Luke's Gospel includes seventeen women found nowhere else. In Luke 8:3 we learn that women were both traveling with and supporting the disciple band during Jesus' ministry in Galilee. The women followed Jesus all the way to the cross, watched him crucified and buried, and on that first Easter Sunday women became the first evangelists. Such pride of place demands equal standing in ministry be given to both men and women. If Mary could be the instrument through whom the Lord's Christ could enter the world, then surely women can be the instruments of announcing that incredible story.

Luke 2:25–40

Theological Perspective

With Simeon's unqualified declaration of *shalom* in the near face of death, decades before Jesus' resurrection, Luke makes clear that life lived in the light of the grace of God is in itself wholly and immediately sufficient for peace even in the face of death, just as it is sufficient for peace even in the face of oppression, including persecution to the point of death.

Luke's portrayal of Anna, not only as religiously exemplary but even as a prophet (!), is part of Luke's sociopolitical struggle against sexism. Luke's society is highly patriarchal, and concern over sexism is clear throughout Luke's Gospel.

So he "grew . . . filled with wisdom, and the favor of God was upon him" (v. 40). The call of the Face of the babe that is the essential and literal power of the babe in the manger is common to all babies. What marks out this baby as the Messiah is the fact that, as he grew, it became clear that here was *agape* incarnate, Immanuel.

The call of the Face of any newborn is incredibly strong. However, as we grow, our Faces (that through which we are seized for others) become increasingly obscured by the fallen dimensions of our faces. Thus it can be difficult to love grown-up friends and neighbors, let alone enemies. What distinguishes Jesus is not the call of his Face from the manger, but the purity of a life lived perfectly in and through *agape*, an *agapeic* purity that resulted in an innocence/sinlessness that sustained the power of the call of his Face even into adulthood.

Moreover, insofar as perfect *agape* perfectly sees through the fallen dimensions of faces to Faces, Jesus was distinguished because he was wholly seized in and by love for the Faces of all, even enemies. Thus, as Luke repeatedly depicts, with the exception of those who hardened their hearts, those who met Jesus were both called by his Face with a power usually manifest through the Faces of newborns, and also, despite the fallen dimensions of their own faces, they saw themselves wholly seen and nevertheless wholly loved, that is, they found themselves held in and by grace.

Ultimately, Jesus' love for all Faces leads him into a struggle against oppression that results in his crucifixion. As love incarnate, with utter faithfulness to *agape*, he thereby signifies as God-persecuted-peasant/prophet-on-the-cross that the power of *agape* surpasses the oppositional powers of the world, that through the power of agape, *shalom* transcends understanding, surpasses even fear of death.

WILLIAM GREENWAY

Pastoral Perspective

we can only because we have been *given* endurance. The end of the comedy is a beginning, but in this comedy what is next is also begun in us. This is best represented in Simeon. His satisfaction in seeing the consolation of Israel and his willingness to depart are not based on a task that he has completed. They are not the result of *his* running the good race or *his* fighting the good fight—for the child that he holds in his arms is not a task that he has completed, but a task (or better, a hope) that God has completed, a promise God has fulfilled for him.

God brings one end to the comedy. God intervenes once again (*deus ex machina*), as God does continually in this court of Christ the King that consists of ancient Simeon and Anna, of dumb Zechariah and barren Elizabeth and their crazy son John, of the carpenter Joseph and the virgin Mary, and of the shepherds, a ragtag crew in motley. The drama and the characters themselves suggest that this consummation, which is also a beginning, is a task and hope God is completing, not in and for kings and counselors, but in and for carpenters, in and for old people who pray even when the hope has gone out of their prayers, in and for confused young women and men, in and for working men and women, in and for those barely hanging on, in and for all caught in this comedy of life. We can endure because God comes wearing not the high and mighty mask of tragedy, but the low face of comedy, the one with the gracious grin.

RICHARD S. DIETRICH

Feasting on the Gospels

to everyone who is awaiting Jerusalem's liberation (the force of the metaphor "redemption"). Yet by the end of the story, even followers of Jesus will speak of deflated hopes and shattered dreams of a people's liberation (24:21). Beyond the crucifixion of Jesus, Jerusalem will not be liberated but instead ravaged by Roman armies; by 70 CE the temple will be a heap of ruins. The world being what it is—economic, political, and military systems being what they are—peace is a fragile promise, an elusive gift. God's work of salvation, freeing and restoring a people and a world, must overcome formidable counterforces, somehow incorporating into the agenda the powers and the cross they will impose on the Messiah.

We inhabit that same world, one in which peace and justice are as elusive as ever. The good news entrusted to us concerns honor for God's covenant people and the light of understanding—gracious welcome too—for all people. Yet the invitation to faith and living hope will be credible in our time only when it helps people to grapple with realities that appear to call faith and hope radically into question— and when the invitation is backed up by demonstrable commitment to enact the good news in sustained communal practices that flow from the saving grace of God. Schooled ourselves through experience to trust in a faithful God, we persevere in hope, even when salvation—in its various guises of liberation, restoration, healing, and peace—appears to retreat. So we add our trusting, hoping, sense-making voices to those of Anna and Simeon long ago.

Growth. No less than other New Testament books, Luke presses heady claims for Jesus, already introduced to the reader at his birth as Messiah, Savior, and Lord (2:11). Yet like anyone else, this Human One must grow through experience, beginning with early childhood and its basic need for acquisition of knowledge—or wisdom, as the text puts it. God's gracious favor rests upon him, a life claimed for the work of salvation that is in store. The next passage will give a glimpse of that growth in discernment and evidence the divine favor in Jesus' life, when he impresses teachers in the temple and articulates his awareness of God as his Father. His ensuing career will extend the same gracious favor of God to others, reaching to our own time and space.

JOHN T. CARROLL

The Promise/Fulfillment Motif. Simeon's song highlights the Lukan theme of promise/ fulfillment. In the Greek the song begins with an emphatic "*now.*" On the one hand, the *now* refers to the coming of the Lord's Messiah. The emphatic *now* signals the dawning of the messianic kingdom; the day that Israel had hoped for and longed for is here at last, and with it the prophetic promises will be fulfilled. On the other hand, the *now* signals that the Lord has kept his promise to Simeon, who has lived to see it all. "According to your word" can refer to God's promises to the prophets and God's promise to Simeon (v. 26), both of which find their fulfillment in Jesus. "*Now . . .* dismiss your servant in peace" is a Semitic way of saying, "Let me die." *Now* that God has done what he promised ("according to your word"), Simeon's life is complete and he is ready to die. That God's promises are always reliable is a pastoral word that people need to hear now as then.

Continuity with Judaism. Everything in this section takes place in the temple and is in keeping with the Law. Simeon is "guided . . . into the temple," where he will see "the Lord's Messiah" (vv. 26–27). Anna has spent a lifetime in the temple, where "she worshiped . . . with fasting and prayer night and day" (v. 37). While areas of discontinuity often tend to get most attention, Luke is intent on showing the continuity, and so must the preacher be today! The church's failure to recognize the importance of its relationship with Judaism has often led to horrific consequences for Jews—persecution, pogroms, even the Holocaust! We can be thankful that over the last seventy years there has been a dramatic reassessment of Christianity's relationship to Judaism and the continuing role of Judaism in salvation history.

A Foreboding Foreshadowing (vv. 34b–35). Simeon's last words are followed by warning (vv. 33–35). This story will not be all sweetness and light. Mary's child will be the "falling" and "rising" of "many" in Israel. The sequence here is important. If "many" is taken in the Semitic sense of "all," then "all" will fall (even Jesus' closest disciples!) before they can "rise." Falling is a state from which one can be raised. Indeed, the "inner thoughts" of people will be revealed. There is surely a pastoral sermon here! Mary's own heart will be broken. As Luke–Acts will demonstrate, the cross at the center is a cross for all!

W. HULITT GLOER

Luke 2:41–52

⁴¹Now every year his parents went to Jerusalem for the festival of the Passover. ⁴²And when he was twelve years old, they went up as usual for the festival. ⁴³When the festival was ended and they started to return, the boy Jesus stayed behind in Jerusalem, but his parents did not know it. ⁴⁴Assuming that he was in the group of travelers, they went a day's journey. Then they started to look for him among their relatives and friends. ⁴⁵When they did not find him, they returned to Jerusalem to search for him. ⁴⁶After three days they found him in the temple, sitting among the teachers, listening to them and asking them questions. ⁴⁷And all who heard him were amazed at his understanding and his answers. ⁴⁸When his parents saw him they were astonished; and his mother said to him, "Child, why have you treated us like this? Look, your father and I have been searching for you in great anxiety." ⁴⁹He said to them, "Why were you searching for me? Did you not know that I must be in my Father's house?" ⁵⁰But they did not understand what he said to them. ⁵¹Then he went down with them and came to Nazareth, and was obedient to them. His mother treasured all these things in her heart.

⁵²And Jesus increased in wisdom and in years, and in divine and human favor.

Theological Perspective

This story, the only New Testament account about Jesus as a child other than the birth narratives, bridges the gap between the infant Jesus' dedication in the temple (2:21–39) and the beginning of his adult ministry. Following Jesus' circumcision and presentation at the temple, his parents returned to Nazareth, where "the child grew and became strong, filled with wisdom; and the favor of God was upon him" (v. 40). Luke then picks up the story just prior to the time when Jesus reaches the age of accountability at thirteen according to Jewish law. He portrays Jesus as a precocious boy who amazed the teachers in the temple and astonished his parents (vv. 47–48). This short, but theologically rich segment raises questions regarding Luke's universal vision of salvation (see 24:47), challenges traditional theologies of "family values," and highlights Luke's Christology.

Overtly, this portion of Luke continues parallels between Jesus and Samuel (Luke 2:52 and 1 Sam. 2:26), and Mary and Hannah (Luke 1:46–55 and 1 Sam 2:1–10) begun in chapter 1. Although it is common for theological reflections on this segment of the Gospel to read it in the context of Judaism, it is possible that in doing so we may have confused the narrative setting with intended audience.[1] Recent

1. Bradley Billings, "At the Age of 12: The Boy Jesus in the Temple (Luke 2:41–52), the Emperor Augustus, and the Social Setting of the Third Gospel," *Journal of Theological Studies* 60, no. 1 (2009): 70–89.

Pastoral Perspective

In this modern day and time we cannot imagine a child, even a tween, lost for three solid days. With all of our technology—cars and cell phones and sophisticated police forces with their search-and-rescue equipment—it is hard for us to imagine how a child could be lost for this long. Losing a child for three days is a long time—long enough for panic, despair, and anger to set in.

We can well understand, then, how Jesus' absence must have felt for Mary and Joseph. We should not be unduly surprised that they do not notice his absence until they have traveled a day's journey from Jerusalem. In the first century, it was common for faithful Jews to travel in large groups to and from Jerusalem to celebrate the Passover, as Luke says they had done every year. Because they were traveling as part of a large group of relatives and friends, Mary and Joseph assumed that Jesus was somewhere among the group. It would not have seemed strange not to see him as they began their journey toward home with their fellow pilgrims.

However, when families regrouped at the end of the first day's walk, Mary and Joseph would have noticed that Jesus was not among the band of travelers. This may have been when panic began to set it. Once they did notice Jesus was missing, they had a day's walk back to Jerusalem to look for him. Once in the city, a very large city for that time, they

Feasting on the Gospels

Exegetical Perspective

This story is found only in Luke's Gospel. No other canonical Gospel has a story about Jesus' childhood. On the other hand, noncanonical Gospels abound with such stories, particularly the *Infancy Gospel of Thomas*, where you find multiple stories of miraculous deeds done by Jesus at the ages of five, eight, and twelve.

Such stories are common in the Greco-Roman world. They express the idea that a great man was assumed to have had a precocious childhood. For example, Cyrus, who was to become king of Persia, is said to have been recognized for his unusual skills at leadership while only ten years of age (Herodotus, *Histories* 1.114). Pythagoras, the famed Greek philosopher, was said to have been renowned for his wisdom while still a child (Iamblichus, *The Pythagorean Life* 10.11). According to Philo, Moses advanced beyond all his peers in learning while still a child (*Life of Moses* 1.21). Many in Luke's audience must have recognized this story about Jesus as a type of story they had heard before about heroic figures.

In Luke's story, Jesus is twelve years old, a pivotal age in the culture for the passage from childhood to adulthood. That is the age at which Epicurus the Greek philosopher is said to have begun his study of philosophy (Diogenes Laertius, *Life of Epicurus* 10.14). It is also the age of Samuel when he began to prophesy, according to Josephus (*Jewish Antiquities*

Homiletical Perspective

This story of twelve-year-old Jesus staying behind in the temple is easily cited as the Gospels' answer to questions about Jesus' childhood, as it is the only canonical trace we have of that period. Extracanonical material tells stories of childhood miracles, but the preacher can do little with those stories. To have a single story as rich with detail as this one allows a preacher to imagine Jesus' childhood as a long and intriguing preparation for his ministry. Yet the placement of this story in Luke also allows the preacher to say more, for the story is an episode of recognition among three such episodes. It displays not only how Jesus was recognized as the Christ in the narrative, but also ways we might describe how the Holy Spirit still promotes such recognition.

The story comes between Jesus' ritual purification in the temple and the long beginning of John's public ministry leading to Jesus' baptism in the wilderness. At the time of his purification, the elderly Simeon and Anna, long faithful witnesses to the people's hope for a promised One, see the infant Jesus and identify him as the one waited for, the Messiah. The family then returns to Nazareth, where Jesus grows in ways needed for him to become the One he is claimed to be.

He will be recognized again twelve years later, although now with potential to reshape the tradition. He is not only listening and learning; he is also

Luke 2:41–52

Theological Perspective

scholarship has highlighted the striking parallels between Luke's narrative and tales of the divinized emperor Caesar Augustus and shown convincingly that the text is intended to demonstrate that Jesus is superior, not just to all previous Jewish prophets, but to the greatest of Roman emperors.

The intended audience for Luke was likely not a group of Jews intimately familiar with the temple and Jewish tradition but late-first-century urban Gentile Christians living far from Jerusalem, long after the temple had been destroyed, in a world dominated by Roman pagan culture. This reading opens the way to a stronger interpretation of what is theologically central to Luke's Gospel—Jesus is not just for the Jews. He brings salvation to all people, all nations. Unfortunately, in the interest of supersessionist theologies, Christians have often tended to downplay Luke's potent message of salvation for all people.

The second theological issue is that of "family values" and Jesus' problematic interaction with his mother. Traditionally, theologians have interpreted Jesus' response to his mother's reproach in terms of verse 49, which is actually a vague and difficult passage to translate. Theologies concerned to find textual support for claims that "family" means the patriarchal relation of man, woman, and children explain away Jesus' disrespectful response by focusing on the later statement that he returned to Nazareth "and was obedient to [his parents]" (v. 51).

Schüssler Fiorenza argues that a valid alternative to the NRSV translation is, "Did you not know that I had to be among the household of my Father?"[2] Jesus' obedience to his parents only lasts until his public ministry begins: the message is that nothing, not even family ties, should be allowed to interfere with obedience to God. Schüssler Fiorenza's translation reveals how God as Father functions to undermine, not support, the patriarchal claims of traditional Christianity. The biological family is now of secondary importance in relation to the call of God (cf. 9:60). A new spiritual family is being called into existence, and that means the demands of earthly family relations are no longer primary.

Another dimension of Luke's treatment of family is related to Mary's obedience without understanding; she has often served theologically as the model for female behavior. In this vein, some have made much of her traveling to Jerusalem for the Passover;

Pastoral Perspective

had to decide where in Jerusalem they would look for Jesus.

I am not sure first-century parents panicked as twenty-first-century parents panic, but I can only imagine the pressure Mary and Joseph felt, fearing they had lost not only their son, but the Messiah whom God had entrusted to their care. Panic may not even begin to describe how they were feeling by the time they discovered their calm and comfortable twelve-year-old seated among the religious leaders in the temple. There is not a parent, guardian, or grandparent unable to relate to this sense of panic that would have overwhelmed Mary and Joseph, and surely their community, until Jesus was found.

One clear pastoral issue that this text lifts up is the concern for the welfare and the well-being of our children and youth. Mary and Joseph were worried about Jesus. Anyone who has children or grandchildren in this twenty-first-century world worries about them. The concern may not be with physically losing a child; more often the fear is figurative. Parents worry about their children losing their way, about losing their faith, about losing their moral compass and values. The text could bring all of these issues up in parents, grandparents, guardians who know what it is like to worry about their young people day in and day out.

Jesus, however, was not worried a bit. Anyone who has ever known a twelve-year-old boy can understand this. What was there to worry about, from his perspective? He was where he wanted to be. Jesus was doing what he wanted to do, what he was called to do. One of the most common questions I have been asked as a pastor is, "What am I to do with my life?" It is a question that almost everyone struggles with at some point along the journey.

Here Jesus offers us an excellent example of following one's true calling—and acknowledging that this can begin at a very early age. Jesus understood his own call and found his way among the teachers in the temple at a very young age. The importance of discerning and following one's true call—and being part of a community that makes room for this—is a second pastoral aspect of this passage. Frederick Buechner says, "The place God calls you to is the place where your deep gladness and the world's deep hunger meet."[1] This deep gladness is surely something that those seeking to grow in faith and in relationship with God are seeking in their lives.

---

2. Elisabeth Schüssler Fiorenza, "Luke 2:41–52," *Interpretation* 36, no. 4 (1982): 399–403.

1. Frederick Buechner, *Wishful Thinking: A Theological ABC* (New York: Harper & Row, 1973), 95.

5.348). In later generations in Judaism, instruction in the Mishnah began at the age of ten and instruction in the Talmud at the age of fifteen (*Pirke Aboth* 5.21).

Luke's story therefore fits a literary type in which a heroic figure exhibits extraordinary characteristics even at an early age. Sometimes, as here in Luke, the elaboration of the story includes as a motif the befuddlement of the parents and/or other adults or childhood peers at the actions of the child. This serves to reinforce the idea that the heroic figure was endowed with powers that were greater than others at the same age. It was assumed that such powers derived not from the earthly parental heritage but from the gods.

The family of Jesus is said to have made a regular practice of going to Jerusalem for the Passover meal (vv. 41–42). During the Second Temple period, Passover was primarily a pilgrimage festival. That is, since sacrifice could take place only at the temple, the Passover meal would normally be eaten only in Jerusalem. The family is therefore being pictured as exemplary in their piety. This fits a theme found throughout Luke's birth narrative. It also foreshadows Jesus' own piety in celebrating the Passover in Jerusalem as an adult, even though it resulted in his death.

The story also spotlights the centrality of Jerusalem in the story of Jesus. As a child Jesus is in Jerusalem, and Jerusalem is where he will end up. Jerusalem is also where resurrection appearances take place (according to Luke; in Mark, resurrection will be experienced in Galilee). According to Acts, Jerusalem is where the church will begin. When Luke wrote, Jerusalem and its temple were in ruins. The piety practiced by the family of Jesus was no longer possible. However, for Luke and his readers, the legacy of the temple and of the teachers of Israel was now being claimed by Jesus.

The story not only draws on classic themes from ancient literature; it also draws on ordinary familial motifs: it dramatizes a parent's worst nightmare, the loss of a child in a strange city. Add to that the age of the child, an age when the independence of adulthood beckons. It is a poignant story that illustrates Luke's skill as a storyteller. Yet it is not meant to be a story about family values; rather, there is a higher meaning in mind. The story functions to define Jesus as an extraordinary child who cannot be held to normal human standards. The concerned response of the parents serves to emphasize that point. The mother of Jesus points out that "your father and I have been searching for you in great anxiety" (v. 48).

engaging and responding in rabbinic fashion. He is Teacher. Then when he is recognized again by John and by the Spirit, he is Son of God. He is first recognized as the one who *fulfills* the promise as Messiah. He is then seen as the one who *interprets* the promise as Rabbi. He is then anointed as the one who *enacts* the promise as God's Son.

We still recognize Jesus in these ways. We may see him as the fulfiller of our unfinished hopes and deepest yearnings. We may find in his teachings the promise of understanding in ways that are both consistent with what we know and altogether new. Finally, we may experience in his Spirit and the ministry of the church a power for individual and social transformation unlike any other.

In addition to looking at Luke's *placement* of this story in the Gospel, we may consider how three themes emerge within this story. Each of them describes a different but complementary analogy by which we might recognize Jesus as the Christ within us and among us today.

One of these is the theme of *wonder*. This encapsulates the intensified emotions of this story. Consider the crowds as they hear Jesus with the teachers and are amazed (*existēmi*, v. 47). This amazement is greater than simply being impressed, for it has the same root as "ecstasy." Seeing this boy learning and teaching among his elders, they are outside of themselves, unsettled, drawn to something they have never seen before. Then consider the parents, particularly Mary, who are described as "*astonished*" (v. 48), *anxious* (v. 48), and *confused* (v. 50). Mary, in the end, *treasures* these things in her heart (v. 51). Their astonishment when finding him back at the temple is different from the crowd's earlier amazement (v. 47). It is more complex—it is overwhelming. They are overwhelmed to the point of being scandalized. Their son is disobedient, even though safe. He is oblivious to their distress, to the point of being put out by it. Theirs has been no ordinary worry, but the fright and suffering (have anxiety, *odynaomai*) of a parent losing a child. There is an intensity here that is mirrored by Jesus' emphatic response.

Here is a child grown up quickly, reminding his parents that he has his own vocation. Although they do not understand his reasons, Mary holds what has happened in her heart. She ponders and waits for the understanding that still eludes her. This is the same treasuring that she is said to have performed since his birth, when others came to her and her baby and were also amazed (2:19). His presence calls out of

Luke 2:41–52

Theological Perspective

since it was not a requirement of Jewish law, her doing so must have been a special instance of motherly devotion. This is an unfortunate misinterpretation. For most of Jewish history, women were not *required* to attend, but they were not prohibited and apparently often did go (1 Sam. 1:7; 2:19). In the first century Rabbi Hillel required women to go, despite the optional nature of the law.[3] Theologically this material cannot support twenty-first-century rhetoric of "traditional family values."

The final theological vein to be mined here is Christology. A careful reading uncovers themes of Jesus' nature as both human and divine. In later centuries, controversy raged over how to understand this, but Luke offers a subtle, elegant portrayal of Jesus' dual nature. The birth narrative has already alerted us to Jesus' origins in the action of the Holy Spirit and his status as Savior, Messiah, and Lord (2:11). Now we see themes of humanity and divinity that will be marshaled in the future to develop Chalcedonian Christology.

Against Gnosticism, we see a very human family traveling to Jerusalem for the Passover. We have a very human teenager becoming so wrapped up in what he is doing with the teachers in the temple that he disregards his parents' wishes and schedule. As a final reminder of his humanity, the segment ends with Jesus returning home and remaining obedient to his human parents as he "increased in wisdom and in years" (v. 52). Against later Ebionite theology, Jesus reminds us that his father is God and his home is the temple. The twelve-year-old shows such spiritual maturity and insight that even the teachers are amazed, and his human parents do not understand. The segment closes by weaving together themes of human aging and hints of supernatural influence as he gains in "divine and human favor" (v. 52).

CHARLENE P. E. BURNS

Pastoral Perspective

For those in denominational traditions that mark the passage to a more mature stage in the journey of faith with a confirmation process, this text is an obvious affirmation of this process during the tween or early teen years. For those traditions that welcome a profession of faith from tweens and early teens, this is also an affirmation. At the ripe young age of twelve Jesus was among the learned leaders of the synagogue, teaching, learning, and growing in wisdom and in knowledge. This story offers an invitation to the twenty-first-century church to provide a place of full inclusion and honest engagement for young people. In a time when so many congregations segregate older and older children from the main worship service, we encounter Jesus, a mere twelve years old, fully engaged in a theological discussion with the religious teachers of his time.

While some might argue that Jesus was not an ordinary twelve-year-old, there is nonetheless an invitation in this story for the church to be welcoming and encouraging of its youth, as these religious leaders were of the young Jesus. Jesus was not shoved aside because he was too young to appreciate what the religious leaders were teaching and discussing. He was not sent out to another room to learn in a way "more appropriate" for someone who was only twelve years old. Jesus was fully engaged in the discussion, in the study, in the life of the community of faith.

This story invites us to reflect upon a wide range of emotions at work in this transitional moment for Jesus, his parents, and his larger community. Amid the jumbled feelings of loss, fear, worry, anger, relief, and joy, we also see a young person breaking free of his everyday life and beginning to discover his true identity and vocation. Risk and fear turn to discovery and wonder. This is a model for each of us as individuals, but also for our communities of faith.

KATHY BEACH-VERHEY

---

3. Charles H. Talbert, *Reading Luke: A Literary and Theological Commentary* (Macon, GA: Smyth & Helwys, 2002), 37–38.

Exegetical Perspective

The assumption behind her statement is that he should be more respectful of his father Joseph. This sets up Jesus to point out that, in fact, he *was* being respectful of his father, namely, his divine Father. This is the dramatic turning point in the story. Up to this point, Jesus had been presumably disrespectful, even disobedient, and needed to be effectively disciplined by his parents. His response is explanatory but not repentant. His is not an example to be followed by other young men. It is a different kind of story.

Jesus' reply to his mother (v. 49) can be translated in more than one way.[1] It can be translated as in the NRSV: "Did you not know that I must be in my Father's house?" After all, he is in the temple, where the spirit of God dwells. Another translation possibility is: "Did you not know that I must be among those belonging to my Father?" This version emphasizes that Jesus is a pious child of Israel. The third translation possibility is: "Did you not know that I must be involved in my Father's affairs?"—or "about my Father's business?" (KJV). This is the preferred translation, because it not only incorporates the other two possibilities but encapsulates the theme of the story: that Jesus is engaging in a serious study of the law with the teachers.

The heart of the story is in verses 46–47. Jesus is still a young boy, yet he has shown himself to be so advanced in the knowledge of the law that he has amazed the teachers of Israel. He is, indeed, more than an astute student or precocious child. He is manifesting his status as Son of God. He is teaching the teachers.

DENNIS E. SMITH

Homiletical Perspective

us as well an openness to wonder, a willingness to be surprised, an intensification of feeling, and the patience sometimes to hold the experience for a time when we might understand more than we do now.

A second theme is in the *rhythm of obedience and restlessness* that winds through this pericope. In the verse before, Jesus' first twelve years in Nazareth are summarized as years of faithful development. He has become strong in both wisdom and divine favor. With the journey to Jerusalem for the Passover, and then his respectful engagement with the teachers, the Gospel reaffirms his obedience to the tradition. Then at the conclusion of the episode we are told that he returns home and remains an obedient child, growing in strength, stature, and favor. He fulfills the expectations put on a faithful Jewish child of his time.

Yet there appears here a restlessness that runs through the Gospels, with Jesus obedient in this way and yet also subversive. He respects his parents, and yet is clear that his sense of vocation trumps his family obligations. Mary speaks of his earthly father (v. 48), and Jesus immediately describes the Holy One as his Father and says his home is in the temple (his "Father's house," v. 49). He honors the teachers, and yet presumes himself to teach, long before given any right to do so. Similarly, our own spiritual formation requires both deep and respectful engagement with tradition *and* openness to where Christ's Spirit might take us in response to the tradition.

Finally, one notes the theme of *slow growth and transformation* in the story. Jesus is always already Messiah, and yet he also grows *into* that role. As Mary protects, holds, and treasures what she sees of her son in her heart, so the Spirit moves in protected ways within us, and within God's people, through the many experiences of grace we receive. Transformation may not be instantaneous. It may grow slowly. Yet even so, it may still become every bit as dramatic as the promise it fulfills.

WES AVRAM

1. Joseph A. Fitzmyer, *The Gospel according to Luke I–IX*, Anchor Bible 28 (New York: Doubleday, 1981), 443–44; Luke Timothy Johnson, *The Gospel of Luke,* Sacra pagina (Collegeville, MN: Liturgical Press, 1991), 59–61.

Luke 3:1–6

¹In the fifteenth year of the reign of Emperor Tiberius, when Pontius Pilate was governor of Judea, and Herod was ruler of Galilee, and his brother Philip ruler of the region of Ituraea and Trachonitis, and Lysanias ruler of Abilene, ²during the high priesthood of Annas and Caiaphas, the word of God came to John son of Zechariah in the wilderness. ³He went into all the region around the Jordan, proclaiming a baptism of repentance for the forgiveness of sins, ⁴as it is written in the book of the words of the prophet Isaiah,

"The voice of one crying out in the wilderness:
'Prepare the way of the Lord,
  make his paths straight.
⁵ Every valley shall be filled,
  and every mountain and hill shall be made low,
and the crooked shall be made straight,
  and the rough ways made smooth;
⁶ and all flesh shall see the salvation of God.'"

Theological Perspective

This passage opens by locating John the Baptist's ministry in history. Luke situates this event by way of a descending listing of those holding earthly power over Palestine at the time: emperor, governor, high priest. During the political rule of these human beings "the word of God came to John son of Zechariah in the wilderness" (v. 2). John preaches the need for "a baptism of repentance for the forgiveness of sins" (v. 3) and paraphrases the book of Isaiah.

Isaiah 40:1–5 is a proclamation of preparation. The people of Israel are to prepare for return from exile and revelation of God's glory to all people. In using this passage, Luke is telling us that, likewise, the people of John's time are to prepare for return from their exilelike existence of failure to live a moral life (as will be shown in vv. 10–14) and be ready to share with "all flesh" in the universal "salvation of God" (v. 6). Theologically, the passage places human governments in proper relation to divine power, presents the last in the long line of Jewish prophets, proclaims the need for baptism, and calls to mind once again Luke's vision of salvation that will extend to all nations and people.

In juxtaposing the names of emperor, governor, and high priest with John's appearance, Luke signals that all temporal power is subject to the heavenly power of God. Politics and religion are human

Pastoral Perspective

Luke begins this story about John the Baptist by recounting who was in charge—or who ordinary folks thought was in charge—at the time. The lengthy list of the Roman political and Jewish religious leaders of the day reminds the readers of the power structures and systems that existed when John the Baptist heard God's call to preach. Yet God's word did not come to the political or religious leaders in the places of power in the city of Jerusalem. The word of God came to John, son of the priest Zechariah, out in the wilderness. The story invites us to follow John into the wilderness, to discover the ways of repentance and transformation.

It is not the custom of most "religious" folk today to incline their ears to wilderness prophets. Most "church folk" are more inclined to listen to the people who would make today's list of leaders—like the list with which Luke begins this pericope. One pastoral consideration in this text is the invitation to listen to the seemingly marginal voices of our time. John the Baptist was outside of the mainstream. He did not make Luke's list of first-century power players. There are leaders and prophets in our time and place too who may not make anyone's "who's who" list but who nonetheless have an important word we need to hear. Luke, through the voice of John, reminds us

Feasting on the Gospels

Exegetical Perspective

In this text Luke takes on and develops the traditional beginning of the Gospel story. According to Mark, John came to "prepare the way." Luke seeks to explain more deeply what that means. He does his research, utilizing as his sources the Gospel of Mark, Isaiah, Q, and the writings of a variety of historians of his day. In his retelling of this story, "preparing the way" is not to be reduced to a preparation for the beginning of the Jesus story. Rather, it is broadened to include the continuation of that story, namely, the institution of "the Way," as detailed in Luke's second volume, Acts (see Acts 9:2; 18:25–26; 19:9, 23; 22:4; 24:14, 22).

The story is based on an early tradition that John, an apocalyptic preacher located in the wilderness of Judea, had been sought out by Jesus to be baptized by him. This part of the Jesus tradition is likely based on actual history, since it also shows up in Josephus, in what appears to be an independent account:

> To some of the Jews the destruction of Herod's army seemed to be divine vengeance, and certainly a just vengeance, for his treatment of John, surnamed the Baptist. For Herod had put him to death, though he was a good man and had exhorted the Jews to lead righteous lives, to practice justice toward their fellows and piety toward God, and so doing to join in baptism. (*Jewish Antiquities* 18.116–17)

Homiletical Perspective

There are several interpretive trajectories here that may be selected, according to the preacher's or teacher's context, interest, and history. One approach might explore the place of this narrative in Luke's vision of salvation history. Another might explore the theological and spiritual significance of the apocalyptic genre hinted at in this passage. Another will draw analogies from John's ministry to ecclesiology and mission, seeing the role of the church in the world as similar to John's role in relation to Jesus.

In the first approach, Luke 3 is taken to signal the beginning of our Lord's earthly ministry. Prior to that, Luke has described ways in which Jesus' birth, purification in the temple, encounter with the temple teachers when twelve, and upbringing in Nazareth predict both his identity as Messiah and his role as rabbi. Yet a third confirmation comes in this chapter, culminating in Jesus' baptism by John and the Holy Spirit's confirmation of Jesus as the pleasing Son of God.

As part of this confirmation, there comes an extensive description of John's ministry. Although often overlooked in preaching that focuses on the story of Jesus, John has a role that is worth exploring. John sets Jesus' ministry into time, aided here by Luke's situating John himself in time. The moment is *religiously significant* in the history of Israel. It is *politically significant* in the history of political

Theological Perspective

endeavors and as such are to be conducted in line with God's plan. The people of John's day have lost focus and, as we shall see in Luke 3:7–14, no longer live lives informed by concern for social justice. As in the past, God has sent a prophet to remind the people of their obligations to God and of their need to return to the ways of God. In the Jewish tradition, the prophet was chosen by God to speak an important message, usually of warning, to the people. The prophets were men and women of great holiness who served as examples of righteousness, and they came to challenge the status quo.

For the Christian tradition, John is the last of the prophets, and he speaks the "the word of God" (*rhēma theou*) that had come to him in the wilderness. Some have argued that Luke's word choice here has theological importance.[1] These interpreters say that Luke uses *rhēma* rather than *logos*—the word used for the preexistent Christ in John's Gospel—because *rhēma* means a revelation received through the Holy Spirit, whereas *logos* signifies a written revelation. Luke, however, uses both terms frequently and apparently synonymously.

In the early fifth century Augustine of Hippo offered a more poetic interpretation of John as "the voice" and Jesus as "the Word spoken"; the voice is only understood by virtue of the clarity of the words spoken.[2] The most significant aspect of this passage for theological reflection, however, is not which Greek term for "word" was chosen by the author, but rather what that "word" compelled John to preach: "a baptism of repentance for the forgiveness of sins" (v. 3).

Historically, theological interpreters have reflected on John's baptism in contrast to baptism in the name of Christ. John's baptism fits within the Jewish purification ritual system as an eschatological act of penance—this is "a baptism of repentance for the forgiveness of sins" (v. 3)—whereas the baptism to come will bring not just forgiveness of sins but also regeneration and entry into the community of believers. As will become clear in the next portion of the Gospel, John's baptism is directly tied to social-justice concerns like feeding and clothing those in need (3:11), marking the return to righteousness.

Augustine of Hippo taught that John functioned as a boundary stone between the Old and New Testaments and between two ages, the sinful era before Christ and the new era inaugurated by him. Adding

1. John MacArthur, *Luke 1–5*, MacArthur New Testament Commentary (Chicago: Moody Books, 2009), 191–98.
2. Augustine of Hippo, *Sermons 273–305A* (III/8), in *Works of Saint Augustine*, trans. Edmund O. Hill (Hyde Park, NY: New City Press, 1994), Sermon 293.

Pastoral Perspective

that God's justice and truth often come to us from unlikely places and characters.

A second pastoral consideration is with the place where John preached: the wilderness. The wilderness is unfamiliar. It is uncomfortable. It generates fear. Few of us choose to go into the wilderness, although most of us find ourselves there more often than we like during our life journeys. Pastors do not like the wilderness any more than do the folks who come to worship hoping to be comforted and affirmed. Yet it is often in the wilderness that God does something transformative, renewing, or inspiring. God often uses the wilderness times of life to teach, to stretch, and to remake God's people.

There is a pastoral invitation in this story to explore the wilderness times and places in our lives and to examine where and how God is present in them. Just as God shaped Israel into a people during their long sojourn in the wilderness, we too are likely to be transformed when we step away from the false securities of our lives. Like the people of Israel, we may complain about the discomforts and threats we encounter in the wilderness. The creature comforts that folks are used to may be absent. The familiar structures of church, the order of worship and the music, the committees and the events that happen year after year, are not present in the wilderness. Still, the word of God came to John in the wilderness. The word did not come to the temple in Jerusalem, nor was it heard in the familiar streets of the city outside the temple, but rather out in the wilderness. We may complain about our rulers—both political and religious—but we prefer the structures that we know and are familiar with to the lawless, unpredictable wilderness. Luke invites his readers, through the voice of John the Baptist, to consider venturing beyond the conventional and into the unfamiliar.

The wilderness seems like a scary place to us and to those who join us in the pews on Sunday mornings. Wilderness conjures up thoughts of harsh conditions, loneliness, hardship, and suffering. However, throughout the story of God's salvation we find example after example of God using wilderness times to bring about renewal, rebirth, clarity, and purpose for God's people. The Israelites complained that they would prefer to go back to slavery in Egypt, rather than learn how to adapt to their new life in the wilderness. Elijah fled to the wilderness only to hear God there in the silence more clearly than he had been able to hear God elsewhere. Even Jesus spent significant time in the wilderness, forty days

Mark interpreted the story of John baptizing Jesus by way of Isaiah 40:3, which proclaimed that the preaching in the wilderness would be a preparation for the coming of the Lord. In Mark, the "preparation" of John consists not only in his preaching in the wilderness à la Isaiah but also in his providing the launching pad for the ministry of Jesus. Luke adapted and expanded this interpretation of John as the "one-who-prepares-the-way." He begins the story of John much earlier in his narrative, with a lengthy interweaving of the story of John's birth with the story of Jesus' birth (1:5–2:20). Here in 3:1–6 he makes two significant additions to Mark's account: he adds a chronological introduction, and he lengthens the biblical quote to include Isaiah 40:3–5. Each addition connects with larger themes in Luke's Gospel and thereby makes an important theological contribution to Luke's story of John.

Luke takes pride in being a consummate researcher. In his prologue, he says he has utilized only the most reliable sources (1:1–4). Here in 3:1–2 he has apparently consulted a variety of historical writings, most prominently Josephus, to set the political context for the preaching of John. This fits a pattern he follows elsewhere in Luke–Acts, in which he often interweaves the story of Jesus with its political context. Sometimes his political references are correct, sometime incorrect (e.g., 2:1–2). Regardless, the political references do more than simply establish the historical setting for the story of Jesus. They also provide a backdrop for a developing theology in regard to earthly rule.

Here the leaders named are largely defined by their commitment to violence and death. Most will play a role in the death of Jesus: Pontius Pilate, governor of Judea; Herod Antipas, tetrarch of Galilee; Annas and Caiaphas, named as high priests; and, by implication, the ruler of them all, Emperor Tiberius. In addition, two of those named will play a role in the death of John, Herod Antipas and Philip, tetrarch of Ituraea and Trachonitis (3:19). Lysanias, however, whom Luke names as tetrarch of Abilene, has no further role in either Luke or Acts. Luke's identification of Annas and Caiaphas as joint high priests is confusing and questionable. Annas was actually high priest from 6 to 15 CE; his son-in-law Caiaphas was high priest from 18 to 36 CE. Later in Luke's story, when Jesus is interrogated, it is by an unnamed high priest (22:54, 66). Still later, after the death of Jesus, Annas alone is identified as high priest (Acts 4:6). Apparently Luke had conflicting information about the high priesthood at this period and was unable to resolve it.

oppression, occupation, and desire for liberation. It is *culturally significant* in the role John takes on to warn, admonish, and separate those who are ready for Jesus' ministry from those who are not.

Luke affirms the religious significance of the moment by presenting John as the one predicted by Isaiah to cry out in the wilderness, whose life and witness will say that the time has come for repentance and redemption. Resonant with the call of prophets in Hebrew Scripture, John takes up the mantle not only of Isaiah, but also of Amos, Hosea, Jeremiah, and more.

Luke also signals the political significance of the moment by situating John within a specific moment in Israel's history: "in the fifteenth year of the reign of Emperor Tiberias" (v. 1). Roman rulers who are impinging upon Israel are named and placed on the map. Interwoven with their rule is the inevitably compromised religious leadership of an occupied people, "during the high priesthood of Annas and Caiaphas" (v. 2).

An astute reader will also note the cultural significance of this moment, recognizing what is in store for John at the hands of worldly power, firebrand that he is. Those already familiar with the story will know this is the context of what lies ahead for Jesus. That Jesus' ministry cannot be separated from John's signifies how embedded the life, work, and teachings of Jesus are in the real world. The tension between the radical rhetoric of John's message and Jesus' language of reconciliation and forgiveness preserves a dynamic germane to Christ's ministry. Mercy judges as it forgives, love reveals as it heals, sacrifice divides even as it reconciles. Mercy, love, and sacrifice win, but not by escaping the difficulties of the moment. It may, therefore, be reassuring to see that religious, political, and cultural dynamics are always present within Christian vision. They may complicate Christian hope, but they will never defeat it.

An affirmation of Christian hope suggests a second approach to this passage, in which the tone of the passage becomes the topic. Here is a glimpse of an apocalyptic sensibility that recurs throughout the New Testament. The late emeritus professor of Bible at the Hebrew University, Shemaryahu Talmon, succinctly summarized the significance of New Testament apocalyptic sensibility when he noted that, in contrast to much (not all) of Hebrew Scripture, one has the feeling throughout the New Testament that "something is always just about to happen."[1]

1. Shemaryahu Talmon, lecture, Hebrew University in Jerusalem, Spring 1985.

Luke 3:1–6

Theological Perspective

to this theme, Colin Brown's[3] interpretation of John's baptism illuminates how Luke's salvation history, begun in the wilderness among the Israelites, focuses first on the life of Jesus and then opens outward again with the universal offer of salvation. Brown argues that perhaps John's baptism was significant not so much as ritual purification through washing in the Jordan as for the symbolic meaning of the Jordan River itself. Luke has used Old Testament imagery extensively to ensure that parallels between John the Baptist and Elijah are seen. Now John the Baptist cries out from the wilderness and travels "into all the region around the Jordan" (v. 3), proclaiming the need for repentance. In ancient times, the Jordan marked the boundary of the promised land. The Israelites' crossing of it in Joshua 3–5 marked their cleansing of "the disgrace of Egypt" (Josh. 5:9), and the river also figures prominently in the Elijah-Elisha stories of 2 Kings, where its crossing sanctifies Elisha as Elijah's successor (2 Kgs. 2:6–14). In performing his baptisms in the Jordan, perhaps John intends his Jewish followers to understand themselves as having crossed into a newly sanctified life.

John's baptism recalls the Jewish meaning of repentance as turning back or returning; it represents the symbolic exodus of a sinful people from Judea and their return as a contrite and sanctified people who may now reclaim the land as a renewed nation. In turning their backs on past sins, those who accepted John's baptism participated once again in the symbolic ending of national disgrace and attained spiritual freedom from the bonds of Roman oppression. John's proclamation from out of the wilderness is, then, a call to moral renewal. As will become abundantly clear in the next passage, this moral renewal centers on social justice; the people had capitulated to Roman rule and in so doing had lost touch with what it means to be the people of God. Theologically this serves to remind us across the centuries that worldly powers must always be subject to God's call for compassion and justice.

CHARLENE P. E. BURNS

Pastoral Perspective

that offered him the opportunity to gain strength and clarity for his mission and ministry on earth.

This story also offers a pastoral invitation for those who feel as if they are lost and alone in the wilderness. There is a word of hope and purpose for those who have not voluntarily entered the wilderness or have no interest in the transformation that God may have for them there. The word of God comes in the wilderness, in strange, unconventional ways, yet promises a new and better tomorrow; for the Savior of the world is both there with us and coming soon to redeem and restore us.

The word of hope to those in the wilderness is that all will be made new. The rough places will be made smooth, and the crooked shall be made straight. The wilderness is not only a place where we are jerked from our comfort zones and challenged to hear God's word, but also the place where the troubled, the hurting, the alienated, the angry, and the forlorn may hear a word of hope and renewal and discover the possibility for rebirth and change. People in the pew may not want to be in the wilderness, but if they are there, this text offers a word of hope and the promise of transformation.

It is hard for God to find us—and for us to find God—when we are surrounded by the comforts and distractions of this world. Perhaps this is why John's speech was so stark, so forthright, and so challenging. In order to join God's people we must come out from the slavery and seduction of this world. John's prophetic word makes clear what is required. In the wilderness places and moments, God is likely to be speaking to us—as God did through John the Baptist—words of challenge and hope and a presence that transforms and renews.

KATHY BEACH-VERHEY

---

3. Colin Brown, "What Was John the Baptist Doing?" *Bulletin for Biblical Research* 7 (1997): 37–50.

Exegetical Perspective

In contrast to the inhabited earth, which is ruled over by earthly authorities, the word of God comes to John in a "desolate, uninhabited land," which is the literal meaning of the word we translate as "wilderness" (*erēmos*). This is a location where "the word of God" can thrive, unthreatened by the dark powers of the urban landscape. It is a harsh land, an appropriate setting for a message of repentance. The term "repentance" (*metanoia*) in broad terms means a "change of mind" or in some contexts "remorse." The baptism of John functions as a ritual sign of commitment to the lifestyle or ethos defined by repentance. The ethos of repentance will be defined in more detail in John's preaching (3:7–14).

Luke has expanded the quotation from Isaiah (Mark ended the quotation with "make his paths straight") and, in so doing, has highlighted its message of political critique. This emphasis becomes clear when one notices its connection and contrast with the elaborate listing of villainous rulers in verses 1–2. For Luke, it is the political landscape that will be smoothed out and straightened with the coming of the Lord, a theme also emphasized earlier in the birth narrative (1:51–53, 70–75). This is also the time "when all flesh shall see the salvation of God" (v. 6), a phrase that gets at one of Luke's primary emphases. The coming of the Lord is the time of "a light for revelation to the Gentiles" (2:32). The rest of the story in Luke–Acts will largely revolve around that theme.

To the secular world, events are numbered by the reigns of rulers. In God's eyes, events are numbered by different criteria, the criteria announced of old by the prophets. Rulers come and go, but the word of God endures, following a different path, a straight path.

DENNIS E. SMITH

Homiletical Perspective

Time is full and ready to break open. This summary suggests the power that apocalyptic sensibility can give preaching. For Luke's John, as for the readers of Luke's Gospel, something dramatic is indeed always just about to happen. This may be a core dynamic within Christian experience in general. For in Christian piety there resides a necessary openness to surprise, an inevitable openness to an active God, and an unavoidable openness toward the future. John's ministry places this openness at the root of Jesus' ministry.

In light of apocalyptic sensibility, a preacher might argue against cynicism, despair, and the compromise of principle for expediency. They betray Christian hope. One might similarly argue against clinging to purely practical solutions to spiritual challenges. One might do this by noting ways in which a purely incremental pragmatism that is free of a deeply expressed hope for true, adaptive, and lasting change leaves individuals, families, congregations, communities, and the world short of what the gospel promises. Hope is worth sacrifice, for something might happen at any moment.

Finally, preachers and teachers more inclined to a mission-oriented interpretation than a theological one might find in John's ministry an analogy to the role of the church in relation to God's mission. Here the church becomes the voice crying in the wilderness to prepare the Lord's way. Isaiah's imagery becomes important here, as Luke uses it to describe John's passion. Differences that hinder the realization of God's vision are to be equalized, just as crooked paths are to be made straight, valleys filled and mountains leveled, and rough ways made smooth (vv. 4, 5). In short, barriers that stand between "all flesh" (v. 6) and God's way for the world are to be dismantled. Only in this way will Jesus' vision of God's realm be made real in this world. Barriers of race, ideology, class, gender, education, and even religion may be hurdles to be overcome on the way to the reconciliation promised in and by Christ.

In light of this mission-interested analogy, one may ask a congregation how they are breaking down barriers in their own lives, whether those barriers are spiritual or practical. One might ask how the congregation itself is doing this work in its own ministries. Finally, one might issue a call to action, inspired by John and in service to Jesus.

WES AVRAM

⁷John said to the crowds that came out to be baptized by him, "You brood of vipers! Who warned you to flee from the wrath to come? ⁸Bear fruits worthy of repentance. Do not begin to say to yourselves, 'We have Abraham as our ancestor'; for I tell you, God is able from these stones to raise up children to Abraham. ⁹Even now the ax is lying at the root of the trees; every tree therefore that does not bear good fruit is cut down and thrown into the fire."

¹⁰And the crowds asked him, "What then should we do?" ¹¹In reply he said to them, "Whoever has two coats must share with anyone who has none; and whoever has food must do likewise." ¹²Even tax collectors came to be baptized, and they asked him, "Teacher, what should we do?" ¹³He said to them, "Collect no more than the amount prescribed for you." ¹⁴Soldiers also asked him, "And we, what should we do?" He said to them, "Do not extort money from anyone by threats or false accusation, and be satisfied with your wages."

Theological Perspective

In keeping with the prophetic tradition, John castigates those who have come for baptism, warning that having been born a "child of Abraham" is no guarantee of salvation. He uses a striking metaphor to drive home the point: if being offspring of Abraham is all God is looking for, God could use the stones to fill out the rolls.

Taken in isolation, the passage seems to advocate what Christians will later call works righteousness or justification through works, but to read it this way one must remove it from the whole story, from the wider context of the "good news." Only when passages like this are taken out of context is it possible to claim scriptural support for theologies either of righteousness through faith alone or through works alone.

The passage fits within Luke's overall presentation of Jesus' ministry as focused on transforming this world into one in which those who *have* take care of those *in need*. It serves to remind believers of their obligation to work for social justice here and now. To claim to be children of God without dealing charitably and justly with others is to sin, clearly to miss the mark. This is not to imply, however, that to follow Christ means simply caring for others. The passage in context is consonant with the scriptural message that without good works, faith cannot be

Pastoral Perspective

A natural reaction when John called the crowd gathered before him a "brood of vipers" would have been collective recoil and flight. Who wants to be compared to a den of snakes waiting to ambush their unsuspecting prey? Instead of recoiling, the crowd remained and repeatedly asked John what they should do (3:10, 12, 14). Had I been labeled as part of a family of snakes, I would not have waited around to hear what would come next from the prophet's mouth. Yet the crowds, who had flocked to the wilderness to hear John's challenging preaching and to be baptized in the river Jordan, remained in his presence and pressed John to explain what he meant by repentance. It seems that John's audience, in all its diversity, really came out to the desert because the people wanted to change.

The crowds who gathered with John seemed to understand, by their questions, that repentance is more than just a wish or a profession of nice words. Repentance is something that is done. It is acted out in the ways life is lived. Repentance is not about looking back at what has gone wrong in the past, but about looking forward to how life may be lived differently in the future, as forgiven and transformed people. True repentance is about change—changing oneself and the world around you, with God's help. Twenty-first-century preachers and teachers would

Exegetical Perspective

This story continues the account in 3:1–6 of John the Baptist's proclamation of God's coming reign. Here Luke provides content to the "voice of one crying out in the wilderness." Giving voice to the preaching of John the Baptist is a fascinating component of the Gospel tradition, in which otherwise only the preaching of Jesus is featured. This tradition apparently originates in the source Q. Luke is here artfully combining Mark, Q, and his own creative addition. The result is Luke's version of the "preparation" theme, in which John introduces the ethos of the new community of God. This theme fits Luke's emphasis not only in the Gospel but also in Acts, where it will be used to define the church in its golden age.

According to Mark, the content of John's preaching could be reduced to the phrase "proclaiming a baptism of repentance for the forgiveness of sins" (Mark 1:4). Josephus, on the other hand, identifies an ethical component to John's teaching: "John, called the Baptist . . . who was exhorting the Jews to life upright lives, in dealing justly with one another and submitting devoutly to God, and to join in Baptism" (*Jewish Antiquities* 18:116–17). Luke's synopsis of the preaching of John has much in common with that of Josephus. Luke follows Mark in characterizing the preaching of John as "proclaiming a baptism

Homiletical Perspective

In the wilderness preparing people for the One who is coming, John's message is sharp and his tone is one of warning. The moment of decision has come, for something is about to happen that will divide rather than unite. No one will be allowed to stand in the middle. You will be on one side or the other. He saw what Christian tradition came to call, using Latin, a *status confessionis*, when fidelity to the God of Abraham depends not upon mere affiliation or mild affirmation, but responding to a moment by uniting word and act in repentance and transformation. There is no more time for patience.

Luke presents John's either-or call as the opening bell of Jesus' ministry. Luke's depiction of the ministry of this wild one in the wilderness may present itself as a historical account of how Jesus came into public view, but it also says something about how everyone must turn to Christ, regardless of whether that turning is quiet or dramatic. It matters not whether one is ready to choose, willing to change, or somehow aware of the significance of a moment. In this narrative, vague acknowledgment of God's rule and Jesus' messianic vocation is not enough. It is an inadequate preparation for discipleship. Something more definitive and decisive is called for.

To reinforce this idea, we should note the irony in the first verse of this passage. John intensifies his

Theological Perspective

genuine, and without charity, there is no justification (Matt. 7:22–23; John 15:2; 1 Cor. 6:9–11; Gal. 5:19–21; Jas. 2:17).

Theologians who read John's call to repentance (and also Paul's discussions of justification) through the lens of post-Reformation theologies often fail to take into account what repentance meant in first-century Jewish circles, including Jesus and his followers. Repentance, then and now, presupposes faith. For Jews, repentance was a crucial expression of the covenantal relationship with God. Every Jew would have practiced acts of repentance before the annual atonement for sins on Yom Kippur, so the content of John's preaching is not new, but perhaps the form of enactment is. To repent is "to return"; in crossing over the Jordan and returning, John's followers indicate that they intend to return to ways of life that conform not to Roman norms but to Jewish covenantal life.

Some post-Reformation readers mistakenly contrast John to Jesus, claiming that John advocated works righteousness but Jesus preached righteousness through faith alone. Carried to its logical conclusion, faith-alone thinking led in the early centuries to antinomianism. In the late fourth century, for example, Jovinian's faith-alone thinking led him to claim that it was impossible to sin after baptism. Augustine of Hippo refuted this claim in his *On Faith and Works* (413 CE) and developed a more complex theology of faith-leading-to-works made possible by prevenient grace. For many centuries following, the language of salvation was grace oriented, and the church was said to be the sole means through which grace comes into the world.

Although in the New Testament grace is spoken of as a gift, the idea that grace is mediated through the church gradually evolved into practices thought to increase one's access to this divine commodity. During the Middle Ages, emphasis on works said to earn grace began to overshadow faith, as in the Roman Catholic Church's sale of indulgences in exchange for reduced time in purgatory for oneself and one's loved ones. In reaction to abuses of the indulgence system, Martin Luther preached a theology of justification by faith.

Luther's Latin phrase *sola fide* became the slogan for reform in the sixteenth century. Some of Luther's followers took this teaching so far that they revived antinomianism, distorting Luther's teachings. Although Luther did argue that works do not in and of themselves lead to justification, as a whole his theology of justification affirmed that genuine faith

Pastoral Perspective

be thrilled if the people who come to worship and education events, small groups, and prayer meetings were so open to this kind of transformation today.

In this passage, John the Baptizer offers to the crowds in the wilderness, and to the followers of Jesus in the twenty-first century, guidelines for living a changed life. For preachers and teachers looking for a "practical" text that ordinary church folks can really wrap their heads around, this passage is a great place to turn. While this encounter with John the Baptist is often read during the Advent season, these verses offer the followers of Jesus Christ a message for all seasons about mission and justice. John linked repentance to the daily practices of peacemaking, sharing resources, and fairness, especially in relationships usually characterized by exploitation and self-interest. He called believers to move beyond lip service and to "bear the fruit" of repentance in their communities and in the world.

Those who genuinely repent will live their lives with a focus not on self, but on others, turning away not only from their former lives, twisted by alienation and violence, but toward deeds of compassion, justice, and love. John also made clear that the time for this transformative repentance is *now*. "The ax is lying at the root of the tree," John warned. The time for believers to bear good fruit is now. Putting off change until tomorrow is not an option, for the tree that does not bear the fruit of repentance is about to be chopped down. Those who are made new in the waters of John's baptism are called into immediate, decisive action.

The crowds who came to John the Baptist in the wilderness seemed to sense the urgency of John's message. A similar sense of urgency should shape our proclamation today. In the twenty-first century the evidence that a new way is needed is all around us. Every passing day seems to bring a multitude of tragedies: a bombing, a plant explosion, a terrible shooting, a devastating hurricane. Around the globe, news reports remind us of continued civil wars, the death of hundreds of low-wage workers in workplace disasters, elected leaders murdering their own people, the ravages and violence of drug trade, and the horrors of human trafficking.

In addition to the stories of tragedy and pain that greet us in every headline, each of us knows of more personal stories of grief and suffering. Often even the Christian response to so much difficulty is to throw our hands in the air and declare it all too complicated to know where to begin to respond. However, we are not called to fix everything, only to

of repentance" (3:3). Like Matthew, however, he goes beyond Mark in providing an excerpt from that proclamation in a text found in exact word-for-word parallel form in Luke 3:7–9 and Matthew 3:7–10, making it one of our strongest examples of the existence and use of Q.

Luke 3:7–9 is a blunt apocalyptic text, promising "wrath" and "fire" for those who do not "bear fruit worthy of repentance," or live a lifestyle that exhibits true repentance. In its basic form, it is a traditional prophetic critique: Israel has gone astray; thus the prophet delivers his message in the wilderness, where Israel was first formed as God's people, rather than in Jerusalem, and calls for Israel to repent. What remains undefined is what the term "fruit of repentance" represents in Luke. The most specific clue to its content is that it stands in opposition to any claim of Abraham as father, which correlates with a key theme of Luke, the Gentile mission, a theme already suggested in the Isaiah quotation above (3:4–6, citing Isaiah 40:3–5). The quotation connects the message of John with the revelation of God's salvation to "all flesh." The Gentile mission theme is also embedded in Jesus' first sermon in Luke, delivered to the synagogue congregation in Nazareth (4:16–30). Here Jesus identifies his ministry as bringing "good news to the poor," then undercuts the audience's expectations by identifying the "poor" as non-Jews (4:18, 25–28).

This theme will be fulfilled in Acts, in which a key turning point in the story is the conversion of the first Gentile, Cornelius (Acts 10–11). In its original historical context, this message in Luke is intended to affirm Gentiles, a group that lacks specific biblical legitimacy as children of God. It is a message that has too often been reduced to supersessionism, the idea that Gentiles take the place of Jews in God's eyes. This is an unfortunate and debilitating development in Christian theology. A more appropriate adaptation of this theme for the modern context is to see in it a strain of universal proclamation that Luke presents as inherent to the gospel, a proclamation of good news to "all flesh."

The next paragraph, 3:10–14, is Luke's own creative addition to the preaching of John and his definition of the term "fruits of repentance." He introduces the paragraph with a question that arises naturally from the previous apocalyptic warning: "What then should we do?" This is a typical segue for Luke (see 10:25; 18:18; Acts 2:37; 16:30; 22:10). It is the point where Luke functions most specifically as an evangelist of "the Way."

message in a way no contemporary preacher would dare. He has little patience even for those who have heard his message and come forward to accept it. Would an evangelist in a stadium watching hundreds coming down from the stands to accept the faith he has preached turn to the very ones coming forward and call them snakes? This is what John seems to do. He questions the honesty of those who have come, insisting they have more to do than just present themselves. Repentance requires more than just inclination, he insists. It requires an ethic, even as it requires the drama of attention, warning, and acceptance. Only the tree that bears fruit will be spared the ax (v. 9).

Perhaps John looks out and sees old divisions still holding among those coming for baptism, with some sheltering themselves from the sun while others burn, or some bullying their way to the front of the line by claiming privilege. Perhaps some are insisting their pedigree exempts them from the full force of John's baptism. They do not need the water, really. They hope they can stand at the edge and let the splash fall on them without ever going in. Seeing this, John doubles down.

The perplexity of the crowds in response to John may be similar to how followers of God have often experienced the tension between law and grace. Are we saved from wrath because we make changes, or are we saved because we simply accept unearned favor? Unable to resolve the tension, we may ask the exasperated question that the crowds asked John: "What then should we do?" (v. 10).

"What then should we do?" is asked three times in these verses. It is first asked by "the crowds" after John criticizes those who claim that their status as children of Abraham is enough to save them. It is then asked by tax collectors and finally by soldiers. The identification of those three groups cannot be incidental.

From one vantage point, these three groups demonstrate the expanding political horizon of this ministry. They begin with the closed group of those who believe they are OK because they have the membership card of righteous oppression under Roman rule. The next group includes those who live in between. They are the tax collectors who move between the occupied Jewish community and the occupying Roman authority. They are agents of the political reality, making decisions of self-interested compromise every day. The third to ask are soldiers, the occupiers. They cannot claim Abraham as their ancestor, nor do they live in between. They wield

Luke 3:7–14

Theological Perspective

leads to good works: "if good works do not follow, faith is false, and not true."[1]

John the Baptist's instructions to those who come for baptism make it clear that genuine repentance flows into acts of social justice. John speaks to the specific ways in which each group that comes to him engages in injustice. When "the crowds" ask what they ought to do to "bear fruits worthy of repentance" (v. 8), he replies that those having sufficient clothing and food must share with anyone having none (v. 11). He tells the tax collectors that they must "collect no more than the amount prescribed for you" and the soldiers that they must cease extorting money through falsely accusing people of crimes they have not committed (vv. 12–14).

Scholars estimate that 90 percent of the population lived in poverty and were subjected to annual taxation rates of 30–40 percent.[2] Jews employed by the government as tax collectors were paid a percentage of what they collected, but it was standard practice to extort additional sums whenever possible. The exploitative soldiers to whom John is preaching are presumably Jewish "police," men employed by the Sanhedrin to enforce Jewish law. This parasitic abuse of fellow Jews was in direct violation of covenantal responsibilities; repentance for tax collectors and for the Jewish police meant turning back to the life of communal justice required by God.

The theological import of this passage touches on issues of faith, justification, and social justice. It is not birth lines but the bearing of "good fruit" that ensures salvation (v. 9); it is not which family we are from but what we do that matters to God. What we do flows from faith, expresses our repentance, and includes sharing of resources, honesty, and just treatment of those over whom we have worldly power. Genuine faith is not opposed to good works, but good works are the integral expressions of genuine faith. What we do reveals whose we are.

CHARLENE P. E. BURNS

Pastoral Perspective

turn around so that we see what God is doing in our midst, conforming our own practices to the reality of God's rule. John's challenge to the crowds two thousand years ago is still the challenge that is before the North American church in the twenty-first century: to repent, to turn around, to live for others, to get involved in the work of restoring relationships. So the question is still the same today: "What are we to do?"

"What are we to do?" It is both a very basic question and a central question for any who take discipleship seriously. As those who have been transformed by the grace and love of Jesus Christ, what then are we to do? Jesus' ministry, which began shortly after his baptism by John, put flesh on John's instructions and shows us living answers to the question. Jesus' ministry was directed to making sure the hungry and the naked had the basic necessities for survival, that all were treated with dignity and respect. Like John, he lifted up honest work done with integrity, taught folks to live modestly while avoiding greed, and reached out to those on the margins of society. Jesus lived and modeled humility and simplicity for the sake of others, all the way to the cross.

"What should we do?" the crowds, the tax collectors, and finally the soldiers ask John. Today John might answer, "Be like Pope Francis, who on his first Maundy Thursday, instead of washing the feet of his fellow bishops in Rome, went out to the local juvenile prison and washed the feet of the young prisoners there, regardless of their religious tradition or gender." "Be like the powerful and well-connected CEO who left corporate America to become the head of a large, Christian nonprofit organization, so that he could devote his energy each day to improving the lives of the poor." "Be like the teenage girl who gave up her allowance so that her elderly neighbor could buy gas to go visit his wife with Alzheimer's in the nursing home miles away."

This is repentance that bears fruit. Repentance for this moment.

KATHY BEACH-VERHEY

1. Martin Luther, Smalcald Articles, 1537, in *Book of Concord*. Part III, Article XIII; http://bookofconcord.org/historical-7.php; accessed Nov. 17, 2012.
2. E. P. Sanders, *Judaism: Practice and Belief 63 BCE–66 CE* (Philadelphia: Trinity Press, 1992), 146–69. Richard Horsley, *Bandits, Prophets, and Messiahs: Popular Movements in the Time of Jesus* (Harrisburg, PA: Trinity Press, 1999), 52–63.

Exegetical Perspective

The answers to the question also draw on typical themes in Luke. The first group addressed, the "crowds," are those who have more clothing and food than they need; they are exhorted to share with those who lack sufficient clothing and food. This group represents the rich, a group often singled out in Luke to be in danger of damnation unless they carry out their responsibility to care for the poor (12:13–21; 16:19–31; 18:18–25). The second group addressed are the tax collectors, a classic category of "outcasts" in Luke, typically paired with a generic group identified as "sinners" (5:27–30; 7:34; 15:1). They are exhorted to collect taxes honestly, as exemplified later in Luke by Zacchaeus, who is also, incidentally, a rich man (19:1–10). The soldiers are the third group to be addressed. These are most likely intended by Luke to be Roman soldiers like the centurion Cornelius, the first Gentile convert (Acts 10–11). They therefore represent Gentiles, and their presence here functions to foreshadow the importance of Gentiles later in the story. They too are exhorted to be honest in their monetary dealings.

In all three cases, the primary issue being addressed has to do with the proper use of possessions. Luke 3:10–14 therefore emerges as the culmination of Luke's interpretation of John's message to "prepare the way." For Luke, "the Way" is another term for the Christian community itself (Acts 9:2 et al.). The phrase "prepare the way" therefore has a double meaning: it refers to the preparation both for the coming of Jesus and for his message, which is fulfilled when the Way emerges. Luke 3:10–14 functions to foreshadow Luke's understanding of the central ethos of the new community of God. In its ideal form, it will be a community in which all possessions are shared and all those in need are cared for (Acts 2:44–45).

DENNIS E. SMITH

Homiletical Perspective

the sword of the world's powers, and yet they too are capable of sensing the moment and hearing John's call. They may have further to go than any of the others, but their journey to change may actually be easier for that reason.

Notably, John does not demand that any of these groups leave their "places." They stay where they are, but they are to be different where they are. Christian ethics has never fully resolved whether conversion requires a change of life-vocation or a transformation within life-vocation.

From those who would claim the protection of status, affiliation, or membership, John demands that generosity replace self-interest. The needs of the other should take greater priority, a higher status, than one's own protection or security (v. 11). This demand is repeated throughout the New Testament.

From those who, like the tax collectors, have learned survival skills in an unjust system, John demands integrity (v. 13). No more stealing, no more gaming, no more "everybody else does it" excuses. They must demand less for themselves so that others may be treated fairly. This call is particularly relevant in our market-driven economy today.

Finally, from the soldiers, whose tool is neither status nor savvy but raw power, John demands respect for others (v. 14). John tells these that the fruit of their repentance, like what he demands of tax collectors, will be seen not in personal gain but in true modesty. They will have less, which will be a holy price to pay for treating others as they deserve to be treated. No more extortion, no more deception, no more threats. They may no longer command by fear. Like John's demands upon the others in his audience, his demand of the soldiers remains relevant in so many places of our world today.

The movement of Christian ethics might be summed up in a strange syllogism: "Be perfect! You can't! You must! With Christ, all things are possible!" This sums up the impossibility at the beginning of faith that can be worked out only in the *life* of faith. We become prepared for discipleship of Christ when we see this clearly, take the decisive step, and expect his grace.

WES AVRAM

Luke 3:15–20

¹⁵As the people were filled with expectation, and all were questioning in their hearts concerning John, whether he might be the Messiah, ¹⁶John answered all of them by saying, "I baptize you with water; but one who is more powerful than I is coming; I am not worthy to untie the thong of his sandals. He will baptize you with the Holy Spirit and fire. ¹⁷His winnowing fork is in his hand, to clear his threshing floor and to gather the wheat into his granary; but the chaff he will burn with unquenchable fire."

¹⁸So, with many other exhortations, he proclaimed the good news to the people. ¹⁹But Herod the ruler, who had been rebuked by him because of Herodias, his brother's wife, and because of all the evil things that Herod had done, ²⁰added to them all by shutting up John in prison.

Theological Perspective

The whole Gospel of Luke is filled with the presence and activity of the Holy Spirit. Our particular text (vv. 15–20) focuses on the active presence of the Holy Spirit as the distinguishing factor in the life and ministry of Jesus. While John baptizes with water, Jesus baptizes with the Holy Spirit and fire. Jesus' life and ministry are Spirit filled. We should not, however, miss the continuity between the baptisms performed by Jesus and the baptisms done by John the Baptist, even as we highlight the distinction, for the Holy Spirit has been at work from the beginning. Moreover, John the Baptist's message of repentance and warning of judgment finds continuity in Jesus. Nonetheless, the presence of the Spirit in Jesus' life and ministry is a prominent and decisive difference.

What does this tell us about Jesus in relation to the Holy Spirit? Our text underscores at the outset the relationship between Jesus and the Holy Spirit. Jesus embodies the presence and power of the Holy Spirit; he is Spirit filled. The Holy Spirit has found a dwelling place in him, and he is its conduit. Only by being such a person can his life and acts reveal the presence and power of God. As one filled with the Holy Spirit, Jesus baptizes with the Holy Spirit and fire. What does it mean to be baptized with the Holy Spirit and fire? What is this kind of baptism?

Pastoral Perspective

John the Baptist put on quite a show, and the people noticed. It is easy to imagine the crowd at the riverbank taking in the spectacle of powerful preaching and multiple baptisms. Excitement would have been in the air as the people wondered who this preacher was.

Quite naturally, the people began to lift John up and to project their hopes and dreams onto him. Scripture says that they "were filled with expectation," and that they asked John whether he was the Messiah come to save them from the oppression of the Romans. John was clearly an extraordinary person; so, in their longing for an end to their oppression and discomfort, the people wondered aloud whether he was the one, *the* extraordinary person. The crowd was looking for a star, a leader to take them away from their troubles, and they looked to John with hopeful eyes. It must have been quite flattering.

Yet John resisted the temptation to accept their praise and to bask in the glory that the crowd offered him. He chose instead to point to Jesus. In a humility that must have taken his listeners by surprise, he directed attention away from his own efforts and instead worked to excite the crowd even further in anticipation of the Great One to follow. He even began to help them reshape their expectations of the

Exegetical Perspective

The author begins this section by distinguishing those filled with messianic expectation (v. 15, "the people," *laos*) from those needing to repent (vv. 7, 10, "the crowds," *ochloi*). The "crowds" initially addressed by John the Baptist included tax collectors (v. 12) and soldiers (v. 14)—segments of the Jewish population most likely not filled with messianic expectations. In the context of the Gospels, tax collectors were Jews responsible for collecting taxes from various areas in Palestine for the Romans. Likewise, "soldiers" here refers to Jews who voluntarily enlisted in the service of Herod Antipas (vv. 1, 19).[1] Jewish messianic expectation during the time of Jesus has to be understood within the context of Jewish life under Roman imperial rule.

Beginning two generations before Jesus and continuing beyond the time of Jesus and the New Testament writers, Rome aggressively expanded and consolidated its imperial power by conquering people of the eastern Mediterranean. While the Roman Empire is touted by many as one of the greatest civilizations in history, the living conditions

---

1. Since the time of Julius Caesar, Palestinian Jews were exempt from service in the Roman army. Some Jewish men, however, did enlist as a means of income (Josephus, *Antiquities* 14.10.6 §204; 18.5,1 §113). In keeping with the characteristic Lukan emphasis on salvation for all nations and people, Luke's version of this scene includes tax collectors and soldiers, neither of whom appear in Matthew's or Mark's version of the story.

Homiletical Perspective

"John the Baptist" is a misnomer. The title fails to capture the importance of his ministry and the significance of his role. Yes, John baptized, a ritual residue of the priestly family business he otherwise eschewed. He was also John the Prophet, claiming God's voice, pointing to what was to come in God's name, pointing out what was ungodly in the moment, and calling out (even name-calling!) those who needed repentance. As we consider this text from a homiletical perspective, it is also important that he was John the Preacher.

The church usually encounters John the Preacher during Advent, preparing the way of the Lord. Worship leaders practicing *lectio continua* may have introduced John in Luke's infancy narrative, where Gabriel's annunciation and Zechariah's prophesy outline what this child would become, the one to "go before" and "make ready" (1:17), the one "to give knowledge of salvation to his people by the forgiveness of their sins" (2:77). The lectionary offers Luke 3:7–18 and the subsequent seasonal themes of expectation and waiting. John proclaimed that "one who is more powerful . . . is coming." John the Preacher pointed to Jesus.

Look up some of the great artistic imaginings of John; they do not all portray John in the act of baptizing Jesus. Dutch artist Hieronymus Bosch

Luke 3:15–20

Theological Perspective

Holy Spirit and fire are synonymous, for fire is one of the metaphors for the Holy Spirit. Fire is one of the four cardinal elements (along with wind/air, water, and earth) associated with the Spirit. Fire can be destructive. Fire burns and kills, but fire also cooks and warms. Its heat actually makes some plants grow, as in jack pine pinecone seed. After a forest fire, the pinecone that has been dormant for years responds to the enormous heat and opens its hard cone. The dreaded fire that destroys gives way to the green vegetation. Fire renews the earth.

The Holy Spirit and fire in our text can be translated as "wind and fire." This translation makes sense as we think of the metaphor of the wind that separates the chaff from the grain, with the chaff ending in the fire (v. 17). The Holy Spirit as fire is a powerful presence of God; it is a presence that demands and effects repentance (turn around; new direction) as well as transformation, which is not just renewal but newness. Yet there is no repentance and newness without judgment. The refining and transforming fire of the Holy Spirit brings judgment to our old ways. The judgment, however, is rendered not for its own sake but for the sake of forgiveness and transformation. Only in this context can judgment be received as good news. The primary purpose is not to burn the chaff (judgment), but to save the grain.

As one who baptizes with the Holy Spirit and fire, Jesus' acts of baptism—that is, of welcoming people into the new community and into the kingdom of God—are characterized by the burning presence of Holy Spirit that effects repentance and judgment as well as forgiveness and transformation. He calls people to turn away from their sins or, to use another metaphor, to turn away from their old ways. These old ways were going to be cast into the purifying fire. Acting on the power of the Holy Spirit, Jesus proclaims the way to new life, the way that also means the destruction of the old self. Newness cannot bypass the refining fire. It is only through the refining fire of the Holy Spirit acting in Jesus the Christ that humanity will acquire a new heart. It is only through the baptism of the Holy Spirit that a new heart is possible, and it is through it that one joins and participates in a community of forgiven sinners (ecclesial community) that is seeking to live life with a new heart.

What is this new heart or center (Latin *cor* and French *coeur*)? It is a heart or center that burns mightily and shines brightly in Jesus the Christ through the power of the Holy Spirit. It is not lukewarm, neither hot nor cold. It has moved away from the sick bay of

Pastoral Perspective

role of the Messiah, pointing them to the baptism of the Spirit and the separation of the fruitful ones from the chaff that oppressed them. John was doing good work, and he was doing precisely what the Lord called him to do; but instead of taking credit for it himself, he diverted the praise directed at him to Jesus.

It is so tempting to accept accolades for the work we do in the service of Jesus and the church. As we pour ourselves out in service, it feels good to have others notice our efforts and praise our endeavors. John's example is a wonderful reminder that the role of good servants of Christ is to deflect that praise to him. As we reach out to the poor and the weak in fulfillment of Jesus' command to love others, we can evangelize in a wonderful and positive way by making it clear that our actions are motivated by the love of Jesus. Verse 18 characterizes John's humble refusal to be the center of attention as one of the ways that he spread the good news to the people. There is an old saying, often attributed to Francis of Assisi, that calls us to preach the gospel always and, if necessary, to use words. John's humility is such a lesson.

Humility, however, is not to be confused with timidity. Although John was very humble in his refusal to accept praise for himself, he did not hesitate to call people away from sinful behavior. His plain and prickly truth-telling extended to Herod, the Roman-appointed ruler of Galilee. Herod was involved in some sordid political intrigue that involved divorce and marriage to his half-brother's wife, and John publicly disapproved of his behavior. In this passage, we learn that the cost of John's truth-telling is his freedom; later it will cost John his life.

John understood that it is important to stand against sinful behavior, particularly if that behavior is exhibited by public figures. John knew that people watch and emulate the behavior of public figures, and he knew that Herod was a lousy role model. Therefore he included King Herod in his call for repentance, refusing to turn a blind eye to Herod's behavior simply because he was a powerful person.

John's example prompts us to consider the ways that we are called to confront sinful behavior in our lives. Practically speaking, most of us simply do not have the occasion or opportunity to point out the adulterous behavior of our political leaders. However, if we have eyes to look for it, most of us encounter sinful economic oppression every day of our lives. When we buy goods that are manufactured in exploitative environments from a retail behemoth that squeezes the life out of local economies so that

Feasting on the Gospels

under the so-called *Pax Romana* were perceived by many of those conquered by Rome as anything but peaceful. Life for many under Roman rule consisted of economic exploitation, oppressive taxation, and military domination. While Jewish tax collectors and soldiers might have fared better than many, most Jewish people sought a deliverer—the Messiah—to free them from the systemic exploitation and oppression of daily life under Roman rule (see 1:67–75).[2] The author of the Gospel of Luke situates the ministry of John the Baptist and Jesus within the context of Roman imperial rule by dating John's ministry to the reign of specific Roman emperors, governors, and rulers (3:1), and by reminding his audience of the evils committed by the Roman tetrarch, Herod Antipas (3:18–20; 9:9; cf. Mark 6:17–29).

While many commentators suggest the association of John the Baptist with the Messiah by "the people" was sparked predominantly by John's eschatological preaching, it seems Luke is suggesting that the moral/ethical preaching of John—presented in the immediately preceding section—influenced the people's perception just as much as (if not more than) John's eschatological preaching. While the Gospel of Matthew contains the same eschatological preaching that is found here in Luke, Matthew does not state that the people were wondering whether John was the Messiah. Only Luke includes the moral/ethical preaching of John the Baptist (vv. 10–14) and, immediately after that preaching, presents the people as wondering whether John was the anticipated Messiah who would come to deliver the Jewish people from Roman oppression.

According to the text, the people wondered but did not ask John if he was the Messiah; his response, however, clearly addressed their wondering. Not only did John make it clear that he was not the Messiah; he implied that Jesus was the anticipated Messiah by identifying Jesus as the one who "is coming" and the "more powerful" one (v. 16). The use of the title "the one who is to come" (see 7:19) reflected a Palestinian Jewish messianic expectation that appears to have crystallized around the beginning of the second century BCE.[3] John declared that he was unworthy to remove Jesus' sandals—a task a disciple would do for his master or a slave would perform when a male visitor entered the house of the slave's master.

painted a reclining John, in the midst of the wilderness, pointing to a lamb in a gentle pool of water. Matthias Grünewald's *Isenheim Altarpiece* depicts John at the foot of the cross, holding an open Bible in his left hand and pointing to the crucified Christ with his right forefinger. John was "sent from God . . . as a witness to testify to the light" (John 1:6–7), as a sign of the inbreaking dawn from on high (Luke 1:78). It was John's job to turn the spotlight on Jesus Christ, pointing not just beyond himself but beyond the accumulation of messianic expectations, to God's new revelation.

It is the preacher's job to point to Jesus Christ as God's new revelation, pointing beyond ourselves and our assumptions and expectations. A sermon on this text might be about sermons themselves, with both the preparation process and the preaching event directed to examining the role and purpose of the proclamation of the Word. Preparing a sermon on this passage calls the preacher to reflect critically and candidly on exactly what she or he is doing. Entertaining? Educating? Preaching the good news? Pandering to popular opinion and culture? Provoking thought and action? Persuading people of God's purposes? Proclaiming Christ, and him crucified? Speaking God's Word or just offering a good word? All or none of the above? Exactly what *is* this homiletic endeavor? Preaching styles will vary by person, culture, and now the incorporation of technology. Yet what is the essential task of preaching? Is it not to be John the Preacher and point to Jesus Christ?

A sermon on this text might open a conversation between preacher and congregation about preaching. Members of the congregation may be practiced in commenting on particular sermon content, but there are larger questions about preaching itself to be posed and explored. What are the operative assumptions and expectations? Where do the preacher's purposes and the congregation's needs and expectations differ? What might need to be corrected or clarified? Is there real or perceived pressure to be entertaining and noncontroversial, thus obstructing the responsibility to educate, the mandate to proclaim, the calling to point to Jesus Christ? This could be a lively discussion!

As a paradigm for preaching, John the Preacher surfaces some of the more difficult dimensions of homiletics. A preacher may identify with John's crying in the wilderness if the distance between the direction of the gospel and the sociopolitical location of the congregation is great. A preacher unfortunately may come to regard her or his congregation

---

2. For a detailed examination and critique of Roman imperialism during the time of Jesus, see Richard A. Horsley, *Jesus and Empire* (Minneapolis: Fortress Press, 2003).

3. See Joseph A. Fitzmyer, *The Gospel according to Luke (I–IX)*, Anchor Bible (New York: Doubleday, 1970), 471f.

Luke 3:15–20

Theological Perspective

spiritual coldness and numbness. Rather, it is a life on fire. With a new heart, it is a life with a burning center and porous borders. Burning center and porous borders are complementary: a fire is possible only when there is a free flow of air. In a similar manner, openness and burning with commitment are complementary. A person with a new heart is both passionately committed to following Christ and open to new transformations. His or her life is characterized by radical hospitality: passionately giving while open to receiving, passionately courageous in making a stand when life is at stake and humbly courageous in accepting mistakes and changing course.

The church, a community that experienced the baptism of the mighty wind and the holy fire of which Jesus became the bearer, is a community that embodies the power of the Spirit, even with all of our human limitations. Apart from the baptism of the Holy Spirit, the church does not inspire and eventually expires. If the church exists by mission as fire exists by burning, the church's life depends on the renewing energy of the holy fire and the enlivening inspiration of the holy breath. The church, the body of Christ, invites and welcomes new disciples and commissions them for mission under the sign and power of the almighty wind and the refining fire. May our churches burn with the fire of Christ, and may we follow with courage wherever the wind of the Spirit leads us.

ELEAZAR S. FERNANDEZ

Pastoral Perspective

we can save a few dollars, we are condoning and participating in sinful behavior through our economic vote. Taking the time to choose fair-trade products and to patronize local merchants amounts to taking a stand against the forces that place profit ahead of people.

However, as was the case for John the Baptist, such a stand has its cost. It is difficult to spread one's dollar as far when a product's price is not the only consideration. It is not as convenient to shop with local merchants who simply cannot afford to stay open continuously. Standing against the economic exploitation of the weak can be expensive and inconvenient, but in such day-to-day witnesses to God's reign, we stand with John in his call for repentance.

We also stand with John and echo his call for repentance when we recognize and confront the economic and political structures that systematically exploit the weak. As the people of God, the gospel gives us eyes to see and ears to hear the immigrants, the oppressed, and the weak who are desperate for relief, just as the oppressed people in this Scripture were. We are given ears to hear their cry, just as John did, and voices to point them to Jesus for hope and for strength. We are called to confront their oppressors, just as John did, pointing out the sin and corruption and using our influence to alleviate it, even if the cost to us is substantial. One greater than us follows and commands us to love our neighbor.

As consumers and as the people of God, we collectively have a very loud voice, a voice as strong as John's. When the one who is to follow John uses his winnowing fork on the threshing floor of our lives, it is the wheat of our grace-empowered efforts to cry out in support of the weak that will fill the baskets, and the chaff of the biggest sale or the cheapest price that will flash to ashes in the unquenchable fire.

LARRY DUGGINS

Exegetical Perspective

The point is to emphasize the superior status of Jesus in relation to John, most likely to undermine the idea that Jesus might have been a disciple of John's, since John baptized Jesus. Further evidence of the author's attempt to minimize the potentially embarrassing and inferior depiction of Jesus as being a disciple of John is reflected in the author's removal of the words "after me" when John declared, "one who is more powerful than I is coming." In both Mark and Matthew, John declares, "The one who is more powerful than I is coming *after me* [*opisō mou*]" (Matt. 3:11; Mark 1:7). Since the term *opisō* is often used in the context of an inferior following after a superior—sometimes as a technical term for discipleship—Luke's omission of the term here seems quite telling (see 7:38; 9:23; 14:27; 21:8 for other occasions of Luke's use of *opisō*).

The evidence that Jesus is the more powerful one is found in the fact that Jesus would baptize the people with fire and the Holy Spirit, while John baptized only with water. In the Gospel according to Mark, John the Baptist declared that Jesus would baptize with the Holy Spirit (1:8); in this Q version of John's declaration, Jesus baptized with fire in addition to the Holy Spirit (v. 16; cf. Matt. 3:11). It is with this fire that Jesus would burn the chaff when he entered the threshing floor of judgment with his winnowing fork in his hand to gather the wheat into his granary (v. 17). The reference here is clearly used as an eschatological image of the sorting out of humans according to their fruitfulness (cf. vv. 7–9).

John's preaching here in this Q material is clearly meant to portray John as the prophet sent to prepare the way for Jesus (3:4; cf. 1:76; 7:24–27) and to emphasize that the *eschaton* has begun and that Jesus is the eschatological Messiah sent by God to usher in the mercy (1:72), justice (vv. 10–14), and judgment (vv. 7–9, 17) of God. According to Luke's Gospel, this news is "good news" for "the people" (v. 18; cf. 2:10–11).

GUY D. NAVE JR.

Homiletical Perspective

as a "brood of vipers" (3:7). Preachers may be overwhelmed by the expectations they are "filled with." They may feel inadequate and unable to respond meaningfully to the "questioning in their hearts" (v. 15). On the other hand, a preacher may come to regard himself or herself as the church's savior. To the disenchanted, the overwhelmed, and the inadequate, Luke's portrait of John offers good news: the Coming One is more powerful and will empower us with the Holy Spirit. To the self-identified saviors John offered the pointed reminder that Jesus was the Christ!

John the Preacher's homiletic style is exhortation. To exhort is literally "to urge out," to give advice that urges action or warning that demands change. Exhortation is what makes the very word "preaching" fall on the contemporary ear as pejorative, carrying an association with judgment and "telling us what to do." Verse 18 makes an unusual pairing of "exhortations" and "good news"! John had rebuked Herod for "all the evil things that Herod had done," and sexual misconduct is on the list. John did not mince words, even when his targets winced at his words. Herod will retaliate by imprisoning and eventually executing John (3:19–20; 9:9). What if the dialogue between this text and sermon calls us to practice John's form of exhortation and speaking truth to power?

Herod Antipas, tetrarch of Galilee and Perea, eventually overstepped his political prerogatives and was exiled as a traitor. In this text, however, the inference is to the impropriety of a sexual relationship with his brother's wife. Perhaps it is no surprise that verses 18–20 are omitted in the lectionary pericope. The church has been lax in calling out the sexual misconduct that occurs in its very midst. Fingers that point to current revelations in the Roman Catholic Church must also, with integrity, turn to every church body and exhort confession, truth-telling, mutual accountability, covenanted change, forgiveness, and reconciliation. John the Preacher points out "evil things" and in the same breath points to the good news of Jesus Christ. He assumes the risk inherent in exhortation. Are preachers willing to accept that homiletic challenge?

DEBORAH A. BLOCK

Luke 3:21–22

²¹Now when all the people were baptized, and when Jesus also had been baptized and was praying, the heaven was opened, ²²and the Holy Spirit descended upon him in bodily form like a dove. And a voice came from heaven, "You are my Son, the Beloved; with you I am well pleased."

Theological Perspective

After Jesus was baptized and was praying, according to Luke, "the heaven was opened" and the "Holy Spirit descended" upon Jesus and "a voice came from heaven" saying, "You are my Son, the Beloved; with you I am well pleased." With this account Luke wants to establish at the outset the primary identity of Jesus: He is the Messiah, the beloved Son of God. In a voice coming from heaven, God confirms Jesus' identity as the chosen one in whom God has found favor. Jesus is the one through whom God is acting in history. His authority is not from any human sovereign, but from God, whom he calls Abba/Father. Reinforcing the confirmation that Jesus is the beloved Son of God is the action of the Holy Spirit, which descends upon Jesus in this moment after his baptism. The presence and power of the Holy Spirit in Jesus is a mark of his identity. He is imbued with the Holy Spirit and acts with the power of the Holy Spirit. Jesus knows of his special relationship to God and knows by heart what this entails.

Jesus as the Messiah whom God has chosen, and who has found favor with God, occupies a central place in salvation history, the story of God's action in history to save human beings and the whole of creation. His appearance, baptism, and ministry must be seen in light of this history of salvation, as a fulfillment of the covenant that God initiated and,

Pastoral Perspective

It is funny to imagine Jesus as simply part of the crowd, but one can certainly be left with that impression as this passage begins. Luke has been discussing the life and ministry of John the Baptist, but he never says that John baptized Jesus. In fact, the baptism itself is not described at all, but mentioned as if it were simply routine and mundane. All the people were baptized, and Jesus also was baptized. Humble Jesus, not asserting himself or suggesting that the Savior of humanity might deserve a cut in line and an audience with the senior, chief baptizer, instead waits his turn and is baptized with everyone else. He quietly withdraws in prayer, and then all heaven breaks loose.

The heavens open and, in one of those rare times in Scripture where the three persons of the Trinity are described as appearing together, Father, Son, and Spirit join in a quiet celebration of affirmation and blessing. The Holy Spirit becomes visible, in bodily form, and settles quietly on Jesus as a dove flutters its wings and gently alights on a perch. The voice affirms Jesus as Son, affirms Jesus as Beloved, and affirms Jesus as one with whom the Father is pleased. The baptism may have been routine, but the aftermath surely was not.

Jesus approaches his baptism with humility and, one can imagine, with faith and trust. He comes

Exegetical Perspective

As a college professor who teaches Introduction to New Testament Studies every spring, I regularly have students read the accounts of Jesus' baptism found in Mark (1:9–11), Matthew (3:13–17), and Luke (3:21–22). I ask them to identify major differences in the three accounts. Without exception, every year students mention the absence of John the Baptist from Luke's account. For those unfamiliar with the story of Jesus' baptism, if all they had was Luke's passing reference to the event, they would have no way of knowing that Jesus was baptized by John.

As stated in the previous commentary on Luke 3:15–20, the author of Luke intentionally emphasizes the superior status of Jesus in relation to John and minimizes any appearance of Jesus being a disciple of John. In Mark, the reference to John's arrest follows Jesus' baptism and temptation in the wilderness (Mark 1:14). The author of Luke has clearly rearranged the Markan source material (cf. Mark 6:17–18). By narrating John's arrest before mentioning Jesus' baptism (vv. 19–20), the author of Luke minimizes the potentially embarrassing and inferior depiction of Jesus being a disciple of John and presents his audience with no mental image of John actually baptizing Jesus. The author also presents the baptism of John as having far less to do with John creating disciples for himself than with John

Homiletical Perspective

A story of Jesus' baptism is woven into the fabric of all four Gospels; in Luke the story is uniquely textured by two emphases, each suggesting a homiletical direction.

"All the People." Luke's account emphasizes that Jesus' baptism was a group event. "When all the people were baptized" (v. 21) echoes the presence of people in verses 15, 16, and 18. Jesus' baptism was not a private, individual experience. From this beginning, Christian baptism has been immersed in the context of human community. To be sure, there are some divine special effects—heaven opened, the Spirit descended, God's voice proclaimed—but there was a common, public experience that Jesus was part of that day. He was one of the crowd, one of the people who came to hear John and receive his baptism, one of us. As the church prays in a Great Thanksgiving for the baptism of the Lord, "Jesus took his place with sinners and your voice proclaimed him your beloved."[1] Luke 3:21–22 both claims the identity of Jesus as God's beloved Son and grounds the church in its sacramental affirmation that all the baptized are also claimed as beloved sons and daughters.

1. *The Book of Common Worship* (Louisville, KY: Westminster/John Knox Press, 1993), 201.

Theological Perspective

in turn, as expressions of the expectations and hopes of the people. The story of Jesus thus presupposes an understanding of the history of failures and betrayals and the violations of the covenanted relation by God's people. Failure to live according to covenanted relations is one way to think about sin: sin is a violation of covenanted relations between human beings and God and a violation of covenanted relations between humans and the rest of creation.

The appearance of Jesus the Messiah is an expression of God's initiative to bring humanity back to the covenant, and he is God's way of fulfilling salvation history. God raised prophets to make sinful human beings turn away from their destructive ways and follow the way of life, but the unrepentant could not bear the message. They killed the messengers. This was also the case with John the Baptist, the last of the prophets and the forerunner of Jesus. Finally, God sent Jesus, the Son of God incarnate, to bring humanity back to the covenanted way of life. He came with full authority from God and the power of the Holy Spirit. His baptism by John the Baptist marked his continuity with the past, while his baptism by the Holy Spirit marked the coming of the new covenant. Jesus, the Son of God, witnessed to the coming reign of God, a reign characterized by the presence of food for the hungry, clothing for the naked, recovery of sight to the blind, and healing for the broken.

Even though our focus has been on the identity of Jesus the Messiah, the account also reveals the identity of God. If Jesus the Messiah is the one in whom God has chosen to dwell and reveal God's self, then we can know God through Jesus. Through Jesus we know that God loves the physical and the material world. The God we know in and through Jesus is the God of history and an active agent in history. This God shares the messiness of history, assumes the form of humanity, and suffers with humanity in order to bring redemption or salvation. Through the prism of Jesus we see the brilliance of a God whose power shines through love and persuasion and not through coercion. In Jesus the Messiah we know of a God who has taken the form of weakness in order to confound the mighty and strong of this world. God in Jesus, the Son of God, is at work through the Spirit, raising new voices, empowering people, and nurturing their hopes. The God we know in Jesus is a God of a new tomorrow whose power is already at work in the world, and faithfully born in Jesus.

As the one in whom God has chosen to dwell, Jesus is in constant communication with God. In the

Pastoral Perspective

to the place where John is preaching a message of repentance and forgiveness of sins, of turning back to the selfless ways of caring for the weak and marginalized. In response, Jesus submits himself to the cleansing ritual. Jesus' thoughts and motivations in offering himself for baptism remain a mystery to us for now, but we have his example to follow. The Sinless One finds it important to demonstrate publicly his trust in God and his desire to live a life aligned with God's will, while dying to the claims of this world upon him.

As we who sin reflect on the example of Jesus, the message of John helps us begin to grasp what Jesus may have been embracing in his baptism. John calls the people to "bear fruits worthy of repentance." He teaches sharing, mercy, fairness, and justice, and he calls on the people to wait in joyful anticipation of the One who follows him. John specifically warns against any claim of entitlement as a child of Abraham, and teaches that those trees that do not bear fruit will be cut down and burned.

Many Christian people have developed deeper understandings of baptism that involve beautiful concepts like new birth, restoration of the soul, and being marked as belonging to Christ, but those understandings have not yet been developed in the time of John. The Baptist offers forgiveness, calls for a turning away from self-centeredness, entitlement, and greed, and turning to a transformed life of treating the poor and the weak with compassion and equity. Jesus responds to that call and makes it his own through his baptism.

God rejoices at Jesus' choice. The Holy Spirit chooses that moment to let her presence in the life of Jesus be tangibly and physically known. The Father chooses that moment audibly to bless the Son and to state God's pleasure in him. God's response is powerful, joyful, and empowering. Dare we imagine that God's reaction to our own baptism will be the same?

Many of us believe that the Holy Spirit comes to us in a special way when we are baptized. Just as the Spirit settled onto Jesus, the Spirit comes to us to empower us to embody the very actions that John commanded and that Paul also affirmed (Gal. 5:22–23). The Spirit empowers us to bear the fruit worthy of repentance that John preached about and that Jesus lived. As the Spirit turns us away from sin, justice, peace, and joy come into our grasp.

God's blessing also is bestowed on us. In Galatians 3:26, Paul reminds us that "in Christ Jesus you are all children of God through faith." We are God's sons and daughters, and in our baptisms we stand in

initiating the formation of a community of God's people and inaugurating God's plan of universal salvation—a plan fulfilled through Jesus of Nazareth (see 1:69, 76–77; 3:3–6; 7:28–30; Acts 10:34–38).

While the author provides no image of John baptizing Jesus, in these two verses he does provide images of Jesus being baptized with "all the people" and of Jesus engaged in prayer. In both Mark and Matthew there is no reference to Jesus being baptized with other people. In Mark and Matthew it appears as though Jesus makes a special trip from Galilee to the Jordan in order to be baptized by John and that Jesus' baptism is an individualized baptism, in which Jesus is the only one being baptized at that moment (Mark 1:9–11; Matt. 3:13–17). As is often the case in Luke, however, Jesus here is depicted as being with and among the people. Luke further conveys this image of Jesus among the people by the differing depiction of Jesus' so-called Sermon on the Mount. In Matthew, Jesus separates himself from the crowds by ascending a mountain (Matt. 5:1); in Luke, however, Jesus teaches among the people (6:17). In Luke, Jesus identifies with the people and unites himself to them, especially the lowly, the outcasts, and those on the margins of society. Jesus' ministry itself is specifically directed to those on the margins (4:18).

Prayer also plays an important role in Luke's Gospel. The first major episode in Luke—the foretelling of the birth of John the Baptist —occurs during prayer (1:10). Jesus' ministry begins with prayer and ends with prayer (23:46). The author of Luke depicts Jesus at prayer more often than any other Gospel writer. Jesus is frequently presented as engaging in prayer at critical moments in his ministry (5:16; 6:12; 9:18; 9:28–29; 11:1–2; 22:32, 39–46; 23:34, 46). It is not surprising, therefore, that in Luke's account of Jesus' baptism the Holy Spirit descends upon Jesus *after* Jesus prays. In Luke, God gives the Holy Spirit in response to prayer (11:13). Prayer is the means of enlisting God's power—power that is given through the Holy Spirit (24:49; Acts 1:8). Prayer is depicted as a constant activity of the church and a precursor to the coming of the Holy Spirit upon the church (Acts 1:14; 2:1–13).

The opening of heaven serves as a prophetic and eschatological expression of divine revelation (see Ezek. 1:1; Isa. 64:1). In Luke, while the heavenly voice speaks directly to Jesus, it does appear that both the heaven being opened and the dove descending upon Jesus are visible to all the people.

The coming of the Holy Spirit upon Jesus prepares Jesus for the "beginning" of his work (v. 23).

This passage provides the biblical framing for the sacrament of baptism, setting our baptism within the story of Jesus' own. Although the sacramental liturgy promises no opening heaven, no descending dove, and the voice often heard is that of a screaming child, yet with water and words the church enacts a scene from the sacred story, believing that the Holy Spirit is acting in our story as well: "(Name), child of God, you have been sealed by the Holy Spirit in baptism, and marked as Christ's own forever."[2] Like Jesus, we are claimed by the Holy Spirit in our baptism, and like Jesus, we are called by our baptism into a community. "All the people" are encouraged to remember their own baptisms, "all the people" are asked to guide and nurture the baptized ones in discipleship, "all the people" are invited to profess their faith together.

Luke's emphasis on the public nature of Jesus' baptism gives foundation to the celebration of the sacrament of baptism in public worship (not Mother's Day brunch!) and gives the preacher an opportunity to counter cultural trends toward "private" or "family" baptismlike events. Preaching on this text also challenges the preacher to counter the domestic sentimentality of much baptismal practice *in* the church with the risky example of Jesus' ministry, a ministry directed to "all the people" in all their need, a call to follow Jesus into the larger community and the life of all the world.

A sermon formed by this text might be richly informed by the actual celebration of the sacrament of baptism. In the Revised Common Lectionary, Luke 3:21–22 has its home on the Sunday celebrating the baptism of the Lord. Here is an occasion that invites joining the Word and sacrament to proclaim the good news. In the Reformed tradition, to take one example, the sacraments follow the reading and preaching of the Word. The Word illumines the meanings of the sacraments, and the sacraments respond to the meanings of the Word. In actual practice, does this integrity exist? The sacrament of baptism has been particularly susceptible to disconnection from both preaching and the liturgical year. It may be offered on dates convenient for the families of those to be baptized or influenced by the culture (Mother's Day!) and placed in the order of worship without regard for its essential partnership with the Word. Even its symbols have been marginalized. Baptismal fonts are tucked into corners and replaced by bowls, hidden away until needed. When the preacher preaches on baptism, what do all the people see?

2. *The Book of Common Worship*, 414.

Luke 3:21–22

Theological Perspective

Gospel of Luke, Jesus is often presented in prayer; as one who calls God Abba or Father, he communicates to God/Abba through prayer. Prayer is a mark of his connection to God, evidence of Jesus' sonship. As the Son of God, it is God's own presence in Jesus that prompts him to pray. To put it differently, prayer is the language of God/Father speaking through this favored one: God is the source of his prayer, God is the receiver of his prayer, and God brings his prayer to fruition.

The Jesus who calls God Abba is the same Jesus who teaches us to call God Abba. The church, a community following the way of Jesus, has been invited to participate in this relationship. We who are followers of Jesus the Christ have been adopted as children of God, the Abba of Jesus. As children of God, when we pray to God, we are praying to our Abba. In the manner that God's own self prompted Jesus to pray, it is also God/Abba who prompts our very selves to pray. Our prayer is God's presence moving through us. We can pray to God/Abba because deep in our hearts we are connected; we are children and heirs to the reign of God. God is urging us to pray, and when we respond with receptivity, we become an opening and a channel of God's saving power in the world. Like Jesus, in praying we run the risk of being used by God as a channel to accomplish God's will for creation.

ELEAZAR S. FERNANDEZ

Pastoral Perspective

that line with his Firstborn. We are God's "beloved," the object of God's deep and undying affection. In the Old Testament, Israel itself is identified as God's beloved, and as God's son and servant. In Isaiah 42:1, one of the passages that echoes in the divine pronouncement here at Jesus' baptism, the one who is the object of God's pleasure and upon whom the Spirit is poured is also set apart for a divine mission, to bring forth justice to the nations. As God has loved Israel and reached out again and again to redeem and restore Israel, even through the ministry of Jesus himself, so God continues to love and redeem us—and to set us apart for mission.

By God's grace, therefore, we too are the ones in whom God is well pleased. In our haste to avoid any semblance of works righteousness and any inkling that we might be able to earn our own salvation, we sometimes forget that through God's grace we are called to please God. God created us in God's image, and gave us the ability to choose. When God's grace touches our lives and we make choices that align with the will of God, God smiles! Just as God weeps with us in our times of pain, God laughs with us in our times of joy. God invites us into concert with God's will, and when grace makes it possible for us to choose justice, peace, and joy, God is well pleased with us.

The baptism of Jesus reminds us of the Baptist's call to care for the poor and the weak. It reminds of the need to repent, to turn away from selfishness and greed. As we follow the example of Jesus' humility, remembering and reembracing our own baptisms or perhaps experiencing baptism itself, we are reminded that the Holy Spirit is with us, that we are children of God, that we are God's beloved, and that we are the ones in whom God is well pleased. So empowered, we are truly God's people in the world.

LARRY DUGGINS

Exegetical Perspective

The Holy Spirit actually anoints and empowers Jesus for his work (4:1, 14, 18; cf. Acts 10:36–38). The phrase "bodily form" is found only in Luke. The fact that the dove imagery has baffled biblical interpreters for centuries has not hindered the production of theological speculation regarding its meaning and significance. Despite all the speculation regarding the dove imagery, the only thing that can be said with any degree of certainty is that the author clearly wants the audience to understand the dove as "bodily" descending upon Jesus. This bodily reference seems to emphasize the reality and concreteness of the dove—and thereby the reality of the Spirit, God's prophetic and creative power. As prayer is prominent in Luke–Acts, the Spirit also plays a distinctly prominent role in Luke–Acts.[1] The author of Luke, more than the authors of Mark and Matthew, highlights the importance of the Spirit; the reference to a bodily descent of the Spirit is in keeping with this emphasis.

The voice from heaven clearly depicts divine approval of Jesus and is most likely meant to echo ideas and sentiments expressed in Psalm 2:7, Isaiah 42:1–4, and possibly Genesis 22:2, 16.[2] While the phrase "You are my Beloved Son" is also found in Mark and Matthew, the use of the phrase here foreshadows and resonates with the Lukan extension of Jesus' genealogy, which results in the identification of Jesus' line beginning at the beginning with "son of Adam, son of God" (3:38). The reality of Jesus' identity as God's "Son" is emphasized here before Jesus embarks on his ministry and journey through Galilee, just as the reality of his identity as God's "Son" is emphasized before he embarks on his ministry (9:35) and final journey to Jerusalem (9:51–19:46).

GUY D. NAVE JR.

Homiletical Perspective

If Luke 3:21–22 evokes a sermon on baptism, it might also provoke the question of where the baptismal font rightly belongs. The Presbyterian Church (U.S.A.) Directory for Worship advises that worship space be arranged to "visibly express the integral relation between Word and Sacrament and their centrality in Christian worship."[3] Negotiate these waters carefully! Preachers must take seriously their role as teachers and question-raisers, and the symbols in our midst—or absent from our midst—may proclaim a message inconsistent with our biblical and liturgical tradition.

"Jesus . . . Was Praying." A sermon on this text might also be shaped by prayer. Jesus at prayer is a signature posture of Luke's Gospel, and here Luke uniquely portrays Jesus praying after his baptism. As the story unfolds, Jesus will pray before he calls the disciples, before his transfiguration, before he teaches his disciples to pray, before his betrayal, and before his death on the cross. Prayer marks Jesus' decisions and transitions. Luke gives us words for "when you pray" (11:2–4), allows us to overhear Jesus' prayer on the Mount of Olives (22:42), and puts us in earshot of his last words, a prayer for the forgiveness of his executioners (23:34). What was his prayer after being baptized?

Every sermon should be shaped by prayer, of course. The preacher rightly prays when first approaching the text; a prayer for illumination upon approaching the pulpit may be too late! In Luke 3:21–22 Jesus is approaching his ministry. In the next verse Luke tells us that "Jesus was about thirty years old when he began his work" (3:23). The transition is marked by prayer. What was Jesus' prayer here? What would Jesus pray? The text invites our deep reflection on the prayers of Jesus as he began his work. We can imagine his prayers for illumination, for openness to God's Word and Spirit, for faithfulness to God's purposes, for a lighted path, for a discernment of God's voice in the noise of the world, and for courage. Faithful to Luke's emphasis on Jesus at prayer throughout his ministry, the homiletic journey with this text might be to pray rather than preach, to create a pastoral prayer that gives voice to the transitions and decisions in our life together, trusting that the Holy Spirit will fall afresh.

DEBORAH A. BLOCK

1. See James B. Shelton, *Mighty in Word and Deed: The Role of the Holy Spirit in Luke–Acts* (Eugene, OR: Wipf & Stock, 2000).
2. The addition of the adjective "beloved" to the allusion to Ps. 2:7 suggests that Jesus enjoys a special love relationship to God as God's Son.
3. *The Constitution of the Presbyterian Church (U.S.A.)*, Part 2: Directory For Worship (Louisville, KY: The Office of the General Assembly, 2011), W-1.3024.

Luke 3:23–38

²³Jesus was about thirty years old when he began his work. He was the son (as was thought) of Joseph son of Heli, ²⁴son of Matthat, son of Levi, son of Melchi, son of Jannai, son of Joseph, ²⁵son of Mattathias, son of Amos, son of Nahum, son of Esli, son of Naggai, ²⁶son of Maath, son of Mattathias, son of Semein, son of Josech, son of Joda, ²⁷son of Joanan, son of Rhesa, son of Zerubbabel, son of Shealtiel, son of Neri, ²⁸son of Melchi, son of Addi, son of Cosam, son of Elmadam, son of Er, ²⁹son of Joshua, son of Eliezer, son of Jorim, son of Matthat, son of Levi, ³⁰son of Simeon, son of Judah, son of Joseph, son of Jonam, son of Eliakim, ³¹son of Melea, son of Menna, son of Mattatha, son of Nathan, son of David, ³²son of Jesse, son of Obed, son of Boaz, son of Sala, son of Nahshon, ³³son of Amminadab, son of Admin, son of Arni, son of Hezron, son of Perez, son of Judah, ³⁴son of Jacob, son of Isaac, son of Abraham, son of Terah, son of Nahor, ³⁵son of Serug, son of Reu, son of Peleg, son of Eber, son of Shelah, ³⁶son of Cainan, son of Arphaxad, son of Shem, son of Noah, son of Lamech, ³⁷son of Methuselah, son of Enoch, son of Jared, son of Mahalaleel, son of Cainan, ³⁸son of Enos, son of Seth, son of Adam, son of God.

Theological Perspective

People, in general, are curious to know their genealogical line. Being able to trace ancestral roots as far back in history as possible satisfies the human longing to connect to one's roots, locate oneself within a longer historical frame, and experience a sense of belonging to a particular human family that stands in continuity with the past. A genealogical search may be motivated by a desire to know the family journey and to pursue its great tradition in response to the present challenges. Others may excavate their genealogy because of some immediate benefits, such as to make a claim to an inheritance or to assert one's superiority over others.

How shall we take Luke's account of the genealogy of Jesus? What are his motivations? To answer these questions we need to consider his main thrust. His genealogy of Jesus is in continuity with his main message. It is his way of establishing the idea that Jesus is the Son of God, which is the final point of Luke's genealogical account. It is his way of establishing the divine origin of Jesus, a theological interest that is inseparable from another interest: the matter of salvation. Luke's genealogy of Jesus, the Son of God, is driven by his concern about salvation. The genealogy that finds its culmination in Jesus as the Son of God points to his essential role in salvation history.

Pastoral Perspective

What was Jesus doing during those thirty years before he began his ministry? Luke does not give us very much information (although more than the other evangelists). He describes the birth of Jesus, the angels and the shepherds, the naming ceremony, and the purification ceremony with Simeon and Anna. We know that the family returned from Bethlehem to Galilee and their own little town of Nazareth. At the age of twelve, we hear that Jesus went to the temple as part of the Passover celebration, where he caused a bit of an uproar. Other than that, Luke does not share a word about Jesus' life until his baptism.

There are several noncanonical Gospels that purport to tell stories of Jesus' youth, including one that has him breathing life into little birds that he formed from mud. Other pieces of folklore suggest that he traveled widely, seeking religious instruction from masters of many traditions. The topic of Jesus' youth and young adulthood has always been a source of interest and curiosity, and has been the subject of much speculation and storytelling.

Perhaps Jesus spent the first thirty years of his life simply living. One can imagine that he spent his youth learning a trade, apprenticed as a carpenter under Joseph. Others speculate that, because he does not appear in the stories of Jesus' ministry, Joseph

Exegetical Perspective

As is the case in Matthew's genealogy, Luke here traces Jesus' ancestry through his father, Joseph. Other similarities between Luke's and Matthew's genealogies include the references to Zerubbabel and Shealtiel in the postexilic period (3:27; Matt. 1:12) and identical lists of names covering the premonarchial period between Amminadab and David (3:31–33; Matt. 1:3–5) and the patriarchal period between Abraham and Hezron (3:33–34; Matt. 1:2–3). Despite these similarities, however, so many significant differences remain that scholars once speculated that Matthew had traced Jesus' ancestry through Joseph while Luke traces it through Mary. Such speculation, however, ignores the fact that Luke never mentions Mary in Jesus' genealogy.

The two genealogies share none of the same names in the monarchial period—with the exception of David—and only two names from the postexilic period. Another difference involves the role of women in the two genealogies. Matthew's genealogy includes four women; while Luke mentions more women in his Gospel than do the other Synoptic writers, Luke's genealogy includes no references to women. Another difference is that Luke's genealogy begins with Jesus and works its way back through Jesus' ancestry to Adam and God, whereas Matthew begins with Abraham and works forward to Jesus.

Homiletical Perspective

". . . Enoch, son of Jared, son of Mahalaleel, son of Cainan, son of Enos, son of Seth, son of Adam, *son of God*" (Luke 3:37–38). Can your genealogy do that? Luke traces Jesus' lineage back to the Creator of the first male creature. Not only will Jesus have a purpose; he will have a pedigree, a history, a relationship not only with ancestors and with the people of Israel but with the Creator of all things. He is, as the previous account of his baptism claims, God's Son (3:21–22), and if anyone somehow did not hear or misunderstood or did not believe the voice from heaven, here is further evidence, all seventy-seven generations of it.

Where is this text in the lectionary? It appears neither in the daily lectionary nor in the Sunday and festival lections for Luke's Year C. The Revised Common Lectionary skips from the baptism of Jesus to his teaching in the Nazareth synagogue (4:14), even holding the intervening episode, the wilderness temptation, for airing on the First Sunday in Lent. The lectionary preacher may feel relieved by the omission. Reading Luke 3:23–38 aloud in the worship service is a challenge. How do you pronounce "Reu" and "Arphaxad" and "Nahshon"? How would you proclaim good news with this text?

Matthew's Gospel also supplies a family tree, in which Jesus descends from the great patriarch

Luke 3:23–38

Theological Perspective

While, on one hand, the genealogy of Jesus points to his divine origin, on the other hand, it also points to his roots and connection to humanity. The Son of God is at the same time the son of Adam; he is the son of humanity. Like the claim that Jesus is the Son of God, the point that Jesus is the son of Adam is motivated by soteriological interest: it is essential to salvation history; it is at the heart of the incarnation. Jesus is of God and sent by God, who was embodied in human flesh to save humanity and the whole of creation. God in Jesus assumes the brokenness and suffering of humanity to save humanity and creation.

One should not, however, be content to speak of Jesus' humanity in generic ways. The generic human being does not exist. To assume humanity is to be part of a family and a tribe, as well as to be tied to a certain locale, with its distinctive geography, culture, and history. This is the case with Jesus, the Son of God. Choices were made prior to his own exercise of choice. We may speak of the choices that were made prior to one's exercise of agency as destiny, which is not the iron jacket of history but the circumstances in which one is born. In the case of Jesus, he was a man who was born in a place called Palestine and whose parents were Mary and Joseph. He grew up in the religious tradition of his parents, and felt called to bear witness to the coming reign of God. His witness offended the religious and political establishments of his time, which carried out the plot to kill him. Jesus was born under the Roman occupation, resisted the occupation, and was killed by the occupation forces.

Luke's brilliant genealogical account, which identifies Jesus as both the divine (Son of God) and the human (son of Adam), provides us with a theological frame to make a creative interpretation of the integration and interweaving of the divine and the human, of transcendence and immanence, of the spiritual and the material, and of the universal and the particular. Luke's genealogy of Jesus offers us a lens that holds our focus so that, as we go deeper into the particular, the specific, the earthy, and the mundane, we need not worry about losing the divine, the transcendent, the grand, and the universal.

Maybe, to our surprise, as we go deeper into the specific and the minute, our horizon opens up and widens: we see the divine in the earthy and the human, the transcendent in the immanent, the universal in the particular, the eternal in an hour, and the cosmos in a grain of sand. Immanence is not the opposite of transcendence; rather, immanence is the transcendent presence of the transcendent God in

Pastoral Perspective

may have died during Jesus' youth or young adulthood, which would have placed on the young Jesus the burden of caring for his mother and his family. Perhaps those first thirty years were filled with learning responsibility, taking care of family, participating in the community, and dealing with life's triumphs and setbacks. Perhaps those thirty years were spent laying a foundation for ministry, so that Jesus' teachings would be well grounded in the reality of living as a working person with responsibilities.

Whatever the reality of the situation might be, Luke chose to complete the framing of Jesus' background for ministry by stating his age and reciting his genealogy. It is as if Luke wanted to be certain that Theophilus, his reader, had every bit of the background he needed to understand fully the fulfillment of prophecy in the life of John the Baptist, and then to understand how John's life played its role in fulfilling prophecy about Jesus. The establishment of the Davidic lineage of Jesus is an important part of that story.

We notice first that Luke's genealogy is full of people who walked closely with God. We encounter David, the king whom God loved, and Boaz, the just protector of Ruth. We see Jacob, who wrestled with God, and Abraham, the father of great peoples. We find Noah, and Methuselah, and Enoch, and then we settle on Adam, the first person, the one who walked with God in Eden. Jesus comes from a long line of the faithful whose exploits and encounters with God fill our Scriptures. As Luke documents Jesus' descent from David, Luke uses the prophecies of Micah, Isaiah, and Ezekiel to validate and support his description of Jesus as messianic king.

It is notable that, among these examples, Luke does not mention the extraordinary women mentioned in Matthew's genealogy. For instance, he omits Bathsheba because he traces a different path of ancestry from David, but he also omits Rahab and Ruth. Perhaps it was not important to Luke's documentation of qualifications that Jesus' ancestry included a prostitute who saved Israel and a foreigner who defined and embodied loyalty.

In the second place, Luke's genealogy is used to establish legal credibility. As if heralding the birth of Jesus by angels was insufficient to establish his credentials as the awaited Messiah, Luke produces the full messianic bloodline to bolster Jesus' case. Even in the face of miracles, we still want to examine his documents. We are often so inclined to focus on the traditional and ordinary ways of establishing validity or authenticity that we can miss or dismiss

Exegetical Perspective

Finally, in Matthew, the genealogy immediately precedes the story of Jesus' birth, while in Luke it precedes the "beginning" of his ministry (v. 23).

While the identification of Jesus as "thirty years old" may have been meant to imply full maturity (Num. 4:3) or to echo the ages of David (2 Sam. 5:4) and Joseph (Gen. 41:46) when they began significant phases in their own lives, it also situates the ministry of Jesus around the middle of the reign of the Roman emperor Tiberius (3:1). Luke's interpretive commentary, "as was thought," when referring to Jesus as the son of Joseph (v. 23), clearly links the genealogy to 1:26–35, where Jesus has already been identified as "Son of God."

As previously stated, the only name shared by Luke's and Matthew's genealogies during the monarchial period is David. Matthew's focus on the Davidic kings of Judah in the period from David to Babylonian captivity (Matt. 1:6–11) serves to authenticate the "kingly" lineage and image of Jesus—"king of the Jews" (Matt. 2:2; 27:11, 29, 37). This kingly image is further highlighted in the birth and infancy narrative found in Matthew, where a star—often used to symbolize the birth of a new king—marks the birth of Jesus. Royal dignitaries from the east follow the star looking for "the child who has been born king of the Jews" and bringing gifts to honor him (Matt. 2:1–12). In contrast, virtually all of the names in Luke's genealogy from David to Babylonian captivity are unknown (vv. 27–31). Luke even traces Jesus' ancestry through David's son Nathan rather than King Solomon (v. 31).[1] It appears that the Lukan genealogy intentionally avoids all of the Davidic kings. Similarly, Jesus' birth in Luke is not depicted as the birth of a king, but rather the birth of one placed in a barn manger among animals—born to poor and destitute parents who could not afford a lamb to sacrifice when Jesus was presented in the temple for purification (2:1–7, 22–24).

While Matthew's genealogy highlights both David and Abraham, two significant figures within Jewish history, neither David's nor Abraham's place is explicitly highlighted in Luke's genealogy. Matthew's genealogy begins with Abraham, while Luke's genealogy goes beyond Abraham, tracing Jesus back through prepatriarchal ancestors to Adam and then to God. Jesus in Luke is not merely the Jewish Messiah in the lineage of Abraham and David; Jesus is the Messiah sent for all people. He is a descendant of

Homiletical Perspective

Abraham. Luke, however, reverses the direction of ancestry, going from the immediacy of Joseph, Jesus' father, "as was thought," to Noah and the covenant with all the earth, to the universality of Adam, the father of humankind. Luke continues to develop the theme of "all the people" (3:21) from the preceding baptismal narrative, now even broadening the earlier definition of "all the people" as Israel, "Abraham and his descendants" (1:55; also 1:73), to "all peoples" as both Israel and the Gentiles (2:31–32). God's family is universal; God's grace is for all humankind. Good news!

What would take a preacher to this text? James McClendon was convinced that lives were the real data for Christian theology; he called it "biography as theology."[1] Persons embody convictions—"tenacious beliefs" in his description—about God. Not only in words, but especially in actions that convey values, visions, and convictions, our lives bring to expression our foundational beliefs about who God is. What difference do those lives make for a community? Christianity turns upon the character of Christ, embodied in the living witness of people and communities of faith. Who are the "fresh exemplars" in our own time? A homiletical approach to this text tells the stories of living witness.

A Service of Baptism. This genealogy might be included with Luke 3:21–22, setting the identity of Jesus as God's Son in the larger picture of God's story with humankind. There are not many Zerubbabels or Amminadabs or Methuselahs at the baptismal font these days, but Jesus' ancestors are not without contemporary namesakes, Joshuas and Nathans, Jacobs and Noahs. A connection might be drawn between the name of a male baptizand and a great-great-great-great-grandfather of Jesus, opening a biblical character to contemporary awareness and example in a sermon, pointing to a story in the Hebrew Scriptures that is unfamiliar to the congregation.

Such a namesake homiletic, however, is limited by the gender exclusivity here. Unlike Matthew, Luke's cloud of witnesses does not include women; and even though Matthew names only four women in his genealogy of Jesus (Rahab, Ruth, "the wife of Uriah," and Mary, Matt. 1:1–17), their stories send signals about the unexpected twists in God's journey with God's people. God makes surprising choices! Luke's

---

1. While it is unclear if the tradition has any bearing on the genealogies found in Matthew and Luke, Zech. 12:12–13 does suggest a possible division in the Davidic line, pitting "the house of David" against "the house of Nathan."

1. James Wm. McClendon Jr., *Biography as Theology* (Philadelphia: Trinity Press Int., 1990).

Theological Perspective

manifold particularities. Immanence is the other side of transcendence. Similarly, if something is universal, it must be particularly present. This is the heart of God's economy of salvation, the heart of the incarnation, and the scandal of particularity. God's universal saving love finds its way into the world only through the particular. If, as we often say, the devil is in the details, God must also be in the details or the particular. In Jesus, the Son of God, God's universal saving love has become particular, particularly embodied in the most destitute and downtrodden, to bring salvation for all.

So, what started out as a focus on the particular—genealogical excavation—finds its end point in generous and hospitable universality. Luke's genealogical excavation, contrary to the ways of this world, functions as a way to subvert the assertion of privilege by virtue of one's ancestral lineage and exclusivist claims. It tells us that we should not equate particularity with exclusivism. The central message of the incarnation—a supreme exemplar of God's particularity—is not God's exclusivity, but God's radical hospitality and particular availability. God has made God's self particular, in order to speak the good news to every time and clime. Rootedness to the local is not a prison house; rather, it is an entry point of connections to the wider world.

We are all located in a specific time and place, and we belong to a certain family and nation, but we can live in ways that embody hearts much wider than our family lineage and national affiliations. It is not a contradiction to love one's family and nation and still love global justice. In fact, loving global justice is the only way truly to love one's family and nation. We may be from various nations, but we have one genealogical root: we are all children of Adam and we are all children of God. Our genealogical beginning and eschatological ending is to live as God's children.

ELEAZAR S. FERNANDEZ

Pastoral Perspective

the indications of credibility and character that come in unexpected or unconventional ways. This conventional kind of thinking allows us to appreciate a coworker or a neighbor who is friendly, cares for his wife and children, and works hard making a living, but nevertheless to support our government's deporting him because his family crossed the border illegally during his childhood. We place a higher premium on appropriate historical and legal credentialing than on significant, firsthand evidence that this person is a good and productive neighbor.

In the third place, we can also look to genealogy and history for disqualifying factors. In vetting Jesus' qualifications to be considered Messiah, the fact that his human bloodline can be traced back to King David was vital. In hindsight, however, that concern seems simply trivial in light of the truth that Jesus' bloodline flows miraculously and directly from the living God. From a legalistic perspective, certain boxes must be checked but can never account for the unusual factors that might provide the best evidence of a person's true identity and character. Does a lifetime of peaceful living and productive citizenship suffice to restore the voting rights of a person convicted of a serious felony in his or her youth?

Reflecting on the genealogy in Luke invites us to examine why we look to Jesus as Messiah. Is it because all of the prophecies are fulfilled in a legally defensible way? Do we see Jesus as the Son of God because we can trace his bloodline back to the first man, whom Luke refers to as "son of God"? Is he the Messiah and Son of God because the whole fabric of his life and ministry reveals this truth to us? Dwelling with the genealogy gives us room to hold both the legal and the experiential evidence up to the light, in order to see how they influence us and affect each other. The genealogy is not the only evidence that Luke presents to establish the true identity of Jesus for Theophilus. It is one of many factors that Luke brings to the table to construct a more complete description of the truth. Perhaps we should keep this in mind as we consider "litmus test" judgments of those around us. What does the complete picture show?

LARRY DUGGINS

the world's first people—before ethnic identities and divisions.

In the Gospel of Matthew, Jesus tells a Canaanite woman, "I was sent only to the lost sheep of the house of Israel" (Matt. 15:24). Jesus is portrayed in Matthew as the anticipated Jewish Messiah sent to deliver the Jewish people. In Luke, however, the Jewishness of Jesus is not as strongly emphasized. The recipients of Jesus' ministry are identified less by ethnicity than by social status. The Jesus of Luke is depicted as one born under Roman oppression—his family travels for days from Nazareth to Bethlehem while Mary is pregnant, because Emperor Augustus has ordered a census. Jesus is born in a manger with no star or royal dignitaries to honor him. He and his family live their lives in poverty on the margins of society. When he delivers his first public address in Luke, he declares it is to the poor that he has been sent (4:16–19). According to Luke, Jesus has been sent not merely to the lost sheep of the house of Israel but to all in need, because he is not merely the son of David and the son of Abraham—he is the Son of God. Luke's genealogy is the only known ancient Jewish genealogy that traces ancestry beyond ethnic identities and human origins all the way back to God, making Jesus a savior for all creation.

The differences between the genealogies of Jesus found in Luke and Matthew clearly demonstrate how theological and literary constructions often take precedence over historical accuracy. As modern readers we should be cautious, therefore, not to be too insistent on making historical arguments based on these genealogies. Even some attitudes in the Bible toward genealogies are quite negative, classifying them with "myths" and emphasizing the worthless and meaningless speculation often associated with genealogies (see 1 Tim. 1:4 and Titus 3:9).

Luke ends Jesus' genealogy with the assertion that his line can be traced to the "son of Adam, son of God," clearly connecting Jesus' genealogy to the words spoken by the voice from heaven at Jesus' baptism and bringing the account of Jesus' preparation to a close before beginning the narration of Jesus' ministry—a ministry that is, like his baptism and preparation, anointed and led by God's Spirit (3:21–22; 4:1, 18–19).

GUY D. NAVE JR.

genealogy does not deviate from a consistent patriarchy, and hearing it read aloud will be a reminder of the cultural distance between text and context in congregations where teaching and preaching have acknowledged and critiqued a patriarchal worldview and embraced a God-given, God-driven gender equality. A sermon on this text might be shaped by asking, "What is wrong with this picture? Who is missing in this family tree?" and offering some answers. A bold and creative preacher might craft a genealogy of women.

Worship Services Celebrating Ordinations or Church Anniversaries. Luke 3:23–38 could be called upon to proclaim the good news of God's steadfast presence and unfolding purpose from the beginning, generation to generation. Sermons on such occasions lift up the faithful witness of our ancestors and challenge the present community to carry the gospel into a new day. A scriptural genealogy opens an opportunity to look at some newer branches of the family tree of faith. What lives might be lifted up as a witness for us and for our children's children? Hebrews 12:1–2 and the image of "so great a cloud of witnesses" might provide a helpful scriptural partner here. Our lives are not only descended from a long line of those who pursued and glimpsed God's promises but are also "surrounded" by their continuing influence.

A Watchnight, New Year's Day, or First Sunday of a New Year Service. A sermon could pair this genealogy with names from those annually published lists of the notable and the notorious who died in the past year. These lists yield figures in politics, the arts, sports, and popular culture; every year the heavens also open to some who have made significant contributions to theology and ethics, who have provided leadership in the religious community, and whose faith has impelled leadership on more secular ground. The preacher who culls the death notices in denominational newsletters and church journals will find an array of "sermon examples" in actual lives that have embodied God's hopes and dreams for humankind, sometimes at great cost with little recognition. Preached into a world that is saturated with celebrity and starved for significance, these exemplars inspire the faithfulness of a new generation.

DEBORAH A. BLOCK

Luke 4:1–13

¹Jesus, full of the Holy Spirit, returned from the Jordan and was led by the Spirit in the wilderness, ²where for forty days he was tempted by the devil. He ate nothing at all during those days, and when they were over, he was famished. ³The devil said to him, "If you are the Son of God, command this stone to become a loaf of bread." ⁴Jesus answered him, "It is written, 'One does not live by bread alone.'"

⁵Then the devil led him up and showed him in an instant all the kingdoms of the world. ⁶And the devil said to him, "To you I will give their glory and all this authority; for it has been given over to me, and I give it to anyone I please. ⁷If you, then, will worship me, it will all be yours." ⁸Jesus answered him, "It is written,
   'Worship the Lord your God,
      and serve only him.'"

Theological Perspective

It has often been said that the temptations in the wilderness increase in spiritual intensity and value, from the simple need of the organism for food through the human drive for earthly power to a direct human challenge to God's nature. The perversions the devil represents in this passage follow and mock the developmental curve of the human spirit. That so many theologians have thought this reveals at least one thing: doing theology has been the privilege of the well fed. Only someone who has never been hungry would treat the pain of physical hunger in so offhanded a manner. The ancient texts we revere as Scripture may have first been circulated orally by ordinary people, but they were *written* by people with bellies full enough that there was time to become literate. Most poor people in those days could not read or write and did not have enough to eat.

However, let us pursue this ancient idea of an ascending order of importance in the temptations on its own terms for a moment: it is true that the fact of our capacity and desire to reflect upon the nature of our being is what makes us human. Animals get hungry too, and they certainly erect hierarchies of power, but they do not ponder the nature and limits of the divine providence once they have eaten their fill. Our capacity even to *desire* spiritual autonomy depends upon our physical needs for food, water,

Pastoral Perspective

This story of the temptation of Jesus is intriguing, even mysterious, to most twenty-first-century people. Few of us know anyone who has fasted for forty days, and fewer have undertaken prolonged fasting ourselves. Not many of us have encountered the devil in so tangible a form as to transport us to a distant city.

However, many of us have been baptized in water in the name of the triune God. Perhaps we have also felt the touch of oil on our foreheads, accompanied by a prayer that the Holy Spirit will fill us and guide us into lives holy to God and loving to our neighbors. Although the ritual may only take a few minutes, baptism is part of a lifelong journey with God and other travelers.

So perhaps we can imagine ourselves taking time on the journey in a quiet place in the presence of God, far from our busy lives. There we can attend to our souls, to the calling of God within us, and to deep questions about life that we often suppress. As difficult as it may be to focus on these central issues, when we do, we often emerge "full of the Spirit" (v. 1), radiant, full of holy joy and good intentions.

Would it not be good if we could return to our homes and our work refreshed, changed forever? Early Christians believed for many years that baptism not only freed them from past sins, but also

9Then the devil took him to Jerusalem, and placed him on the pinnacle of the temple, saying to him, "If you are the Son of God, throw yourself down from here, 10for it is written,

  'He will command his angels concerning you,
    to protect you,'
11 and
  'On their hands they will bear you up,
    so that you will not dash your foot against a stone.'"

12Jesus answered him, "It is said, 'Do not put the Lord your God to the test.'" 13When the devil had finished every test, he departed from him until an opportune time.

Exegetical Perspective

Luke carefully introduces the identity of Jesus at the outset of the Gospel. Birth, adolescence, baptism, and genealogy give way to one final episode before the inauguration of Jesus' public ministry: temptation. The Greek verb translated "to tempt" in verse 2 (*peirazō*) implies hostile intent. Repeatedly Jesus is approached by the devil with temptations to become other than the Son of God he is created to be.

The tradition of Jesus' temptation is widely attested in early Christian literature (see Heb. 2:14–18; 4:15 and instances of testing in John 6:14–15; 7:1–9; 12:27–28), but the temptation account is a Synoptic scene. Mark introduces core elements such as the Spirit, the wilderness, forty days, and Satan in his characteristic Cliff's Notes rendering (Mark 1:12–13). Matthew and Luke follow Mark's placement of the scene and build upon Mark's account, utilizing a common source. While Matthew's and Luke's accounts have much in common, key differences underscore the function of the scene in Luke. Most importantly, while Matthew and Luke share the same three temptations, their sequencing differs. Matthew moves from bread in the desert to the pinnacle of the temple to a high mountain, anticipating the conclusion of Matthew's Gospel on a mountain in Galilee. In Luke, the final two temptations are reversed, so that the climactic moment occurs at

Homiletical Perspective

Rembrandt drew several depictions of the devil tempting Jesus. In one of them the two look like friends. They appear to be ambling down a country road, deep in conversation. The devil is a half step behind Jesus. His head is skeletal, but there is an urgent, deeply human look on his face. He is reasoning with Jesus, not menacing him. One of his wings is thrown over Jesus' shoulder in an almost familial manner. He leans in, mouth open slightly, eyes on Christ, speaking quietly, a heavy stone in his hands. He holds the stone out as if it were a gift. "If you are the Son of God, command this stone to become a loaf of bread" (v. 3).

It is a scene of powerful intimacy. Despite his wings, Satan does not look monstrous. He looks reasonable. Most of our temptations are. Rembrandt captures this truth powerfully. It is easy to identify with Jesus in his drawing, just as it is easy to identify with Jesus in this pericope. Perhaps too easy. Jesus is tempted to sacrifice the truth of who he is for material gain, prestige, power. We have all faced such temptation. As a result preachers are tempted to use these verses as a platform from which to talk about humanity.

We should resist this impulse. We should let the story reveal something new about God, instead of simply reminding us of things we already know

Luke 4:1–13

Theological Perspective

and shelter being adequately met; we will not lift our eyes higher than our own empty plates if these basic needs are not met. Yet lift our eyes we will, as soon as we are able, and we will question everything. This is so universal a human quality that we assign ages to it. Age four is the year of "Why?" about the world. The working of God's will occupies the minds of seven-year-olds in ways different from the ways in which five-year-olds consider it. Young adults jettison their childhood God with enough regularity that even churchgoing parents may not be particularly alarmed by their rebellion. "It is a stage," they tell each other consolingly, as they remember their own youthful agnosticism.

That human sorrows like poverty and hunger can cramp the spirit's growth is no reason for us to deny the power or worth of that growth. Indeed, one attending to the spiritual life can and should draw the moral imperative that every human being has the God-given right to attend to it as well. What keeps my brother or sister chained to a never-ending search for the next meal should also keep me from the unreflective enjoyment of my own wider horizons: my spiritual freedom is intimately connected to my neighbor's well-being. The church has recognized this for centuries in the pairing of spirituality and service to the poor, to children, to the sick. Almost all convents and monasteries, whose main spiritual task is prayer, also exercise some kind of specific and intentional ministry to those in need.

The idea that contemplation and activism are somehow exclusive of one another is neither useful nor accurate; few mystics, modern or medieval, would recognize the separation of one from the other as having anything to do with their vocation. Even the prayer lives for which they are revered are understood to be prayer on behalf of the world. The most cloistered solitary is *active*: active in intercessory relationship with the workers outside her enclosure.

Here then is the temptation the devil left out: he does not tempt the love that forms the second half of the Great Commandment common to all the Abrahamic faiths: love God and love your neighbor. The temptations in the wilderness are self-absorbed, aimed at Jesus alone: his hunger, his lust for power, his equality with God. Yet if the incarnation has any meaning at all, it must surely mean this: Jesus does not permit himself to stand alone. His love is saving love, inclusive of every man, woman, and child who has ever lived or ever will live. The devil does not tempt Jesus' saving love in this story. He does not

Pastoral Perspective

that they could hope to live righteously for the rest of their lives; but as time passed, realism set in. Christians have learned (no matter Charles Wesley's sung prayer that God would "take away the love of sinning"[1]) that living in holiness is not as easy as we might hope.

Therefore, at the very time when it seems we have risen to new spiritual heights, something usually conspires to draw us down to earth again. Other inner voices—some call it the devil—attempt to lure us away from our identity as baptized children of God. Hence, what happens next in Luke's text is not really surprising, even if it may not be so easy to find analogies in our own lives to the temptations Jesus endured.

We would hardly blame anyone famished from fasting forty days for doing anything necessary to get food, but Jesus resisted the devil, who said, "If you are the Son of God, command this stone to become a loaf of bread" (v. 3), subtly trying to undermine the divine word at Jesus' baptism: "You are my Son, the Beloved; with you I am well pleased" (3:22). *If you are a child of God, if you are the son or daughter of God, then prove it, then take advantage of it. Work a little magic!* Jesus answered, "It is written, 'One does not live by bread alone'" (4:4, quoting Deut. 8:3). What in our lives at the office, at high school, at home lures us to forget who we are as children of God and tempts us to trade in our inheritance in Christ for a few crumbs of bread?

Next the devil offers Jesus the glory and power of ruling all the kingdoms of this world, if only Jesus will worship him (vv. 5–7). We would like to think that, like Jesus, we would quickly refuse the devil's offer: "It is written, 'Worship the Lord your God, and serve God only'" (4:8, quoting Deut. 6:13). Active Christians would not necessarily succumb in order to rule over millions of people or have access to untold wealth, but we might be seduced by seemingly good reasons. Perhaps we would be willing to bend our sense of ethics in order to make a positive difference in the world, to solve problems, or to help others. Perhaps, like the pastor who is too busy doing "ministry" to pray, or the church treasurer who cooks the books to make it appear his family is a leading giver, our desire for recognition could lure us away from our values and the worship of God. This tricky temptation to gain power may play on our greed, our good intentions, or our weak

---

1. Charles Wesley, "Love Divine, All Loves Excelling," in *Glory to God* (Louisville, KY: Westminster John Knox Press, 2013), 366.

the temple, a locus of salvation for Luke and the site where the Gospel begins and ends. Thus Luke's narrative of temptation not only marks the beginning of Jesus' ministry, but also reveals much about how it will proceed.

References to Jesus' identity as the Son of God form bookends for Luke's account, appearing in the first and final temptations. The divine sonship attached to Jesus throughout his birth and adolescence and then proclaimed decisively from heaven at his baptism is now the focus of temptation in the wilderness. Jesus' status as *the* Son of God is reinforced by Luke's description in verse 1 that he is "full of the Holy Spirit," which descended at the Jordan and will continue to play a prominent role throughout Luke–Acts. The phrase "full of the Holy Spirit" occurs more than a dozen times in Luke–Acts (see references to Peter, Stephen, Barnabas, and Paul), but never in Matthew, Mark, or John. Jesus is "led by/in the Spirit" (v. 1), reflecting relationship and solidarity shared with the Spirit (like Simeon in 2:27), as opposed to Mark's description that "the Spirit drove him into the wilderness" (Mark 1:12). Jesus' identity is further emphasized through the devil's repeated use of "If you are the Son of God," which not only acknowledges Jesus' identity but also seeks to exploit it and offer an alternative vision for Jesus to embody. While Jesus never engages the "if," he is asked to deliberate about what divine sonship means. Jesus decides what it means to be Jesus.

The story proceeds in a triadic pattern typical of Jewish folklore (employed again by Luke in Peter's denial in 22:54–62 and the threefold taunting of Jesus in 23:35, 37, 39). First, the devil approaches him when he is already hungry with the temptation to command a stone to become bread. Unlike Matthew, Luke's account describes a single stone, and thus may be conceived as an individualistic temptation for Jesus to feed himself. In the second temptation, the devil offers authority and glory of "all the kingdoms of the world." Whereas Matthew describes the kingdoms of the *kosmos* ("world") Luke uses the politically laden noun *oikoumenē*. For Luke, *kosmos* typically refers to creation (9:25; 12:30), while *oikoumenē* generally refers to the political order (as in 2:1; 21:26; Acts 17:6). Luke conceives of a struggle between two kingdoms. The social-political order previously presented as under the charge of Rome (2:1; 3:1) is here revealed as a counterkingdom ruled by the devil, whose authority now dangles before Jesus. In the final temptation, the devil takes Jesus to Jerusalem and there, in this cultic center so vital to

about ourselves. Samuel Wells makes this argument forcefully in an essay about Lenten preaching. He writes that this passage "has a tendency to lead either into the Scylla of exploring our personal temptations to multiply food, jump off temples, and rule the world, or the Charybdis of setting up our petty greed, lust, and pride as some kind of equivalent to God's choice in Christ never to be except to be with us; two equally absurd, but frequently practiced homiletical directions."[1]

If we follow Wells's advice, sidestepping our dominating fixation on humanity should help us preach about God. In this passage Jesus chooses a certain way of being, one that makes the cross inevitable, even as it contradicts many of the assumptions we bring to our understanding of God.

One way to read the devil's three temptations is to view them as corresponding to our preferred definitions of divinity. Every congregation is at risk of projecting its own particular definitions onto heaven and then mistaking them for God. Sooner or later, every congregation is guilty of this mistake. Every Christian is too. We want God to be all-powerful in each of the realms the devil tempts Jesus. We want God to hold ultimate authority in every arena, be it economic (the bread in vv. 3–4), political (the kingdoms in v. 5), or spiritual (the miraculous power in vv. 9–11). However, to each of these Jesus says no.

In a congregation that risks idolizing charitable giving or social justice, a preacher might explore the fact that in this lesson Jesus refuses to feed the hungry. We may want God to side with our efforts toward achieving economic parity, but in this instance Jesus fails to get on board. In a congregation that equates God with nationalism, a preacher could explore the fact that in this lesson Jesus declines to become the ruler of *any* nation. We may want to believe that God is the force behind our nation's power, but Jesus refuses to wield such authority. Finally, in a congregation that wants to believe God is a master of the supernatural, a preacher might explore the fact that Jesus tells the devil he will not indulge in such performances.

Imagine if he had. If Jesus had agreed to any of the devil's offers, he would have become an ancient revolutionary, a skillful politician, or a beloved magician. He would have become an unusually powerful person—which is not really that unusual. Every age is replete with powerful people. A preacher might

---

1. Samuel Wells, "Lenten Preaching in the United States," *Journal for Preachers* 36, no. 2 (2013): 10.

Luke 4:1–13

Theological Perspective

say, "Worship me and I will not destroy the people you love: your parents, your disciples, your friends, that innocent mother and baby, the defenseless old man you passed on the road here." He tempts Jesus' divine power, but stops short of even trying to tempt the divine love.

The temptations introduce the questions that will absorb the better part of the church's theological attention in the first four centuries of its existence: Who is God? What can we assert about God's nature? How does Jesus relate to God the Father? However, they attempt to answer these questions in a vacuum: the same limitations apply to the three temptations as apply to the creeds, the fruits of those first few centuries of Christian thought. In the creeds, speculative attempts to describe God echo down the ages to us. They try to tell us who God is, but they do not even try to tell us who *we* are, what we should do, or what is the nature of the good in human affairs. There is no moral theology in the creeds, and there is none in the three temptations of Jesus in the wilderness.

If we were writing the creeds today, they would be very different documents. They would make an attempt to link human behavior to the nature of God, rather than considering the divine nature on its own. If we were writing the creeds today, they would contain ethics as well as systematic theology. If we were writing Gospels today, the same: we would imagine Jesus tempted ethically, in the spirit of what we have come to call the Great Commandment. In the wilderness, Jesus gathers strength for the life that awaits him beyond the wilderness. It is a painful but fruitful time, and he emerges not only into self-knowledge, but into an activism that will take many forms in the short years remaining to him: healing, teaching, and confronting the unjust power structures of his world.

BARBARA CAWTHORNE CRAFTON

Pastoral Perspective

self-esteem and lead us away from worshiping God and living out our baptismal covenant. How important it is to remain grounded, as Jesus was, in who we are as children of God, supported by Scripture that reminds us to worship only the Holy One!

Still the devil persists, this time spiriting Jesus away to the pinnacle of the Jerusalem temple, with Scripture as a weapon: "*If* you are the Son of God, throw yourself down from here. God will command angels to protect you . . . so that you will not dash your foot against a stone" (vv. 9–11, quoting Ps. 91:11–12). Jesus says, "Do not put the Lord your God to the test" (v. 12, quoting Deut. 6:16). In other words, trust God, but do not test God's love by taking a foolhardy risk, then crying for rescue. "I know I did not study for this test/prepare this sermon/practice this music, but get me through, God, by your Spirit." Seek a deeper relationship with God, based on love and prayer, not only on frantic emergency calls or tests to prove God's goodwill.

Temptation takes many forms. The reasons we succumb are as diverse as our life stories. This means that interpreting this passage calls for close reading of the contexts in which the worshipers live, so that the congregation can make connections with this familiar yet mysterious passage. While any practice that leads us away from God and our authentic selves may deserve exploration, reflection on this passage should not be trivialized (for example, by jokes about consuming chocolates hurriedly if Valentine's Day precedes the beginning of Lent). Instead, teaching and preaching should explore what it means to worship God fully with our lives and how to discern the divine will when making decisions, based in our identity as children of God who are called and gifted by the Holy Spirit to live out our baptismal faith in the world.

RUTH C. DUCK

Exegetical Perspective

the Gospel of Luke, the devil quotes from Psalm 91 in an effort to persuade Jesus: "throw yourself down from here."

All three temptations invite palpable displays of power. Each engages a different dimension critical to competing conceptions of Messiah—the material/economic, the political, and the religious—thereby forcing a decision over what it means to be the Son of God.

To understand Jesus' response, the text invites the reader to look back. Among its many echoes, the details and themes of the passage link the temptation of Jesus to the wandering of Israel. Like Israel, Jesus is hungry in the wilderness. He is also tempted to "fall down and worship," but no golden calf is minted. The setting, the symbolism of forty days, the character of the three temptations, and the replies of Jesus, all taken directly from Deuteronomy, point to the trials of Israel, with one critical difference: whereas the children of God at times succumbed to their trials, the Son of God emerges faithful, true, and strengthened in his identity.

The temptation also prompts a look ahead, foreshadowing the entire narrative. Jesus leaves the wilderness having faithfully determined the scope of his identity as the Son of God, which he will embody throughout the remainder of the Gospel. In his ministry, as in his temptation, he moves from the wilderness to the mountain to the temple, and along the way gracefully meets the economic, political, and religious challenges before him. The devil meanwhile, after departing "until an opportune time" (*kairos* or "special time" in v. 13, as opposed to the *chronos* time of v. 5), later reenters the story and claims Judas Iscariot (22:3), thereby setting in motion the mechanics that ultimately lead to Jesus' death. In Luke 23:37 the "if" returns to the narrative ("let him save himself if he is the Messiah of God"; see also 23:35 and 23:39). Perhaps remembering his strength in the wilderness, Jesus prays resolutely in the garden, "Not my will but yours be done" (22:42). Once again, no angels appear outside Jerusalem to bear him up beyond the risk and the trauma. Yet, as the Gospel concludes, the resurrected Son of God is triumphantly "carried up into heaven" (24:51).

ALAN P. SHEROUSE

Homiletical Perspective

consider contemporary figures that fall into the devil's categories and then ask whether anyone will remember their names in two thousand years, let alone sing hymns to them in worship.

This text appears on the first Sunday of Lent. This means that it is the first step in the season's relentless movement toward the cross. Had Jesus responded differently to the devil, his story would have ended differently. By refusing to practice human power, Jesus made himself vulnerable to human power. For centuries Christianity has suggested that this is because he was born to suffer. A sermon on this story could explore the fact that this lesson suggests otherwise. It suggests that the form of strength God chooses to practice is quite different from all of our human understandings of strength and is therefore subject to them. We tend to think of Jesus practicing a steely resolve in this lesson. However, it could be argued that he is choosing weakness.

This is not to say that the story reveals God's permanent incapacity. If one wants to make that sort of claim, it is best saved for Good Friday. Just as God cannot be boxed into our presuppositions about strength, God cannot be limited by our understanding of weakness. As noted above, one can imagine Jesus choosing to practice traditional forms of power. Indeed, there are times in his ministry when he does so. This story does not make abstract claims about the true nature of God. It simply shows Jesus making a choice. He refuses to define his ministry with the kind of power we tend to idolize. This suggests that such power contradicts the love that God is revealing through him. In order to reveal that love at the end of Lent, Jesus must practice it at the season's onset.

MATT FITZGERALD

Luke 4:14–20

¹⁴Then Jesus, filled with the power of the Spirit, returned to Galilee, and a report about him spread through all the surrounding country. ¹⁵He began to teach in their synagogues and was praised by everyone.

¹⁶When he came to Nazareth, where he had been brought up, he went to the synagogue on the sabbath day, as was his custom. He stood up to read, ¹⁷and the scroll of the prophet Isaiah was given to him. He unrolled the scroll and found the place where it was written:

¹⁸ "The Spirit of the Lord is upon me,
  because he has anointed me
    to bring good news to the poor.
He has sent me to proclaim release to the captives
  and recovery of sight to the blind,
    to let the oppressed go free,
¹⁹ to proclaim the year of the Lord's favor."

²⁰And he rolled up the scroll, gave it back to the attendant, and sat down. The eyes of all in the synagogue were fixed on him.

Theological Perspective

No wonder all eyes are fixed on Jesus when he finishes reading. In choosing this passage from Isaiah to read in his hometown synagogue, he announces the year of the jubilee, that all-bets-are-off year described in detail in Leviticus 25. Debts forgiven, slaves freed, bad real-estate transactions redeemed—economic, agrarian, and even domestic life in the year of jubilee will be quite unlike life as most people live it, which is why scholars have had their doubts about whether the jubilee was ever actually observed in ancient Israel.

Scripture is much more full of hope than of journalism: peace on earth proclaimed when there is no peace, the inversion of unjust power hierarchies proclaimed while they are all still firmly in place. At first glance, it all seems a bit premature: will we not look foolish, hymning our liberation while we are still in chains?

Yet the proclamation of liberty always precedes its actual birth. In 1776, the American Declaration of Independence resolved "That these United Colonies are, and of Right ought to be Free and Independent States; that they are Absolved from all Allegiance to the British Crown, and that all political connection between them and the State of Great Britain, is and ought to be totally dissolved." It is worth noting that this assertion marked the *beginning* of the struggle

Pastoral Perspective

This story of Jesus' inaugural sermon drawing on Isaiah 61:1–2 is so familiar that it may be difficult to hear it freshly. Many Christians have rightly taken it as a statement of their mission, just as Jesus took Isaiah's words as his call, but hearing the text in this way may lead us to miss some aspects of the text.

Do we focus on the content of the call (bringing good news to people who are living in poverty or in prison, or who are blind or oppressed), without considering the Spirit who is upon us, anointing us to carry out these missions? If so, we may not be attending to the specific gifts and vocations for which we (as churches or individuals) are being called and anointed. We may forget how Jesus tells the disciples to wait for the Spirit: "You will receive power when the Spirit has come upon you; and you will be my witnesses in Jerusalem, in all Judea and Samaria, and to the ends of the earth" (Acts 1:8).

Though the ministries of Christ usually require more wisdom, strength, and talent than we possess on our own, "the Spirit and the gifts are ours" (to quote the beloved hymn by Martin Luther). Notice that the passage begins by saying that Jesus returned from his forty days in the wilderness and his tempting by the devil "filled with the Spirit" (v. 14). Why do we attempt to live as Christians without seeking the guidance, gifts, and strength that the Holy Spirit

Feasting on the Gospels

Exegetical Perspective

Jesus' appearance in his hometown synagogue and his first public words inaugurate his ministry in Luke. The reader knows what the crowds do not: Jesus has been declared the Son of God at his baptism, confirmed as such through his lineage, and bolstered in his identity through temptation in the wilderness. The synagogue scene reiterates that the son of the carpenter is in fact the Son of God. Taken as a whole, verses 14–30 form in Luke a mission statement for Jesus' life, encompassing who Jesus is, what his ministry is about, and how people will respond to him. The scene is Luke–Acts in miniature.

The importance of this episode for Luke is revealed in its placement. Unlike Mark (6:1–6a) and Matthew (13:53–58), who locate an appearance of Jesus at the Nazareth synagogue later in his Galilean ministry, Luke places this expanded story at the beginning.

As the story shifts from Jesus' temptation to his public ministry, Luke uses an introductory statement similar in form to 4:1: Jesus returns to Galilee "in the power of the Spirit" (a phrase used more than a dozen times in Luke–Acts but not used in the other Gospels). The Spirit that descended on Jesus at baptism (3:22) and filled him prior to temptation (4:1) now empowers him. Despite the antagonism of the

Homiletical Perspective

This passage moves us from Jesus' rejection of the devil to Jesus' rejection by the people of his hometown synagogue. These seven verses are book-ended by high drama. Initially they seem wanting in comparison to the stories on either side. Indeed, this passage can be read as nothing more than transition from a conversation with Satan to the edge of a wildly raucous worship service. These verses are the silence in between. Luke seems to be catching his breath (and allowing the audience to catch theirs), winding down from Christ's temptation, even as he winds up for the next confrontation. Nevertheless, God is at work in the quieter moments of Scripture too. This passage does more than simply move Jesus into Galilee. It affirms the full power of the Spirit in Jesus' person and the Spirit-infused content of his proclamation.

In the first verse of chapter 4 Luke tells us that after his baptism Jesus is "full of the Holy Spirit." One might imagine that his encounter with the devil would leave him empty, but in verse 14 Luke echoes the claim of 4:1 and affirms that Christ's tank remains full. Once again Jesus is "filled with the power of the Holy Spirit." This suggests that denying what the devil had to offer gave Jesus more of what he really needed.

In case we doubt Luke's claim, the next verse gives evidence of the fact that Jesus is brimming over

Theological Perspective

for independence, not its end. The end was still seven bloody years away. All political ideas live in the human imagination before they become flesh in the human community. So it is with all prophecy.

So it also is with Jesus: he proclaims liberation and healing before it comes to pass. His very life will come and go, looking for all the world like a failure: picked up by the authorities, convicted in a sorry excuse for a trial on a trumped-up charge, tortured and then executed, his followers in hiding. No first-century king or emperor bites the dust because of him. Israel does *not* get free—indeed, within a few decades the temple will be destroyed, and the Jews will be scattered to the four winds.

What, I wonder, are they thinking while their eyes are "fixed" on Jesus? Waiting for him to explain, I suppose, his choice of this scriptural passage for his first day back in the synagogue of his childhood. This moment takes place on the Sabbath, which means that people expect to hear some teaching on the Scripture they have just heard him read. Certainly they are aware of the implications of the jubilee passage. Messianic expectation is consistently high in Israel at the time of Jesus: more than one charismatic leader has already been proclaimed as the anointed one. "Perhaps our own Jesus is the One. Perhaps the time has come for our deliverance. Perhaps this is a message, a coded alert for us to rise up and overthrow the Roman oppressors." There is even some specific expectation that the uprising will begin in Galilee. "Just let him say the word," at least some of his hearers may be thinking, "and we will follow!"

Take a step back, and two thousand years have passed. Both Christians and Jews have had to reinterpret what the coming of Messiah means—not once, but many times. Some of Jesus' contemporaries expected a cataclysmic victory over the powers of darkness, and expected it soon. Most of them probably took his crucifixion as yet another dashed hope. One can only guess at their feelings the day the temple fell. What now? Surely some remembered another passage in Isaiah, in which their chosen-ness is revised to form the image of the Suffering Servant. Who would ever have considered *that* a Messiah? No Jew would. Christians adopted it, forced to do so, as their expectation of an immediate second coming fell back and back before the forward march of history. From the radical eschatology of the young Paul ("We will not all fall asleep, but we will all be changed, in a moment, in the twinkling of an eye!" 1 Cor. 15:51–52*),* which was already beginning to give ground by the time of his death, to the bitterly

Pastoral Perspective

brings? What wilderness in our hearts must we engage to emerge filled with the Spirit?

We also may be missing the communal aspects of the call. The call that Jesus embraced was not a solitary mission, but the task of whole communities and ultimately the whole church throughout the world. Isaiah's Servant of God (who speaks in 61:1–2) should be understood not as an individual but as representative of the people of Israel. The church finds its call as it continues the ministry of Jesus, drawing on the varied gifts of its members. None of us has all the gifts. No one individual or congregation has all the responsibility to do all of the ministry (or every kind of ministry) to which the worldwide church is called in Jesus Christ.

For several years I studied congregations who were reaching out across cultural groups to minister to their neighborhoods and embody full Christian hospitality. I came to realize that, while all churches are called to provide a gospel welcome, some have a particular charism or anointing to build bridges in new ways, welcoming the multiversity of the church in God's tomorrow. Not every church is called to a special ministry with autistic children, or to serve meals to homeless people, or to share in partnership with a church in another country. Each church should seek out its particular callings, sometimes leaving behind ministries that were thriving in years past but are now lacking energy.

If we trust the Spirit and see ourselves as part of a larger community, the next step is to make concrete these callings that sound so good in the abstract. Could your church partner with underfunded schools to forge new futures for young people, thus bringing good news to the poor? Could your church become a leader in mainstreaming people with visual disabilities so that they can participate more fully in worship, in ministry, and in society? While this might not literally mean recovery of sight to people who are blind, it could remove cultural barriers that make the lives of people with disabilities more difficult. Could your church give practical support (clothing, job training, meals) to a shelter for people escaping abusive homes? These are ways to bring liberty to the oppressed.

In recent years, churches have debated the ethics of the death penalty, and a number of religious groups have urged its abolition.[1] While some Christians (notably practicing Catholics) have opposed

1. See deathpenaltyinfo.org, accessed Feb. 14, 2013, link on religion and the death penalty, and "Illinois Bans Capital Punishment," NYTimes.com, March 9, 2011, accessed Feb. 14, 2013.

devil, he has been strengthened through his forty days in the wilderness.

Proceeding into Galilee, Jesus is said "to teach in their synagogues" (v. 15). The imperfect form of the verb (*edidasken*) connotes a recurring activity. Twice Luke says that on the basis of his teaching, Jesus gains renown ("a report about him spread" and "[he] was praised by everyone," vv. 14–15). Given Jesus' growing acclaim, it is reasonable to assume that he is withholding some of the jarring eschatological and christological implications of his message until he appears in his hometown.

Focus narrows in verse 16 as Jesus moves from Galilee to Nazareth, "where he had been brought up." The pluperfect form—"had been brought up"—suggests an extended absence. Focus sharpens further as Jesus moves from the town to the synagogue, where his "customary" appearance reinforces Luke's presentation of him as a devout Jew, circumcised (2:21), presented in the temple (2:22), and taking part in Passover (2:41–51). In cultic terms, Jesus has moved from the temple (4:9) to the synagogue. His movement mirrors that of postexilic Judaism from the "high places" to the local spaces of worship. This historical development forms a foundation for the worship practice of early Christians, like those in Luke's audience.

Inside the synagogue, the meticulous pace of Luke's narration signals the importance of the moment. Action slows. Every motion is described. Luke writes that Jesus "went" in and "stood up to read." The scroll "was given" to him. He "unrolled" it. He "found" the place (vv. 16–17). The string of verbs creates suspense and draws attention to verses 18–19, which follow. The literary structure also directs attention to verses 18–19, as verses 16–17 and 20 form a frame around the reading from Isaiah. In verses 16–17 Jesus *stands*, he *is handed* the scroll, and he *unrolls* it. In verse 20, the order is inverted: he *rolls up* the scroll, he *hands* it to the attendant, and he *sits*. The parallel rising and falling actions stress Jesus' reading from Isaiah as the climactic moment.

After the scroll is handed to him, Luke is careful to note that Jesus "found" the desired passage. His first recorded public words in the Gospel are not arbitrarily chosen. His reading is a modified excerpt from Isaiah 61 with a flash of Isaiah 58. Consistent with the centrality of the Spirit in Luke's Gospel, the first public words from Jesus' mouth are, "The Spirit of the Lord." The first three phrases in the reading again tie the ministry of Jesus to the work of the Spirit: "The Spirit . . . is upon me . . . because [the

with the Spirit's power. He goes from town to town, teaching in many different Galilean synagogues and he is "praised by everyone" (4:15). This is hard for any preacher to imagine. Jesus talks to multiple congregations, and there is not a single disgruntled listener. There are no failed anecdotes, no wavering attention, no crying babies, no cell-phone distraction. It is tempting to write off Luke's claim as an exaggeration, but a preacher might use this verse to explore the difference between our Sunday morning attempts to get at the Word and Jesus' embodiment of it. Whether God shows up when we preach is not up to us. As Karl Barth says, "What human utterance concerning God aims to be when it is intended as proclamation is not grace, but service of grace."[1] Meanwhile, Jesus is grace. We point toward the love of God. Jesus is the love of God. This must have made his preaching electric.

Fallen human beings are still capable of missing his point. So perhaps Jesus selects pleasing texts for his supersuccessful Galilean preaching tour. It is not likely, but even if it is so, he tries a different tactic when he gets home to Nazareth—or he has one foisted upon him. His old neighbors do not let him preach on an easy psalm. They thrust Isaiah straight into his hands.

We must wait for the next lesson to hear what Jesus does with the verses that he reads, but they speak for themselves. Any preacher could get in trouble with the phrases in Jesus' selections from Isaiah.

In contemporary America, the most dangerous thing in Isaiah might be the proclamation of release to the captives. In sermon notes for this text, Lauren Winner cites a *New York Times* article that states, "The United States has less than 5 percent of the world's population. But it has almost a quarter of the world's prisoners."[2] We imprison more people than any other nation on earth. Some of us benefit from this fact, and most of us are complicit with it. This means that most of us are both indicted by the Scripture Jesus quotes and frightened by the idea that God intends to do something about it.

Early in my work as a pastor, I visited a death-row inmate convicted of killing a teenage girl. At the time of my visit he had been awaiting his execution for twenty-one years. When we spoke, he talked about grace incessantly. Eventually I asked him if his sense

---

1. Karl Barth, *Church Dogmatics*, I/1, *The Doctrine of the Word of God, Study Edition* (London: T. & T. Clark, 2010), 49.
2. Lauren Winner, "Visiting Prisons," The Hardest Question Blog, thq. wearesparkhouse.org/featured/epiphany3cgospel.

Luke 4:14–20

Theological Perspective

resigned revisionism of Elie Wiesel as he reflects upon the Holocaust, Messiah moves the goalposts again and again, and mortals struggle to regroup.

Christians and Jews alike have carried diverse messianic hopes for the end time into the modern age, some continuing to look for a supernatural army of the heavenly host to bring the world to a cataclysmic end, some for a transcendent figure to subsume material existence in spirit, some for an ongoing spiral of evolutionary change, some for a marriage of quantum mechanics and theology unimaginable just fifteen years ago. It is good, then, for us to remember how we first receive the messianic hope in the Gospel of Luke: justice and healing for those who suffer illness and wrong. Many Jews today might say that we ourselves are the messianic hope, the vehicle by means of which will come any deliverance we can expect. Many modern Christians would agree: "Thy kingdom come," we pray, "thy will be done." Today we understand this eschatological hope to be not only about God's agency, but about our own.

Paul speaks of the church as the body of Christ. In the body, all the parts depend on each other in order to continue. They feel each other keenly, display the loss visibly when one part is severed from the rest. This image of the church as the body of Christ provides a way for us to think of messianic hope: *we are in Christ already*. We are permanently part of the living Son of the living God, whose membership in the divine fellowship is as indelible and as intertwined as is our membership in him. What might this understanding of the church mean for the justice and healing Messiah will bring? It means that *even now* we participate in a oneness of which we are only dimly aware. Among many other things, it must also mean that our participation in the repair of the world in even the smallest way ("to the least of these my brethren") furthers the messianic hope.

BARBARA CAWTHORNE CRAFTON

Pastoral Perspective

the death penalty as a part of an ethic of reverence for life, others have come to oppose it because of defects in criminal justice systems. In 2000, Governor George Ryan of Illinois suspended the death penalty when it was discovered that, of twenty-five people who had been on death row in that state, thirteen had been wrongly convicted; in 2011 (under Governor Pat Quinn), this temporary ban became Illinois law. Not only has DNA analysis made it more possible to reverse convictions, but also it is becoming increasingly clear that the problem of false convictions (sometimes due to prosecutors' suppression of evidence) is systemic throughout the United States. This situation provides many ways for churches to bring release to captives. They may engage in debate about the death penalty, advocate its abolition, volunteer or financially support groups such as the Innocence Project, which provides support and legal assistance to people who maintain that they have been falsely convicted.[2] While Christians may have different opinions on these issues, these concerns deserve consideration by all churches and particular ministries by some.

We are familiar with campaign speeches that set out a lengthy agenda and ads about unnumbered products that promise to change our lives for the better. Often they are only talk. Jesus' inaugural sermon was also bold in what he laid before his hearers, but his words and actions truly made a difference in human lives. This is the incarnation—the Word become flesh: a community of welcome, reconciliation, and sharing that respects the human dignity of poor people, of women, of foreigners, of children, of all. We too are called to incarnate the Word, each in our own way, guided and empowered by the Spirit.

RUTH C. DUCK

---

2. See http://www.innocenceproject.org/fix/What-can-I-do.php, accessed Feb. 14, 2013.

Exegetical Perspective

Spirit] has anointed me. . . . [The Spirit] has sent me." The threefold repetition of "me" strengthens the sense that Jesus claims Isaiah's prophetic description for himself.

The citation of Isaiah 61:1–2a agrees verbatim with the LXX, with three notable modifications. Luke drops reference to "the day of vengeance of our God" (Isa. 61:2b), thus omitting the tone of judgment found earlier in the Gospel in the preaching of John (3:17). Also omitted from Isaiah are the words "to bind up the brokenhearted" (Isa. 61:1). Further, Luke adds the phrase from Isaiah 58, "to let the oppressed go free," which, taken together with "release for the captives," announces the ministry of Jesus as a ministry of freedom from bondage.

Echoing the songs and sighs for justice and redemption heard throughout Luke's infancy narratives, Luke presents the primary themes of Jesus' ministry. Jesus' ministry will encompass "good news to the poor," whom Mary in the Magnificat imagined would be lifted up (1:52–53). In days to come, Jesus will announce God's blessing on the poor (6:20) and factor the poor into his teaching, more so in Luke than in any other Gospel (7:22; 14:13, 21; 16:20, 22; 18:22; 21:3). Jesus' ministry will further proclaim release for the captives from the various forms of demonic, economic, social, and political bondage that oppress them. Jesus will also restore sight to the blind, not only at a physical level, but also figuratively reviving the prophetic vision of the year of the Lord's favor.

Having carefully established who Jesus is, Luke now employs Isaiah to describe all that Jesus will do. The proclamation in the synagogue will become for Jesus the thread that follows him through the entirety of his ministry. When messengers from John ask the critical gospel question—"Are you the one who is to come, or are we to wait for another?" —Jesus will prove his answer by reiterating the substance of what he declared in the synagogue: "Go and tell John what you have seen and heard: the blind receive their sight, . . . the poor have good news brought to them" (7:19–22).

Having announced his mission, Jesus returns the scroll and sits down. Again, every movement is described. Tension mounts. The eyes of the synagogue, and no less the eyes of the reader, are "fixed on him" (v. 20) in anticipation of what is to come.

ALAN P. SHEROUSE

Homiletical Perspective

of grace had overwhelmed his sense of guilt. He said, "The gospel requires us not simply to be sorry, but to be transformed by our sorrow. For me, this is a daily transformation." For this prisoner, guilt and grace stood in tension. Forgiveness had not erased the memory of his sin, yet he insisted over and over again that Christ has freed him from it.

He said, "I will never forget my crime. But there has to come a point where you receive forgiveness and then forgive yourself. Not to justify your actions, but to accept God's love. . . . It does not matter where you are. It is who you are that matters. I am a person who is loved and forgiven by God." Then he rattled the chains that tied his wrists together dismissively. As if they did not matter.

I jumped back from the table. Our conversation was over. Not because this killer had done something violent, or said something awful, but because he had claimed the love of God as his own. He claimed that Jesus had already set him free. I could not stand it.

I stepped into that prison with my heart in my throat, anticipating the worst of the worst. Instead I found a broken sinner, redeemed and pieced back together by the love of God. Instead of a monster I found grace, a power strong enough to transform monsters into gentle men. I could not tolerate it.

What does it mean to believe in a God who opposes imprisonment, be it behind bars of iron or bars of guilt? It is good news to the captives, but those of us who think that we are free tend to receive it as the opposite. Is it any wonder Jesus' next words will cause things to spin out of control so quickly?

MATT FITZGERALD

²¹Then he began to say to them, "Today this scripture has been fulfilled in your hearing." ²²All spoke well of him and were amazed at the gracious words that came from his mouth. They said, "Is not this Joseph's son?" ²³He said to them, "Doubtless you will quote to me this proverb, 'Doctor, cure yourself!' And you will say, 'Do here also in your hometown the things that we have heard you did at Capernaum.'" ²⁴And he said, "Truly I tell you, no prophet is accepted in the prophet's hometown. ²⁵But the truth is, there were many widows in Israel in the time of Elijah, when the heaven was shut up three years and six months, and there was a severe famine over all the land; ²⁶yet Elijah was sent to none of them except to a widow at Zarephath in Sidon. ²⁷There were also many lepers in Israel in the time of the prophet Elisha, and none of them was cleansed except Naaman the Syrian." ²⁸When they heard this, all in the synagogue were filled with rage. ²⁹They got up, drove him out of the town, and led him to the brow of the hill on which their town was built, so that they might hurl him off the cliff. ³⁰But he passed through the midst of them and went on his way.

Theological Perspective

As the previous passage challenged us to consider the nature of messianic hope, this one collides with the cherished notion of Israel's chosen-ness. Once the people realize the direction in which Jesus' thought is heading—that their status as Israelites is not a determining factor in God's love—things go south in a hurry. At first, "all spoke well of him," but within a few verses they have all united in an effort to run him off a cliff.

The god who meets Abraham beneath the stars and promises him virtually numberless descendants is just that—Abraham's god. The mature development of monotheism as a coherent theology still lay in the future. Genesis assumes the existence of other gods, and there are many passages in the Hebrew Scriptures that suggest that there certainly *are* some, though none of them is as strong as the god of Abraham. By the time of Jesus, though, it has been clear in Israel for centuries: there is only one god, and that god is the God of Israel. The other gods—and by now the children of Israel have lived for a long time in a political system in which the emperor himself is considered to *be* a god—are not gods at all, but spiritual beings more on the order of demons, or even completely imaginary beings.

The unfolding of the idea of monotheism over several centuries had direct bearing on both the

Pastoral Perspective

"Today this scripture has been fulfilled in your hearing" (v. 21). Jesus' amazing words remind us that Scripture is not merely a record of the past or a collection of wise teachings; through the continuing work of the Spirit, these cherished texts are active, inspiring new insights and actions. Thus the act of reading the Bible in worship should not be taken lightly, but lovingly and carefully prepared. Scriptures can be proclaimed so clearly and expressively (through the spoken word, or also through dance or visual arts) that they speak as powerfully as any sermon.

Although Scripture may be active, especially when proclaimed with power, we are not always ready to receive the Word, especially when it comes from an unlikely source, for example, the son of Joseph the carpenter. The people in Jesus' hometown, Nazareth, have mixed feelings. They are amazed at how well Jesus reads in their synagogue service, but it seems that the talk about him on the street is not good: people are grumbling that he does not do the mighty works of healing he has done in other towns. (The parallel passage in Matt. 13:58 says, "And he did not do many deeds of power [in Nazareth], because of their unbelief.")

Jesus confronts them: "Truly I tell you, no prophet is accepted in the prophet's hometown"

Exegetical Perspective

With the eyes of all in the synagogue fixed on Jesus and the words from the scroll of Isaiah ringing in their ears, Luke moves to the second half of the episode inaugurating Jesus' public ministry. Jesus has outlined the content and character of his ministry as good news and release on behalf of the poor and oppressed. Those gathered in Nazareth, along with the reader looking in, now anticipate the implications of this message. How, when, and, most critically, for whom will this hopeful change will occur?

After he is seated, Jesus proclaims a sermon in a sentence: "Today this scripture has been fulfilled in your hearing" (v. 21). The first public word spoken by Jesus in Luke, outside of his Isaiah reading, is "today." The word appears twelve times in Luke, connoting imminence and immediacy (e.g., 2:11; 13:32–33; 19:5, 9; 23:43). Jesus embodies what he proclaims. The fulfillment of the Scripture and realization of the Isaianic hopes are present in him.

The fulfillment is described as coming in the "hearing" of those gathered. Having referenced their "eyes" (v. 20), Luke now moves to the ears. The fulfillment that was seen by the crowds at Jesus' baptism is now heard in his proclamation in the synagogue. Fulfillment is a present, sensory reality.

Initially enthused by his proclamation, all those gathered "spoke well" of Jesus (v. 22). The

Homiletical Perspective

It is a mistake to conflate Luke's account of Jesus' rejection in Nazareth with the story Mark and Matthew tell. In their versions he evokes his neighbors' anger with the claims he makes. Familiarity has bred contempt, and they cannot believe he is the One he says he is. In both of these Gospels Jesus is rejected for his audacity. He evokes something similar to but more intense than the kind of incredulity you feel when a belatedly precocious adolescent tells you that he intends to be elected president. "*Really*. Aren't you the carpenter, the son of Mary?"

This dynamic is absent from Luke's version of the story. The townspeople are not angry because Jesus claims to be the realization of God's power. They are angry because he is not using that power the way they want him to use it. Unlike their counterparts in Mark and Matthew, Luke's Nazarenes do not want less Jesus. They want more. When they cannot have more, they try to kill him.

Before that happens, Jesus explains his unwillingness to work the wonders he has worked elsewhere by recalling miracles of Elijah (1 Kgs. 17) and Elisha (2 Kgs. 5). In 1 Kings the heroic prophet raises a dead child on what looks like the strength of his own empathy, crying out to God for a miracle with an intensity that leaps off the page. As 1 Kings has it, Elijah shouts, "'O Lord my God, have you brought

Theological Perspective

notion of covenant and that of chosen-ness, which follows from it. The older arrangement, expressed in the divine claim of Exodus 6:7, "I will take you as my people, and I will be your God," raises certain questions unanswered, once the God of Abraham is identified as the ordering and generative power of the entire universe. It is no longer a private matter. Is this God of the Hebrews also the God of those who do not acknowledge him? Are those outside of the covenant somehow included in the plan and, if so, how? We have hints that it is so in the Hebrew Scriptures: God calls the king of Persia "Cyrus…my shepherd" (Isa. 44:28) for instance, though Cyrus is neither a Jew nor a follower of the God of Israel. Yet the human drive to exclude is a strong one, and nowhere is it stronger than in matters of religion, in which defining the community by defining who is not a member serves as a convenient intellectual shorthand for a more rigorous examination of faith. "Who are we? That is an easy one: we are not *them*. We are *us*." The people in the synagogue that day are comfortable with their privileged status, and they do not respond well to Jesus' questioning it.

The notion of Christian chosen-ness is just as stubborn. Once "Israel" became, to Christian ways of thinking, a spiritual community rather than an ethnic one, Christians were willing and able to adopt the whole body of its exclusivity as their inheritance. The earliest Christians struggled with the universalizing implications of their faith, but they did not do so for very long: by the end of the first century CE, the universalizing implications were accepted, and the idea that Christianity was simply a sect of Judaism and that therefore Gentile converts needed to undergo circumcision was no longer viable or even very interesting.

It would become axiomatic to Christians as the centuries unfolded that the centerpiece of their faith would be the reward of heaven and the punishment of hell, that the saving work of Christ was primarily about this drama in the afterlife of each individual, and that the algorithm for sorting through the enduring question of who is in and who is out was faithful membership in and service to an ever-more-powerful church. The radical freedom of God as Lord of history would be as thoroughly domesticated among medieval Christians as it had been among first-century Jews: "Salvation is only possible through our community. We possess utter and concrete certainty about how it is attained."

For generations of Christians, this certainty has colored everything: the nature of Christian initiation

Pastoral Perspective

(v. 24). He goes on to remind them of miracles Elijah and Elisha did for people from other countries. Their bewildered admiration of a local kid who has done well changes quickly to murderous rage. Why the dramatic change? Perhaps they expected him to defer to his elders rather than to speak out with such boldness. Maybe they were offended by his direct challenge of their whispered attitudes. Were they disappointed to learn they were not first in line for Jesus' miracles, and reluctant to remember how the prophets did wonders in Lebanon and Syria? What, then, of ourselves? Can we remember times when we have refused to pay attention to an unlikely source? Have we been slow to see God at work among people of backgrounds different from our own?

Fast forward to the twenty-first century, with its endless conflicts among nations, political parties, and church factions. In such times, people are quick to demonize one another, and slow to imagine they could learn from someone from another party or faction. Yet churches could be centers of respectful conversation, wellsprings of deep dialogue that leads to discernment. We could hear the Spirit's voice in one another's speech and see Scripture fulfilled before us. Perhaps then we would be more able to answer our call to bring and be good news. We might even be surprised at miracles happening among us.

The most surprising part of this astonishing passage comes in the last verse. In their rage, the people drove him out of town, hoping to throw him off a cliff. "But he passed through the midst of them and went on his way" (v. 30).

Perhaps Jesus escaped this angry mob as a miracle of nonviolence, of overcoming violence through the power of love. In some lectionaries, Luke 4:21–30 is scheduled near the time when we remember Martin Luther King and his commitment to social justice through nonviolent resistance. He himself learned about nonviolence from Mahatma Gandhi, the great Indian leader who succeeded in leading India to freedom with little bloodshed, through the nonviolent power of what he called "love-force." Gandhi wrote that love is "not merely a negative state of harmlessness, but . . . a positive state of doing good to the wrongdoer, while refusing to cooperate with the wrong."[1] Dr. King wrote, "When I speak of love I am not speaking of some sentimental and weak response. I am speaking of that force which all

---

1. Mahatma K. Gandhi, *Non-Violent Resistance* (New York: Schocken, 1951), 161.

verb—*martyreō*—occurs eleven times in Acts and generally suggests acclaim or positive testimony. The favorable reaction of the congregation is underscored by Luke's use of *thaumazō* ("to be amazed"). In light of these positive connotations, the question from the crowd—"Is not this Joseph's son?"—can safely be interpreted as a statement of approval, rather than a skeptical jab. Luke, more than the other Gospel writers, has already accentuated Jesus' identity as Joseph's son (in 2:48 and in 3:23, in the genealogy, directly before Jesus' temptation), and the Nazarenes reaffirm this status.

However, the omniscient author again invites the reader to share in the irony of what the crowds do not know. Much more than the corporeal son of Joseph, Luke is emphatically presenting Jesus as the Son of God through description of his birth, adolescence, baptism, temptation, genealogy, and now an instance of hometown testing. The limited perspective and presumptions of the townspeople are coming into conflict with the self-understanding and messianic consciousness of Jesus.

Acting out of his identity as Son of God, Jesus seems to bristle at the restricted vision of those gathered and their misstep in mistaking his identity. He begins his reply in the form of a pronouncement, thus offering a correction to their assumptions. "Doubtless you will quote to me . . . ," Jesus says, anticipating the reaction of his listeners with the omniscience so typical of Luke's characterization. The ancient maxim "Doctor, cure yourself" recalls the earlier temptations to prove himself ("throw yourself down," 4:9) while anticipating later taunts for Jesus to save himself from death on the cross. Jesus perceives the desire of his hometown crowd to be given priority in the fulfillment at hand. "Truly I tell you," Jesus announces, calling for special attention, "no prophet is accepted in the prophet's hometown" (v. 24).

The aphorism firmly locates Jesus within the prophetic tradition, building upon his use of Isaiah and anticipating his upcoming references to Elijah and Elisha. Jesus invokes Israel's second greatest prophet and his student in order to recall their respective roles in bringing about God's deliverance to Gentiles (see 1 Kgs. 17 and 2 Kgs. 5). As he did earlier in the episode, Jesus appeals to Scripture to build his case. While neither Elijah nor Elisha displayed an orientation toward the Gentiles over against Israel, Jesus demonstrates that even in the Hebrew traditions the scope of God's salvation extends beyond Nazareth—and beyond Israel—to encompass the Gentiles.

calamity even upon the widow with whom I am staying, by killing her son?' Then he stretches himself upon the child three times and cries out to the LORD, 'O LORD my God, let this child's life come into him again'" (1 Kgs. 17:20–21). Voilà, the child rises. The widow needs a miracle, and Elijah gives her one. Doubtless, every person Jesus addresses in that synagogue knows well both this story and the counterpart featuring Elisha (4:27). We can be equally confident that many of them stand in need of the miraculous just as desperately as did the widow of Zarephath or Naaman the Syrian.

However, Jesus will not work one. He has done wonders in Capernaum, but there will be none in Nazareth that day. Pressed for an explanation, Jesus turns the stories from 1 and 2 Kings like a dagger: "There were many widows in Israel in the time of Elijah . . . yet Elijah was sent to none of them except to a widow at Zarephath in Sidon" (vv. 26–27). God grants miracles, but not to every person who needs one, not even to God's own chosen people. Neither does Jesus. It is that fact that enrages his listeners. The congregation becomes a mob. Jesus is grabbed and dragged to the edge of a cliff.

Preaching this difficult passage should be easy. At least it should not be hard to help our listeners identify with those who react so violently to Christ's original unwillingness. Contemporary churchgoers have modern ways of expressing anger over our unmet needs, modern methods of dragging Jesus to the cliff, muttering against him in tones that may be more muted, but are no less devastating for their subtlety. Those first-century Nazarenes are not the only ones who do not receive what they need from God.

Nearly every time we preach, we stand before those who need a miracle. It seems that Christ hands them out arbitrarily. When he disappoints them, Jesus' first listeners rush him violently. In our day we tend simply to retreat. Many leave their childhood faith behind and place all their trust in pleasure or science or profit. Meanwhile some churchgoers give up, while going through the motions. We sing the hymns and say the prayers, without really believing that God can step into our midst.

I once heard a marital counselor say that when it comes to a relationship's long-term viability, indifference is more dangerous than anger. Sometimes it can seem that we have grown indifferent to a God who often seems to let our needs go unmet, a Christ who disappoints our expectations.

In verse 30 we see that even though Jesus will not work the miracles his listeners want, he works one

Luke 4:21–30

Theological Perspective

by baptism, the efficacy of confession, what salvation is, and, most importantly, to whom it would and would not be given. A rendering of the Last Judgment was prominently displayed in every European cathedral, with particular painterly attention lavished on the colorful fate of the damned. "God lives in this institution, and only here. Behold what awaits you if you should be foolish enough to stray from it or to disobey the commands of its leaders."

The enraged crowd of Luke 4:29–30, observant Jews to a person, could not stomach the idea of their God extending to someone outside their circle the same favor that they themselves enjoyed. We have not changed much in the two thousand years since that day. Many among the faithful are still made nervous by the suggestion that salvation is possible outside the church; this has nibbled at the edges of the institution for a century or more. Roman Catholic theologians since the Second Vatican Council have been kept busy explaining just how this might be so, and theirs has been an anxious dance indeed.

Surrounded as we are by centuries of corporate life bearing witness to Christ's presence in the church, it can be hard for us to remember that Jesus most probably did not imagine himself to be founding a church at all, certainly not an institution with the layers of history and the intricate hierarchy the church now displays. His point here in the fourth chapter of the Gospel of Luke is just the opposite of what the church has long claimed: salvation is not only possible outside the church; it might depend on being able to see membership in the gathered community as the beginning, rather than the fulfillment, of what it means to be chosen of God.

BARBARA CAWTHORNE CRAFTON

Pastoral Perspective

the great religions have seen as the supreme unifying principle of life. Love is somehow the key that unlocks the door to ultimate reality."[2] Could it be that the love of God was the shield that led Jesus safely from the hostility of his neighbors? What would it be like to practice nonviolent, powerful love in our homes, our churches, our country, and our world, walking away rather than responding to violence with violence?

Perhaps Jesus escaped the crowd by means of the miracle of people helping one another, as people pitched in and helped Jesus feed hungry hordes on another day. There must have been some people in the crowd who remembered that God had commanded, "You shall not murder." Perhaps his mother and father, sisters and brothers had been at the synagogue. (Certainly when I preached in a Presbyterian church in a little Tennessee town near where most of my relatives lived, parents, aunts, and cousins showed up, although few of them were Presbyterian.) Jesus' cousins might have disguised him in their clothes or massed around him so that he was hard to find. If we think of Jesus as a solitary miracle worker in this passage, we may miss the possibility that his presence called out love in others who were there that day. When we think of how he sent out newly minted disciples to preach and to heal, we realize that Jesus was always about bringing people together to do ministry together. This too is love-force.

"Today this scripture has been fulfilled in your hearing." The Spirit of God is upon Christians today, anointing us to proclaim good news and to be good news in the midst of poverty, oppression, imprisonment, and any physical condition that diminishes our lives. What particular things can we do to make a difference? God is at work in our city or village, and also in towns far away, among people of many faiths, bringing miracles as people minister together. In our common ministry, we will discover that Scripture is fulfilled in our hearing and our living, through the power of love.

RUTH C. DUCK

2. Martin Luther King, "Beyond Vietnam," speech printed in *Sojourners* 12, no. 1 (Jan. 1983): 16.

Exegetical Perspective

The scope Jesus describes reflects Luke's already-universalizing tendency, as seen in the birth narratives and most recently in the genealogy, which does not stop with Abraham as in Matthew, but traces Jesus' lineage all the way back to the universal figure of Adam. The scene looks ahead to the work of the church in Acts after Pentecost, as the fulfillment moves from Israel to all nations. Jesus is therefore affirming release for all the captives and good news for all who are poor, not simply those in his hometown—or "home country," as the noun (*patris*, vv. 23, 24) can also be translated. As is typical in Luke, Jesus' speech is realized in the actions that follow immediately, as the conflict initiated by the prophet's teaching escalates among the prophet's hometown residents.

As Simeon had foreseen (2:34–35), the Son of God incites opposition from the outset of his ministry. Luke describes the gathered crowd as "filled with rage." The phrase appears in Acts 19:28 to describe a riotous crowd's response to the growing acclaim of Paul and expansion of the movement. It also bears some resemblance to the phrasing used to describe the crowd enraged at Stephen when he accuses the people of having rejected Jesus (Acts 7:54–58). The same rage that will lead to Stephen's death now wells up in the Nazareth crowd that drives Jesus out of town. The scene recalls his final two temptations in Luke. Again Jesus demonstrates his identity as Son of God as he passes through the crowd without incident and resolutely continues on his way, ultimately finding his home not in Nazareth, but among "the poor, the crippled, the lame, and the blind" (14:13).

The passage concludes with an imperfect verb (*eporeueto*) describing Jesus' continuous action: "He was going on" (NRSV "went on his way"). The verb (*poreuomai*) appears throughout Luke to describe Jesus' journey toward Jerusalem and the cross. Luke's foreshadowing is further evident in his reference to a hill outside Nazareth, where no such hill exists. Topographical invention reveals theological intention. The message Jesus inaugurates in Nazareth will expand and intensify throughout his ministry, and the rage of the opposing crowd will escalate along with it. While he goes on his way on a fictional hill outside Nazareth, on a real hill outside Jerusalem he will not part the crowds.

ALAN P. SHEROUSE

Homiletical Perspective

nonetheless. Driven out to the edge of town, standing on a cliff, at risk of dying well before his work is done, Jesus "passed through the midst of them and went on his way." Endangered by the crowd for refusing to show his power, he then uses his power to evade the danger. Christ the ironist strikes again. He dodges their rage as deftly as he dodges their need.

All of this suggests that we simply cannot box Jesus into our definitions, our expectations, or our crises. Our need may be real. It may even be desperate, but Jesus will not be neatly defined as one who satisfies us by fitting every contour of our need—which is to say that Jesus will not always be what we need. He will not always be what we want. He will rarely be what we expect. However, he will always be God and God is free. I imagine that some jaws drop and the faith of at least a few grows when he slips through that ancient crowd and its members realize that their desire to kill Jesus will also go unsatisfied.

The question to ask our congregations is this: Will Jesus be able to elude contemporary indifference as easily as he escaped first-century anger? Of course he will. As Christian Wiman says, "If every church crumbles to dust, if the last believer in the last prayer opens her eyes and lets it all finally go, Christ will appear on this earth as calmly and casually as he appeared to the disciples walking to Emmaus after his death."[1] Our disappointment may be strong, but God is stronger still. If we recognize this fact and let Christ be God on his own terms, our appreciation for his power may grow. Perhaps then our faith will increase, even as our expectations are dashed and our disappointment burns.

MATT FITZGERALD

---

1. Christian Wiman, *My Bright Abyss: Meditation of a Modern Believer* (New York: Farrar, Straus & Giroux, 2013), 11.

³¹He went down to Capernaum, a city in Galilee, and was teaching them on the sabbath. ³²They were astounded at his teaching, because he spoke with authority. ³³In the synagogue there was a man who had the spirit of an unclean demon, and he cried out with a loud voice, ³⁴"Let us alone! What have you to do with us, Jesus of Nazareth? Have you come to destroy us? I know who you are, the Holy One of God." ³⁵But Jesus rebuked him, saying, "Be silent, and come out of him!" When the demon had thrown him down before them, he came out of him without having done him any harm. ³⁶They were all amazed and kept saying to one another, "What kind of utterance is this? For with authority and power he commands the unclean spirits, and out they come!" ³⁷And a report about him began to reach every place in the region.

Theological Perspective

The difference between power and authority is a critical one. Having power, knowing how to use power correctly, and being authorized to use power are distinct issues. In the text from Luke, there is no dispute about Jesus having power or his knowing how to use it. The ongoing tension and a primary problem throughout his ministry is the question of authority.

What is the relationship between authority and power? Authority involves recognized agency, the *right* to take an action, to prevent an action, or to reward and punish actions of others. Authority legitimates the use of power.

Everyone has a relationship with authority. As young children begin the process of self-differentiation from their caregivers, they learn to negotiate between the "me" and the "not me." Once there is any separation between the "me" and the "not me," the issue of authority is invoked. Who can tell me what to do? Whose voice should I heed? Who has the right to determine the law of the land? Who has the right to say this reading of a tradition or a text is the correct reading, or at least a better reading than the alternatives? In a social system, some entities, such as the courts and the police, are acknowledged as having authority by almost everyone. However, even in a tightly controlled society, the

Pastoral Perspective

Demons and unclean spirits? Literal devils sound bizarre to our modern ears, yet many of us are acquainted with evil. We have experienced events in our lives ranging from the disturbing to the traumatic. As a pastoral psychotherapist, I have sat with survivors of abuse and assault that have shaken me. I have seen the horror of encounters with the demonic reflected in my patients' eyes. Literal devils may not exist, but in our God-given freedom to choose the good, we are also given the freedom to participate in evil, which often appears as a rupturing of relationships and gash in the goodness of creation.

Probably much, if not most, of the evil we do is not our conscious intent—although some people may even choose to do evil in a bid to grasp idolatrous power for themselves. The majority of us do not choose evil and prefer to think of ourselves as good. Yet we have internalized the wounds we have suffered, big and small, and they continue to live on inside us as wounding aspects of our inner selves. What better metaphor might be used for these internal wounds than to understand them as our inner demons?

We want to be good people, and so our first impulse is to say, "Whatever is bad in me, I want to get it out!" We turn to a variety of "exorcists" for this purpose—from self-help books, yoga classes, and

Exegetical Perspective

This account relates Jesus' teaching at the synagogue in Capernaum and subsequent healing of a man "who had the spirit of an unclean demon" (v. 33). It mirrors Mark 1:21–28 quite closely, although the omission of Mark's disparaging reference to the scribes in Mark 1:22 may reflect Luke's emphasis on Jesus' continuity with Judaism. It is the first of six stories of Jesus' early ministry in Galilee (4:31–5:16). All of these read like illustrations of Isaiah 61:1–2, which Jesus reads and claims to fulfill in Luke 4:16–21. Indeed, there is some reason to believe Luke intended them to read as such, since the Capernaum stories seem to be out of sequence. Luke 4:23, for instance, assumes that Jesus' miraculous deeds at Capernaum are already well known, yet we do not in fact hear about them until 4:31 and following.

The fact that this story follows the one about Jesus' rejection at the synagogue in Nazareth (4:16–30) points up a contrast in the people's response to him. Whereas Jesus is rejected in his hometown of Nazareth, he seems to be quite popular in Capernaum. Both stories are set in synagogues, but the response of the crowd could not be more different. In Nazareth, Jesus' listeners find him well spoken and speculate on his being Joseph's son, but they completely miss the significance of his announcement that the Isaiah passage has been fulfilled in

Homiletical Perspective

In Luke 4:14–30, Luke sets out the great vision that is filled out in the Gospel of Luke and the book of Acts. The ministry of Jesus signals that God is in the process of ending the old, broken age and is moving toward replacing that old world with the Realm of God. The ministry of Jesus not only indicates this transition has begun but also embodies it: the Realm is partially prefigured through the work of Jesus and will become fully manifest after Jesus' return. The miracles demonstrate that the claims of Jesus and the church are true: the Realm really is at hand.

The preacher might follow the movement over the last generation in preaching to let the function of the text suggest the function for the sermon. From the perspective of Luke 4:18–19 and 4:24–27, the miracles performed by Jesus in the Gospel and by the church in Acts are both signs that point to the presence of the Realm and acts that embody the qualities of the Realm. In a sense a miracle is a mini-apocalypse, in which the restoration of the Realm of God (represented in this text by a person released from possession by a demon) replaces an element of the old and broken world (represented in this text by a person possessed by a demon).

Such a sermon would have two essential parts. First, it would help the congregation understand the function of unclean spirits in the world of the

Luke 4:31–37

Theological Perspective

authority to exercise power over another involves the other's internal assent. Hence, even in oppressive societies, officially authorized powers are subject to unauthorized questions, even rejection by individuals or groups.

In the contemporary world, one of the practical questions is, "Shall I recognize any authority outside myself or outside my interest group?" As you read this theological reflection, no doubt elections are being held somewhere in which voters will authorize certain persons to lead them nationally, regionally, or locally. In democratic societies, elections formally and legally authorize the exercise of power, even though sometimes socially legitimated power may still lack authority in someone's mind.

In Luke 4, the evangelist opens Jesus' ministry with stories about his power and authority. When Jesus arrives in Jerusalem at the close of his earthly ministry, the religious leaders demand, "By what authority are you doing these things?" (20:2). Neither his opponents, human and demonic, nor his allies question Jesus' power—his *ability* to do. Jesus heals, exorcises, and forgives. Nevertheless his opponents and allies differ deeply regarding his *authority*. In the wilderness testing, Satan tries to become the source of Jesus' authority. When Satan shows Jesus all the world's realms, Satan tells him, "To you I will give their glory and all this authority; for it has been given over to me, and I give it to anyone I please. If you, then, will worship me, it will all be yours" (4:6). Jesus' hometown folks authorize him to compliment but not to critique; after his critique, the outraged gathering tries to throw him from a cliff. The people who receive his ministry in Capernaum are amazed at his power and authority, astounded by his teaching and the power of his word. He speaks a word and the demons obey.

Clearly Luke wants his readers to know that Jesus is authorized by God. He is the Christ, through whom the reign of God is wedging into the world. God empowers and authorizes Jesus by means of the Spirit to exercise power over the demonic and unclean spirits that make human beings ill and imprison body or spirit.

Note the sequence in Luke as he seeks to establish Jesus' authority in his readers' minds. Jesus returns from his baptism in the Jordan "full of the Holy Spirit" and is led by the same Spirit into the wilderness testing. After successfully completing his tests, Jesus, "filled with the power of the Spirit," returns to Galilee. He announces his call in the Nazareth synagogue, and the hearer is immediately shown the

Pastoral Perspective

life coaches, to psychotherapists and even our clergy. However, exorcism always fails if all we are trying to do is banish the parts of ourselves we wish we did not have, without understanding the unconscious function they still perform for us deep in the psyche, and what pain they bear for us.

This Gospel story shows us a different kind of exorcism—not one of pure banishment, but one of *forging a relationship* with the demonic. Like our own demons, this man's demon cries out for attention. Our demons may cry out by "acting out," sabotaging us or our relationships, or causing us to crash down steep cliffs of addiction in an effort to satisfy deep longings, to heal pain, or to seek elusive pleasure. If we listen to Augustine or C. S. Lewis,[1] we may be able to be somewhat more friendly toward our demons, because in their thrashing about for attention, they are revealing to us our incompleteness and unhealed sufferings, as well as the deepest longings of our life—to be restored to harmony with "the Holy One of God" (v. 34).

Jesus neither ignored the man's demon nor tried to stuff him back inside the man to shut him up. He accorded the demon agency (literally): "*Silence yourself, and come out*." Carl Jung observed that it is only when we go into the depths of our own psyche and confront the parts of ourselves we wish were not there—the Shadow[2]— that we can experience growth and transformation. As small children, we internalized the hurts we experienced, by necessity taking in the aspects of parents and other caretakers who wounded or neglected us, in order to create a psychic bond with them while we were literally at their mercy. These internal figures served a protective function—they helped us by taking evil into ourselves to project the good onto those on whom we depended. If our unconscious had not had the capacity to encapsulate badness and blame within ourselves, the outer world might have been unbearable. In adulthood, however, these inner figures often have outlived their usefulness. We find that we cannot trust other people, or we fear intimacy, or we hurt others before they get the chance to hurt us first.

It does no good to try to deny or eject these demons through some back door of the psyche. They cry out to be brought into the light—even the light of the living God. When we do hear their cries—as Jesus did in this story—we are able to learn how they

1. C. S. Lewis, *The Screwtape Letters* (San Francisco: Harper Collins, 1996), ix.
2. C. G. Jung, "Psychology and Religion" in *Psychology and Religion: West and East*, ed. and trans. Gerhard Adler and R. F. C. Hull, Collected Works of C. G. Jung, vol. 11 (Princeton, NJ: Princeton University Press, 1970), 131.

Exegetical Perspective

their hearing (4:21). This seems to annoy Jesus, who goes on to cite two instances of prophets who were similarly underappreciated in their hometowns and went on to perform miracles in foreign locations, where they *were* appreciated (4:25–27). At this, the crowd becomes enraged and attempts to throw Jesus off a cliff (4:28–29).

In stark contrast to this, the crowd at the Capernaum synagogue responds, not to his public speaking ability or his pedigree, but to the content of his teaching and his obvious authority (v. 32). While Luke does not record any verbal exchanges with the Capernaum crowd, he really does not have to; Jesus' actions speak louder than words. His teaching is followed immediately by the healing of a man possessed by an unclean spirit. This is precisely the kind of demonstration of power he refuses to do in Nazareth.

Demon possession and exorcism may be difficult subjects for many postmodern readers to get their heads around, but it would be a shame to let this get in the way of recognizing the liberating force of this miracle. In Jesus' day, demons were seen as the source of most mental and physical illness. As Fred Craddock points out, "we have not, by the announcement that we do not believe in demons, reduced one whit the amount of personal and corporate evil in the world. The names of the enemies have been changed, but the battles still rage."[1] The fact that Jesus has the authority and power to banish such forces demonstrates that he has equal authority and power to banish whatever possesses us.

There is much to be learned from the verbal exchange between Jesus and this man's demon. The demon seems to be the one who initiates the exchange, since Luke makes no mention of the afflicted man seeking to be healed, and Jesus simply responds to the demon's outburst. Luke leaves us with the impression that the demon has overheard Jesus teaching in the synagogue and recognizes him immediately. The fact that the demon uses Jesus' name could be seen as a kind of power play, assuming an unwarranted level of intimacy. This is intimacy of a "know your enemy" variety. The demon knows that Jesus stands for everything he and his fellow demons stand against. They are oil and water—polar opposites—and so the demon's opening salvo is simply to scream, "Let us alone! What have you to do with us, Jesus of Nazareth?" (v. 34). As soon as he

1. Fred B. Craddock, *Luke*, Interpretation series (Louisville, KY: John Knox Press, 1990), 66.

Homiletical Perspective

Gospels. Second, the sermon would help the congregation recognize the exorcising, Realm-creating power of Jesus, at work today, and would explore how the congregation can respond to that power.

Taking this approach the preacher could begin by exploring the origin and function of unclean spirits (demons) in Judaism in the Hellenistic age. In those days many people thought of unclean spirits as distinct beings who were associates or territory managers of the devil, much as angels were associates of God. Demons inhabited individuals and institutions and sought to disrupt God's purposes in those single and corporate lives and to bring them into the domain of the devil.

The ancient Jewish theologians who moved in this direction were performing the oldest function of religion by trying to make theological sense of life. They reasoned that the brokenness of the old age is so fractious that it could only be the result of an outside power: the devil and associates (unclean spirits). Many congregations today do not believe in the existence of a devil or unclean spirits as distinct entities but see the figures of the devil and the unclean spirits as representing distortions of life by forces and systems that are bigger than individuals or communities and over which we do not have direct and simple control.

The preacher could see the ancient figures of the devil and the unclean spirits as equivalents of systems that distort God's purposes for life, such as racism, sexism, classism, anti-intellectualism, and homophobia. While such systems are not personal beings that occupy the hearts and minds of individuals and communities, they function much as the devil and the unclean spirits did in the world of the Bible, in that they distort our sense of reality so that we act in ways that are racist, sexist, classist, and so on. Individuals and groups sometimes fall victim to these systemic forces without making a conscious choice to do so. Individuals and communities essentially become captive to such systemic distortions of life.

The preacher who takes such a route would help the congregation recognize unhealthy systems as contemporary equivalents of the devil and the unclean spirits and explain how these unhealthy systems control our values and behaviors.

Further, the sermon could alert the congregation to how people today encounter the exorcising, Realm-building power of God. Racism, as noted, is a contemporary equivalent of demonic possession. At Christian Theological Seminary, where I serve, we are confronting the demon of racism. Trainers help

Luke 4:31–37

Theological Perspective

difference between Jesus' having power and authority and the people's differing levels of acceptance of what he claims he is empowered and authorized to do. Then, in Capernaum, the hearer is shown what an authorized Jesus can do. The message throughout Luke 4 is that God has given Jesus authority over unclean spirits to proclaim the good news in word and deed, fulfilling a vision of what "good" means, as caught in the words of Isaiah 61.

In contemporary society, we talk about authenticity, by which we often mean being self-authorized, being one's own person, or acting true to oneself. This is decidedly not Luke's perspective. Jesus is sent by God in the power of the Holy Spirit. He is on a mission not of his own making or authorization (4:43). Being authentic for Jesus means fulfilling a God-given, God-authorized life. In Greek, the word for "authority" is *exousia*, literally "from being." Jesus' authority is an expression of living from the wellspring of his being; and his being, Luke wants to be clear, is derived from God and God's purposes.

The opening stories of Jesus' ministry in Luke are, therefore, christological claims. Luke links Jesus' ministry to Third Isaiah's call to proclaim a jubilee year when people will be released from all the evils that bind humankind. Luke's claim is that Jesus is authorized by God to proclaim such a year and, in proclaiming it, to inaugurate God's reign. Later in the Gospel, Jesus' opponents will question by whose authority he exorcises, heals, and forgives. In fact, is not the issue of Jesus' authority—who authorized him and what he was authorized to do—at the heart of confessing Jesus as the Christ or being unable to make that confession?

During political campaigns in the United States, we have become conditioned to the phenomenon of campaign strategists creating worlds with or without facts. Using words that appeal emotionally to a particular demographic population, strategists fabricate fictions that are plausible because they align with a person's dispositions and biases. The contrast to the figure of Jesus as presented by Luke could not be starker: a man who speaks the truth with power and authority, says what he does and does what he says, and uses the healing and freeing power given to him to bring close the reign of God.

GARY PELUSO-VERDEND

Pastoral Perspective

once protected us and how they are now ready to depart, if we are ready to bear the hidden hurt and knowledge they once bore for us. They may throw us down for one last time (just as therapy is often not a pleasant process!), but then they will truly depart without doing us further harm.

In Greek, the "unclean spirit" is *akathartos*, related to the words *kathairō*, "to cleanse," but also "to prune," and *katharizō*, "to purify," but also "to heal." The skilled gardener knows that in order to prune one must know how to preserve the life-sustaining buds on each branch, however unruly. We cannot be healed or cleansed from the stains that life has left on our souls without first recognizing them for what they are—the marks of the messy, impure, and wild hurts of life upon our own selves. In recognizing our own imperfection, our own unruliness, we are less likely to act out that brokenness and wildness on others, or to project it onto them while denying it in ourselves.

This passage in Luke follows soon after Jesus is tempted by the devil in the wilderness, thereby confronting his *own* demon. This temptation narrative from Luke's Gospel assures us that however painful the process of bringing our inner demons out into the light of day, Christ has trod the path of recognition and confrontation before us. Christ bears the spiritual authority to know our inner demons, to command them, and ultimately to heal them—thereby liberating us to live our lives more fully in the light of God.

PAMELA COOPER-WHITE

Feasting on the Gospels

asks the question, an awful possibility seems to occur to him and prompts another question, "Have you come to destroy us?" Perhaps the answer is obvious, because he finishes with what, from any other lips, would be a moving confession of faith: "I know who you are, the Holy One of God" (v. 34).

Earlier in the passage, the crowd notes that Jesus "spoke with authority" (v. 32). Now, with a few authoritative words, Jesus rebukes the demon and sends him packing. No gimmicks or fancy incantations are necessary—only the word of the Holy One of God. Notice too that the rebuke comes in two parts. The first is "be silent." Jesus is not about to let some show-off demon decide how and when his identity is to be revealed. The second part of the rebuke is the command, "Come out of him." The demon obeys without a word, though perhaps the fact that he throws the man to the ground could be seen as a last, petulant flourish. Maybe he is just in an awful hurry to leave. In any case, the man is unharmed and blessedly free from his demon houseguest.

The crowd not only witnesses this, but overhears the exchange with the demon. They are understandably amazed and wonder, "What kind of utterance is this? For with authority and power he commands the unclean spirits, and out they come!" (v. 36b). The "out they come!" remark testifies to the apparent ease with which Jesus has dispatched the demon. Also significant, however, is their use of both the words "authority" and "power." This reflects their growing sense of awe. After hearing Jesus teach, they recognize that he speaks "with authority" (v. 32). After seeing him heal the man with the demon, they recognize both his authority and his power. It is no wonder, then, that word begins to spread about him in "every place in the region" (v. 37). The stories that follow bear witness to both his growing reputation and his determination to oppose all those "forces that hurt, cripple, oppress, or alienate human life."[2]

CAROL M. BECHTEL

Eurocentric members of the community confront our racist assumptions and behaviors. In the process, people of European origin in the community seek to turn away from racist attitudes and practices and to manifest more Realm-like qualities of living.

The fact that the exorcism in this text occurs in a synagogue presents the preacher with another intriguing preaching possibility. Just as the demon is in the synagogue itself, the preacher could encourage the congregation to explore the possibility that unclean spirits are at work in the congregation and in the larger church. For instance, without conscious awareness, the church often operates according to the same dynamics of racism, sexism, classism, nationalism, and similar distortions as the larger culture.

According to Luke 4:36, the crowd is amazed at the exorcism, but they do not understand that the exorcism is a sign of the inbreaking of the Realm of God. They ask, "What kind of utterance is this?" (v. 36). The sermon might help the congregation recognize moments, events, and social movements that bring the Realm into practical expression but that the congregation may not recognize as such. How does the congregation ask, "What kind of utterance, event, or movement is this?"

Many congregants today are unfamiliar with the world of the Bible. As part of a teaching moment at the time of the reading of the Scripture lesson (or during the sermon itself), a preacher who uses PowerPoint could project a map of northern Galilee showing Capernaum in relationship to the Sea of Galilee, Nazareth, and Jerusalem. The projection could include the ruins of the synagogue at Capernaum as they are today. Such pictures, used with permission, are readily available on the Internet. The preacher should explain that the ruins now visible are from a synagogue built in the fourth century CE, but that archeologists think the fourth-century synagogue is on the site of the earlier one. The preacher could also project an artist's renderings of both the outside and inside of the first-century synagogue. This material might help the congregation enter the world of the text by imagining the scene.

RONALD J. ALLEN

2. Craddock, *Luke*, 66.

³⁸After leaving the synagogue he entered Simon's house. Now Simon's mother-in-law was suffering from a high fever, and they asked him about her. ³⁹Then he stood over her and rebuked the fever, and it left her. Immediately she got up and began to serve them.

⁴⁰As the sun was setting, all those who had any who were sick with various kinds of diseases brought them to him; and he laid his hands on each of them and cured them. ⁴¹ Demons also came out of many, shouting, "You are the Son of God!" But he rebuked them and would not allow them to speak, because they knew that he was the Messiah.

⁴²At daybreak he departed and went into a deserted place. And the crowds were looking for him; and when they reached him, they wanted to prevent him from leaving them. ⁴³But he said to them, "I must proclaim the good news of the kingdom of God to the other cities also; for I was sent for this purpose." ⁴⁴So he continued proclaiming the message in the synagogues of Judea.

Theological Perspective

There is something important to be considered here in Luke's repeated use of the word "rebuke." When Jesus heals Peter's mother-in-law of a high fever, he "rebukes" the fever (v. 39), as if the woman were held captive by the fever, and the fever leaves her. In the previous passage, Jesus rebuked the demon that held the man captive (4:35). In the following passage he rebukes the demons who try to out him as the Son of God, the Christ (v. 41).

In our day, the word "rebuke" is rarely used outside of a narrow set of contexts. If you type "rebuke" into a search engine, the top hits include mostly definitions and biblical citations. Click on the latter and you will find expositions of biblical passages where the word is used or applied to contemporary Christian behaviors. Then there are a few references to politicians rebuking an action or policy of another, using the word in the sense that combines criticism and rejection.

The narrow set of contexts today where the word still is used includes Scripture and the communities of faith formed by Scripture. In these contexts, to rebuke means much more than to criticize or reject; it has significant theological importance. The Greek word for "rebuke" is *epitimaō*. *Timaō* means to honor or punish; thus, to rebuke signifies an action by one in a position to judge, to name and by

Pastoral Perspective

So many demons, so little time! When I am weary, this story reads like a comforting morality play for the overworked, the burned out, and the codependent! It is comforting to realize that even Jesus got tired.

All too often, as Christians we exhort one another to practice sacrifice as the cardinal Christian virtue: "Deny yourself, take up your cross and follow me." We point to Jesus' sacrifice on the cross as the pattern for a life of sacrificial love. Women, perhaps especially, have been told to care selflessly for spouses and children, to be the emotional weather vanes for the family system, and even to put up with abuse, in the name of Christian sacrifice. Reading the Gospel of Luke, we do not find Jesus to be the model of a holy doormat. When Jesus finally does give up his life at the end of Luke's Gospel, it is because he had the courage and the utter, intimate confidence in the power of God's Spirit within him to proclaim good news to the poor and liberation to the captives. It is this courage and confidence we should pray for and seek to embody, rather than a distorted story of sacrifice that glorifies suffering for its own sake and redeems no one.

This story in Luke's Gospel serves as evidence that we are not called to a pallid selflessness, but to a life in which we must discern daily how best to use the gifts and talents God has given us. There is a helpful

Exegetical Perspective

This passage contains the second, third, and fourth stories in a set of accounts centered on Jesus' early ministry in Galilee (4:31–5:16). All of them are linked, not only by itinerary, but by theme. Jesus' identity, authority, and power are paramount, but we learn of these through his acts of compassion, healing, and liberation. Jesus' growing popularity elsewhere in Galilee stands in stark contrast to the rejection he experienced in Nazareth (4:16–30). Yet these stories should also be seen against the background of the temptation narrative in 4:1–15. Over and over again, he demonstrates his determination to use his power not for selfish gain, but to alleviate the suffering of others. Although fame often follows him, it is not something he seeks for its own sake. In fact, one gets the sense that Jesus' burdens grow right along with his popularity.

Luke relates Jesus' healing of Simon's mother-in-law in 4:38–39 (cf. Mark 1:29–31 and Matt. 8:14–15). Although this is the first time we have encountered Simon in Luke's Gospel, Luke seems to assume Simon needs no introduction. (In Mark, there is no need to introduce Simon, since we have already met him and heard the story of his call, along with that of his brother Andrew and their fellow fishermen James and John in Mark 1:16–19.) Neither does Luke elaborate on why Jesus goes to Simon's house after

Homiletical Perspective

The congregation that first heard this story in Luke was filled with people who were similar to many people today: they were in danger of losing the hope of the gospel. This situation was understandable. Jesus' early followers believed that Jesus would return soon. Two generations later, when Luke wrote Acts, many had become discouraged. They were in conflict with some Jewish leaders, and the Roman Empire still held sway. They were anxious and confused. Some had already given up the hope of Jesus' return.

In response, Luke piles miracle stories, one upon another, reinforcing the claim that the ministry of Jesus embodies the Realm of God (Luke 4:16–18, 24–27). Later, Luke emphasizes that God empowers the apostles and the church to continue Jesus' witness to the Realm in their times and places. Reports such as Luke 4:38–44 function as idealized memories that are paradigmatic for later times. As miracles once testified in abundance to the presence of the Realm of God at the time of Jesus, so manifestations of the Realm continue to occur in the later church.

Some congregations today are in situations similar to that of Luke's community: diminished, discouraged, hesitant in witness. The preacher might remind the community that a dynamic past is more than occasion for nostalgia; it can be a resource for

Luke 4:38–44

Theological Perspective

naming "make it so." Authors of both Testaments in the Bible reserve the word mostly for God, and New Testament witnesses extend the authority to rebuke to Jesus as well. In contrast to the Word of God that births life, "the reproving Word . . . calls down destruction. . . . *Epitimaō* becomes a technical term for the powerful divine word of rebuke and threat."[1] *Epitimaō* carries this technical meaning in Luke's fourth chapter. To rebuke is to speak a word whereby an evil power is defeated, overpowered, and brought "into submission." Said differently, *epitimaō* means to issue a command that delivers persons from the forces of disease and death that bind them.[2]

The act of rebuking is a necessary part of the gospel Jesus proclaims. As the text before us illustrates, it is understood that Satan saps the life of God's children through illness and demonic possession. Satan's empire, or Rome's empire, controls this world. In order to make room for God's empire, the powers of this world must be rebuked: denounced, pushed aside, rejected. As proclaimer of God's empire, Jesus is empowered to rebuke the occupying empires. Thus, to proclaim and to rebuke are two sides of the same coin, two dimensions of the Christ's power to usher in the empire of God.

Given the biblical meaning of the word "rebuke," and with its authorized use limited primarily to God and to God's Christ, consider the question: what is the relationship between Christ's authority to rebuke and the authority of the church, as the body of Christ, to rebuke? In other words, does Christ authorize today's church to rebuke, to command in a way that delivers?

If the reader's reaction to the question is anything like this writer's, the answer is a combination of near-rejection ("Rebuking seems so harsh!") and curiosity ("What would it mean to 'command in a way that delivers'?").

First, there is the issue of whether "rebuke" is too harsh. Note that, in these three instances in Luke, Jesus does not rebuke a *person* but malevolent *forces*, such as diseases and demons that are bad for human beings. If a rebuke is properly used to deliver someone in bondage, then perhaps it should be aimed only at those forces and, when fitting, those persons who ensnare, bind, and enslave. One can imagine the church rebuking the practice of calling an individual an "illegal," or rebuking lies that obscure the facts,

Pastoral Perspective

little saying: "Say no, to say yes," or "Say no, so you can say yes to something greater." Jesus could have kept on healing people in Capernaum—there seems to have been no shortage of demons there! If he had stayed and kept rebuking the bad spirits, he no doubt would have earned considerable gratitude from the good people in Simon Peter's town. However, Jesus was unerringly focused on his mission: "I must proclaim the good news of the kingdom of God to the other cities also, for I was sent for this purpose" (v. 43). Easy for him to say, we think—after all, he was the Messiah!

How do *we* know when to say no, so that we can say yes to something greater? How do we know what is lesser and what is greater—especially when people are clamoring for us to do what they want, right here, right now? This takes discernment. It is perhaps easy to say no to things we find distasteful or wrong. How do we know when to say no to things that are actually good?

Augustine, who wrestled with temptation and the slippery slope from desire to concupiscence, stressed repeatedly that evil is not a thing or a force that we can easily recognize and engage in battle. He is best known for his idea that evil is the absence of good (*privatio boni*).[1] He had a more nuanced view of evil as well—that evil can be a mistaking of lesser goods for greater ones. Evil for Augustine was often too *much* of a good thing: evil happens when hunger becomes greed, desire becomes lust, authority becomes coercion, pleasure becomes an idol, and confidence becomes the delusion of complete self-control.

Is there an analogy here for too much caregiving? What happens when our compassion, originally funded by God's grace, becomes an overweening need to be needed? When our desire to care becomes a desire to be seen as caring? When does genuine sacrificial love become the narcissism of the self-proclaimed martyr? When does a genuine feeling of fulfillment in doing good subtly slide into self-aggrandizement? Discernment is tricky precisely because the "devil" all too often comes disguised as an angel of good (see 4:1–13).

Our choices—even our choices for something apparently good—can lead to evil through lack of understanding the bigger picture. What are the unintended consequences of our choices? If I respond to

---

1. "Epitimaō," in Gerhard Kittel, ed., *Theological Dictionary of the New Testament*, ed. and trans. Geoffrey W. Bromiley (Grand Rapids: Eerdmans, 1964), 2:623–26.

2. Joseph A. Fitzmyer, *The Gospel according to Luke*, Anchor Bible 28–28A (New York: Doubleday, 1981, 1985), 1:546, 550.

1. See Augustine of Hippo, *On the Free Choice of the Will* [De libero arbitrio], trans. Thomas Williams (Indianapolis/Cambridge, UK: Hackett, 1993); see also Pamela Cooper-White, *Many Voices: Pastoral Psychotherapy in Relational and Theological Perspective* (Minneapolis: Fortress Press, 2007), esp. 117–32.

leaving Capernaum's synagogue. Reading between the lines, it seems logical to assume that Simon is at the synagogue and invites Jesus to return home with him afterwards. Perhaps, as he does with Zacchaeus, Jesus simply invites himself (19:5). In either case, there is strong reason to believe Simon has witnessed the way Jesus heals the man who is possessed by a demon (vv. 33–35).

When Jesus arrives at Simon's house, he is informed that Simon's mother-in-law is suffering from a high fever. While Luke does not say that this fever is "demon induced," in that day evil spirits were commonly understood as a possible or even probable cause of physical ailments. Luke's description of the healing parallels the earlier healing in one particularly impressive regard: Jesus "rebuked" the demon (cf. v. 39 with v. 35). In contrast with Mark's account, there is no touch involved (Mark 1:31)— only the authoritative command of the One whose authority demons seem to recognize and fear. The fact that Simon's mother-in-law "immediately" gets up and shows hospitality to her guests demonstrates the completeness of her cure. She does not even need to convalesce.

Right on the heels of this story is another (vv. 40–41) about further healings that take place in what we are intended to assume is the same evening (cf. Mark 1:32–34 and Matt. 8:16–17). The fact that people begin to bring their sick relatives and friends to Jesus "as the sun was setting" reflects the fact that the Sabbath is now over (see v. 31), and people are once again allowed to carry things—which they have been forbidden to do on the Sabbath. It is clear that reports of Jesus' healing powers have indeed begun to spread (v. 37), and one gets the impression people are just waiting for the last ray of the sun to disappear so they can rush their ailing loved ones to this incredible healer. There is, evidently, no prohibition against carrying good news to one's neighbors about what one has seen in the synagogue!

Here, Jesus heals by both touch ("laying his hands on each of them," v. 40) and by word. As before, he rebukes the demons and they flee. Once again (see vv. 34–35), the demons are not inclined to go quietly. While the demon in the synagogue declared Jesus to be "the Holy One of God," this set names him as "the Son of God." Jesus stifles them in both cases, but here Luke elaborates and tells us that Jesus "would not allow them to speak, because they knew that he was the Messiah" (v. 41). It is an explanation that raises as many questions as it answers. Is Jesus concerned that people have too many preconceived

what the church can be and do in the present. Contexts and ministries may change, but a church that once made a vital witness can do it again in a new time and place.

Scholars note that Luke–Acts contains an impulse toward the restoration of the social situation of women in the Realm of God. This theme is reinforced by Luke 4:38–39 when Jesus heals Simon's mother-in-law. The preacher could use this association, especially in dialogue with the pictures of women across Luke–Acts, to help the congregation recognize the continuing repression of women and opportunities to join movements for liberation today.[1]

Luke sometimes demonstrates the egalitarian impulse in the Realm by presenting women and men in pairs: 4:31–37 (a man) and 4:38–39 (a woman). How can the congregation move toward mutually supportive relationships among women and men? The preacher might point out that, even with Luke's egalitarian intent, the woman here is shortchanged in the space given to her in comparison to the length of the story about the man.

Some congregants puzzle over whether miracles actually occurred in antiquity, and whether they occur today. Some wonder why God would heal only a few people in antiquity while not healing others. Some ministers today report poignant encounters with parishioners who are in extremis or who have family or friends in such circumstances. Such folk sometimes wonder why God does not directly heal them or their loved ones.

The preacher could develop a sermon that straightforwardly discusses such matters. A minister who believes that such miracles not only occurred then, but also occur now, would need to offer a rationale for that confidence and explain why some people receive miracles and others do not. A minister who thinks the miracle stories derived from an ancient mythological worldview would compare and contrast the place of miracles in ancient and contemporary worldviews, and help the congregation identify ways the miracle stories help us recognize God's presence and purposes today. Ministers from both theological poles need to help the congregation name where and how they believe God is active today, and how to respond faithfully. Preachers from both viewpoints share the common claim that the miracle—whether literal or metaphorical—offers a glimpse of God's Realm.

---

1. For an approach to preaching on themes that span Luke–Acts, see Ronald J. Allen, *Preaching Luke–Acts*, Preaching Classic Texts (St. Louis: Chalice Press, 2000).

Theological Perspective

or rebuking social norms that encourage bullying. When used in this way, the practice of a rebuke seems fitting rather than harsh.

If the act of rebuking can be understood in this way, then curiosity may lead us to realize that, in fact, congregations actually do a great deal of rebuking, in particular as the body of Christ engages in two common practices. The first is the practice of baptism. Some contemporary baptismal liturgies have retrieved the ancient connection between baptism and rebuke:

> Do you renounce the spiritual forces of wickedness, reject the evil powers of this world, and repent of your sin? . . . Do you accept the freedom and power God gives you to resist evil, injustice, and oppression in whatever forms they present themselves?[3]

In this and all similar baptismal liturgies, the church, in effect, rebukes: commands in a way that delivers.

A second place that the church often rebukes is prayer. Christians from many traditions recite a rebuke to the empires of this world, from rote, frequently unmindfully, every time they pray the Lord's Prayer, the Our Father. When Jesus told his followers to pray, "Your Empire come, your will be done, on earth," every hearer knew there was already an empire occupying this world. Jesus' prayer rebukes the empire that denies daily bread to a people endemically hungry and that burdens people whose dignity is sullied by crushing debt in a system designed to keep them indebted.

So, to answer the question about whether or not the church has been given the power to rebuke: if we consider the liturgy surrounding the sacrament of baptism and the weekly recitation of the Lord's Prayer, one must at least acknowledge that the church continues Christ's work of rebuking and praying to be delivered from the evil powers that bind human beings.

GARY PELUSO-VERDEND

Pastoral Perspective

this request today, who might suffer for it tomorrow? If we spend our time overresponding to querulous complaints, what gets neglected? If I overfunction in taking care of someone's needs, how might I actually be failing them in other ways? If we say yes to this or that interesting project, what other work are we failing to accomplish? If I spend all my time dealing with pastoral needs of people within the congregation, what advocacy might I be neglecting in the public square—or vice versa? If we remain mostly in a reactive mode, what proactive visioning are we failing to engage?

Discernment takes time. That is why Jesus went to a solitary place at daybreak. It is a balancing act. We do not disappoint people heartlessly, or simply ignore others' pain. We can follow Jesus' example and exercise some triage. Jesus did attend to those who presented themselves to him for healing, but he also had to draw a boundary for the sake of the greater good to which he was called. Jesus knew he would be disappointing people in Capernaum as he had just done earlier in Nazareth, but by taking a step back from the clamor of the villagers in one place, he was able to recall his mission "to the other towns also."

This is finally about discernment of vocation. Just because we *can* do something does not mean that we *should*—even if it is something at which we are good. In the novel *Evensong*, Gail Godwin wrote, "Something's your vocation if it keeps making more of you."[2] To what are *you* called, and how will your day-to-day choices hinder you or keep you on the path God has set uniquely before *you*?

PAMELA COOPER-WHITE

---

3. *The United Methodist Hymnal* (Nashville: United Methodist Publishing House, 1989), 34.

2. Gail Godwin, *Evensong* (New York: Ballantine, 2000), 12.

notions of what the Messiah is supposed to be? Is he reluctant to sully such news by having it come from such unworthy sources (see Acts 16:16–18)? It is impossible to tell. What is certain, however, is that those around Jesus are gathering information and impressions of him. Perhaps Jesus simply wants to give them a chance to draw their own conclusions.

In verses 42–44, Jesus leaves at daybreak for a "deserted place" (see also Mark 1:35–39). We are not told why he does so, but it is not hard to imagine his needing a break. He starts the Sabbath teaching in the synagogue, after all, and spends until well after sunset healing people and dispatching demons. Perhaps we should also remember the last time he is in what could be translated literally as "a desert place." Luke uses the same word to describe the setting of Jesus' temptation in 4:1. There he rejected the devil's seductive promises of fame and power. Now, just a short time into his ministry, he has both fame and power. Yet, they are byproducts of his ministry and not the reasons for it. In any case, the location is theologically suggestive.

In Mark, it is Simon and his companions who seek Jesus out with the news that "everyone is searching" for him (Mark 1:37). In Luke's account, however, there are no disciples to run interference for Jesus. The crowds look for him, find him, and try to prevent him from leaving them. He breaks the news that he cannot stay, but has to bring the good news of the "kingdom of God" (the first appearance of this phrase in Luke) to other cities as well. The section concludes with a reference to his "proclaiming the message in the synagogues of Judea"—here used in a general sense to refer to Palestine as a whole, not simply the southern territory of Judah (cf. Luke 1:5).

CAROL M. BECHTEL

In Luke 4:42–44, the crowd at Capernaum wants to prevent Jesus from leaving them. They want him to continue what he was doing in Luke 4:31–41. The mission of Jesus, however, is not confined to Capernaum and environs. He must go to other cities to announce, teach, and embody the Realm. This forward movement is the pattern for the church in Acts. The church cannot stay in the comfort of Jerusalem and Judea but must go through Samaria on its way to the ends of the earth (Acts 1:8). The mission of Jesus is needed everywhere life is broken.

Many congregations have a desire similar to the desire of the crowd in Capernaum. When we experience the renewing power of Jesus in our immediate world, we want to have Jesus stay with us. A congregation's focus can easily center on Jesus meeting our needs and healing our brokenness. We can become so absorbed in our own situation that we forget to look at the needs of the world through the eyes of Jesus.

Today, as in the time of Luke, Jesus presses ahead to take the announcement of the Realm of God to communities that also need its restoring power. The preacher might explore ways in which the congregation can join Jesus in witnessing to the Realm "to other cities also." For today's congregation, other cities may include, literally, other cities, states, and nations where the restoring power of God's Realm is needed. Under homiletical management, "other cities" might also include other neighborhoods or other social groups with which the congregation typically has little contact. Indeed, a dying congregation is sometimes reborn when its vision shifts from its own diminishing circumstances to mission.

Relatively few parishioners today can picture life in Palestine in the days of Jesus. As part of a teaching moment in connection with the public reading of the Scripture lesson or as part of the sermon, a preacher might project a picture or drawing of a Palestinian house similar to the one in which Simon may have lived. People today are often struck by how small and dim such places were. The visual presentation could include historically informed representations of people with "various kinds of diseases." The preacher might also show a slide of a "deserted place" in the semiarid area around Capernaum. Such information may help the congregation get a feel for the world of the text.

RONALD J. ALLEN

Luke 5:1–11

¹Once while Jesus was standing beside the lake of Gennesaret, and the crowd was pressing in on him to hear the word of God, ²he saw two boats there at the shore of the lake; the fishermen had gone out of them and were washing their nets. ³He got into one of the boats, the one belonging to Simon, and asked him to put out a little way from the shore. Then he sat down and taught the crowds from the boat. ⁴When he had finished speaking, he said to Simon, "Put out into the deep water and let down your nets for a catch." ⁵Simon answered, "Master, we have worked all night long but have caught nothing. Yet if you say so, I will let down the nets." ⁶When they had done this, they caught so many fish that their nets were beginning to break. ⁷So they signaled their partners in the other boat to come and help them. And they came and filled both boats, so that they began to sink. ⁸But when Simon Peter saw it, he fell down at Jesus' knees, saying, "Go away from me, Lord, for I am a sinful man!" ⁹For he and all who were with him were amazed at the catch of fish that they had taken; ¹⁰and so also were James and John, sons of Zebedee, who were partners with Simon. Then Jesus said to Simon, "Do not be afraid; from now on you will be catching people." ¹¹When they had brought their boats to shore, they left everything and followed him.

Theological Perspective

Luke's interweaving of the call of the first disciples with the story of the miraculous catch of fish is theologically intentional. The author begins the story with "once," a word that functions like "once upon a time," signaling that this is not a chronological narrative but is a story told to make certain theological claims.

In the Gospels, miraculous harvests and catches of fish are signs of the advent of the empire of God. Luke's telling of the miraculous catch of fish involving Peter will remind readers of the very similar narrative in John 21. In John, the resurrected Jesus, unrecognized by the disciples, leads the disciples to a great haul of fish. The fish are cooked for breakfast. Then Jesus passes the mantle of ministry to Peter and the disciples and instructs Peter to keep his sheep. In Luke, the author inserts the miraculous catch story to make christological claims at the *outset* of Jesus' public ministry, as he is calling his first disciples. Jesus has the power and authority to change people's lives.

In Luke's narrative, even before submitting his life to following Jesus, Peter calls him Master and Lord. However, the miraculous catch evokes an even more profound response from Peter. His fearful command to Jesus, "Go away from me, Lord, for I am a sinful man" (v. 8), recalls the beginning of First Isaiah's

Pastoral Perspective

"Life is what happens to you while you're busy making other plans."[1] The disciples did not receive their calling from Jesus while they were in a designated sacred space like the synagogue, or even while they were in prayer or contemplation in their own homes. Their call did not come while they were quietly listening for it but, rather, at the end of a long, sweaty work session, when they were discouraged and ready to pack it in for the day. They were not doing anything grand or holy; they were just washing their nets. Along came this itinerant preacher and healer. He was probably a nuisance after a long night of hard labor, but they dutifully showed their respect to the rabbi and shoved the boats back in the water to carry him out a little way from shore, as he asked. Perhaps they had witnessed his healings or stood astounded by his exorcisms or listened to his sermons. We do not really know. Maybe there was something he said that caught their attention, impressed them enough to take him halfway seriously when he said, "Put out into the deep water" (v. 4). They wearily told him that this was not a good place for fishing—nothing good was going to happen here. Only then, in the midst of weariness and pessimism, did Jesus show

---

1. Variously attributed; quoted by John Lennon in "Beautiful Boy," track 7 on the *Double Fantasy* album with Yoko Ono (New York: The Hit Factory, 1980).

Exegetical Perspective

This passage contains the fifth in a set of six stories centered on Jesus' early ministry in Galilee (4:31–5:16). All six contain elements of the miraculous, but this narrative is unique in that it also includes the calling of three of Jesus' first disciples: Simon (later called Peter), James, and John. While the first four episodes in the set are described as happening over a two-day period (4:31–37 at the Capernaum synagogue earlier in the day; 4:38–40 at Simon's house after the healing at the synagogue; 4:40–41 at or near Simon's house after sunset; and 4:42–44 in a "deserted place" early the next morning), this account has a less specific chronology. The fact that it involves characters we have just met, and that the story is set at what Luke calls "the lake of Gennesaret" (v. 1; otherwise known as the Sea of Galilee) suggests that we are to understand it as having happened shortly after the events just described.[1]

The story begins with Jesus preaching to a crowd. This has happened twice before in recent narrative memory. The first time was in Nazareth, when the crowd turned into a mob and tried to hurl him off a cliff (4:16–30). The second time was in a "deserted place," where the crowd tracked him down

1. Verse 44's reference to "Judea" does not necessarily imply that Jesus left Galilee at this point to travel south to Judah. "Judea" is sometimes used as a general term to refer to the whole of Palestine (see Luke 1:5).

Homiletical Perspective

As the story in Luke's fifth chapter begins, Simon (Peter) and others involved in fishing are cleaning their nets after being on the water all night without success. Jesus teaches a large crowd from a boat. While Luke does not report the content of this teaching, the immediate context (4:14–44) prompts us to think Jesus announced and interpreted the presence and future of the Realm of God.

When Jesus finishes his teaching, he instructs Simon to take the boat into deep water and to let down the nets. The haul is so large that additional workers are needed, and even then the boats are in danger of sinking. As the encounter ends, Jesus indicates that henceforth Simon will catch people. Here is a story leading to a sermon or two about the mission of the community and the place of the apostles as authorities within that community.

The ancient listener would hear a reference in the "deep water" to the power of chaos (as in Gen. 1:1). Chaos, of course, threatens God's purposes of order, security, and blessing. The extravagant size of the haul points to the abundance of the coming Realm of God. Jeremiah long ago used the image of "catching people" to speak of those who serve God's purposes (Jer. 16:16–18).

Luke uses this passage to urge the congregation to put its net into the chaos of its own difficult

Luke 5:1–11

Theological Perspective

vocation (indeed, the lectionary pairs the two Scriptures in Epiphany, Year C). In Isaiah 6:5, Isaiah sees a vision of the Holy and responds in fear, "Woe is me! I am lost, for I am a man of unclean lips, and I live among a people of unclean lips."

Comparing Isaiah's call and Peter's call yields an interesting similarity as well as some differences. The similarity is the human response to the Holy. Rudolf Otto, in his famous book *The Idea of the Holy*, wrote of the Holy as the experience of Other, an experience both terrifying and fascinating. He illustrated the human response to the Holy by commenting on Isaiah 6 and Luke 5. Otto judged that neither Isaiah nor Peter is responding in moral terms, as if either of them has personally committed grievous sins of which they are now acutely aware.[1] Rather, the spontaneous reaction of the creature when in the presence of the Holy is to feel the profound contrast between the sacred and the profane. In Jesus' holy presence Peter feels the weight of profane human life. "Profane" is not a moral term but simply means outside the temple, that which is not holy. In this reading, Peter's and Isaiah's exclaimed confessions of being sinful are actually expressions of awe and praise, visible demonstrations of respect for the Holy.

The differences between these two call stories are at least as interesting as the similarity. Both Isaiah and Peter confess their unfitness for whatever the Holy has in mind for them. In Isaiah's case, the seraph touches the incense coal to his lips to remove the guilt and sin. The deficiency or impediment to Isaiah's ministry is removed; he can now fulfill his calling. In Luke, the writer provides the better case for Otto's argument that Peter's confession of guilt is more an exclamation of awe and respect and inadequacy in the presence of the Holy than it is a confession of guilt. Jesus would forgive the sins of many in Luke's narrative, but he does not offer absolution to Peter. Rather, Jesus invites Peter to drop his fear. Whatever Peter means by "I am a sinful man," Jesus responds not with a moral cleansing but with the invitation, "Do not be afraid." Those words are the divine response in Scripture to human beings gripped by the *mysterium tremendum*.

The other interesting contrast in these two call stories involves each man's reaction to the recognition of being in the presence of the Holy. Isaiah declares he is "lost." The contrast between holiness and profanity (himself and his people) is so

---

1. Rudolf Otto, *The Idea of the Holy*, trans. John W. Harvey (London: Oxford University Press, 1923; 1958 ed.), 50–59. In Isa. 6:7, the author writes that Isaiah's sin and guilt are removed, which might imply a moral cleansing.

Pastoral Perspective

them something amazing and new: a sign of holy abundance, a surplus of nourishment in the midst of seemingly barren waters. Simon felt unworthy of such abundance. Jesus said not to fear it; it was a sign of the new vocation that was being set before him and all the disciples. With newfound faith, they got up and went to "fish for people"—to lead lives renewed in trust and service.

Our vocation too comes to us in the midst of our everyday life and work—not apart from it or before we even get started doing things with our lives. That is not to say that we do not sometimes need to take quiet time apart to reflect and discern, as Jesus himself did in the previous chapter in Luke. However, God does not wait for the times when life is settled and still to call us. God finds us wherever we are, whatever we are doing, and shows us something—often with the very materials of our everyday lives and work. God uses the details of our particular time and place to catch our attention and throw us a new challenge. We think we are just humming along, doing what we always do, and suddenly we see something that causes us to wonder: what in my life would need to change in order to be the new person God is calling me to be?

This sounds good, but it is not always as obvious as in this story from Luke. How do we actually know when God is beckoning us toward a new future, a new form of service? No messenger shows up with a ton of shimmering fish to throw on our desk or workbench! Like the disciples, we do have to do something to receive our calling. The disciples, weary as they were, agreed to put their boats back in the water at Jesus' behest. Like them, we have to be open to the voice of the stranger, the wandering Wise One in our midst. He may come in the form of a literal stranger, someone unknown to us, from whom we might prefer to turn away, or in the form of a friend who provokes us with a word we did not expect or want to hear. He may come in the form of an inner voice we would prefer not to acknowledge, or a part of ourselves that we have silenced in order to keep peace with ourselves or others, but at the expense of not deepening our lives. We have to practice paying attention to the strange and the surprising, because strange and surprising messages really do come to us, virtually every day, and they may bear an unlikely holy word for us in answer to our weary questions. Just when we are most prone to wonder, "Is this all there is?" or "What do I do now to get out of this rut?" Jesus comes and drops something sloppy and squirmy into the midst of our

and "wanted to prevent him from leaving them" (4:42–44). The contrast between the two incidents is ironic—one crowd wants to get rid of him (permanently!) and the other cannot bear for him to leave. There is an element of risk—if not outright danger—even in the second incident, however. This is a crowd that has witnessed or heard rumors of Jesus' miraculous healings (see 4:31–41), and they track him into the remote area to which he has deliberately retreated. When they find him, they want "to prevent him from leaving them" (v. 42). Jesus explains that he has to "proclaim the good news of the kingdom of God to the other cities also" (v. 43), but the memory of how quickly the Nazareth crowd turned into a mob adds an element of anxiety for us as readers.

In both of these previous stories, Jesus "escapes" unharmed. However, they play on our minds when Luke tells us in 5:1 that yet another crowd is "pressing in on him to hear the word of God." This time Jesus creates some breathing room by asking Simon (who is there cleaning his nets with fellow fishers James and John) to put out a little way from shore (vv. 2–3). The "off-shore pulpit" makes it easier for Jesus to conclude; when he is finished speaking, he simply asks Simon to row him out into deeper water. If this story were to follow the pattern of the previous two, it would be over, but Luke gives this one a surprise ending.

Jesus tells Simon to let down his nets for a catch. We can hear the weariness and skepticism in Simon's voice when he answers, "Master, we have worked all night long but have caught nothing" (v. 5a). One imagines a shrug prior to his next words: "Yet if you say so, I will let down the nets" (v. 5b). Somewhere in the space between these two telling sentences, Simon must have reviewed what he has witnessed Jesus saying and doing in previous days. Simon has seen Jesus healing people and casting out demons with a word (4:33–37, 40–41). Jesus has cured Simon's own mother-in-law of a fever (4:38–39). Simon has heard Jesus preach and teach with unprecedented authority on more than one occasion (probably in 4:31–32; possibly in 4:42–44; and certainly in 5:3–4). In light of who is giving the orders, Simon abandons his skepticism and obeys.

The catch, of course, is miraculous. Even with the aid of James and John in a second boat, they can hardly handle it and the boats threaten to sink. At this, Luke tells us that "when Simon Peter saw it, he fell down at Jesus' knees, saying, 'Go away from me, Lord, for I am a sinful man!'" (v. 8). Note that Luke uses the name Simon Peter for the first time—which

moment in history, and to expect a manifestation of the Realm of God (represented by the eschatologically sized catch). In Acts, Luke hints that Gentile life, with its idolatry, exploitation, and violence, is a form of chaos (e.g., Acts 4:25–26). Hence, Luke 5:1–11 anticipates the mission of Luke's community, especially inviting Gentiles into the community of the Realm of God.

The preacher could encourage the congregation to let down its net into the chaos of its moment in history, in other words, to engage in mission even when the prospects for ministry are no more promising than they were for Simon and his partners when they fished all night to no avail. Yet, when Simon does what Jesus says, a manifestation of God's Realm follows.

With respect to this story authorizing the ministry of the apostles, Luke typically distinguishes between the "apostles" (the Twelve) and the larger group of "disciples" not included in the Twelve. In a limited sense, Luke does not regard the call to Simon in Luke 5:1–11 as paradigmatic of the call to all disciples. Rather, Luke uses this story to certify the leadership of Peter and the apostles as reliable guides for Luke's congregation, in view of the fact that the community to which Luke wrote was conflicted over which viewpoints and directions for mission to regard as authoritative. For example, should they engage in the Gentile mission?[1]

In Luke–Acts, Jesus is the major authority and model for the church's witness to the Realm of God. Jesus calls and prepares the Twelve to represent his authority and continue his ministry after the ascension. Luke 5:1–11 is the first step in establishing the authority of Simon, who eventually authorizes the Gentile mission by welcoming the first Gentile into the church (Acts 10:1–11:18). Simon lowers his net into the world of Cornelius, and the centurion becomes a part of the community of God's Realm.

Today's church is vexed by questions of authority. In the early twenty-first century some authorities and sources that claim to be normative say yes with regard to certain issues and no to others, while other authorities say just the reverse. This text suggests a sermon on authority in the church. The preacher might reflect on the nature of apostolic authority within Scripture, beginning with how Jesus and the apostles functioned as authorities for the Lukan

---

1. Luke likely wrote about 80–90 CE to an urban congregation outside of Palestine. For more information, see Ronald J. Allen, *The Acts of the Apostles*, Fortress Biblical Commentaries for Preaching (Minneapolis: Fortress Press, 2013), 1–28.

Luke 5:1–11

Theological Perspective

profound that Isaiah can see nothing in his future but obliteration. Note that Peter asks or commands Jesus to "go away." Peter's command to Jesus, even though it ends with his unworthiness, could suggest that he retains a sense of his own power and freedom. He is not obliterated by the encounter with the Holy but tries to defend himself against it. In Isaiah's case, it is hard to imagine that he sensed any real choice. Standing in the midst of the presence of the Holy One of Israel, how could he feel anything but inadequate and, once "cleansed," overpowered and available? Peter chooses. The difference may imply contrasting theological anthropologies.

There is another matter that might be addressed theologically, namely, the juxtaposition in the story between what the disciples-to-be are doing when Jesus arrives and their action at the end of the story. When Jesus arrives on the scene, the fishers are tired and empty handed. No fish in the boat translates to empty stomachs and purses. Jesus asks for the boat and begins to use the boat to fish for people. After Jesus finishes speaking to the crowd, the fishers make the miraculous catch. Rather than processing the haul for market or making a cooking fire, the fishers as disciples "leave everything" and follow Jesus. Jesus' first catch is the fishers! After fishing all night, and landing the catch of their lives, they leave it all on the beach.

Imagine walking away from the biggest deal, from the greatest offer of promotion you will ever receive, from a lottery jackpot—because you have just received a better offer. Besides, the fishers may be hungry; but there is no nourishment here. Compare the fish flopping on the beach in Luke 5 to John 21, where the disciples and Jesus eat a piscine eucharistic breakfast. Luke may want the hearer to know that more valuable treasure and lasting soul food are ahead for those who drop what they are doing to follow the Christ.

GARY PELUSO-VERDEND

Pastoral Perspective

too-small lives. The surprising catch becomes nourishment, if we let it.

Like the disciples, we also have to throw our nets out into the *deep* waters. Shallow, tentative paddling is not allowed if we are to discern where God is calling us. This requires us to take risks. We could fail and come up with nothing. The boat could capsize. The nets we have fashioned for our safe, contained selves might break under the weight of our unlived lives. Jesus tells us, as he tells Simon and the others, not to be afraid. When we risk what we have known for the sake of responding to God's call on our lives, we will be given all the abundance we need and more. Living into our vocations may well bring hardships, even suffering (as Peter certainly came to know), but there is a kind of suffering and "quiet desperation" that also comes with keeping our lives small.

We will know that we are on the right path, as the disciples do, if we can sense that the new life of service beckoning us, despite the risks, is one that offers sustenance and joy. Who are the people God is giving us to fish, and what is the glorious catch that awaits us if we hear and act upon God's unlikely, holy invitation?

PAMELA COOPER-WHITE

may signal that the shift in Simon's vocation from fisher to disciple has already begun. Even more significant, however, is Simon's consciousness of his own sin. His plea echoes that of the prophet Isaiah when he finds himself in the presence of the Holy One of Israel and cries, "Woe is me! I am lost, for I am a man of unclean lips" (Isa. 6:5). Simon may be repenting of his initial skepticism, but one suspects it is much more than that. Simon has finally begun to sense whom he is dealing with here. His response confirms what the demons have blurted out earlier, namely, that Jesus is none other than "the Holy One of God" (4:34; cf. 4:41).

Jesus reassures Simon by telling him that from now on he will be "catching people" (v. 10). One wonders just how reassuring this is, but Peter, James, and John follow nonetheless.

Luke's version of this story differs significantly from its counterparts in Matthew 4:18–22 and Mark 1:16–20. In Matthew and Mark, the calling of the first disciples takes place earlier in Jesus' ministry— just after the stories of Jesus' baptism and temptation. In Luke, these disciples are not called until after they witness Jesus in action. While one could lament the loss of a certain "shock value" that is a feature of Matthew and Mark's version (the disciples "immediately" leave their nets and follow Jesus on the strength of a one-sentence invitation and—evidently—his compelling presence), Luke's version has the advantage of making a lot more sense. Further, Luke allows his readers to identify with the disciples as they gradually gather information and form an impression of who Jesus is. When Luke finally announces in verse 11 that the disciples "left everything and followed him," we are much more likely to do so ourselves.

CAROL M. BECHTEL

community. In addition, other sources of authority and how they relate to Scripture in the contemporary community could be explored.

Peter responds to the manifestation of Jesus' power by declaring his own unworthiness (v. 8). In this respect, Peter is like many Christians today in having a vivid awareness of his own limitations (v. 8). Who am I to confront the church or the city council or the government with the possibilities of the Realm of God? What can our little congregation do to affect racial reconciliation or the systemic causes of poverty or world peace? Yet the text offers a powerful response. Because Jesus is in the boat with us, the power of God's Realm is already at work through us. Indeed, Jesus gives us far more power than we can imagine (see Eph. 3:20). We simply need to do what Jesus says: put down our nets into the chaos of life.

Some people today are troubled by the picture of the first apostles leaving everything to follow Jesus. Should we, likewise, leave everything? Luke, of course, does not intend for all disciples to become itinerants, as were Jesus and the apostles in the Gospel of Luke. As we see, particularly in Acts, discipleship can be fully practiced in one's own life setting.

Luke presumes that God is ending the fractious, broken age of the present and initiating cosmic restoration through the Realm of God. As long as Simon and his companions are fishing, they are the equivalents of middle-class business leaders enmeshed in the old age with only as much security as the old age could promise: they fish all night and come up empty. Jesus, however, calls Simon to leave behind the familiarity, values, and behaviors of the old age (with its idolatry, exploitation, manipulation, injustice, scarcity, violence, and death) and to live now as if the Realm of God is already present (with the living God, mutual solidarity, justice, peace, love, and life). The sermon could help the congregation recognize that following Jesus means leaving behind reliance on the old-age fishing business and, instead, joining Jesus on the way to God's Realm, trusting in the values and practices of the Realm as the way toward a security promised in an eschatological world.

RONALD J. ALLEN

Luke 5:12–16

¹²Once, when he was in one of the cities, there was a man covered with leprosy. When he saw Jesus, he bowed with his face to the ground and begged him, "Lord, if you choose, you can make me clean." ¹³Then Jesus stretched out his hand, touched him, and said, "I do choose. Be made clean." Immediately the leprosy left him. ¹⁴And he ordered him to tell no one. "Go," he said, "and show yourself to the priest, and, as Moses commanded, make an offering for your cleansing, for a testimony to them." ¹⁵But now more than ever the word about Jesus spread abroad; many crowds would gather to hear him and to be cured of their diseases. ¹⁶But he would withdraw to deserted places and pray.

Theological Perspective

Might it be that a great deal of what passes for "prayer" among modern Christians is a theologically unsound activity?

Prayers of praise and thanksgiving are fine. Meditation and contemplation are usually pretty safe. Even intercessory prayers cause no problems when, for example in common worship, we say that "we pray for . . . ," without providing much specificity about what we want to happen.

Too often, though, intercessory prayer includes more detail: "Please, God, would you . . . ," followed by whatever it is we believe should happen, or hope will happen, or simply wish would happen. Dear God, please heal my friend of his disease. Please God, guide the hands of the surgeon so that this operation will be successful. Please do not let my daughter be killed in the war. Do not let our house get foreclosed. Help me keep my marriage together. Help me overcome all those problems at work. Please fix these broken relationships. Please, God, make my life better, or at least tolerable. Please.

It is easy to push this kind of wishful thinking into the realm of excess and parody: "O Lord, won't you buy me a Mercedes-Benz." Everyone (including the singer of the song) seems to recognize the silliness of that request, but the difference between that and "please do not let our house go into foreclosure"

Pastoral Perspective

What are we to make of our urgent longing to be healed, yet our resistance to believing that God can and does choose to heal us? Many pastors have heard congregants say they just cannot bring themselves "in this day and age" to pray for God's healing for themselves or a loved one. Why this reluctance? The culprit is modern medicine, whose miraculous ways can be explained by science and therefore, by proxy at any rate, seem reasonable to the rest of us. For many faithful people, a sensible reliance on medical practice during times of illness has eclipsed any reliance on God, whose healing ways are beyond our ability to fathom. When we or a friend or loved one is ill, we may end up turning to faith halfheartedly, if at all, reducing God to the role of backup medical provider.

We are offered help for our modern dilemma in the story of the leper who announces that Jesus can heal him if he so chooses. The first part of this aid can be seen in the story's setting. Immediately prior to this text, Jesus orchestrates a huge catch of fish; the sight instantly converts Peter, James, and John. Peter, like Isaiah before him (Isa. 6:5), throws himself down in the presence of the Divine and asks for forgiveness. The context for the conversation is an ordinary task that is suddenly infused with mystery and bounty. Following our text, another miraculous

Feasting on the Gospels

Exegetical Perspective

By cleansing the leper Jesus yet again implements the mission he claimed in Nazareth in 4:18–19. His stated purpose is to convey to captives and the oppressed what Luke twice in those verses terms in Greek *aphesis* (variously translated as "forgiveness," "release," "liberation," "freedom"). The leper is thus one sufferer in a group of many who have already been or will be beneficiaries of Jesus' *aphesis*. Among them are the possessed man (4:33–37) and Peter's mother-in-law, who is literally "constrained by a high fever" until it "releases" her at Jesus' behest (4:38–39, my trans.), as well as countless other ill and possessed people (4:40–41). After the leper, still more will have their chance at *aphesis*, including the paralyzed man (5:17–26), whom Jesus heals and whose sins are forgiven (5:20), as well as his sinful dinner companions (5:27–32), for whom Jesus states, "I have come" (5:32). Luke is driving home the point through these proof stories that Jesus meant what he said in 4:18–19, that with his arrival a new brand of "forgiveness" or "liberation" is at work.

The case of a man with leprosy is particularly well tailored for a mission that caters to the oppressed, for in the biblical tradition lepers are socially ostracized. In Leviticus 13–14 "leprosy" covers a myriad of skin maladies, none of which is the same as what the biomedical profession today identifies as

Homiletical Perspective

When Jesus reached out to touch the "leper," it was more than an empathetic gesture. The whole gospel is about Jesus identifying himself with those who are shunned by society. Though sinless, he was baptized with penitent sinners as though he were one of them. He sought out the company of outcasts, even sharing meals with those cast out by religion. He died on a cross between criminals, the kind of death that Deuteronomy describes as "under God's curse" (Deut. 21:23). For Jesus to touch the leper was to stretch over a chasm that separated the clean from the unclean, those who were in from those who were out, and put Jesus himself at risk of being counted among those to be feared and despised.

The preacher might develop a sermon that highlights the fact that if Christians want to be where Jesus is, they will find themselves, in one way or another, in the same corner as the feared and despised. Being "in the same corner" requires, at the very least, the willingness to raise a voice of advocacy, the church speaking up for contemporary society's version of lepers.

We may admire Jesus for his capacity for human sympathy, but he is more than a role model for those who would cultivate a gift for human kindness. Unfolding a sequence of snapshots to reveal Jesus' character, Luke would have the church understand

Luke 5:12–16

Theological Perspective

is a difference determined only by the price tag and our own sense of luxury versus necessity. When we pray for something that we want to happen, what exactly are we doing? What effect do we think it has on God?

These questions are the source of my trouble with prayer. I remember, for example, the student who stood up in the seminary chapel and said, "Thank you for your prayers. My tests were negative, and I know it is because you were praying so hard." As a theology professor, my first thought was, I really hope you did not learn that theology of prayer from me.

Consider, for a moment, the implications of that claim. It would be bad enough if we imagined that we (that is, those who prayed so hard) actually determined the results of the biopsy. Do we imagine ourselves endowed with paranormal capacities, bending spoons, and forcing certain chemical reactions to occur? For Christians, though, the claim is stronger (and worse): not that our prayer makes things happen, but that *God* makes things happen, and that we *cause* God to make things happen because we pray so hard.

That claim creates an enormous theological problem. If God is God, then we cannot *cause* God to do anything. God is not subject to our whims or our entreaties or even to our powers of persuasion. God does not listen to the person who is praying the loudest and make decisions based on our level of ardor. Simply put: we do not cause things to happen by wishing that they would happen and then praying for them to happen. We just do not.

This story from Luke's Gospel offers us an alternative theology of prayer. We hear of a man stricken with leprosy—truly a horrible disease with all kinds of disastrous social consequences along with the physical ones. In the ancient world, at least, it would be hard to imagine someone more pitiable, someone more in need of healing. Yet observe what happens: "When he saw Jesus, he bowed his face to the ground and begged him" (v. 12)—begged him for what? Surely, to be healed. Please, Jesus, heal me. Save me from this ugliness, this wasting away, this disease that will, in time, cause my limbs to disappear. Heal me from this stigmatizing condition that isolates me from others. Save me from this. Please.

That, at any rate, is what I would want to say—part of me, at least. Another part of me would scoff at myself, wondering how I imagined that the enthusiasm of my prayer would cause God to alter my state. Do I really think that I can cause God to act for my benefit? That my rhetorical flourishes and loud cries, my evocation of sympathy and pity

Pastoral Perspective

healing becomes the focus of conflict between Jesus and the Pharisees about proper healing procedure (5:17–26).

Like the Pharisees in that encounter, our own understanding of healing is framed by the false choice between God's care and the more "correct" avenues (Sabbath laws/modern science) in which healing ought to take place. This story provides preachers and teachers with the opportunity to remind parishioners that, far from being a supernatural onlooker, God desires our healing and chooses to provide it, though not always in the way we desire.

The leper makes one of the most direct appeals to Jesus in the Gospels, begging to be made clean. Then as now, being made clean refers to a great deal more than physical healing; it often involves being reconciled to God and to the community. Other texts take us down similar pathways, so it might be wise to focus here on the divine choice to heal rather than on secondary topics. Preachers have already spent many words on the fact that Jesus' touching of the leper ends his social isolation. Amy-Jill Levine and Marc Zvi Brettler have gone a long way toward correcting negative portrayals of the Jewish community of Jesus' day as one that isolated the ill and withheld both connection and compassion.[1] The man in this story appears not to have a condition that requires him to remain apart, given that he greets Jesus within the boundaries of an unnamed city. Jesus' choice to touch the man may well speak more to the man's connection with his religious community than to his being some kind of exception within it. Indeed, Luke may be using some of the details in the story to establish that Jesus is a follower of the law with a full set of rabbinic credentials; he is going to need them in the following sequence of scenes, in which he comes into open conflict with the Pharisees.

Jesus sends the healed leper off to make the proper thank-offerings before the priests. Nothing is said to indicate that the healed leper tells anyone other than the priests what has happened to him, yet the word spreads anyway. The divine desire to be healed is uncontainable. Even Jesus cannot silence the news of his healings, although he will suffer the consequences of being sought out by the crowds and will need to get away by himself to pray. This little moment alone, which we appreciate for its glimpse of Jesus at prayer, reminds us that even Jesus must

---

1. Amy-Jill Levine and Marc Zvi Brettler, *The Jewish Annotated New Testament, New Revised Standard Version* (New York: Oxford University Press, 2011), 110.

Exegetical Perspective

leprosy (Hansen's disease). Even mildew or mold is considered leprous in Leviticus, so that houses and clothes can become infected as well (Lev. 13:47–59; 14:34–53). When a priest diagnoses a person to have contracted one of these epidermal disorders, he or she is considered ritually unclean and so must live alone and outside the Israelite camp. This person must, moreover, assume the guise of a mourner, with disheveled hair and torn clothes, who cries out, "Unclean, unclean" (Lev. 13:45–46). Even the Judean king Uzziah, whom God made leprous for his hubristic attempt to usurp the priestly role, lived thereafter in a separate house, excluded from his own court as well as the temple (2 Chr. 26:21).

In commenting upon these Levitical laws Josephus, a Jewish historian writing near the same time as the author of Luke, underlines how sternly they prohibit lepers from entering cities, treating them as "differing not at all from a dead person." Elsewhere, he describes lepers as lone wanderers, who call no village or city their home, and underlines that those who live with or "touch" them will themselves be considered unclean. Laying his hands upon the ill is one of Jesus' typical gestures of healing (4:40). When he touches the leper (5:13), he exhibits a willingness to cross a social boundary and reach out to one deemed unclean. He thereby risks being designated by others as unclean.

Jesus' readiness to converse with lepers is not entirely an anomaly in the ancient world. Josephus recognizes that in many nations lepers are not socially shunned, but are free from reproach, hold high offices, and enter temples freely. Evidently the leper Naaman, whom Elisha cured, is an example of one such highly placed leper, for he is a successful general in the army of the king of Aram (2 Kgs. 5:1; see Luke 4:27). These few examples make it clear that the attitude toward lepers was by no means uniform in antiquity and varied between, and likely within, the many cultures and nations that comprised the Roman Empire. Even Josephus implies that by adopting a more lenient and accepting attitude toward lepers the Levitical laws might have practiced more *philanthrōpia* ("humane treatment"). Jesus' outreach to this infected man, whom he is willing to touch, is thus not without precedence in certain ancient cultural spheres, even as it may have grated against others.[1]

Having touched the unclean leper, Jesus goes on to affirm the Levitical parameters. He orders the

1. Josephus, *Jewish Antiquities* 3.261–68; *Against Apion* 1.281–2.

Homiletical Perspective

that in Jesus we sense the heartbeat of God. This is why we turn to Jesus and trust his word for us: so that the rhythm of our own hearts might match that of the divine heart.

A quite different homiletic approach would be to ask why God permitted the leper to get sick in the first place. Why is there such a thing as disease? Why so much human misery? We ask those questions, sometimes desperately, and experts of various kinds offer biological, psychological, and sociological answers that satisfy a speculative curiosity but fail to settle the spirit. The experts may be right, but our spirits are quieted only by the heartbeat of God, as the child is quieted in its mother's embrace. The God revealed in Christ is not just sympathetic, but makes a home with those in distress, sharing it as though it were God's own distress. That is exactly the message the figure on the cross holds before our eyes.

If God can make the sick well and the broken whole, why is it that we pray for miracles and do not get them? It would be a mistake to blame those who pray, as though their faith must not be as strong as that of the leper in Luke's story. Of course, there are instances of unexpected remissions and spontaneous healings, but there is no recipe that leads directly to the results we want for ourselves and those we love. We may trust that God is not indifferent without knowing exactly how God's compassion will work itself out in individual cases. However, if these stories are not intended to promise miraculous cures for those who need them, what does it mean today that the Gospels report Jesus healing the sick, making the broken whole, restoring people to their right minds, and raising the dead?

The Christian hope rests in the conviction that the mighty acts by which Jesus freed people from afflictions serve as a preview and foretaste of a healed creation. God's redemptive project is not just about who goes to heaven. It is nothing less than a new heaven and earth, God's ultimate redemption. However sickness and hurt became a part of the created order, God's project is not just random "fixes" here and there, handed out especially to the faithful. Rather, God's project is nothing less than the repair of the disruptive disorder that disfigures the creation as we know it. The healing of the leper carries this promise: God will fashion a new creation, in which no one will be sick or fearful of contamination or rejected as an outcast.

When Jesus dismissed the leper and sent him to the priest, "as Moses commanded," the man had already been healed. Jesus did not send him to the

Luke 5:12–16

Theological Perspective

on God's part, would change God's plans? I cannot imagine believing in a God who was subject to such whims, or who made decisions about sickness and health on the basis of how strongly the sufferer argued for healing.

The man in this story does none of these things. He does not plead for healing, but neither does he scoff at the idea that Jesus might decide to heal him. He finds a path that affirms God's power to heal while also affirming God's sovereignty in not making those decisions based on our individual desires. He does this by making a statement of faith—a theological statement, in fact, and one of some profundity: "Lord, if you choose, you can make me clean."

This statement cuts some of the toughest theological knots surrounding the complexity of prayer. The man makes no attempt to force God's hand; he does not even express his own wishes. He simply affirms that healing—all healing—is ultimately in God's hands. In a sense, he is affirming one of the key phrases of the Lord's Prayer as we usually say it: "your will be done." Interestingly enough, this phrase is not in Luke's version of the prayer (11:2), but only in Matthew's version (Matt. 6:10.) Nevertheless, the idea is common throughout the New Testament: the ultimate goal of all our prayer should be that God's will be done.

As it happens, Jesus does heal: "I do choose. Be made clean" (v. 13). While we celebrate the healing, we easily forget that the man *did not ask* to be healed; he simply affirmed God's power to do so. If our own forays into intercessory prayer are to be anything more than magical spoon bending or attempts to conform God to our will, then they too must take this form: "If you choose, you can . . ."

That is more than enough.

DAVID S. CUNNINGHAM

Pastoral Perspective

make his desires known to the God who chooses to heal. Through prayer he remains intimately connected with the source of his own healing power.

The exchange between Jesus and the leper at the beginning of the story includes the powerful repetition of the phrases "If you choose," and "I do choose" (vv. 12b, 13). The preacher might want to echo this repetition in the structure of the sermon, or the teacher might want to emphasize this repetition in the classroom. The leper is described as bowing to the ground and begging Jesus for healing. He is participating fully, both physically and emotionally, in his own request. God must not be portrayed as handing out healing based on the sincerity or urgency of our pleas. Whose plea for healing is not urgent, after all? Nevertheless, there is some insight to be gained about prayer and healing from the total trust and confidence of the leper, whose attitude is vastly different from that of the dubious parishioners described at the beginning of this essay.

In the text the leper receives the direct physical healing that he seeks, yet he likely receives other forms of healing as well, some of which might not be readily knowable. Those who do turn confidently to God for healing—alongside doctors, ministers, or other human agents—know all too well that earnest prayers for healing are seldom answered in the ways we choose. Many ills are healed only in death. Yet what pastor does not have stories to tell of unexpected healings that have accompanied illness and even death?

Might our preaching or teaching on this text enable someone to murmur gently, "I do choose," while undergoing CAT scans or MRIs, or awaiting surgery? What effect might the mantra "I do choose" have on an addict at a 12-step meeting, a resident of rehab, or a person consigned to the labyrinths of mental-health care? The one who wrestles on behalf of others with this text has the chance to convey God's passionate desire to heal us from all manner of ills, including the disease of rampant distrust in God's presence and power.

CATHERINE E. TAYLOR

leper, "Show yourself to the priest, and, as Moses commanded, make an offering for your cleansing" (5:14). Jesus here directs his reentry into the community at large. He specifically cites Leviticus 14:1–32, which stipulates an eight-day period of sacrifices and rituals whereby the cured leper is gradually restored to society. The leper is thus quite literally one cast out whom Jesus grabs and pulls back into the social fold.

This is not the only place in Luke's Gospel where lepers profit from Jesus' *aphesis*. On his way to Jerusalem Jesus meets ten lepers. The fact that they "kept their distance" (17:12) speaks to their marginalized status. Jesus also tells these lepers to show themselves to the priests in accordance with Leviticus 14:1–32, and on their way their leprosy is cured (17:14). Jesus does not touch them in this case and does nothing to circumvent the Levitical laws. Rather, he once again confirms the ritual process stipulated there for a cured leper's reincorporation into the community. The touching of the first leper certainly opens Jesus to the charge that he is himself unclean and may have raised the eyebrows of some (though not all); but for the most part his deliverance of *aphesis* to lepers remains within the horizons of the Levitical laws.

The leper is in fact only one category of social outsider to whom Jesus will pay heed throughout this Gospel. Others include sinners, the poor, blind, crippled, and deaf (5:32; 7:22; 14:13, 21). Not only is this care for outsiders and the marginalized a part of Jesus' declared mission (4:18–19; 7:22); it is a task he directs his followers to undertake as well (14:12–27; 15:3–32). The narrator, finally, issues another notice that this event is actually quite typical, for "many crowds would gather to hear him and to be cured of their diseases" (v. 15). This is a reminder that the leper is one of many recipients of Jesus' energetic work of *aphesis,* and that hence the mission laid out in 4:18–19 is flourishing.

JEFF JAY

priest for healing, but for certification that he was free of disease and for restoration to the community through a ritual with water. He was no longer to be held at arm's length, an outsider, one who bore in his person an unnamed but fearsome disorder. The rite reversed his alienation and brought him back from something like a living death to new life.

The preacher will understand that the water ritual described in Leviticus 14 was not, of course, Christian baptism. Nevertheless, it is possible to discern in the rite certain similarities with the sacrament. In particular, one notes the intention to transfer someone from death to life, bringing near the person who has been "far away" (Acts 2:39) to be integrated into the community. In both the Leviticus rite and in baptism, water plays a role. It is as though that which is disfiguring and alienating in human beings, whether actually or potentially, might be drowned, and a new person might emerge. We will then, with the help of the Spirit, be enabled to see the person through God's eyes, as one who is indeed fresh and clean and new, whom we recognize and embrace as sister or brother.

It is curious that Jesus, having healed the leper with a word, "ordered him to tell no one." Why? The preacher will be aware that every story in the Bible is both told and understood in a larger context. The leper's story cannot be understood except as part of the narrative as a whole, from Jesus' ministry with the afflicted and the poor to his death and ultimately his resurrection, which serves as God's promise of a transfigured creation. Taken by itself, Jesus' action could identify him as just another faith healer, a magician or worker of miracles. Making sense of the healing requires waiting for the whole story, in which the leper's piece of it, combined with others, signals a down payment on a new creation.

RONALD P. BYARS

Luke 5:17–26

¹⁷One day, while he was teaching, Pharisees and teachers of the law were sitting near by (they had come from every village of Galilee and Judea and from Jerusalem); and the power of the Lord was with him to heal. ¹⁸Just then some men came, carrying a paralyzed man on a bed. They were trying to bring him in and lay him before Jesus; ¹⁹but finding no way to bring him in because of the crowd, they went up on the roof and let him down with his bed through the tiles into the middle of the crowd in front of Jesus. ²⁰When he saw their faith, he said, "Friend, your sins are forgiven you." ²¹Then the scribes and the Pharisees began to question, "Who is this who is speaking blasphemies? Who can forgive sins but God alone?" ²²When Jesus perceived their questionings, he answered them, "Why do you raise such questions in your hearts? ²³Which is easier, to say, 'Your sins are forgiven you,' or to say, 'Stand up and walk'? ²⁴But so that you may know that the Son of Man has authority on earth to forgive sins"—he said to the one who was paralyzed—"I say to you, stand up and take your bed and go to your home." ²⁵Immediately he stood up before them, took what he had been lying on, and went to his home, glorifying God. ²⁶Amazement seized all of them, and they glorified God and were filled with awe, saying, "We have seen strange things today."

Theological Perspective

This passage, like the one that precedes it, raises questions about how human beings can, or should, go about communicating their desires to God. In the previous passage, a man with leprosy approaches Jesus and does *not* ask, as we might expect, that his disease be healed; instead, he makes a statement of faith: "If you choose, you can make me clean" (5:12). Jesus' act of healing seems to occur, not in response to the man's desires, but in response to his faith.

In this passage, the same theme occurs: again, the person in need of healing does not ask for it. In fact, he does not say anything at all until after the healing has occurred. He is paralyzed, apparently confined to his bed and perhaps unable to speak. Nor are any words forthcoming from the men who are carrying him. We can only surmise that they simply want to get the paralyzed man into Jesus' vicinity—given that they go to extreme lengths to reach this goal. In doing so, they give us one of the most memorable and evocative scenes in the Gospels.

Although the man's friends do not say anything, they communicate clearly through their actions. If we were staging this story as a play and wanted to give them a few lines of dialogue, either before or during the process of lowering the man into the crowd in front of Jesus, what would we have them say? This kind of thought experiment leads us into

Pastoral Perspective

Strange things happen to people who let go of the need to conform or the need to control. They may find themselves healed of their affliction and able to perceive the activity of God taking place around them in new ways.

Certainly this story from Luke 5 bears multiple readings. It can be approached from the perspective of people who are willing to break through seemingly insurmountable barriers to obtain healing for a friend or loved one, though the four men disappear from the scene just after Jesus commends their faith. One such barrier may be the need for healing itself to manifest in a particular way. However, once that barrier has been scaled or broken through, whatever form of healing *has* taken place may suddenly become recognizable as something for which to give God glory (v. 25).

The story is also a fruitful platform for an examination of Jesus' healing power, which Luke attributes to God and describes almost like a companion who is "with" Jesus. The wording may lead some hearers to wonder if God's healing power may not always have been as potently available to Jesus as it is on this occasion. The preacher or teacher can experiment with ways to encourage congregation members to think of Jesus' healing power as a companion of their own. Might his power be more available

Exegetical Perspective

Luke continues to advance several of the motifs that appeared when Jesus healed the leper (5:12–16). In this text, Jesus heals a paralyzed man, who, as such, likely fared only slightly better than the leper in terms of the ways he was hustled off to societal peripheries because of his disability. Elsewhere, the "lame" join other social outsiders, including lepers, the poor, crippled, deaf, and blind (7:22; 14:13, 21). In Acts, which is the second volume to Luke, the paralyzed man whom Peter heals is very poor, and his condition has reduced him to the status of a beggar (Acts 3:1–8). In some other early Jewish texts the paralyzed and other disabled people are likewise socially excised. According to Leviticus, they are among those who have a "blemish" and, along with the blind, mutilated, hunchbacks, dwarves, and others, are not permitted to make offerings as priests (Lev. 21:16–24). In a text from Qumran (i.e., one of the Dead Sea Scrolls) the paralyzed and the lame, together with the blind, deaf, mute, or anyone with a "blemish," are excluded from the congregation of the elect, whom they may address only in private.[1]

The paralyzed man's physical separation from Jesus because of the intervening crowd may in fact

1. 1Q28a (1QSa; Florentino García Martínez, *The Dead Sea Scrolls Translated: The Qumran Texts in English* [Leiden: Brill, 1994], 126–28).

Homiletical Perspective

American religious culture has not been as patient with the mysterious ways of God as Scripture is or actual human experience requires. We want to know how it all works. The early frontier preacher Walter Scott and his colleagues evangelized the unchurched by spelling out a simple formula for salvation that could be ticked off on the five fingers of one hand: faith, repentance, and baptism, resulting in the forgiveness of sins and the gift of the Holy Spirit. The first three things humans could do, while God would do the others. The tradition of nineteenth-century revivalism was equally straightforward. The preacher's task was to stir in the sinner an awareness of his or her sin and perilous condition before God, leading to repentance that triggered God's grace offered in Christ. Sometimes God does indeed work in predictable sequences—but not always.

A sermon on this text might make the case that God's grace is neither mechanical, always working in the same way, nor reducible to a formula as simple as making a "decision for Christ." In Scripture, sometimes people approach Jesus with faith that he can heal them. After such a healing, Jesus may say something like, "Your faith has made you well." On the other hand, sometimes Jesus transforms the circumstances of someone for whom there is no evidence of faith at all, for example, restoring the Gerasene

Luke 5:17–26

Theological Perspective

a deeper understanding of the story, by making us attend to the motives, desires, and assumptions of the characters.

Would they reveal themselves as wanting to fulfill certain desires? That is, do we imagine the men talking about wanting the man to be healed? Might their conversation have more to do with Jesus and their belief that he can perform the healing? Depending on what we choose, we might imagine these men as similar to the leper in the previous passage (who simply makes a statement of faith), or we might find them simply wanting God to fulfill their desires. These two alternatives express two very different theologies of prayer—so it matters which of them we choose.

One approach focuses on our own desires: we want healing to occur, so we will take whatever actions are necessary to bring it about. The goal in this case is to convert one's own desires into divine action, asking God to grant our wishes. Even though this perspective seems to put a great deal of faith in God, it actually seems to attribute any positive outcomes to our own facility and power: we somehow imagine that, through the strength and ardor of our prayer, God is persuaded to act in a particular way. In addition to undermining God's sovereignty and endowing ourselves with magical superpowers, this approach comes very close to the ancient Christian heresy of Pelagianism. This was the view, against which Augustine and others argued so strongly, that seemed to put us in charge of our own salvation. Pelagianism was the belief that our own good character, good deeds, and ardent prayer would contribute mightily to our salvation.

The alternative, which was compellingly affirmed by Augustine and reinforced by many other theologians over time (Martin Luther, in particular) is that God alone is in charge of our salvation and our healing. Our role is to believe in that truth. This approach leads us to imagine that the men who are carrying the paralytic are acting on the basis of faith. They believe that Jesus has the power to heal, so they work hard to make sure their paralyzed friend gets to him. He cannot get there on his own, so they need to carry him. The crowds are too great to push a way through, so they need to go up to the roof and lower him in. They do all this, not in order to make their wishes come true, but because they believe in Jesus.

This approach is further validated by Jesus' reaction to the presence of the paralyzed man. Jesus does not make any reference to what the man's friends want, or to the fulfillment of their desires. Instead,

Pastoral Perspective

to them at some times than at others? If so, why? How would such companionship fare in the face of critique by family or friends? Most parishioners know people who are good at being actively engaged in their own healing, and might benefit from the paradigm of companionship as a way to harness the power of God's healing in their own lives. Yet the evangelist appears to be less interested in persistent friends, obstacles to healing, or even the healing of the paralytic per se. Luke uses the story primarily as the setting for a confrontation between Jesus and the Pharisees.

The Pharisees' opening question in verse 21, "Who is this who is speaking blasphemies?" is the very first question they ask in Luke's Gospel. The tone of the encounter sets the stage for the deepening animosity that is to come (5:29–32; 7:36–50; 11:37–52; 14:1–24). The text is unclear as to whether the question is actually voiced, or just a feeling shared by the Pharisees after witnessing a remarkable healing. The narration has already gone to some lengths to alert readers to the presence of a veritable convention of religious elites who "had come from every village of Galilee and Judea and from Jerusalem" (v. 17). We are thus primed for some kind of interaction between them and Jesus. He either overhears or intuits what is going on in their hearts, and openly engages them. This too is a plot point worth pondering at some length: every insistence on conformity with community norms that goes unchallenged will also go unchanged.

Given that this is the first encounter in Luke between Jesus and the Pharisees, there is no way to know how much tension to ascribe to the exchange. It might have sounded to a witness like intellectual banter between a wandering rabbi and strict religious devotees. Given the tradition of questioning and counterquestioning that was the way of teaching and learning in the Jewish community, the idea is not implausible. Levine asserts that Luke's overall presentation of the Pharisees is "puzzling, inconsistent, and complex," and that "at best" this exchange might indicate that they simply misunderstood Jesus.[1]

Jesus, however, does not misunderstand the Pharisees. Either he, or the narrator, makes it plain that forms and conventions do not matter as much as authority and compassion. Jesus then reissues his healing command in a more conventional form.

1. Amy-Jill Levine and Marc Zvi Brettler, *The Jewish Annotated New Testament, New Revised Standard Version* (New York: Oxford University Press, 2011), 110.

dramatize his overall fringe status. He is not a part of the crowd, and they in turn bar him from the center, where Jesus is working. If it were not for the ingenuity of the men, who lowered him into Jesus' presence after climbing on the roof (vv. 18–19), this social outsider would have remained precisely that: on the outside, without access to needed healing. Jesus attributes this to "their faith" (v. 20), which is the first use of this term in Luke's Gospel, here employed to describe those who bring one who is outside inside, where, they trust, healing will occur. These unnamed men are the first examples (besides Jesus) of those who act on behalf of people at the social periphery. This will be one of the major demands Jesus places on his followers in subsequent chapters. It will be his followers' task to centralize the marginal (14:12–14, 16–24). In turn, Peter, Philip, and Paul will rise to meet this challenge in the earliest days of the church when they too extend their healing powers to the "paralyzed" and "lame" (Acts 3:1–8; 8:7; 9:32–35; 14:8–10).

Yet paralysis is only one aspect of this man's social stigma. Jesus also deduces from his disability that he is a sinner, for Jesus' first words to him are "your sins are forgiven you" (v. 20). Later, Jesus equates forgiveness with curing the paralysis, and the man's subsequent ability to walk serves as proof that Jesus' forgiveness is efficacious (vv. 23–24). Behind this text there lies the assumption that physical disabilities and other ailments are punishments for sinful behavior. While this is jarring in terms of contemporary medical sensibilities, the fact is that understanding infirmity to be the result of moral or ritual failure is common (but by no means the rule) in antiquity. The link appears elsewhere in the New Testament when, for example, the apostle Paul suggests that many Corinthians are falling ill because they are eating the bread and drinking "the cup of the Lord" in a way that is unworthy (1 Cor. 11:27–30). Also in John the disciples ask Jesus point-blank whether a man born blind sinned himself or whether the sin was his parents' (John 9:1–3). In another text from Qumran the Babylonian king Nabonidus suffered from a malignant inflammation and was banished from his community for seven years. The Babylonian gods did not respond to Nabonidus's prayers for deliverance. It was not until he prayed to the God of Israel that he was healed, but only after a Jewish exorcist forgave him his sins.[2]

The connection between sin and ill health is only a more specific version of the broader assumption that suffering constitutes divine punishment for

2. 4Q242 (4QPrNab ar; Martínez, *Dead Sea Scrolls*, 289).

demoniac to his right mind (8:26–39), or healing the woman in the synagogue who has been bent over for eighteen years (13:10–17). Then there are instances of Jesus' healing someone whose faith is unknown, in response to an appeal from a third party, for example, healing Jairus's mortally ill daughter (8:40–55) and, in this text, healing a paralyzed man who has been carried to Jesus by his friends.

On the wall of the baptistery in the church of Dura-Europos, the very earliest church building ever recovered (about 235 CE), there is a fresco that pictures the healing of the paralytic. The scene is painted on other early baptisteries as well, signaling that Christians in early times understood that God's grace may work indirectly as well as directly. The preacher knows that faith is not a go-it-alone project. It always involves other people. Even the person who is converted to Christian faith by reading the Bible all alone has been carried to Christ by the community to whom the Scriptures have been given and who has treasured them from generation to generation. Can the congregation identify those who have carried them to faith or those whom they might help to carry?

Another homiletic approach might begin with a question: "Is it possible to have faith on behalf of another person?" In our individualistic culture, the answer would seem to be no, but the question might best be answered by someone who has experienced a crisis of faith. Perhaps there is someone who has suffered a terrible loss, a deep disappointment, or witnessed a profound injustice. Maybe another is in a state that monastics describe as "anomie," a kind of numb indifference. If these persons simply slink off on their own, separating themselves from the community of faith, the likelihood is that the last spark of faith will eventually be extinguished.

If, instead, they go to worship, even though they may be spiritually and emotionally removed, the faith of the community reveals its sustaining power. At any given service of worship, there are present both those whose faith is strong and those whose faith is weak or has even vanished. The strong support the weak until the weak become strong, and then, as necessary, they exchange roles. The grace that is exhibited in Jesus Christ is at work in many ways. As in the story of the friends who bring the paralytic to him, Jesus even responds to the faith of those who serve as supporters and advocates for one who may or may not believe. Who have been your supporters and advocates?

A peculiarity of this pericope is that Jesus first addresses the paralytic saying that his sins are

Luke 5:17–26

Theological Perspective

the text says that "he saw their faith," and on that basis acts to forgive the man's sins.

As if to reinforce the point, the story goes on to give the counterexample of those who do not have faith. The scribes and the Pharisees do not express their own desires, either; they do not suggest that they *do not* want the man to be forgiven or healed. They simply have a different belief: a belief that Jesus does not have the authority to do these things. Two different faiths: one, that Jesus' goodness and power mean that it will be worth the effort to get their friend into his vicinity; the other, that no one on earth, not even Jesus, has the power to forgive sins. Neither group tells Jesus what they want; they simply express their differing faiths.

How do we approach Jesus? Do we think about what we want to happen—the wounds that we want healed, whether our own or those of others? Do we come to God with a wish list of our most deeply held desires? Do our prayers take the form of Christmas shopping lists, with every sentence beginning with "I want"? Do we, rather, come to Jesus asking that God's will be done?

I like to imagine that the man's friends really have no idea what will happen when they bring him to Jesus. Some may think he will be forgiven, others that he will be healed, and still others may be uncertain or even doubtful. In one respect, however, they are united: they think that it will be a good thing if they can bring the man into the presence of Jesus.

May our own prayers take that same shape: "Yes, I have written out a few wish lists in my life. For now, though, I want to leave them behind. I simply want to dwell in your presence. My greatest desire is that your will be done."

DAVID S. CUNNINGHAM

Pastoral Perspective

Once again, it is not possible to tell from the narrative if the paralytic was healed the first time Jesus spoke or the second. Are there times as individuals, or in the lives of congregations, when we have already been offered forgiveness and healing by God, but we will not know it until we respond to the command to take up our beds and walk?

Many survivors of one of the deadliest school shootings in the United States discerned God's healing action among them as they overheard their own comments about the event. The tragic shooting deaths of thirty-two students and faculty at Virginia Tech took place in 2007, four years before I arrived as a pastor in the Blacksburg community. The most common stories shared by parishioners were never about the shootings, but about the way individual students and residents resisted intense pressure from reporters who wanted them to make negative statements about the university and its handling of the attack in the first hours. For the worldwide media that descended on Blacksburg, there was only one way to tell and sell a tragic story: portray as much conflict as possible. Yet students and residents did not feel conflicted about the university administration or the first responders. They voiced admiration for how events were handled and directed their most negative comments at the behavior of the press. Even the youngest students on campus resisted being swept up by the media. On the whole, the community demonstrated caring and compassion for the victims' friends and families and for one another that allowed healing to take root and grow.

The passage from Luke 5 ends with all parties expressing amazement, awe, and a shared sense that something strange has taken place. Whatever tensions arose between Jesus and the Pharisees, they are gone; everyone present glorifies God (v. 26). Too often we avoid slowing down in sermons or in the classroom to savor such moments of unity in the Gospel texts. Like the reporters who descended on Blacksburg, we are attuned to looking for points of conflict, rather than celebrating shared amazement. Parishioners may benefit more from lessons in how to embrace what is strange than from yet another take on healing. There is always a chance that within what is strange to us, some kind of holy healing is already taking place.

CATHERINE E. TAYLOR

Feasting on the Gospels

moral and/or ritual deficiencies. This is a hallmark of Deuteronomic theology and is the prophetic response to the destruction of Jerusalem by the Babylonians in 587 BCE. Luke is by no means immune from this broader pattern, for he interprets the destruction of Jerusalem by the Romans in 70 CE as divine punishment for the rejection of Jesus among the Jewish leadership (13:34–35; 19:41–44; 20:9–18). Here, as with the case of paralysis, suffering is understood as divine retribution for sins.

Recognizing the link this text makes between paralysis and sin illuminates how this story develops another major Lukan theme, namely, Jesus' outreach to sinners. In the subsequent episode, Jesus will dine with sinners and, in response to grumbling Pharisees, will declare that he has come precisely "to call sinners to repentance" (5:29–32). The Pharisees' objection in 5:21 arises from the fact that Jesus bypasses the priestly methods for atonement prescribed in Leviticus (Lev. 4:1–5:13). This very sequence unfolds repeatedly throughout Luke (7:36–50; 15:1–32; 19:1–10), as Jesus shows himself devoted to the possibility that all sinners can transform their lives despite Pharisaic critiques.

His words to the paralyzed man, "your sins are forgiven you" (v. 20), also recall Jesus' stated mission in 4:18–19. The Greek verb translated "to forgive" in 5:20 and 23 is *aphienai*, whose root (*aphe-*) appears twice in its noun form in 4:18, where Jesus promises "to proclaim *aphesis* to the captives" and "to send the oppressed away in *aphesis*" (my trans.). In both cases *aphesis* may be translated as "release, freedom, or liberation," but also as "forgiveness," which would make the connection with 5:20 and 23 explicit. By healing the paralyzed man and forgiving his sins, therefore, Jesus carries out his stated purpose. He frees a person who has been marginalized by his disability and extends God's forgiveness to another of the sinners for whom he has come (5:32). He thus delivers to this "captive" and "oppressed" man *aphesis*, with the full range of this word's possible connotations.

JEFF JAY

forgiven. What does sin have to do with his paralysis? Sometimes the Bible leaves the impression that afflictions must be punishment for sin. The preacher recognizes that such a view might be strangely comforting, since it seems to make of suffering something we might be able to avoid by good behavior. While afflictions are not necessarily caused by sins real or imagined, a guilty conscience can certainly manifest itself in physical or emotional symptoms. On more than one occasion (e.g., 13:1–5), Jesus denied that there was a necessary link between misfortune and sin. Did Jesus know something about the paralytic's story that Luke has not handed on to us? If not, why is his first response to the friends' intervention to declare that the paralytic's sins are forgiven?

It may matter that among those crowded into the house where Jesus was that day were "Pharisees and teachers of the law" who had come from "Galilee and Judea and from Jerusalem." It was a teachable moment for them and for us. The issue would seem to be Jesus' authority and identity. What we see in Jesus' declaration of forgiveness and later his command to the paralytic to "stand up . . . and go home" is that Jesus is able to do divine things with only a word. In this case that word, incarnate in Jesus, liberates and heals, whether as a release from guilt or traumas past, or release from a physical anomaly that has frozen the afflicted man in place. Where Jesus is, the rule of God becomes evident. When he speaks, God's will is done. His voice manifests itself as God's voice. His word is always a healing word, even when it does not have the effect of removing the presenting affliction. The sick and even the dying may experience the kind of healing that gives strength to endure in hope.

The preacher addresses many like the paralytic, who are physically healthy yet frozen in place, paralyzed by fear, anxiety, the experience of failure, or simple uncertainty. The same word that released the paralytic will also support and free them—sometimes through the support and encouragement of friends in faith.

RONALD P. BYARS

Luke 5:27–39

²⁷After this he went out and saw a tax collector named Levi, sitting at the tax booth; and he said to him, "Follow me." ²⁸And he got up, left everything, and followed him.

²⁹Then Levi gave a great banquet for him in his house; and there was a large crowd of tax collectors and others sitting at the table with them. ³⁰The Pharisees and their scribes were complaining to his disciples, saying, "Why do you eat and drink with tax collectors and sinners?" ³¹Jesus answered, "Those who are well have no need of a physician, but those who are sick; ³²I have come to call not the righteous but sinners to repentance."

³³Then they said to him, "John's disciples, like the disciples of the Pharisees, frequently fast and pray, but your disciples eat and drink. ³⁴Jesus said to them,

Theological Perspective

In this passage that ends a series of three, people display their faith in Jesus (or lack thereof). They are motivated by a variety of circumstances, and their faith is demonstrated in a variety of ways. In all three vignettes, most of those who express their faith in Jesus say nothing at all. The one man who does—the man with leprosy who is first mentioned in verse 12—does not approach Jesus with a demand or a request, but simply with a statement of faith. In the second passage, a paralytic is lowered through the roof of the building by a group of people who say nothing. In the present passage, Levi abandons his tax booth and follows Jesus without saying a word.

The relative silence and reserve of people who express their faith in Jesus stand in contrast to the loquaciousness of the skeptics in the crowd. These voices have been growing steadily over the course of the chapter; they first make their voices heard at verse 21, when they question Jesus' ability to forgive sins. They find themselves silenced into amazement by Jesus' response to their doubt; but a short time later, they (or another group of similar persuasion) give voice to their concerns over the kind of company that Jesus keeps and the way that his followers behave.

What should we make of this contrast—this relative silence of those who believe in Jesus as opposed

Pastoral Perspective

"Who are you really, Jesus?" That may be the larger question behind the Pharisees' queries in the wake of Levi's banquet, a question that still rings true for many of the faithful in our congregations today. Most Christians can fill in the blank with the expected answers—Son of God, Redeemer, Savior— but until we wrestle with the question as if we were sitting with Jesus at the same table, our answers may remain rote and thin.

The Pharisees are not sitting with Jesus at table, but they have seen him there, eating with the wrong crowd. The occasion was a banquet thrown by Levi, the tax collector whose instant conversion opens the story. Those who have been in the pew for any length of time will likely remember at least one sermon that outlined why being a tax collector in Jesus' time was a highly profitable yet despised job. It involved collaboration with Rome and corruption in the form of fleecing of one's neighbors. Even so, many people resist stories in which someone leaves everything to follow Jesus after scarcely a glance. Walking away from a six-figure salary is harder and harder for people living in a competitive consumer culture to fathom.

Unless the preacher or teacher wants to focus attention on Levi's conversion, he or she may need to help people get past their skepticism by allowing

"You cannot make wedding guests fast while the bridegroom is with them, can you? ³⁵The days will come when the bridegroom will be taken away from them, and then they will fast in those days." ³⁶He also told them a parable: "No one tears a piece from a new garment and sews it on an old garment; otherwise the new will be torn, and the piece from the new will not match the old. ³⁷And no one puts new wine into old wineskins; otherwise the new wine will burst the skins and will be spilled, and the skins will be destroyed. ³⁸But new wine must be put into fresh wineskins. ³⁹And no one after drinking old wine desires new wine, but says, 'The old is good.'"

Exegetical Perspective

The Pharisees find Jesus' sinful codiners offensive (v. 30) and critique his neglect of devotional fasting, which is incongruent with the practices of John and the Pharisees (v. 33; cf. 7:31–35). The rift between Jesus and the Pharisees thus deepens as two fresh controversies arise in addition to the prior conflict over Jesus' right to forgive sins (5:21–25) and the subsequent skirmishes regarding the Sabbath (6:1–11). In 5:36–39 Jesus grapples with these disharmonies in two parables that underline the incompatibility between the old and new. A piece of cloth is not torn from a new garment and used to patch an old one, for the patch will shrink, and in the end both garments will be ruined (v. 36). Likewise, new wine is not put into old wineskins, for the old skins will burst, and the new wine will be wasted (v. 37). In a sense Jesus owns up to the inevitability of tension, conflict, and fissure when the old meets the new. These metaphors reiterate what Simeon foresaw already in the infancy narrative (2:33–34), namely, that Jesus will provoke collision and strife, as is abundantly evident in the surrounding controversies.

One exegetical question that emerges here is, with which side of the old-new dynamic does Jesus identify his own work and teaching? It is true that for Luke Jesus' overall ministry is old in the sense that it is rooted in, even the fulfillment of, Israel's history

Homiletical Perspective

Some days it requires little stretch of the imagination to picture walking away from a job at the drop of a hat—especially if the call to do so should come from a trustworthy person who invites us to chuck it all and join him in an unfolding adventure! What if Jesus were to call us? What if he *does* call us? If we should discern his call, perhaps through the voice of another, or through some circumstance that sharpens our awareness, would we experience that call as a relief, or an obligation?

The preacher might begin a sermon with such a question. For Levi, one might imagine that it was both. It was a relief to change sides, but it would cost him something.

When Levi, feeling good about his decision, gave a party for Jesus, some respectable establishment types complained to Jesus' disciples about the disreputable company Jesus kept. Had he no concern for his reputation? He responded by comparing himself with a physician, whose vocation was to be there for those who most needed care.

Surely we in the church are not the "well" who have no need of a physician, are we? One homiletic question is this: Is the church, gathered around Jesus, meant to be mainly concerned with preserving the supposed purity of its own members? Should we build the walls high and guard them so as not

Luke 5:27–39

Theological Perspective

to the actively vocal nature of those who question his authority? Is it simply that obedience and faithfulness can be carried out in silence, whereas skepticism requires us to give it voice? Are we being pointed toward a more profound claim, a claim about the importance of faith and trust among those who have no voice?

In the dominant cultural milieu of twenty-first-century North America, we are taught to stand up for ourselves, to give voice to our concerns, and to express our feelings. This comes easily enough for some of us; I, for example, am a college professor, so I can talk for hours at the drop of a hat. For others, though, this cultural expectation can be fear inducing; it even leads some people to isolate themselves to avoid facing an ever-more-interactive world. What is it like to feel that one has very little to say—particularly in a world in which everyone talks nearly all the time?

My focus here is not so much on those whose voices have gone unheard (because of political oppression, say, or cultural marginalization); rather, I am thinking of those who just do not want to say that much. Perhaps they feel that the world is already too filled with words; perhaps they simply feel more comfortable listening to what others have to say. Are we sometimes guilty of assuming that such persons have little to offer, or that they are not full participants in our world? Should it not be acceptable to listen quietly to the world, without feeling the need to speak and intervene at every possible moment?

These three passages all celebrate the quiet presence of such persons. The leper who speaks only an affirmation of his faith in Jesus, the paralytic and his friends who say nothing as they come into Jesus' presence, and Levi's silent decision to follow Jesus: all are examples of people who are fully engaged with the world, yet without feeling the need to express every single thought that crosses their minds. They contrast rather sharply with those who loudly and frequently express their doubt, disapproval, or concern about Jesus' actions and about those with whom he associates.

In fact, the relative silence of Jesus' followers may be part of what provokes the skeptics to express their doubts. In Jesus' day, as in ours, silence creates a vacuum that some kind of sound will likely fill. If no one is actively and loudly expressing faith and confidence, this provides a good opening to those with decidedly different views.

Still, that does not necessarily argue for a more vocal form of faith. Luke points us to something

Pastoral Perspective

the opening scene to function as Luke probably intends: as evidence of how electrifying a face-to-face encounter with Jesus was for at least some of the despised and marginalized people he most wanted to reach.

The gathering Jesus attends at Levi's house is the first of many scenes in Luke's Gospel that take place at table or in the context of a meal. Luke presents no less than four table scenes in which the Pharisees question Jesus' methods and motives, with the stakes becoming higher at each succeeding meal (5:29–32; 7:36–50; 11:37–52; 14:1–24). As the first of these meal scenes, however, there is nothing in the back-and-forth between Jesus and the Pharisees to warrant a deeply negative description. It might simply have been a fact-finding mission on the Pharisees' part, leading to an earnest theological exchange. What change does imagining the conversation as relatively civil make in how it might be preached or heard?

If yours is a congregation that has heard the Pharisees described time and again as unfeeling and rigid, or solely obsessed with forms, a sermon or lesson that begins from a more informed historical perspective could challenge that stereotype and—more importantly—save listeners from the sin of pigeonholing the Pharisees the way they have been repeatedly accused of pigeonholing others. From this side of the cross, every meeting at table with Jesus has deep significance, as does the openness of his invitation, then and now. He would have included the Pharisees. Asking how well we maintain the openness of Christ's table would be very much in keeping with the text.

Although biblical literacy is on the decline, Jesus' comment about "the well" not needing a physician (v. 31) will be overly familiar to at least some people in the pews, preventing them from noticing, perhaps, that in this scene Jesus includes the Pharisees among the well. Further, Jesus does not disagree with the Pharisees' description of his table fellows as "sinners," but casts himself as a physician healing the sick. The intimacy and enjoyment involved in the cure may have been what raised the Pharisees' eyebrows, not a disagreement about who was in and who was out.

Meals evoke images of family in our contemporary context. They are the setting for both conviviality and the day-to-day deepening of emotional bonds. This meal was in fact a banquet, which suggests lavishness and bounty. The question about why Jesus' disciples' do not fast suggests that the

and Scriptures. In the birth stories (1:46–55, 67–79), the genealogy (3:23–38), and Jesus' inaugural sermon in Nazareth (4:16–20) Luke makes it clear that God's ancient purpose is fully active in the person of Jesus. Later, the resurrected Jesus will instruct his followers that the passion and resurrection occurred in accordance with the Torah, prophets, and Psalms (24:25–27, 44–45).

The fact that in Luke Jesus' story is in reality an old story clothed with the prestige of Jewish antiquity has led some to interpret Jesus' words in 5:36–38 as an affirmation of the old against the new. On this reading Jesus turns the tables on the Pharisees. Although his actions may appear novel, he argues that they are in fact quite in keeping with what is old; and that it is rather the teachings of the Pharisees that are unjustifiably novel and out of tune with the fulfillment of the ancient Scriptures and God's larger purposes for Israel. This is why, in accordance with the tastes of the day, Jesus affirms that old wine is better than new, which no one wants to drink (v. 39).[1]

While this reading accurately highlights how much pain Luke takes to root Jesus' ministry in Israel's ancient traditions, so that Jesus is not an entirely novel phenomenon, it is equally important to consider that novelty is by no means negative in Luke–Acts. In fact, the Greek adjective *kainos*, used to describe the "new" garment in 5:36 and the "new" wineskins in 5:38, appears only one other time in Luke, when Jesus speaks of the "new covenant" during the Last Supper (22:20). Ironically, the new covenant is itself an old concept, from Jeremiah 31:31–34, where God foresees a new covenant for Israel, whose sins God will forgive. This will replace the old covenant, which Israel had broken, resulting in the destruction of Jerusalem by the Babylonians in 587 BCE.

According to Luke, Jesus declares his own death to be the commencement of the new covenant, just as Jeremiah had predicted (22:20). Later in Acts, the philosophers, whom Paul meets in Athens, characterize Paul's teaching about Jesus and the resurrection as *kainos* ("new") (Acts 17:19, 21). In these texts, therefore, Jesus, his death, resurrection, and future judgment, are all deemed novel, and positively so, yet this newness always carries the all-important imprimatur of antiquity.

In light of these observations, it is likely that Jesus is associating his own work and teaching with the

to risk contamination by association with people whose moral and ethical behavior is dubious—even notorious? Some churches seem to believe so, and one result is that Christians tend to be suspected of being smug scolds, not to mention hypocrites. Is the church intended, rather, to be gracious as a sign of divine grace, both more realistic about ourselves and our own failures, and more likely to turn our faces toward our neighbors, whoever they may be, than away from them?

In every religion there are people of good character. No one could impugn the piety of the Pharisees or accuse them of failing to respect the rules. We admire people like that. However, if there is a downside to such earned respectability, it may be that it becomes tempting to compare ourselves with others and find the others wanting. In this case, the Pharisees succumbed to the temptation to find fault: "John's disciples, like the disciples of the Pharisees, frequently fast and pray, but your disciples eat and drink" (v. 33).

Now, in retrospect, John and his disciples look pious, while Jesus and his disciples look like party animals! Fasting can be a good thing, but you do not expect the guests at a wedding to fast, do you? There is a time for celebration, and one of those times is certainly while the bridegroom is mingling with the guests and receiving their toasts and good wishes. The bridegroom, clearly the long-awaited Messiah, is Jesus. Where Jesus is, there is the Messiah, and where the Messiah is, God's kingdom is being manifest, at least in that moment. The preacher's opportunity here is to highlight the fact that the church is a meal-keeping community in which Jesus is the host. Therefore the meal is a festive one, meant to serve as a sign of God's ultimate reign, when they shall come "from east and west, from north and south" (13:29) to eat together in the kingdom.

Jesus offers a "parable" about the problem of trying to combine the new with the old. Note first the reference to a garment. In the New Testament we find images of being "clothed" with Christ in baptism (Gal. 3:27), and "putting on Christ" (Rom. 13:14). At some point, the preacher may point out that this metaphor about conversion became a ritual act that involved removing the old clothes and dressing the newly baptized in a white garment. Neither the "old garment" nor "old wineskins" represents Judaism. Jesus honored Israel's tradition, prayed as a Jew, worshiped in the synagogue, quoted his own Jewish Scriptures. Nor is Jesus making a sweeping statement that old and new are always incompatible, incapable

---

1. Joel B. Green, *The Gospel of Luke*, NICNT (Grand Rapids: Eerdmans, 1997), 249–50.

Theological Perspective

quite profound by observing that people sometimes express their faith in quiet ways. Those who come to Jesus do not need to prepare themselves with a carefully constructed argument as to why they deserve his attention and help. They do not need to find the right words or the right power brokers in order for God to respond to whatever characterizes their lives—whether that be suffering (the leper), incapacities (the paralytic), or just the banalities and annoyances of one's work (Levi collecting taxes). They do not need to pay for access or "know the right people." They just need to be in the presence of Jesus and to believe that he has something to offer.

Perhaps this is our modern-day version of Jesus' claim that "those who are well have no need of a physician." By analogy, we might make reference to those who have plenty of money, plenty of access to expertise and power, and plenty of other resources at their disposal. This is not to say that such persons have no need of God; in fact, they often discover that their money, power, and influence fail to provide the kind of help that they have sought. Those who have never had those resources at their disposal, those who find themselves at the margins of society, may recognize their needs sooner, and take a more direct route into the presence of Jesus. Those who already have much may take longer to discover that the apparently "needy" people who have clustered around Jesus are having a pretty good time: a feast in the presence of the bridegroom.

It is a bit counterintuitive, living in a culture that so celebrates the power of words and the tools of influence, to imagine a fabulous party being enjoyed by those who have little and who say little. That is the essence of the "great reversal" Jesus proclaims, in which the first arrive last, only to discover that the last are already there.

DAVID S. CUNNINGHAM

Pastoral Perspective

Pharisees were worried not simply about Jesus eating with outcasts; they also were upset that Jesus and his disciples were having such a good time! Jesus brings up the family image himself when he comments about the importance of enjoying time with the bridegroom while he is present.

Bridegrooms, and brides as well, mean a new family is about to be formed. Newness and the formation of a new family run though the parable Jesus gives as his final response to the Pharisees. He is not using the parable to refer to the church; Jesus must not be ripped out of his Jewish context. Given the church's poor record in this regard, actually acknowledging Jesus to be the first-century Jew that he was would be such a new perspective to some that it might make the point the parable makes about wineskins. However, Jesus is heralding newness: newness in relationship with God, newness with regard to one another, newness in regard to the practices of faith. At the same time, the parable of the Wineskins also maintains at least some regard for the old. One reason for not using a new piece of cloth on an old garment is that the match would be poor and render the old garment shabby; or, if the new patch were to shrink, the garment would be torn. The new garment sacrificed for a patch would also be wasted. Again, saying that new wine would burst old wineskins implies at least some regard for maintaining the integrity of both.

Whatever else Jesus' use of the parable may imply, he is cut from old, recognizable cloth, but he is doing and bringing new things. The final line of the parable, however, tells the truth about how unwelcome newness usually is. It will not do for the preacher or teacher to try and remove the ambiguity from the parable itself or from the final, perplexing line. Parables are meant to startle and stir up thought. The challenge is to present them in ways that keep the ambiguity and the mystery intact.

CATHERINE E. TAYLOR

new in 5:36–38. On this reading, Jesus is arguing that the Pharisees react critically because their old and entrenched ways and views are incompatible with his new and fresh approach. Jesus thus speaks critically in 5:39 of those who prefer old wine to new, for it is to be expected that people will in general prefer what is vintage and be closed to what is not.

From the point of view of the fledgling church, these parables provide a way to understand newly emerging institutions and theological innovations. They also help to explain the general rejection experienced by both Jesus and subsequent followers. Within the immediate context of Luke's Gospel, moreover, Jesus' analysis of novelty's inherent incongruence with the old also provides commentary on the two preceding controversies. In both, Jesus does in fact introduce an innovation to which the Pharisees strongly object.

First, Jesus dines with tax collectors and other sinners. The Pharisees are actually correct to question this practice, for it is inconsistent with both early Jewish and Greek writers, who commonly advise the righteous to avoid associating with people of lesser character (e.g., Prov. 1:8–19). Even Paul quotes the Greek comic poet Menander approvingly, "Bad company ruins good morals" (1 Cor. 15:33).

Second, the disciples of Jesus do not fast. The Pharisees' question again is a fair one, for fasting was also a common practice among devout Jews, as Raphael affirms in Tobit 12:8: "prayer with fasting is good." The Pharisees themselves are also examples, since they fast twice weekly (18:12).[2] On both counts Jesus justifies his fresh approach, for he has come precisely to help sinners to repentance (v. 32). Furthermore, "wedding guests" do not fast while the bridegroom is with them, although, alluding to the passion, they will fast when the bridegroom is taken away (vv. 34–35). The parables in 5:36–39 are one more way of ratifying innovation and verifying that old-school objections, together with the conflict that ensues, are totally within expectation.

JEFF JAY

of being reconciled. Rather, the "old" represents the kind of religious conventionalities that narrow the Pharisees' perspective and our own.

The "new" is not just the unprecedented or whatever is novel. As new clothing for the baptized represents new life, wine is served as a symbol of the coming kingdom. Both signal the kingdom that has drawn near, God's future dominion having become present in Christ. The "new" in this saying refers, then, to Christ in his kingdom, the revelation and present manifestation of God's sovereign rule. "New wine" is too dynamic to be contained by boxing it into superficial respectability that is characterized by scorn of the neighbor masquerading as genuine piety.

The Christian life appropriately includes times of fasting, self-examination, and penitence; but because the crucified One has risen, and because his resurrection serves as God's promise that Christ's kingdom shall one day fill the whole earth, it is not only about penitence. The Christian life is always eucharistic; that is, it is a life of studying, rehearsing, and cultivating the art of gratitude, of thanksgiving, and of rejoicing. There is still evil, injustice, and cruelty in the world. The eucharistic life does not require that we pretend not to see these things or that we simply bow passively before it. Christians together are called to find ways to manifest the healing that the Great Physician offers to all, both those who already have their lives together, and those whose lives are in disarray.

It is grace, the preacher might remind us, that Levi must have met in Jesus, giving Levi the courage to trust him enough to turn his life around. It is grace rather than scolding that should overflow the church's life and work. Grace is the balm that makes repentance possible, that heals, and that chases away despair.

One sermon on this text might rest its weight on verse 39, which suggests that when one develops a taste for the old religious conventionalities, that is, the pure folks disdaining the impure, the "new wine" of the kingdom will be hard to swallow. "And no one after drinking old wine desires new wine" (v. 39). Better to cultivate a taste for the new.

RONALD P. BYARS

---

2. For avoiding sinners and fasting in ancient literature, see Adela Yarbro Collins, *Mark*, Hermeneia (Minneapolis: Fortress Press, 2007), 190–200.

Luke 6:1–11

¹One sabbath while Jesus was going through the grainfields, his disciples plucked some heads of grain, rubbed them in their hands, and ate them. ²But some of the Pharisees said, "Why are you doing what is not lawful on the sabbath?" ³Jesus answered, "Have you not read what David did when he and his companions were hungry? ⁴He entered the house of God and took and ate the bread of the Presence, which it is not lawful for any but the priests to eat, and gave some to his companions?" ⁵Then he said to them, "The Son of Man is lord of the sabbath."

⁶On another sabbath he entered the synagogue and taught, and there was a man there whose right hand was withered. ⁷The scribes and the Pharisees watched him to see whether he would cure on the sabbath, so that they might find an accusation against him. ⁸Even though he knew what they were thinking, he said to the man who had the withered hand, "Come and stand here." He got up and stood there. ⁹Then Jesus said to them, "I ask you, is it lawful to do good or to do harm on the sabbath, to save life or to destroy it?" ¹⁰After looking around at all of them, he said to him, "Stretch out your hand." He did so, and his hand was restored. ¹¹But they were filled with fury and discussed with one another what they might do to Jesus.

Theological Perspective

This pericope focuses on two confrontations Jesus has with the Pharisees. Each confrontation underscores Jesus' uniqueness and what the Sabbath looks like in this new covenant. The first occurs when Jesus' disciples pluck grain on the Sabbath, a clear violation of Sabbath law. When the Pharisees object, Jesus recalls the story in 1 Samuel 21:1–9 of David eating the sacred bread set aside for the priests. Jesus does not argue that David's acts were lawful. In fact he points out that David's acts were "not lawful" (v. 4) and appears to equate the disciples' acts to David's. In essence Jesus does not address the question of whether the acts are unlawful; rather, he redirects their question when he states: "The Son of Man is lord of the sabbath" (v. 5). This rejoinder places Jesus in clear parallel and juxtaposition with David.

Immediately our attention is drawn to Jesus' place in the lineage of David as the leader and king of Israel, but Jesus surpasses David because he is the actual "'lord" of the Sabbath. In this claim, Jesus announces his special relationship both to the Sabbath, as its lord, but also to the covenant as a whole. The Sabbath was integral to the covenant. God established and observed the first Sabbath at creation, and on this seventh day humanity entered the creation by joining God in a day of rest. God's first day for humanity included no work, but rather consisted of

Pastoral Perspective

When I was growing up, I would often spend a week or two during summer vacation staying with my grandparents in Pittsburg, Kansas. After grudgingly concluding that television was not just a fad, Nonna and Pop bought a little black-and-white set that stood against the wall in their living room. We enjoyed endless games of dominoes and checkers, but at certain times I wanted to lie in front of the TV undisturbed. That was the hour of the first televised revivals with an energetic preacher named Oral Roberts who held forth only a hundred miles from Pittsburg.

His first name alone suggested that he was a speaker who thought he had a lot to say. What fascinated me, though, was what happened after the sermon. That is when he would call on the Holy Spirit to stir anyone with a need—physical or spiritual—to come forward for healing. He had a handheld microphone that he used to astonishing effect. The mike allowed him to capture the crowd's attention, focus them on a particular person, call that person's name, and then with a boisterous beseeching prayer, to lay on his right hand and enact the healing.

The scene of a particular woman who had come forward on crutches is still vivid in my mind, in part because reruns of this video clip appear in some documentaries of Pentecostalism. She walked away

Exegetical Perspective

Gleaning Grain on the Sabbath. The biblical episode that Jesus appeals to is Abimelech's allowing David and his troops to eat of the so-called bread of the Presence in 1 Samuel 21:2–6. Luke's point is that human welfare is more important than purity regulations.

Most modern scholars hold that Luke here rewrites Mark 2:23–28, but there are a few significant differences. Mark 2:26 wrongly named the priest Abiathar, not Abimelech as in 1 Samuel. Luke does not make the same mistake, insofar as the name of the priest is entirely missing in his account. More remarkable is his omission of Mark 2:27a: "The sabbath was made for humankind, and not humankind for the sabbath." This sentence in Mark introduces the saying that does appear in Luke: "so the son of man is lord even of the sabbath" (Mark 2:27b, my trans.). Here "son of man" probably is not a title for Jesus but refers in general to humankind. By way of contrast, the NRSV capitalizes "Son of Man," on the assumption that it is a title for Jesus. It surely is a title in Luke's version, which seems to reflect a pre-Markan stratum of tradition.

What concerns us here is the fact that the Gospel of Matthew likewise does not name the priest who offered David the bread of the Presence or Mark's introduction to the final aphorism, similarities most likely not coincidental, which raises an intriguing

Homiletical Perspective

This section on Jesus' attitude toward the Sabbath is a continuation of the story begun in the previous chapter of Jesus' exchanges with the scribes and Pharisees. Although Luke will escalate the energy of the conflict as Jesus nears Jerusalem, at this point in the story it would be useful in preaching to correct some of the stereotypes about scribes and Pharisees, and to note that their function in the narrative is to present pointed questions that allow Luke to expand on Jesus' teachings and their implications. It is only at the end of this part of the story (v. 11) that they are "filled with fury" and begin to plot.

How one keeps the Sabbath was a much more loaded question in Jesus' day than in our own. One strategy for the preacher is to use this pericope to explore how the Sabbath was originally defined and expanded in the Hebrew Bible, what it meant to the Pharisees and to other people in Jesus' day, and what it means to us now. It is noteworthy that the discussion in Exodus 20:8–11 and Deuteronomy 5:12–15 focuses less on the duty of the individual to observe a Sabbath rest than his duty to allow his servants and even beasts of burden to have a day without work. There is nothing in the written Law about simply eating or "doing good" as in the Gospel story. It is also noteworthy that the scriptural record on keeping the Sabbath is fundamentally related to God's

Luke 6:1–11

Theological Perspective

humanity joining God in observation of the completion and goodness of the creation.

The Sabbath foreshadows God's fulfillment of the covenant in the life, death, and resurrection of God's Son as the act of God's provision for the salvation and reconciliation of humanity. Just as God's creation was complete and good aside from any participation from humanity, so also God's covenant is complete and good aside from humanity's affirmation. Rather, God invites humanity to rest in God's provision of a good creation and, looking forward, in observance of God's completed covenant in the sacrificial life, death, and resurrection of God's Son.

In declaring himself the lord of the Sabbath, Jesus announces both his authority over the Sabbath and his place as the fulfillment of God's promise. Jesus is both the lord and the fulfillment of the Sabbath. In observance of the Sabbath, Jews pause to acknowledge that which God has provided and to celebrate the faithfulness of God, who will fulfill all that God has promised. In this declaration Jesus positions himself as that one for whom Israel may and must give thanks as the provision of God, as the fulfillment of God's promise of redemption. As the lord of the Sabbath, Jesus is the fulfillment of the promise in which Israel has been trusting and resting since the exodus.

However, Jesus also pronounces himself the "Son of Man" who is lord of the Sabbath. This phrase must not be overlooked as a marker of who the Son of Man is. While he is the promise of the Sabbath, Jesus is also the man who in his flesh is the union of God and humanity. Just as David was the leader God chose and appointed king of Israel, so Jesus is the true human king of Israel whom God chose from before foundations of the world to be the Lamb slain. He is not only the fulfillment of the Sabbath; he is also the true king of Israel who leads by surrendering his life, and who creates a new covenant with his very flesh and blood. In Jesus' humanity God has joined God's self in covenant with all of humanity. As the Son of Man who is also lord of the Sabbath, Jesus is the union of God and humanity, the master and fulfillment of God's covenantal promises.

The second Sabbath confrontation occurs as Jesus is teaching in the synagogue, when a lame man comes to be healed. The Pharisees see this as a test: will Jesus dare to defile the Sabbath by healing on the Sabbath in defiance of the law? Instead, Jesus sees this as an opportunity to reveal what it means that he is lord of the Sabbath. In healing the lame man, Jesus poses a question to the Pharisees for which

Pastoral Perspective

after the prayer, her crutches lying on the floor of the platform while Oral shouted, "See what the Lord can do?!"

At age ten I was hooked on the drama. I also thought I had been given a strong whiff of chicanery. The drama felt like a setup to me. More than the question of whether the healing was real was the issue of its manipulative staging. To my young mind, the woman seemed more like a victim than a victor.

I have a similar visceral reaction to the story of the man with the withered hand. The setup of the story is the same in all three Synoptic Gospels, with scribes and Pharisees on one side of a synagogue and Jesus on the other. Jesus, of all people, calls to the man, who almost surely would have been lingering unseen at the edge of crowd, to "come and stand here" in front of him. At first, Jesus fails even to address him directly, asking the scribes and Pharisees if it is fitting to practice an act of healing on the Sabbath. When he looks around and they do not respond, Jesus utters his only other words to the man, "Stretch out your hand," and the man's hand is restored.

That he was healed is great, but it still seems utterly manipulative. The man is being used to dramatize some bigger point. He is a pawn in a dispute among religious authorities. I just do not like this.

I also do not like that the story makes me feel like a flop. Oral Roberts took the story to heart; if he wanted to find a model for his public healings, he could certainly find it in Luke 6. Moreover, he could argue that Jesus passed on this healing power to his apostles, who enjoyed the fruits of the Spirit continually as reported in Acts. So why not in mid-twentieth-century Oklahoma? Meanwhile, in my forty years as an ordained minister and professor, I have never healed anyone. To put the failure another way: the Holy Spirit has never healed anyone in my pastoral presence, in the resonance of my words, in the flailing of my gestures, or in the wake of my wildest hopes and most fervent prayers.

With that miserable thought, I have now made this Gospel story be about me—which it is most clearly not. Hitting that wall is the beginning of insight.

Awakened from my self-absorption and skepticism, I see something here that I never noticed before. Jesus' healing is born out of silence. True, he asks out loud whether it is "lawful to do good" on the Sabbath. After that, nobody says anything. I wonder how long that moment lasted. I wonder how deep the silence was.

question: did Luke know the accounts both in Mark 2:23–28 and Matthew 12:1–8? If he did, one would have to explain why Luke ignored Matthew 12:5–6, for which Luke has no equivalent. "Or have you not read in the law that on the sabbath the priests in the temple break the sabbath and yet are guiltless? I tell you, something greater than the temple is here. But if you had known what this means, 'I desire mercy and not sacrifice,' you would not have condemned the guiltless" (Matt. 12:5–7).

An alternative position, one I have advocated elsewhere, is that the story at hand appeared already in the lost Gospel often referred to as Q.[1] In my reconstruction of the *Logoi of Jesus* (the likely title of the lost Gospel) the incident about gleaning grain on the Sabbath appeared as the third controversy in a sequence of four that culminated in the dispute about Jesus' healing on the Sabbath. Luke follows the same sequence (as did Mark and Matthew). If this is the case, Luke would have seen this story both in the lost Gospel and in Mark and seems to have preferred the former. This allows modern interpreters to monitor the evolution of this story, and many others, in early Christian literary tradition, in this case from the *Logoi of Jesus* to Mark and from both to Luke. Again, if this is the case, Luke's original contributions are modest; often, however, they are interpretively important, as we now shall see.

The Healing of a Man with a Withered Hand. Matthew, Mark, and Luke each contain a version of this story; Luke's generally shares most with Mark 3:1–6, but there is reason to suspect that he also knew of the account in Matthew 12:9–14 or, more likely, a version of it that already appeared in the lost Gospel. To understand why, one needs to turn to a similar story in Luke 14, where one finds the following parallels with Matthew's account of the healing of the man with the withered hand.[2]

Matthew 12:10–11	Luke 14:1b–5
. . . a man was there with a withered hand, and they asked him, "Is it lawful to cure on the sabbath?" so that they might accuse him.	They were watching him closely. Just then, in front of him, there was a man who had dropsy. And Jesus asked the lawyers and Pharisees,

1. Dennis R. MacDonald, *Two Shipwrecked Gospels: The Logoi of Jesus and Papias's Exposition of Logia about the Lord*, SBLECL 8 (Atlanta: Society of Biblical Literature, 2012), 148–50 and 209–11.

2. For a more comprehensive treatment, see *Two Shipwrecked Gospels*, 150–51 and 201–2.

act of creation and to God's freeing the people from slavery.

A preacher will want to emphasize what the Sabbath was intended to honor, and how it might be connected with concern for the whole community. Jesus' understanding of keeping Sabbath can be interpreted as a return to the original values of the Mosaic Law, and not a radical break from his people's tradition. What should be avoided is the implication that for Christians to follow Jesus means turning our backs on all the virtues of Jesus' own Jewish background.

One fruitful direction for a homily would be to continue asking what the Sabbath means and to look hard at our own practices. How do we—as individuals, as a church community, as a culture—honor God's creative acts, including creation's seventh day, when God rested? Does our hyperactive lifestyle wind up imposing a burden on others in our families or our community? How do we define and enjoy a holy rest? How do our answers to these questions relate to Jesus' teaching and modeling?

Another direction for the preacher is to continue exploring the engagement between Jesus and the Pharisees and how that could relate to our own understanding or practice of our faith. One might start with the assumption that the Pharisees were like us, religious people trying to find conscientious and practical ways to relate to God as we understand God. If we start there, what can we discern about the Pharisees' agenda in questioning Jesus? Try out a variety of approaches. Were they simply curious about Jesus? If they were not intentionally distorting the meaning of the Sabbath, were they afraid of something? Did Jesus' methods or teachings threaten their status in their community? Did Jesus challenge the Pharisees' own faith? As people who had made it their mission to interpret God's Law as clearly as possible—so it could actually be followed perfectly—did Jesus represent to them a loosening of the structure that would make the whole thing tumble down or fall apart?

Think about the religious ideas and practices that make us nervous, particularly those of us who are "regulars" in church, who believe we know what is expected. What have we experienced as rocking our boat? Is there some measure of status we maintain by holding to our own structures of belief or ways of faith? When someone voices a view different from ours, are we fearful that they present a threat to our security? Do their questions pose a legitimate challenge to our own faith system?

Luke 6:1–11

Theological Perspective

they are likely unprepared. Rather than debating them on nuances of the law, Jesus asks if it is lawful to "do good or to do harm" on the Sabbath.

Jesus' question omits a third option, that of "doing nothing." From the outset, Jesus rules this option out; we are asked only if it is lawful to "save life or destroy." By omitting this third option, Jesus challenges the notion that inaction is acceptable in the face of another's physical need. According to the text, the Pharisees sought to hide behind the Sabbath as an excuse to avoid feeding the hungry and healing the broken in body. Upon revealing himself as the Son of Man who is himself lord of the Sabbath, Jesus equates inactivity in the face of need with destruction of life, and indifference to suffering with actively doing harm.

In announcing this mandate to serve and help others on the Sabbath, Jesus takes the further step of redefining the understanding of proper observation of the Sabbath and his posture as the lord of the Sabbath. As the Son of Man who came to seek that which was lost, Jesus heals the lame man, placing his physical needs at the forefront. Jesus' action demonstrates that the faithful observance of the covenant can no longer take the form of inaction in the face of human need. Those who would observe the new covenant will do so in loving service of human need, not in indifferent neutrality that ignores and avoids. Just as Jesus heals the lame man on the Sabbath, even in the synagogue, so our observance of the Sabbath and thankfulness to the lord of the Sabbath takes the form of serving the sick, feeding the hungry, and caring for the marginalized and outcast.

KEITH ERRICKSON

Pastoral Perspective

This I can relate to. How many pastoral moments have been silent ones, spaces opening where there were no words?

"I can't believe she's dying—I can't even imagine life without her."

"Cancer happens to other people, not to me."

"I thought we had a strong family, and now he's leaving me?"

So, Pastor Frank, what do you have to say to that? Not much. Who does?

Actually, the question concerning lawfulness was not all of Jesus' question: "Is it lawful to do good or to do harm on the Sabbath, to save life or to destroy it?" Wait! When would it ever be lawful to do harm, or worse, to destroy life? The law to which Jesus appeals here is the covenant, the mitzvoth, the commandments for living in a godly way in community with God's people. Why single out the Sabbath? When would it ever be God's will that we do harm?

Again, silence. It would be nice to think that at least one person who was listening, at least one hearer who was pondering Jesus' question, got it. Maybe someone among them realized in the silence that the group confronting Jesus was double-minded. They were righteous and godly and angry and violent all at once. The silence exposed the collision of their Sabbath piety and their furious fantasies of doing something about this Jesus. They did not dare break the silence in their mindless rage.

As for the man with the withered hand, he says not a word the whole time. Even when his deepest longing is being realized—to be restored not only to the full use of his right hand but to full participation in his community—he says nothing. Surely he knows then that silence makes room for grace. If God's grace could be for him, then surely God's grace is for the angry righteous too, if only they will listen. This is the Sabbath, after all.

THOMAS EDWARD FRANK

Exegetical Perspective

"Is it lawful to cure on the sabbath?"

He said to them, "Suppose one of you has only one sheep and it falls into a pit on the sabbath; will you not lay hold of it and lift it out?"

"Is it lawful to cure people on the sabbath, or not?" But they were silent. So Jesus took him and healed him, and sent him away. Then he said to them, "If one of you has a child or an ox that has fallen into a well, will you not immediately pull it out on a sabbath day?"

One explanation of these parallels, and the one that I prefer, is that the lost Gospel already contained the story of the healing of the man with a withered hand and that Matthew retained it more conservatively than Mark or Luke. One therefore might reconstruct the original story (*Logoi* 3:25–28) as follows:

> He entered a synagogue on a Sabbath, and behold a man was there with a withered hand. And they were observing him closely, saying, "Is it permitted to heal on the Sabbath?" And he said to them, "Who of you whose ox falls into a pit on a Sabbath will not grab it and bring it out?" And they were not able to respond to these things. He said to the man, "Stretch out your hand." His hand stretched out and was restored like the other one.

Be that as it may, Luke knew of this tale from Mark (and perhaps also from the lost Gospel and Matthew) and used it for his own ends, not only here in chapter 6 but also in 13:10–17 and 14:1–6 (the healings of a woman bent over with age and a man with dropsy). The Synoptic evangelists made good use of the story to contrast Jesus' healing on the Sabbath with pharisaic restrictions on such activities. However, it is clear that many Jewish leaders actually would have agreed with Jesus on this issue. As was the case with the story of gleaning on the Sabbath, this story makes Jesus a teacher who places human welfare ahead of rigid observations of religious law.

DENNIS RONALD MACDONALD

Homiletical Perspective

Are there questions we do not dare ask, because we fear they would start the snowball rolling downhill? Do we turn away from the challenges that other traditions offer, out of fear that we might be influenced by them and even agree with them? Where do these other systems or traditions come from? Are we made nervous by the deluge of information we now receive all the time, about faith and beliefs from around the world? How comfortable are we holding to the Christian faith we have been taught, when an enormous part of the world's people believe something else? Can some continue to claim scriptural inerrancy or others insist on Christian uniqueness?

Indeed, we live in a time when we are being battered with information and opinions that question many aspects of our tradition. This may confuse many of the people who come together to worship in community. One way to address the confusion might be to return to Jesus' challenge to the scribes and Pharisees: "Is it lawful to do good or to do harm on the Sabbath, to save life or to destroy it?" (v. 9). Jesus is moving the focus of the discussion from the issue of work versus rest to the notion of acting out of concern for one's neighbor. He is saying that the Law, as the Pharisees and scribes might understand it, is not the matter at hand; healing is.

To keep the Sabbath holy is to participate in God's act of creation. That means to find ways to rest from the hyperactivity so prevalent in our world. It also means to act, when we are called upon, on behalf of life, because any act of love is fundamentally an act of creation. Tradition and religious practice are not ends in themselves, says Jesus, but need to be in the service of something greater, which is a commitment to live in harmony with God's creative power of love.

LINDA LEE CLADER

Luke 6:12–16

¹²Now during those days he went out to the mountain to pray; and he spent the night in prayer to God. ¹³And when day came, he called his disciples and chose twelve of them, whom he also named apostles: ¹⁴Simon, whom he named Peter, and his brother Andrew, and James, and John, and Philip, and Bartholomew, ¹⁵and Matthew, and Thomas, and James son of Alphaeus, and Simon, who was called the Zealot, ¹⁶and Judas son of James, and Judas Iscariot, who became a traitor.

Theological Perspective

Immediately following the Sabbath confrontations during which Jesus declares himself lord of the Sabbath and demonstrates what Sabbath observance means, Luke tells us that Jesus chooses twelve apostles. In this pericope we find that Jesus first teaches about faithful service, then equips and sends out his followers on a mission to lead and serve in like manner. As Luke tells the story, God's gracious self-revelation is closely and immediately followed by Jesus' calling a company of apostles.

In verse 12 we are told that Jesus went out to a mountain to pray and "spent the night in prayer to God." This draws a parallel to Exodus 19:16–25, when Moses ascended Mt. Sinai and returned with the Ten Commandments. In that story Moses approached the very presence of God, and God gave Israel the Ten Commandments. In drawing upon that story, Luke shows that even as Jesus approaches the presence of God in prayer, Jesus' posture as the Son of Man means that Jesus himself is the unique intermediary between God and humanity. As the perfect union of God and humanity, Jesus himself serves humanity as the sacrifice offered to enter the Holy of Holies, and Jesus himself performs the priestly mediation between God and humanity. There no longer remains the question of how sinful humanity can possibly approach the presence

Pastoral Perspective

Every congregation I have ever been a part of, as visitor, member, or pastor, has held up the twelve apostles as exemplars of Christian faith and discipleship. The Twelve are depicted in stained-glass windows and wood carvings of an imagined Lord's Supper; they are studied as models of redemption and included as characters in countless Lenten dramas, even though we know virtually nothing about any of them. Entire novels and screenplays have been written to fill out all the missing information. Above all, the apostles are put forward as people to imitate. In particular, we should aspire to join them in their calling.

Few people, in my recollection, have ever been particular about whether they speak of the Twelve as "apostles" or "disciples." The terms are used interchangeably. While the former suggests someone sent as a witness, the latter suggests someone learning, being formed in life and wisdom under the influence of a teacher. They are not the same calling, but most people seem to think they are.

This assumption that apostle and disciple are the same opens the way for pastors and church leaders to urge everyone to follow the example of Jesus' disciples and be like them, especially in their apostolic witness. The confusion is reinforced by the zeal of evangelical Protestantism and its singular focus on

Exegetical Perspective

The List of the Twelve. The apostle Paul already
knew a tradition that Jesus' closest associates numbered twelve, and he even names a few of them. It
would appear, however, that he was unaware that
one of the Twelve betrayed Jesus, insofar as the risen
Jesus appeared to all of them (1 Cor. 15:3–5). The
earliest Christian document to give the names of the
Twelve is the Gospel of Mark (Mark 3:13–19), which
resembles Matthew 10:2–4. Luke 6:12–16, however,
is significantly different.

In the first place, Luke apparently added that
Jesus went to the mountain to pray, in keeping with
his emphasis on prayer elsewhere in the Gospel.
Two other differences between the lists in Mark and
Luke strongly suggest that the latter author saw an
even earlier list in the lost Gospel. Only in Mark
does one find that the sons of Zebedee shared a
name that Jesus gave them: "Boanerges, that is, Sons
of Thunder" (Mark 3:17). Curiously, Matthew too
omits this half verse and agrees with Luke in linking
the two pairs of brothers (Peter/Andrew and James/
John). This agreement probably was not an accident;
they agree because they share a common source or
because Luke knows Matthew.

Notice also that unlike the lists in Matthew and
Mark, Luke's ends with two Judases: "Judas [the
son of] James, and Judas Iscariot, who became a

Homiletical Perspective

The parallels to this passage in Matthew (10:1–4)
and Mark (3:13–19) offer some suggestions about
how to approach Luke's story of the selection of the
Twelve. One difference among the accounts may
reveal a particular emphasis in Luke's narrative;
another may suggest the grounds for an imaginative
journey beyond the passage itself. What a preacher
should probably avoid is letting the twelve names
generate twelve short stories: listeners will tend to
become more interested in keeping track of how far
they have gotten through the list than in arguments
for the identity of Simon the Zealot or Judas son of
James.

The most striking difference between Luke's version of this incident and those of the other Gospels
is the emphasis Luke places on prayer. As many
commentators have observed, Luke describes Jesus
praying before important moments in his ministry,
such as at his baptism by John (3:21–22) and on the
mountain of the transfiguration (9:28–36). Luke
continues the emphasis in the Acts of the Apostles,
notably when Matthias is chosen to replace Judas
(Acts 1:15–26) and when Paul and Barnabas are
commissioned (Acts 13:1–3). In the current passage,
Luke emphasizes Jesus' nightlong prayer before his
decision by placing the prayer on a mountain, symbolically a place particularly close to God.

Luke 6:12–16

Theological Perspective

of God, for in Jesus' flesh God and humanity are united. In Jesus' humanity dwells the fullness of the godhead bodily; as a result Jesus is able to make intercession for humanity in his priestly ministry.

Luke wants readers to note that Jesus was on the mountain in prayer "to God." This signals that Jesus' calling out of the Twelve is not to be an arbitrary choosing of friends or even an assembling of the most qualified for the job. Jesus isolates himself in prayer to seek the will of the Father in ordaining those who will be called out into mission. In his prayer to God Jesus illustrates the continual presence and communication humanity may enjoy with God. While Jesus' relational indwelling with the Father is indeed unique, it is also prescriptive and illustrative of the believer's indwelling relationship. Jesus himself is fully human, and in Christ's humanity God chooses to be in covenant with all flesh. Jesus' unique relationship with God the Father enables him to remain in perfect communion with God, and via our cohumanity with Christ, we are incorporated into Jesus' unique relationship with the Father and are therefore privileged to remain in pure communion with God. Jesus' remaining in prayer to God is illustrative of the life of prayerful communion we as believers are enabled and empowered to live. Jesus' remaining in prayer to God prior to his calling out of the Twelve both demonstrates and empowers believers likewise to remain in prayer to God.

Jesus calls followers to an active participation in God's mission. Rather than delineating a detailed description of what being called out to be an apostle entails (that will follow in Luke's Acts of the Apostles), it seems sufficient in Luke's Gospel to fill out our understanding of apostleship by describing the tasks and mission of the apostles. Initially we are invited to follow the apostles as Jesus not only lays claim to their lives, but also empowers them to serve God and humanity.

In selecting twelve apostles from a community of disciples, Jesus draws a parallel with the calling out of the twelve tribes of Israel. Just as the twelve tribes were physically constitutive of the nation of Israel, so the Twelve called out by Jesus will bear witness in themselves to God's new covenant and salvific work. In addition, just as the formation of the nation of Israel is constitutive of the covenant, so also the sending out of the twelve apostles represents the advent of the new covenant.

In naming all twelve apostles Luke highlights the specificity and diverse nature of Jesus' apostles. Jesus purposefully chooses fishers and "Sons of Thunder"

Pastoral Perspective

Matthew 28:19–20. My own denominational tradition has burdened itself for a generation now with the slogan "Making disciples of Jesus Christ." Almost no earnest conversation ever probes the meaning of this phrase, even though devout Christians have many different ideas about what faithful discipleship means in today's world. There seems to be little concern over the English verb "make" that is used to translate a Greek imperative, even though we live in a culture of industry and consumption that reduces any such verb to a synonym for production. I hear virtually no discussion of the implication here that the church is composed of individuals who have been "made," and that a congregation's vitality depends on those "made" going out to find new individuals to "make" after they come in the doors.

In short, the final test of "being a true disciple," in today's evangelicalism, is to make new disciples, which is simply another way to say "being an apostle." My denomination even asserts that every lay member, not to mention pastor, is called to carry out the Great Commission, even though only the apostles (the eleven remaining, that is) were on the Galilean mountain where Matthew has Jesus giving his command. Luke has Jesus charging "the eleven and their companions" gathered in a room in Jerusalem (24:33) to be "witnesses"—not the entire crowd of disciples who have been following him around.

The evangelical logic here escapes me. Luke clearly has the twelve apostles chosen from among the crowd of disciples. Obviously not everyone receives Jesus' calling to be one of the Twelve. This does not make the nonrecipients inferior disciples. They just have a different calling, and what a blessing that is! The apostle Paul makes that clear in his many discussions of the diversity of gifts and the need for each of them in the body of Christ (see 1 Cor. 12).

I wonder what would happen if evangelical Protestantism would lay this particular burden down. It is certainly deadweight in the average congregation. The pulpit gives the preacher a spectacular vista from which to view the variety of God's people. As I have looked out on the panorama of my own congregation, I know that we are not all called to the same work. In addition, I know that the pews hold many people who are not sure why they are present at all, who may have a question or a longing but no definite direction, who like the aspirations in our songs and sermons but are not so sure about the truth of it all. For that matter, I could say the same about myself most Sundays, even as I lay out my pages of homiletic notes.

Feasting on the Gospels

betrayer" (v. 16, my trans.). To bring the number of disciples up to the traditional twelve, Luke had to omit Thaddeus, who appears in Matthew 10:3 and Mark 3:18. A similar list appears in Acts 1:13, where again Thaddeus is missing, replaced by "Judas the son of James."

Elsewhere I have argued extensively that Luke saw three lists of the Twelve: in addition to Matthew 10:2–4 and Mark 3:13–19, he saw a list in the lost Gospel (*Logoi* 3:29–33).[1] In the lost list he would have seen the brothers paired (as in Matthew: Peter/Andrew and James/John), as well as Philip, Bartholomew, Thomas, Matthew, James the son of Alphaeus, Thaddeus, Simon the Cananaean, and Judas the son of James. When Mark rewrote the list, he gave James and John the sobriquet Boanerges to connect them with the Dioscuri, the sons of Zeus, the Greek god of thunder. The parallels between the Boanerges and the Dioscuri are striking. Like James and John, Castor and Polydeuces were sailors who negotiated with Zeus their postmortem glorification (see Mark 10:32–45).

This evangelist also transformed "Judas the son of James" into Judas Iscariot. Why? Only two people in the ancient world ever were called "Iscariot": Judas, one of the Twelve, and his father Simon (John 6:71; 13:2, 26). The origin of this sobriquet has been the object of myriad suggestions, none of which has gained wide consensus. I hold to the view that Mark created the nickname from the Greek word for "into" (*eis*), and the Aramaic word for city (*qirietha'*), in which case Iscariot would mean "into-the-city." When viewed in light of Mark's story about Jesus, the epithet "Iscariot" warns the reader that it is in the city Jerusalem that Judas will betray Jesus, as in 10:33a: "See, we are going up to [*eis*] Jerusalem, and the Son of Man will be handed over to the chief priests and the scribes, and they will condemn him to death."

The word "Iscariot" also evokes Homer's "Melanthius, son of Dolios [Blacky, son of Deceitful]," Odysseus's disloyal slave, who would have betrayed his master to Penelope's suitors if ever he learned that the hero had returned. The first time one encounters Melanthius in the epic, he is in transit from the fields into the city (*Odyssey* 17.182–213).

From the field to the city
Odysseus and the noble swineherd hurried to go.
. . . .

1. Dennis R. MacDonald, *Two Shipwrecked Gospels: The Logoi of Jesus and Papias's Exposition of Logia about the Lord*, SBLECL 8 (Atlanta: Society of Biblical Literature, 2012), 140–42 and 203.

Luke connects prayer with the Holy Spirit, and the evangelist's particular interest in the action of the Holy Spirit offers an important dimension to consider. From the inspired prophetic utterances in the infancy narratives, through Jesus' baptism by John, time in the wilderness, and citation of the passage from Isaiah in the synagogue in Nazareth, the Spirit is active, directing the working out of God's plan in Jesus. Then, in the book of Acts, Luke goes on to represent the Spirit as the propelling energy in the continuation of God's mission in the early church, signaled by the Spirit's dramatic descent at Pentecost. It is not "cheating" to read this emphasis back into the Gospel, and doing so underlines Luke's particular agenda. Luke clearly identifies the Spirit as the connection between the earthly ministry of Jesus and the acts of all the apostles. In a sense, his narrative does not end with the final chapter of the book of Acts, and someone might ask where the call to apostleship has spread, even to the present time.

Unlike Matthew and probably Mark, Luke says that Jesus "named" the twelve disciples "apostles." Note that someone listening to this lesson read aloud might not know that in Luke's narrative Jesus has already "called" the individuals whom he names "apostles" here. The many people following Jesus are all disciples until this moment: the "naming" of the Twelve is an important step toward Jesus' carrying out his mission of teaching and healing. He now has an inner circle of friends who will have particular responsibilities and face particular challenges.

Another step in this direction might be to ask about the differences between a "disciple" and "apostle." Will any listeners be worried about the many disciples who were *not* "named" as "apostles"? Later in Luke's narrative (8:1–3) the Twelve are mentioned along with "some women who had been cured of evil spirits and infirmities," three of whom are mentioned by name. Is there a hierarchy of discipleship? Are the two words designations for two ways to be faithful servants of Jesus and the community? Can anyone be a disciple or an apostle, or do they need to wait for a call or a naming?

The Twelve have been named apostles, and that naming has happened after Jesus prayed all night on a mountain. Is this a pattern that could be useful in a contemporary context? A preacher might expand on Luke's interest in Jesus at prayer and the presence of the Spirit by drawing connections between the preacher's immediate community and their apostolic mission in the here and now. To what extent and under what circumstances has this community

Luke 6:12–16

Theological Perspective

as well as a tax collector (Matthew) and Judas Iscariot. In drawing from people of diverse backgrounds with a range of socioeconomic and educational backgrounds, Jesus illustrates what the body of Christ on earth is and should look like. The body of Christ is a great feast to which all are welcome, and Jesus intentionally calls those who outwardly may not initially appear "properly dressed" or may not be the most prominent or influential in society. In mirroring the kingdom of heaven, the church is purposefully a mixed bag of society that reaches across races, ethnicities, and socioeconomic barriers and to which God compels "the poor, the crippled, the blind, and the lame . . . so that my house may be filled" (14:21, 23).

Jesus' choice to call out Judas, "who became a traitor" (v. 16), was not a mistake. The life, death, and resurrection of the Son of Man was God's original will and plan. That Judas was included in the original Twelve was neither a regrettable oversight by Jesus nor an inability on Jesus' part accurately to assess Judas's character. Judas's inclusion and subsequent betrayal were an integral aspect of God's original will and determination for the Lamb of God slain from the foundation of the world. Therefore Judas, "who became a traitor," was numbered among the Twelve.

To put the matter another way, the inclusion of Judas demonstrates that the reconciliation accomplished by Jesus' atoning death and resurrection was not God's reaction to an unforeseen turn of events, or a Plan B. The betrayal of Jesus by Judas was as instrumental to God's economy of reconciliation as the birth and resurrection of Jesus. God loves humanity with an eternal love, and God willed from all eternity to reconcile humanity to himself through the sacrificial life, death, and resurrection of the God-man, Jesus Christ. Even a betrayer like Judas had an essential part to play.

KEITH ERRICKSON

Pastoral Perspective

What a relief it would be to read Luke differently. Jesus goes off to pray alone, spending a night on the mountaintop in prayer with God. What if Jesus is spending these hours not evaluating the gifts of each individual disciple, but weighing his own vocation? Is this the moment truly to begin a community? Is the time at hand to name a new community of witnesses to the reign of God?

At daybreak Jesus is ready. I imagine him running down the path, tearing through the brush, leaping the rocks, and breathlessly shouting to his disciples to come around. Yes, this is the day. This is the time for a new community. You Twelve, you have a particular role here as witnesses in this community of disciples. Everyone listen to me! We have places to go and people to see and God's work to be done in showing the world what the reign of God is like. The Gospels do not even all agree on the names of the Twelve. Did names matter so much when it was a community of diverse gifts that was being formed?

Now my imagination knows no bounds. I see myself leaping down the steps and off the platform. I am shouting to the congregation, "We all came here for different reasons, but the point is, we are here. If you do not feel like singing today, let us sing for you. If you just cannot pray today, the congregation will offer you a spacious silence and say the words. We are a community of witness. We are not all the same; we have many gifts and callings. God has given them all and will use them all. God has a place for you here."

Will this make my congregation less evangelical? It seems to me that, freed from the weight of everyone trying to be like Peter, Andrew, James, and John, less freighted with the righteousness of bringing in the kingdom through our own discipleship, the congregation will flourish in the exercise of its many gifts. Jesus prayed for a community to form. Maybe our congregation can be one too.

THOMAS EDWARD FRANK

Exegetical Perspective

And when, as they walked down the bumpy road,
they were near the city;
. . . .
there Melanthius, son of Dolios, met them
as he was driving his goats, the most prized of all the
   herds,
as dinner for the suitors.
                    (*Od.* 17.182–83, 204–5, and 212–14)

Later in the epic Melanthius always appears in a negative role, supplying the suitors with goats, pouring wine for their feasts, and arming them to fight Odysseus. Similarly, throughout the Synoptic Gospels, including Luke, Judas "Into-the-City" switches loyalties and leads an armed crowd to arrest Jesus.

It therefore would appear that Mark saw "Judas, son of James," in the lost Gospel and created "Iscariot," and Matthew followed suit. Luke could have seen at least two, perhaps three lists, and noticed that Judas, the son of James, seems to have fallen to the side; that is, he took this character and Mark's Judas Iscariot to be different men and included them both, but omitted Thaddeus. Why he omitted Thaddeus has been something of a mystery; some have suggested that heretical groups appealed to him as a transmitter of esoteric traditions about Jesus especially in Syria. Many other interpreters, however, think that Thaddaeus and Judas, the son of James, were one and the same person.

Several names in Luke's list play significant roles in Luke's two-volume work, most notably Simon Peter, James, John, and Judas. Apart from the list of the disciples in Acts 1:13, Andrew, Philip, Bartholomew, Matthew, Thomas, and James the son of Alphaeus are noticeably absent (the Philip in Acts 8 is not one of the Twelve). The Gospel of John gives some attention to Philip and Thomas, but is silent about Andrew, Bartholomew, Matthew, and James the son of Alphaeus. This silence would not last long; later Christian authors provided some of these characters their own Acts and martyrdoms.

Luke rightly preserved the literary location of the list as it appeared in the lost Gospel, where Jesus, like Moses, ascends a mountain with his twelve most intimate associates (iconic for the twelve tribes of Israel), to whom he then presents a sermon crafted as an alternative to Jewish law.

DENNIS RONALD MACDONALD

Homiletical Perspective

been "named" something specific in connection with the mission of Christ? Who or what has done the naming? How does the community's experience of common worship resonate with Luke's connection between prayer and mission? What examples of the direction or urging of the Holy Spirit can be identified in the life of this worshiping community?

Continuing a bit on the issue of naming, one could look at Simon Peter in particular. Matthew simply says "Simon, called Peter" (Matt. 10:2), while Mark seems to emphasize the naming by saying "he laid upon Simon the name Peter" (a parallel phrase comes a verse later, when Jesus also "laid the name Boanerges, that is, Sons of Thunder," on James and John (Mark 3:16–17, my trans.). Luke uses the same words for naming the apostles and naming Simon Peter, the only one of the evangelists to do so.

How far is it legitimate to push this verbal echo? Could someone say that being named an apostle might be at least the linguistic equivalent of being named "Rock" or "Rocky"? Indeed, we have become so used to hearing Peter's name as an actual given name that we may need to be reminded that it looks suspiciously like a nickname, like "Sons of Thunder." We might come up with some other instances of nicknames that have taken over for the original given name, John "Chrysostom" ("golden-mouthed"), for example.

A playful preacher might invite the people assembled to reflect on nicknames they have carried at one or another time in their lives. Which ones did they "lay upon" themselves? Which were assigned them by parents or family or friends? Were there any who took public enough stands to receive a nickname in the press (local or national)? Did the nickname affect their self-definition, or arise from it? Did the nickname somehow shape their future?

Finally, if they imagined Jesus giving them a nickname, what might it be?

LINDA LEE CLADER

Luke 6:17–26

¹⁷He came down with them and stood on a level place, with a great crowd of his disciples and a great multitude of people from all Judea, Jerusalem, and the coast of Tyre and Sidon. ¹⁸They had come to hear him and to be healed of their diseases; and those who were troubled with unclean spirits were cured. ¹⁹And all in the crowd were trying to touch him, for power came out from him and healed all of them.

²⁰Then he looked up at his disciples and said:

"Blessed are you who are poor,
   for yours is the kingdom of God.
²¹ "Blessed are you who are hungry now,
     for you will be filled.
"Blessed are you who weep now,
     for you will laugh.

Theological Perspective

After the Sabbath confrontations, and upon his prayerful calling of the twelve apostles, Luke tells us of the Sermon on the Plain, which parallels Matthew's Sermon on the Mount (Matt. 5–7). The order of these three pericopes is telling. The calling of the Twelve is followed by Jesus' healing and teaching the multitudes. Luke's account first describes Jesus' interaction with his circle of disciples and followers and immediately connects it to Jesus' outreach ministry. The order of Luke's account demonstrates that while Jesus' life and ministry were intrinsically linked to God's historic covenant with the house of Israel, they were also extended to all people and nations. God's love for and presence with those "inside" the covenant is connected to, and demonstrates God's relationship with, all those "outside" the covenant.

Another key element of Luke's account is found in verses 18–19, where we are told that a multitude from near and far was there "to hear him [Jesus] and to be healed of their diseases." It is important to note that the mixed crowd not only had an expectation of and faith in Jesus' teaching, but also had expectations about the reach of his power. Luke again makes the point that the crowd included people from locations within the range of Jesus' ministry and people from locations that were without. Given the locations mentioned in this text, we may assume that the

Pastoral Perspective

Matthew has Jesus on top of a mountain delivering the Beatitudes; Luke has him coming down from the mountain where he has been praying, to stand on a level place. Matthew puts Jesus on a mountain in Galilee to give his last charge to the disciples (Matt. 28:19); Luke has him appearing in a room in Jerusalem where the disciples have gathered (Luke 24:36). Sermon on the Mount or Sermon on the Plain? Great Commission or presence in the breaking of bread? Which will it be—the elevated Jesus or the Jesus among us?

No juxtaposition in the Gospels could make any clearer what a difference one's perspective makes. If I am looking up at Jesus, above me, like Moses on a mountaintop between earth and heaven, the Beatitudes appear as a higher law, a covenant made with a community to which I aspire to belong. In Matthew the blessed are poor "in spirit;" they hunger and thirst "for righteousness." The Beatitudes are presented as a framework of disciplined living through which I can grow in right relation with God and neighbor.

If by contrast I am looking at Jesus on my level, with Jesus looking up at me because he has knelt down to touch someone sick or lame (6:20), the Beatitudes appear to be immediate, everyday, inseparable from the joys and sufferings of life. In Luke the

²²"Blessed are you when people hate you, and when they exclude you, revile you, and defame you on account of the Son of Man. ²³Rejoice in that day and leap for joy, for surely your reward is great in heaven; for that is what their ancestors did to the prophets.
²⁴ "But woe to you who are rich,
     for you have received your consolation.
²⁵ "Woe to you who are full now,
     for you will be hungry.
    "Woe to you who are laughing now,
     for you will mourn and weep.
²⁶"Woe to you when all speak well of you, for that is what their ancestors did to the false prophets."

Exegetical Perspective

The Setting for the Sermon on the Plain. Luke 6:1–49 has affinities with Matthew's Sermon on the Mount (Matt. 5–7), and some scholars hold that one best explains them as evidence of independent redactions of a lost Gospel, Q or the *Logoi of Jesus.* The lost Gospel and Matthew both present Jesus giving his inaugural sermon on a mountain, but not Luke, who has Jesus and the Twelve descending from the mountain, evocative of Moses giving the commandments to the twelve tribes after descending Mt. Sinai. Luke's scene also recasts Mark 3:7–10, where crowds come from "Judea, Jerusalem, Idumea, beyond the Jordan, and around Tyre and Sidon" to be healed.

Luke 6:20–26: Beatitudes and Woes. Matthew 5:3–12 and Luke 6:20–23 present Jesus blessing groups of the righteous. Luke may well have known of the Beatitudes in Matthew, but surely he did not create his version by abbreviating what he found there. Matthew's version not only is significantly longer; it displays a secondary, spiritualizing interpretation.

Matthew 5:3–12	Luke 6:20b–23
³ "Blessed are the poor in spirit,	^{20b} "Blessed are you who are poor,

Homiletical Perspective

Everyone listening to this reading should be squirming about now. Luke may have crafted a nice balance between blessings and woes, but the woes have the upper hand, coming at the end of the reading. Stop here. Do not go on with Jesus' further teachings on how to relate to friends and enemies, for if the assembly is listening, they are stuck weighing their own lives and experience against those woes.

Maybe Jesus is not really talking to us today. Maybe this is one of those stories that is so culture bound as to be irrelevant to our situation. A person could certainly squeeze out of Jesus' trap that way. Probably some of the listeners are already trying that. Maybe the preacher is tempted to take this route, as well.

Maybe some of us have quickly tried to remember the part of the speech about the blessings, recalling how often we have heard about God's unconditional acceptance and love. That part is more familiar to us anyway, from the times we have heard Matthew's Beatitudes (Matt. 5:3–12, minus any woes) quoted in films, songs, and other popular media. We strain to recall the positive message, and ignore the warnings.

The problem is that if we want to identify with the categories of disciples who are blessed, then we have to come up with evidence that we are the oppressed—the poor, the hungry, the mourning, the

Luke 6:17–26

Theological Perspective

crowd was a diverse mix of Jews and Gentiles and that Jesus taught and attended to the needs of all without discrimination or favoritism.

In turn, we see that Jesus' ministry did not prioritize teaching to the exclusion of healing and was not marked by a bifurcation of spiritual and physical. For Jesus the spiritual was bound up with the physical, and the physical embodied the spiritual; the two were inexorably intertwined. Jesus knew no preaching or teaching ministry that ignored the economic and physical reality that envelops us all. Luke prefaces the Sermon on the Plain with his account of Jesus healing "them all" to emphasize the interconnection of the physical with the spiritual in Jesus' mission.

Luke's account of the Sermon on the Plain parallels four blessings with four woes in which Jesus transformed and recalibrated what the dominant religious tradition considered the formula for God's blessing and presence. In the traditional formula, one could identify those whom God blessed and favored with his presence by their continued wealth, privilege, well-being, and societal acceptance, while those whose lives were marked by continuous struggles, who experienced hunger, wept, and were shunned by society were surely rejected and shunned by God. The socioeconomic societal structure was understood to correspond with God's acceptance and favor; the presence and favor of God was evident in a person's largesse, quality of life, and reputation.

Enter Jesus, who declares the kingdom of God in his very person. Jesus declares that the poor, those who hunger, those who weep, and those who are hated and excluded are actually blessed by God, while the rich, those who are full now, those who laugh now, and those who are well connected and loved by all are the object of God's woe. This is the man who institutes a new covenant between God and humanity and, through the self-giving love that he is, fulfills the law and the prophets.

Jesus radically challenges the dominant tradition of what God's presence and blessings look like. As he identifies God's blessing with the poor and hungry, Jesus not only connects his ministry with the marginalized, but also paints an unexpected picture of who God is. Gone is the image of the God of strength and power who identifies with the influential, who blesses the privileged, and whose presence is signaled by riches and political strength.

Rather, just as Jesus is the perfect union of God with humanity, his presence and ministry to the sick, the lame, and the outcast demonstrate God's solidarity with those who are hungry and weep. The

Pastoral Perspective

blessed are just plain poor and hungry. I cannot look past them to see something loftier; Jesus is blocking my view.

No pure in heart in the Sermon on the Plain. This is a gospel for hard living, in the down and dirty mess of kids without food, dead husbands, and a broken leg that will not let me walk to till my field or carry water back home from the well. You who are rich, enjoying big meals with hearty laughter and good times, enjoy it while you can, because it does not last and you too should offer a caring hand to the poor.

What a difference perspective makes. In Matthew, I sense Jesus looking down, inviting me to come up and see the big picture— a new covenant community of pure hearts and hunger for righteousness. In Luke, I sense Jesus is looking up at me, as if to say, what are you doing right this minute? People are sick and dying right here, tormented by spirits. They have come from all over the land, from the coast to the river, from south to north as far as you can go in a few days' journey. Will you get down here with me and help?

Luke makes clear that the Beatitudes are not about righteousness in general. The Beatitudes are not about our aspirations to godliness. They are about a community of disciples standing with the grieving, the poor, and the hungry of the land—as Jesus does. They are about practicing the presence of Jesus through acts of care and compassion. Luke insists that the Christian life begins with ministry, not with belief. Luke asks us to follow Jesus into the crowd, to learn about him not from parsing his teachings for every word of higher law and eternal truth, but from working alongside him.

Luke summons Christians to begin with practice, to learn Christ's way by doing. What a relief this is for Protestants raised on the demands of correct doctrine and perfected character. We seem to have an endemic trait of arguing over words, trying to get our creeds perfected, and debating imponderable questions about who will be saved and when. We have preached, cajoled, admonished, and reprimanded, drawing on the Beatitudes for both assurance and judgment, as we try to define what righteousness is. So fervently have we struggled to get this right that we regularly end up making the Beatitudes about us.

Luke will not let us settle for that. Just as I despair over never really being pure in heart or, worse, of being content with my own double-mindedness, knowing that I talk peace while in my heart of hearts

for theirs is the kingdom of heaven.

for yours is the kingdom of God.
21 Blessed are you who are hungry now, for you will be filled. Blessed are you who weep now, for you will laugh.

4 Blessed are those who mourn, for they will be comforted.
5 Blessed are the meek, for they will inherit the earth.
6 Blessed are those who hunger and thirst for righteousness, for they will be filled.
7 Blessed are the merciful, for they will receive mercy.
8 Blessed are the pure in heart, for they will see God.
9 Blessed are the peacemakers, for they will be called children of God.
10 Blessed are those who are persecuted for righteousness' sake, for theirs is the kingdom of heaven.
11 Blessed are you when people revile you and persecute you and utter all kinds of evil against you falsely on my account.
12 Rejoice and be glad, for your reward is great in heaven, for in the same way they persecuted the prophets who were before you."

22 Blessed are you when people hate you, and when they exclude you, revile you, and defame you on account of the Son of Man.
23 Rejoice in that day and leap for joy, for surely your reward is great in heaven; for that is what their ancestors did to the prophets."

Luke's version likely came from the lost Gospel whose author was informed by Isaiah 61:1–2. Reconstructions of the lost Gospel invariably include the Beatitudes and accept Luke almost verbatim.[1] Scholars part ways, however, with respect to the woes. Did both evangelists see the woes in Q (or *Logoi*), but Matthew omitted them, or did Luke create them to match the blessings? The following columns display their inverted parallelism: poor/rich; hungry/full; weeping/laughing:

---

1. See Dennis R. MacDonald, *Two Shipwrecked Gospels: The Logoi of Jesus and Papias's Exposition of Logia about the Lord*, SBLECL 8 (Atlanta: Society of Biblical Literature, 2012), 214–15.

hated. For some listeners, that may not be a great stretch. There are, undoubtedly, people in any congregation who are suffering, usually in secret. However, many in the congregation are not suffering, and in North America the congregation as a whole seldom suffers collectively. A shrewd solution is to claim that contemporary Christians are the offspring of those formerly poor, and to lean back on a triumphalist interpretation of the work of Christ. Christians have certainly tried this approach for most of our history; but in the context of this text, that is really just another form of denial.

To distance ourselves from the people of the woes, we have to argue that we really are not all that rich, fat, happy, or well-liked. Most of us will claim not to be rich, so we might benefit from a few reminders of places or peoples who live in extreme poverty, or who have spent their lives under military or other forms of assault. If the preacher decides to linger on the discomfort this part of Jesus' sermon invites, it will be particularly important to recall consciously where the pain and suffering is in this assembly, and to avoid a cavalier dismissal or categorization of oppression and prosperity. Someone in the assembly is hurting, and someone else is indifferent to the suffering of others. People change roles from time to time. The preacher needs to keep all of these variables in mind.

At this point it would be all too easy to begin patting ourselves on the back for the charitable work we have done, as though this is a feather in our cap. Perhaps we have taken not just the consolations but also the challenges of the gospel seriously, and we have devoted ourselves to significant ministries and mission activities. Those of us who hear many sermons and are more or less familiar with Scripture have heard the challenges about giving away our money and serving the poor. Even so, we may have found ways to make excuses, to rationalize our prosperity or our indifference. Our text begs us to stay with the discomfort, and to avoid engaging in any form of denial.

Remember whom Jesus is addressing at the start of this preaching. He has just named the Twelve of his inner circle and has returned from the mountain to a crowd of disciples and assorted others. Luke says these others have come in search of healing and to hear Jesus. They have been healed of their illnesses, both physical and mental, and now Jesus begins to respond to their hunger for good news. His sermon begins with what sounds like good news for all the oppressed and poor and hurting, and then it explodes.

Luke 6:17–26

Theological Perspective

wealthy and privileged regularly question and mock Jesus for ministering to and maintaining a presence with the sick, the poor, and the outcasts. However, just as his humanity reveals God in the flesh, so his ministry to the marginalized reveals God's solidarity and presence with those whom society has forgotten. God's strength is revealed in weakness; God's overabundant riches are made known in poverty; God's powerful presence is made known in the one who has no place to lay his head (9:58).

This God, though whole and lacking nothing, determines Godself to be one with needy humanity in a radical configuration of who God is. This God is not a distant overlord who remains detached from sinful and imperfect humanity. Rather, this God chooses to be one with humanity in God's very Son and to be with humanity as the rejected one. This God determines that God's Son alone will know and understand what it means to be truly cast out with those whom society deems cast out of God's blessings and favor. As a result, God is uniquely able to identify with the outcast and marginalized in society. God's eternal unification with needy humanity in the God-man is a determination and revelation of who God is, and results in a demonstration of God's continual blessing and presence with the needy and marginalized among society. The God who died a criminal's death is the very God who is present with the poor, needy, and marginalized.

Jesus declares to the multitudes that God stands with those whom society stands against, and that God is both revealed and hidden in the poor, hungry, and outcast who experience lack. In a radical reconfiguring of God's blessing and woes, Jesus challenges the contemporary notion not only of whom God blesses, but also of who God is. The revelation of this God is at once strange, radical, and challenging; nevertheless, it is this God whom the Son of Man reveals in his teaching and healing ministries to all people.

KEITH ERRICKSON

Pastoral Perspective

I am aggressive and angry—in short, just as I get stuck in the conundrums of bad faith and inconsistent character—here is Luke to relieve me of my illusory pilgrim's progress. Just act, just serve, just help; and faith will follow. You do not have to know already what can be learned only by serving.

That is why congregations are always discovering, whether dishing out the potatoes in a soup kitchen, changing the bandages of the wounded, or taking care of the kids while the widow gets her house in order, that they are being ministered to far more than they are ministering; that their own need for transformation is most obvious when they are with people they thought were the needy ones; that the Jesus they assumed they were taking with them to the site of ministry is already there ahead of them. What a relief it is as well, to know that my congregation is not responsible for bringing Jesus along, much less for explaining him—only for following him into the crowd of suffering and hope.

The Jesus looking up at us in Luke seems already to know that we who have enough prefer to avoid the poor, because they remind us how close we are to the edge of want. Jesus on his knees with a paralyzed man seems already to know that our own fears of illness and death keep us at arm's length from the sick. Jesus inviting us to join him seems already to know that we—our lives, our faith, our being with God—will be transformed in the dust of the plain.

Jesus came down the mountain. On a level place, he blessed the tumultuous crowd. His words were for these real and hurting people, the actual hungry and poor of the land. That is why, if I stand with the poor, the grieving, and the sick, I might have a chance to see Jesus.

THOMAS EDWARD FRANK

Exegetical Perspective

Luke 6:20–23

[20] "Blessed are you who are poor, for yours is the kingdom of God.
[21] Blessed are you who are hungry now, for you will be filled.
Blessed are you who weep now, for you will laugh.

[22] Blessed are you when people hate you, and when they exclude you, revile you, and defame you on account of the Son of Man.
[23] Rejoice in that day and leap for joy, for surely your reward is great in heaven; for that is what their ancestors did to the prophets."

Luke 6:24–26

[24] "But woe to you who are rich, for you have received your consolation.
[25] Woe to you who are full now, for you will be hungry.
Woe to you who are laughing now, for you will mourn and weep.
[26] Woe to you when all speak well of you,

for that is what their ancestors did to the false prophets."

Several considerations favor attributing the woes to the lost Gospel.[2] First, at the end of the sermon in both Luke and Matthew, one finds the parable of the house built on rock, which will stand, and the house built on sand, which will fall (Luke 6:46–49; Matt. 7:24–27). If the sermon began with blessings and woes, the result would provide elegant bookends. Second, the lost Gospel elsewhere uses woes with a minatory force (e.g., Luke 11:39, 42, 43, 44, 46, 47, and 52, each of which has a parallel in Matthew). Third and most decisively, if Matthew indeed expanded and heavily redacted the Beatitudes in 5:3–12, he would have been obligated to revise the woes as well, a task that would have required making them parallel to the blessings.

In any case, the Beatitudes and woes in Luke's sermon provide a fitting introduction to the sermon that follows. Jesus, as a new Moses, blesses his disciples for the hardships they have endured on his behalf and promises them rewards in his kingdom. Similarly, he predicts punishments for the rich and complacent. The trope of the two houses at the end of the sermon reinforces the blessings that come from heeding Jesus' teachings and the woes that come from hearing the teachings but disregarding them. Thus readers, ancient and modern, critical of wealth and privilege have found in Luke's Beatitudes and woes sources of inspiration.

DENNIS RONALD MACDONALD

Homiletical Perspective

The healings and the prophetic explosion are part of the same movement, the foretaste of the coming reign of God. From early in his Gospel (1:46–55), Luke has identified God's reign with reversals of fortune and power, and Jesus' declaration of his own mission, in the language of Isaiah, links healing with good news to the poor and release of captives (4:18–19). The promised reign of God does bring healing—not only physical healing for individuals, but a healing of the corruption and greed that mark human society. That would be good news for the people of Jesus' own day, oppressed under foreign occupiers and betrayed by their own leaders. How good is that news for us today?

This question demands that the preacher consider whether the good news of Jesus is the same from one century to the next, and from one social context to the next. Assuming that in fact it is the same, the homiletical message appears to be clear: no matter who we are—how rich or poor or successful or oppressed—we cannot be confident that our worth or the meaning of our lives depends on our position in society. We cannot claim that either our prosperity or our poverty is a reward or a curse from God. We can never assume we are only the blessed or only those who might expect the coming woes. Our lives as individuals and communities are complex; we are both sinners and the saved.

A sermon on this reading needs to explore the discomfort and neutralize the denial triggered by the blessings and woes. Ultimately, though, it needs to point to the grace of God. We can never "get it right" or be secure in our own power or status. Rather, we can be secure in our faith in God's justice, a justice rooted in God's delight in us, and in all of creation.

LINDA LEE CLADER

---

2. *Two Shipwrecked Gospels*, 215–16.

Luke 6:27–36

²⁷"But I say to you that listen, Love your enemies, do good to those who hate you, ²⁸bless those who curse you, pray for those who abuse you. ²⁹If anyone strikes you on the cheek, offer the other also; and from anyone who takes away your coat do not withhold even your shirt. ³⁰Give to everyone who begs from you; and if anyone takes away your goods, do not ask for them again. ³¹Do to others as you would have them do to you.

³²"If you love those who love you, what credit is that to you? For even sinners love those who love them. ³³If you do good to those who do good to you, what credit is that to you? For even sinners do the same. ³⁴If you lend to those from whom you hope to receive, what credit is that to you? Even sinners lend to sinners, to receive as much again. ³⁵But love your enemies, do good, and lend, expecting nothing in return. Your reward will be great, and you will be children of the Most High; for he is kind to the ungrateful and the wicked. ³⁶Be merciful, just as your Father is merciful."

Theological Perspective

In Luke 6:27–36, Jesus calls his hearers to a radical type of Christian reciprocity, the dynamics of giving and receiving in relationships. In doing so, he raises issues of authentic discipleship, the integration of Christian attitude and action, the tension between eschatological hope and present suffering, and mission. The key verse is "Love your enemies" (v. 27b), which is elaborated in verses 27c–36. In this passage, Jesus constrains his hearers to reimagine reality. He calls them to choose God's reciprocity over the world's by employing divine mercy as the foundational principle for interchanges between God, Christian disciples, and others.

The central imperative, "Love your enemies," is a paradox. How can one love those whom, by definition, one hates? (The primary meaning of the root of the Greek word for "enemy" is "to hate.") This three-word command upends any ordinary definition of reciprocity. It certainly does not fit into the categories known to Luke's readers: gift, exchange, and retribution.[1] In the first type, a powerful benefactor gives out of largesse to less fortunate inferiors, to elicit praise and indebted thanks. In the second, social equals, such as friends or business partners,

Pastoral Perspective

This text is a gift to every congregation. It bears ripe fruit for congregants taking up the challenge to follow the Golden Rule. The woman in the third pew lives a different life from the man in the seventh, with far different joys, hopes, concerns, and challenges. Yet the text, which is found in Luke's Sermon on the Plain, speaks to both of them, just as it speaks to all of us. When we allow ourselves to live faithfully into its commands, we grow as individual people of faith and as a Christian community.

The minister can focus on what this text means to the individual, church, or local community, but it also provides an opportunity to speak to the kind of justice and love that "turns the world upside down." The Sermon's audience includes congregations around the world and also nations and governments that identify themselves as Christian. In these contexts, the text speaks to entire groups of people as much as to individuals, leaving the door open for the minister to home in on national and international issues when preaching or teaching this text.

Turning the other cheek can be used to wrestle with the decision to enter a war and engage in military retribution. Offering the coat can be a helpful metaphor when evaluating a nation's response to domestic and global poverty. The enemies that we are to love are not limited to the neighbor who has

1. See Alan Kirk, "'Love Your Enemies,' the Golden Rule, and Ancient Reciprocity (Luke 6:27–35)," *Journal of Biblical Literature* 122, no. 4 (2003): 667–86.

Exegetical Perspective

Luke's Sermon on the Plain (NRSV "a level place," 6:17) here in chapter 6 is much shorter than its parallel, the Sermon on the Mount (NRSV "mountain," Matt. 5:1) in Matthew 5–7. Together the many similarities and the equally many variations between the two versions of the sermon suggest that both can be traced to a common source (probably what scholars call the Q document), rather than to any direct literary dependence of one on the other.

In Luke, the sermon serves as the theological basis of the "ministerial training program" found in 6:19–9:6. During this part of the Gospel the twelve "apostles" whom Jesus called out from the larger group of "disciples" were prepared by teaching and apprenticeship for the mission on which they would be sent out by themselves (9:1–6). The sermon is composed of a variety of teachings that can be grouped in four sections, each with a thematic focus and structure. The first is the collection of blessings and woes discussed in the previous section of this commentary (6:20–26). The second, which is the focus of this portion of the commentary, deals with relationships with enemies and benefactors (6:27–36). The third (6:36–42) deals with mercy and judgment and the fourth (6:43–49) with the importance of personal integrity. The third and fourth sets of teachings are treated in the next two sections of

Homiletical Perspective

In these verses, the writer of Luke presents Jesus articulating the ethical commitments that his followers are to live out in their relationships with each other and with God. The so-called Sermon on the Plain—of which these verses are a part—begins in verse 17, where "a great crowd of disciples" and people from far away gather around Jesus. They have come from the coast and the city to hear him. He is besieged.

Following his pronouncement of blessings (on the oppressed and wanting) and woes (on the privileged and satisfied), Jesus summarizes in almost bumper-sticker fashion what he has just said so that people will remember and be bothered by it. We do remember, and we are bothered: "Do to others as you would have them do to you." In response, we either agree that this is a logical basis on which to structure relationships, or believe that if other people at least treated us as Jesus said they should, our lives would be more pleasant.

One way to wrestle with this text in the pulpit is to examine Jesus' ethical position more closely to understand what it requires of us. The troubling aspect of Jesus' admonition is not the Golden Rule itself, impossible as it is to obey. That rule, in fact, may seem relatively easy compared to the command with which Jesus begins his teaching: "love your

Theological Perspective

exchange mutual benefits. In the third, one unjustly takes from another, eliciting retribution in response, as the victim is able.

Jesus plainly addresses the third type of interaction in verses 27c–30 and clearly forbids retribution, even proportional retribution. Those who have been wronged are not only to refrain from vengeance but to love the wrongdoer. Christians are to exhibit this love through action as well as attitude. Mere inner compunction, like the regret a soldier may feel after killing an enemy, is insufficient. Those who hate, curse, abuse, strike, or rob Christians receive in return good, blessing, prayer, the other cheek, and more goods. You shall know they are Christians by their love, enacted.

At first glance, Jesus appears to reject reciprocity outright. One Christian tradition, represented in Matthew's Gospel, sees Jesus as calling for a disinterested perfection above and beyond reciprocity's concerns. Matthew 5:45 illustrates this with God's indiscriminate blessing of sun and rain falling on good and evil alike. Matthew's motive for love of enemy plays out strictly between God and the believer, who strives to be perfect as God is perfect. Not so Luke. He pulls his readers' eyes from God to neighbor by inclusion in verse 31 of the Golden Rule, prototype of earthy social reciprocity in Christian, Jewish, and Greek literature.

In most contexts, the Golden Rule is a balance scale for common social reciprocity, type two above. It is launched from self-interest, calculated to elicit some fair personal benefit ("credit" in vv. 32–34), and predicated on the other party's reasonable response. The Rule has Christian ethical significance only in context, however. In Luke's context, the three verses before the rule ignore acting in self-interest and shun calculations of a positive response from one's enemy. On the contrary, the enemy's response is irrelevant in the given examples. Indeed, in verses 32–34, disciples who practice reciprocity based on expected gain from equals are indistinguishable from sinners. Social reciprocity among equals cannot establish Christian credentials.

What significance, then, does the Golden Rule have in Luke's setting? First, it confirms reciprocity between all persons as somehow part of Christian formation. Second, though self-interest is excluded, consideration of the other's benefit, even the hateful other, is depicted as Christian. Third, those who imitate Jesus are called to initiate new reciprocal possibilities. They do not passively absorb evil; they actively "Do unto others . . ."

Pastoral Perspective

never returned our lawn mower, but to sovereign states or militaristic splinter groups that have been viewed with distrust or been the objects of national animosity for centuries. What are the social or political policies that can begin, however imperfectly, to respond to Christ's command? What is the duty of the Christian who is both a citizen of the world and a child of God blessed by grace?

That being said, the Sermon on the Plain and the Golden Rule will challenge not just the collective body of a congregation, but individuals in particular circumstances. How would one address this text when ministering to someone desperately seeking pastoral care in the context of a conflicted relationship? How would one address this text with an uncertain eighth-grade confirmand, standing with one foot in faith and the other outside the door of the church?

To begin, we should not dismiss a literal reading of the text. A number of scholars contend that the ethical commands of Jesus, specifically in Luke, are not meant to be read as symbolic "cheeks" or "coats" but quite literal ones. They are not instructions to be heard and then interpreted. They are to be heard and then obeyed. More importantly, however, is the fact that for most people, a moment of actual abuse, theft, and deceit makes Jesus' command more real than an abstract theological discussion of the text, no matter how powerful it might be.

Thus out of real-life situations, inevitable problems arise. Congregants come to the preacher with the most tragic of tales—the marriage broken up by addiction, the mother who abandoned her children for reasons both understandable and tragic, the question of how to respond to an abusive father, to name just a few. Do we forgive? Do we offer our own vulnerability as a sign of God's love? What is the gospel to a child who is bullied in school when the strength of a turned cheek communicates only weakness and vulnerability? There is no justice in submitting ourselves to abusive relationships as though abuse equals obedience to Christ's command.

Remaining in destructive relationships is the "world turned upside down," but not in the way that a loving Christ would ask of us. The Golden Rule does state that we are to do to others as we would have them do to us. We would, of course, hope that they love us. However, none of us is strong enough to endure the exact opposite of love and offer our honest and fullest love in return. This is the discernment of the Holy Spirit. We must believe that in the Lukan text, Christ's Sermon on the Plain, there was this commentary. (The attentive reader will notice that I have included verse 36 in both the second and third sets of teachings. That is deliberate, since it is a bridge that can function equally well as a summary of the guidance for relationships with enemies and benefactors or as an introduction to the discussion of mercy and judgment.)

The section addressing relationships with enemies and benefactors changes the rules in a dramatic way. Normal social interactions tend to be reciprocal. We normally treat others the way they treat us. If they have done us harm, the normal human response is to try to get even, and if they are in a position to benefit us, we work to curry their favor. The general principle that one should love one's enemies and treat them and benefactors the same frames this counterintuitive section of teachings (vv. 27, 35). The verses enclosed within that frame elaborate on how the other person's actions should *not* determine one's own conduct in a relationship. Instead, the norm for one's behavior is the very nature of God (v. 36): be merciful, as God is merciful.

The first group of teachings (vv. 27–28) and the concluding summary (v. 31) give general guidelines for how one should behave. They are stated in the plural, as instructions to apply in any situation. The intervening verses (vv. 29–30) give three examples of specific experiences that might occur in one's daily life, and they are stated in the singular. The first refers to a slap on the cheek, which is an attempt to humiliate rather than to do harm. In the response that is counseled, the offended person refuses to be humiliated, but instead takes control of the situation from the offender, who now must decide whether to continue what has become a game. The second example (v. 28b) could envision either a robbery or the commandeering of one's property by a soldier, which was permitted in the occupied areas of the Roman Empire. Again, the "victim" would refuse to remain a victim, but instead would threaten to humiliate the "perpetrator" by stripping naked in front of (usually) him. The final example (v. 30) assumes the common occurrence of begging, by which the poorest of the poor survived. One should give generously to them, according to this teaching, without calculating either a return of what one has given or a reciprocal favor by which the recipient could repay the "debt" incurred. These instructions bring the general principles down to the specific interactions of daily life, as a prelude to the concluding instruction in verse 31, that changes the key to behavior from what one *has experienced* from another person, to what one *wishes* they would do.

enemies," a command that is much more demanding than treating people in the way we want to be treated.

Jesus requires of us what may very well be at the crux of God's grace: love your enemies. Do not retaliate. Do not look for ways to "give them what they deserve." Do not engage in revenge, or even remember what made you so angry yesterday. Do not desire towers of bricks to fall on those who have acted hatefully toward you, even if somewhere in Scripture it says that this is a just reward. Do not desire that the children of your enemies be killed. Do not curse those who curse you.

Notice that the preceding sentences are all negatives that, in fact, express the essence of what Jesus is saying in this text. However, Jesus' own words are not spoken in negatives. Jesus' words do not concern what we must avoid, but what we are to do. The distinction made by Luke's wording of Jesus' Golden Rule points to the world of difference between an ethic that existed before Christ and the one we have from him.

Jesus said, "Love your enemies, pray for those who abuse you." These are specific actions that the best of us are incapable of doing fully, even on our most charitable days. Case in point: Do our congregations actually pray for our enemies on Sundays in the intercessions? How many times, if you have included prayer for enemies on Sunday, have you heard about it later? "Say, pastor, praying for our enemies? We have soldiers in harm's way, you know." We might try to get by with praying "for our enemies" in a way that asks for horror to befall them. Jesus, however, is about to get even more specific.

Jesus forces us to try on the shoes of the other person: "Do to others as you would have them do to you." Not only does Jesus not let us off the hook; his words about how to treat those who are the most difficult turn us into the very people who may well be someone else's enemies.

In previous centuries and in varying religions, the Golden Rule was phrased in negative terms. It was called the Silver Rule: "Do not do to others . . ." A similar construction comes from Seneca, a Roman philosopher who lived during Jesus' lifetime: "Expect from another what you have done to another."[1] While Jesus' language uses an active verb, Seneca's formulation is passive. Seneca's language is about waiting to get what you deserve. If you have

---

1. Seneca, Epistula 94.43, quoted in John Topel, "The Tarnished Golden Rule (Luke 6:31): The Inescapable Radicalness of Christian Ethics," *Theological Studies* 59, no. 3 (Sept. 1998): 482.

Luke 6:27–36

Theological Perspective

What hope have Christians that such risky reciprocity may produce a worthwhile outcome? Luke's early interpreters found the answer in Jesus. Ambrose in the fourth century reminded those struggling to love their enemies to read this text and see Jesus, who, though hated, cursed, abused, struck, and stripped, loved his enemies and opened a new possibility for them through mercy offered in spite of persecution. Ambrose could not read this command without remembering Jesus' prayer from the cross for his enemies' forgiveness, Luke 23:34. Cyprian linked Stephen's dying prayer, Acts 7:60, to both the Sermon on the Plain and the cross.[2]

In following Christ, Christian disciples enter a radically new reciprocal giving and receiving with God and others. Disciples who selflessly love their enemies will receive adoption as children of God as they, who have received divine mercy, give mercy to others (vv. 35–36). As noted above, in Matthew perfection is the goal of love of enemies, but in Luke's redaction, mercy is the essence of God's reciprocal dealings with the world. In both Gospels, victims of evil take nonretributive initiative. In Luke, this counterintuitive response springs from mercy. Those who have received God's mercy counter evil by giving mercy to the ungrateful and wicked "expecting nothing in return" (v. 35). In doing so, a new relational future is made possible as one's enemies are placed in a previously unimagined reality.

God's reciprocity in this passage corresponds to type one above, a benefactor rich enough to give gifts to inferiors who are too poor to repay. Only God is rich enough in mercy to give love away, even to the wicked and ungrateful, without concern for return benefit, even gratitude. Christian disciples, recipients of God's superabundant mercy, are victims turned rich benefactors. They regift that mercy to their persecutors. In God's economy, the taker becomes the indebted inferior; the robbed becomes generous contributor.

Finally, mission is bound up in God's reciprocity. The enemy who receives mercy is to the disciple as the disciple is to Christ, an undeserving inferior granted mercy but not required to reciprocate. By the disciples' love gift, the enemy is confronted with the potential for a new relationship. Receiving mercy, enemies are offered an opportunity to participate in the economy of divine reciprocity.

WILLIAM LOYD ALLEN

Pastoral Perspective

no real notion of a nine-year-old beaten daily by an alcoholic father. Christ does indeed love us, and when we are called to love our neighbor, then we are also called to a healthy and safe love of self as well.

While we pray that the difficulty of the confirmand rarely includes wrestling with abuse, it is not unlikely that in these moments of faith formation, they read the Sermon on the Plain as Christ asking too much of them, or even Jesus being unrealistic in his instructions. Our youth, after all, are being guided by the church into their own life of discipleship. What happens when they run up against the discomfort of the Golden Rule?

First, the minister should take their discomfort at face value. As adults in our congregation wrestle with Christ's commands at each stage of life, the youth in particular might find significant difficulties with the text in the light of bullies, cliques, and the ever-changing relationships of adolescence. It is no secret that young people want to know what they "need to do" in order to pass the trial of completing a writing assignment or making the cuts for the basketball team. When the youth of our church ask what it is that they need to do in order to be Christian, responding with Luke 6:27–36 will likely earn this response: "That's impossible!"

It is not an incorrect response. Perhaps what Jesus expects of us is meant to be taken literally, but his commands can never fully be accomplished, even by those of us who try to follow him. For our youth and congregation, our best answer may be to strive toward perfection together, and celebrate his mercy in the grace that meets us halfway.

JONAH K. SMITH-BARTLETT

---

2. All classical sources are quoted from *Ancient Christian Commentary on Scripture, New Testament III, Luke,* ed. Arthur A. Just Jr. (Downers Grove, IL: InterVarsity Press, 2003), 104–9.

Exegetical Perspective

The second block of teachings (vv. 32–34) deals with the more difficult situation of one's relationships with potential or actual benefactors. To repay one favor with another is the normal coinage of human relationships, and that is all the more true in the sort of "patronage" system in which both Jesus and Luke lived. In such a system, both one's social status and one's economic circumstances would hang on what one owes to others and what one is owed by others. In Luke's Gospel an important aspect of the good news encountered in Jesus was that such calculations would no longer determine one's social or economic status. Luke discusses these changes in the economic language of borrowing and lending (vv. 32–34), and then shifts to the more strictly relational language of loving and doing good (v. 35a).

The concluding motivation—a promised reward, and a new identity as children of God (v. 35b)—sets the stage for the theological affirmation that God too is kind, not only to those who are morally good and appropriately pious ("grateful"), but also to the ungrateful and the wicked. In short, one is to live into the image of God in which humankind has been created—a goal repeated in the verse about God's mercy (v. 36) that both looks back over this section and anticipates the teachings on mercy and judgment that follow (6:37–42).

Identity precedes ethics. To put it another way, reminders of who God is and thus who we are form the theological foundation for the apostles' ministerial education, which Luke's community and we are invited to overhear. What seems at first to be a collection of teachings about how the apostles should behave under the lordship of Jesus—that is, a collection of teachings about ethics—turns out to be instead a discussion of their identity as apostles sent out in Jesus' name to continue his ministry. That is our story too, in the chain of the generations that Luke knows as the "church," which links those first followers to Luke's community, and on to us as well.

SHARON H. RINGE

Homiletical Perspective

done a good thing for someone, you can expect good in return. If you have been nasty, you may expect the ax to fall in due time. It is a description of what happens in our relationships. It is about reciprocity: you scratch my back, and I'll scratch yours; or, more ominously, you will get what is coming to you. This is, quite honestly, how we live when we do not pray for our enemies.

Jesus' formulation of the rule is miles from this. Jesus is not describing what is but what should be. All the revenge plots, suicide bombings, and broken relationships would be done away with if the human race not only heard Jesus' words but really listened and obeyed. "Do to others . . ." means "love your enemies." This is a radical ethic, forcing us to admit that we are unworthy servants in the face of its command.

Finally, the command does not insist we drum up positive *emotions* about our enemies. The preacher's task is to proclaim that love is an *action*. You can love your enemy without liking your enemy. Feelings have no bearing on our capacity to express love for our enemies. Love of enemy means living in the hope—and acting toward the possibility—that your enemy's life can be conformed to the goodness God desires for all people. We are to pray for those who abuse us so that what is amiss in our relationships can be healed. This love and prayer—adherence to the Golden Rule—is about turning what could continue to destroy persons and communities into actions that have in them the potential for healing beyond what we can imagine.

Jesus' command to love and pray for those we disdain becomes for us a vision of God's intent for human life—what God's actions are, in fact, toward us. We do not, through God's mercy, "get what we deserve." Instead, we are made "children of the Most High" (v. 35). Jesus names us members of God's family.

MELINDA A. QUIVIK

³⁷"Do not judge, and you will not be judged; do not condemn, and you will not be condemned. Forgive, and you will be forgiven; ³⁸give, and it will be given to you. A good measure, pressed down, shaken together, running over, will be put into your lap; for the measure you give will be the measure you get back."

³⁹He also told them a parable: "Can a blind person guide a blind person? Will not both fall into a pit? ⁴⁰A disciple is not above the teacher, but everyone who is fully qualified will be like the teacher. ⁴¹Why do you see the speck in your neighbor's eye, but do not notice the log in your own eye? ⁴²Or how can you say to your neighbor, 'Friend, let me take out the speck in your eye,' when you yourself do not see the log in your own eye? You hypocrite, first take the log out of your own eye, and then you will see clearly to take the speck out of your neighbor's eye."

Theological Perspective

In the previous section, Jesus has just told his hearers to love their enemies and shower them with mercy. Should sinners get off scot-free, then? "No!" is the answer Jesus anticipated from some of his hearers. If God was not up to seeing justice done, they were. Such sentiment, akin to the elder brother's protest in Luke 15:30 ("but this son of yours . . .") is portrayed in Iris DeMent's hit song, "God May Forgive You (But I Won't)."

In a preemptive response to this way of thinking, Jesus issues another imperative in Luke 6:37–38a: "Do not judge . . . Forgive . . ." Jesus' point in Luke is twofold: First, judging will put your eyes out; second, forgive and your eyes will be opened to see God's purposes, your own good, and some sinners saved. In making this argument, Luke touches upon issues of justice and forgiveness, judgment and authority, church discipline and Christian community, Christian leadership and humility, and the character of spiritual guidance.

"To judge" can mean to form an opinion as to whether a person is in accord with Christian principles. Alternatively, "to judge" can carry the juridical sense of passing sentence on the guilty, as a courtroom judge condemns criminals to prison terms. In verse 37, Luke uses "judge not" in the second sense, making this clear by his use of the parallel, "do not

Pastoral Perspective

In this text, Jesus instructs the disciples about how to be teachers. Through a bit of determination and a lot of imitation, they can go out into the world and teach others. By seeing Jesus and then following in his ways, they will begin to hear, understand, and live the gospel they have been given to proclaim, rather than being like teachers who are no more than "the blind leading the blind" (cf. v. 39).

In Luke's scene we have the original teacher (Jesus), the teachers-in-training (the disciples), and the blind that need to be guided (the people), some of whom might become followers of Jesus. We need look no farther than the book of Acts to see how the role of teacher becomes institutionalized by those who were first called Christians. The Twelve, whose job in the community was to preach and teach the Word of God, could not spend their time waiting on tables (Acts 6:2). If they were responsibly to serve the Word and to pray, they needed to give the Word their complete devotion. Perhaps the seeds of this understanding of a minister's role, what some traditions still call "teaching elder," were sown in these verses of Luke's Gospel.

The contemporary church has further professionalized the role of those whom Luke identifies as guides for the blind. Today ministers and other church leaders spend a minimum of three years in

Exegetical Perspective

This reading continues Luke's version of Jesus' first sermon, contained in chapter 6 (the Sermon on the Plain, 6:17). As with the other parts of the chapter, most of the teachings in this section are found somewhere in Matthew, although not all are part of his version of the sermon. The many similarities and the equally many variations suggest that both can be traced to a common source (probably what scholars call the Q document), which both evangelists reworked to serve their purposes. In Luke that purpose appears to be to present the theological basis of the "ministerial training program" found in 6:19–9:6. During this part of the Gospel, the twelve "apostles" whom Jesus called out from the larger group of "disciples" are being prepared by teaching and apprenticeship for the mission on which they will be sent out by themselves (9:1–6).

The verses that are the focus of this part of the sermon (vv. 36–42) comprise the third section of the sermon, which deals with mercy and judgment. I have included verse 36 in both the second and third sections, since it is a bridge that can function equally well as a summary of the guidance for relationships with enemies and benefactors (part 2) and as an introduction to the discussion of mercy and judgment (part 3). In the first case God's values and actions are to be the norm for our human behavior.

Homiletical Perspective

It is useful to begin consideration of the verses in question with a reminder of the escalating intensity of what comes just prior in the text. Chapter 6 began with Jesus' teaching that "the Son of Man is lord of the sabbath" (6:5), in defiance of the religious leaders' outrage that the disciples had gleaned in the field and that Jesus had healed a man's withered hand on the Sabbath. Following his pronouncement of blessings and woes in the Sermon on the Plain (6:17–49), Jesus utters a series of statements concerning the radical nature of what is demanded of his disciples, culminating in the command to love our enemies (6:27–36). Now in verse 37 Jesus insists that we are not to judge. A clear-eyed person will agree that these are impossible commands.

Would Jesus ask the impossible of us? If this question became the sermon's theme, it would be fruitful to focus on our fundamental inability to obey God's will for us, and on God's overflowing mercy in the face of our failing. The sermon might lift up Jesus' command as a vision he offers to us—of a life free of the debilitating consequences of revenge, because freedom is grounded in mercy.

The assembly would need, in either case, to hear the sermon address Jesus' stern requirement, "Do not judge, and you will not be judged," because it is a necessary and ubiquitous theological thorn. This

Luke 6:37–42

Theological Perspective

condemn," and its opposite, "forgive." In each case, guilt is assumed, because forgiveness is unneeded where no sin exists. In other words, Jesus does not forbid forming an opinion regarding others' faults; indeed, he assumes the validity of so doing in verses 37 and 41–45. He does, however, prohibit condemnation on the basis of such discernment.

At the heart of these two ways, judging and forgiving, lie two conflicting motives. Judging seeks separation of sinners from the righteous in order to dispense just punishment. Forgiving seeks (re)union by inclusion of sinners in loving community through the costly work of reconciliation.

In these verses Jesus speaks mostly about the negatives of judging. He forbids judging, in order to avoid being judged (v. 37). Since "no one is good but God alone" (18:19b), the inevitable result of a culture of judgment, secular or ecclesiastical, is universal condemnation. A world bent on justice through judgment fulfills the anonymous maxim "An eye for an eye and a tooth for a tooth leaves the whole world blind and toothless." The generosity that is forgiveness, on the other hand, strives to create an overflow of goodness (v. 38). Judging operates on an economy of scarcity: purity's borders must be defended. Forgiveness promotes an economy of abundance: invite all into loving community, and depend on God's generous measure (v. 38b).

Jesus next demonstrates that those who judge others are ipso facto doubly blind: blind, first, to God's example and, second, to their own faults. Luke 6:39–40 combines an old saying about the blind leading the blind with another about disciples following their master. Judgmental disciples implicitly claim authority to condemn, but their master, Jesus, models forgiveness rather than condemnation. Luke argues that Jesus' disciples should not usurp his authority, but imitate his example. Disciples who act otherwise are leaders blind to God's ways. Any who accept such vigilante leadership, even if sanctioned by official religious or political structures, tumble blindly into trouble, like Pieter Bruegel's subjects in his 1568 painting *The Parable of the Blind*. Those whom God forgives and who extend forgiveness to others envision a future beyond retributive justice.

Classic expressions of these two types of leadership are the characters Javert and Valjean in Victor Hugo's 1862 novel *Les Misérables*. Rather than open his eyes to the bright future made possible by Valjean's forgiveness, Javert chooses to plunge blindly into oblivion.

Pastoral Perspective

seminary, preparing themselves to be "fully qualified . . . like the teacher" (v. 40b). Biblical studies, theology, pastoral care, and homiletics are a few of the requirements that equip "teachers in training" to be faithful leaders of God's people. The downside of this ordering of our common life is that people become accustomed to leaving the interpretation of Scripture and the teaching of the young to the "experts." Having invested time, money, and prayerful discernment in the training of those who are called to lead the congregation, members are reluctant to take responsibility for ongoing Bible study, and parents abdicate the role of being their children's Christian educators.

Framing Jesus' words about guides and teachers are words about exercising judgment within the community. Like parentheses, Jesus' instructions about judgment, forgiveness, and responsibility at the beginning of this text, and his observations about specks, logs, and the removal of both from one's eyes at the end, become all the more important in light of the relationship between clergy and congregation.

Whether because of the outward signs of a minister's office—the minister's robes, stoles, and presence behind the pulpit on a Sunday morning as well as the clergy collar worn during the week—or the inward authority assumed because of their theological training, ministers often symbolize, for better or worse, the first person people think of when they hear the word "Christian." This is not a role that ends with the benediction on Sunday morning. It follows ministers wherever they are, whenever they encounter others in their community, whatever the circumstances in which they find themselves. Fair or unfair—it may at times be a difficult burden to bear—those whom Jesus calls to be "guides" and those called to ministry today bear the responsibility of being the face of Christian discipleship to those both inside and outside the church. This reality is written into the small print of every ministerial call. Therefore congregations and their communities often hold under the proverbial microscope the behavior, politics, and lifestyle choices of their ministers. This is most often done out of love, when congregants young and old alike look to their ministers as role models or sources of encouragement in the Christian life.

This modern context makes the implications of the Lukan text all the more important to understand. Church leaders and clergy should recognize their own shortcomings before they turn, even in love, to challenge the people of their churches. To put it very simply, a minister cannot preach on forgiveness when the congregation knows that outside of

Feasting on the Gospels

The second case looks at the situation from the human perspective, such that what we are willing to offer to others in matters of mercy and judgment will determine what we receive from God.

Both perspectives are troubling. In the first case, divine perfection (which Matthew in his parallel in 5:48 names as such: "Be perfect, therefore, as your heavenly Father is perfect") is unattainable and therefore an unrealistic standard by which to judge human behavior. Perhaps a more helpful way to view it is not as a standard but, rather, as a guide for our human journeys through life, like the North Star that served to guide escaping slaves on their journeys to freedom.

In the second case (spelled out in vv. 37–38), the claim is that our behavior shapes God's own action. That second perspective leads us into consideration of how it is that God's transcendent, omniscient, and immutable self (as later doctrine would summarize it) can be determined by the actions of finite humanity. In fact we are plunged into the latter dilemma by the "triple tradition," for the same pattern of reciprocity is expressed in Mark 4:24, as well as in Matthew 7:2 and Luke 6:37–38. Clearly the Synoptic traditions insist that we take seriously our role in shaping God's action, not just by our prayers, but by our own actions that set the standard for God's. This parity between God's action and ours is echoed also in Luke 11:4 (par. Matt. 6:12), the petition for forgiveness in the Lord's Prayer. (That same view of how human actions shape God's can be seen in the much-maligned Letter of James, which by that evidence certainly merits welcome into the heart of the canon.)

Luke continues in chapter 6 with what he calls a *parabolē*. In this instance that word seems to refer to a series of three proverbs whose truth is assumed to be self-evident (vv. 39–42), instead of to the brief narratives with unexpected twists and turns that we usually think of as parables. In the first of the proverbs (v. 39), the point is apparent, but the underlying assumption needs to be flagged for further reflection. In fact, as persons in the disabilities community are quick to state, one blind person can be an excellent guide for another in familiar territory. Even in unfamiliar territory, those who are blind have learned coping mechanisms to keep themselves safe, to the point where one blind person can sometimes be a more reliable guide for another than a sighted person who is less aware of her environment would be.

That proverb is followed in verse 40 by a second proverb that is "true" in that it reflects the common

admonition against judging allows for the making of distinctions. It does not ask us to pretend that there are no differences between one thing and another. Judgments must be made in ways that the sermon could illustrate. We "judge" all day long concerning the use of our time, whether to believe something, which direction to go in order to accomplish a task or foster a relationship. These judgments are worthy and necessary. Jesus' admonition about judging is more specific and simultaneously bigger than the smaller judgment calls a person makes daily.

Jesus' command against judging follows the admonition to love one's enemies. The sermon could examine how judgment is put into a particular context and given a certain logic, pressing toward how it is that we attain enemies in the first place. We judge an action taken against us as threatening, and we judge the person who has threatened us. We render judgments on those who get in our way, who oppose us, who are, in fact, our enemies. It is the way of human beings to refuse to love our enemies; it feels good to judge those who deserve it. Opposition seems to enhance our self-esteem. The pedestal—of my own construction—on which I usually stand grows taller when I can look down upon someone who is obviously not measuring up.

All of these ways of judging are worthy fodder for a sermon and, in fact, need to be included in order to make plain the need for our self-examination. Jesus' command to love our enemies is integrally connected to refraining from judgment, raising compelling questions the sermon could take up. How are we to reconcile this command with the obvious reality that the world is filled with people with whom we are in competition and with whom, by definition, we are in conflict? By what measure do we judge? By what measure are we to judge?

Although Jesus does not tell us how we are to achieve this, he makes four impossible demands that give shape to the kind of judgment his followers must avoid. He tells us: do not judge or condemn; forgive and give; do not break relationships; but nourish them. To help us understand the seriousness of this ethic, Jesus says we will be judged ourselves according to the criteria we use in judging others: "for the measure you give will be the measure you get back" (v. 38). In other words, the criteria we use for our actions become the criteria by which we will be acted upon; and the criterion or "measure" we are to use is not our own but the measure of God's mercy.

Justice is not a neat amount that, according to our deeply flawed comprehension, is simply "meted out."

Luke 6:37–42

Theological Perspective

Those who judge others are blind to their own faults as well as to God's example. Judgmental Christian leaders who create public scandal by committing the very sins they vociferously condemn in others are commonplace. Psychologists call this bias projection. Desert monks of the early church compare such a person to a monk who does not grieve over his beloved's corpse, but leaves it to weep loudly over a stranger's.[1] As Leo Tolstoy wrote, "Everyone thinks of changing humanity, and nobody thinks of changing himself [or herself]."[2] Hypocrites are not necessarily aware of their hypocrisy. Many log-eyed leaders are sincere and committed servants of ethical practices in Christian communities, communities that reward their counterproductive, judgmental public zeal.

Jesus said, "First take the log out of your own eye" (v. 42). He knew that if misguided judges could grasp their own faults, they would more readily accept God's forgiveness and more likely offer it to others. As in basic airline protocol, put your oxygen mask on first; then help others. The traditional antidote for log-eyed Christians is the spiritual discipline of self-examination. The prime example is Ignatius Loyola's *examen*, which he urged Jesuits to practice even if they abandoned all other forms of prayer. Others include spiritual guidance, *lectio*, and psychotherapy. When Christian leaders and congregations blindly ignore such practices, sinners are more often harmed than helped. The practice of forgiveness also benefits from self-examination, which can help prevent denial and lessen humiliation, and can even reveal the kinds of misunderstanding that make the need for forgiveness moot.[3]

In sum, the spiritual process we can follow is purgation, illumination, and union. Unity with God, self, and others begins with the purgation of judgmental elements blocking the light that illuminates the truth(s) within ourselves, truth(s) we can handle only if we are forgiven and forgiving. This is at the heart of what Jesus commands in Luke 6:37–42.

WILLIAM LOYD ALLEN

Pastoral Perspective

church the minister is not forgiving toward others. A minister cannot preach on love when the congregation knows that outside of church the minister is not known for being a person who leads with love in the community.

Surely ministerial leaders today are anything but perfect. How then can ministers create genuine community when they know how far short of the ideal they fall? Can ministers admit, from the pulpit and elsewhere, that they have logs or specks in their eyes, and that even though their witness to the gospel attempts to be faithful, it is distinctly possible that their witness will be flawed? In some congregations this admission might be troubling; in other congregations, the humanity of the minister is a saving grace to those who themselves live outside the "expected lines" of Christian perfection. Church leaders too have Eden in their past, the promise of forgiveness in their present, and the peaceable kingdom in their future.

Although ministers need to come to terms with their own limitations, this is never a reason to shy away from a bold witness, including a challenging prophetic witness in the pulpit, a Bible study, a pastoral visit, or a child's classroom. The partial blindness in a minister's eyes and the imperfect witness of a merely human being devoted to the Word and prayer should never be an excuse for failing to bear witness to the gospel. In fact, to bear witness to the gospel in the midst of human imperfection is to lend testimony to God's grace and the divine power that is made perfect in weakness. As minister and congregation set out on their journey of faith as a community, with much patience and prayer, they might do so in the hope that their sight becomes a bit clearer and that God's grace is ever more evident with every step along the way.

JONAH K. SMITH-BARTLETT

1.Abba Poeman, quoted in *The Book of the Elders: Sayings of the Desert Fathers: The Systematic Collection*, trans. John Wortley (Collegeville, MI: The Liturgical Press, 2012), 136. See esp. chap. 9, "One Should Guard against Judging Anybody."

2. Leo Tolstoy, *Letters to Friends on the Personal Christian Life* (Christchurch, Hampshire, England: The Free Age Press, 1900), 29.

3.See Bobby B. Cunningham, "The Will to Forgive: A Pastoral Theological View of Giving," *Journal of Pastoral Care* 39, no. 2 (1985): 142.

Exegetical Perspective

social assumption of a hierarchy of status in which a "disciple" is inferior to the teacher he follows. In a world that now is apt to speak of teachers and students as "colearners," that attribution of relative status should also be named for the contextually conditioned assumption that it is. In fact, Luke already leads us in that direction in verses 41–42, when he continues with another image-enriched saying that could be considered a third *parabolē* in the chain.

The self-evidence of this third saying depends not on social assumptions about blindness or about the relative value of teachers and students, but rather on a functional criterion. The absurdity of trying to see anything with a log in one's eye is compounded by the image of a person hampered in that way trying to help someone whose eye is irritated by a speck of dust. Taken literally, the "hypocrisy" or pretense of the would-be helper is laughable. As a metaphor, though, it holds a mirror to many human projects, especially those of members of the dominant groups in a society who have all the answers for others but are unaware of obstacles to their own perception.

The three *parabolai* risk leading us into the deep weeds of social convention and prejudice. Taken together, though, they propel us back to the sayings about reciprocity of verses 37–38. These sayings push us to transpose the Golden Rule into a more complex key, especially when joined to verse 36. Instead of being a simple (albeit difficult) guide for human behavior, they become a meditation on the foundational affirmation of both fact and vocation, that humankind is created in God's image.

SHARON H. RINGE

Homiletical Perspective

Justice is a quantity of forgiveness beyond belief. When Jesus tells us to give and give and then give more, his criteria for judgment obliterate our sense of what is fair. Our paltry measurements do not even find themselves on God's scale. The only true measure of judgment is mercy.

The preacher will want to portray the great chasm between the human ways of reacting to enemies and God's way. Depending on the assembly's capacity for truth-telling, the preacher might show that in every conflict—from the personal to international—each side tends to see the other as the enemy. Because God, in contrast, sees all parties in need of forgiveness, Jesus sets before everyone the transforming power of love.

The second part of this text is a parable that offers many possibilities to the preacher. How often in the culture is the image of the "blind leading the blind" evoked, and likewise the admonition that a disciple is not above the teacher? Both sayings speak to human self-awareness about what one knows and what one does not know, as well as to the leadership roles assumed in a community by those who certainly do not see themselves as others see them. Therefore Jesus goes on to suggest that we need to judge ourselves honestly and realistically before we ever presume to judge another. A sermon might explore how the church can become a community where people may name the logs in their own eyes and even ask for help in removing those logs! Perhaps an exploration of the function of the prayer of confession in the service of worship, as well as the possibility of honest confession of sin among members, might invite people to begin with self-examination before they turn to consider the faults of their neighbors, not to mention their enemies.

MELINDA A. QUIVIK

43"No good tree bears bad fruit, nor again does a bad tree bear good fruit; 44for each tree is known by its own fruit. Figs are not gathered from thorns, nor are grapes picked from a bramble bush. 45The good person out of the good treasure of the heart produces good, and the evil person out of evil treasure produces evil; for it is out of the abundance of the heart that the mouth speaks.

46"Why do you call me 'Lord, Lord,' and do not do what I tell you? 47I will show you what someone is like who comes to me, hears my words, and acts on them. 48That one is like a man building a house, who dug deeply and laid the foundation on rock; when a flood arose, the river burst against that house but could not shake it, because it had been well built. 49But the one who hears and does not act is like a man who built a house on the ground without a foundation. When the river burst against it, immediately it fell, and great was the ruin of that house."

Theological Perspective

The Sermon on the Plain ends with two parables in Luke 6:43–49. They address hearers of Jesus' hard sayings who have decided to come to Jesus (v. 47) and call him "Lord" (v. 46). These parables serve a purpose similar to that of the exhorters in America's frontier revivals, where after the preacher's sermon, an exhorter would rise to urge, encourage, and warn the congregation to respond rightly. The concluding images of fruits and foundations in Luke's sermon exhort believers to realize the necessity of personal transformation and active obedience, so that their initial positive response may yield the fruits of the kingdom (vv. 43–46) and survive the flood of future hardships (vv. 47–49). In this conclusion to the sermon, Luke raises issues of conversion, the relationship between Christian being and doing, and the perennial question faced by every generation of disciples who have been attracted to Jesus and his teachings: Who is up to this task, and how can it be achieved?

The history of the interpretation of the Sermon on the Plain (and its parallel, Matthew's Sermon on the Mount) tells the story of disciples caught between the Charybdis of unattainable demand and the Scylla of unimplemented idealism.[1] If Jesus'

1. See Loyd Allen, "The Sermon on the Mount in the History of the Church," *Review and Expositor* 89 (1992): 245–62.

Pastoral Perspective

For a number of reasons, it is not easy to run a confirmation class, not the least of which is the fact that some of these beloved young people can easily list five to fifteen places where they would rather be. Nevertheless, the youth of the church need to hear the good news as much as the rest of the congregation, and they both understand quite clearly and respond readily when the gospel is made relevant to them. Moreover, young people who participate in the church's ministry benefit from the invaluable experience of belonging to a community where there is no competition with their peers, no letter grade from a teacher, and no one standing in judgment of their personal stories. The confirmation class is, at its best, a space where students will come to see how God meets them in their unique lived experiences.

Still, not every student participates in the same way or at the same level. So it is not uncommon for youth ministers to find themselves breathing a sigh of relief, sensing a weight lifted off their shoulders, or even noting a sense of joy when that one particular child enters the room. She is the one who does not whisper to her friends while you are explaining the exodus. He is the one who asks creative questions about discipleship. They show up a half hour before the Confirmation Sunday service with bagels and coffee. How can a minister help but compare and

Exegetical Perspective

This section of the commentary continues with the fourth section of Luke's sermon in chapter 6, commonly known as the Sermon on the Plain (6:17) and a parallel to Matthew's Sermon on the Mount (Matt. 5:1) in Matthew 5–7. The similarities and differences between the sermons in Matthew and Luke point to the likelihood that they can be traced to a common source, particularly what scholars commonly refer to as the Q document (for the German word *Quelle,* "source"). Luke's version of the sermon serves as the important theological basis of the "ministerial training program" found in Luke 6:19–9:6. In this section of the Gospel the twelve "apostles" Jesus called out from the larger group of "disciples" were prepared by explicit teachings and by Jesus' example for the mission on which they would be sent out by themselves, both while Jesus was still with them (9:1–6), and even more dramatically in the life of the church in the years ahead.

The sermon consists of a variety of teachings that can be grouped in four sections, each with a thematic focus and structure. The first is the collection of blessings and woes discussed earlier in this commentary (6:20–26). The second section deals with relationships with enemies and benefactors (6:27–36). The third set of teachings (6:36–42) speak to mercy and judgment. The fourth grouping (6:43–49),

Homiletical Perspective

This text has two images of the life of faith—those of a tree and a house—that by their compatibility extend what has gone before them in this Gospel. Together they offer us a fuller understanding of who we have become because of Jesus' life, death, and resurrection. Were we to give titles to the preceding sections of Luke 6, we would see that Luke 6:27–36 concerns "Loving One's Enemies"; Luke 6:37–42, "Not Judging"; and Luke 6:43–49, "Integrity." These teachings form a pathway for those who seek to follow Jesus. Whereas the first two sections demand of us specific practices, in Luke 6:43–49 we see the vision that undergirds them. Luke tells us that when the practices become second nature, one becomes the kind of person that Jesus likens to a tree bearing good fruit and a house built on a solid foundation.

It may be difficult for us to hear the point of these admonitions if we are honest about our inability radically to alter our normal human responses to people who thwart us. We do not do the thing we yearn to do, as Paul reminds us; we do the things we do not want to be doing (Rom. 7:15). It is a daily struggle to overcome our broken selves.

Additionally, we may find it difficult to hear Jesus' point about the image of the tree and its fruit, because the words "good" and "bad" get in our way. For many people, it is too simplistic to say that a

Luke 6:43–49

Theological Perspective

imperatives are to be obeyed unconditionally, Christians will fail and be humiliated in the eyes of the world. If they are unworldly ideals, the Christlike life is compromised, or even emptied of content. The author of the second-century sermon *2 Clement* realized this long ago and wrote: "For when the heathens hear God's oracles on our lips, they marvel at their beauty and greatness. But afterwards, when they mark that our deeds are unworthy of the words we utter, they turn from this to scoffing and say that it is a myth and a delusion" (*2 Clem.* 13.3).

Christian interpreters wrestled with these problems from the beginning. Before Constantine, they generally urged disciples to obey the commands literally and suffer the consequences in emulation of the crucified Christ and other martyrs. Sixteenth-century Anabaptists and later Leo Tolstoy took a similar "Christ against culture" view.

The post-Constantine church typically asked for real implementation of Jesus' teachings but used two main strategies to explain why most disciples failed in the attempt: Jesus meant the sayings either for another time or for other people. The former interpretation is exemplified by modern-day dispensationalists and Albert Schweitzer's interim ethic. Each argues that the hard sayings had full force only in a past age. The second strategy dominated Christian interpretation from Augustine to Luther, when the church tended to teach that the sermon's commands were to be taken literally in every age, but not by everyone. Some sayings were meant only for an elite spiritual minority, such as monks, priests, and nuns. Most Christians could not wholly live in such stark contrast to the world, but could take steps in the right direction. While one may not be able to lend to all who ask, all should give alms to the poor. While everyone should follow the basic "precepts" of the sermon, only a few spiritual elites were under obligation to follow literally the harder sayings, or "counsels."

Luther and the mainline Protestant reformers, who emphasized the equality of all believers, reinstated the view that every directive of the sermon should be attempted by every Christian. In their inevitable failure, believers would be driven inward to realize the grace offered in the Beatitudes. This interiorization of the demands of the sermon finds its extreme in what Harvey K. McArthur calls the "Attitude-not-Acts" approach of modern liberals such as Rudolf Bultmann.[2] The sermon is not a

2. Harvey K. McArthur, *Understanding the Sermon on the Mount* (New York: Harper & Bros., 1960), esp. chaps. 4 and 5.

Pastoral Perspective

contrast these superstars with the youth who whisper now and again or who do not have much to say about discipleship at all. Ministers naturally celebrate the good confirmands. These are the good trees, and as Jesus said, they bear good fruit.

In actuality, Jesus is speaking in much broader terms than whether or not children—or congregants for that matter—show respect and politeness during classes, worship services, and pastoral care calls. He is speaking about the kinds of fruit borne by human actions both in the church and in the larger world. Bad fruit cannot be produced by a good tree, and good fruit never falls from a bad tree. What people do and what they produce reveals what is in their hearts. Jesus' teaching is clearly meant to extend beyond the doors of the church to all corners of the world.

There is, however, a problem in the simple identification of persons or actions with bad fruit or good fruit. That problem is the imperfect and flawed assessment that one person makes of another. We can hear the saying "you can tell a tree by its fruit" and agree with its truth, but we are not expert botanists of the human condition. Luke 6:43–45 is much better understood when it is paired with the pericope that precedes it. We must take the log out of our own eye before we can take the speck out of another's. We must carefully judge our own moral makeup before we can begin to identify the signifiers of the heart that produce good, the heart that produces evil, and the context of the abundance of the heart that is spoken by the mouth.

Verses 46–49 abruptly change the subject from the DNA makeup of the good person and the evil person to good acts versus ambivalent inaction. Here human beings are given complete agency. Whether that freedom to act is comfortable or afflicting is a very important question to ask of individuals and congregations.

The congregant who comfortably acts on the word of Christ is likely a very recognizable presence in the church. She might have a regular pew on Sunday. She might participate in the Bible study. She might be a Stephen minister. She might even go on mission trips where she, quite literally, helps to construct strong foundations upon which houses can be built and rebuilt. Christ called her to praise, and she obeyed. Christ called her to build her faith in community, and she followed. Christ called her to care for her neighbors, and she tended those who were close as well as those who were far off. No rising river, whether it be the passing of a loved one or the critique of nonbeliever, can shake her faith.

Exegetical Perspective

which is the subject of this commentary, addresses the importance of personal integrity. The core of this latter section parallels the concluding section (Matt. 7:16–27) of Matthew's Sermon on the Mount (Matt. 5–7) and is amplified by the incorporation of material found as Matthew 12:33–35. In and of itself, this is unremarkable, as most of the teachings in this chapter of Luke's Gospel are found somewhere in the Gospel of Matthew, though not all are part of either's version of this important sermon.

The section begins with a series of commonsense affirmations (vv. 43–44) that evoke the lyric "So, Plant a carrot, Get a carrot, not a Brussels sprout."[1] Both the kind and the quality of a plant's produce reflect the kind and quality of the parent plant: good fruit from a healthy plant, poor fruit from a sick plant, figs from a fig tree, and grapes from a grape vine—no gambles, and no surprises. (At least that is the assumption, though clearly Jesus or the author of this text never visited my garden!) This is an ethical parallel to the theological affirmation of the author of the Gospel of John, that one's identity is determined by one's source or origin (e.g., John 3:1–15), just as Jesus' nature (as Spirit) and actions reflect his origin "from above." In other words, for good or ill the whole person holds together in the integrity of identity and actions.

The theme of integrity continues in the logic that underlies Luke 6:45. Though Luke does not have a parallel to the teachings on the sources of ritual defilement found in Matthew 15:1–20 and Mark 7:1–23, since for most of his audience Jewish purity laws were not an important concern, Luke addresses an ethnically and religiously more diverse audience with a similar affirmation. That affirmation is the importance of the coherence of a person's values and resulting behavior. That affirmation is shared by many Hellenistic philosophers as well as by other writers of what would become the New Testament. In summary, the values or "treasure" held in a person's heart are expressed in and determine one's behavior.

The final clause of Luke 6:45, "for it is out of the abundance of the heart that the mouth speaks," brings Luke into harmony with the Letter of James on the power of speech (or as James says in 3:2–12, "the tongue"). Indeed, Luke's continuation of the sermon in 6:46 (par. Matt. 7:21) with the affirmation of the need to complete one's verbal confession of

Homiletical Perspective

tree or a person is bad. We all have failings; no one is all good or all bad. New Testament scholar Luke Johnson offers a translation of verse 43 that is more easily grasped: "A sound tree does not produce rotten fruit." A "sound" tree is stable, referring to the ancient conviction that "character precedes action."[1] A sound or solid tree is one that bends with the wind, is flexible, yielding excellent or average fruit, along with fruit that would not win awards for great color or shape. Being "sound" is multifaceted, while being "good" or "bad" suggests a univocal judgment. That a person might be sound like a tree may give us a way to understand Jesus' calling to us to stand on firm ground as we face each day's choices moment by moment. What we do toward ourselves and others comes out of the "treasure of the heart," what Luke calls a "storehouse" (v. 45). Character is formed from what is stored up through our interactions with others. In the end, the point is that a tree—in whatever shape it finds itself—yields fruit commensurate with character and its capacities.

The other teaching concerning the house is considered a parable because in it "a comparison is made between God's kingdom, actions, or expectations and something in this world, real or imagined."[2] Of the two types of parables—narrative and simile—this is a simile. It offers, again, a portrait of someone who not only hears Jesus' words but lives in accordance with them. If you act on what you hear from God's Word, you will build on a foundation that will not fall apart under stress. Your foundation will be embedded in immovable rock.

The preacher may want to explore with the congregation the dimensions of the passage that pertain to life's regular and very difficult challenges. We are all subject to trials in our work and with family, civic responsibilities, environmental choices, health, and private spiritual struggles. The strain and tumult of life is depicted as flood water against which the house—the person (or community) you have become as a result of the values on which you have based your actions—will either stand or fall. Anyone who has been faced with rising waters, whether life threatening or not, knows how hard it is to confront something as unmanageable as water that has breached its banks. You cannot scoop the water up; it keeps coming. Listening to the divine Word as the guide to life, the source of strength, and the measure

---

1. "Plant a Radish" from *The Fantasticks*, Tom Jones with Harvey Schmidt (New York: Applause Theatre Book Publishers, 1990).

1. Luke Timothy Johnson, *The Gospel of Luke* (Collegeville, MN: The Liturgical Press, 1991), 113–14.
2. Arland J. Hultgren, *The Parables of Jesus: A Commentary* (Grand Rapids; Eerdmans, 2000), 3.

Luke 6:43–49

Theological Perspective

map to be followed, but an attitude of free response to God, which can produce other equally valid ways of action.

The two parables under consideration speak directly to the persistent polarities in this history of interpretation that either see Jesus' sayings as a prompt for an internal attitude adjustment or view the sermon as a list of external acts creating Christian identity—Christianity as inward faith or Christianity as outward works.

The first parable (vv. 43–46) demonstrates from nature that good fruit comes only from good trees, and by analogy good works can come only from good people. What comes out of a person, whether word or deed, reveals the heart's nature. An inward conversion to Christ's likeness is essential to being children of God. Being merciful aligns one with God's mercy; being forgiving aligns one with divine forgiveness (6:36–37). Only transformed hearts can live transformed lives. Christian attitude matters.

However, the sermon continues, attitude is not all that matters. Jesus points to the inconsistency of those who believe in the sufficiency of the credo "As long as I am sincere in my desire to serve God . . ." If desire alone is truly sufficient, why do those who pray sincerely, "Lord, Lord," not do as Jesus says (v. 46)? In the second parable (vv. 47–49) Luke draws on an image from building construction to focus on the human initiative that must accompany spiritual conversion. In classic biblical two-ways fashion, this parable contrasts the way of life (those who dig a good foundation on the bedrock of Jesus' words) and the way of death (those who have no such foundation). Matthew's parallel treatment of this parable (Matt. 7:24–27) emphasizes what the house is built upon: rock, not sand. Luke stresses the builder's active initiative: dig a foundation, and dig it deep. There are no two ways about it. The disciples who survive the flood of judgment rising with God's coming kingdom will be those who hear Jesus' words and dig, dig, dig to build a life of action upon them.

The details of such discipleship are debatable, but the mutual involvement of heart and hands is not. The Sermon on the Plain ends with encouragement and challenge, hope and warning, exhortation to dependent faith and human initiative.

WILLIAM LOYD ALLEN

Pastoral Perspective

She is not in the minority in terms of her life of discipleship, but with her complete confidence in those things of God that cannot be shaken, she does stand in the minority of Christian believers. For a majority of churchgoers, especially those who are younger and whose faith is still in a period of gestation, because a solid foundation has yet to be built, their faith is often and easily shaken. Whether due to the devastation caused by a hurricane, an unhealthy church relationship in the past, or even the difficulty of believing in the resurrection, much less in God's ever-present grace, our congregants are not expert contractors, carpenters, or roofers of a faith that can withstand the storm. Sometimes good people can hardly hammer the nail straight: they cannot find their way through a difficult relationship or a particularly vexing challenge to faith.

In the final verses of this text, notice how Christ differentiates between those who act and those who choose not to act. Christ does not differentiate between those who act perfectly and those who act imperfectly, stumbling and making mistakes along the way. All are called to action by the God in whose grace each may be confident. All are called to act on his words by the God who is fully aware of each one's shortcomings and deep need of the church's assurance that, in spite of human failure and sin, Christ loves them still.

In modern sociological terms, Christ's words in this text give credence to both nature and nurture. As for nurture, houses with strong foundations that are set alongside houses lacking foundations underscore how each bears a responsibility to the other as together they seek to live the life of Christian discipleship. As for nature, because Jesus understood the complexity of how people in general and Christians in particular grow, grace abounds.

JONAH K. SMITH-BARTLETT

Exegetical Perspective

"the Lord" by its embodiment in action also echoes James's famous declaration of the need for both faith and works (Jas. 2:14–26).

The integrity of hearing and acting on the teachings of Jesus is emphasized in two ways. The first is by the device of "end stress," namely, its position as the concluding point in the sermon. The second is its amplification in a memorable parable about two builders (vv. 47–49). While the parallel in Matthew 7:24–27 allows for the role of good fortune in happening to build on solid rock instead of on unstable sand, and for the vicissitudes of the weather, Luke's version of the story attributes the good or bad outcome to the care and attentiveness of the builder. Matthew labels the two builders "wise" and "foolish," but Luke simply describes their contrasting actions. One digs down through whatever the topsoil, in order to reach solid rock on which to anchor the house. The other simply uses the material that happens to be on or near the surface. An audience like Luke's, which surely included householders and artisans, would immediately catch on to which builder (and, more importantly, which course of action) they should emulate.

That easily remembered and even more easily grasped story draws to a close Luke's foundational text for the training program Luke presents for those who will have to carry on Jesus' ministry on earth after his crucifixion, resurrection, and ascension to heaven. As this final section of the sermon makes clear, these words will need to take on flesh, first in the example of Jesus' own ministry in their midst, and then as they complete their apprenticeship with him, and finally as they carry that ministry forward in their new times and places, and with new congregations.

SHARON H. RINGE

Homiletical Perspective

for choices, builds our capacity to "keep on keeping on" when we daily face a world that opposes God. Listening to God's Word gives power to stand firm and endure.

Vital to the preaching of this text is the preacher's focus on how God's power is at work even, or especially, when the task seems impossible. Because these images are so focused on what the tree must do and what the home builder is about, it could be easy to miss where and how God is at work in forming stable lives that will produce good fruit. Must we conclude that the good fruit and the solid foundation are ours alone to produce? No, the one who speaks to us is also the one whose Word forms and reforms us. The preacher must, however, ask where God is active in these verses and seek the answer not only in what is explicit but in what is implicit. The preacher may note that the "good treasure of the heart," the "storehouse," is a gift from the one who speaks to us words of promise and challenge.

Finally, the sermon may want to explore the stark proposal that Luke presents here: God enables us to do what Jesus commands of us. Through the Word of God, through listening and internalizing it, we become a people building on a "rock" that will not be destroyed. The house that is foundational for our character as people—who love our enemies, pray for our abusers, and bear good fruit—is built by God's own love for us in Christ Jesus.

MELINDA A. QUIVIK

Luke 7:1–10

¹After Jesus had finished all his sayings in the hearing of the people, he entered Capernaum. ²A centurion there had a slave whom he valued highly, and who was ill and close to death. ³When he heard about Jesus, he sent some Jewish elders to him, asking him to come and heal his slave. ⁴When they came to Jesus, they appealed to him earnestly, saying, "He is worthy of having you do this for him, ⁵for he loves our people, and it is he who built our synagogue for us." ⁶And Jesus went with them, but when he was not far from the house, the centurion sent friends to say to him, "Lord, do not trouble yourself, for I am not worthy to have you come under my roof; ⁷therefore I did not presume to come to you. But only speak the word, and let my servant be healed. ⁸For I also am a man set under authority, with soldiers under me; and I say to one, 'Go,' and he goes, and to another, 'Come,' and he comes, and to my slave, 'Do this,' and the slave does it." ⁹When Jesus heard this he was amazed at him, and turning to the crowd that followed him, he said, "I tell you, not even in Israel have I found such faith." ¹⁰When those who had been sent returned to the house, they found the slave in good health.

Theological Perspective

Key theological themes and interests emerge in Luke 7:1–23. The first focuses on the people who appear in the three passages: the crowds who gather around Jesus, the disciples who accompany Jesus, and those specifically identified, namely, the Roman centurion and his servant, the widow of Nain, and John the Baptizer, along with John's two messengers. Luke's advice to them all, and to us, is to listen, watch, and wait, in faith. A second thematic interest that emerges in this chapter is that of Jesus' identity and purpose. Luke emphasizes Jesus' participation as a healing presence and as the Awaited One/Messiah (with the caveat that the fullness of his mission to deliver the people is not yet at hand). The third theme concerns the nature and character of God. In these texts the evangelist depicts God through the lens of Jesus' unconventional wisdom teachings and his spiritually empowered activities as a healer and renewer of life.

Beginning with the people who encounter Jesus in Luke 7:1–10, the Roman centurion, his slave, the intermediaries between the centurion and Jesus, and the anonymous onlookers all play important roles in the scene. Along with Jesus, the Roman centurion is focal in that he initiates contact with Jesus. That he is a Gentile is notable because it signals a central concern for Luke, namely, his emphasis on

Pastoral Perspective

Our North American culture sits uncomfortably with the notion of *authority.* For decades bumper stickers and social critics have encouraged us to "Question Authority!" As individuals, we pride ourselves on our ability to think critically, to judge for ourselves, to make our own way in the world. We are wary of institutions labeled "authoritarian," for we fear the arbitrary exercise of power. Yet the word "authority" lies at the heart of this passage and begs to be given a new hearing.

As our passage opens, Jesus has just delivered an unsettling sermon to his disciples and the crowds who have come to hear him and to be healed. In that sermon he asserts that the world's hierarchies are not God's hierarchies. He instructs his followers to abandon the calculation of self-interest and live with *mercy* as their guiding principle. Finally, he rounds out his discourse with the challenge: "Why do you call me 'Lord, Lord,' and do not do what I tell you?" (6:46). In the Sermon on the Plain, Jesus stakes a claim for his own authority.

Having concluded that teaching, Jesus enters Capernaum, where he is met by a delegation of local religious leaders. They have come to plead the case of a Roman benefactor, who has heard about Jesus and who desires that Jesus come to heal a slave, who is near death. The elders argue that the Roman

Exegetical Perspective

Following the Sermon on the Plain (6:20–49), which parallels the Sermon on the Mount in Matthew 5–7, Jesus goes to Capernaum. In the sermon, Jesus has spoken of loving one's enemies (6:27–36), being non-judgmental (6:37–42), and doing good (6:43–49), all of which could be applied to the present narrative. This story is also contained in Matthew 8:5–13 and so is part of the double tradition, that is, the so-called Q material that appears in both Matthew and Luke but is absent from Mark. It is also part of the minor interpolation of material (6:20–8:3) that Luke adds to his use of Mark, his other major source. The focus of Luke 7:1–10 is on Jesus' ministry to Gentiles, something to which Luke has alluded and something that has caused Jesus to be vilified earlier in the Gospel (4:25–30).

Mark's Gospel makes clear that Jesus' home during his public ministry is in Capernaum (Mark 2:1), but in Luke it seems to be just another town in Galilee to which Jesus travels. This is not Jesus' first visit. He has previously preached to Jews in the synagogue there and healed a demon-possessed man (4:31–37). Interestingly, mention is made of Jesus' activities in Capernaum in 4:23, but there is no account of his ministry there until 4:31. The story in Luke 7:1–10, however, has to do with a Roman centurion (Gentile)—who serves as a model example of faith in Jesus—and his slave.

Homiletical Perspective

Every culture functions according to a social contract. There are expectations for the powerful and those dependent on them, expectations for insiders and outsiders, expectations for patrons and recipients. Some expectations are implicit, some explicit, but they are real nonetheless. In Luke 6, Jesus sets out the social contract for life together in God's reign. In Luke 7, this reign immediately comes into contact with the norms and values of the Roman Empire.

To connect the modern reader to this text, one might explore examples of our own culture's social contract: the give-and-take of those in power and those who are dependent on that power. Some readers know intimately what it means to rely on others—employers, professionals, politicians, or even personal caregivers. They are keenly aware of what it means when those over them act with integrity, responsibility, and generosity. They also know what it is like when those with power abuse it for their own gain. Medical, legal, and clergy malpractice; political graft and corruption; corporate fixation on short-term profit at any price; abuse and neglect by guardians: these are all-too-familiar stories.

Other readers will approach this story from the perspective of a position of authority. Parents and teachers, nurses and lawyers, police officers and politicians, business owners and bankers all know what

Luke 7:1–10

Theological Perspective

Jesus' significance for "the other." Although it is not completely clear that the centurion is a "God-fearer" (meaning a Gentile who respects and even practices the Jewish faith), Luke indicates that he is cognizant of Jesus' healing power and sends his delegates in the hope that Jesus can heal his servant.

It is not too much to think here about all those who, in our day and time, choose to check "none" in surveys about religious affiliation and who stand outside of Christian tradition as people who are not "of us." In recent years these "others" have come to represent an increasing percentage of the population. These modern-day Gentiles—often derided as unbelievers, agnostics, atheists, secularists, and sometimes apostates—are precisely the audience insiders need to engage, as Jesus does the centurion's delegates. Although separate from the institutional church, many of today's religiously unaffiliated are "seekers" who are open to spiritual truth that enlightens and heals.

The nameless servant is the quintessential "Nobody." He plays no active role in this story, except that he is the object of the centurion's, and eventually Jesus', concern. His name is unknown; he represents the "huddled masses" who long for health and healing. He represents those who hopelessly hope for help. The centurion, like the Samaritan of Luke 10:25–37, reaches out on the servant's behalf and seeks aid for him. Jesus is the hope in this crisis of illness, the one to whom literally anyone, even the gravely ill, can turn in time of need—whoever they are and wherever they are. Additionally, both the gathering crowd who witness Jesus' response to the delegation, and the delegates themselves, represent other nameless persons who are privy to this healing drama. Although we know nothing of their responses, we do know that the healing power of God can be a vibrant testimony of God's love and care for those whose eyes are open and whose hearts are receptive.

A second theological interest that emerges in this text centers on Luke's portrait of Jesus. Here and in the next passage (7:11–17), Luke sets the stage for the interview about Jesus' identity that the two inquirers sent by John initiate with Jesus (7:18–23). In the present passage Luke discloses key characteristics of Jesus the Messiah. First, Jesus is approachable. The delegation sent by the centurion is received by Jesus in the spirit of hospitality, congeniality, and openness. Luke's Jesus makes no distinctions among those whom he encounters. Second, Jesus listens. He receives the delegates and ponders their request.

Pastoral Perspective

centurion deserves Jesus' attention because of his demonstrated support of the local community. Jesus does not reply but does accompany the leaders as they set out for the centurion's house. The reader does not know whether Jesus has been persuaded by the elders' argument or is simply practicing the mercy he has preached.

Before they reach the house, though, Jesus is met by a second delegation. This commission, made up of the centurion's friends, does not attempt its own argument. These companions have not composed a rationale to persuade Jesus. Rather, they have been entrusted with the centurion's own words, which they now report in the first person. They re-present their friend to Jesus.

In contrast to the elders' presentation, the centurion's words make no claim of personal merit. The centurion does not locate his request in any matrix of social obligation. He does not profess to be worthy of Jesus' care. The centurion leans, instead, on a profound confidence in the power and the mercy at work in Jesus. The centurion does not need for Jesus to come to him. He does not need to touch, or to see, or even to hear Jesus. He needs only for Jesus to choose; he needs only for Jesus to say the word—even from a distance.

The centurion seems able to trust in the efficacy of Jesus' decision because as an officer the centurion knows what it means to be part of something larger than himself. He knows what it means to take direction and to offer direction, to be charged with responsibility and to commission others. He explains that he too is a person "set under authority."

We may bristle at the analogy. In similar fashion Luke's listeners may have recoiled at the thought that an occupying army's chain of command might serve as an analogy for God's way of working in the world. Yet Jesus equates the centurion's confidence with exemplary faith, faith the likes of which he has not found in Israel. In telling the story this way, perhaps Luke is reminding his readers that nothing in their experience is beyond God's redemption or God's holy use.

In the end, the centurion trusts in the power and the healing love enfleshed in Jesus, and perhaps that is the key to our reclamation of the word *authority*. To assert Jesus' authority is not to suggest a coercive power. Rather, to trust in Jesus' *authority* is to affirm his intimate connection to the *Author*, the originator, of all life. When the centurion entreats Jesus, "Only speak the word, and let my servant be healed" (v. 7), he affirms Jesus' connection to the one who

Exegetical Perspective

The slave is gravely ill, and the centurion is concerned because the slave is quite valuable (*entimos*, v. 2). The centurion's anxiety seems to be a matter of protecting his property more than personal attachment to the slave. That is to say, he is worried about the financial loss or loss of work output that he might incur if the slave dies. In Matthew it is not certain whether it is a slave or the centurion's child (*pais*, Matt. 8:6, 8, 13) about whom the centurion is troubled, and the slave/child is not about to die, but is suffering great pain from some kind of paralysis.

In Luke's narrative, two groups intervene with Jesus on behalf of the centurion. The Matthean account has no such intervention. There the centurion approaches Jesus himself (Matt. 8:5–6). First, having heard about Jesus' healing ability, the centurion in Luke sends a delegation of Jewish elders with his request that Jesus come to his house and cure his slave. The elders are from the synagogue that the centurion built (v. 5). Later the reader discovers that the centurion sends emissaries because he feels unfit to speak with Jesus directly (v. 7). In other words, it is out of humility, not a sense of self-importance, that he sends others in his stead.[1] The elders in Luke's account are only too happy to champion the centurion's cause, because he has shown great affection for the Jewish nation, not least by building a synagogue for them. The centurion may or may not be a God-fearer, but is certainly a benefactor of the Jewish community. In contrast to the centurion's view of his worthiness, the Jewish community thinks he is eminently deserving of Jesus' help. After hearing the Jewish elders' plea for the centurion, Jesus agrees to go with them to his home.

As they approach, the centurion sends a second delegation, consisting of friends, to meet them. As Luke Johnson has pointed out, in Hellenistic society, "friends" could be "political allies or associates . . . or the patrons of a powerful benefactor."[2] Even though the centurion has asked through the Jewish elders for Jesus to come, his friends pass along a different message, namely, that Jesus should not enter his house because of his (the centurion's) unworthiness. He asks Jesus simply to say the word and let his slave be healed. As is customary for commanders, the petition is grammatically imperative. One might say, therefore, that the centurion commands Jesus to refrain from coming into the house and to heal the slave sight unseen. In a reversal of perspectives, Jesus

1. Luke Timothy Johnson, *The Gospel of Luke*, Sacra pagina 3 (Collegeville, MN: Liturgical Press, 1991), 118.
2. Johnson, *Luke*, 118.

Homiletical Perspective

it means to carry responsibility for others. They bear the weight of others' dependence on them: children in their care, clients who require their expertise, citizens who rely on their fairness, employees and investors who depend on their business decisions.

The story of the centurion appealing to Jesus reveals the social contract of that day. This centurion (like Cornelius in Acts 10) enjoys a position of political tenure, military stature, social achievement, and financial security. With so much clout, this man is in a prime position to abuse his privilege—which, as historians note, happened often. According to Richard Horsley, the Roman occupiers "terrorized people into submission . . . through the ruthless devastation of the land and towns, slaughter and enslavement of the people," and "crucifixion of people along the roadways or in public places."[1]

Yet not all occupiers were brutal. This centurion is extolled by the Jewish elders as one who is "worthy," as "one who loves our people," and who "built our synagogue for us" (v. 4). Perhaps he is even a God-fearer. As a broker of the patronage of the emperor, he has acted with integrity, using his power for the benefit of his clients. He is an ethical, admirable, and faithful administrator of his authority. That a Gentile—an outsider, and especially one who has the means to abuse his power—should conduct himself in such an uprightly manner is a lesson to all of us who strive to be moral in our daily navigation of our own social norms.

Remarkably, this centurion goes much further than ethically fulfilling the social contract of his day. *He fulfills the higher standards of the social contract of the kingdom of God*—a social contract laid out in the Sermon on the Plain just prior to this passage. These standards, notes David Gowler, "include loving your enemies, doing good to those who hate you, blessing those who curse you, and praying for those who abuse you (Luke 6:27–28). They include turning the other cheek, giving to everyone who begs from you, and being merciful just as God is merciful (Luke 6:29–30, 36). They include not only calling Jesus 'Lord, Lord,' but also doing what he taught (Luke 6:46)."[2]

Later in Luke, the contrast between the empire's social contract and that of the kingdom of God is laid out even more plainly: "The kings of the Gentiles lord it over them; and those in authority over

1. Richard Horsley, *Galilee: History, Politics, People* (Valley Forge, PA: Trinity Press, 1995), 116.
2. David B. Gowler, "Text, Culture, and Ideology in Luke 7:1–10: A Dialogic Reading," in Vernon K. Robbins et al., *Fabrics of Discourse* (Harrisburg, PA: Trinity Press Int., 2004).

Luke 7:1–10

Theological Perspective

Listening to the needs of the people—all people—is a touchstone of messianic ministry. The proclamation of the good news comes in response to the particular request of the centurion. Human need is met by caring love and healing. Third, Jesus responds to the needs of others with understanding and hope, for here he announces that the servant is already recovering. Fourth, the remarkable healing power of Jesus surprisingly transcends the physical distance between the healer and the ill servant.

This fourth factor invites theological reflection on the efficacy of intercessory prayer. The power of healing is unhindered by space or time. How many have experienced the sort of comfort and hope in time of need derived from knowing that people of faith were praying for them around the globe! I remember a Pentecostal couple in northern Georgia who fasted and prayed for my own healing. An agnostic lawyer in North Carolina "thought kind words" on my behalf during a life-threatening bout with lymphoma. The power of healing prayer transcends distance.

Luke 7:1–10 also illumines the nature and character of God. It foreshadows one of Luke's seminal concerns: the universal concern of God for all people. It also depicts a caring Jesus who, as a healer, makes whole the sick and the bereaved, in order to reveal the character of the Messiah and the restoration and renewal of all things in the messianic age. Those who have witnessed and received the caring Jesus now wait with hopeful patience for the fullness and coming power of the kingdom of God.

The healing of the centurion's servant illustrates precisely what David Bartlett observed about Luke: "For Luke, the point clearly is not simply to present informational truth but to present theological truth, saving truth, the truth about the way God acts in history."[1] The healing of the servant points to the fact that God continues to act in human history.

DONALD W. MUSSER

Pastoral Perspective

speaks all creation into being. Likewise, later in Luke when Jesus shares his authority with his followers, he invites us, by extension, into the intimacy he shares with the one he calls *Abba*.

Three concluding observations:

1. I have had heartbreaking conversations with active church members nearing the end of their lives, who have suffered mightily from a sense of "unworthiness." This passage implores us to give up our need to be accounted "worthy." God's mercy extends to the whole of creation—we do not have to earn it—and our need to be considered "worthy" can get in the way of our trusting God and the community of faith with the real story of our lives. To live into the promise of God's mercy is to discover the capacity to extend mercy to others. To live into the promise of God's mercy is to discover joy.

2. The centurion is a Gentile. He stands outside the acknowledged community of faith in his day. We all know persons who are estranged from or do not feel welcomed by our own communities of faith. The role played by the centurion's friends in this passage invites us to imagine ways in which we might be called to give voice to the longings and perspectives of those who stand outside our communities, but also long to know God's mercy and healing.

3. Affirming that we belong to the body of Christ implies that we too are persons "set under authority" (v. 8). In what ways is our life in community fueled by the mercy of God, and in what ways are we still guided by calculations of self-interest? How are we making room for the next generation to assume this authority?

MARGARET LAMOTTE TORRENCE

---

1. David Bartlett, *Fact and Faith* (Valley Forge, PA: Judson Press, 1975), 53.

Exegetical Perspective

has shown himself willing to enter the house of a Gentile, while the centurion has demonstrated sensitivity to Jesus' position as a religious Jew who might consider a Gentile home to be unclean.

Following this is a curious passage about the centurion's military chain of command. On the one hand, he is subordinate to higher authority; on the other hand, he commands those below him. He compares his own position to that of Jesus ("I also am a man set under authority, with soldiers under me," v. 8). The passage does not make clear under whose authority Jesus is (God's?) or who is subject to him (disease?). Joseph Fitzmyer has argued that the centurion's statement is "meant to enhance the power of Jesus' command"—Jesus prescribes and his orders are obeyed.[3] In any case, Jesus admires the centurion for what he has said, especially the acknowledgment that Jesus could heal his slave without entering the centurion's home. Jesus tells the third group in the narrative, the crowd that has followed him to the centurion's home, that this Gentile has demonstrated more faith in him than any of his Jewish coreligionists.

The story ends with the centurion's friends returning to his house to find the slave in good health, even though it is not reported in the narrative that Jesus has uttered any word of healing. The Jewish elders have interceded and convinced Jesus that the centurion is fit to receive his assistance, but the fact that the centurion has sent them in the first place and his trust that Jesus need not enter his home to cure his slave emphasize the centurion's faith as the main factor in the healing.

WILLIAM SANGER CAMPBELL

Homiletical Perspective

them are called benefactors. But not so with you; rather the greatest among you must become like the youngest, and the leader like one who serves" (22:25–26).

This is precisely how the centurion behaves. He uses his power not for his own benefit, but to intercede on behalf of his slave (v. 2). He humbles himself, asking first for his clients, the Jewish elders, to intervene for him (vv. 3–4), then sending his friends to intercede (v. 6). He, who has all of the authority and power of the empire behind him, does not consider himself worthy to bring Jesus into his house, recognizing that a righteous Jew would be defiled entering the house of a Gentile (vv. 6–7). Finally, he recognizes that the power Jesus wields in his "kingdom" far outweighs the power of the empire's reach. The centurion calls Jesus "Lord" (v. 6), and—from his own experience of authority—recognizes the unconstrained power Jesus enjoys (v. 8).

Gowler writes,

> It is through his humbling of himself as "not worthy" and the characterization of himself as—even as a centurion who is an agent of imperial power—inferior to Jesus, that the centurion reaches a state of honor far beyond what the Jewish elders had described. Jesus is "amazed" and praises the centurion: ". . . not even in Israel have I found such faith." The real "miracle," then, is not the physical healing of the centurion's *doulos/pais*; it instead is the faith of this centurion.[3]

The challenge for us today is not only to behave justly according to our social contract, whatever our position of power or powerlessness, authority or dependence. Jesus invites us instead to recognize the limitations of our social contract and to reach to a higher order of life, the higher order that Jesus embodies: "Let the same mind be in you that was in Christ Jesus, who, though he was in the form of God, did not regard equality with God as something to be exploited, but emptied himself, taking the form of a slave, being born in human likeness. And being found in human form, he emptied himself, and became obedient to the point of death—even death on a cross" (Phil. 2:5–8).

CHRISTINE CHAKOIAN

---

3. Joseph A. Fitzmyer, *The Gospel according to Luke I–IX*, Anchor Bible 28 (Garden City, NY: Doubleday, 1981), 653.

3. Gowler, "Text, Culture, and Ideology."

Luke 7:11–17

¹¹Soon afterwards he went to a town called Nain, and his disciples and a large crowd went with him. ¹²As he approached the gate of the town, a man who had died was being carried out. He was his mother's only son, and she was a widow; and with her was a large crowd from the town. ¹³When the Lord saw her, he had compassion for her and said to her, "Do not weep." ¹⁴Then he came forward and touched the bier, and the bearers stood still. And he said, "Young man, I say to you, rise!" ¹⁵The dead man sat up and began to speak, and Jesus gave him to his mother. ¹⁶Fear seized all of them; and they glorified God, saying, "A great prophet has risen among us!" and "God has looked favorably on his people!" ¹⁷This word about him spread throughout Judea and all the surrounding country.

Theological Perspective

This passage continues to expound upon central Lukan themes. The previous text (7:1–10) saw Jesus respond to the deathly illness of the centurion's slave and restore him to health. In this text, Luke broadens the picture of Jesus as a miracle worker by portraying him not only as a healer of the sick but as one who resuscitates the dead. The recipient of renewed health (the centurion's servant) and the recipient of a new life (the widow's son) are totally dependent on the compassionate concern of Jesus, who is God's agent of life-restoring power. As Jesus responds to the needs of both an ill Gentile and a poor grieving widow and mother suffering the loss of both her husband and son, these stories concretize Jesus' ministry to the sick, the outsider, and the hopeless.

The story of resuscitation that Luke recounts in Luke 7:1–10 focuses on Jesus as a worker of miracles. Here, Luke's reference to Jesus as Lord (*kyrios*, v. 13*)* goes a step further and underscores the extraordinary power that Jesus possesses in his person. It is this power that enables him to do the seemingly impossible, that is, to bring the widow's dead son back to life. However, the Lukan Jesus is not only powerful; he is also the exemplar of compassion, who acts on behalf of the most downtrodden. In this scene, it is the twice-grieved widow to whom Jesus ministers.

Pastoral Perspective

A few months ago, I officiated at a funeral on a Saturday morning and a wedding on the same Saturday afternoon. The wedding had been on my calendar for a long time; it was scheduled to take place at the bride's home. The death that precipitated the funeral, on the other hand, was unexpected. I had been in the deceased man's home just the day before he died; we had laughed together over a football game.

When that long Saturday finally was over, I remember thinking that if the bride had planned to be married in the sanctuary instead of at home, the paths of those two congregations would have crossed. One crowd, dressed in wedding finery, full of joy and anticipation, would have met another crowd weighed down by grief, mired in loss. I wondered how those two groups would have experienced each other's presence. How might they have understood differently the central event of their own day, if they had been forced to encounter the other's experience?

In the passage at hand, which is closely tied to the one that precedes it, Jesus travels from the relatively large and prosperous city of Capernaum, to the small village of Nain. Capernaum has been the setting for dramatic confrontations, revolutionary new teachings, and amazing acts of healing. There a capacity crowd has pressed in to hear Jesus' words and to

Exegetical Perspective

Luke 7:11–17 is unique to Luke's Gospel. As was the case in Luke 7:1–10, this story is located in the minor interpolation (6:20–8:3) that interrupts Luke's use of the Gospel of Mark. This section of the Gospel combines material that is exclusive to Luke with material that Luke shares with Matthew (the Q material). Jesus travels to Nain immediately (my trans.; *egeneto en tō exēs*, lit. "it happened in the next [time]") after healing the gravely ill slave of the centurion in Capernaum (v. 11). Nain was located in southern Galilee approximately twenty-five miles south of Capernaum, that is, about a day's journey away. A large crowd travels with Jesus, presumably those who followed him to Capernaum (7:9), as well as a number of his disciples.

As he approaches the city gate, Jesus and his entourage come upon a funeral procession leaving the city. This would not be unusual, because burials during this period were mostly in caves (interment) or trench graves (burial) located outside the city. The preparation of the deceased person for burial involved washing the body, anointing it, and wrapping it in linen or other fabric. The use of coffins was uncommon; normally the corpse was carried to the gravesite on a litter or bier (*soros*, v. 14), as is the case in this passage. The deceased man would not have been dead long. As a rule, burial occurred

Homiletical Perspective

The story of the raising of the widow's son is unique to Luke, yet it evokes other stories from Scripture. For the modern Christian reader, the raising of Lazarus in the Gospel of John often comes to mind. However, for the earliest followers of Jesus, a different memory is stirred: the story from 1 Kings 17:10–24, when the prophet Elijah raises the son of the widow of Zarephath in Syria. Jesus has already brought this story to memory in his inaugural sermon at his home synagogue (4:26). God's mercy to the outsider has just been reinforced in the healing story of the centurion's slave (7:1–10); now God's mercy to the poor will be reinforced in this resurrection story.

The parallels between the two resurrection stories are many. In both, the encounter occurs at the gate of the city—the place at which the elders gather to adjudicate justice. In both, the woman is widowed, and the son appears to be her only male relative, and therefore her only source of economic security. In 1 Kings 17 the family is overtly portrayed as impoverished; in Luke 7, the economic dependence of the woman on her only male relative in presumed. In both cases, the man of God is moved by the plight unfolding in front of him. Elijah cries out to the Lord in protest of the calamity brought on the widow (1 Kgs. 17:20–21); Jesus is deeply moved

Luke 7:11–17

Theological Perspective

Enduring the death of her husband, she has lost any economic security she might have attained through her marriage. Now, with the death of the son, upon whom the widow was likely dependent for her material needs, she has lost everything. Tears are streaming down her face as Jesus, along with his disciples and other followers, engages the funeral proceedings. Imbued with spiritual power and heartfelt empathy for the widow, Jesus acts on her behalf. He speaks to the widow as a prelude to his impending and seemingly impossible evocation to her dead son, and he quiets the crowd with words akin to what we hope to convey when we say to someone, "Do not cry" (v. 13). Then, with the mourners in rapt attention, he addresses the corpse and pronounces with authority: "Young man, I say to you, rise!" (v. 14).

As impossible as it seems, the widow's son rises to life at Jesus' command. Jesus then presents him to his mother, lifting her from grieving tears and incipient poverty. In a double sense, both the mother and son are restored to life. The mourners stand as awed observers, probably in unbelief at what they have witnessed. A holy fear grips them. A strange but wonderful miracle has happened before their very eyes, and it has shaken the foundations of a world in which the dead do not rise. Overwhelmed, they recognize that in Jesus they are in the presence of a contemporary prophet who mirrors the characteristics of Elijah, on whom much messianic theology focused. In this set of healings, a new age, a renewed understanding of divinity, and a proclamation of a new way of living are unveiled. Luke views Jesus as the prophet of this new world.

The passage yields theological themes that are relevant to the faith community, particularly to congregational life and ministry. The first is the power of divine compassion to bring healing, restoration, and renewal to those who languish in suffering and utter hopelessness. Jesus exemplifies this kind of compassion, and his actions make clear that real human suffering is the object of God's concern. Just as Luke so vividly illustrates and emphasizes the inspiring results of God's compassionate intervention among the bereaved, the broken, and the belabored, so does the narrator enable us to see that reaching and empowering those who suffer must be on the agenda of congregational ministry. Divine concern for human suffering should manifest itself in faith-filled human action and intervention.

The church, therefore, is called to make known in real ways God's compassion for all people. Congregations may be led to consider more closely how

Pastoral Perspective

experience his power. Luke tells us that when Jesus and the disciples eventually leave Capernaum, a large crowd follows them out. One might imagine that this crowd is excited, curious to see what will happen next, yet probably not expecting much from its passage through Nain.

As they approach the village, Jesus and his followers are met by another crowd in a very different mood. The disciples may have heard this second crowd before seeing them, keening as they made their way toward the community's burial grounds. The corpse they carry is that of a young man. The crowd supports a solitary woman, his mother, whose grief is unrestrained.

How easy it would be for Jesus simply to stand aside, to make room for the grief-stricken procession to pass. Instead, when Jesus sees the woman, he has "compassion for her" (v. 13). Luke suggests that Jesus feels the woman's pain in his gut. His response to her is visceral.

As a woman now without husband or son, this grieving widow *is* the *poor*, the *hungry*, the *weeping*, and *excluded* that Jesus has just described in the Sermon on the Plain (6:17–49). With no male relative to secure her place in a patriarchal culture, she is lost. Jesus has just assured his listeners that such persons are *blessed*. What can that mean? As he lifts his hand to stop the funeral procession, Jesus illustrates his sermon. We watch the Beatitudes come to life as Jesus tells the woman to weep no more.

Without hesitation, Jesus reaches for the dead man's litter. He makes himself ritually unclean by handling the stuff of death. He willingly forfeits his ritual status out of compassion for another.

When Jesus speaks to the dead man, though—commanding him to rise—he goes beyond any miraculous healing that the crowd observed in Capernaum. They have seen healing before, but they have never watched as life is restored to a corpse. When the young man sits up and begins to speak, the two crowds unify in a response of fear. They, and we, must wrestle with who this Jesus is.

Luke reports that the crowd glorifies God, saying, "A great prophet has risen among us!" (v. 16). For the first time in Luke's Gospel, Jesus is labeled a prophet. It is an appropriate designation, because details of this story parallel an ancient story of the prophet Elijah restoring the life of a woman's dead son (1 Kgs. 17:17–24), but the parallels are not exact. While Elijah pleads for God to act on the dead boy's behalf, Jesus speaks directly to the young man who has died. Jesus' authority includes the capacity to

within twenty-four hours after death, both because the warm climate would accelerate decomposition and in order to avoid as much as possible ritual defilement.

The deceased man is also the only son of a widow.[1] The implication is that he is her only child. The widow likely was supported by her son, and his death puts her in a difficult position financially. A widow in Israel was not provided for out of her deceased husband's estate. Inheritance went first to sons, then daughters, then others on the husband's side of the family. Since this was the family's only son, the entire estate would have passed to him. In this case, the considerable crowd of mourners (including some perhaps hired) who accompany her to the gravesite suggests that the family is prominent in the community and likely has financial means.

Luke includes two additional stories in which Jesus heals an only child. One is the narrative about Jairus, the ruler of the synagogue, who pleads with Jesus to come to his house and cure his only daughter from a grave ailment (8:40–56; par. Matt. 9:18–26; Mark 5:21–43). There is also a crowd with Jesus then and much weeping (klaiō, 8:52). Weeping connects this account to other parts of the Gospel, for example, the beatitude "blessed are you who weep" (6:21), the woman who washes Jesus' feet with tears (7:38), Peter weeping after denying Jesus (22:62), and the women Jesus meets on the way to his crucifixion (23:27–31). Unlike the story of the centurion's slave in 7:1–10, Jesus does enter Jairus's house to resuscitate the child. Another narrative about the healing of an only child is the story of the possessed boy (9:37–43; par. Matt. 17:14–20; Mark 9:14–29). Responding to the father's appeal, and again witnessed by a large crowd, Jesus exorcises the demon and returns the boy to his father, just as he returns the son to his mother in verse 15.[2]

Jesus is moved with compassion (splanchnizomai, v. 13) for the widow. Luke uses this word in two other passages, the parables of the Good Samaritan (10:33) and the Prodigal Son (15:20). Both passages are found only in Luke. In addition, both also describe merciful acts on the part of the story's protagonist. The Samaritan renders aid to the man who has been robbed and left for dead on the side of the

with compassion (splanchnizomai, v. 13). In both cases, when the son is raised, the first sign of life is the sound he makes (v. 15; 1 Kgs. 17:22 LXX).[1] In both cases, the same words are used to describe the actions of Jesus and Elijah returning the son into the widow's care: "He gave him to his mother" (v. 15; 1 Kgs. 17:23).

Finally, both close with similar proclamations confirming the identity of the healer as God's prophet. At the end of the story in 1 Kings 17, the widow announces, "Now I know that you are a man of God, and that the word of the LORD in your mouth is truth" (1 Kgs. 17:24). At the end of the scene in Luke, the crowd proclaims, "A great prophet has risen among us!" and "God has looked favorably on his people!" (v. 16). In the Gospel, when messengers from John the Baptist come to question whether Jesus is "the one to come," Jesus is able not only to point to healing the sick and bringing sight to the blind, but also to say that "the dead are raised" and "the poor have good news brought to them" (7:22).

For the modern reader as for the early Christian, these are not merely accidental parallels. They are harbingers of good news, and each could be the focus of a sermon.

First, just as God once visited the people in the time of the corrupt King Ahab, God visited the people again in the era of Greco-Roman corruption. This same God continues to visit us through the ongoing presence of the Spirit (see Acts 2ff.). God will not leave us alone, but will come to us again and again with power—especially when the powers and principalities of the world are most perverted.

Second, just as Elijah comes to help the Syrian widow at Zarephath, in spite of her being foreign and poor, so Jesus comes both to heal the outsider Greek centurion's slave (7:1–10), and to raise the son of the poor widow at Nain. God will continue to stand at the gate of justice, remembering those whom the world has forgotten, rejected, or rendered invisible in their wretched physical need.

Third, just as Elijah pleads with God on behalf of the widow of Zarephath in her calamity, Jesus does not remain unmoved, but reacts to the grief of the widow of Nain with deep compassion. God will not stand aloof, disregarding the abject sorrow and broken hearts of the people.

Yet for those of us who hear this good news in our time, there is still more at stake than receiving God's mercy and another sermon to be preached.

---

1. The structure and language of this passage echo Elijah's raising of the widow of Zarephath's son (1 Kgs. 17:17–24; see Luke 4:25–26; Luke Timothy Johnson, *The Gospel of Luke*, Sacra pagina 3 (Collegeville, MN: Liturgical Press, 1991), 118, 120; Joseph A. Fitzmyer, *The Gospel according to Luke I–IX*, Anchor Bible 28 (Garden City, NY: Doubleday, 1981), 656.

2. The phrase is identical to that in the Elijah resuscitation story (1 Kgs. 17:23); Johnson, *Luke*, 119.

1. Robert C. Tannehill, *Luke* (Nashville: Abingdon Press, 1996), 127.

Luke 7:11–17

Theological Perspective

to become increasingly proactive agents of compassion, healing, and renewal. Just as Luke recounts the stories of those whose lives were changed by Jesus, sharing the stories of those whose lives have been touched by God, especially in the local congregation and community, can be a profound source of inspiration and motivation to the followers of Jesus.

Second, despite skeptics in the past and in our own time, Luke challenges us to be open to possibilities that seem extremely unlikely. Luke's Jesus causes us to rethink the everyday assumptions, expectations, and approaches that we often bring to Christian ministry, and to embrace larger possibilities and perspectives. In this same vein, Marcus Borg cautions us not to see Jesus as a sage of conventional wisdom but, rather, to view Jesus as a purveyor of a subversive and alternative wisdom. Cultural wisdom often stems from secular assumptions that run counter to the gospel's focus and intent. Jesus' activity inspires his followers to look beyond business as usual to see and seek the ways of God which transform reality.[1]

Finally, we must not lose sight of how Luke locates this story in the context of Jesus' identity as Messiah. Already it is clear from the stories of the centurion and the widow that a Spirit-infused congregation of followers of the messianic Jesus ought to become compassionate agents of hope and healing to the broken and belabored. The way of Jesus is unconventional, and often is counter to cultural norms and conventional wisdom. God acts in ways that are beyond our understanding and our expectations and contrary to a typical modern notion of God's absence in time as voiced by Borg: "We . . . tend to image reality as ultimately indifferent. . . . Reality is a vast 'cosmic soup' . . . [that] is indifferent to human purposes and hopes."[2] By contrast, Jesus' unconventional wisdom reveals a world where God is actively present in astonishing power and love. Luke bids us enter into that world, the realm of God that Jesus preaches, teaches, and embodies throughout the Gospel narrative.

DONALD W. MUSSER

Pastoral Perspective

speak words of life, to make the dead rise. Jesus is a prophet, and Jesus is more than a prophet.

I began this essay by describing a particular Saturday on which I officiated at one friend's marriage and another friend's funeral. News of that death came late one evening during the preceding week. After taking the call, I grabbed my car keys and headed to my friend's house. As I arrived, the EMTs were closing the doors to the ambulance and preparing to drive away. I assumed that I had missed my opportunity to hold my friend's hand one last time; I assumed that his body lay in the back of their vehicle. When I entered the house, I discovered family members and neighbors gathered in the living room. It was a few minutes before I realized that my friend's body, still warm, lay on the floor of his bedroom, a few feet away. The ambulance had left empty, after failing to revive my friend. So we all moved to be with him: family and friends, neighbors, a health-care worker and her dog. We sat on the bed, we knelt on the floor; in jeans and pajamas, perfectly dressed, we formed an unlikely congregation as we anointed his body with oil and our tears, and gave him back to God.

I expect to carry that image with me for a long time. For me, that motley assembly is a picture of the body of Christ, still reaching out in compassion, even in the face of death. It moved me to learn that different incarnations of that little group had assembled in that house many times over the years. A few years before my friend died, his wife had succumbed to cancer, so the EMTs were quite familiar with the address. Although I had never been to the house at night, this little crowd of neighbors and friends had been gathering there in the darkness for years, every time an alarm sounded. They looked like Jesus to me, always moving toward the pain, toward the death, bringing life.

MARGARET LAMOTTE TORRENCE

---

1. This rich distinction is found in Marcus Borg, *Meeting Jesus Again for the First Time* (New York: HarperCollins, 1995), 69–95.
2. Borg, *Meeting Jesus*, 168.

Exegetical Perspective

road, and the father forgives his wayward son before the son even arrives home to ask for forgiveness. Luke refers to Jesus as "Lord" (*kyrios*, v. 13) here. In Luke's Gospel, this title is used for both Jesus and God. When the narrative calls Jesus Lord, therefore, it has christological overtones, connecting Jesus to God and Jesus' power to God's.

When Jesus comes forward and lays his hand on the bier, which renders him ritually impure, the pallbearers stop. Jesus calls out, "Young man, I say to you, rise!" (v. 14). The term for young man (*neaniskos*) refers to someone between the ages of twenty-four and forty. Thus the dead man is about the same age as Jesus at his execution. Luke uses the word for "arise" (*egeirō*) a number of times in a variety of ways, including healing stories; for example, he tells the paralytic man to "rise [*egeirō*], pick up [*egeirō*] your stretcher, and go home" (5:23–24). It is also the term used of the raising of Jairus's daughter (8:54) and, not surprisingly, Jesus' own resurrection (24:6, 34).

The young man sits up and speaks, and *phobos*—which here means awe and reverence—seizes all those present. Quite a large contingent of Jews witnesses Jesus' raising of the widow's son, and they all glorify God for lifting up (NRSV "has risen," *egeirō* again) a great prophet and for aiding (NRSV "looked favorably on," *episkeptomai*, v. 16) God's people, assistance that is prophesied in Zechariah's prayer (1:68, 78). Jesus calls himself "prophet" (4:24; 13:33). Others refer to him this way as well (9:19; 24:19). Jesus is able to perform powerful deeds as did the prophets of old, Elijah and Elisha, and like them he is willing to minister to Gentiles (7:1–10) and women, groups that might be considered outcasts (see 4:16–21; 7:18–23).[3]

The passage ends with the notation that the report of this episode goes out to all of Judea and the surrounding countryside. This repeats a pattern in Luke (4:14; 4:37; 5:15; also 3:3). The Gospel leaves no doubt that Jesus' fame is spreading throughout the areas in and around the regions of his public ministry.

WILLIAM SANGER CAMPBELL

Homiletical Perspective

If we are to follow in the way of Jesus, then we will *participate in the continuation of that mercy to others.* This is what Jesus tells us, his disciples, to do: not just to love God, but to "be merciful, just as your Father is merciful" (6:36). It is not enough to call him "Lord, Lord"; we are also to act on the words he tells us (6:46–47).

What does it mean to be faithful to Jesus' word in this story? It means doing what Jesus did, in his name and by his power.

It means striding into the halls of power, especially where power has been corrupted—in the backroom deals of political alliances, in the whispered secrets of insider trading, in places of greed and favors, nepotism, and professional abuses. It means having our own eyes open in places where justice should be accomplished—in the modern equivalents to the city gate, like the courtrooms and police stations and legislatures, where the poor are vulnerable to overloaded systems and inadequate resources. It means having our hearts moved with compassion in scenes where poverty and grief prevail—in the wake of private tragedy or natural disaster, in the silent ache of those left behind by addiction or destitution, in the invisible isolation of aging or mental illness or job loss.

We may not be able to raise the dead in Jesus' name and return them to their mothers' arms. However, to the extent that we can have compassion on the brokenhearted, seek justice for the vulnerable, and stand up to the powers and principalities, we will have begun to fulfill the prophet's will for our lives. Blessed are we who are called to follow in his footsteps.

CHRISTINE CHAKOIAN

---

3. Johnson, *Luke*, 120.

Luke 7:18–23

¹⁸The disciples of John reported all these things to him. So John summoned two of his disciples ¹⁹and sent them to the Lord to ask, "Are you the one who is to come, or are we to wait for another?" ²⁰When the men had come to him, they said, "John the Baptist has sent us to you to ask, 'Are you the one who is to come, or are we to wait for another?'" ²¹Jesus had just then cured many people of diseases, plagues, and evil spirits, and had given sight to many who were blind. ²²And he answered them, "Go and tell John what you have seen and heard: the blind receive their sight, the lame walk, the lepers are cleansed, the deaf hear, the dead are raised, the poor have good news brought to them. ²³And blessed is anyone who takes no offense at me."

Theological Perspective

Asking questions is a formative aspect of faith. Some of the fondest memories of parents are the questions their children asked. Cemeteries evoked questions about death. A "missing" grandparent spawned questions about the afterlife. The communion cup and bread led to curiosity about why Jesus had to die as he did. The symbol of the cross that was on Mommy's necklace became an opportunity to explore images of death and resurrection. Maturity brought forth further questions about God's love and our suffering, about the validity or invalidity of "other" faiths, about child abuse and hypocrisy.

Questions seek answers. As faith grows and develops, the answers are modified, clarified, added to, subtracted from, reaffirmed, and, sometimes, rejected. As we mature in our journey, and as we grow to grapple with the substance of the Word, old questions will reemerge, new questions will arise, and our answers will remain firm or evolve accordingly.

In Jesus' day, the dynamic of ongoing questions and answers was foremost in the faith and practice of pious Jews. Judaism was in an upheaval as it sought to understand how it should respond to Roman occupation. Should the Jews acquiesce and submit peacefully to Rome? Should the Jews, instead, resist violently and seek to overthrow the Romans? Was

Pastoral Perspective

With so much amiss in our world—personally, politically, environmentally—John's question to Jesus still hangs in the air today: "*Are you the one who is to come, or are we to wait for another?*" (v. 19b). Have we misunderstood? If you are the Messiah come into the world, why is there so little justice, so little peace, so much damage? "*Are you the one who is to come, or are we to wait for another?*" The Scriptures offer few more poignant questions.

John's whole life—from the promises offered before his conception until his imprisonment under Herod—was spent preparing the way for the coming Messiah. Once jailed, John must have waited eagerly for reports of God stirring in the world, setting things right. His followers were eager to be his eyes and ears and bring news back to him, but their reports were not what he expected. Wealthy/Gentile/ Roman occupying officers having their servants healed by Jesus? Grieving widows the center of his attention? Had Jesus sold out? Had he gone soft? Had he lost his way? As John imagined the possibility of his own impending death, did he wonder if all of his sacrifice had been wasted?

To his credit, John faces his dilemma head-on. He sends two of his followers to Jesus. They carry John's question, and John's name, with them. When the followers arrive, the sounds and smells and sights

Exegetical Perspective

Luke 7:18–23 consists of material shared with Matthew's Gospel (Q; Luke 7:19, 22–23; par. Matt. 11:2–6) and material unique to Luke's Gospel (7:18, 20–21), and is part of the minor interpolation (6:20–8:3) that Luke adds to Mark's Gospel. Matthew says that John heard about Jesus' work, but does not mention how (Matt. 11:2). Luke's version of the story makes clear that John's disciples report the news to him. As in Matthew's account, John is in prison in Luke (3:19–20). He has generous visitation privileges, however, as his disciples can see him whenever he or they wish, and they can carry messages back and forth freely. John's disciples are mentioned elsewhere (5:33; 11:1; Mark 6:29; John 3:25–26), but in Luke only here do they play an active role. The phrase "reported all these things" (*apēngeilan . . . peri pantōn toutōn*, v. 18) connects this passage with the ones before it, in which Jesus cures the centurion's slave (7:1–10) and resuscitates the dead son of the widow of Nain (7:11–17), but it also generally includes all that Jesus does and teaches.

John selects two specific disciples, perhaps because of their trustworthiness, to send to the Lord with John's question, "Are you the one who is to come [*ho erchomenos*], or are we to wait for another?" (v. 19). The inquiry brings to mind John's prophecy about the

Homiletical Perspective

Although the Matthean version of this story appears in the Advent lectionary, the Lukan parallel is absent. Preaching this text detached from the focus of Advent presents rich possibilities.

This brief passage follows immediately after two healing narratives: Jesus heals the slave of a centurion (who by birth as a Greek is outside the circle of the chosen). Then he resurrects the son of a Jewish widow (who, without husband or son, is doomed to be poor). Moreover, the second story mimics with intricate detail a story about Elijah (1 Kgs. 17). In response, the crowds are awestruck, praising God, and proclaiming that Jesus is a great prophet sent by God to help the people (7:16). Immediately, news about Jesus spreads throughout the region.

The news reaches John the Baptist through his disciples. He in turn sends two of them back to Jesus to question him directly. (According to Deut. 19:15, reliable witness requires a minimum of two men.) They are to ask of Jesus "Are you the one who is to come, or are we to wait for another?"

Their timing is impeccable. Jesus had "just then" (literally "in that hour") cured many. John's disciples were no longer relying on others' testimony, but seeing with their own eyes the healing work of Jesus (v. 21).

What are we to make of John's question, posed through his disciples? Often we assume that it is

Luke 7:18–23

Theological Perspective

there any hope that religious and political freedom could be achieved? If so, then by what means? Sectarian voices from Sadducees, Pharisees, Essenes, and ultranationalist Zealots debated the questions, and conflicting answers vied for the people's affirmation and allegiance.

Of the many questions asked in the synagogues, in the temple, among sages in the Sanhedrin, and among Jews in village gatherings of the elders, none was more important than a question about messianic expectations. Although some in first-century Judaism embraced the hope that a godly deliverer would arise in their midst, expectations nevertheless varied and questions remained. Who was the one to deliver the people from their oppression? How would the Messiah enact deliverance? What signs would give clues to the Messiah's identity and demeanor? These questions percolate throughout Luke 7:18–23. Luke's answers are among the most important in his Gospel and, indeed, in the entire New Testament.

The most pertinent theological question in the text comes from the lips of John the Baptist, who speaks from his prison cell by way of two of John's disciples who bring his question to Jesus. That John asks this question at all is significant. He has known Jesus longer than any of Jesus' followers. By baptizing Jesus in the Jordan River, he had a seminal role in the launching of Jesus' ministry. His life story and the biography of Jesus coincide, not just because they share in a wider family history, but because the burning questions of messianic identity and messianic activity consumed both of them. From Luke's birth narrative we know that John is to play a major role in the narrative about Jesus. John's role as messianic forerunner heightens the import of the question posed by his delegates. It is time for the question to be answered.

While Luke clearly connects the identity of the Messiah to Jesus, Luke does not express Jesus' identity in mere words. He also illustrates Jesus' nature through his actions. Luke portrays Jesus as a compassionate healer and worker of miracles whose focus is on the vulnerable (children and widows), the outcast (the Gentile centurion), and the invisible ones (the nameless souls in the crowds). Luke not only underscores the works of the Messiah; he also prompts those of us who confess Jesus as Messiah to "go and do likewise." We are to be compassionate laborers with all those who are poor, sick, weary, and fearful.

Although scholarly discussion of the intent and motive of John's question may well be worthwhile, it

Pastoral Perspective

surely overwhelm them: everywhere poor women, crippled men, sick children needing Jesus' help. Finally, though, the messengers get a chance to pose their challenge. They repeat John's question verbatim: "*Are you the one who is to come or are we to wait for another?*" Does all activity cease for a moment as the words leave their mouths?

When Jesus responds, he does not offer a tidy answer for John's disciples to memorize and carry back to their teacher. If only it were so easy. Instead, Jesus commissions the messengers as witnesses. They are to go back and report to John what they have seen and what they have heard. That will mean, first and foremost, that they must take in the suffering around them. They must stop and see the pain on their neighbors' faces; they must make time to hear the hard stories of strangers. In the process they also will see the hope that is born in someone who is given a second chance: a chance to walk, a chance to see, a chance to live in community after long years of isolation, a chance to live again. Jesus charges the messengers to describe and interpret to John the chaos and cacophony that surround him everywhere he goes.

We are not privileged to overhear the conversation that takes place between John and his disciples upon their return. We do not know how John reacts. As his followers describe blind persons receiving the gift of sight, does John sense that his disciples might, themselves, now see the world in a new way? Does he long for fresh vision himself?

We also do not know whether the messengers report Jesus' parting benediction: "And blessed is anyone who takes no offense at me" (v. 23). It does not matter; those words are meant for more than John. I suspect most of us are offended by Jesus, if we take his life at all seriously. We are slow to give up our privileged places; we do not want to cede too much control; we still imagine we might secure our own futures; we still judge our neighbors. God's upside-down economy has no place for our plans; it offends us.

When I came through seminary, I studied Luke with a thoughtful professor who occasionally punctuated his lectures with the question, "And when the heavens open, is that a *good* thing?" We never discussed his question; it just hung in the air. His query still encourages me to consider how much Jesus disrupts my comfortable life, my settled expectations. His question still prods me to ask, "How much am I—how much are we—willing to yield to this new life?"

one who is coming in Luke 3:16 (*erchetai*).[1] Jesus will emphatically answer John's question momentarily. Referring to Jesus as "Lord" (*kyrios*) has christological implications here as it did in the previous passage (7:13), connecting Jesus to God and Jesus' power to God's (see, e.g., 4:18 and 6:46). The word for "wait," *prosdokaō*, is important for Luke, occurring six times in the Gospel and five times in Acts, and only five times in the rest of the NT. Here the term lifts up the theme of expectant waiting found in Luke 3:15.

In the section of the pericope that is absent from Matthew (vv. 20–21), the two disciples arrive at Jesus' location. They identify themselves as messengers from John and repeat the Baptist's question verbatim, repetition that emphasizes its significance. While they are there— *en ekeinē tē hōra*, "at that hour," v. 21 (a phrase used elsewhere in Luke to mark important narrative moments [2:38; 10:21; 12:12; 13:31; 20:19; 22:53; 24:33],[2] though the phrase is slightly different in these verses: *autē tē hōra*; "in that very hour")—they are able to witness firsthand Jesus healing many people from illnesses, which he has done before (4:40; 6:18; see also 9:1), from suffering (NRSV "plagues"), and evil spirits. Again, this recalls the two preceding passages (7:1–10; 7:11–17). Luke often speaks of unclean spirits (4:33–36; 6:18; 8:26–39; 9:38–42; 10:17–20; 11:24), but mentions evil spirits only two other times: when he speaks of the women he healed, including Mary Magdalene, Joanna, and Susanna among many others (8:2), and when he mentions the unclean spirit that brings other spirits more evil than himself to inhabit the man (11:24–26). Nevertheless, for Luke, there appears to be no difference between evil spirits, unclean spirits, and demons (4:33–36, 41; 7:33; 8:2; 8:26–39; 9:1; 9:38–42, 49–50; 10:17–20; 11:14–23; 13:31–32). What is clear is that Luke's world is inhabited by all of them and that Jesus is graciously giving (*charizomai*, v. 21) sight to many blind people.

Afterward, Jesus responds to John's two disciples. They are to return to John and report to him—as they had done previously (7:18)—what they had just seen and heard Jesus say and do. The list of Jesus' deeds that follows in verse 22 has allusions to Isaiah and contains wonders attributed to Jesus elsewhere in Luke. First, the blind are given sight (Isa. 29:18;

1. According to Joseph A. Fitzmyer (*The Gospel according to Luke I–IX*, Anchor Bible [Garden City, NY: Doubleday, 1981], 663), it may also reflect an early tradition concerning Jesus' identity as Elijah returned, taken from Mal. 3:1. See Fitzmyer's discussion of *ho erchomenos* on pp. 665–67, as well as that of Frederick W. Danker, *Jesus and the New Age: A Commentary on St. Luke's Gospel*, rev. ed. (Philadelphia: Fortress Press, 1988), 163–64.
2. Luke Timothy Johnson, *The Gospel of Luke*, Sacra pagina 3 (Collegeville, MN: Liturgical Press, 1991), 122.

a question born of doubt; that somehow he who once believed has grown skeptical. Robert Tannehill observes:

> There has been no indication in Luke that John recognized Jesus as the fulfillment of John's prophecies. Therefore, John's question does not represent the weakening of previous belief but the hopeful exploration of possibility. The possibility occurs to John because of his disciples' report concerning "all these things" that Jesus has been saying and doing. John raises a question that others, too, will raise concerning the implications of Jesus' work for an understanding of Jesus himself and his future role.[1]

What a different enterprise it is to imagine John's question as a "hopeful exploration of possibility." Instead of throwing John in with the naysayers and skeptics, we are invited to come alongside him as fellow seekers.

One homiletical path is to encourage questioning as a part of faith. John's question—whether Jesus is the One who saves the world—is still germane to many. Today, as then, there are corrupt political powers in place; religious leaders still disappoint and fail us; the poor are still crushed and the powerful protected, the fraudulent rewarded and the vulnerable broken. Is Jesus the world's savior, and if so, how?

Jesus' answer is to point to ways in which he is fulfilling the messianic promise of Isaiah 61:1–2 proclaimed early in his ministry: "He has sent me to preach good news to the poor, to proclaim release to the captives and recovery of sight to the blind, to liberate the oppressed" (4:18). Whenever we see such evidence—or better yet, participate in such activity, as the body of Christ today—we are witnessing God's promises unfolding.

A second question we might ask is this: Why is there still suffering? Why did Jesus not unseat the powers and principalities, and sweep out the pompous, legalistic religious leaders for good? Perhaps Jesus had this disappointment in mind when he told John, almost parenthetically, "Blessed is anyone who takes no offense at me" (v. 23). "Blessed" (*makarios*) reminds us of the Beatitudes, which overturn our usual expectations of what counts as blessing. "Blessed are the poor," for example, and "blessed are the hungry" (6:20–21). True to form, what follows is startling. Literally it means "blessed is anyone who is not scandalized/caused to sin/made

1. Robert C. Tannehill, *Luke* (Nashville: Abingdon Press, 1996), 129.

Luke 7:18–23

Theological Perspective

is notable that Luke, as theologian, does not inquire into this matter. His intent is to focus on the nature of messianic ministry. By including illustrations from Jesus' activities with the Gentile centurion's servant (7:1–10) and the deceased child of the Jewish widow (7:11–17), Luke points toward the "person" and "power" of the One about whom John asks. Implicit in Luke's narrative are intimations of a caring God who compassionately engages the sick, the dead, and the grieving. As the people of this God, we are to go and do likewise.

Is Jesus then Elijah, the prophet at the onset of the messianic age? Indeed, he is, for Jesus is a *nabi* (the Hebrew term denoting a spokesperson for God). Moreover, beyond the content of Jesus' preaching and teaching, he is a doer of truth, embodying a spiritual power that evokes mighty and astonishing deeds.

John has sent two men to listen to Jesus and to observe his activities. John is most interested in Jesus' actions. Jesus' answer to John's inquiry is framed completely in those things that have happened in his ministry, namely, the healings, exorcisms, and resuscitations. It is as though Jesus says, "By my deeds, John, you know who I am." Today, far too many contemporary churches fail to communicate clearly who we are as the people of God. Christian communities talk about faith rather than acting in faith; they maintain beautiful sanctuaries rather than showing hospitality; they espouse ethical values rather than acting ethically in the world; they study the meaning of discipleship rather than being Jesus' disciples.

The text ends with a beatitude from the lips of Jesus. He announces that blessing will fall upon those who do not reject him and his actions. Here, to receive Luke's Jesus is to bear witness to the age-old promise of God to Abraham (Gen. 12:1–3): that all people who become children of God by faith will both be blessed and become a blessing to others. We are to be blessings to one another and to all people, especially those in greatest human need. We are to enact our identity as a blessed community, living in the spirit and power of our Messiah, Jesus.

DONALD W. MUSSER

Pastoral Perspective

For Jesus commissions *us* as witnesses too. We must make our own choices about what we will see and what we hear, and how we will tell the story. One obvious implication: if the locus of Jesus' activity in the world is among the poor and suffering, then that is where we need to spend our time—if we want to see Jesus—if we want to have a story to tell.

I am comforted by the knowledge that even though John was filled with the Holy Spirit, he also was filled with questions. The life of faith is not devoid of doubt or disappointment. We should not expect that it will be otherwise.

I am challenged too by what John does with his question. He takes it to Jesus. Following the ancient model we see in the Psalms, John offers himself in dialogue, just as he is. He does not beat around the bush; he asks his question. I sometimes wonder if our practice of being polite with God and each other robs our worship of such authenticity. What would it look like if, instead of keeping our own counsel, we offered in community the questions that burn in our hearts and keep us awake at night? How might God grow us up? How might God transform and use us?

Jesus said, "Those who are well have no need of a physician, but those who are sick; I have come to call not the righteous but sinners to repentance" (5:31–32). Only as we expose our own ignorance, confusion, and need—only as we allow our own pain to see the light of day—do we make space for God to meet us in those broken places.

MARGARET LAMOTTE TORRENCE

Exegetical Perspective

35:5; 42:18). Jesus will again heal a blind man near Jericho later in Luke's Gospel (18:35–43). The lame walk (Isa. 35:6), another cure that Jesus explicitly performs (5:17–26). Lepers are cleansed, a healing that Jesus brings about in Luke 5:12–16 and 17:11–19. The deaf hear (Isa. 29:18; 35:5; 42:18), the only malady on the list that Jesus does not address in Luke. The dead are raised (Isa. 26:19; see also Sir. 48:5). This brings immediately to mind the miracle at Nain narrated in the preceding passage (7:11–17); but it recalls as well the healing of Jairus's daughter (8:40–56; par. Matt. 9:18–26; Mark 5:21–43). Finally, the poor have good news preached to them (*euangelizomai*, Isa. 61:1). Its placement at the end of the list indicates that Jesus' messiahship is centered on preaching good news to the poor, although Luke notes several times that Jesus preaches good news to others than simply the poor (4:43; 8:1; 16:16; 20:1). This verse also echoes Jesus' reading of Isaiah 61:1 in 4:18: he brings good news to the poor, release to the captives, recovery of sight to the blind, freedom to the oppressed, and the year of the Lord's favor. Jesus responds that the prophecy is fulfilled in him (4:21).

The passage closes with Jesus speaking of the blessedness (*makarios*) of anyone who does not take offense at him (v. 23). Joseph Fitzmyer argues that what Jesus is saying here is that John and others must deal with the fact that he has not come in the way they might have expected (3:16–17).[3] It also contrasts those who accept Jesus, whatever their conception of messiahship is, with those in the Gospel who are offended by him, for example, Jesus' neighbors from Nazareth who are so outraged that they attempt to kill him (4:28–29) and the Jewish leaders who take offense at what Jesus says and does throughout the Gospel.

WILLIAM SANGER CAMPBELL

Homiletical Perspective

to stumble" because of me. (It is the only instance where "offense" [noun *skandalon*, verb *skandalizō*] is used other than 17:1–2: "Occasions for stumbling are bound to come, but woe to anyone by whom they come! It would be better for you if a millstone were hung around your neck and you were thrown into the sea than for you to cause one of these little ones to stumble.")

Jesus is warning us that our faith may stumble over our unfulfilled expectations of what the Messiah should be and do. If we hope the Messiah will sweep in with power and might, we will be disappointed. However, if we look for a Messiah who enters into the suffering of the world, then we will be blessed beyond our imagination. Jesus keeps company with the outcast instead of the powerful; rules with humility instead of power (Phil. 2:1–11); is crowned with thorns instead of majesty (Matt. 27:29). Later, the apostle Paul set out the competing hopes for the Messiah this way: "We proclaim Christ crucified, a stumbling block to Jews and foolishness to Gentiles, but to those who are the called, both Jews and Greeks, Christ the power of God and the wisdom of God. For God's foolishness is wiser than human wisdom, and God's weakness is stronger than human strength" (1 Cor. 1:23–25).

A third homiletical approach might be to consider *our* responses to the questions of those around us. When John asks, "Are you the one who is to come?" (v. 20), Jesus instructs his followers to "Go and tell . . . what you have seen and heard" (v. 22). Whether we are facing innocent questions of faith from our children, skeptical questions of faith from our friends, or indifferent questions to faith from our culture, we are invited to respond with our own testimony. It is not enough simply for us to watch what the Lord is doing in our lives. As we are reminded at the end of Luke's Gospel: "You are witnesses of these things" (24:48). In the face of the world's questions, it is our privilege to testify to the ongoing work of the Messiah.

CHRISTINE CHAKOIAN

3. Fitzmyer, *Luke*, 664–65, 668.

Luke 7:24–35

²⁴When John's messengers had gone, Jesus began to speak to the crowds about John: "What did you go out into the wilderness to look at? A reed shaken by the wind? ²⁵What then did you go out to see? Someone dressed in soft robes? Look, those who put on fine clothing and live in luxury are in royal palaces. ²⁶What then did you go out to see? A prophet? Yes, I tell you, and more than a prophet. ²⁷This is the one about whom it is written,

'See, I am sending my messenger ahead of you,
    who will prepare your way before you.'

²⁸I tell you, among those born of women no one is greater than John; yet the least in the kingdom of God is greater than he." ²⁹(And all the people who heard this, including the tax collectors, acknowledged the justice of God, because

Theological Perspective

Luke 7:24–35 helps readers understand both who John the Baptist is and who we ourselves are. The Gospel of Luke does not define these identities independently, as if they could be understood on their own terms. It rather takes them up in the wake of a series of stories that reveal more and more about who Jesus is. John's identity, like our own, can only be understood in relation to Jesus.

The stories in the first part of Luke 7 present Jesus as the fulfillment of the hopes of a long prophetic tradition. Jesus named these hopes when he taught in the synagogue in Nazareth. Reading from the scroll of Isaiah, he said, "The Spirit of the Lord is upon me, because he has anointed me to bring good news to the poor. He has sent me to proclaim release to the captives and recovery of sight to the blind, to let the oppressed go free, to proclaim the year of the Lord's favor" (4:18). Here Jesus is healing the sick and giving sight to the blind (7:21). In Nazareth Jesus reminded the people of the miracles that Elijah did in raising the son of the widow of Zarephath (4:26) and that Elisha did in curing the leprosy of Naaman the Syrian (4:27). Now Jesus has raised the son of a widow (7:11–17) and cured the servant of a centurion who, like Naaman, was a military leader for a foreign power (7:1–10). Jesus is embodying what he proclaimed in Nazareth: "Today

Pastoral Perspective

This well-known scene unfolds as John the Baptist languishes in jail. Having posed to Jesus the question of whether or not he is "the one," John's emissaries are headed back to John, carrying the scriptural clues to Jesus' identity. Jesus then turns and poses to the crowd questions about John's identity. What did you go out to see? A man easily swayed? No. A luxurious man? No. A prophet? Yes, but even "prophet" sells him short. So then, who is John? Jesus' answer is a stunning tribute: John is the greatest man alive. If this is true, Jesus' next affirmation is even more stunning: the least person "in the kingdom" is greater than John. Those who enter God's new realm—that is, Jesus' disciples—receive a healing even John cannot imagine, a freedom even John cannot grasp, a joy even John cannot deliver.

Something new is afoot, and John is not part of it, except by way of preparation. Jesus' forerunner may be the greatest man alive, but he is not the agent of God's new thing. There can be no clinging to what came before, even to John. No matter how worthy the past may have been, you have to let it go. It would be natural for Jesus to want to stay with his much-admired cousin, to console him, perhaps even to try to spring him from jail; but Jesus' mission requires relinquishment. If he does not tear himself away, if he hitches his wagon to a beautiful but fading star, if he

they had been baptized with John's baptism. [30]But by refusing to be baptized by him, the Pharisees and the lawyers rejected God's purpose for themselves.)

[31]"To what then will I compare the people of this generation, and what are they like? [32]They are like children sitting in the marketplace and calling to one another,

'We played the flute for you, and you did not dance;
we wailed, and you did not weep.'

[33]For John the Baptist has come eating no bread and drinking no wine, and you say, 'He has a demon'; [34]the Son of Man has come eating and drinking, and you say, 'Look, a glutton and a drunkard, a friend of tax collectors and sinners!' [35]Nevertheless, wisdom is vindicated by all her children."

Exegetical Perspective

Having answered John's questions, John's students return to their master while Jesus addresses "the crowds" on the subject of John the Baptist.

The three questions in Luke 7:24–26 comprise an *anaphora*, a rhetorical figure that repeats the same word or words at the beginning of successive clauses or sentences to achieve emphasis. Did the people who came to John come out to watch the river grasses blow (v. 24) or to glimpse people dressed in finery (v. 25)? No, they went out to see a prophet; and what they saw was much more than a prophet (v. 26).

The teaching about John in Luke 7:24–28 is almost word for word the same as in Matthew 11:7–11, including the quotation of Malachi 3:1, which Mark inserts at the beginning of his Gospel and attributes to Isaiah. (See also Exod. 23:20.) Luke 7:24–28, therefore, comes from the sayings source commonly called Q, which contains sayings of Jesus and John the Baptist that are in Matthew and Luke but not in Mark. Likewise, the comparison of the present generation to a group of disagreeable children in Luke 7:31–35 (Matt. 11:16–19) is from Q.

Between the two blocks from Q, Luke has a short narrative about the tax collectors who received John's baptism and the Pharisees and lawyers who rejected it (vv. 29–30). Matthew, on the other hand, has a saying about John as the coming Elijah (Matt.

Homiletical Perspective

A homiletical reading of this "John and Jesus" text brings into consideration the remarkable oppositions Luke has embedded here. Three are especially important to note as we move toward a strategy for preaching this text:

Those grounded in religious certainties and moral strictures are not the just, but are among those who have rejected God's purposes. Those reflecting the justice of God are sinners who have come to the Jordan, repented, and been baptized by John.

The children in the marketplace are likened to "this generation," who will neither join in the celebration of Jesus and the forgiven, nor mourn with John over the sins of such a generation. The opposition, then, is between those who neither dance nor mourn and the redeemed, who have responded to both flute and dirge.

In a second reference to children, Jesus speaks of wisdom being "vindicated by all her children" (v. 35). They will abound and be blessed, encompassing a vast and diverse new family of God.[1]

This much is clear: an ironic twist has taken place. Insiders put themselves outside the realm of

1. One commentator summarizes this polarity nicely: "By concentrating on insiders, the opposition narrows the possibilities for wisdom's nurture; Jesus, through his outreach to publicans and sinners, brings many outsiders under her tutelage" (Frederick W. Danker, *Jesus and the New Age: A Commentary on St. Luke's Gospel* [Philadelphia: Fortress Press, 1988], 168).

Luke 7:24–35

Theological Perspective

this scripture has been fulfilled in your hearing" (4:21).

John the Baptist sends messengers to ask Jesus if he is "the one who is to come," or if they should wait for another (7:20). Luke's narrative has already made clear the answer: "the blind receive their sight, the lame walk, the lepers are cleansed, the deaf hear, the dead are raised, the poor have good news brought to them" (7:22). Jesus is indeed the fulfillment of the hopes of the prophets, the one John and his disciples have been waiting for.

If Jesus is "the one who is to come," then who is John? In this passage Jesus asks the crowds a series of questions that elicit the answer. Did they go into the wilderness to see "a reed shaken by the wind" or "someone dressed in soft robes" (vv. 24, 25)? No. They went to see a person whose unwavering desire to prepare the way of the Lord led him to a life of deep austerity. They went to see a prophet—and, Jesus says, "more than a prophet" (v. 26). As important as the prophetic tradition has been, John is not just one more prophet. He is, Luke writes in a mash-up of Malachi and Exodus, the "messenger" who will prepare the way of the Lord (v. 27). With this, Jesus ratifies John's own statement of his mission to "prepare the way of the Lord" (3:3–6). John is who he says he is; and when he is understood in relation to Jesus, it becomes clear that his mission is even more timely than he thought it was.

Having worked through an understanding of Jesus to a deeper understanding of John, Luke now turns to the people he calls "this generation" (v. 31). Jesus and John divide this generation in surprising ways. Those who might seem righteous, the ones Luke identifies as Pharisees and lawyers, reveal their inner resistance to the one who is coming when they refuse John's baptism. Those who seem less likely to share in the reign of God—people like the centurion of 7:1–10, the tax collectors of 7:29, and the notorious sinner who will bathe Jesus' feet with her tears in the very next story (7:36–50)—are revealed to be faithful through their responses to Jesus and John.

Luke brings the identities of John, Jesus, and this generation together with an analogy to children who will neither dance to festive music nor weep with those who are mourning (vv. 31–32). This generation resists what it sees as the asceticism of John and the prodigality of Jesus. In saying that John eats and drinks too little, and Jesus eats and drinks too much (and with the wrong people!), Jesus' opponents unintentionally reveal their true selves. Their resistance exposes their attachment to the present age. In their

Pastoral Perspective

lives backwards into what might have been, he will miss what the Spirit does next. Painful and as seemingly heartless as it appears, John must stay in jail. Jesus must leave him there and go on.

There is wisdom here for Christians stuck in reverse gear in their personal or communal lives, insisting on formulas and solutions that were good for their time, but not for now, and who are unwilling to see good in anything new. There is wisdom too for nostalgic congregations that hold back from change, for fear of appearing ungrateful for their forebears' contributions and sacrifices. The text may also speak to the general human experience of loss—those great and little deaths that, when borne in the spirit of Christ, temper the soul with grief while rendering it more responsive, more agile, and more fully free. The pastor will help her people taste the good fruits of letting go of what was and what might have been, for the sake of the kingdom's encompassing joy. She will do so, however, without playing down the difficulty of this kind of faithfulness. Listeners need to be assured that just as "leaving John in jail" was probably one of the hardest things Jesus had to do, God knows that letting go of the past's hold on us is one of the most difficult things we ever do.

This text presents a different set of opportunities for the pastor in the questions, accusations, and aphorisms with which Jesus confronts the crowd. Here an exasperated Jesus lays bare his listeners' contradictory, self-seeking judgments of his identity, authority, and ministry. What did you go out to see? Did John fit or defraud your expectations? What about me? Did you expect one thing and get another? Do you even know what you want? Will you ever be satisfied?

Here we encounter the debate among Jesus' contemporaries about what sort of liberation and what sort of liberator God has in mind for God's people. Jesus' questions may be read as a commentary on the sort of confused spiritual expectations that lead to disenchantment, and even to cynicism and hypocrisy. As the object of his detractors' clashing notions of godliness and competing images of the Messiah, Jesus decries their habit of discounting the message because of the messenger's failure to conform to their assumptions.

The pastor may wish to linger on this theme. After all, hardly a person in the pews has not foolishly sought perfection in a spouse or a child, a coach or a politician, and been hugely disappointed. How many have passed up life-changing opportunities because they had a different future in mind, or

Feasting on the Gospels

11:12–15), a saying that bears some resemblance to Luke 16:16.

We could believe that Luke 7:24–35 is one large quotation from Q, consisting of two blocks, except for the fact that both Matthew and Luke have additional material between those blocks. The material in Luke 7:29–30 does not come from Q; but Matthew's intervening material, based on its similarity to Luke 16:16, might owe something to Q.

Who was John? The answer of Luke 7:24–28 comes in a series of oppositions: John is not only a prophet, but he is also something greater than a prophet (v. 26). In Luke 7:27, John is the messenger foretold in Malachi 3:1, but Luke does not call him Elijah as Matthew does (Matt. 11:14). Even though John is the greatest human born of a woman, he ranks below even the least in God's kingdom (v. 28). The expression "among those born of women" reflects the Semitic origin of this expression (Sir. 10:18; Job 11:12 [Greek only]; 14:1; 15:14; see Gal. 4:4). The phrase simply means "people." The comparative form *mikroteros* ("lesser") requires the superlative ("least") in English translation: "*least* in the kingdom of God." NT Greek demonstrates the relative infrequency of the superlative degree in the Koine.

Luke 7:29–30 stands between the two blocks of Q material (vv. 24–28 and vv. 31–35) and in context continues Jesus' teaching in verses 24–28. In these two verses, we learn that by rejecting John's baptism, the Pharisees and lawyers have already turned their backs on God's will and in so doing already stand against God, even before Jesus' appearance.

Recall the parable of Lazarus and the Rich Man (16:19–31), in which the destitute Lazarus died and went to be with Abraham, while the heedless rich man died and found himself in Hades (16:19–23). At the end of the story, seeing that Abraham was not going to send Lazarus to Hades to relieve him, the rich man begged Abraham to send Lazarus to the rich man's five brothers to warn them (16:27–28). This request was unnecessary because the five brothers had the instructions of Moses and the prophets. If these instructions were unable to bring the five brothers to repentance, then a resurrected Lazarus would not do so either (16:27–31).

Likewise, in Luke 7:30, the Pharisees and lawyers did not have to await the coming of Jesus to turn their backs on God's call in Jesus. If they have not heard John, who was "more than a prophet," then they will not hear Jesus. This short saying takes us directly into the figure of the troublesome children (vv. 31–35).

God by way of their pride and prejudice, while those condemned as outsiders are now among wisdom's children, by way of repentance and a joyful openness to the gospel. Perhaps most tragic of all are the nonchalant, the blasé, and the self-centered ones, who neither mourn nor dance.

Turning to the task of shaping a sermon, the abundance of oppositions within the pericope offers fertile soil for a number of focused sermons or a narrative homiletical plot as proposed by Eugene Lowry.[2] While each stage will be briefly interpreted as we move through the narrative, within each stage are multiple sermonic possibilities.

Conflict. The sermon begins with an invitation to the listeners to enter into the stress and turmoil of one of the text's oppositions. What if some aspect of the great chasm between liberals and evangelicals is developed, with particular reference to the congregation's own faith location? Is the congregation firmly and fiercely located on one side or the other of this schism? Or is this parish huddled down in a "no-man's-land" somewhere in the middle? The focus could be on a topic such as worship wars, sexuality, or doctrinal standards. In any case, the preacher will need to bring the dominant issue to concrete expression.

Another issue that could be explored here is the point of view that the preacher forms for the listeners. Clearly Luke is deploying this particular Jesus tradition to caution his church from siding with those who reject the justice of God. In other words, the sermon should not use the opening conflict in the passage to valorize its hearers while demonizing others. Do not all of us in some way or other try to turn gospel back into law?

Complication. Here, the preacher may invite the congregation to reflect on the deeper spiritual issues of passivity and self-absorption. Ironically, the overheated battles of the religious extremes are intertwined with those who remain quite detached, caring neither to dance nor mourn. Overdone zeal too often provides others with rationalization for simply backing away from any position at all. Life devolves into a concern for self and one's own "lifestyle." Since this kind of passive nonengagement is borne out in churches and society at large, the preacher may draw on both ecclesial and secular examples to illustrate the problems and cost of social passivity and self-absorption. Members of the household of faith as

2. Eugene L. Lowry, *The Sermon: Dancing the Edge of Mystery* (Nashville: Abingdon Press, 1997).

Luke 7:24–35

Theological Perspective

response and relationship to Jesus, they show themselves for who they really are.

There is great theological significance in the recognition that we come to know ourselves and others through contact with Jesus. To say that Jesus reveals the truth is not just to say that he is a teacher of doctrine. It is to say that encounters with Jesus bring out the deepest truths of people, institutions, movements, and more. Thus the text raises questions about what the coming of Jesus reveals about our own identities. Looking to the story of John, can we come to a better understanding of what we have been doing all along? Listening to the story of the children in the marketplace, can we discern the roots of our own resistance to Jesus in our childish and conflicted responses?

We can also examine the ways in which these identities speak to the relation of this age to the reign of God. No one in this age is greater than John the Baptist, Jesus says. His greatness comes not because he brings in the reign of God, but because he prepares a way for it. Yet however great he may be, he is still less than the least person in the reign of God (v. 28). That reign, then, is not established by even the greatest forerunners. It is so much greater that the best people, efforts, and hopes of this age cannot compare to it. The risk in proclaiming such transcendent hope is that it can be cast over the far horizon, with no transforming connection to the present. The gift of John the Baptist is to discern the profound nearness of the reign of God—and the need to prepare the way for its consummation. Readers are enjoined to take up the work of John, looking for the concrete actions in this age that prepare the way of the Lord.

TED A. SMITH

Pastoral Perspective

refused rich gifts because their wrappings were ordinary, or because they were smaller than they imagined rich gifts should be? Search committees choose new leaders to solve their congregation's problems, and when salvation proves elusive, they are the first to heap piles of withering criticism on the ones they themselves called. The centering-prayer crowd discounts the faithfulness of the social-justice types as mere activism; the social-justice types suspect that the prayerful bliss of the devout is sheer pious evasion. When the God of our childhood, our projections, and our unexamined needs resists our manipulations, we say, "There is no God." The pastor might wish to introduce her people to Christian practices that fashion habits of discernment, self-knowledge, and openness to the upending surprises of God.

Spiritual restlessness may also be an appropriate theme to explore. Many of the curious people who went out to "look at" John in the wilds are now looking at Jesus. Will they stick with him, or will they eventually "look for another"? Who knows? The next guru just might be "the one." There is nothing intrinsically wrong with human seeking. Some of the greatest figures of the Christian tradition have been restless souls. Augustine of Hippo worked his way through several philosophical schools and religious sects before making a baptismal commitment. The pastor will take seriously the disquiet and strivings of the seeker and so-called spiritual-but-not-religious people; but he might also use the text to encourage the oft-neglected virtue of staying put. To be forever in hot pursuit of the next great thing may be a sign of immature faith that attempts to fill the unfillable need to finally possess "the answer."

Jesus' questions echo: Do you really know what you want? Do you really know what you need? The pastoral minister might help restless, seeking souls settle in long enough to stop seeking "the answer" and instead respond to "the love"—the divine love that will not let them go.

MARY LUTI

Exactly who is "calling out" (*prosphōnousin*) to whom in verse 32 has been a subject of debate, but the word *allēlois* ("to one another") makes it clear that some of the children are calling out childish taunts: "you did not dance" and "you did not weep." The image is of quarreling children, not an antiphony of opposing complaints. All the time, the children sit, doing nothing but arguing. The people of this generation are like the quarreling children, giving foolish excuses for following neither John nor Jesus. Their reasons blatantly contradict one another, but logic hardly matters to these quarrelsome children.

The picture of quarreling, pouting children explains the aphorism in verse 35, "Wisdom is vindicated [*edikaiōthē*] by all her children." The only difficult thing about the saying is the simple *kai* ("and") that begins the verse. The NRSV's translation "nevertheless" is misleading, as is "yet" in the RSV. While it is true that *kai* can sometimes be an adversative conjunction, such is not its main function. Since "this generation" is clearly not acting wisely, responding neither to John the Baptist nor to Jesus, then they are like troublesome children who do nothing but sit around and gripe at each other. They are not demonstrating the wisdom expected of them. They are, rather, like the Pharisees and lawyers who did not accept the baptism of John (v. 30). The simple "and" (*kai*) makes complete sense as introducing an ironic description of the children's behavior.

Mention of "wisdom" (*sophia*) in verse 35 raises a question about what "wisdom" means here. Is this wisdom the proverbial wisdom of Proverbs 10–31? Against that interpretation is the fact that wisdom in Luke 7:35 is wisdom personified, whose children vindicate her. Is she then the creative wisdom of Proverbs 8:22, Wisdom 7:22–8:1, and Sirach 24:1–34? No. Wisdom's role in creation is absent from Q's small proverb. Wisdom in verse 35 is the personified wisdom of Proverbs 7:1, wisdom calling her children to obey her commandments so as to live. The focus is on actions, the actions of this generation compared with the indifferent, quarrelsome actions of the children.

FRED L. HORTON

well as some of our secular friends seem to pride themselves in their lack of engagement with great issues confronting the world today. For congregations where the demographics center on baby boomers, perhaps a reference to an episode of *Seinfeld* will help expose this stance of life being "about nothing."

Sudden Shift. The opening conflict in Luke 7:24–35 has invited the listeners into an even deeper, more complicated location. If the preacher has chosen to engage in the considered analysis suggested by Lowry, the stage is now set for the hearing of some good news that will abruptly halt the downward spiral of stages one and two and provide this sudden shift. Within our text in Luke, the good news is about the justice of God, through which repentant sinners respond to the invitation to become wisdom's children. Becoming wisdom's children, of course, is an achievement of divine grace in Christ and not based on our worthiness (see 7:2–10).

The need for concrete imagery remains and, since we are "naming grace," our strategy for illustration will need to shine more brightly than the images and examples deployed in the first two stages. Since this stage embodies a sudden shift, the image should be mobile rather than static and communal rather than individualistic. Has the congregation recently found itself surprised by grace in an ethnically or economically diverse experience? Recall that experience here.

Unfolding. Here Lowry proposes a new location for the listeners in which they begin "settling in to tomorrow."[3] Once again, the focus here will need to remain mobile and communal. Moreover, since we have dispensed with hardened religious exclusionary convictions as well as noncommittal neutrality, we may well be invited to listen once more to the children in the marketplace. They invite us, as appropriate, to mourn, and, in the fullness of time, to dance. One image comes to mind that may invite the congregation to do both—a funeral in the traditional New Orleans practice. Invite the congregants to join in the procession of mourners, led by the brass marching band. What is buried in our baptisms other than our old selves, what is washed away other than our sins? Then invite the congregation to join with the other marchers as they return in a joyful procession, perhaps led by Louis Armstrong singing and playing "O When the Saints Go Marching In." Who knows, the congregation may even dance.

RICHARD L. ESLINGER

3. Lowry, *Sermon*, 87.

Luke 7:36–50

³⁶One of the Pharisees asked Jesus to eat with him, and he went into the Pharisee's house and took his place at the table. ³⁷And a woman in the city, who was a sinner, having learned that he was eating in the Pharisee's house, brought an alabaster jar of ointment. ³⁸She stood behind him at his feet, weeping, and began to bathe his feet with her tears and to dry them with her hair. Then she continued kissing his feet and anointing them with the ointment. ³⁹Now when the Pharisee who had invited him saw it, he said to himself, "If this man were a prophet, he would have known who and what kind of woman this is who is touching him—that she is a sinner." ⁴⁰Jesus spoke up and said to him, "Simon, I have something to say to you." "Teacher," he replied, "speak." ⁴¹"A certain creditor had two debtors; one owed five hundred denarii, and the other fifty. ⁴²When they could not pay, he canceled the debts for both of them. Now

Theological Perspective

Early in Luke's Gospel Simeon tells Mary that her son Jesus will "be a sign that will be opposed so that the inner thoughts of many will be revealed" (2:34b–35a). Simeon's words are fulfilled throughout the Gospel, but they are illustrated to striking effect in Luke 7:36–50.

Jesus comes to the house of Simon, a Pharisee, for a meal. While he is reclining at the table, a woman the text identifies as a sinner enters the room, bathes his feet with her tears, wipes his feet with her hair, kisses his feet with her lips, and anoints his feet with ointment. Simon says that if Jesus were really a prophet—if he were really the kind of person Simeon says he is—then he would know that this woman is a sinner. Jesus tells a story that makes clear just how well he knows the woman—and Simon.

Simon, like the one in Jesus' story who has been forgiven a small debt, does not show Jesus much love. He does not even fulfill the basic duties of a host. He offers Jesus no water for washing, no kiss of welcome, and no oil for his head. The woman, on the other hand, offers something like an ecstatic parody of the work of a host. She uses tears instead of water to wash Jesus' feet, gives him endless kisses of welcome on his feet, and anoints his feet with valuable ointment. Forgiven a great debt, she shows great love. With Jesus' arrival, the outward appearance

Pastoral Perspective

The interconnected and overlapping themes of judgment, pardon, gratitude, love, and hospitality in this text invite the pastor to a rich feast of possibilities. The scene is a dinner at Simon's house at which Jesus is a guest. When Simon invites him, he has to know that Jesus' fame as a prophet is clouded. Even Jesus had heard what people are saying about him—"a glutton and drunkard, a friend of . . . sinners" (7:34). Nevertheless, Simon is perplexed when a sinner follows him right into his dining room. It is hard for Simon to credit Jesus as an authentic man of God when a notorious woman with loosened hair is weepily kissing his feet in what seems to the modern reader to be an over-the-top display of affection.

It may be hard for many of us too. The pastor may wish to explore the notion, ingrained in some Christians' minds, that "godly" and "sinner" are completely separate categories, and that the proper life work of a Christian is to move out of the latter and into the former. Whether in "soul-winning" churches where mixing it up with sinners is required in order to save them or in "progressive" churches where the gospel is judged by current standards of political correctness, everyone knows the difference between good people and bad. You cannot be good unless you are a Christian like us. You are not in God's good graces if you support the wrong political

which of them will love him more?" [43]Simon answered, "I suppose the one for whom he canceled the greater debt." And Jesus said to him, "You have judged rightly." [44]Then turning toward the woman, he said to Simon, "Do you see this woman? I entered your house; you gave me no water for my feet, but she has bathed my feet with her tears and dried them with her hair. [45]You gave me no kiss, but from the time I came in she has not stopped kissing my feet. [46]You did not anoint my head with oil, but she has anointed my feet with ointment. [47]Therefore, I tell you, her sins, which were many, have been forgiven; hence she has shown great love. But the one to whom little is forgiven, loves little." [48]Then he said to her, "Your sins are forgiven." [49]But those who were at the table with him began to say among themselves, "Who is this who even forgives sins?" [50]And he said to the woman, "Your faith has saved you; go in peace."

Exegetical Perspective

The placement of the story of the woman who shed tears on Jesus' feet, dried them with her hair, and then anointed them with oil is hardly accidental or unrelated to the idea of the vindication of wisdom's children in verse 35. While the story has striking similarities to Mark 14:3–9, Matthew 26:6–13, and John 12:1–8, the function of the story sets it apart from the accounts in the other three Gospels. For Luke, the anointing of Jesus' feet is not a preparation for Jesus' burial, as it is in Mark 14:8, Matthew 26:12, and John 12:7. In fact, Luke's story occurs early on, during Jesus' ministry in the Galilee (3:1–9:50), and has no obvious association at all with the death and burial of Jesus.

Following immediately upon the comparison of the tax collectors and others who received the baptism of John with the Pharisees and lawyers, who did not (7:29–30), there is no question that the word "Pharisee" in verse 36 ties these two lections together. For his part, the Pharisee acts like the grumpy children in verse 32, protesting sullenly to himself that Jesus could not be a prophet because a prophet would not suffer such anointing from a sinner (v. 39). Jesus' parable of the Two Debtors, together with the subsequent dialogue with Simon in verses 40–47, explains the woman's actions and shows her behavior as the intimate and faithful act

Homiletical Perspective

The narrative of the woman and Simon the Pharisee follows naturally upon the opposition-laden discourse of John and Jesus. The woman represents one of wisdom's children by displaying unfettered gratitude for Jesus' forgiveness of her sins. While Luke portrays Simon as someone who may yet "reject God's purpose" (7:30), it is nonetheless possible to see him as a more open character than commentators generally allow. As one interpreter argues, "It is important that Simon is presented as an open character, who might still learn from Jesus and accept what he is saying."[1] As the dinner host, Simon may be seen as a representative member of the religious establishment—the Pharisees in Luke's day, the church in ours—someone torn between strict religious convention and the grace-filled life of those who know the forgiveness and peace of their Savior.

The plot of the Lukan story proceeds through a number of miniscenes. David Buttrick's "mode of immediacy"[2] would therefore offer real promise to the preacher as a means by which to proclaim this

1. Robert C. Tannehill, *Luke* (Nashville: Abingdon Press, 1996), 138.
2. The mode of immediacy for David Buttrick is the way of shaping a sermon's sequence of moves that is grounded in the field of understanding evoked by the biblical text. See Richard L. Eslinger, *The Web of Preaching: New Options in Homiletical Method* (Nashville: Abingdon Press, 2002), 159–61. Also see David Buttrick, *Homiletic: Moves and Structures* (Philadelphia: Fortress Press, 1987), 333–63.

Luke 7:36–50

Theological Perspective

of the virtuous host melts away. Inner thoughts are revealed. Simeon's words are fulfilled. The contrast between Simon and the unnamed woman, and the deep connections between forgiveness and love that the contrast reveals, are at the theological center of this passage.

For centuries Christian interpreters have conflated Luke's story of the woman who washes Jesus' feet with similar stories in Matthew 26:6–13; Mark 14:3–9; and John 12:1–8. The stories share some significant common features: a woman washes Jesus' feet at a banquet and wipes them with her hair. An objection is raised. Jesus rebukes the objector and defends the woman. All of this happens—at least in the stories in Matthew, Mark, and Luke—in the house of someone named Simon. However, the differences between Luke's story and the stories in the other Gospels are far more significant. In the stories of Matthew, Mark, and John, there is concern about the cost of the ointment or perfume used to anoint Jesus. No such concerns are expressed in Luke. In Matthew, Mark, and John, the story is positioned in close relation to Jesus' death. The anointing anticipates the care the women will show for his crucified body.

Luke relates the story less to Jesus' death and much more to his ministry—and the divergent responses that his ministry evokes. For Luke, it matters very much that the woman is a sinner and the man supposed to be hosting is a Pharisee. In other versions, there is no mention of sin in relation to the woman. While the host is named Simon in all the Synoptics, Matthew and Mark identify Simon as a leper. Only Luke takes pains to establish him as a Pharisee.[1]

These contrasts bring Luke's telling of the story into sharper relief. It is not an anticipation of Jesus' death. It is not a conflict between extravagant worship and care for the poor. It is a story with themes that are central to Luke's Gospel: Jesus eats and drinks with sinners, evoking different responses from people who understand themselves to have been forgiven much and people who understand themselves to have been forgiven little, or not at all.

These themes relativize the importance of debates about the order of salvation presented in this passage. Debates about whether the woman loved Jesus because she had been forgiven or received forgiveness because she loved Jesus have raged with particular intensity since the Reformation. The story has

1. For a more complete contrast of the stories, see Luke Timothy Johnson, *The Gospel of Luke*, Sacra pagina 3, ed. Daniel J. Harrington (Collegeville, MN: The Liturgical Press, 1992), 128–29.

Pastoral Perspective

party. You are unwelcome if you are on the opposing side of any given social issue.

Judgments like these are legion. They are also futile; for if godliness does indeed require moral purity, Jesus is not the only one who does not make the grade. Everybody is in trouble, including Simon, who has not yet learned what Jesus teaches—namely, that God's lines are blurry; sin and repentance connect us more tightly to God than moral uprightness; and it can be really bad to be too good. The pastor can draw on Luke's portrayal of Simon's confusion and Jesus' ease in the woman's presence to comfort and encourage the condemned and self-condemning, and to help the self-satisfied break through their illusion that "we" have nothing in common with "them."

In some congregations, weekly rituals of confession are the means by which all acknowledge a shared human condition in need of merciful help, and all celebrate the divine love that will not let us go. In others, however, the confession is suppressed so that the liturgy will not make people feel bad about themselves. No matter how often Christians read in Scripture that the one who sins and repents causes celebration to break out in heaven (15:7), some of us still refuse to make God happy in that way. Most pastors are painfully aware, however, that on any given Sunday there are parishioners in their pews who have repeatedly repented, in ways great and small, public and intimate.

These humbled souls identify intimately with the unnamed woman shedding tears of grief and gratitude on Jesus' feet. They may not make an outward show of their relief at having been unaccountably pardoned and restored, but the moving drama of Simon's house is playing out within them nonetheless. The pastor can validate their story as the Christian story by his or her adept handling of this text, creating space for testimony about the many times we too could have found ourselves barging into Simon's house, perfume in hand, to reverence the Healer "who saved a wretch like me."

Although some churches provide space for emotional, public altar calls and other "come to Jesus" moments, many do not tolerate displays of even tepid emotion, especially if checkered lives might be laid bare in the process. Sinners in these fellowships have learned to clean up before arriving so as not to disturb the shiny fiction that "we are all good and decent people here" who have never done anything bad enough to require the gift of mercy. This text gives the pastor a chance to explore a congregation's self-understanding, even perhaps to invite people

that it is. In this encounter and dialogue, the woman shows the actions of the offspring of wisdom.

Given this close tie between the story and Jesus' teaching about the children of wisdom, it would be easy to conclude that the story is from L, Luke's own special source. That conclusion, however, hardly explains the significant points of contact of verses 36–50 with Mark's account of the anointing in the house of Simon the leper (Mark 14:3–9//Matt. 26:6–13) on the one hand, and John's account of Mary's anointing Jesus' feet in John 12:1–8 on the other. In Mark, Matthew, and Luke, the accounts treat the unnamed woman as an uninvited guest. In Mark and Matthew, the woman anoints Jesus' head (Matt. 26:7; Mark 14:3), not his feet. Yet in Luke 7:38 and John 12:3 Jesus' feet alone receive the ointment. In Luke, the woman dries his feet with her hair. It is only in John that the reader knows the woman's name (John 12:3). Finally, in all three Synoptic Gospels, the woman carries the ointment in an alabaster vase. These connections are intricate and do not admit of a simple explanation.

Support for the origin of Luke's story in L comes from its unique features. Only in Luke is the woman a "sinner" (*hamartōlos*, vv. 37, 39), a term that does not necessarily suggest prostitution but does refer to some kind of questionable behavior known to the people of her city. To make this woman out to be a prostitute and then to support this idea with the fact that she lets down her hair to dry Jesus' feet goes far beyond what the text says. Loosened hair was a sign of shame or mourning for a woman in first-century Palestine (*Sotah* 7a, *Bava Qamma* 90a, *Yevamot* 116b), not seduction. Either shame or mourning or both would be appropriate to the context in Luke.

The instruction to Simon is likewise unique. The host in verses 36 and 39 is an unnamed Pharisee, but in verse 40, Jesus directs his question to somebody named Simon. This change could mean that the parable of the Two Debtors in verses 40–44 originally circulated independently, but against that conclusion is the fact that Jesus mentions Simon and the woman of the story together in verse 44. The question as to which debtor would be more grateful for the forgiveness of his debt has a foregone conclusion, but Simon's reply is unnecessarily wary and even petulant: "I suppose [*hypolambanō*] the one for whom he canceled the greater debt" (v. 43).

Some evidence for Luke's sources is equivocal. Luke 7:48–50 reminds us of Mark 2:5–12, where Jesus forgives the sins of a paralytic and perceives that the scribes in attendance question his authority

word. The moves of the homiletical plot could be sketched as follows:

Introduction. It is important to shape an introduction that contrasts the woman's behavior with the careful hospitality of Simon. He invites Jesus to dine with him and his guests, and the event is carefully scripted according to the dining conventions of the day.

Move 1. The sermon sets the homiletical plot in motion: "Enter a woman, stage right. She heads directly for Jesus, reclining there at the table. Immediately she kneels, tears washing away dust and dirt, long hair drying feet, kisses, and anointing. Everything done in abandon; no hint of reserve or propriety. All is grateful adoration."

Imagery: If the congregation is blessed with a liturgical dance ministry, a dancer could embody the woman's joy, deep sorrow, and release in a brief performance. Perhaps the preacher could depict a gospel choir singing "O Happy Day (when Jesus washed my sins away)."

Move 2. The sermon proceeds to the next move: "It was to be expected. After all, Simon had trained to observe distinctions like those that exist between clean and unclean, sin and righteousness. So a thought arises from deep in his soul, ready to be spoken: 'If this man were a prophet, he would have known what kind of woman . . .' The logic is deeply ingrained. Once we know what kind of woman, what kind of person, then we would hold ourselves in careful caution. One does not want to get too close. Besides, what would people think?"

Imagery: Perhaps a little story may be appropriate here. One tells of a woman in a small town. Her dilapidated house has a leaky roof and the siding is in shambles. She is confined to the house except for making visits to her doctors, does not go to church, and has a shady past. A church member brings her plight to the board of deacons. Could the church repair the roof and siding? The deacons meet in solemn deliberation. The next day, they tell the church member their decision. The woman did not deserve the church's intervention. There would be no repairs to this woman's house.

Move 3. "Jesus responds to the interior thoughts of his host. 'Simon,' he addresses him, his voice caring and even parental. Then the parable is heard by Simon, the woman, and everyone else in the house. 'Two debtors,' one owing a year and a half's wages,

Luke 7:36–50

Theological Perspective

been pressed into service for arguments about the respective roles of grace and works. Each side can find support in the text. The story concludes with Jesus telling the woman that her faith has saved her. Then after the woman washes Jesus' feet, Jesus says, "Therefore, I tell you, her sins, which were many, have been forgiven" (v. 47a). Forgiveness seems to flow from her action. Yet the very next clause presents the other view: "hence"—because she has been forgiven—"she has shown great love" (v. 47b).

The story Jesus tells about the two creditors also fits well with an interpretation in which divine forgiveness precedes and evokes a response of human love (vv. 41–43). One could account for these differences through a history of composition, as François Bovon suggests.[2] What is most important is that arguments for both sides can be found, and that the story in its canonical form does not work especially well as "evidence" in a doctrinal dispute that took shape centuries after its composition. The theological thrust of the passage is not especially interested in the mechanics of forgiveness.

Instead, the richest theological claims of the text emerge from what both sides of these debates have in common: a sense of the deep connection between God's love for human beings, made manifest in forgiveness, and human love for God, made manifest in adoration. The relevant contrast is not between faith and works, but between the woman who shows great love and the Pharisee who offers Jesus a tepid welcome. A theologically rich discussion of the passage might ask what the present community shares with Simon. It might trace the connections of adoration and forgiveness in the life of the woman and the lives of the people gathered in worship. It might seek to describe the intimate, embodied, and extravagant love the woman shows Jesus—and even risk evoking such expressions of love in the present.

TED A. SMITH

Pastoral Perspective

to consider that the best thing any church could hope for is to be filled with weeping sinners—people whose lives are marked by the humility that comes from knowing the judgment they deserved, but did not receive. It is the actions of the forgiven in the church and the world that are characterized by the most merciful tenderness and the most amazed thanksgiving for the graciousness available to all in Christ.

If the sinful woman's anointing of Jesus is the emotional heart of the text, only slightly less so is Jesus' frank conversation with his host, in which he contrasts the woman's outpouring of loving attention to Simon's aloof withholding. Here we learn that Simon's inclination to look askance at the woman and doubt Jesus' moral character is intimately tied to his failures as a host. There is a whiff of stinginess about him; his lack of largesse in moral matters and his ungenerous welcome of Jesus—no water and no kiss (vv. 44–45)—are at root the same. When Jesus receives the woman and her extravagant care, he reproaches Simon's parsimonious spirit, long before he tells him the story of the generous creditor.

Jesus' parable about debt forgiveness evokes the biblical jubilee, the year of the Lord's magnanimity, when the canceling of one another's debts signals a more encompassing adjustment of human relationships. Through the redistribution of wealth we rediscover one another not as debtors and creditors, but as beloved kin. To forgive debts—moral as well as financial—is to exercise the generosity that loving much entails. The story of the sinful woman in Simon's house turns out in the end to be a call to mission. Thus the pastor will help focus her congregation outward, in a spirit of identification with sinners, withholding none of the mercy we ourselves have received.

MARY LUTI

2. François Bovon, *Luke I: A Commentary on the Gospel of Luke 1:1–9:50*, Hermeneia, ed. Helmut Koester (Minneapolis: Augsburg, 2002), 297.

Feasting on the Gospels

Exegetical Perspective

to do so. His final statement to the woman in Luke 7:50, however, is word for word the beginning of his parting statement to the woman with the hemorrhage in Mark 5:34, Matthew 9:22, and Luke 8:48: "Your faith has saved you." Following this, Luke 7:50 and 8:48 have "go [*poreuou*] in peace." Mark 5:34 has "go [*hypage*] in peace."

The best explanation is that the author of Luke did indeed find the story of the woman anointing Jesus in his sources, where it already showed features we also see in Mark and John. For example, "Your faith has saved you" in Mark 5:34, Matthew 9:22, and Luke 8:48 can be grammatically either masculine or feminine. Indeed, the dismissal could easily be a liturgical expression put on the lips of Jesus in L. The use of "go" (*poreuomai*) in Luke 7:50 (L) would account for the presence of the same verb in Luke 8:48, where Luke's source, Mark 5:34, read "go away" (*hypagō*).

Luke avoids "doublets," dual versions of the same story in the tradition. For instance, Luke 9:10–17 has the feeding of the five thousand from Mark 6:30–44, but nothing in Luke corresponds to the feeding of the four thousand in Mark 8:1–10. Likewise, Luke does not contain the anointing in Bethany, even though the account was in the author's source, Mark 14:3–9. It would be uncharacteristic of the Third Gospel to have included both 7:36–50 and a parallel to Mark 14:3–9.

We see the vindication of Wisdom's children (7:35) through the faithful and loving actions of the woman who anointed Jesus' feet (vv. 36–50). Her overwhelming display of love differs sharply from Simon's overwhelming indifference to the most basic duties of hospitality. Her loving action gains for her both forgiveness of her many sins (v. 47) and healing/salvation (v. 50). By contrast, Simon's treatment of Jesus demonstrates little in the way of love and so holds little hope for either forgiveness or salvation.

FRED L. HORTON

Homiletical Perspective

the other owing a couple of month's pay. When neither could pay, the creditor forgave both. Then Jesus adds the big question to the little parable: 'Which of them will love him more?' Simon's answer is a bit hesitant, but honest. It is the one who owed more. That one, forgiven the huge debt, would display much more affection and gratitude. In spite of the slight difficulty in choking out the answer, the Lord responds to Simon, 'You have judged rightly.' Welcome to wisdom's household."

Imagery: A young couple adopts a boy born with AIDS. Who rejoices in this: those who assert that the disease is God's judgment, or the loving adoptive parents?

Move 4. Finally, the sermon can ask the congregation to consider key questions: "Who then is the true host? To be sure, Jesus is the guest, but the identity of the host has become a bit confused. Still addressing Simon, Jesus asks, 'Do you see this woman?' That in itself is a profound question. For those like Simon, it has become second nature not to see those people who do not measure up to certain moral and religious standards. Jesus asks Simon and the 'church of Simon,' do we see this woman? Good question. Then the Lord tallies the various actions of the woman and of Simon in regard to the matter of hosting. Simon: no water provided for Jesus' feet when he entered; the woman: 'bathed my feet with her tears.' Simon: no kiss; the woman: a ceaseless kissing of Jesus' feet. Simon: no anointing of Jesus' head with even supermarket olive oil; the woman: a lavish anointing of Jesus' feet with costly ointment.

"The values of these acts of hosting are added up and the results mirror the debts that were forgiven. The woman's score is about a year and a half's worth of gratitude. Simon scores in the low two months' range. Can Simon even take in the massive reversal that has taken place? 'See this woman?' If so, can Simon see that she is the one who has assumed the role of a gracious host at this banquet?"

Imagery: The intention is to call to mind examples of communal expressions of gratitude (especially examples by outsiders). These might include the warm and heartfelt welcome to church members extended by prisoners who are participating in their Cursillo, Tres Dias, or Walk to Emmaus.

The sermon's conclusion, then, invites the listeners to join with "this woman" in lavish praise of the Lord. The congregation is also invited to join with those whom Christ welcomes into the joy of his reign.

RICHARD L. ESLINGER

Luke 8:1–3

¹Soon afterwards he went on through cities and villages, proclaiming and bringing the good news of the kingdom of God. The twelve were with him, ²as well as some women who had been cured of evil spirits and infirmities: Mary, called Magdalene, from whom seven demons had gone out, ³and Joanna, the wife of Herod's steward Chuza, and Susanna, and many others, who provided for them out of their resources.

Theological Perspective

It is tempting to read Luke 8:1–3 without stopping to notice what it says. There is no dramatic action. It can feel like a utilitarian bridge between the great story of the woman who anoints Jesus (7:36–50) and the famous parable of the Sower (8:4–15). Yet it is the passage's location that hints at its deeper significance. Luke 8:1–3 brings to a close the "little interpolation" in which the author inserts material into the larger narrative framework that he takes over from the Gospel of Mark. As the end of this insertion, Luke 8:1–3 distills crucial elements of Luke's distinct understanding of the gospel. This little summary and transition is not a passage to be skipped.

Verse 2 says that "some women" are with Jesus. Luke gives names of three of them: Mary of Magdala, Joanna, and Susanna. He also writes that there are "many others," and that they provide material support for the community gathered around Jesus. This same group of women, Luke says, keeps watch with other disciples as Jesus is crucified, accompanies the body of Jesus to the tomb, and tends to it with spices and ointments (23:55). Mary Magdalene, Joanna, and other women are the first to learn of Jesus' resurrection. They run to share the news with the male disciples (24:1–12). Luke's mention of the women suggests their significance for the way Luke understands the ministry of Jesus and the church that arose from it.

Pastoral Perspective

In this short passage, we see a peripatetic Jesus, on the move "through cities and villages . . . bringing the good news of the kingdom of God" (v. 1). The time is short. God's new era is imminent, and no distance or trouble can slow its proclamation or its proclaimer. If he were traveling alone, this headlong Jesus might forget to eat or sleep; and he might run out of money. Fortunately, he is not alone. The Twelve and "some women" are "with him" (v. 2). Among the Twelve, we know of only one who has communal duties: Judas, who keeps the accounts. It is the women who ante up to pay the bills (v. 3). It would not be far-fetched to imagine that they also do the cooking and the weekly wash.

Those who exalt traditional gender roles use this text as evidence that God intends women to serve men's needs in the background, so that men may do God's work in the foreground without a mundane care. The text does not require this view, however. It is instructive that the women in this passage do not send supportive checks from back home. Rather, they supply the group up close, in the daily unfolding of their own *sequela Christi* ("following of Christ"), exemplifying obedience to Jesus' insistence on dispossession for all who would follow him as disciples.

Because Luke describes the accompanying women as people cured or exorcised (v. 2), it is tempting to

Exegetical Perspective

The author has treated us to several surprises in the collection of pericopes in Luke 7:18–8:3. We learned in 7:29 that "all the people" who submitted to John's baptism included an unlikely group, tax collectors. In 7:31–34, we learned that "this generation" sullenly refused to respond to either John the Baptist or Jesus; but we also learned to our surprise that some, at least, accepted them (7:35). When Jesus had dinner with a Pharisee (7:36–50), it is no surprise that Jesus and the Pharisee fell into a debate; but the debate was about the surprise of a weeping woman interrupting their dinner to anoint Jesus' feet. Yet this sinful woman, not the Pharisee, gained forgiveness. The exceptions have proved the rule. The baptism of tax collectors emphasized that baptism was for "all the people." The woman who bathed Jesus' feet with her tears was not the only person who could receive divine forgiveness, but her relief showed that forgiveness was not just for the religious elite.

We now come to the last surprise.

In Luke 8:1–3, women are the only followers who receive any real attention, not because they were the only faithful followers of Jesus, but because the social restrictions of first-century Palestine made a large following of women improbable for a teacher like Jesus. Our passage about the "many others" (Greek: feminine plural) who accompanied and provided for

Homiletical Perspective

This pericope provides a narrative marker for Luke's readers. Material about Jesus' ministry is summarized by way of restatement—Jesus is doing those things that Luke first announced in Luke 4:18–19—and provides an important and new insight into the community that follows Jesus. Three women, named along with the Twelve, are accompanied by "many others." The women serve as benefactors and also testify by their presence to the startling and unique nature of the good news of God's reign.

One approach to shaping a sermon on this new page in Luke's story of Jesus is to turn to David Buttrick's "mode of reflectivity."[1] We will identify a series of homiletical moves designed to guide the community's reflection as it attends to the Scripture passage. These moves may be sketched as follows:

Move 1. The sermon sets the stage for the congregation's reflection: "Jesus will not cease proclaiming the good news. He moves along through cities and villages, everywhere bringing the good news of the

---

1. The mode of reflectivity does not organize the sermonic plot immediately upon the movement and sequence of the biblical text. Rather, the respective moves of the sermon will shape a field of meaning within congregational consciousness that is evoked by the text or contemporary context. See Richard L. Eslinger, *The Web of Preaching: New Options in Homiletical Method* (Nashville: Abingdon Press, 2002), 161–63. Also see David Buttrick, *Homiletic: Moves and Structures* (Philadelphia: Fortress Press, 1987), 365–90.

Luke 8:1–3

Theological Perspective

Luke describes at least some of the women as having been "cured of evil spirits and infirmities" (v. 2). Leaving their homes to follow Jesus, they embody the Lukan ideal of faithful response. Like the Twelve, they are "with Jesus" (v. 1), "providing for them [Jesus and the community around him] out of their resources" (v. 3). Some commentators have taken this as a complete description of the discipleship of the women, as if they do nothing more than provide financial support for the preaching and healing ministries of men. Women might be "deaconesses"—the word shares a root with the word translated by the NRSV as "providing for"—who simply support the ministries of others. Yet there is nothing to suggest that Luke's description of the women is meant to be comprehensive. On the contrary, Luke describes the women doing much more than paying the bills. They follow Jesus to the cross. They anoint his body. They keep watch, receive the good news of Easter, and proclaim that news to others. Mary, Joanna, Susanna, and other women respond to Jesus in ways that lead them into rich, complex ministries.

Christian commentators are right to celebrate the faithfulness of these women. They are right to argue that the stories of these women show how Jesus calls women to discipleship and how women have long responded with ministries that demand recognition from the whole community. Moreover, these stories can be proclaimed as good news without resort to the caricatures of Second Temple Judaism that have poisoned too many Christian sermons and commentaries. Those arguments depend on portraits of Judaism as especially repressive of women and of Jesus as a boundary-breaking liberator who invites women into roles they have never played before. Contrary to these portraits, Amy-Jill Levine notes the women with Jesus

> all had freedom to travel and access to their own funds. The women who provided him support, such as Mary and Martha (see Luke 10:38–42; John 11–12), not only had access to their own funds but could also own their own homes. Women frequented synagogue gatherings and the Jerusalem Temple, and neither place had balconies where the women were to be relegated.[1]

In calling women to play significant roles in the life of the new community around him, Jesus does not make a radical break with Jewish practices of his day. That does not mean that Jesus' call to women, and the faithful responses of women, are not good

1. Amy-Jill Levine, *The Misunderstood Jew: The Church and the Scandal of the Jewish Jesus* (San Francisco: HarperSanFransisco, 2006), 143.

Pastoral Perspective

assume Jesus had healed them and that their decision to follow him was a highly emotional one. Apart from promoting stereotypes, this assumption ignores the fact that Jesus esteemed many women for their faith and love before he cured them or someone for whom they pleaded. Gratitude is a powerful emotional motivator, not to be ignored; but the careful reader will not sell women short by describing these women in emotional terms. He will see in them what Luke surely does: called disciples, equipped by their faith to follow in the Way.

Although women in progressive congregations rarely hear a traditional application of this text from the pulpit, many have experienced the assumptions that undergird it. Women of every conviction, class, and condition continue to struggle with external and internalized expectations and demands, as well as with society's unequal valuation of their work. The pastoral minister might reflect on the impossible binds women find themselves in when it comes to gender roles and to the kinds of work and service that matter most.

A sensitive minister will not imply that background service is inferior to foreground leadership, however. From a pastoral standpoint, affirming the gifts and sacrifices of women and men who choose supportive roles is not only to do justice to their contributions; it is also a way to temper any impulse to lead or stand out that is not grounded in readiness to serve in more hidden ways too. Nonetheless, the pastoral minister will be willing also to address the frustration and grievance many women feel when their call to leadership goes unrecognized or their gifts go unused, even as they are left holding the full bag of responsibility for meeting the needs of others, making others looking good, or attending to details so that everything turns out well.

Some listeners may feel queasy at the mere mention of women in Jesus' entourage. After all, nothing in the text suggests that the women follow him at a decent distance, or that they modestly repair to roadside inns at night while Jesus and the Twelve rough it under the stars. That women are "with him" raises questions pious Christians generally suppress—touchy questions having to do with what we normally mean when we talk about "providing" for real human beings with real bodies and real physical, spiritual, and emotional needs.

We are not obliged to think of the text's "providing" as a monthly allowance passed immaculately from Susanna's hand to Judas's purse. Rather, we may—perhaps we must—imagine that the resources

Exegetical Perspective

Jesus and his disciples (v. 3) would have likely been jarring to Luke's readers.

These women included, but were not limited to, women "who had been cured of evil spirits and infirmities" (v. 2). One of them, Mary Magdalene, had received healing from seven demons. Notice how our writer omitted Jesus as their healer, an omission implying that the women did not follow Jesus only because of his healing power. Luke mentions two other women by name: Joanna, well married to Chuza, an estate manager (*epitropos*) for Herod Antipas (v. 3), and Susanna (v. 3), who is of no known rank but has the dignity of a personal name. These women made provision "out of their resources" (*ek tōn hyparchontōn autais*, v. 3, literally "from what belonged to them"), suggesting strongly that they were women of some means, a likelihood also implied by the high rank of Joanna, wife of Chuza (v. 3). This suggestion of wealth goes hand in hand with the likelihood that such women would have the leisure to accompany Jesus around the Galilee.

Mary Magdalene means "Mary of Magdala," a reference to a town on the west coast of the Sea of Galilee near modern Mejdel. Aramaic *magdala'* or *migdala'* means "[the] tower"; so the town's name probably refers to a prominent structure there. That this Mary received healing from seven evil spirits is a matter otherwise found in New Testament literature only in Mark 16:9, where the non-Markan writer has used the expected *ekballō*, "throw out," to refer to the exorcism of her demons. Luke does not identify Mary Magdalene with the sinful woman who anointed Jesus' feet in Luke 7:36–50.

Mary Magdalene (v. 2) and Joanna (v. 3) find additional mention in Luke 24:10, where the writer includes them with "Mary the mother of James, and the other women." Mary Magdalene plays a role in all the Gospel accounts of the death and resurrection of Jesus (Mark 15:40, 47; 16:1; Matt. 27:56, 61; 28:1; Luke 24:10; John 19:25; 20:1, 11–18); but she plays the least prominent role in Luke, having only two mentions (8:2; 24:10), both of which put her in the company of Joanna and other women.

Does the participle *diēkonoun*, "serve" (NRSV "provided for," v. 3), which describes what the women did, suggest doing household services like cooking in addition to providing material support? The verb in Luke–Acts sometimes means household chores. For instance, the Twelve in Acts 6:2 complain that they should not have to relinquish God's word to serve (*diakonein*) tables. Further, the service that Peter's newly healed mother-in-law performed for

Homiletical Perspective

kingdom of God. Along with Jesus, in every age, those called to follow are graced with the same commission: proclaim the good news. This mission is always a journey. It is what we do; it is who we are." (Note: It is important not to set up a "then-now" dichotomy between Jesus' ministry and our own as disciples. Keep the same present tense for both Jesus' words and actions and those of his church today.)

Imagery: A concrete and vivid example needs to be provided of a vital mission church, preferably one sponsored in part by the congregation or its judicatory. Perhaps members or pastors of the congregation have visited the new church. For example, one congregation in Ohio supports Amen United Methodist Church in Cambodia. This vital community of new Christians is mainly young—because of the "killing fields" horrors of the recent past—and fervent in their service and joy.

Move 2. The sermon continues to encourage reflection: "Look at Jesus' entourage, those who are following him. Yes, there are the Twelve and along with them are the women followers; some are named, but Luke reports that there were 'many others.' Among the women who follow Jesus is Mary of Magdala, healed of seven demons, now freed from such oppression. Then Luke points out Joanna, wife of Herod's steward, a woman of considerable influence and means. Susanna is also mentioned, but apart from her being among those who follow along with the Twelve, Luke refrains from commenting on her status. There are, of course, the 'many others.' (We could also provide the names and ministries of some of the other women, as we do on All Saints' Day [Sunday]. They include Felicitas and Perpetua in the very earliest years after the New Testament; Scholastica, the fourth-century sister of Benedict; medieval mystics and counselors like Catherine of Siena and Hildegard of Bingen; John Wesley's mother, Susanna; Sojourner Truth, abolitionist; Mother Teresa of Calcutta; and the list goes on. The preacher is invited to amend the listing of these women saints by referring to those in her or his own church tradition.) All are among those 'many others' who are following Jesus."

Imagery: The urgency now is to provide the listeners with an "eyewitness account" of one of the women saints who are among those following Jesus. Perhaps a church mother within the congregation who has joined the great cloud of witnesses should be celebrated. In any event, the description of her ministry and witness will be concrete and well imaged.

Luke 8:1–3

Theological Perspective

news. It simply means that the good news comes not in comparison to an imagined Judaism, but in the fact of the call of women and the shape of their response.

For Luke, the women's willingness to share their possessions is a sign of the depth of their participation in the community, not of their restriction to some limited, supporting role. Luke makes clear how much he values the sharing of possessions in Acts 1:13–14 and 2:41–47. Mary, Joanna, Susanna, and the other women anticipate this distinctive mark of faithfulness in Luke's vision of the church. The willingness of these women to share possessions challenges our own understandings of what it means to be church.

The women also seem to have left whatever family they have in order to follow Jesus. Like the Twelve, they seem to be traveling with Jesus without spouses, parents, children, or other family members. Joanna, at least, is married; but she seems to have left her husband, Chuza, in Herod's court. In this too the women serve as models for discipleship. Jesus leaves his own family, and when they come to him later in this chapter, he responds with a new understanding of kinship: "My mother and my brothers are those who hear the word of God and do it" (8:19–21). Likewise, in Luke 9:59–62, Jesus rebukes a man who says that he will follow Jesus as soon as he has buried his father and a man who simply wants to say goodbye to the people at his home.

The call to follow Jesus demands immediate response. It may require leaving behind families made through birth or marriage, to join the new family gathered around Jesus. Again, the women are exemplary disciples. What matters is not just the fact of the women's discipleship, but the challenge that the particular content of their discipleship poses to the church today. What would it mean for the community gathered around Jesus to take precedence over other family ties? The call of Jesus—and the faithful responses of these women—presses just such difficult questions on followers of Jesus today.

TED A. SMITH

Pastoral Perspective

the women shared included many human forms of love, loyalty, service, and commitment. If stewardship sermons routinely ask us to share more than our money by giving generously of our whole selves; and if self-gift in affection and accountability is an ideal among us in the church, why should it be any different in that first church of traveling companions?

One need not go the route of the *The Da Vinci Code* or *The Last Temptation of Christ* to impress on listeners the possible incarnational implications of these women's companionship. Perhaps the most pastorally important thing is that, simply by reporting that they provided for Jesus' needs, the text forces us to discover that Jesus actually had needs. He had a body. He needed to change his tunic, brush his hair, wash his face, fill his rumbling stomach, empty his bowels, and sleep at night. He had an emotional and spiritual life. He needed people to talk to and worry with and touch, to sing with and pray with and love. He needed light and air and beauty. For some of these things, he also needed money.

To flesh out the church's often disembodied Savior is a task of great pastoral urgency in a world that routinely denies goods and services to meet the most basic requirements of millions of bodies, casually violating their integrity in the most horrific ways. It also matters to people in the pews who daily shoulder the care of bodies in their professions and families, or whose own bodies require the constant attention of generous providers.

A Jesus without needs, or a Jesus sublimely indifferent to them, is an ineffectual judge of crimes against the body. He has little to say to the embodied human condition. He can only suggest we rise above our troubles and pains, our needs and limitations, our desires and feelings, and get on with it. The pastoral minister will introduce her listeners to the Jesus the generous women knew, a human being who needed the care they gave him from the first bright days of his preaching to the day they went to sweeten the stench of his battered body in the grave.

MARY LUTI

Exegetical Perspective

Jesus and his entourage in Luke 4:39 was certainly household labor, as was the household labor Martha complained about doing in Luke 10:40 while her sister Mary sat at Jesus' feet. Yet in other Lukan contexts, the verb *diakoneō* is nonspecific. See Luke 22:26–27 and Acts 19:22 (NRSV "helpers"). Serving Jesus and the Twelve "out of their resources" in verse 3 is less than specific, however, and might include anything from material support to the preparation of meals.

All three verses come from the author's hand and not from a source like Mark or L, as shown by several Lukan features in the narrative. The pericope begins with the secondary Hebraism *kai egeneto*, "and it happened," followed by an expression of time, a typical Lukan feature (NRSV "soon afterwards"). The expression of time is the unusual Greek expression *en tō kathexēs*, "in order," which occurs five times in Luke–Acts but occurs nowhere else either in the New Testament or in the Septuagint. *Diōdeuō*, "go through" (v. 1), occurs twenty times in the Septuagint, but in the New Testament only here and in Acts 17:1.

The women had found relief from "evil spirits and infirmities." Neither with respect to "some women" nor in the verse's specific reference to Mary Magdalene does the author use the customary verb *ekballō*, "cast out," of the exorcisms; rather, he subsumes the exorcisms under the general rubric of healing. The only possible non-Lukan use of "heal" in reference to exorcism is Matthew 17:16, 18, but only if we regard the boy's malady, "being moon-struck" (*selēniazetai*, Matt. 17:15, NRSV "epileptic"), as a case of demon possession. Luke 6:18 and Luke 8:2, however, unambiguously employ the verb "heal" (*therapeuō*), not "cast out" (*ekballō*), in reference to exorcism.

We hear from this company of women again. Luke tells us that it was "the women who had come with him from Galilee" who witnessed the burial of Jesus and returned on the first day to do their final service for him (23:55–24:1). These women are the first witnesses to the empty tomb (24:2–3) and to the proclamation of the heavenly messengers, that Jesus had risen (24:4–5). Mary Magdalene and Joanna reappear as part of this company and go with them to announce Jesus' resurrection to doubting disciples (24:10–11).

FRED L. HORTON

Homiletical Perspective

Move 3. "The procession is unique, a 'singularity,' as physicists would say. Nowhere else would such a strange collection of people be journeying together. Men and women, rich and poor, all led by Jesus. The message he announced was singular, too—the good news of the kingdom of God. It was blossoming as they traveled; embodied in those who traveled together with him. However, if this evangelical procession was unique, it was linked together with other singular acts of God. The angel Gabriel came to a town in Galilee called Nazareth, to a virgin named Mary. 'Greetings, favored one' (1:28), the angel announced. God was coming to a manger. At the Jordan, Jesus also came to John to be baptized. A voice came from heaven, 'You are my Son, the Beloved' (3:22), and the Beloved began his work among us. His journey continued, although at the end the Twelve betrayed, fled, were scattered. The Lord 'descended to the dead' and then as promised rose in glory. The women who had come to grieve at the place of death heard the words of life: 'He is not here' (24:5).The ultimate singularity—the Lord is risen indeed.'"

Imagery: The Orthodox icons of the nativity and the women at the tomb both point to this singularity of Christ. The babe is wrapped in swaddling clothes that look much like the graveclothes heaped up in the tomb. Heaven is opened in both, and the Spirit descends. Mary—the "God-bearer"—gives birth to the Child while at the empty tomb the women watch in amazement at Christ's triumph over death.

Conclusion. "So proclaiming the good news is a matter of who we are as disciples, whom we include, and what we say and do. The good news of the kingdom of God, the good news to the poor, is release to the captives, recovery of sight to the blind, and deliverance to all who are oppressed. Thus the year of the Lord's favor is proclaimed. The kind of community that embodies and proclaims this good news has everything to do with God's inbreaking reign. Only a singular, even unique community can bear testimony to the mystery that in Christ God comes—in a manger, at the Jordan, to the cross, on the Emmaus road, at Pentecost, and, when the Eucharist is celebrated, 'in this Holy Meal.'"

RICHARD L. ESLINGER

Luke 8:4–15

⁴When a great crowd gathered and people from town after town came to him, he said in a parable: ⁵"A sower went out to sow his seed; and as he sowed, some fell on the path and was trampled on, and the birds of the air ate it up. ⁶Some fell on the rock; and as it grew up, it withered for lack of moisture. ⁷Some fell among thorns, and the thorns grew with it and choked it. ⁸Some fell into good soil, and when it grew, it produced a hundredfold." As he said this, he called out, "Let anyone with ears to hear listen!"

⁹Then his disciples asked him what this parable meant. ¹⁰He said, "To you it has been given to know the secrets of the kingdom of God; but to others I speak in parables, so that

'looking they may not perceive,
and listening they may not understand.'

Theological Perspective

Far from treating this parable as a way to classify people into categories of the spiritually mature or the morally saved, the parable invites us to acknowledge that our hearing and believing God's Word does not have to do with how much we know but with the God who sows the kingdom of God among us and in us.

Two Reformed doctrines may be helpful. The first doctrine has to do with true faith. Sixteenth-century Reformers spoke of true saving faith that consisted of three parts: *notitia* (information), *assensus* (belief), and *fiducia* (trust). These can be demonstrated with the following sentences: That is a chair (*notitia*); I believe that chair can support me (*assensus*); I trust the chair can support me, so I will sit in the chair (*fiducia*). The first aspect is a superficial acknowledgment of raw data; the second aspect is the acknowledgment that the stated information is true; the third aspect is an internalized trust that the information is not only true in a general, abstract sense, but that its truthfulness has touched the soul and heart to the point of trusting.

The second doctrine has to do with Scripture. When the Reformers spoke of the doctrine of *sola Scriptura*, apprehension of the truths of Scripture rested upon God's initiative in two places: in Scripture itself and in the reader/hearer. Concerning God's

Pastoral Perspective

The films *House of Sand and Fog* (2003) and *Crash* (2004) captured my full attention from the beginning to the end, and resonated in me within the days that followed. As I tried to understand what was powerful about those movies, I came to realize that my mind had made a straight correlation between those fictional stories and the urban setting where I live today. Moreover, the movies contained many of the same sensitive lessons that I have learned from real-life incidents and personal experiences. This regularly happens when we listen to good, concrete, shocking, inspiring stories that make us consider our own lives. Such shocks of recognition become important pedagogical moments in our lifelong learning experiences and encourage us to respond.

Jesus had spoken about what it takes to believe, or to have faith, challenging his disciples and those who approached him to make radical moves toward the kingdom of God and all its implications. He pictured faith by showing them how the faith of an individual that owned a name, a heart, a story, and countless existential questions, no matter who she might be, is much above the Pharisee's ethics, morals, and religious discourses and logic (7:36–50). This was the kind of faith that led a sinful woman to wet his feet with her tears, then wipe them with her hair, and gently kiss and pour perfume on his feet. That

[11]"Now the parable is this: The seed is the word of God. [12]The ones on the path are those who have heard; then the devil comes and takes away the word from their hearts, so that they may not believe and be saved. [13]The ones on the rock are those who, when they hear the word, receive it with joy. But these have no root; they believe only for a while and in a time of testing fall away. [14]As for what fell among the thorns, these are the ones who hear; but as they go on their way, they are choked by the cares and riches and pleasures of life, and their fruit does not mature. [15]But as for that in the good soil, these are the ones who, when they hear the word, hold it fast in an honest and good heart, and bear fruit with patient endurance."

Exegetical Perspective

Parables are a difficult literary form to study. Their everyday images and their familiarity can lead the reader to feel overly comfortable with them and certain of their meanings. Parables in their original setting within Jesus' ministry, however, were intended to make the hearer uncomfortable by their unexpected use of common images or the shocking outcome of everyday situations. The renowned scholar C. H. Dodd defined a parable as "a metaphor or simile drawn from nature or common life, arresting the hearer by its vividness or strangeness, and leaving the mind in sufficient doubt about its precise application to tease it into active thought."[1]

The three-part structure of this passage supports Dodd's definition. The uncertainty raised in the mind of Jesus' hearers by the parable itself (vv. 4–8) leads to a question and response that explains the inconsistent results of speaking in parables (vv. 9–10), as well as an interpretation of the parable (vv. 11–15).

The parable depicts a mode of planting that shocks in its wastefulness. Most seed bears no fruit. The parable takes the risky nature of the process for granted, although it concludes with a matter-of-fact assertion that some did fall on good soil. Joachim Jeremias, a prominent parable scholar, highlights the

1. C. H. Dodd, *The Parables of the Kingdom* (New York: Charles Scribner's Sons, 1961), 5.

Homiletical Perspective

"What is a parable?" This was the question posed to me by an elder as I stood on the chancel steps before the session with my sixth-grade confirmation class as we were being examined for church membership. I replied with my memorized answer: "A parable is an earthly story with a heavenly meaning." Decades later, I believe this definition of a biblical parable still holds true, as long as the "heavenly meaning" does not become *too familiar*, thereby getting lost in the earthly story. Acting out the literal meaning of the word "parable"—"places alongside" or "tosses against"—the story mixes the familiar from everyday life with the unfamiliar "secrets of the kingdom of God"; a sower, seed, birds, rocks, and soil rub up against the choked, snatched, fallen-away, held-fast, and fruit-bearing Word of God. The results are less of a corresponding harmony, and more of an intentional discord. What was once familiar is no longer so. The hearer, once easily located in an accustomed setting, becomes dislocated in relation to the God's kingdom and God's Word. So great is the unfamiliarity, the unease of dislocation, when Jesus calls out, "Hello, is anyone listening?" (a loose translation of verse 8, perhaps in response to the awkward silence and blank stares on faces), the disciples could only reply, "What does it mean?"

Luke 8:4–15

Theological Perspective

initiative in Scripture, the doctrine of the perspicuity of Scripture meant that the message of holy Scripture as God's Word written is clear and lucid, compelling in its witness to the triune God revealed in Jesus Christ through the Holy Spirit. The inherent perspicuity of Scripture is what Reformed scholasticism termed *principium cognoscendi internum* (internal source of knowledge). Concerning God's initiative upon the reader, the doctrine of perspicacity meant that a reader can apprehend and penetrate the message of Scripture but that the totalizing effects of sin had so infiltrated the mind and heart of humanity as to cause Scripture's message to be obscured.

Since perspicuity connotes clearness of the text, and perspicacity connotes clearness of understanding, the Reformers were suggesting that lack of comprehension was our fault, not the text's. Therefore God's initiative is continually needed. Without the illuminating assistance of the Holy Spirit, human beings cannot grasp the otherwise perspicuous nature of Holy Scripture. The Holy Spirit not only provides comprehending power, but regenerates the heart to be fertile soil to receive the seed that is sown, what is termed *principium cognoscendi externum* (external source of knowledge).

Two common interpretations of the parable before us call to mind these Reformed doctrines of faith and Scripture in that both find fault with the soil for the lack of harvest. The first interpretation describes the four soils as four different types of hearts/people. One soil/heart allows worldly cares to choke the young plant; another cannot resist the influence of evil; a third has no depth and so the seed/word cannot take root; the fourth is good, fertile soil. Another interpretation sees three types of soil that are exposed to the seed but finally do not have true saving faith. Somehow there was temporary acceptance (*assensus*), but not ultimate, enduring trust (*fiducia*).

While both interpretations place fault on the deficiency of the hearers and readers, each does so from a particular angle of vision. The first interpretation sees immaturity in the hearers/readers, requiring "stronger" faith (quality) or "more" faith (quantity); somehow we have not been serious enough about the Word of God. The second interpretation separates humanity between those who were intended to receive the Word and those who ultimately were not, a division between those "elect" and the "nonelect." Both interpretations emphasize the *notitia*, the contents of the faith and outward evidence of saving faith.

Pastoral Perspective

event exemplified how differently he and the Pharisees understood and related to sinners. Here was a real, face-to-face experience of life that caused each character—Jesus, the disciples, and the Pharisees—to respond to the very concrete, observable faith of "[a] woman in the city, who was a sinner" (7:37).

Now, with the parable of the Sower (vv. 4–15), Jesus pictures faith and discipleship from a different angle. Note again that Jesus sees not from a decontextualized, otherworldly perspective, but from within a recognizable this-worldly context. He shifts from an unexpected experience to a familiar real-life analogy full of significance for those who believed and those who decided not to respond to the gracious, inviting, and salvific message of the gospel. This parable is not fictional imagination or simply a story that illustrates one of his many teachings. Jesus' story is based on the life experience of a particular sower of his time that is applicable to our time. In one sense, this parable speaks out of personal knowledge—that of Jesus, that of his hearers, as well as yours and mine—and the life struggles that may prevent people from responding in faith.

In uncovering the meaning and applicability of the parable, we see first that there are different places where seeds may fall as the sower goes out to sow his seed—on the path, on rocky ground, among thorns, and on good, fertile soil—and the differences of soil and environment are what make the whole difference.

Second, one realizes that Jesus depicts an all-embracing, merciful God who does not sow different seeds, as if the God of salvation were careless enough to intentionally make some of them incapable of germinating. If this were the case, then anyone who receives the seed would experience the inevitable placebo effect. Either the person would be given a seed incapable of generating anything because there is nothing in it, or a seed less effective and weak, or a seed that would prove to be remarkably fruitful—an extra-strength type of seed. No! A just, graceful, merciful, all-embracing God sows the seeds created to be absolutely the same, full of God's own word, with a passionate heart full of harvesting hope.

The seeds that are the gospel contain abundant and eternal life, ready to flourish. They are ready to infuse a powerful life that brings salvation here and there, for now and then, depending on the response of faith of those who hear the gospel message. The response contained in this parable is characterized as the "word" and associated with something that is

Feasting on the Gospels

contrast present in the parable between the frustrations of the sower's labor and the rich harvest that ensues.[2] As Luke retells the parable, it is the image of a tremendous produce, "a hundredfold," that remains in the hearers' mind. Unlike Mark 4:8 and Matthew 13:8, where the resulting yield varies, here the fullest outcome is certain for those seeds that find fertile ground. Yet the specific situation to which this agricultural image relates is never made clear in the parable. The hearer is left "in sufficient doubt about its precise application."

In the second section of the passage, the uncertainty of the listener is expressed in the doubt of Jesus' disciples, who ask Jesus the meaning of the parable (v. 9). Although verse 10 has been interpreted as a problematic interlude on the purpose of parables that postpones Jesus' response to the disciples' question, it makes more sense to read this verse as an explanation of why parables can be difficult to hear and comprehend. As such, it functions as a response to the disciples' question, when one recognizes that the "meaning" of the parable is bound up in the difficulty of hearing and understanding the word.

When Luke's language is compared to his source, Mark 4:10–12, it becomes clear that the common (though difficult) conclusion derived from Jesus' statement in Luke 8:10—that the purpose of the parables is to obfuscate the message, for all except his inner circle—cannot be supported in Luke's retelling. First, there is no narrative transition that separates the disciples and those closest to Jesus from the listening crowd (unlike Mark 4:10). The intended audience for his teaching, therefore, may be much wider than in Mark. Second, Luke does not include Mark's divisive language of "insiders" and "outsiders," distinguishing only between those who hear him and "others" (v. 10). Third, commentators have noted that the Greek phrase translated "so that" (v. 10) can be used to express the consequences of an action, as opposed to its purpose. Reading the phrase in this way would deny that Jesus *intended* his parables to confuse, although this *may* be the outcome. This reading parallels the situation in the parable—in some cases what one sows bears fruit; in others it does not.

The passage concludes with Jesus' explicit interpretation of the parable. Many commentators identify this interpretation as allegorical (i.e., particular elements within the story are assigned specific symbolic meanings). They argue that such allegorical interpretations were the additions of later editors

2. Joachim Jeremias, *Rediscovering the Parables* (New York: Charles Scribner's Sons, 1966), 119–20.

Luke's parable of the Sower—what does it mean? In constructing a reply for today's hearer, the preacher is presented with various options in sermon form and method. A popular approach treats the parable as a contemporary allegory with clear one-on-one correspondences with characters, objects, and events in the story. Here the sermon is like a morality play where warnings are given to the congregation about the specific dangers of initially hearing the Word but losing your salvation by succumbing to temptation; experiencing initial joy but withering because of a lack of rootedness in God's Word (a neglect of Bible study, daily devotion, and worship); and not bearing fruit because faith is in a chokehold by life's distractions, demands, and pursuits of riches and pleasure. By contrast, those who hear *and* bear fruit are lifted up as models of fortitude, honesty, a good heart, and patient endurance. Illustrations of those who bear fruit are often named from Christian history or from the life of the congregation. Implied or stated, the sermon's concluding charge is to be fruitful bearers of the Word.

Although the intent of such a sermon is to serve as a warning against laxness and to encourage fruitful virtues, it should be noted there are no signs of repentance in the parable and no restoration from a change of heart. Who wants to identify with a faith that is hopelessly devoured, parched, or choked? The danger for the hearer is that the "rub" between heaven and earth is always for the person who is not attending church that Sunday, or for the person in the balcony, or even in the pew next to you, but never for yourself. Such a sermon seems to call forth a response like that of the Pharisee in an upcoming parable of Jesus: "I thank you that I am not like other people" (18:9–14).

To avoid the pitfalls of dividing the hearers between *us* and *them*, another familiar option for the sermon is to internalize the seeds and their landing place as being the inner landscape of one's journey toward an abundant life of faith. Such sermons usually focus more on the first half of the parable with its ambiguity between seed and soil, and less on the literal explanation in the second half, downplaying it as either a later addition or as one possible interpretation. Whereas the first model portrays others as examples of what happens when one gives into temptation, is inattentive, and is distracted from God's Word, this model identifies and addresses the seasons in our lives when it seems that faith is being pecked away, withering, or being choked. The reassurance and hope of such a sermon is that even

Luke 8:4–15

Theological Perspective

Yet the parable's starting point is not on the content of the faith but its origins: the sower—God—whom the Reformed scholastics called *principium essendi*, the principle of being, the very foundation of life. God speaks, God sows, God creates, God enables us to apprehend what God is saying.

Jesus was prompted to tell this parable about the kingdom of God to the throngs of people who were following him as he traveled through cities and villages. Every step he took multiplied the number of his followers. Luke 8 begins by including in that throng the twelve disciples and the three women who provided key assistance on Jesus' itinerant ministry. The parable invited hearers to inspect their intent in following Jesus. Was it out of curiosity? Was it because of the glamour of Jesus' wonder-working miracles? Was it, in the words of the Westminster Catechism, "to glorify God and to enjoy God forever"?

At this point in the Gospel, all in the throng may have thought that they were receiving God's word in the depth of their hearts. By the end of the story, the same "throng" will include Judas the betrayer, doubting Thomas, and Peter the denier. Likewise, the world of seven billion people cannot be pigeonholed as good soils or bad soils. Neither can we categorize one another as mature or immature. What experience demonstrates is that seasons of our lives show us the varying degrees to which our hearts bear fruit and also times when we are choked up by the cares of the church and world.

The kingdom of God is sown in us as we live in response to the promises of the kingdom and the ethics of the kingdom marked by love, compassion, and service. The kingdom of God is sown in us as the Spirit of God works in our hearts to disclose to us the transformative work of God in the world and in our lives, prompting us to participate in that work. The kingdom of God is about God, who reveals God's self, who sows God's own heart in us, so that our lives will move in response to God's heart. God's heart pulses and longs for the world to hear and receive God's Word that is love and to live into it. For that to happen, the Spirit furrows the soil, waters it, and causes it to bear fruit.

NEAL D. PRESA

Pastoral Perspective

beyond human measurement and comprehension, but nonetheless is among us: God's kingdom.[1]

The fact is that some hear the message of the powerful and transforming good news but because of the many obstacles to the word, never get to the point of fully believing in their hearts, enduring in their joy, or being fruitful in their faith. The obstacles may present themselves in many forms: evil forces, weakness as they face ordeals, concerns, anxieties, and times of testing as well as possessions, false expectations, and the pleasures of life. These obstacles can be overwhelming for any of us, and they do overcome and swallow some who lack the ability to perceive and understand the word, even though they look and listen.

God's word reaches deep into our human soil, and we, both men and women, by grace alone and through the work of Holy Spirit in us, are the agents of listening, understanding, responding, and doing. The problem is that some embrace the message of salvation, but then fail to sustain their response to and practice of God's word. That is why Luke not only focuses on the differences between failure and success in the seeding of the word of God through witnessing by words, deeds, and signs the transforming power of the Gospel message. He also focuses on the word of God represented by the seeds and how people receive them and respond to them.

Christians find much confidence not only when they see themselves taking part in the very same story that God is still telling and revealing, in and out of every human reality of any given context, but also in the power contained in the preaching of the word of God. When we respond and persevere, "The story of God's . . . revelation in Christ [becomes] our story too."[2] Although God's word has the power of bringing our lives and ministry to fruition at surprising levels, it needs to find the proper soil: eyes that look and perceive, and ears that listen and understand.

L. WESLEY DE SOUZA

1. Darrell L. Bock, *Luke 1:1–9:50*, Baker Exegetical Commentary on the New Testament (Grand Rapids: Baker Books. 1994), 722.
2. Bernard T. Adeney, *Strange Virtues* (Downers Grove, IL: InterVarsity Press, 1995), 102.

Exegetical Perspective

who domesticated the original message of the parable within Jesus' ministry. Yet this is not certain. Assigning meaning to specific elements of a parable was not foreign to parables within Jewish tradition.

Brad Young argues for a distinction between meaning assigned by the storyteller to certain elements of the parable and the elaborate symbolization that defines the later Christian allegorical method of interpretation.[3] Contrast, for example, the parable of the Vineyard in Isaiah 5:1–7, in which only the major narrative elements have been assigned meaning (the vineyard is Israel, and the grapes are its people), with Augustine's allegorical interpretation of the parable of the Good Samaritan, in which every detail of the story, down to the two coins paid to the innkeeper, represents a broader concept or distinct application. Jesus' interpretation of the parable appears to fall somewhere between these two extremes. Regardless of the origin of this interpretation, a reader of Luke's Gospel must engage it and consider how it clarifies the particular meaning of the parable presented in Luke's narrative.

In verses 11–15, Jesus identifies the sown seed with the word of God. As the seed falls on various types of soil resulting in various yields, so the word of God is heard by people who respond to it in various ways. The dangers to the seed are associated with obstacles that hinder the growth of the word within the hearer. In each case, the word falls upon listening ears, but in most cases healthy fruit does not develop. As in the parable itself, the interpretation reiterates the risky nature of sowing seed, but with the interpretation Jesus clarifies the association he expects his audience to make. The act of planting mirrors the act of hearing the word. Finally, despite the risks, there will be hearers that produce results and a plentiful harvest.

This interpretation raises a challenging question: does the association of listeners with types of soil that are affected by unavoidable hazards imply an inevitability to their failure to hear the word that releases them from accountability? This question highlights the difficulties inherent in interpretations of the parables. By assigning meaning to all elements of the parable, the listener can be distracted from its focus: the fruitful harvest that arises from hearing. It is this point that is expanded throughout chapter 8.

DEBORAH THOMPSON PRINCE

Homiletical Perspective

in the most desolate times in our lives, new life has begun and is taking root, and eventually we will see its growth and harvest its benefits.

The problem with this approach is that the parable's heavenly unease is collapsed into the comfortable familiarity of a hoped-for common experience. The sermon becomes more familiar than the parable, thereby losing the rub between the "secrets of the kingdom of God" (v. 10) and our lives. In this parable, there is no sense that we can nurture the seed within us so that it may grow. In each negative example, the seed dies or is fruitless. As much as we would hope for it, in this particular parable, there is no gardener "to the rescue" who shoos away threats, refreshes with a good watering, digs out the weeds, and leads us to a fulfilling and productive life.

The challenge of familiar parables is that they foster familiar sermons. Perhaps the parabolic rub of the story for today shifts the focus away from the outer or inner life of the individuals, and toward the fertile environments of Christian community. Questions of "What kind of seed am I?" or "What kind of seeds are they?" give way to "How can we, as a community of Christ, be good soil for the widely scattered Word of God, seeded and entrusted to our care?" In this reversal, questions of salvation are replaced with questions of Christian welcome, nurture, discipleship, and growth: How can we be a community where the love of Christ takes deep root in us? How can we provide respites of living water for those who have hit rock, are parched and withering? How can we quote Jesus, "Let anyone with ears to hear listen!" unless we give our ears to those scattered along our way? Perhaps, then, individual voices of "I thank you that I am not like other people" will grow into a chorus, thanking God for seedtime, harvest, and "all good gifts" of Christ-centered community.

MICHAEL A. BROTHERS

---

3. Brad Young, *Jesus and His Jewish Parables* (New York: Paulist Press, 1989), 6–7, 103–5.

16"No one after lighting a lamp hides it under a jar, or puts it under a bed, but puts it on a lampstand, so that those who enter may see the light. 17For nothing is hidden that will not be disclosed, nor is anything secret that will not become known and come to light. 18Then pay attention to how you listen; for to those who have, more will be given; and from those who do not have, even what they seem to have will be taken away."

19Then his mother and his brothers came to him, but they could not reach him because of the crowd. 20And he was told, "Your mother and your brothers are standing outside, wanting to see you." 21But he said to them, "My mother and my brothers are those who hear the word of God and do it."

Theological Perspective

As a young adult in a Filipino American congregation, I regularly sang Graham Kendrick's 1987 hit song "Shine, Jesus, Shine" at church retreats and evangelism committee meetings. The point of the singing was to encourage all of us to shine with the faith that Jesus has given to us, to show it in words and in works to the world, so all may see the light and come to the saving knowledge of Jesus Christ.

This text emphasizes not so much evangelism or outward proclamation on the part of the church, but listening. Here listening is equated with truly hearing, hearing with receiving, and receiving with shining. Jesus goes a step further and says that those who truly listen, who have heard and received and are shining, are those who do what the Word of God says. These, he says, are his family members.

Jesus reframes what has been commonly understood to be an evangelistic call. The narrative setting for these sayings of Jesus is Luke–Acts, written to a postresurrection Lukan community that is coming to understand its place and identity in God's mission in the known first-century-CE world. Liturgical scholar Gordon Lathrop sees in the Lukan narrative a running theme of exodus—or as Luke characterizes the theme, Jesus' "departure" (also *exodos* in the Greek). This wordplay is unique among the Gospels. Jesus'

Pastoral Perspective

My grandfather, Pedro Inácio de Souza, was an outstanding storyteller. His stories were mostly improvised, or he elaborated old stories anew, verbalizing and imaginatively dramatizing them. His stories are the richest memories I keep of him. As I recall the time he moved into our home to live with us, one particularly meaningful detail comes alive again: Before we would each go to sleep, he would place a kerosene lamp on a stand while telling me his stories. I was young and a few times I fell asleep without hearing the end of the stories. Most of the time, though, he was the one who fell asleep before ending his story, lamp still burning. His voice would become softer and softer; his last sentences started weakening, his utterances turned broken, and then his voice became inaudible and confusing until he stopped speaking. That was it! I was often left with only my imagination and the light from the kerosene lamp illuminating the wall of my bedroom.

He did not need to use a kerosene lamp in our shared bedroom, because we had electricity and a lightbulb, but he was born and raised by that light and never saw the need to employ the light switch. Therefore, despite the smell of kerosene that filled the entire house and my father's insistence that there was no need for such an old-fashioned and "ineffective" way of lighting the room, Grandpa followed a

Exegetical Perspective

This passage concludes the teaching segment that began with the parable of the Sower (8:4). Together with the parable and its interpretation, this section forms a narrative arc that emphasizes the relationship between hearing and doing.[1] An initial reading of these verses may lead to the conclusion that they are a haphazard collection of Jesus' sayings (vv. 16–18) with a pronouncement story (vv. 19–21) added for good measure. However, their presence immediately following the parable of the Sower brings the careful reader to a full realization of Jesus' lesson that true hearing yields a remarkable harvest.

The three distinct sayings in verses 16–18 each employ an oppositional set of circumstances. The first saying is sometimes labeled the parable of the Lamp, but it is better described as a proverb, as are the other sayings in this passage. The first saying continues the parable of the Sower's focus on the positive result that can come from a commonplace action. In this case, the commonsense response to having a lamp is to use it to provide light, not to hide its benefit from those who need it. The second saying restates the message in a general form that brings out the theme of hiddenness and revelation. The first two sayings share an emphasis on visibility and employ

1. Patrick E. Spencer, *Rhetorical Texture and Narrative Trajectories of the Lukan Galilean Ministry Speeches* (London: T. &T. Clark, 2007), 114–27.

Homiletical Perspective

Whether or not the preacher perceives these sayings of Jesus as being disconnected or connected will determine the sermon's message, shape, and intended hearers. If they are treated as a collection of disconnected sayings, categorized together because of loose word or image associations, then the preacher may be offered four separate sermon possibilities: (1) The light of Christ is not hidden but shown forth so that others may see the light. (2) All that is hidden and is in secret will be disclosed, become known, and come to light through Christ. (3) How we listen to the Word of God informs what we will receive and exposes what we never had in the first place. (4) The family of Jesus is made up of those who hear the Word of God and do it. If these truly are a random collection of Jesus' sayings, then the preacher is faced with the choice between preaching four minisermons as detached verse-by-verse expositions, and preaching on one saying, thereby ignoring the others and the surrounding biblical context.

However, the fact that these sayings appear elsewhere in Luke (11:33; 12:2; and 19:26) shows that they are grouped together here for a purpose. If we believe there is intent in this collection and meaning in its placement, then the passage as a whole becomes a continuation of the previous parable of

Luke 8:16–21

Theological Perspective

journey to Jerusalem is akin to Moses' leading Israel to a new land,

"If this is so, then for Luke the risen Lord is still the journeying one, still gathering people into the kingdom, still being refused and opposed, but also still the one coming to be received by the current assemblies of Christians—like the stranger in the Emmaus account and like the traveling preachers."[1]

Key to this journey is "hospitality given or refused to the traveler."[2] The identities of fellow travelers are those whom Jesus regards as "my mother and my brothers"—those who hear the Word of God and do it. This is not about revving up people in an evangelism conference to hand out gospel tracts and expecting people to say the sinner's prayer and know the Four Spiritual Laws. This is about receiving a word from our brother, Jesus, recognizing the light of his risen presence among us, and doing his will as we receive him and his word (cf. Luke 24:15, 28–29, 36–37; Heb. 13:2).

How do we receive a word from Jesus and recognize his risen presence among us? We confess that God is, at the same time, fully absent and fully present. The Luke–Acts narrative comes from a community that lived in the postascension reality of Jesus' bodily absence. We confess in the Apostles' Creed that Jesus Christ "ascended into heaven, and is seated at the right hand of God the Father Almighty; from thence he shall come to judge the quick and the dead." Yet the One who is fully absent is also fully present in the time between ascension and the Parousia; such present absence is made divine presence through the Word and the Spirit. As Michael Horton warns, the full absence of Jesus Christ does not mean that the church is called to somehow continue the incomparable, incommensurate ministry of Jesus Christ, or relegate to itself what only Christ can do. Rather, the church testifies through the gifts of the ministry of Word and Sacrament to the presence of the risen, ascended Christ among us through the Holy Spirit.[3]

Such concurrent tension of the fully absent/ fully present Lord keeps us humble and drives us to wait upon the initiative of God to reveal God's self. Moreover, it keeps us attentive to continually listening, receiving, and following the Word of God that is being given to us on the journey. This militates against any sense of ecclesiastical triumphalism that

1. Gordon Lathrop, *The Four Gospels on Sunday: The New Testament and the Reform of Christian Worship* (Minneapolis: Fortress Press, 2012), 111.
2. Lathrop, *Four Gospels*, 110.
3. Michael Horton, *Covenant and Eschatology: The Divine Drama* (Louisville, KY: Westminster John Knox Press, 2002).

Pastoral Perspective

well-defined ritual of lighting and extinguishing the fire of the lamp. He would go to the kitchen in his pajamas, strike a match and gently light the tip of a short stick, and walk back to the bedroom. Then he would stretch his body toward the ceiling, so that he could reach the lamp's wick high on the wall. After waiting a few moments to ensure the wick could support the fire by itself, he would step away and, finally, lie back on his bed with his hands under the nape of his neck, and start his stories.

My grandfather's lamp-lit stories became mine. As I listened to them intently, particularly those that were biblically inspired, that kerosene lamp seemed gradually to gain strength, as if the fire grew in its reach and depth. That lamp had a revealing power that seemed to bring truths and secrets, good and bad, into light. It infused meaning to the detail of the room and our lives as no lightbulb could, giving the impression that nothing was more powerful or illuminating than being under my grandfather's lamp and stories. It was as if my mind and soul were part of those stories that generated redeeming moments of pure grace. These stories eventually became my main source of motivation to respond to the faith.

In much the same way, Jesus' teaching through proverbs and the imagery of a lampstand (vv. 16–18) reminds us that nothing will remain obscure, hidden, shadowed, unknown, or unredeemable by God. We believe that Jesus is the light of the world, the discloser of secrets, the revealer of eternal and cosmic truth, and the tender of human hearts. He is the teller of our stories. John reiterates what Luke exposes about Jesus' teaching: "In him was life, and the life was the light of all people. The light shines in the darkness, and the darkness did not overcome it" (John 1:4–5). Sooner or later, all will know his revealing light through the knowledge and response to his word announced by those who know his transforming love.

Jesus' word is all about the story of the God who encounters human stories and generates a new, cosmic, redeeming story—a new creation. Those "who hear the word of God and do it," whose sins have been forgiven, experience a profound sense of community in love and obedience. They become like a family composed of beloved relatives (vv. 19–21) that share the very same blood and story: that of Christ. We invite one another to fellowship in the kingdom of God, making the light of Christ shine in the darkness of our own stories.

Jesus spelled out the secrets of the kingdom of God by telling stories. As Jim Wallis puts it in one of

light imagery. The visual imagery makes an interesting pair with the accent on hearing that permeates both the previous passage and the one immediately following these two sayings (v. 18a). The mark of true hearing is its visible result.

Furthermore, Jesus' statement that nothing is secret that shall not be made known supports the broader perspective evident in Luke that the "secrets of the kingdom of God" (8:10) are not limited to insiders, who are fortunate to receive private explanations from Jesus (contra Mark 4:10–11, 34). As noted in the commentary on the previous passage (8:4–15), Luke avoids Mark's divisive language of insider and outsider and conveys that it is one's ability to hear that affects one's reception of the "secrets of the kingdom of God." Because Luke does not follow Mark in moving from a public to a private setting immediately after the parable, the reader must assume that it is the entire audience, the "great crowd" who had gathered from "town after town," who heard the parable and also Jesus' extended interpretation on the true nature of hearing. The wide audience supports the prominent theme in Luke of the universality of Jesus' message and purpose. All listeners, then, are potential hearers who can share in the secrets of the kingdom and share in the production of its visible results.

The third saying of Jesus is separated from the first two by Jesus' defining statement, "Then pay attention to *how* you listen" (v. 18, my emphasis). This statement identifies the central concern of the larger teaching segment (8:4–21). Hearing involves action. Whether the image is the growth of a seed planted in good soil or the placement of a lamp, there is always an action that produces a bountiful and enlightening outcome. Luke's particular insistence in the dynamic quality of hearing is evidenced by his modification of Mark's statement, "Pay attention to *what* you hear" (Mark 4:24, my emphasis). Mark's phrase emphasizes the inanimate substance of hearing; Luke emphasizes its living character. Authentic hearing results in a situation changed for the better, whether a tremendous harvest, a light-filled room, or the full disclosure of what was previously unknown.

The final proverbial saying punctuates this revelation about hearing: the one who knows how to hear will receive even more, for its outcome will be great. However, for those who do not have this knowledge or ability, even what they think they have will be lost, as nothing will come to fruition.

Luke's inclusion of verses 16–18 after the parable of the Sower parallels his source, Mark. From

the Sower, a showing and telling of what it means to hear and live out the word of God in Christ's community.

As in the preceding explanation of the parable of the Sower, this section mixes hearing with image and gesture. Right before these sayings, we are told that the ones who hear the Word of God and hold it close to the heart in honesty, sincerity, and love are in "good soil." They are the ones who will bear fruit over the long haul with "patient endurance." Unlike the "secrets of the kingdom of God," this fruit is not hidden from the public. Neither is it scarce among the thorns, to be found only with "patient endurance." As stated in Jesus' parable, fruitfulness is a fully visible and conspicuous "hundredfold." Although the Word is held fast in the heart, its fruitfulness and overabundance are public; it cannot be concealed, hidden, or kept private, even if one would try. It is like the light from a lamp, which is never hidden or kept secret, but is put on a lampstand so that all who enter may see and benefit from its light.

The following verse, "For nothing is hidden that will not be disclosed, nor is anything secret that will not become known and come to light" (v. 17), is usually seen as a continuation of the exposing light of the lamp and treated as a small digression from hearing and bearing fruit. However, when also seen as an introduction to what follows, it becomes a wake-up call to the consequences of *how one listens* to the Word of God. Nothing will remain secret; even our motives will be revealed. The kind of hearing that is honest, sincere, and loving will increase a hundredfold. Conversely, listening that is self-deceptive, self-serving, defensive, and cynical takes away what seemed to be there in the first place. Like neglected seed, what was originally given is plucked, trampled, scorched, and choked by a closed posture of hearing and an absent response.

In stark contrast to complacent, concealed, and inactive listening, Jesus' encounter with his family becomes an opportunity to display active hearing that is public and lived out in community. Active listening takes effort rather than assuming familiarity; it reshapes commitments rather than assuming the continuation of comfortable arrangements. In fact, such hearing and doing create a new community, a new family not only for Jesus but *for its members as well*. In the community of Christ, we become for each other mother, father, sister, and brother.

These sayings of Jesus can serve as voice guides for the sermon's structure:

Luke 8:16–21

Theological Perspective

sees itself as the flashlight of Christ upon the world. On the other hand, it infuses the people of God with hope that we have not been abandoned, but that the Holy Spirit, who is the Spirit of Christ, truly and fully unites us to our risen and ascended Lord, to one another, and to all of God's people in all times and places. The hiddenness of God's presence is revealed in the Holy Spirit, evidence to us that every good and perfect gift is from God and sufficient for the journey.

This reframes what "incarnational" means. Incarnational does not necessarily mean making physical what/who is spiritual. When carried into an ecclesiastical triumphalist posture, incarnational ministry quickly devolves into describing the church, its offices, ministries, and instrumentalities as "the hands and feet of Jesus." Incarnation, at least postresurrection and postascension, means discerning the light of the Holy Spirit who illumines the power and Word of God in Jesus Christ in the lives of living, fleshy, real people bearing witness to resurrection power and hope in their words and deeds. If anything, the term "incarnational," at least as it is used in a Christian context, ought to drive us toward understanding that the material world and the spiritual world are not different worlds: rather, the material and the spiritual truly exist only in their interpenetration of each other.

It follows that incarnational ministry is never about just providing for material needs or simply pointing to spiritual goods. Incarnational ministry recognizes that people are both embodied and inspirited and that both body and spirit yearn for nourishment. This is wise instruction for pilgrims on the journey, for Jesus' mother and brothers and sisters who, like our forebears, see the cloud by day and the fire by night. "My mother and my brothers are those who hear the word of God and do it."

NEAL D. PRESA

Pastoral Perspective

his recent online posts, "Stories are what change the world, more than just ideas."[1] We must keep in mind, however, not only that stories have power but that we must attend to the light under which they are told. The light of our stories is the revealing redemption all can derive from listening and responding to Christ's work on the cross. This is why listening to God's story and telling it to others under the power, guidance, and grace of the Holy Spirit makes the light of Christ enlightening. We encounter and touch every human being within our reach, connecting ourselves with his or her concrete stories of suffering and happiness, pains and hopes, rejection and love.

My grandfather's way of living and teaching through tales and proverbs had a clear pedagogy: telling stories of life, offering lessons stemming from experience. Jesus used the same pedagogy when he wanted his followers to perceive the signs of the kingdom he preached about and their own participation in and response to God's economy of salvation. Jesus was not only the best storyteller one may ever know, but also the protagonist of the greatest story ever told.

Jesus' intention was to reveal God's kingdom, using simple language verbalized in human categories that enhanced imaginative thinking and response. This is why he often departed from what life had to say, and parables like the Good Samaritan, the Prodigal Son, the Lost Coin, the Lost Sheep, and the Shepherd, the Thief, and the Doorkeeper demonstrate it. Through them, he inspired his listeners and us about the truth of the gospel, the signs and mysteries of the kingdom, and the practices of faith.

L. WESLEY DE SOUZA

---

1. Jim Wallis, "Stories That Change the World," available at http://sojo.net/blogs/2013/04/25/video-stories-change-world; accessed on Sept. 25, 2013.

Exegetical Perspective

this point on, however, Luke deviates from Mark, highlighting his unique emphasis throughout this passage. Whereas Mark follows up the parable of the Sower with other seed parables (Mark 4:26–32), Luke concludes with a pronouncement story (vv. 19–21). When Jesus' mother and brothers come to see Jesus, but cannot reach him because of the crowd, the disciple's announcement of their presence offers Jesus the opportunity to make a statement identifying his true family as those "who hear the word of God and do it" (v. 21).

This statement does not necessarily exclude Jesus' family members from those who hear God's word and act on it. In fact, the phrasing may imply that Jesus' mother and brothers are to be included in this group. In either case, Jesus insists that his family is not defined by traditional ties, but by one's ability to hear truly, which means hearing in a way that brings about visible results through action.

Luke's modifications of Mark strengthen the connection between the various sections of the narrative unit and highlight his distinct perspective on the active nature of hearing and its inseparable relationship to results. First, because the parable of the Sower stands on its own and is not followed by other seed parables, it brings into stark focus the relationship between the parable and the various sayings of Jesus that follow it and function to interpret it. Second, Luke counters Mark's interest in distinguishing between insiders and outsiders by broadening Jesus' audience (8:4 and 8:9) and omitting Mark's conclusion that Jesus' disciples received private explanations that outsiders did not (Mark 4:33–34).

Throughout this short teaching section in Luke, Jesus proclaims that the possibility for authentic hearing and the fruitful action in which it results is sown widely and displayed publicly. Not all will hear in this manner; there is a real risk that spreading God's word will not be successful, and, for many, the secrets of God's kingdom will remain perplexing. Just as certain, however, is the reality that those who do hear will produce a rich harvest, providing light and clarity to the world, and so will be mothers and brothers of Jesus.

DEBORAH THOMPSON PRINCE

Homiletical Perspective

"Some fell into good soil, and when it grew, it produced a hundredfold."
". . . So that those who enter may see the light."
"Nothing is hidden that will not be disclosed."
So "pay attention to *how* you listen."
"For those who hear the word of God and do it" are "my mother and my brothers," my father and my sisters.

Images and stories that live out these sayings can be interjected as the hearer is led from fruitful abundance to the new family of Jesus Christ.

Such a sermon would speak well to occasions of initiation: baptism, confirmation, and reception of new members. However, it should not be instruction for the newly baptized or confirmed about the responsibilities of being hearers and doers of the Word. It is not a reminder to parents of the importance of education for learning *how to listen* to God's Word. Nor is it a charge to new members that active listening means more than pew-sitting once a week, once a month, or once a year. This sermon is not for the initiates but for the community that listens with attention and action, holds up a light as a welcome to whoever has been scattered their way, and responds with sayings of their own: "See what love the Father has given us that we should be called children of God; and we are!"[1]

In a church I once served, a staff member brought to my attention the plight of a young woman who grew up in the congregation. She was in a troubled situation in a distant state and needed someone sent from the church to provide help. After I reminded the staff member that we had not seen her since high school, and that we cannot rescue everyone, she firmly stated, "She was baptized in this church. We made a promise!" She was right, of course, and help was sent. In hearing and doing the Word of God, we become family—and family is for life.

MICHAEL A. BROTHERS

1. First John 3:1 is often used as the Declaration in the sacrament of Baptism.

Luke 8:22–25

²²One day he got into a boat with his disciples, and he said to them, "Let us go across to the other side of the lake." So they put out, ²³and while they were sailing he fell asleep. A windstorm swept down on the lake, and the boat was filling with water, and they were in danger. ²⁴They went to him and woke him up, shouting, "Master, Master, we are perishing!" And he woke up and rebuked the wind and the raging waves; they ceased, and there was a calm. ²⁵He said to them, "Where is your faith?" They were afraid and amazed, and said to one another, "Who then is this, that he commands even the winds and the water, and they obey him?"

Theological Perspective

I was born on the Pacific island of Guam. Although I grew up in the San Francisco Bay area, I have visited Guam several times, and on every occasion I am awed at the power of the island's beauty, the blue Pacific waters that surround it, and the sheer force of the waves that carry surfers from crest to shore, providing a picture-perfect backdrop to paradise.

When I hear the vehemence with which representatives of island nations such as Fiji and the Philippines call upon global policymakers to take urgent action to curb global fuel emissions and their adverse effects on climate change and rising sea levels, I understand their dire plight. The very waters that provide livelihood and recreation could be the source of the islanders' ultimate destruction. These island nations are calling policymakers to make wise choices.

In 2004, when Banda Aceh, on the Indonesian island of Sumatra, was struck by a massive tsunami, my thought raced to two scriptural passages: God's promise to Noah never to use water to destroy the earth, and today's lectionary passage on calming the Sea of Galilee. If I were a pastor in Sumatra, I do not know how I could preach either passage. For Sumatrans, as with any islanders, the water is our world. In facing the loss of thousands upon thousands of people who encountered death in the

Pastoral Perspective

One of the many expressions I learned when I first moved from Brazil to the United States was the legal term "act of God": "An event that directly and exclusively results from the occurrence of natural causes that could not have been prevented by the exercise of foresight or caution."[1] It is legally assumed that natural catastrophes such as violent winds, tornadoes, floods, earthquakes, tsunamis, and storms are uncontrollable. No one is liable for or guilty of the distress visited on people's lives when inevitable accidents happen as a result of these events.

Interestingly, the expression seems not to be legal in its inception, but theological: God is both the perpetrator and the controller of disasters. This is an easy and quick way to cast all responsibility for existential misfortune on God, the divine scapegoat. In Brazilian Portuguese, the term to explain such uncontrollable forces of nature does not characterize them as acts of God and so does not infer that God generates and acts in catastrophes. Legally speaking, Portuguese refers to *fortuitous events*, which suggests a more fatalistic perspective. Here the responsibility is not yours, mine, the insurance company's, or God's, but something that is more than human yet

---

1. "Act of God," in *West's Encyclopedia of American Law*, edition 2 (The Gale Group. 2008); accessed April 30, 2013. Available at http://legal-dictionary.the freedictionary.com/act+of+God.

Feasting on the Gospels

Exegetical Perspective

A new day (v. 22) marks the break in chapter 8 between a collection of Jesus' teachings (vv. 4–21) and a series of miracles (vv. 22–56). This passage tells the story of the first of these miracles, the stilling of the storm. Here Luke continues to follow Mark 4:35–41 by linking this nature miracle with other displays of Jesus' power to heal and to save. Luke, however, edits Mark's timeline. While Mark connects Jesus' teaching and acts of power, Luke provides a distinct break in time and space between these two forms of Jesus' ministry. In Mark, Jesus' teaching occurs while he is on the water in a boat (Mark 4:1), and it is in the evening of that same day that he and his disciples cross the Sea of Galilee, where a series of miracles take place (Mark 4:35). Luke, on the other hand, places Jesus' teaching clearly on land on one side of the lake. It is not until an unknown later day, "one day," that Jesus tells his disciples to take him across to the other side. This offers a marked break from the previous passage, based on both a new setting in time and a distinct separation between Jesus' activities on each side of the water.

Although counterintuitive, Luke's editing may promote a connection between Jesus' teaching and acts of power, but in a way that reflects Luke's particular perspective on how they are related. In the previous two passages, Jesus uses the parable of the

Homiletical Perspective

It will be easy for the preacher to get lost in the storm. Luke's sparse telling of the story may seem like an invitation for its imaginative retelling by the preacher: "Bright sun reflects on the mirrorlike lake, where there is just enough of a breeze to move the sailboat to its destination and just enough of a gentle rocking that Jesus could take a nap. The rudder cuts through the smooth surface like knife on glass. Suddenly, glass becomes shook foil as a windstorm sweeps down the lake, catching the sailboat in its path and its passengers unaware.[1] Waves bat the boat back and forth like a ball between cat's claws. As the boat fills with water, the disciples fill with fear. Yet Jesus is still asleep! Does he not know? Can he not hear? Does he not care? Over howling wind and crashing wave, the disciples shout out to Jesus 'We are going under. We are going to die!'" We know the rest of the story. We know how it ends, with the ending of the storm—by Jesus. We have heard this sermon before.

Yet this was no storm of the imagination that prompted the disciples to wake Jesus, shouting, "Master, Master, we are perishing!" (v. 24). The "wind and the raging waves" (v. 24) were real. The

---

1. The image "shook foil" is from "God's Grandeur," in *Poems of Gerard Manley Hopkins* (London: Oxford University Press, 1967), 23.

Luke 8:22–25

Theological Perspective

midst of rushing currents, battered communities and grieving loved ones can find little consolation in the Noahic covenantal promise or in the messianic authority over the Galilean storm that raged on the lake and the storm that raged in the fearful hearts of the disciples.

What can the church possibly proclaim in the midst of tragedy, both while the storm is raging and after it has subsided? Like us, prior generations have attempted to answer the "Why me?" or "Why us?" questions in the midst of tragedy, when an omnipotent, benevolent, omnipresent God ought to be both able and willing to save and prevent death.

The disciples' predicament and consequent plea, "Master, Master, we are perishing" (v. 24), were met with Jesus' awaking from his slumber, calming the storm, and inquiring of them, "Where is your faith?" (v. 25). Jesus' query implies that if the disciples' faith were fully active, fear would not have paralyzed them, and they would have been able to steer the ship away from the choppy waters. Does Jesus' question perhaps also imply that a fully active faith on their part would have given them the power and apostolic authority to calm the storms themselves?

Reformed theologian Gregory Love has recently critiqued past attempts at answering the question of theodicy.[1] Prior explanations privileged God's divine plan at the expense of real, affective human suffering, as if somehow tragedy were an instrument used by a God who had a master plan to save humanity from evil, sin, and destruction. Other explanations respond to our own experience of suffering with the belief that God's salvation was affected by the necessary violent death suffered by Jesus Christ to satisfy the wrath of God.

Greg Love sees five models at work in our attempts to come to terms with what appears to us to be gratuitous human suffering: emancipation, hospitality, divine justice, reorientation, and restoration. Each of these dimensions may be God's response to human tragedy, evil, powers and principalities, and systemic forces that stifle life. They demonstrate God's ongoing work of loving humanity, with Christ's own death as an inevitable outcome to the violent ethics of a world that did not care for God's *shalom*. God is not paralyzed by violence or surprised by it, but responds in ways that display the power of God's love to free, to welcome, to right wrongs, to reorient us to God's grace, and to restore

Pastoral Perspective

not divine in nature and accepted as predetermined and inevitable.

Questions are frequently asked when nature shows its uncontrollable fury: Is the ultimate power in God's hands or in the hands of nature? Is God hidden in some sort of unreachable corner of the universe, while we are helplessly confronted by disasters and catastrophes? Is God even out there? If so, what is God's role in all of this? Why does God not intervene? Does God even care whether we are in perilous danger?

These are real, legitimate questions. We all have raised them when the circumstances of life suggest that we have been left alone to face fortuitous events: when our boat is being swamped and the Divine seems to be hidden, remote, asleep, or careless. Honest as these questions may be, are they the only questions to be asked and the only conclusion available? Do we instead reveal our distrust, suspicion, and lack of faith in God when we ask *who* is *where, when,* and doing *what* while "acts of God" take place?

Luke's narrative of Jesus calming the storm (vv. 22–25) suggests that he and his disciples formulated questions differently from those asked in today's skeptical world. Perhaps, in the dire situation aboard their rocking boat, they had no time "to analyze the divine by human rules."[2]

In this story that involves both nature and the people gathered on a small, fragile boat, Jesus is concerned about the disciples' trust and discernment: is there any reason to keep faith when we are in the midst of emotional storms and adrift in a sea of disillusionment? Jesus' focus is on the appropriate response of his disciples' faith. After rebuking the wind and the raging waters, Jesus asks them, "Where is your faith?"

The disciples, on the other hand, shift from a pessimistic conclusion later proved wrong—"Master, Master, we are perishing!" (v. 24)—to a question full of surprise, fear, and amazement, followed by quite a different statement that nourishes and strengthens their faith: "Who then is this, that he commands even the winds and the water, and they obey him?" (v. 25). The disciples' question in the calm after the storm expresses what Jesus intends for them truly to learn about his power and authority over all creation.

Luke's story is like a parable about the meaning and the all-encompassing promise of the kingdom of God or the reign of God made manifest in Jesus

---

1. Gregory Anderson Love, *Love, Violence, and the Cross: How the Nonviolent God Saves Us through the Cross of Christ* (Eugene, OR: Cascade Books, 2010).

2. Darrell L. Bock, *Luke 1:1–9:50*, Baker Exegetical Commentary on the New Testament (Grand Rapids: Baker Books, 1994), 758.

Exegetical Perspective

Sower (8:4–15) and a collection of sayings and a pronouncement story (8:16–21) to teach his listeners the meaning of true hearing, which is hearing in a way that brings about visible results through action. The indeterminate time delay between Jesus' teachings and his acts of power may be intended to mirror the delay between the sowing of the Word (the hearing) and the harvest (the result evident through one's actions). In this way, chapter 8 provides a clear example of the essential link between hearing the Word described by Jesus' teaching (vv. 4–21) and its bountiful fruit, evident in the string of miracles that concludes the chapter (vv. 22–56).

Furthermore, the harvest of life that is achieved through Jesus' miracles will be repeated through the actions of the disciples when, at the outset of chapter 9, Jesus gives them "power and authority over all demons and to cure diseases" and sends them out "to proclaim the kingdom of God and to heal" (9:1–2). The chapter exhibits a progression from the teaching that sows the Word, to the master's example of the great harvest that will occur through those that hear it, to the disciple's opportunity to practice what they have learned. Of course, the disciples "are still apprentices. The later narrative shows that Jesus still has much to teach them."[1]

Luke's vocabulary reinforces this reading. In the midst of the storm, the disciples call out to Jesus, "Master, Master, we are perishing!" (v. 24). The Greek word translated "master" (*epistatēs*) is found only in Luke. The Greek word would bring to the reader's mind a commander, an overseer, or a trainer of youth. Four of the six times that the disciples address Jesus as Master in the Gospel of Luke are concentrated in chapters 8 and 9, and in all cases the passages display Jesus' power to command nature or to heal (5:5; 8:45; 9:49; 17:13) or, in the case of the transfiguration, to reveal that God's power is present in Jesus (9:33). The range of meaning promotes the dual emphasis present in this passage: the exhibition of Jesus' command over nature and the example that this command provides his followers.

The first use of "master" is during an earlier miracle on the Sea of Galilee, when Jesus calls his first disciples (5:1–11). Indeed, these passages focus on the faith of the disciples, often highlighting its underdevelopment. Every time the disciples call Jesus Master, the story displays their struggle to understand Jesus and his message. In the stilling

---

1. Robert Tannehill, *The Narrative Unity of Luke–Acts: A Literary Interpretation*, vol. 1, *The Gospel according to Luke* (Philadelphia: Fortress Press, 1986), 215.

Homiletical Perspective

threat to their lives was real. Jesus did not chastise the disciples for getting worked up over nothing. Unlike Matthew and Mark, Luke states emphatically, "they were in danger" (v. 23). In Luke, the *storm* is rebuked, not the disciples.

It is easy for the preacher to get lost in the storms of today, including the real-weather storms that sweep across the country with increasing frequency. Literally at the preacher's fingertips, there are ample images, video clips, and statistics of devastation and loss in the aftermath of storms. Hurricanes, tornadoes, firestorms, and floods are as close as a phone, tablet, or laptop. With so much at hand, the preacher may be tempted to make quick and easy parallels between the storms of today and the storm that threatened to overtake the disciples.

Yet the congregation does not need the preacher to portray for them the perils of a storm. People in the pew have seen the same images from the media, and some can speak for themselves that "*they were in danger.*" I think of the widow in our congregation who lost her husband in a recent hurricane. Her very presence in worship is a stark reminder that not everyone is rescued from danger and that not all storms are quelled before loved ones have perished.

It is easy for the preacher to get lost in the storms of the congregation. When preparing this sermon, one need not search the Web to find events that crash in on you and take you by surprise. The preacher need only to look out from the pulpit to see families and individuals whose lives are rocked by financial difficulties, battered by abuse, blown asunder by broken relationships, and sinking from sickness of body, mind, and soul. If the stories told from the pulpit are only those of the quelled storms with happy endings, then the rescue of others can seem like rebuke for those currently caught in raging waves with no sight of calm ahead.

It is easy for Jesus to get lost in the storm. Students of literature may remember that the main components of a narrative are plot, setting, character, and sometimes dialogue. However not all stories emphasize all components equally. Perhaps this story does not call for an imaginary retelling of storm, peril, rebuke, and calm. Nor is its focus on the storms of our lives. Perhaps the lack of detail in plot and setting is to emphasize *character*, to focus on Jesus through dialogue. Instead of plot and story, dialogue can become the sermon's framework in this conversation about destination, danger, direction, and identity: "Let us go to the other side of the lake." "Master, Master, we are perishing!" "Where is your

Luke 8:22–25

Theological Perspective

a purposeful framework of hope to the human heart in the midst of chaos.

Reviewing Love's schema, the restoration model of the atonement is applicable to the story before us. The restoration model shows how God respects the free will of humanity while giving humanity reason to live again because of God's desire to fulfill *shalom*. God knows the end, but the route to the end is indeterminate. God works with human choices; thus, human decisions matter.[2]

Jesus' query to the disciples was not a game of "gotcha." Their decision to react the way they did in the midst of the storm mattered. They were responsible for their panicked response. When I traveled to the Holy Land a few years ago, I saw how small those fishing boats are and how a gusty wind in the Sea of Galilee can easily cause ripples of water to turn into tumultuous waves. At least four of the disciples were experienced fishermen. Perhaps it was a false sense of security, knowing that their Teacher was there beside them and could rescue them at any moment. Regardless of the fact that Jesus was in the boat, these disciples needed to own their choices. They may not have been able to control the weather any more than any of us can control so much of the tragedy that befalls us. However, anchored in faith, we can check the course that we have chosen, our responses along that course, and the decisions we have yet to make along the journey.

Taking tragedy, human response, and God seriously is not a matter of diminishing or ignoring the affective fear and confusion that accompany storms, as we see with the disciples. Neither is it a matter of offering simplistic platitudes about what God might be up to. The more difficult place, and the more excellent way, is to attend to the complex interplay of God, humanity, and event. Then, as we seek to interpret that relationship for others in our congregations, classrooms, and other ministry contexts, we will find ourselves being reoriented to the One who abides and abounds with us in life's storms.

NEAL D. PRESA

Pastoral Perspective

Christ. He is the creator of all things, and his power and authority are over people, disease, demons, death, and even fortuitous events like the storms—actual and emotional—in our lives. There is no other way to access and to respond to Jesus' power and authority but in faith. We, as disciples of Jesus Christ, were granted the gift not only of believing and knowing the mysteries of the kingdom and the knowledge of God's salvation brought through Jesus of Nazareth, the Son of God, but also confiding in his power and authority. Paul describes the mystery of the kingdom as being "Christ in you, the hope of glory," which is "foolishness to those who are perishing, but to us who are being saved it is the power of God" (1 Cor. 1:18).

We face a tough reality. One of the biggest challenges of today's Christianity is the crisis of confidence in the content, meaning, authority, and power of the God who is in Christ. Today's crises of faith are often based on our distrust in and skepticism of the Word of God. This raises many other questions: Is there any future for a faith that falls short of trusting Jesus' power and authority? How confident are we in the power of the message of Jesus' cross? Is the Lord of all the source and object of our faith, so that we may rest in his power and authority?

In the parables and sayings preceding this story, Jesus tells us that where we plant the seed of the gospel has ultimate consequences, as does our confidence in the power of the seed to produce results. Then he shares a saying that spells out the mysteries of the kingdom of God, inviting us to believe that he is the light of the world, the discloser of secrets, the revealer of eternal and cosmic truth, and tender of the human heart. Now, by commanding the storms to subside and calming the waters, he teaches that we must trust his power and authority even in the midst of turmoil that may cause fear, anxiety, a sense of helplessness, lack of control, and abandonment. Like the disciples on the boat in the Sea of Galilee, what is at stake in our own lives is this: Do we trust and rest in Jesus' power and authority?

L. WESLEY DE SOUZA

---

2. Love, *Love, Violence, and the Cross*, 268–69.

of the storm, however, Luke has modified Mark's description of how the disciples approach Jesus when the storm erupts. The disciples in Luke do not question Jesus' care for them; they only inform him of the dangerous situation (v. 24). The disciples' failure fully to comprehend Jesus is still evident, but Jesus' response does not imply their faith is lacking, only still in progress. Luke also chooses to describe the disciples' reaction to Jesus' power over the water in a way that tempers the outright fear of the disciples in Mark 4:41. Luke employs a favorite term, "amazement." Although this word consistently reflects an element of uncertainty, it also implies a glimmer of understanding, as does the question that concludes the episode and recognizes that Jesus is in command (v. 25).

This passage also evokes the common motif of the sea[2] as a symbol of chaos and danger that only God can control. The image of God subduing the waters is ubiquitous in the Hebrew Bible, from the stories of creation and the exodus of the Hebrew slaves from Egypt to the Psalms (e.g., Pss. 29:3–4; 65:7; 89:9; 107:23–32). Water was valued and feared: necessary for the sustenance of life, and yet with great destructive potential. Although the Sea of Galilee was not large, its geographic relationship to the surrounding hills meant it was not uncommon for storms to arise quickly on the lake and surprise fishermen or those traveling from one side to the other.

The example that Jesus sets his disciples—that actions empowered by God will result in salvation from danger—fulfills the message of the teachings that precede this miracle, while also clearly indicating that Jesus truly reveals the power of God's kingdom in the world through word and deed. If his followers will only hear this word, their actions too will result in the harvest of God's kingdom on earth.

DEBORAH THOMPSON PRINCE

faith?" (v. 25) "Who then is this, that he commands even the winds and the water, and they obey him?" (v. 25) In response to the dialogue, the sermon becomes antiphony:

"Master, Master, we are perishing," we cry out.
The church responds, "In life and in death we belong to God."[2]
Followers of Jesus ask, "Who then is this?"
The congregation responds, "This is Jesus Christ, the Messiah, Lord, and Savior, God with us."
"Where is your faith?" we are asked by Jesus.
Preacher and congregants respond, "Our faith is here, with you! God abiding with us in calm and storm! God who will never abandon us. God leading us to our destination."

As a sung response to the sermon, the hymn "Eternal Father, Strong to Save" may come to mind. Whereas people are more familiar with the first verse of the "Navy Hymn," the second verse particularly speaks of Jesus calming the storm: "O Savior, whose almighty word the wind and waves submissive heard, . . . O hear us when we cry to thee for those in peril on the sea." A similar plea is made in "Jesus, Savior, Pilot Me": "Thou canst hush the ocean wild; boisterous waves obey thy will, when thou sayest to them, 'Be still!'" However, both of these hymns draw their inspiration from Matthew's and Mark's telling of the story. Appropriate to Luke, a fitting response to Jesus' question, "Where is your faith?" is the hymn "Abide with Me": "I triumph still, if thou abide with me."[3]

MICHAEL A. BROTHERS

2. From A Brief Statement of Faith, Presbyterian Church (U.S.A.), 1983.
3. See The Presbyterian Hymnal; Hymns, Psalms, and Spiritual Songs (Louisville, KY: Westminster John Knox Press, 1990), 562, 543; The Baptist Praise Book (1871), cyberhymnal.org.htm/j/s/jspilotm.htm.

2. Luke prefers to use the term "lake" or "water" to refer to the Sea of Galilee. From his geographical perspective, the "sea" is the Mediterranean Sea.

Luke 8:26–39

²⁶Then they arrived at the country of the Gerasenes, which is opposite Galilee. ²⁷As he stepped out on land, a man of the city who had demons met him. For a long time he had worn no clothes, and he did not live in a house but in the tombs. ²⁸When he saw Jesus, he fell down before him and shouted at the top of his voice, "What have you to do with me, Jesus, Son of the Most High God? I beg you, do not torment me"—²⁹for Jesus had commanded the unclean spirit to come out of the man. (For many times it had seized him; he was kept under guard and bound with chains and shackles, but he would break the bonds and be driven by the demon into the wilds.) ³⁰Jesus then asked him, "What is your name?" He said, "Legion"; for many demons had entered him. ³¹They begged him not to order them to go back into the abyss.

³²Now there on the hillside a large herd of swine was feeding; and the demons begged Jesus to let them enter these. So he gave them permission.

Theological Perspective

The opening sentence of this passage reminds readers of Jesus' boundary-breaking ministry. Having calmed the storm on the lake (demonstrating his power over nature), he and the disciples continue sailing to the other side, "the country of the Gerasenes, which is opposite Galilee" (v. 26). Commentators generally agree that this is Gentile territory. Jesus' foray into this area is brief; however, it underscores the directions the gospel will travel in the future.

As soon as Jesus steps on dry land, he is met by a man "who had demons." The detailed description of the affliction that has assailed the man for a lengthy period of time is no less daunting than the storm that had assailed the disciples. Evidently, people from the city had tried to subdue the man from time to time, using chains and restraints, but to no avail. He was forced into the wilderness, where he lived among the tombstones, isolated from the community, naked and homeless, more dead than alive.

One interesting aspect of this passage is how quickly Jesus assesses the situation and rids the man of his demons. Beset by the demons, the man is unable to verbalize his own needs. By the time the man falls at Jesus' feet, however, Jesus has already commanded the demons to leave him. In the passages that follow this story, Jesus will heal a

Pastoral Perspective

The latter part of Luke 8 consists of four narratives of Jesus' power over naturally occurring storms (8:22–25), demons (8:26–39), sickness (8:43–48), and death (8:40–42, 49–56). This second story of Jesus' power, the healing of a man possessed by Legion, draws a clear delineation between the community and the wilderness and offers at least five occasions where this boundary is crossed, which is good news.

First, Jesus crosses into the wilderness (at least from a Jewish perspective) by traveling to the country of Gerasenes, a place inhabited by Gentiles. This is the only passage recorded in Luke where Jesus brings salvation to the Gentiles and, therefore, echoes the earlier prophetic voices about his ministry: Simeon in the temple, who proclaimed Jesus would be "a light for revelation to the Gentiles" (2:32), and John the Baptist, who announced that "all flesh shall see the salvation of God" (3:6).

Second, as Jesus steps onto foreign land, he is immediately met by a demon-possessed man, who embodies the alienating wilderness of despair and fear. With Jesus' arrival, he will be restored and empowered to return to his kinfolk. In his stark nakedness, beyond the bounds of civilization, residing with the dead in the wilderness, we vividly see torment physically manifested in this man's isolation and abandonment from community. So powerful is

³³Then the demons came out of the man and entered the swine, and the herd rushed down the steep bank into the lake and was drowned.

³⁴When the swineherds saw what had happened, they ran off and told it in the city and in the country. ³⁵Then people came out to see what had happened, and when they came to Jesus, they found the man from whom the demons had gone sitting at the feet of Jesus, clothed and in his right mind. And they were afraid. ³⁶Those who had seen it told them how the one who had been possessed by demons had been healed. ³⁷Then all the people of the surrounding country of the Gerasenes asked Jesus to leave them; for they were seized with great fear. So he got into the boat and returned. ³⁸The man from whom the demons had gone begged that he might be with him; but Jesus sent him away, saying, ³⁹"Return to your home, and declare how much God has done for you." So he went away, proclaiming throughout the city how much Jesus had done for him.

Exegetical Perspective

Immediately after Jesus' sermon in chapter 6, Luke dramatizes the real meaning of that message. He chooses some stories in which the main characters are a foreign military official and his male servant (7:1–10); a widow whose fatherless child had died and was being buried (7:11–17); the poor to whom the good news was preached (7:18–23); an ill-famed woman who "attends" a meal offered to Jesus by a Pharisee (7:36–50); and an important group of women who followed Jesus and were serving him and his disciples (8:1–3).

Through this selection of characters and events (healing, resurrection, preaching, restoration to dignity, service), the author points to the most important elements of his perception of Jesus' ministry: this is in a theology rooted in the OT tradition where God cares for the downtrodden and those who are marginalized. God is the God of the foreigner, the widow, the orphan, and the poor. Indeed, Luke adds a new category to those who are under God's particular protection: the woman.

After Luke's exposition of such an important aspect of Old Testament–infused theology, and after another sermon by Jesus, the subsequent stories reveal something of what it means to be a follower of Jesus: blood relations cannot replace obedience to God's message, and being a disciple does not free

Homiletical Perspective

The story of the Gerasene demoniac is the longest and most elaborate exorcism in the New Testament. Luke's skillful retelling of the story from Mark concludes by persuading a preacher to interpret it (v. 39). Some swineherds have reported what has taken place to "the people of the surrounding country" (v. 37), but they do not understand the meaning of those events. Jesus is in Gentile territory. Smell those pigs? These Gentiles do not understand what has happened. They are simply afraid and eager for Jesus to leave (v. 37). They need an interpreter. As Luke tells it, wanting to be Jesus' disciple is not enough: the man from whom the demons are cast out is instructed, "Return to your home, and *declare* how much God has done for you" (v. 39). The word translated "declare" (*diēgou*) is related to the word Luke uses to describe his own ministry in the first verse of his Gospel, "Since many have undertaken to set down an *orderly account*" (*diēgēsin*, 1:1). The exorcised man is to do what Luke is doing: declare what happened and provide an "orderly account" of it. That will require, as we shall see, a theological interpretation (v. 39).

If any narrative can benefit from an "orderly account," it is the biography of the Gerasene demoniac. The story is full of disorder; this is artfully composed confusion, but chaos nonetheless. The

Luke 8:26–39

Luke 8:26–39

Theological Perspective

woman who can only reach out to touch him and a child whose father must request such healing on his behalf. We are often urged to bring our prayers before the God who knows our every need. Here Jesus acts on the need of the man despite his inability to ask.

Jesus is also quick to acknowledge the presence and power of demons in his world. Exorcising such demons was a primary focus of his healing ministry. In the centuries that have followed, scientific and medical advances have done much to explain and find cures for a number of those natural phenomena and illnesses described as "demon-possessed" in Jesus' time. Some folk might scoff at the presence of demons today.

Yet one has only to discuss this passage with folks from majority-world countries or with those who have been forced to the fringes of society in our country to recognize the presence of the demonic in our time. Often powerless under government regimes (legions) that oppress and economic realities in which the rich prosper and the poor languish, many of our brothers and sisters do battle with the demonic every day.

Colleagues who recently traveled in Ghana described a service of exorcism they attended there. In a country where life often seems chaotic and out of personal control, folks prayed that their brother would be released, delivered from the demons that bound him. African American colleagues whose ancestors were themselves shackled understand the insidious power of the demonic and can give a face to it. Korean colleagues who have struggled for their faith have given a name to such demonic, repressive powers: *han*. *Han* describes the deep, internal pain and grief caused by suffering or injustice. Even young adults in America who have grown up under the influence of the Harry Potter series concede that there is evil in the world that may not be explained or halted. Mention demons to them, and they picture Dementors, those darkest of creatures who can suck the soul out of a person. Although they can be subdued for a time, they cannot be destroyed.

In his commentary on Luke, Justo Gonzáles urges us to reclaim Jesus' respect for the demonic.[1] That evil exists is a reality and mystery. Certainly events of history such as the Holocaust and lynchings remind us that evil is palpable. The unending reports of mass shootings in schools and at malls as well as bombs left on city streets are grim reminders that we have

1. Justo L. González, *Luke* (Louisville, KY: Westminster John Knox Press, 2010), 69–72.

Pastoral Perspective

this man's plight that he cannot stay in community, even when chained and shackled to it. Yet even in this extremely dislocated location, Jesus enters to heal the broken and restore a lost one to the community.

A third discernible border is between health and malady, as witnessed with the location of the herd. The swine are home on the hillside, grazing in the pasture. After the demons are allowed to enter them, they are driven to their death in the watery chaos of the Sea of Galilee. This environmental boundary crossing, where the healthy livestock are infected with the demons, is a troubling one. In it, there is a loss of animal life, a financial loss, and perhaps even an end to the swineherds' livelihood, as well as a loss of a potential food source for the community. Particularly disturbing is the fact that it is Jesus who gives the demons "permission" to cause such destruction (v. 32). Perhaps pastorally it is instructive to know that restoration costs all of us something—not only the one restored, but also the community at large. For instance, a church might find reaching out to the poor and destitute to be costly when those who are socially and economically different attend worship, fellowship hour, and even retreats. This inclusion is likely to cost social comfort, financial resources, and maybe even reputation.

A fourth boundary is between the isolated, splintered man created by the crowd of demons and the restored, united community. The one who would "break the bonds" of the community "and be driven by the demon into the wilds" (v. 29) is now sitting gently at Jesus' feet (v. 35). The one who could not be contained and was driven mad by the myriad of demons has crossed the boundary from chaotic insanity to being clothed (in Christ; cf. 2 Cor. 5:1–5 and Col. 3:1–11) and in his right mind (cf. "sober judgment" in Rom. 12:3).

The fifth boundary is the return of the man to his own community. Jesus refuses the man's request to remain with him on his travels and, instead, directs him to return to his home "and declare how much God has done for you" (v. 39). The crossing of this final border is the restoration of his full humanity, not only for his sake, but for his community's as well, as he is the community's sole witness of God's boundary-crossing, demon-exorcising, life-saving grace.

Traversing this final boundary will be challenging, though. When the community sees that the man is restored, "they were afraid" (v. 35), and it will be against such fear that the man will have to contend

us from the torments of life. Rather, obedience and hardship connect us to Jesus, the one who commands even the winds and the waters (8:4–25).

Over against this background, the healing of the demon-possessed man in Gerasa is told. Consider the scenery of the narrative setting and the details of the story to understand its meaning. Jesus and his disciples arrived on the east bank of the Sea of Galilee, which was the land of the Gerasenes. The Gerasenes lived southeast of the Sea of Galilee, in Decapolitan territory, where there was a strong foreign presence. Gerasa was a very prosperous city, conquered by Pompey for the Romans in 63 BCE. The pagan (Roman) presence is significant, especially in this context, preceded as it is by the healing of a centurion's servant.

Luke now confronts us with a man who said that his name was "Legion" (v. 30). The term, shared by the Roman military, signals the presence of the foreign, the oppressive, and the destructive. What can it mean that the man was controlled by forces so destructive that he could not distinguish between his own identity and the legion of demons? As the Roman legions conquered and took possession of non-Roman territories, so the legion of demons had taken possession of that man. The man suffered not only possession, but a kind of existential schizophrenia marked by the confusion between the singularity of his own personal identity and the plural meaning of his name. (See the change of pronouns in vv. 28–31.) In this, the man represents the condition of Gerasa under Roman control and perhaps the condition of all humanity under sin: foreign powers consistently express themselves in confusions about and the dismantling of identity.

The pagan presence is further stressed by the presence of a herd of pigs nearby (v. 32). No religious Jew bred pigs, since these were impure animals. Perhaps this is evidence of another aspect of Luke's theology: the universality of the gospel. Even those who were in pagan territories and were considered "impure" by others, became recipients of the good news.

Luke underlines a new detail: the man who came to the encounter with Jesus was "from the city" (v. 27) but was no longer there. Cities are places of the living; the demoniac now resided among the dead—not in a house, but in the tombs. He was from the place of human community, but he was now living in solitude. He belonged to a place that provided shelter and comfort, but now he was living in the land of nakedness (v. 27). Even more, he had totally lost control over his own person in such a way that

apostle Paul writes to the Corinthians, "God is a God not of disorder but of peace" (1 Cor. 14:33). Here God's emissary, Jesus, encounters the profound disorder of the forces allied against "the LORD and [God's] anointed" (Ps. 2:2). The situation of the demoniac is chaotic. The man dashes about naked, divested of the human dignity of clothing. People have tried to care for him, restraining him with chains and shackles, but even that was not enough; the demons burst the chains and drove the man from his community into the wilderness (v. 29). Now he lives on the farthest margin of human society among the tombs, among the dead and just barely alive. This is what meets Jesus as he steps from the boat. The demoniac falls down before him, an appropriate posture in meeting the holy, but the initial veneration is shattered with the demoniac's coarse shout. The chaos and contradiction of the man's life are on full display.

Some ancient miracle tales thrilled listeners with elaborate struggles between exorcist and demon—we might recall recent superhero movies that are all chases and fistfights—but there is none of that here. The demon(s) know who Jesus is, know instantly they are overmatched, and beg for mercy: "I beg you, do not torment me" (v. 28). Although they belong to chaos and disorder, they try to negotiate a peace with Jesus. Curiously, they beg Jesus not to return them to "the abyss," the place of death and demons. With the kingdom invading creation, they cannot go home again. They are as homeless as the man they inhabit.

Perhaps to our surprise, Jesus accommodates them and allows them to remove themselves from their victim and enter into a herd of swine. That could have been an amusing and appropriately satisfying conclusion to the story—the ironic fittingness of unclean spirits making themselves at home in unclean hogs—but the chaotic mania of the demons cannot leave well enough alone. They bear their confusion with them wherever they go. The herd of swine, apparently going peacefully about their piggy business beforehand, now go berserk, dash madly over a cliff, and drown in the lake. From Western movies like *Red River* we may be familiar with cattle stampedes, but swine stampedes? If pigs were runners, our bacon would look different. Their frenzied charge into the water evidences the pandemonium that cannot stand against the salvation of God.

That we should listen to this story with amusement is not incidental. It may not evoke knee-slapping laughter, but we smile at the humor. Here

Luke 8:26–39

Theological Perspective

not eradicated evil or its causes. Admitting that there are powers in this world and in our lifetime that we cannot control or conquer saves us from trivializing their effects. Only Jesus Christ has the power to conquer the demons.

In his hymn "A Mighty Fortress Is Our God," Martin Luther acknowledged the presence of demons in the world, a world that is "with devils filled." Their activity in repressive regimes and their unrelenting violence against the innocent may seem to undo us. Yet we know the final outcome. Their doom is sure. The forces of evil may sometimes run amuck and appear to have control, as the legions held sway over the man. The incarnation reminds us that even in the face of such evil, God is also on the loose. That power will prevail.

Finally, note the way in which Jesus departs the scene. News of the exorcism has spread, and people come from the city to see for themselves. They are filled with fear. Just as they may not have had a good explanation for the demons that possessed the man, they now cannot explain what has happened in his healing. All of the people ask Jesus to leave, and he does. He does not try to argue with them or insinuate himself further into their lives. In just a few verses, he will instruct his disciples to leave the villages where they are not welcome. Here he does the same.

The man who has been cured wants to join the disciples, to travel with Jesus. Instead, Jesus gives him two instructions: First, as a sign of restoration and an invitation to reconciliation, Jesus sends the man back to his own people, the Gerasenes, even though it is not clear how open that community will be toward him. Second, Jesus instructs the man to tell others what God has done for him. Before he sends out his own disciples, Jesus commissions a Gentile to proclaim the good news. The boundary-breaking ministry that he had foretold in Luke 4:18 is once again being fulfilled. The man goes his way, his appearance and testimony witnessing to the one who sets captives free.

EDNA JACOBS BANES

Pastoral Perspective

if he is to restore trust. Often we are afraid of those who have been healed by the power of God, maybe even more so when that person declares how much Jesus has done for them. Flannery O'Connor once wrote, "You shall know the truth, and the truth shall make you odd."[1] Once we are restored by the power of God to blessed community (with God, self, and neighbor), we are indeed odd when viewed by society's norms; but the good news is that we are no longer possessed by demons, misshapen desires, addictions, or other restraining boundaries.

One of the pivotal pastoral questions from this text is, "How are these boundaries traversed?" Again and again, the passage points to the power of Jesus. Jesus decides to travel to the other side of the lake, where the Gentiles live (8:22). Jesus is the one who addresses "Legion" and grants them permission to enter the herd (vv. 30–32). Jesus is the one who restores a "man of the city" (v. 27) to his right mind, clothes him in grace, and commands him, "Return to your home, and declare how much God has done for you" (v. 39). Only by the power of Jesus are these boundaries navigated.

This is obviously good news for those who are tormented and driven out of community. The grace of the passage, though, is for all who need to cross over to well-being: those who are obsessed by the rise and fall of their pensions; those who are chained to addiction; and those pastors who fall into the seductive trap of being a congregation's savior. The grace of this story is not only for outcasts, but for each and every one of us.

DAVID G. FORNEY

---

1. Flannery O'Connor, personal correspondence, widely attributed. See Ralph C. Wood, *Flannery O'Connor and the Christ-Haunted South* (Grand Rapids: Eerdmans, 2004).

Exegetical Perspective

he disrespectfully shouted at Jesus (v. 28) in spite of the fact that Jesus was trying to liberate him from his condition. Moreover, he had such an extraordinary physical strength that no one—not even the man himself—was able to control his actions (v. 29).

The last part of this story poses some disturbing problems to modern readers. On one hand, Jesus' liberating power was clearly manifested; on the other, Jesus' "dialogue" with the demons and giving them "permission" to enter the herd of pigs raises some serious questions: What does it mean that Jesus could command demons? Or that he gave permission to them? What does it mean that demons could enter pigs as easily as persons? Why would demon-possessed pigs have chosen to drown?

Contrast the man, postexorcism, with his earlier chaotic life. As a result of his contact with Jesus, the man was now "sitting at the feet of Jesus" (v. 35), rather than running through the deserted places of verse 29. Now he was clothed rather than naked. Now he was in his right mind rather than mentally disturbed. At the end, he was sent, transformed, back to the community of the living: "return to your home, and declare how much God has done for you" (v. 39). The healed man made a request to Jesus. The answer was negative (vv. 38, 39). To follow Jesus meant to go away in obedience. He simultaneously returned home and became a missionary to a land that was new for him.

What is the meaning of Jesus' dialogue with the demons? If, according to popular belief, the demons needed physical bodies to express themselves, does it make sense that they entered into the pigs to destroy the animals and remain, at the end, without bodies? Does Luke want us to be concerned about the pigs after all? Should we, rather, be concerned about the pigs' owners, who are financially hurt by these events? Why did not Jesus send away the demons to their own destiny at once (as it finally happened)? Is the death of the pigs just a symbol of the value of human beings in God's eyes, over profit and over any unclean animals, even if they are part of the creation?

PLUTARCO BONILLA A.

Homiletical Perspective

are the powers of darkness lined up against Jesus, and their demise is comic. John T. Carroll of Union Presbyterian Seminary writes, "With high drama, and not a little humor, the narrative pictures the destructive—and ultimately self-defeating—fury of evil forces, which are powerless . . . before Jesus."[1] The opposing forces can look most impressive. The name "Legion" indicates not only "many demons had entered him" (v. 30), but that they are in formation like the powerful legions of Rome.

Their apparent order is illusory. They bring only disorder and destruction. This disorder, moreover, bears the seeds of its own destruction. It cannot be sustained against the peace of God. From beginning to end of the story of the Gerasene demoniac, Jesus is clearly in charge, his triumph is assumed, and we hear the victory song of Psalm 2, which acclaims that the One "who sits in the heavens laughs" at those who "take counsel together, against the LORD and [God's] anointed" (Ps. 2:4, 2). The Lord can laugh because the Lord knows that chaos and disorder have no future and the victory belongs to a kingdom of peace. In the meantime we can enjoy the laughter of Christ's victory; we can draw checks and chuckles from the treasury of the kingdom.

In the meantime there is work to be done. The man from whom the demons are cast is ready to follow Jesus in the company of the disciples, but Jesus has other work for him to do. Hearing a story about demons can engross us; we become interested in all the wrong things, enticed by the lure of evil and distracted from the truth. Jesus tells the man: "Return to your home, and declare how much God has done for you." Luke explains that "he went away, proclaiming throughout the city how much Jesus had done for him" (v. 39). This description of preaching is at the heart of Luke's Gospel: hearing what Jesus has done, we hear what God is accomplishing in the coming of the kingdom.

PATRICK J. WILLSON

---

1. John T. Carroll, *Luke: A Commentary* (Louisville, KY: Westminster John Knox Press, 2012), 194.

Luke 8:40–56

⁴⁰Now when Jesus returned, the crowd welcomed him, for they were all waiting for him. ⁴¹Just then there came a man named Jairus, a leader of the synagogue. He fell at Jesus' feet and begged him to come to his house, ⁴²for he had an only daughter, about twelve years old, who was dying.

As he went, the crowds pressed in on him. ⁴³Now there was a woman who had been suffering from hemorrhages for twelve years; and though she had spent all she had on physicians, no one could cure her. ⁴⁴She came up behind him and touched the fringe of his clothes, and immediately her hemorrhage stopped. ⁴⁵Then Jesus asked, "Who touched me?" When all denied it, Peter said, "Master, the crowds surround you and press in on you." ⁴⁶But Jesus said, "Someone touched me; for I noticed that power had gone out from me." ⁴⁷When the woman saw that she could not remain hidden, she came trembling; and falling down before him, she declared in the presence of all the people why she

Theological Perspective

Just as Jesus was met by the man with demons the moment he arrived at the shore of the Gerasenes, so he is met by folks on the shoreline as soon as he returns to Galilee. The intensity of his ministry has increased; this time there is a crowd that presses around him. A man named Jairus emerges from the crowd. He is a leader in the synagogue. Despite his standing in the religious community, he, like the man with the demon, falls at Jesus' feet. His young daughter is dying, and he begs Jesus to come heal her.

On the way to Jairus's house, Jesus is interrupted by the touch of a woman in the crowd. She has suffered from a blood disorder (hemorrhaging) for twelve years, the exact number of years Jairus's daughter has been alive. During that time, she has spent all of her resources trying to find a cure. Unlike the daughter, she has no one to take her concerns to Jesus. Once again, she takes action for herself; she appropriates the healing no one else has been able to give her. As one who has been on the fringes of society for many years, she is not bold enough to break through the crowds to demand Jesus' attention. Instead, she reaches out and touches the fringe of his garment.

The results are immediate. After all these years, she knows her body and senses that she has been healed. Jesus must also have a good sense of his

Pastoral Perspective

These last two healing stories of chapter 8 are part of a set of four stories of Jesus' power over naturally occurring storms (8:22–25), demons (8:26–39), and, now, over sickness and even death (8:40–56). With each demonstration of Jesus' sovereignty, we witness the intention of his power to restore humanity. The storm is calmed to save the disciples from drowning. The demons Legion are driven out to a watery grave to return the Gentile man to himself and his community. Now, in these final two stories, a woman is restored to health, and a young girl is brought back to life. Jesus has command over the material world, over the realm of the powers and principalities (including the psychological ones), over physical health, and ultimately over death itself. Surely, Jesus is the long-awaited one, the one described in the previous chapter: "the blind receive their sight, the lame walk, the lepers are cleansed, the deaf hear, the dead are raised, the poor have good news brought to them" (7:22).

Following Mark's lead, Luke couples these two stories. Reading these stories in parallel (rather than serially or as stand-alone narratives) gives the preacher or teacher an illuminating lens through which to view Jesus' healing ministry. By holding these two stories together, we discover, in the first place, that healings are interruptions. Clearly, a

had touched him, and how she had been immediately healed. [48]He said to her, "Daughter, your faith has made you well; go in peace."

[49]While he was still speaking, someone came from the leader's house to say, "Your daughter is dead; do not trouble the teacher any longer." [50]When Jesus heard this, he replied, "Do not fear. Only believe, and she will be saved." [51]When he came to the house, he did not allow anyone to enter with him, except Peter, John, and James, and the child's father and mother. [52]They were all weeping and wailing for her; but he said, "Do not weep; for she is not dead but sleeping." [53]And they laughed at him, knowing that she was dead. [54]But he took her by the hand and called out, "Child, get up!" [55]Her spirit returned, and she got up at once. Then he directed them to give her something to eat. [56]Her parents were astounded; but he ordered them to tell no one what had happened.

Exegetical Perspective

To the four main categories of persons about whom the Old Testament says not only that the authorities of the people of Israel should take special care but also that God is their God—the widow, the orphan, the foreigner, and the poor—Luke has added a new category: the woman (see 7:1–8:4). This very fact is particularly stressed in these two intermingled stories.

Luke sometimes inserts a story within another story in an extended narrative. That is, for example, how he recounts the parallel narratives of John's birth and Jesus' birth. The same literary technique is found in the last part of chapter 8, immediately after the account of the healing of the Gerasene man. In embedding stories within stories, Luke simultaneously reinforces a narrative understanding of life and provides contexts for the two stories by playing them off against each other.

These new stories are healing stories. From the outset, we see that significant details are paralleled, whether by similitude or by contrast in the overall description of events. The following particulars are relevant: (1) two females are the recipients of Jesus' action of healing; (2) one of them is a grown adult; the other is a youngster; (3) a man comes to Jesus to intercede for his daughter; a women herself takes the initiative in search of her own well-being;

Homiletical Perspective

Retelling these stories of Jairus's daughter and the woman with a hemorrhage, Luke interprets the text in Mark 5:21–43. Matthew trims these stories (Matt. 9:18–26) to their essentials to emphasize Jesus' growing notoriety as a wonder-worker (Matt. 9:26). Luke also believes Mark needs editing, but Luke places these two stories within the grand, expansive story of God's salvation invading human life in Jesus Christ. Luke introduces that story with Simeon's aria Nunc Dimittis—"my eyes have seen your salvation" (2:30)—and that saga continues as Jairus and an unnamed woman see in Jesus something hopeful drawing near, breaking in, while others only laugh.

Perhaps Jairus, the leader of the synagogue, and the woman with hemorrhages have heard of Jesus as a healer and wonder-worker. They have heard something about Jesus; that much is clear from the way they approach him. They have problems no one can do anything about, but perhaps Jesus can. Jesus accompanies Jairus to his home; but, before he can get there, a hopeless woman interrupts him.

When salvation approaches, things are made new—including us and the way we are named. The woman with hemorrhages is unnamed but unquestionably unclean. Her uncleanness is contagious (Lev. 15:19–24), though her ailment is private. Luke knows his Septuagint well, and in this instance he

Luke 8:40–56

Theological Perspective

body, for he realizes that power has gone out of him. As focused as he might have been in journeying to Jairus's house, he is also aware of the needs of those around him. He does not chide the woman for reaching out, interrupting his travel, or wasting his time. Instead, he allows her to testify before the crowd and calls her Daughter.

As he is speaking to the woman, someone from the crowd interjects to tell Jesus that Jairus's daughter has died. Jesus continues to the house, however. His presence is always powerful, even in the face of death. Folks have gathered around the home to lament and perhaps to offer their support. As the woman in the crowd has touched him, he touches the girl, taking her by the hand and commanding her to get up. She does.

One theological theme of these stories is the movement from isolation to community. The woman with the hemorrhage may be in a crowd but has no doubt lived much of her life alone. Her illness may have prevented the normal circumstances of marriage and family. Not only does Jesus restore her to health; he restores her to her community. The young girl is surrounded by community but is no longer part of it, for she has died. In restoring the girl to life, Jesus also returns her to full participation in that community. An interesting aspect of Jesus' healing ministry is its emphasis on community. The miracles of healing are never to be enjoyed by the recipients alone but are to be shared in the community to which they return. Despite rejections he has experienced in his community (4:29), Jesus still trusts the communities of his day, and ours, to welcome those who have been outcast and to aid in the recovery of those who have been ill or disabled.

Another theme is Jesus' ability to respond to a variety of people from many different stations in life. He reaches out to young and old alike. He heals folks who are brought to him, and others who are not able to make their request face to face, but can only touch the fringe of his garment. We sense the boldness of the father in prostrating himself before Jesus and the uncertainty of the woman, who approaches him from behind with fear and trembling. Jairus may be wealthy; the woman's resources have all been spent. Jesus does not differentiate between them but methodically restores them to health and life.

Jesus also responds to their healing in different ways. The woman is allowed to tell others what he has done for her. Yet he cautions the family of the young girl not to tell anyone. These examples are instructive for his disciples who are part of the

Pastoral Perspective

healing interrupts the illness. In the cases of Jairus's daughter, the widow's son (7:11–17), and Lazarus (John 11:1–44), Jesus' power interrupts death. Reading these two stories together, we see even the process of a healing being interrupted. As Jesus is heading to Jairus's house to attend to his daughter, he is detained by a woman who has suffered from hemorrhages for twelve years. Holding these two narratives together, we find that healings are not linear or logical. They cannot be put on our calendars or understood sequentially—mainly because, as Isaiah proclaims, "my thoughts are not your thoughts, nor are your ways my ways, says the LORD" (Isa. 55:8).

As pastors, we can help name the divine interruptions in people's lives. By grace, our routines of sin are broken, twelve years of bleeding is finally ended, the flow of addiction in our lives is dislodged, our vitriolic language is silenced, and ultimately our deep sleep in the grave will be interrupted by the sound of the last trumpet. By God's incarnational interruption in Jesus Christ, humanity will be transformed from death to life, "in a moment, in the twinkling of an eye, at the last trumpet" (1 Cor. 15: 52). In this passage, we see that healings take place both along the journey (in the marketplace) and at the final destination (in the child's bedroom). The interruptive nature of healings is only one of several facets a preacher or teacher might want to explore when viewing these two stories in parallel.

In the second place we discover that healings are a serious matter and that they are laughable. Jesus stops midstride after the woman is healed and asks, "Who touched me?" (v. 45). Healings are not casual or impersonal. So Jesus presses the issue, "Someone touched me; for I noticed that power had gone out from me" (v. 46). It seems that Jesus would wait all day until she came forward; when she finally does so, she receives the blessing: "Daughter, your faith has made you well; go in peace" (v. 48). Healings are also laughable matters. When the household hears Jesus declare that Jairus's daughter is not dead but sleeping, "they laughed at him" (v. 53). Perhaps the laughter was mockery or embarrassment or anger at such a cruel joke, but we often laugh at things we do not understand and cannot control.

In the third place we notice that healings invite us to reach out and grab hold of new life personally, and healings are given on behalf of those whose hands no longer work. The faith of the woman—believing, hoping, wishing desperately that if she can but touch Jesus' garment, she will be healed—is faith for us to emulate. She squeezes through the nearly

Feasting on the Gospels

Exegetical Perspective

(4) the woman is desperate because of her ceaseless and unending suffering; the girl's father is desperate because his daughter is about to die; (5) the woman has spent all her financial resources on physicians who could not heal her; the girl's father is a very important person in the community since he is a prominent man in the synagogue; (6) touching plays a very important role in the stories: in one story, the woman touches the fringe of Jesus' garment; in the other, Jesus touches the girl when he takes her hand; (7) this distinguished man has to wait to see his petition fulfilled, while that anonymous woman is instantly cured; (8) both the man and the woman must undergo a test: the man sees that Jesus does not hurry to his house but instead stops to ask a seemingly silly question, and the woman, ashamed, feels impelled publicly to confess the reason why she has done what she has done; (9) fear overtakes both the woman and the girl's father; but (10) in both cases faith overcomes fear; (11) both stories have a happy ending: the woman is sent in peace, and Jairus's daughter receives her life back and her parents are ordered to give her something to eat; (12) the woman had suffered twelve years from hemorrhage; the youngster was twelve years old.

The narrative also stresses some significant elements that are found in previous stories: First, in the case of the demon-possessed Gerasene, the house (*oikos*) is the place of life, where the person finds and gives love, protection, and dignity and where community is created (8:27, 39); for this same reason Jairus asks Jesus to go to his house, since a girl was there in need of protection and life,[1] and sustenance (8:55). In reading these Gospel stories we see that the house plays a very important role in Jesus' ministry: he teaches in houses (5:17–26), and in houses he heals the sick (4:38–39); he accepts invitations to eat in the house of a Pharisee (7:36) and in the house of a publican (5:29), and in both houses he confronts his adversaries; Martha and Mary welcome him in their house (10:38–42). It is no surprise, therefore, that when Jairus asks Jesus to go to his house, Jesus immediately agrees to accompany him.

Second, after the Gerasene man is healed, his local fellow countrymen find him "sitting at the feet of Jesus" (8:35), the typical position of a disciple before his or her master (cf. Mary's position, "who sat at the Lord's feet," 10:39). In this other story, when Jairus approaches Jesus, "he fell at Jesus' feet" (v. 41) in an attitude of supplication and humbleness,

Homiletical Perspective

may compliment his listeners by assuming they know Leviticus 15 as well. Here, where "the crowds surround . . . [and] press in" clamoring for Jesus' attention (v. 45b), this woman is an affront to social hygiene. Reading intertextually with Leviticus 15:19–31, we understand that socially her name is "Unclean" and "Uninvited," but instead Jesus speaks to her, calling her "Daughter." It is a term of affection and kinship, and it echoes through Luke's story.

Mark may tell the story with something of a sneer at the physicians who have taken the woman's money to no avail, but in Luke's telling of the story, the woman is simply beyond the help of what constitutes modern medicine in the first century. She is hopeless. When another "woman with a spirit that had crippled her for eighteen years" (13:11) appears, she is an interruption to the Sabbath, but Jesus names her "a daughter of Abraham" (13:16). The citizens of Jericho know Zacchaeus as "one who is a sinner" (19:7), and Luke invites us to explore our own prejudices by telling us "he was a chief tax collector and was rich" (19:2); but then Jesus declares "he too is a son of Abraham" (19:9). When Jesus calls us, he calls us by names we have forgotten we had and, in that process, creates something new in us.

Before Jesus can finish talking with her—"while he was still speaking" (v. 49)—messengers arrive from Jairus's home to declare that his daughter is hopeless as well. She is dead. There is nothing left to be done: "do not trouble the teacher any longer" (v. 49).

The teacher, however, has not finished the lesson. Jesus' response to the news of the child's death is threefold: "Do not fear. Only believe, and she will be saved" (v. 50). Luke adds the language of salvation to Mark's "Do not fear, only believe" (Mark 5:36). This seems improbable enough, but when Jesus announces, "Do not weep; for she is not dead but sleeping," the howls of laughter really begin (v. 53). People know about death. They know it is permanent. People may survive near-death experiences, but if they survive, that was not really death. The people gathered at Jairus's house know about death. They are paid mourners. François Bovon speaks of "the laughter of these people who are, in part, professionals."[1]

In his Gospel, Matthew remembers "the flute players" (Matt. 9:23) hired for the rituals of mourning. These are the experts; they have seen it all and they laugh. Luke is an evangelist, a preacher of good news; these "experts" are *kakangelists,* purveyors of

---

1. In Matthew the situation is even more dramatic: when the leader of the synagogue approaches Jesus, his daughter had already died (Matt. 9:18).

1. François Bovon, *Luke 1: A Commentary on the Gospel of Luke 1:1–9:50,* trans. Christine M. Thomas (Minneapolis: Fortress Press, 2002), 340.

Luke 8:40–56

Theological Perspective

crowd. As they observe him respond to each individual in a unique way, they see how they are to minister to the myriad requests that will soon be part of their calling. Jesus may be surrounded by a crowd, but every person there is still an individual. Jesus sees and responds to each of them and each of us as unique creatures. As one children's song goes, we are all "precious in his sight."

There is also the theme of the breaking down of barriers in this passage. Those who live on the margins of society are emboldened by the actions of the woman. As the woman is able to break through the crowd to touch Jesus, so they are encouraged to break down barriers that would prevent their full participation in ministry of Jesus today.[1]

Previously there has been an increase in crowds surrounding Jesus. In these two healings, the activity of Jesus' ministry increases. He is on the move—across the lake and back, working among the crowds, traveling to Jairus's house. Several actions occur "immediately" or "at once." One healing story interrupts another. There is an implied urgency as the Galilean ministry nears a close and Jesus prepares to head toward Jerusalem. We know what will face Jesus there, but these two healing stories plus the exorcism that precedes them have established the strength of Jesus. He has power over demons and death itself. The chaos and confusion that will accompany his trial and crucifixion will not be the final word. Another way has already been set in motion.

EDNA JACOBS BANES

Pastoral Perspective

suffocating crowd to find healing for herself. No one else helps her, so she takes matters in her own hands. In the other instance, Jairus, the father, is the one who seeks out Jesus' healing touch on behalf of his daughter. Clearly it is not the daughter's faith that makes her well, but her father going out to find and plead with Jesus to save her (vv. 41–42). What is the same in both miracles are the drive to be made well and believing Jesus has the power to make it so.

In the fourth place, healings are for both the righteous (Jairus, the synagogue leader) and the unclean (the hemorrhaging woman; see Lev. 15:25). For twelve years, the woman was not allowed to enter the synagogue over which Jairus presided. Yet both their prayers are granted. By referring to Jairus by name and socioeconomic status, we see that the sun and the rain fall on the righteous and on the unrighteous (Matt. 5:45). Jairus's house is not immune to suffering because of his religious status. Yet the expectation in that house is that God will hear his prayer. We expect that the woman's prayers, presumably twelve years' worth, go unheard. Yet the good news of this passage is that, in Jesus Christ, God knows and hears our immediate needs and our long-suffered needs, whether we are counted as righteous or unclean. Why? Because God desires to make all things whole and does so through Jesus Christ.

Finally, healings are both public matters, where crowds surround us (vv. 42, 45), and private matters (v. 51). Ironically, Jesus demands to know who was healed by touching him in the middle of the crowd, thus calling public attention to a healing that could have gone unnoticed. In the same breath he orders those who witness the daughter's healing to tell no one (v. 56).

When we read these two stories together, we are reminded that God's restorative acts are not formulaic but truly contextual, fitting our particular wounds and our particular ways of coming to God for care.

DAVID G. FORNEY

---

1. For example, see Musa W. Duba, "*Talitha Cum* Hermeneutics of Liberation: Some African American Women's Ways of Reading the Bible," in *The Bible and the Hermeneutics of Liberation*, ed. Alejandro F. Botta and Pablo R. Andiñach (Atlanta: Society of Biblical Literature, 2009).

Exegetical Perspective

even though there is a crowd welcoming Jesus and he, Jairus, is a leader of the synagogue! The demon-possessed Gerasene has been liberated from the forces of death that were destroying him; on the other hand Jairus is imploring Jesus for his daughter's liberation from death, and in order to attain this goal he does not pay attention to what the people will say about his action of falling at Jesus' feet. As a contrast, and given the nature of her illness, the woman suffering from a hemorrhage "came up behind Jesus and touched" the border of his cloak (v. 44). However, she also has to make a public confession.

Third, the Gerasene's fellow countrymen "kept [him] under guard and bound [him] with chains and shackles, but he would break the bonds" (8:29), and "no one could cure" the woman suffering from a hemorrhage (v. 43). In both cases Jesus was the liberating power.

There is yet another interesting contrast: even though he is a very important man in his community, Jairus has to wait to see his daughter brought back to life. However, when Jesus finally holds the girl's hand, the girl immediately (*parachrēma*) receives her life back. The same word is used to describe the healing of the woman as soon as she touches Jesus' garment. The "time" of Jesus' work does not always coincide with our personal desires. God's time is God's time, not ours.

As the Gerasene is sent by Jesus back to his home (*oikos*) and to his community (*polis*, "city") to tell his own people what God/Jesus (8:39) has done for him, so the parents of the girl are ordered to give her something to eat (v. 55). Blessings received should be transmuted into service rendered.

PLUTARCO BONILLA A.

Homiletical Perspective

bad news. They know what is possible and what is not. They throw cold water on Jesus' words. They are like the idolaters Isaiah describes, utterly confident in their professionalism and craftsmanship: "They do not know, nor do they comprehend; for their eyes are shut, so that they cannot see, and their minds as well, so that they cannot understand" (Isa. 44:18). We are well acquainted with people so expert in their knowledge and finally so expert in their hopelessness that they cannot entertain the possibility of God interrupting their certainty. Knowledge merely funds cynicism. They know only enough to despair. They think of themselves as realistic, tough minded, nobody's fools. They know how to manage the numbers. They know about death, though life is notoriously more complex and confusing. They simply do not know and cannot recognize the power of God's salvation breaking into their midst. Later, Jesus will pray for people like these: "Father, forgive them; for they do not know what they are doing" (23:34).

If Jesus notices their laughter, Luke gives no sign of it. Instead, Jesus gets to the business of salvation that the coming kingdom promises: "Child, get up." "Child" is a word sometimes used to speak of relationship: Jesus connects himself to both the old woman and the young girl through his words: "my child" and "daughter." The last word is not the bleakness of a hopeless situation but "child" and "daughter." Luke Powery, dean of Duke University Chapel, has noticed how in the African American church's language, "Life-giving salutatory metaphors of language are ultimately rooted in the life-giving Holy Spirit who specializes in welcoming the *other*."[2] Salvation is breaking in as Jesus enters one place after another. New language and new names are required to speak of the new thing God is doing, and that is the task of the preacher.

PATRICK J. WILLSON

---

2. Luke A. Powery, *Spirit Speech: Lament and Celebration in Preaching* (Nashville: Abingdon Press, 2009), 16, emphasis Powery's.

Luke 9:1–9

¹Then Jesus called the twelve together and gave them power and authority over all demons and to cure diseases, ²and he sent them out to proclaim the kingdom of God and to heal. ³He said to them, "Take nothing for your journey, no staff, nor bag, nor bread, nor money—not even an extra tunic. ⁴Whatever house you enter, stay there, and leave from there. ⁵Wherever they do not welcome you, as you are leaving that town shake the dust off your feet as a testimony against them." ⁶They departed and went through the villages, bringing the good news and curing diseases everywhere.

⁷Now Herod the ruler heard about all that had taken place, and he was perplexed, because it was said by some that John had been raised from the dead, ⁸by some that Elijah had appeared, and by others that one of the ancient prophets had arisen. ⁹ Herod said, "John I beheaded; but who is this about whom I hear such things?" And he tried to see him.

Theological Perspective

Although Jesus had chosen the disciples earlier (6:12–16), their role until now has been one of observing and learning. Now he will send them out on their own. The summary of their preparation, Jesus' instructions to them, and their subsequent journeys provide an excellent theological framework for the mission trips congregations undertake today.

Jesus had issued his call only after spending a night in prayer and discernment (6:12). Since then, the disciples had been engaged in an extended period of discernment and pastoral formation. They had traveled with Jesus, learning from his teachings and preaching. His Sermon on the Plain (Luke's version of the Sermon on the Mount) had set the stage for the ministry of reversals in which they would be engaged. The parable of the Soils would be useful to them as they encountered different levels of acceptance.

Accompanying Jesus as he healed and exorcised evil spirits, they learned about that ministry. Observing Jesus' various reactions to those who came to him for healing or help, they honed their people skills. Noting the aid Jesus extended to a member of the Roman military (7:2), a sinful woman (7:37), and a widow (7:12), they began to understand the inclusive nature of his work. Just as Jesus was groomed for his ministry as he matured in wisdom and knowledge (2:52), so they were being prepared to minister in his

Pastoral Perspective

While teaching a seminary course on leadership, I often asked the students if they wanted power for their ministry. Few ever raised their hands. If a hand did go up, it was usually the hand of an older student. Of course there are many reasons why students did not raise their hands. Power was not the reason they had come to serve. Power as they had experienced it, both inside and outside the church, was experienced in destructive ways. Yet is this power true power? Theology professor Alan Lewis taught his classes that "the gospel does not abhor power but *reconceives* it radically. . . . The question is not *whether* but *how* power is distributed and used within the church."[1]

In this passage from Luke, we are offered two ways to think about power: one that transforms not only our lives but also the lives of those to whom we proclaim the gospel, and another that corrodes the well-being of the individual and the community. I would like to think that those students who did not raise their hands were thinking of this corrosive use of power, and that those who did raise their hands understood power through the lens of the gospel's radical reconceptualization.

1.Alan Lewis, in *Incarnational Ministry*, ed. C. D. Ketter and T. H. Speidell (Colorado Springs, CO: Helmers & Howard, 1990), 119.

Feasting on the Gospels

Exegetical Perspective

The previous stories were clear manifestations of Jesus' power to transform the lives of those who met him, since they were persons in need. All the disciples—or, on some occasions, three of them—were eyewitnesses to these demonstrations of power. The purpose of their witnessing these deeds was not only for them to observe some spectacular accomplishments, but also to be trained in order to be ready to fulfill their own responsibilities as Jesus' disciples. They had already heard Jesus' teachings and had seen ill persons cured, a man and a young girl brought back to life, a demon-possessed man restored and sent back to his community, and now they—the disciples—were bestowed with power and authority.

The order in which this empowering takes place and its meaning as expressed by the evangelist are important. He says that Jesus called the Twelve and then (1) he gave them power and authority (2) over all devils (3) and to cure diseases, (4) and sent them (5) to proclaim the kingdom of God (6) and to heal those who were sick (vv. 1–2). Power is mentioned first, but it was not a gift of power for the sake of power or power centered in the persons who were going to manifest it. It was not power for domination, but for service—to cure those who were under the power of demons or of diseases. It was power in the context of the kingdom.

Homiletical Perspective

Jesus has encountered demons—not just a few but a cohort so numerous as to be named Legion (8:30). He had healed people in situations others had deemed hopeless (8:43) and raised a child from the dead (8:53–54). Now he sends the Twelve out to do the same and proclaim the kingdom.

Does this seem premature? We are only in the ninth chapter of Luke's story, and much more is yet to come. The disciples have not yet heard the parable of the Good Samaritan (10:25–37), learned to pray (11:1), or heard the parables of Luke 15 that describe God's search for the lost—a search they now are called to make their own. Far distant from their line of vision is the unveiling of God's purpose in the crucifixion of Jesus. How can Jesus expect these novices "to proclaim the kingdom of God and to heal" (v. 2)?

As if Jesus' expectations are not daunting enough, he magnifies the disciples' vulnerability by insisting they make no preparations: "Take nothing for your journey, no staff, nor bag, nor bread, nor money—not even an extra tunic" (v. 3).

A friend was preparing a series of sermons for a large conference, her first such engagement. "I am scared to death," she admitted, "and I keep having these awful dreams!" "You are standing there preaching naked?" I guessed. She moved as if she needed

Luke 9:1–9

Theological Perspective

name. Now he invested them with authority, bestowing on them some of the same power he had felt leave him when the woman touched his hem (8:46).

In their journeys, they were to travel simply. They were to leave behind the usual travel supplies such as money, a walking cane, or a clean change of clothes. Such unencumbered travel emphasized their dependence on God to provide. Extra provisions might prove distracting. They were to seek housing in each town. There they were to stay, sharing the lifestyle of that household, and not seek better accommodations. Although theirs was a ministry of proclamation and healing and they were imbued with the same power and authority they had experienced in Jesus' ministry, they were not to force this ministry on everyone. If they faced rejection, they were not to argue or persuade; rather, they were to leave that place and travel elsewhere, shaking dust from their feet rather than their fists as a sign of their rejection.

Although their mission work is not described in detail, it appears to be one of enculturation. This method of evangelism encouraged mission workers to live among the people for an extended period of time, getting to know them and adapting to their customs, rather than forcing one's own viewpoints or beliefs on the hosts. Paul would later follow in this example of the disciples, often living with local residents for months at a time as he preached the gospel. His ministry in Athens, when he used one of their unknown gods to expound on the gospel, is illustrative of enculturation (Acts 17:22–34).

Douglas John Hall considers this type of missional work an expansion of the ancient practice of hospitality.[1] One accepts others where they are and works with them to discover the truth and beauty of the gospel that is already present. Rather than taking the gospel of Jesus Christ *to* them, we find the Christ *in the midst of* them.

Brian McLaren describes the work as a movement, ministering with people rather than witnessing to them: "What did the movement do? They traveled from village to village, much like a political campaign, spreading their message, looking for 'people of peace' and networking them together, feeding the hungry, healing the sick, offering hope to the depressed, promising freedom for the oppressed, confronting the oppressors and conversing with questioners and critics."[2]

1. Douglas John Hall, *Why Christian* (Minneapolis: Fortress Press, 1998), 147.
2. Brian McLaren, *Why Did Jesus, the Buddha, and Mohammed Cross the Road? Christian Identity in a Multi-Faith World* (New York: Jericho Books, 2012), 233.

Pastoral Perspective

Luke 9:1–9 explores both of these exercises of power: the use of power by the Twelve to bring the good news and cure diseases in the world (v. 1), and Herod's use of power to poison the community for the sole reason of retaining his position (vv. 7–9). The disciples' use of power is instructive to individuals and the community, because it directly participates in God's work. Herod, on the other hand, self-servingly wields power, lopping off the head of "the prophet of the Most High" (1:76). Luke connects God's redemptive, healing power—"the tender mercy of our God, the dawn from on high" breaking upon us (1:78)—with the service of the Twelve. That power turns "the people of Israel to the Lord their God" (1:16) and turns "the hearts of parents to their children" (1:17). That bright dawn exposes sin's powerful corrosiveness, including Herod's tyranny. One promotes the gospel; the other promotes the self.

Theologian Karl Barth wrote that "unqualified power is *per se* the power of negation, destruction, and dissolution. The man [*sic*] who is obedient to the command of God self-evidently cannot and will not desire this power."[2] Herod's use of power was unqualified, as his beheading of John the Baptist attests. Without question, Herod was a brutal ruler of his people. Yet that is not the only unfortunate consequence of his unqualified use of power. Herod's use of power negates his ability to see Jesus when he finally gets the chance in the twenty-third chapter of Luke. Here Herod states, "John I beheaded; but who is this about whom I hear such things?" Consequently, "he tried to see him" (v. 9).

In chapter 23, Herod "was very glad, for he had been wanting to see [Jesus] for a long time, because he had heard about him and was hoping to see him perform some sign" (23:8). Herod's negative, destructive, dissolutive power blinds him in the end from seeing the incarnation of the good news standing before him. He wants to see a miracle, a form of entertainment, but only sees a silent, passive man. Consequently, "even Herod with his soldiers treated him [Jesus] with contempt and mocked him" (23:11). Jesus' authority, even when silent and passive, exposes inhumane and oppressive powers such as Herod's.

It is not coincidental that these two accounts of power immediately follow Jesus' comprehensive demonstrations of power over nature's storms (8:22–25), over demons (8:26–39), and over sickness and

2. Karl Barth, *Church Dogmatics*, III/4, ed. G. W. Bromiley and T. F. Torrance (Edinburgh: T. & T. Clark, 1990), 391.

Exegetical Perspective

This is clearly expressed in the Gospel by the fact that as the disciples went out to do what Jesus had commanded them to do, they first evangelized (v. 6) and healed the people of the villages.[1] Those manifestations of power were both for the benefit of the people and as a confirmation of the truth of the disciples' proclamation: that the kingdom of God was already present and demanded repentance. The two elements—boon and testimony, on the one hand, and the requirement of repentance, on the other—could not and cannot be separated.

As the healed Gerasene man was sent back to his house, as Jesus bid the cured woman farewell in peace (to return to her own community), and as the synagogue leader asked Jesus to go to his house, so the disciples, obedient to Jesus, went to the villages to proclaim the good news and to heal those in need of health. Communities of human beings (house, hamlet, village, town), in need of the good news of the kingdom, play an important role in Luke's narratives. "No man is an island," wrote John Donne: human beings become persons in the community of human beings. This is the reason why Jesus' impact in the life of a person causes this person to go back to his or her community to live there as a disciple of the new Master.

After empowering his twelve disciples, also called "apostles" (or "sent-out ones") in Luke 6:13, Jesus gave them some instructions as to how they should behave in carrying out the mission. Most of these instructions have to be understood in Jesus' social and cultural context. One fundamental element that has to be taken into account is the ancient concept of hospitality. The command not to take anything with them (neither staff, nor haversack, nor bread, nor money, nor a spare tunic) and to stay in one house ("whatever house you enter, stay there," v. 4) was dependent on a quality that was characteristic of the people of Israel and others in the ancient Near East: the virtue of hospitality. When Jesus' disciples were not welcome, they were to shake the dust off their feet as they left the village (v. 5), "as evidence [that is, as rejection and warning] against them" (see Acts 13:51).

These commands involve a paradox. The Lord gave power to his disciples, but they had to live as powerless witnesses, depending for their living on the hospitality of others who could deny it to them. This ultimately means that they had to depend on the One who had sent them.

1. This same perspective reveals itself in the promise of the Holy Spirit made to the disciples by the resurrected Jesus: "But you will receive power when the Holy Spirit has come upon you; and you will be my witnesses" (Acts 1:8).

Homiletical Perspective

to cover herself, blushed, and whispered: "How did you know?"

This is the way we are sent: vulnerably. Charles Campbell, now professor of homiletics at Duke Divinity School, points to "naked street preaching" as emblematic of the proclamation of the kingdom.[1]

When do we ever know enough "to proclaim the kingdom of God"? In a seminary library, you find whole sections, shelves of books, on "the kingdom of God"—thick books too. When you had read all of those—if you could possibly read them all—would you be prepared to speak of "the kingdom of God"?

This appears to be a preacher's dilemma more than anyone else's. Congregations assume that the command "to proclaim the kingdom of God and to heal" applies to those who are professionally employed by the church. Some people are called to speak and teach about the things of God, and others feel it a sufficient sacrifice to show up on Sunday morning and sit in the pews and listen. Faithful church members gladly whip up a batch of cookies for the bake sale or scramble eggs at the night shelter, but they shy away from putting into words why they feel compelled to do such remarkable things. Jesus' sending, however, is not confined to clergy. "I do not have any problem talking about faith in Sunday school," a member confessed, "but when it comes to coffee break at work . . ."

The disciples are summoned to speak nonetheless, and in speaking, something happens beyond our preparations and calculations. Thomas G. Long explains: "A common misunderstanding is to think that talking about faith means getting our belief system all worked out in advance before we open our mouths. . . . To the contrary, saying things out loud is part of how we come to believe. We talk our way *toward* belief, talk our way from tentative belief through doubt to firmer belief, talk our way toward believing more fully, more clearly, and more deeply."[2] Later in Luke, Jesus teaches disciples how this works: "Make up your minds not to prepare your defense in advance; for I will give you words and a wisdom" (21:14–15).

As we are sent "through the villages," we are not—as we might suspect and as we fear—left to our own resources. The mission "to proclaim the kingdom of God and to heal" is initiated by Jesus' command,

1. Charles Campbell, "The Preacher as Ridiculous Person: Naked Street Preaching and Homiletical Foolishness." Inaugural Address, Columbia Theological Seminary, Decatur, GA, March 29, 2005.
2. Thomas G. Long, *Testimony: Talking Ourselves into Being Christian*, The Practices of Faith Series (San Francisco: Jossey-Bass, 2004), 6; the emphasis is Long's.

Luke 9:1–9

Theological Perspective

There is energy in the concluding description of the disciples traveling through the villages, proclaiming the good news and healing the people they met. However, the passage itself ends on an ominous note and offers a stark reminder of the challenges of such endeavors. Herod enters the scene.

Herod appeared earlier in this Gospel as Luke described the ministry of John the Baptist (3:1). Evidently the Baptist did not mince words as to the character of this ruler, rebuking him for the evil he had done. His harsh criticism had landed him in jail (3:19–20). Here Herod admitted, almost offhandedly, that he had beheaded John (9:9). Despite the demise of the prophet, the good news John was preparing the people to receive had not gone away.

Perhaps the crowds Jesus was attracting also attracted Herod's attention. Maybe the increased activity of the disciples traveling throughout the villages caught his eye. Whatever the reason, he was beginning to worry again—like the devil who had left the scene until an opportune time (4:13), Herod will continue to be a threat, appearing here and there in Luke's Gospel, until he participates in another execution, this time by crucifixion.

There is one other detail in these brief verses about Herod that is intriguing. Evidently the mission of the disciples enjoyed some success, for Jesus' reputation was spreading and people were talking. Luke says that Herod was perplexed, confused. In trying to pinpoint who this disturber of his peace might be, Herod listened to the folk around him. They were saying that Jesus might be Elijah, or one of the ancient prophets come back to life, or John raised from the dead. Their speculations and confusion as to the person of Jesus would be mirrored by those closest to Jesus in a few short verses (9:18–20). Herod wanted to see Jesus, Luke tells us. As Jesus set his face toward Jerusalem, he would have his opportunity.

On the heels of the disciples going out to share the good news of this Jesus, the confusion of both Herod and the disciples reminds us how easy it is to misinterpret the gospel we may enthusiastically proclaim.

EDNA JACOBS BANES

Pastoral Perspective

death (8:40–56). Luke links Jesus' sovereign power with humanity's capacity to participate in the gospel. Hence his use of the conjunctive adverb "then" (v. 1) to link Jesus' power with that of the ministry of the Twelve. The world has plenty of examples of Herod's use of power. All we need to do is look at the weekly headlines for contemporary examples. What is unmistakably unique is the radically reconceived power that Jesus gives his followers. Once the Twelve witness Jesus' transforming power in all realms, they journey out to proclaim and to heal "everywhere" (v. 6).

One last contrast between the Twelve and Herod is their respective appearances. Herod, with his regalia, signet ring, banquet halls, and money as afforded him as the ruler of Galilee, is distinctively different from the disciples, whose garb is the garb Jesus commanded: "Take nothing for your journey, no staff, nor bag, nor bread, nor money—not even an extra tunic" (v. 3). By their looks, Herod and the Twelve visibly declare which power they bet their lives on: Herod on humanly conceived power, and the Twelve on God's power. In the end, Herod will even try to dress up Jesus for the part: "then he put an elegant robe on him" (23:11). Yet the power of God is seen when Jesus is crucified, without any badge of office or staff or bag or bread or money.

What might this passage say to Christians today? The minister might want to help the congregation understand and live into the reality that, in God's reign, power is very different from our human notion of power. As Christians, we are sent into the world without the usual accoutrements signifying how potent we are. Rather, we are called to rely solely on God's provision. We are commissioned powerfully to participate in bringing the good news and healing diseases everywhere, not by our own doing, but only by the power of the One who sends us. Maybe it is here that each of us can raise our hand and go.

DAVID G. FORNEY

Exegetical Perspective

One particular feature of Luke's narrative is that, like Mark but over against Matthew (Matt. 10:5), he does not mention the prohibition to enter Gentile territory or any Samaritan town (Matt. 10:6). Luke thereby stresses the universal vision of Jesus' mission. As a matter of fact, this universality of Jesus' whole ministry—deeds and teachings included—is manifested in this Gospel from its very beginning (e.g., in the Nunc Dimittis, 2:29–32) and throughout the complete text, as revealed in the role Samaritans play in different kinds of narratives that are found only in Luke: in parables, as the parable of the Good Samaritan in 10:29–37, and in healing stories, as the miracle of the ten lepers, in 17:11–19 (note the explicit clarification in v. 16, "And he was a Samaritan"). The healing of the demon-possessed man (8:26–39) is another example, since the man lived in a territory inhabited by Gentiles, and he later "went away, proclaiming throughout the city how much Jesus had done for him."

Herod Antipas (see 3:1) heard about this news and wished to know who that man was who was doing such wonders. He did not accept current interpretations, and did not believe that John, whom he had beheaded, had risen from death (vv. 7–9). So he tried to see Jesus. It probably was only a wish out of curiosity. Herod would not see Jesus until Pilate passed Jesus over to him (23:6–13). The interview was disappointing, for Jesus kept silent, and Herod treated him with contempt. Mere curiosity was not—and is not—enough motivation to have a real encounter with Jesus.

PLUTARCO BONILLA A.

Homiletical Perspective

is enabled by Jesus' power and authority, and is an extension of his bringing salvation to God's people. Luke has just shown us the power and authority of Jesus' word—"Daughter, your faith has made you well; go in peace" (8:49) and "Child, get up" (8:54)—and now Jesus shares that power and authority with the Twelve.

We feel alone so often and wonder how much we can trust this power and authority, especially when it comes to Jesus' command: "and heal." We look dubiously at faith healers and know very well that we do not have the power to heal, but we overlook the power of the Word of God to bring healing. Most pastors have a file of notes and letters from parishioners thanking them for their sustaining strength during sickness and grief. The people who write this way are not thinking about sermons practically directed to "Dealing With Breast Cancer" or "Caring For Your Alzheimer's Patient" or "Getting Over Grief," as much as they are about the week-to-week faithfulness of the church in putting forth the gospel message that provides strength, patience, power, healing, and hope. The Word of God in Jesus Christ brings healing, wholeness, and salvation, as Luke makes clear, and we are given that Word of God to share with each other.

We do not understand the power and authority of the Word of God in our world, but Jesus gives his disciples power and authority nonetheless. We are more familiar with the limits of our own abilities and training, and we imagine boundaries to the Word of God. How amazing that God means for God's Word to be spoken through us! We cannot imagine this power that works in our weakness. Luke tells us that the disciples "went through the villages, bringing the good news and curing diseases everywhere" (v. 6). As they went on their way, they discovered the deep truth of their message they did not know beforehand.

PATRICK J. WILLSON

Luke 9:10–17

10On their return the apostles told Jesus all they had done. He took them with him and withdrew privately to a city called Bethsaida. 11When the crowds found out about it, they followed him; and he welcomed them, and spoke to them about the kingdom of God, and healed those who needed to be cured. 12The day was drawing to a close, and the twelve came to him and said, "Send the crowd away, so that they may go into the surrounding villages and countryside, to lodge and get provisions; for we are here in a deserted place." 13But he said to them, "You give them something to eat." They said, "We have no more than five loaves and two fish—unless we are to go and buy food for all these people." 14For there were about five thousand men. And he said to his disciples, "Make them sit down in groups of about fifty each." 15They did so and made them all sit down. 16And taking the five loaves and the two fish, he looked up to heaven, and blessed and broke them, and gave them to the disciples to set before the crowd. 17And all ate and were filled. What was left over was gathered up, twelve baskets of broken pieces.

Theological Perspective

The feeding of the five thousand is the only miracle story found in all four Gospels. While Mark and Matthew have two multiplications, Luke reports only one. In Luke's narrative, this miracle is sandwiched between two episodes: Herod's question, "Who is this about whom I hear such things?" (9:9), and Peter's confession, which answers Herod: "The Messiah of God!"(9:20). In the narrative structure of Luke's Gospel, the miracle prepares the reader to identify Jesus and his commitments from the perspective of the kingdom of God.

The feeding of the five thousand is part of Luke's food theme in his Gospel. One commentator has observed that in Luke's Gospel Jesus is often either going to a meal, at a meal, or coming from a meal.[1] Reference to food is found in each and every chapter of the Gospel. It appears in various forms in references to table fellowship, hospitality, the hungry in the Sermon on the Plain, fasting, messianic banquet, feeding the five thousand, imageries of harvest, good fruit and bad fruit, eating on Sabbath, eating with tax collectors, Jesus accused as a "glutton and drunkard," the "last" meal with his disciples before crucifixion, and the meal at Emmaus.

1. Robert J. Karris, *Luke: Artist and Theologian* (New York: Paulist Press, 1985), 47.

Pastoral Perspective

This passage opens with the disciples returning and "[telling] Jesus all they had done" (v. 10). They were newly back from casting out demons, curing diseases, and proclaiming the mission of God—the very mission of the Twelve that Jesus had sent them on that begins chapter 9. Up until this point in Luke's Gospel, the disciples have played only supporting roles. They had been doing ministry with Jesus in the previous chapter, but now they step out onto their own, actively participating in his ministry, becoming full partners. Can you imagine them returning filled with stories of what they saw and what they had done in his name yet without him? Like elders or deacons returning from their first communion with a homebound member, or a mission team just back from work in Mozambique, or small-group facilitators reporting on their kick-off meeting, the Twelve could not wait to share the hardships and headaches of the wondrous kingdom things they had seen and done.

How much they must have been looking forward to their retreat at Bethsaida. We learn from John's Gospel (1:44) that it was the hometown of Peter, Andrew, and Philip. There is nothing better than a retreat to a familiar place.

For years our staff has gone on retreat just before Thanksgiving, right before the Advent avalanche

Exegetical Perspective

The story of the feeding of the five thousand is the only miracle told in all four Gospels, a clear sign of its significance. To the physically hungry in need of daily bread, the feeding would be a tangible sign of the fullness of God's salvation. To those familiar with the Scriptures of Israel, the story stands in continuity with God's gracious provision for Israel in the wilderness and points forward to the messianic banquet when even death itself will be "swallowed up forever" (Isa. 25:6–8).

This passage is part of a larger unit (9:7–50) that serves as a narrative transition from Jesus' ministry in Galilee to the suffering and death that await him in Jerusalem. By omitting a significant amount of material from Mark's version (Mark 6:45–8:26), Luke's "orderly account" flows smoothly from Herod's question—"Who is this about whom I hear such things?" (9:9)—to a series of stories that provide an answer from three different perspectives.

Jesus has given his apostles "power and authority over all demons and to cure diseases" and "sent them out to proclaim the kingdom of God and to heal" (9:1–2); they now report back to Jesus, although Luke offers no details of their report. Instead, Jesus withdraws "privately" with the apostles to a place that only Luke identifies as Bethsaida, most likely on the northeastern shore of Lake Gennesaret, outside

Homiletical Perspective

This passage unfolds the miracle of the feeding of the five thousand as a lesson in practicing hospitality in the most challenging conditions and surprising contexts. This text is preceded by Jesus sending out the Twelve on a mission of healing and preaching the good news of the kingdom of God. Note how this initial ministry connects the work of healing to that of proclamation: to speak the gospel is to enact good news in the life of the poor, sick, neglected, and marginalized. The mission comes with instructions for the disciples to rely on the hospitality of strangers to provide for their needs. As the disciples return from their mission to debrief with Jesus, they find themselves surrounded by a crowd following Jesus.

At the center of this text, the disciples and the listeners face the classic question: Can we practice what we preach? Are we able to extend the hospitality that we have received and from which we have benefited, when we encounter strangers in other settings? The text carries with it a sense of irony that the disciples, who have just returned from depending on the hospitality of others, immediately want to send the crowd away in the face of an assumed scarcity of resources. Jesus refuses to acknowledge this response as a legitimate option: "You give them something to eat," he orders. The instructions prompt the disciples to inventory their available supplies. Here

Luke 9:10–17

Theological Perspective

The abundance of references in Luke's Gospel is more than an acknowledgment that food is a basic necessity of life. The food motif underscores an important *theological* perspective: Luke's commitment to justice for the poor, the hungry, and the marginalized. Food is a gift of God, a blessing that needs to be shared and not hoarded. For Luke, sharing food is unmistakably related to Eucharist, a public enactment of sharing practiced in the early church with profound implications for Jesus' commitment to God's justice in the world.

This feeding miracle is set in a lonely or "deserted place" where food is impossible to find. The story, perhaps, is an implicit answer to the question of Psalm 78:19–20: "Can God spread a table in the wilderness? . . . Can he also give bread, or provide meat for his people?" The psalm was itself a commentary on stories in Exodus 16 of God feeding the people of Israel. Luke's inclusion of this feeding miracle may be an indirect allusion to that prophetic tradition. The feeding miracle expresses God's fidelity to his hungry creation and the OT promise of a "banquet" (Isa. 25:6) being fulfilled *here and now*. It also fulfills the earlier promise announced in Jesus' sermon: "Blessed are you who are hungry now, for you will be filled. . . . Woe to you who are full now, for you will be hungry" (6:21, 25). In Jesus, God has truly fulfilled his promise of feeding God's creation.

While Jesus ultimately performs the miracle of feeding the crowd, one cannot miss noticing his prior command to his disciples, "You give them something to eat" (v. 13). Put differently, it is much more emphatic: "You *yourselves* give them something to eat." The text invites the reader to consider the social implications of this command. The disciples find five loaves and two fish among themselves, not from the crowd, and Jesus uses this food to perform the multiplication. Interestingly, Luke makes no reference to the compassion of Jesus found in Mark (6:34); rather, Jesus "welcomed" all those who came to him. The meager amount of food available among the disciples becomes the source for the satisfaction of all.

The social dimension of the miracle is reflective of the practice of distribution of the food to the needy in the early church, as indicated in Luke's narration of the Acts of the Apostles (Acts 6:1). The disciples are thus part of a continuing miracle; they are bearers of Jesus' mission of feeding the needy and hungry, called to extend the promise of God's justice for the hungry in the world. The leftover food in the baskets is an indication of the abundance of food in

Pastoral Perspective

hits, for a few days of contemplation, faith formation, and fellowship. The retreat center is on a mountainside with a beautiful western view down a valley filled with cattle fields and hiking trails. We would not leave that place for love or money! Yet our text insists that ministry is done in the midst of ongoing interruptions. Indeed, the church needs to be reminded, just as the disciples learned, that God often presents us with greater ministries cloaked in the garb of more pressing needs. Jesus steps away from the planned script of the retreat and allows the feeding of the multitudes to become a fuller expression of a shared ministry of preaching and healing.

A pastoral dimension worth noting from Luke's telling of the feeding of the multitudes is the way Jesus interacts with the disciples. Mark's Gospel gives us an unflattering portrait of the Twelve, who invariably are missing the point or messing up; in contrast, Luke takes pains to show them in a positive light. Even their voicing of concern for the crowd's welfare in the middle of the wilderness ("deserted place," v. 12) is a sign of compassion. After going on to voice their own legitimate concern about the logistics of feeding so many, they follow Jesus' instructions in organizing the crowd. What can the congregation learn from this text about working together on what seems to be an overwhelming task?

Our congregation learned a great deal about working together on a seemingly overwhelming task when major flooding hit our city. After the flood, someone asked whether we might become a host site for the denominational disaster-assistance work. What would that mean for our ministry? Youth and Sunday school space had to be converted to bunk rooms. Shower facilities had to be added. Administrative and support staff work had to be redistributed, and the budget was affected in ways we could not easily predict. Ongoing ministry to the homeless had to be strengthened and shifted to different parts of the building. Over the next eighteen months, we welcomed more than two thousand people in work teams who came to serve those in need in our city. It was a tremendous interruption to have "house guests" for that year and a half. However, it was also an amazing gift of God. What was clearly an "interruption of need" became an entry point for meaningful ministry and hospitality for many in our congregation.

Likewise, the text raises important questions for the congregation about God's ongoing concern for the poor and hungry. The setting of the scene in the wilderness draws our memory back to the feeding

the jurisdiction of Herod Antipas. Bethsaida would offer a familiar place of respite, if, as John says, it is the home of the fishermen-disciples Philip, Andrew, and Peter (John 1:44).

Luke, however, omits Mark's account of Jesus' desire to provide a retreat for the disciples and offers instead a more comprehensive understanding of Jesus' compassion on those who follow him into the deserted place by saying that Jesus "welcomed them and spoke to them of the kingdom of God, and healed those who needed to be cured" (9:11). In Luke–Acts those three actions will be at the heart of Jesus' ministry and at the core of the apostolic mission in his name (then and now): hospitality, proclamation of the reign of God, and healing.

Toward evening, the Twelve come to Jesus, urging him, "Send the crowd away." Theirs is not an expression of hostility or rejection of the crowd. More likely it is a reasonable, realistic expression of concern. The people need to find lodging (only in Luke) and food before nightfall, neither of which is available in a "deserted place." The phrase (*erēmō topō*) calls forth images of the Lord's feeding of Israel with manna on its desert journey to the promised land. Readers of Luke's Gospel would also remember that it was in the wilderness (*erēmō*) that Jesus was tempted to be merely a bread-Messiah (4:1).

The feeding of the five thousand sets Jesus within the prophetic tradition of Israel. Note the similarities to 2 Kings 4:42–43: "Elisha said, 'Give it to the people and let them eat.' But his servant said, 'How can I set this before a hundred people?' So he repeated, 'Give it to the people and let them eat, for thus says the LORD, 'They shall eat and have some left.'"

Echoing Elisha, Jesus tells his disciples, "*You* give them something to eat." Their response is understandable, although a bit ironic. The disciples clearly do not have the resources to meet the needs of such a large crowd, especially since earlier Jesus had commanded them to take "no staff, nor bag, nor bread, nor money" (9:3) on their missionary journey. Besides, how could they possibly "go and *buy* food for all these people," if they had obeyed Jesus' command to take no money?

Luke numbers the crowd at "about five thousand men." Like so much else in the passage, the number is symbolic. The New Testament scholar Sharon Ringe notes that the number five signifies completeness in Jewish literature and ten is a symbol of fullness, so, "Five thousand—five times ten, times ten, times ten—should not be understood as an actual estimate of the size of the crowd, but as a

the text invites all listeners to widen our horizons and enlarge our expectations. What do we have to offer the world around us? The preacher may want to encourage the congregation to take inventory of the gifts that we bring (and which we often take for granted).

The disciples' quick inventory of the situation yields few resources for them to draw on: five loaves and two fish. This text may offer a particularly striking word to mainline Protestant congregations who have grown weary of living in the shadows and memories of the good old days. The text gives the preacher the chance to subvert the dire expectations of those who define congregational health solely in terms of the size of the congregation. Rather than rely on statistical comparisons with the past, which often lead to a sense of despair, the text invites us to rely on the power of God to respond to the hunger of the throngs of people who live around us. Shrinking membership rolls, budget shortfalls, and declining endowments need not confine the possibility of ministry for the church in the twenty-first century. Instead, the gospel gives us lenses of hospitality that allow us to see and experience the world around us in new ways. Here hospitality is embodied, not simply in terms of welcoming people (as something that we in the church do for those outside the church), but more particularly in terms of accepting the gifts that others bring with them, even when they challenge and transform our assumptions and expectations.

It may be particularly helpful to note the disciples' reluctance to recognize the gift of people and resources that are available. Rather than expecting the crowd to look and act like themselves (as disciples and insiders), Luke interprets the crowd as a gift rather than a threat. It is the crowd that responds to Jesus' message and the crowd who will provide the initial resources that become the basis of Jesus' miracle. In an increasingly multicultural, global society, the text offers us a chance to see the crowd around us a source of blessing that will lead us to encounter the miracle of the gospel in new ways.

Lest we reduce this Gospel reading solely to a tale of community activism, Luke keeps the focus clearly on Jesus. It is Jesus who gives the orders, both to collect food and to seat this extended gathering. Then Jesus receives the offering that the disciples have collected. Luke describes Jesus' action in the classic fourfold eucharistic pattern that is used throughout the Gospel and Acts: Jesus takes, blesses, breaks, and gives the food to the disciples to share it with all in

Luke 9:10–17

Theological Perspective

the world—enough to satisfy all of God's creation, if only the disciples can practice sharing that abundance with others.

The eucharistic symbolism in the pericope is evident when Jesus takes the bread and fish, looks up to heaven, blesses, breaks, and gives them to the disciples to set them before the crowd. The blessing of the food before any meal is a normal practice in Jewish tradition. Nonetheless, the parallels between the narrative structures of the feeding miracle and the meeting of the risen Christ on the road to Emmaus make the liturgical and eucharistic symbolism unmistakable. The feeding miracle and the Eucharist are inextricably related. The feeding miracle, it appears, is a public enactment of the Eucharist practiced in church.

Luke, given his social commitments, portrays Eucharist as a profound symbol of the social commitment of the early church, rather than as a liturgical ritual enacted within the confines of the church. Eating and drinking the body and blood of Jesus Christ in the Eucharist is inseparable from sharing God's abundant blessings upon us, especially the gifts of food and water, with those who are needy and hungry. The miracle of the feeding of the five thousand is to be read not as a past event that Jesus did, but rather as a present expectation that followers of Christ are called to undertake in today's world.

Those of us living in affluent societies where food is so abundantly available may have some difficulty in appreciating the motif of food in Luke's Gospel. The food industry in consumer societies pushes for conspicuous consumption, especially of the fast-food and junk-food variety, and yet we have also become diet conscious and look for healthy and nutritional food. After all, food not only nourishes life, but also creates obesity. In affluent societies we hoard food and waste it, unmindful of the needy and hungry. Food is a perishable commodity, like manna in the wilderness. Millions of tons of food every day is wasted for lack of proper storage or discarded from our refrigerators. For those living in situations of famine and scarcity of food, Luke's food motif has a profound meaning. Luke's story of the feeding miracle challenges the contemporary disciples of Christ to extend that miracle in today's world!

J. PAUL RAJASHEKAR

Pastoral Perspective

of God's people as Moses led them out of Egypt. Just as God's miraculous provision of manna and quail provided sustenance to God's people, how might this new situation provide the setting for another mighty act of God? What if the prevailing needs of the poor and hungry in our communities and, indeed, around the world, challenged our congregations to search for opportunities to do more than we think we are capable of doing? Might we find ourselves in the place where God provides far more abundantly than we can imagine?

One interpretation of this passage popular among the miracle-averse is to explain the multiplication of the loaves and fish as an instance of people sharing the stashes of food that they had been hiding, but sharing only after being shamed into it. Although the abundance of food may in fact have come from that kind of sharing, this interpretation downplays and flattens out any sense of the miraculous. Instead of inviting the congregation to explore God's freedom to act in startling ways and expand human expectations, this interpretation focuses on the shaming aspects of the narrative and presumes that we can solve our own problems.

If the story is about the sin of hoarding resources, then the preacher is given permission to use shame as an acceptable motivational method for changing human behavior. However, that shifts the focus of the story away from God's act of grace, to behavior that emphasizes human self-sufficiency. God is pictured as some kind of therapist or coach trying to get the recalcitrant and greedy to do the right thing. Has our view of God become that small?

The connections of this text with the Eucharist are explicit in the use of the liturgical words "took," "blessed," "broke," and "gave." It is a reminder that our worship is inseparable from our service to Luke's "least of these." As Fred Craddock observes, "Apart from feeding the hungry, the Eucharist becomes a ritual detached from life, just as feeding the hungry, apart from the Eucharist, is not fully satisfying."[1] A pastoral perspective will help our congregation integrate such a vision.

GUY D. GRIFFITH

---

1. Fred Craddock, *Luke*, Interpretation series (Louisville, KY: John Knox Press, 1990), 126.

Exegetical Perspective

number signifying that 'everyone' was present." For Luke, this would suggest that here, symbolically, "the whole church is present, prepared to receive the holy supper."[1]

The feeding of the five thousand also points forward to the messianic banquet in the kingdom of God and to its foretaste in the Christian Eucharist. All the Gospel writers in their accounts of the feeding emphasize the same liturgical actions by Jesus, as he takes the loaves and fish, looks up to heaven (the posture of prayer), blesses, breaks, and gives them to the disciples. Luke will use the same verbs at Jesus' last meal with his disciples before his death (22:19) and at the first meal of the risen Christ at Emmaus (24:30). Well before the composition of Luke's Gospel, the words had provided the basic rubrics of the Eucharist (1 Cor. 11:23–24).

As Jesus gives the broken bread and fish to the disciples to give to the people, Luke says that "all ate and were filled." There is less emphasis in the text on a miraculous multiplication of the loaves and fish and more on there being enough for all. *All* who hunger are filled, as the beatitude of Jesus had promised (6:21a).

Not only is the crowd "filled"; there are twelve baskets of "broken pieces" left over. The rich symbolism continues. If the "broken pieces" (*klasmata*) are understood symbolically in reference to the bread of the Eucharist, the "twelve baskets" can symbolize the sufficiency of the communal meal, not only for the twelve disciples (i.e., the church), but for the twelve tribes of Israel as well. Here Luke symbolically affirms that, in the ministry of Jesus, God provides fully for the needs of Jews and Gentiles alike.

Herod asks, "Who is this?" Luke replies, in effect, that this is he who provides abundantly for all God's people, until all are fed in body and soul in the reign of God.

ALLEN C. MCSWEEN JR.

Homiletical Perspective

the crowd. There is not only enough for everyone to eat; there are twelve baskets left over. With this detail, Luke reinforces his claim that the gospel is a bountiful resource that confounds our skepticism and far exceeds our minimal expectations.

In addition, the text challenges the careful, and sometimes antiseptic, way that we practice Communion in our congregations. How frequently do our congregational and/or denominational rules place barriers to the radical hospitality of the gospel where all are fed? Does the minimalism of current eucharistic practice (often limited to a crouton of bread and a sip of juice/wine) reinforce a theology of scarcity? On this point, the diverse communion practices of the early church may prompt us to reevaluate our current patterns. The ancient eucharistic use of bread, wine, water, oil, vegetables, salt, milk, honey, cheese, olives, fish, and full meals[1] may provide important models for ways in which current eucharistic practice can begin to embody a theology of plentitude and live up to the claim that this is the joyful feast of the people of God. Preaching on texts of abundance provides an opportunity to broaden our experiences of Communion by describing and reclaiming the meal practices of the early church.

Finally, ministers who rely on the hospitality of congregations and communities for their livelihood also face a classic conundrum when reading this text: Can we preach what we practice? Will we hear and unfold this text in a way that challenges the listeners (especially ourselves) to recognize the resources that we often overlook? Could this be an opportunity when those outside the inner circle will provide the means by which God will feed us and teach us new ways of faithful discipleship? Once again, the text invites all who gather to turn our gaze upon the risen Christ who gathers among us in order that we may learn to rely on God's presence in the gift of the Spirit, who leads us into a future far more abundant than we can imagine.

PAUL GALBREATH

---

1. Sharon H. Ringe, *Luke*, Westminster Bible Companion (Louisville, KY: Westminster John Knox Press, 1995), 133.

1. Paul Bradshaw, *Eucharistic Origins* (Oxford: Oxford University Press, 2004), 59.

¹⁸Once when Jesus was praying alone, with only the disciples near him, he asked them, "Who do the crowds say that I am?" ¹⁹They answered, "John the Baptist; but others, Elijah; and still others, that one of the ancient prophets has arisen." ²⁰He said to them, "But who do you say that I am?" Peter answered, "The Messiah of God."

²¹He sternly ordered and commanded them not to tell anyone, ²²saying, "The Son of Man must undergo great suffering, and be rejected by the elders, chief priests, and scribes, and be killed, and on the third day be raised."

²³Then he said to them all, "If any want to become my followers, let them deny themselves and take up their cross daily and follow me. ²⁴For those who want to save their life will lose it, and those who lose their life for my sake will save it. ²⁵What does it profit them if they gain the whole world, but lose or forfeit themselves? ²⁶Those who are ashamed of me and of my words, of them the Son of Man will be ashamed when he comes in his glory and the glory of the Father and of the holy angels. ²⁷But truly I tell you, there are some standing here who will not taste death before they see the kingdom of God."

Theological Perspective

Luke records no reaction from the crowd that participated in the miracle of the feeding of the five thousand in the preceding pericope (9:10–17). This may be intentional, setting the stage for Jesus' question, "Who do the people say that I am?" and Peter's confession. Peter's response is actually a response to the question posed earlier by Herod, "Who is this?" (9:9). Jesus, it appears, is unimpressed with the popular responses of the crowd, and hence the question is now specifically directed to the disciples: "Who do *you* say that I am?"

That question has founded christological discourses throughout history. Every generation of disciples has sought to respond to the question in its own context and culture. Yet Peter's impulsive response remains a classic statement of the identity and ministry of Jesus: "The Christ of God." All Peter knew was that Jesus seemed more wonderful than any of the other comparisons would suggest. Note that Luke omits additional materials and excludes any praise or rebuke of Peter (contra Mark 8:27–32 and Matt. 16:6b–19). In Luke, the "identity question" elicits three different responses: the crowd's, then Peter's, and then Jesus' own. It is followed by the first formal prediction of Jesus' passion.

Theological reflections on this pericope may take many directions. Whether the episode is a product

Pastoral Perspective

The question of Jesus' identity is central in Luke's Gospel and in the life of the church. Twice before (8:25; 9:9) Luke has posed the question "Who is Jesus?" Neither time was an answer given. Now, after the Twelve have returned from their mission and participated in the feeding of the multitude, Jesus asks them the question. He first wants to know what the crowds are saying: What is the word on the street? It is a nonthreatening inquiry that all the disciples could easily answer. Then he asks the existential question: "Who do you say that I am?" (v. 20a).

It must have become quiet in a hurry. James and John probably looked down at their sandals and kicked pebbles; maybe Judas coughed uncomfortably; Matthew began balancing the checkbook. Perhaps the rest looked to Peter, their leader, to answer for them. He did, saying, "[You are] the Messiah of God" (v. 20b). In other words, the disciples responded as many in our churches would today, standing by silently, waiting for the leader to answer the question.

In Georgia there is a Presbyterian new church development beginning its worship life in a Seventh-day Adventist church. This unusual arrangement has given rise to a joke among Presbyterians: "What do you get when you cross a Seventh-day Adventist with a Presbyterian?" The answer: "You get someone

Exegetical Perspective

Luke 9:7–50 serves as a transition from Jesus' ministry in Galilee to the suffering and death that await him in Jerusalem. In this difficult and theologically loaded passage, we come to the heart of that transition and the confessional center of the Gospel.

Luke signals the importance of the scene by replacing Mark and Matthew's emphasis on the event's geographic and political location in the region of Caesarea Philippi with an emphasis on the event's temporal and spiritual significance: it occurs at a time "when Jesus was praying" (v. 18). Throughout the Gospel of Luke, the decisive events in the life of Jesus are set in the context of prayer: at his baptism (3:21), in choosing the Twelve (6:12), at his "transfiguration" (9:28), and in the garden of Gethsemane (22:41).

Earlier in Luke (9:9) Herod had asked of Jesus, "Who is this about whom I hear such things?" Now Jesus asks the same question of his disciples: What is the word on the street about who I am? Their answer is almost identical to what had been reported to Herod (9:7–8). In popular speculation, Jesus is viewed in prophetic categories, as perhaps John the Baptist or Elijah or one of the prophets raised to life again. Note that the resurrection of one of the "ancient prophets" of Israel is not considered odd or impossible but popularly expected!

Homiletical Perspective

When Jesus shows up, it is rarely in the way we expect him to look. This text underscores this observation by taking note of the confusing expectations among those following Jesus. Luke follows the story of the miraculous feeding of the five thousand with this account of Jesus' questioning the disciples about people's perceptions of his identity. At stake in this text is the ongoing question of how we picture Jesus and understand his identity. It is an important question for the preacher to hold up before the congregation. For example, when I was growing up in small, white congregations, it never even occurred to me that Jesus was a person of color. This dark-skinned Jesus challenged my prejudices and carefully constructed social world. Jesus was much more likely to hang out on the other side of town than to want to eat in polite society at our table. How we picture Jesus has significant implications for our theology.

The text interprets the question of identity in terms of the interplay between the disciples' recognition of Jesus and their own sense of self. The call to follow Jesus as one sent by God provides a new understanding of self. The text unfolds in terms of our response to Jesus' ministry of teaching, healing, and feeding. The recognition of God's presence among us leads to the possibility of seeing ourselves in a different light. Rather than placing ourselves and

Luke 9:18–27

Theological Perspective

of the early church's creedal reflection on Jesus, Jesus' own attempt to verify how he was perceived in response to the deeds he was performing, or Jesus seeking a communal affirmation of his ministry and vocation, all are worthy of theological explanation. In Luke's narration, the "identity question" is not about a correct response so much as an attempt to explicate that identity and what it means. Peter's profound answer, "The Christ [or Messiah] of God" required a definitive interpretation in order to avoid possible misunderstandings of that title. Jesus may be the Messiah, but he is also a suffering Son of Man; he will be recognized as Messiah insofar as he is seen as the one destined for suffering and death. Identity leads to destiny.

Luke then subtly shifts the question of Jesus' identity into the question of the identity and calling of the disciples. The identity and vocation of Jesus' followers is invariably bound up with Jesus' own identity and vocation. Jesus' fate will also become the fate of his disciples. The disciples are warned that discipleship is costly and might include suffering and death, as well as the triumph of the resurrection. Taking up the cross is a metaphor that reminds believers of the price of discipleship. Luke, by adding the word "daily," wants to emphasize that the demands of discipleship are a lifelong struggle and commitment more than a specific act of public witness.

Put differently, taking up the cross and following Jesus mean adopting a self-expending posture that seeks to affirm life in all its fullness. It involves a readiness to renounce one's own life. This is not a glorification of suffering for its own sake or self-mortification, nor does it imply that suffering has a redemptive significance in itself. The suffering that disciples endure is a reflection of the suffering of the Messiah. The cross, in a true sense, is a life-giving event rather than a life-denying act. It is ultimately an act of love for the sake of the people of the world, not an act of self-martyrdom.

Thus reference to "denying" one's self does not mean giving up pleasures and comforts but, rather, putting on a "crucified mind" that seeks to uphold and affirm the values of God's kingdom. This is the challenge of Christian discipleship today. Confessing Christ amid trials and tribulations, persecutions and opposition to the Christian faith (as Christians have experienced from time to time in different periods of the church's history and still continue to experience in many parts of the world) demands not a "crusading mind" but rather a "crucified mind."

Pastoral Perspective

who shows up on your doorstep, but does not know what to say." Many in the church have difficulty knowing what to say about Jesus.

In an age of increasing religious pluralism, the singularity of Peter's confession leaves many in our congregations stammering. Sit in adult Bible studies, and you encounter confusion over Christology. Some are reacting to the overstretching triumphalism from the religious right that presents Jesus as a first-century Superman. Others find the miracles too otherworldly and, like Thomas Jefferson, take a razor to the offending texts, making Jesus into a rabbi to be followed for his remarkable ethical teaching. Luke's account of Peter's confession provides the pastor with a platform for substantive teaching that may begin to help the persons in the congregation learn how to "name the name" and what to say when they do.

Part of that teaching will focus on helping the congregation understand what kind of Messiah Jesus will be. Jesus' prediction of the passion, the way of suffering that leads to the cross (v. 22), presents teachers with the opportunity to help congregations see the radical reinterpretation of the Messiah: not as a conquering warrior but as a Suffering Servant. Of course, most of those in our congregations, so saturated with the culture's obsession with success, would prefer to hear about Jesus' victory over sin and death than confront his suffering on the cross. How many who sit in our pews move directly from the cries of "Hosanna" on Palm Sunday to "Alleluia" on Easter, without ever encountering Good Friday's cry of dereliction? Yet it is precisely the *via crucis,* the way of the cross, that Jesus invites his followers to travel.

Indeed, Jesus calls those who want to be his followers to "take up their cross daily" (v. 23). Among the Synoptic Gospels, Luke is the only one that includes the word "daily." It is a reminder that following the Lord is not just an emotional assent made by a campfire at a long-ago youth group retreat. Rather, discipleship is a long slog over a lifetime. In the words of the Presbyterian Confession of 1967, it is about "bearing witness on good days and evil days."[1] Self-denial and cross bearing are out of fashion in a therapeutic culture supported by a service economy. Yet this type of sacrifice is at the heart of the church's witness to the One who carried the cross.

As examples of those who have lived cruciform lives, often we use people such as Dorothy Day and her ministry among the poor, or Mother Teresa and

1. *The Constitution of the Presbyterian Church (U.S.A.),* Part I, Study Edition, Confession of 1967, 9.23 (Louisville, KY: Licensed to Geneva Press by the Office of the General Assembly of the Presbyterian Church (U.S.A.), 1999), 324.

Exegetical Perspective

Immediately, Jesus pushes the question beyond gossip and speculation to a deeply personal, confessional level: "But who do *you* say that I am?" The "you" is emphatic! Peter answers directly, perhaps for the others as well as himself: "The Messiah [*Christos*] of God" (v. 20). In Mark, Peter says simply, "You are the Messiah." Matthew adds the theological confession, "the Son of the living God." Luke omits Matthew's positive affirmative of Peter as "the rock" on which the church would be built (Matt. 16:18), as well as the rebuke of Peter in both Matthew and Mark, and keeps his focus on the meaning of the confession for the life of discipleship.

Yet first Jesus emphatically commands them "not to tell anyone" (v. 21). Why are they not (or not yet) to confess him publicly as Messiah? Is it because of the political, triumphalist baggage the title Messiah inevitably carried? Even more, is it because Jesus cannot rightly be understood as Messiah apart from the suffering, rejection, death, and resurrection that in the purposes of God he must undergo (v. 22)? The word translated as "must" (*dei*, v. 22) carries the connotation not of fate or victimization but of that which is in accord with the ultimate will of God. Luke uses the term *dei* frequently, especially as Jesus tells of the suffering and execution that await him. Luke insists that Jesus cannot properly be confessed as the "Christ of God" apart from the whole of his birth, life, death, resurrection, and ascension, all rooted in the saving purposes of God.

Following Mark, Luke says that the one who "must suffer many things" is the "Son of Man." In the Synoptic Gospels, "Son of Man" is the phrase used most frequently by Jesus in referring to himself. The meaning of the phrase, however, is unclear. It is often used to refer to humanity in general or as an indirect way of saying "I." Other times it is used by Jesus to refer to the apocalyptic figure who comes with power and glory to usher in the kingdom of God (v. 26). For our purposes, two things stand out. (1) The title "Son of Man" was more ambiguous and carried less political baggage than "Messiah," thus leaving greater room for Jesus' own definition of the term. (2) Jesus most often used the title "Son of Man" in reference to himself when speaking of his impending suffering and death. Luke insists that Jesus' way of being "the Messiah of God" links by divine necessity his passion and resurrection, his suffering and glory.

The same is true for all who would follow him. With three imperatives, Jesus insists that all who would be his disciples must "deny themselves and take up their cross daily, and follow [present tense:

Homiletical Perspective

our needs at the center of the universe, the gospel invites us to reorientation. This shift in perspective is pictured as a gradual awakening on our journey of discipleship.

In his recent commentary on Luke, John Carroll notes the distinctive link throughout the Gospel between prayer and identity. Luke alone inserts prayer into the narrative of Jesus' baptism (3:21) as a way of connecting the act of praying with the revelation and disclosure of Jesus as God's beloved Son. Similarly, only Luke places the story of the calling of the disciples as an outgrowth of Jesus' night of prayer on the mountain (6:12).[1] Thus it is no coincidence for Luke that the conversation between Jesus and the disciples about his identity occurs in the context of prayer as they listen in on his prayer.[2] The act of prayer is connected with Jesus' own understanding of his identity and ministry.

The disciples respond to Jesus' inquiry about his identity by repeating the rumors circulating among the crowd. Some see Jesus as Elijah or another of the great prophetic figures from the distant past. Here Luke underscores the ongoing importance of the prophetic tradition lying at the heart of Jesus' ministry. Others in the crowds identify Jesus with John the Baptist, a reformer who challenged the status quo approach of the Jewish leaders in Jesus' era. Jesus' inquiry, though, is more than a survey of the rumor mill. Jesus presses the disciples further. While others connect Jesus with prophetic figures from the distant past or reformers of the recent past, Jesus asks the disciples for their own observations about his identity. Here, in the middle of Luke's Gospel, after witnessing Jesus' healing and teaching ministry, Peter responds, "You are the Christ, the Messiah" (v. 20). This textual turn models the existential move that the gospel always places on its listeners. The gospel is not simply about the report and speculation of other people; it is ultimately about our own response to Christ's claim on our lives.

It is not only contemporary hearers of this text who take offense at Jesus' message of taking up the cross and losing one's life. The earliest hearers of this message would have also taken exception to Jesus' teaching. The command to take up the cross, the Roman Empire's instrument of death, carries with it images of humiliation and shame. In the context of an ancient society rooted in honor and shame, the

---

1. John Carroll, *Luke: A Commentary* (Louisville, KY: Westminster John Knox Press, 2012), 210.
2. Note that "catechumenate" (the practice of making disciples) means to overhear.

Luke 9:18–27

Theological Perspective

Christian discipleship is not a call for voluntary self-abnegation in defense of the Christian faith. Living as we do in a religiously pluralistic world, the crusading mentality that Christians have displayed in the past may today appear less compelling.

This pronounced religious pluralism in our midst has often exacerbated profound tensions and inter-religious conflicts. Pluralism, paradoxically, often provokes religious exclusivism and the hardening of commitments. Yet today we are also far more sensitive to the religious claims of others than in the past and careful not willfully to offend others, even when we differ from or disagree with them. Christian identity and discipleship in this new context call for a renewed understanding of what it means to profess Christ today.

Jesus' call to "deny oneself and take up the cross" today involves practicing a "theology of the cross," as Martin Luther suggested. It means to take on a posture of humility and vulnerability rather than a crusading attitude in relating with others. Christian discipleship is, after all, a *positive* witness to Christ and what Christ has meant for the well-being of humanity in relation to God's kingdom, not a *negative* witness against others. We do not need to deny others or their religious claims and convictions in order to uphold our exclusive commitment to Christ.

We need not always define our Christian identity over against others but, rather, seek to confess our faith in relation to them. This by no means implies that Christ's disciples are to be ashamed of the exclusive claims of our faith. Nor is this cause for a false pretense of humility in relating with others. It does, however, imply recognizing that the redemptive suffering of Christ does not exclude anyone, for it embraces all, whether they confess the name of Christ or not! Christian discipleship is a privilege, not a claim to Christian superiority.

Discipleship, then, is about losing oneself and taking the risk of vulnerability for the sake of Christ! The posture of a "theology of the cross" in dialogue with others is the most appropriate way of confessing and following Christ today. Our identity must indeed bear the marks of Jesus' identity in our witness and human relations.

J. PAUL RAJASHEKAR

Pastoral Perspective

her care for those in India's slums, or Dietrich Bonhoeffer and his leadership of the Confessing Church, or Martin Luther King Jr. and his witness throughout the civil rights struggle. Yet it is not only the extraordinary who are called to bear the cross, but all of us. In spite of the culture, congregations yearn to hear of those who have borne the cross and are unashamed of Christ, of witnesses who sat where they now sit in a sanctuary and who broke bread as they now break bread at Christ's Table. Surrounded in this way by a cloud of witnesses, the text becomes a clarion call to each individual and to the gathered community of faith: "those who want to save their life will lose it, and those who lose their life for [Jesus'] sake will save it" (v. 24).

One other dimension worth noting is Luke's setting of the pericope. Matthew and Mark set Peter's confession in the region of Caesarea Philippi, the political and religious center north of Galilee. This setting draws our attention to the conflict Jesus' followers will have when they confess him as Lord, over and against the political and religious leaders who do not. Luke, however, is silent about the setting, instead emphasizing that the encounter comes in the context of Jesus' prayer life: "Once when Jesus was praying alone, with only the disciples near him, he asked them . . ." (v. 18). What does Luke's context imply about the dynamic role of prayer in Jesus' life and ministry, and how does that pattern inform and instruct his followers?

An exploration of the ways in which intentional prayer informs and strengthens our ministry, enlarges our capacity for compassion, and allows us to hear and respond to the cries of those in need may be a helpful corrective to the popular understanding of prayer as only personal. At every turn the church must reject the "subjective captivity of the Gospel."[2] Confessing with Peter that Jesus is "the Messiah of God" means he is Lord of all.

GUY D. GRIFFITH

---

2. Fred B. Craddock, *Luke* (Louisville, KY: John Knox Press, 1990), 247.

Exegetical Perspective

keep on following] me" (v. 23). The confession of Jesus as Messiah is empty apart from following personally his cruciform way of being Messiah. Discipleship is not a matter of saying the right words, nor is it a singular act of heroic commitment. For Luke, discipleship is an ongoing way of life ("daily"), and the self-denial of discipleship is not a matter of denying the self various things, but of putting the cause of Christ ahead of all the desires of the self.

Furthermore, the "cross" that is to be borne is more than a hardship that must be endured, like a chronic illness. It is the result of the decision to "take up . . . daily" the life of self-giving love, even at the cost of one's life.

In all the Synoptic Gospels, Jesus insists paradoxically that the desire to save one's life will result in losing it, and the losing of one's life for his sake will lead to its being saved. The verbs "will lose" and "will save" in the future tense indicate that the life of costly discipleship will find its ultimate vindication only when the Son of Man "comes in his glory" (v. 26b).

In Luke, Jesus concludes by saying, "there are some standing here who will not taste death before they see the kingdom of God" (v. 27). Here we come to the final exegetical challenge in this difficult passage. Mark says they will "see that the kingdom of God has come with power" (Mark 9:1). Matthew says they will "see the Son of Man coming in his kingdom" (Matt. 16:28). Luke's abbreviated saying appears to place more emphasis on a present foretaste of the kingdom in anticipation of its final coming. For Luke the reign of God is present in the ministry of Jesus, glimpsed in his transfiguration, experienced in his resurrection, yet still awaited in its eschatological fullness.

Herod asks, "Who is this?" Luke replies, this is the Christ of God, the suffering Son of Man, who calls his followers daily to a life modeled after his own cruciform love, until he comes in glory.

ALLEN C. MCSWEEN JR.

Homiletical Perspective

message of the cross is profoundly countercultural and contrasts with the hope, values, and expectations of the listeners. Jesus counters this expectation by noting that ultimately true honor comes not from family/clan acceptance but from God's welcome and embrace.

This hard saying of Jesus carries within it the preacher's challenge to remain faithful to the portrait of Jesus presented in the Gospel. Even though the text includes a reference to resurrection, Jesus does not associate the images of success with either his own ministry or those of his followers. Instead, Jesus closely links the life of discipleship with suffering. To be a follower of Jesus is to place oneself alongside those who suffer. In the midst of suffering is the possibility to encounter the presence of God. Vulnerability prompts us to rely on God rather than our own resources.

One interesting note is that Jesus puts the discussion of the cost of discipleship in terms of loss and gain. Preachers may find this language, which so parallels the vocabulary of today's market economy, is helpful in unfolding the claims of this text, since it invites the listener to a closer examination of the commitments made by the market economy. Does purchasing a fancy new sports car actually deliver on the implied promise of youth and virility? Does a new wardrobe every year satisfy the heart's longing or provide a sense of meaning in life? Jesus invites us to take careful inventory of our lives in order to determine if the chimerical images and phony promises of the advertising world lead to a life of wholeness.

In contrast, faithful discipleship is about learning to lose one's life, beginning in the waters of baptism, where we die to the self and are raised to walk in newness of life. This alternative perspective recognizes that our sole hope is not in terms of gaining the world and losing ourselves in the process, but in learning to rely on God to provide us with new life. Once again, Jesus appears as the one who overturns the table of expectations, in order to point us to the true source of life.

PAUL GALBREATH

Luke 9:28–43a

²⁸Now about eight days after these sayings Jesus took with him Peter and John and James, and went up on the mountain to pray. ²⁹And while he was praying, the appearance of his face changed, and his clothes became dazzling white. ³⁰Suddenly they saw two men, Moses and Elijah, talking to him. ³¹They appeared in glory and were speaking of his departure, which he was about to accomplish at Jerusalem. ³²Now Peter and his companions were weighed down with sleep; but since they had stayed awake, they saw his glory and the two men who stood with him. ³³Just as they were leaving him, Peter said to Jesus, "Master, it is good for us to be here; let us make three dwellings, one for you, one for Moses, and one for Elijah"—not knowing what he said. ³⁴While he was saying this, a cloud came and overshadowed them; and they were terrified as they entered the cloud. ³⁵Then from the cloud came a voice that said, "This is my Son, my Chosen; listen to him!" ³⁶When the voice had spoken, Jesus was

Theological Perspective

Luke's unfolding narrative of Jesus' identity finds its climax in the transfiguration story. Earlier in the chapter, Herod had raised the question "Who is this?" (9:9), and following the miracle of the feeding, Jesus himself had raised the question about his identity (9:18, 20). Peter's inspired response (9:20) is now complemented by the testimony of the voice of God: "This is my Son, my Chosen; listen to him!" (9:35).

Scholars have debated whether the transfiguration episode is a postresurrection appearance projected back into an earlier phase of Jesus' ministry. Such an interpretation is implausible. The temporary nature of the change in Jesus' appearance, the location, and the conversation with Moses and Elijah suggest that it anticipates those postresurrection stories. The closest parallel to this story is Jesus' baptism, which also features a heavenly voice announcing Jesus' identity: "You are my Son, the Beloved; with you I am well pleased" (3:21–22). The difference between the baptismal revelation and the transfiguration is that the former is addressed *to* Jesus and the latter is a testimony *about* Jesus directed to the disciples. The intense private experience of baptism finds a public affirmation in the transfiguration narrative. The transfiguration story thus represents a decisive validation of the identity and vocation of Jesus, confirming Peter's impromptu declaration of Jesus'

Pastoral Perspective

Throughout Scripture God's self-disclosure happens on mountains. God gave the sacred name and commandments to Moses on Mt. Sinai (Exod. 3:1ff.; 20:1ff.) and spoke to Elijah on Mt. Horeb (1 Kgs. 19:11–18), and Jesus revealed the most complete teaching about the kingdom in the Sermon on the Mount (Matt. 5–7). Here, on another mountain, Peter, James, and John receive confirmation of Jesus' identity and are given guidance in their formation as disciples before they are sent out to bear witness to the gospel. In this pivotal passage in the Gospel, Jesus' focus turns toward the waiting confrontation in Jerusalem that will lead to the cross. The passage is also pivotal in the sense that it draws the church's attention to the areas of identity, mission, and formation.

The transfiguration grounds Jesus' identity firmly in continuity with faithful Israel. Moses the lawgiver and Elijah the preeminent prophet symbolize for Luke that Jesus the Messiah—who would suffer, be crucified, and rise on the third day—is the one to whom both the law and the prophets point. Only Luke, among the Gospel writers, allows us to overhear the conversation in which they "appeared in glory and were speaking of his departure" (v. 31). This departure is literally Jesus' "exodus" (Greek *exodos*), that is, his journey to the cross that would lead

found alone. And they kept silent and in those days told no one any of the things they had seen.

³⁷On the next day, when they had come down from the mountain, a great crowd met him. ³⁸Just then a man from the crowd shouted, "Teacher, I beg you to look at my son; he is my only child. ³⁹Suddenly a spirit seizes him, and all at once he shrieks. It convulses him until he foams at the mouth; it mauls him and will scarcely leave him. ⁴⁰I begged your disciples to cast it out, but they could not." ⁴¹Jesus answered, "You faithless and perverse generation, how much longer must I be with you and bear with you? Bring your son here." ⁴²While he was coming, the demon dashed him to the ground in convulsions. But Jesus rebuked the unclean spirit, healed the boy, and gave him back to his father. ⁴³And all were astounded at the greatness of God.

Exegetical Perspective

At the turning point of his Gospel, as Jesus sets "his face to go to Jerusalem" (9:51), Luke addresses the question of the identity of Jesus from a variety of perspectives. Herod has asked, "Who is this?" (9:9). Jesus has asked his disciples, "Who do you say that I am?" (9:20). Now God provides the definitive answer: "This is my Son, my Chosen; listen to him!" (9:35).

The story of the transfiguration of Jesus follows the announcement of his passion, his call to the daily discipleship of self-denial and cross bearing, and his promise that "some standing here . . . will not taste death before they see the kingdom of God" (9:27). Now Peter, John, and James are given a fleeting glimpse of the glory to come, which leaves them speechless.

Mark and Matthew set the story six days after the previous episode, but Luke sets it "about eight days after these sayings" (v. 28). That could simply be a way of saying "about a week later." It could also be a foreshadowing of the resurrection on the eighth day (the first day of the New Creation) as well as an allusion to the feast of Tabernacles (Lev. 23:33–43), with its solemn assembly on the eighth day. The meaning of the time reference is unclear. What is clear is that the whole narrative is shaped by and permeated with images from the Old Testament (e.g., mountain, cloud, altered appearance). By means of these images

Homiletical Perspective

Consider the dualistic categories that we often use to describe aspects of Christian faith: spirituality versus social action; retreat versus engagement; pietistic devotion versus real-life ministry. This extended version of the transfiguration allows no such separation to take place. While sometimes we read the transfiguration story as an exercise in religious escape, Luke carefully holds together this mountaintop experience with the challenges of daily service and ministry. Gaining a stronger sense of Christian identity and vocation is bound together with the struggle for peace and justice in the world around us.

The narrative begins with Jesus taking Peter, James, and John up the mountain to pray. Preachers will need to wrestle with the question of biblical (il)literacy among members and visitors in their congregation, as lying beneath this Gospel text are important touchstones from Hebrew Scripture. The mountain offers a geographical reference to significant episodes in the lives of Moses and Elijah, who are pictured in prayer alongside Jesus and the disciples. Moses ascended the mountain to intercede with YHWH and to establish a covenant between God and Israel culminating in the gift of the Ten Commandments (see Exod. 34, which includes a description of Moses' shining face as a sign of his communion with God). At the end of his life, Moses

Luke 9:28–43a

Theological Perspective

messiahship (9:20). The fact that it is witnessed by the inner circle—Peter, John and James—accompanied by an explicit heavenly admonition, "Listen to him," indicates that the intent of the narrative is to convince the disciples to pledge sole allegiance to Jesus.

The transfiguration story appears as a moment of reassurance to the disciples, who are anxious about their future. After hearing predictions about how Jesus will be rejected by the authorities and put to death, the disciples experience a sense of gloom and doom, distraught over their chosen vocation. Perhaps they grapple with the awfulness of what is revealed to them. When Jesus takes three of his closest disciples up the mountain to pray, it may be a clue or an ominous sign of an impending disaster. When they see him pray, they can sense that Jesus too must be grappling with the reality of a terrible destiny ahead of him.

Perhaps Peter's newfound awareness of Jesus as the "Christ of God" has no depth, and the meaning of his confession has not really sunk into his own mind. It is one thing to confess Jesus as the Christ, but this Christ is so different from Peter's instinctive expectation that it is hard for him to realize the truth. The parallel account in Mark records Peter's shock and vehement protest (Mark 8:32) indicating his inability to comprehend that the one anointed by God must suffer, experience death, and be raised again to be the Savior.

The spiritual experience at the mountain must bring a sense of relief. The sense of gloom and doom suddenly vanishes; instead, the disciples see a radiant Jesus, his glory showing through. They are dumbstruck to see Moses, through whom came the law of God, and Elijah, one of the greatest prophets of the OT, in conversation with Jesus. Both Moses and Elijah were prophets who suffered rejection and persecution, yet each was vindicated by God. Their presence confirms the prediction of Jesus' own suffering and death, but also assures his future vindication. Moses and Elijah are the right persons for the conversation with Jesus about his departure to Jerusalem, for they, themselves, were rejected prophets and figures of suffering. Now here they are on the mountain bearing witness to Jesus as the one who fulfills and surpasses their roles.

For the three disciples, it is undoubtedly an overwhelming experience. They have a glimpse into the greatness and glory of Jesus—not the glory of greatness as the world counts greatness, but the glory of one who is ready to take upon himself the

Pastoral Perspective

to the deliverance of God's people, every bit as much as Moses' bringing the children of Israel out of Egyptian bondage did.

However, key to Jesus' identity is not that he is simply another in the line of Jewish prophets or a deliverer like Moses. Rather, the text claims that he is the fulfillment of all that was hoped for and promised by the Scriptures. That claim is echoed in the words at the beginning of the book of Hebrews: "Long ago God spoke to our ancestors in many and various ways by the prophets, but in these last days [God] has spoken to us by a Son" (Heb. 1:1–2).

Likewise, the theophany, God's voice from heaven affirming, "This is my Son, my Chosen; listen to him!" (v. 35), echoes the experience of Jesus' baptism (3:21–22). For Luke, both the baptism and transfiguration establish Jesus' identity and call the disciples— the church—to ground their life, their work, and their witness in him. Just as the voice from the cloud commands the disciples to listen to Jesus, so this passage invites the pastor and congregation to explore who they say he is in light of this claim, a confession that is the foundation of the congregation's identity.

Many in our congregations hear this text and want to talk about their own "mountaintop experiences." Some will tell of spiritual "thin places," where they have experienced closeness to the divine presence. Others, following Peter's impulse to "make three dwellings" (v. 33), will want to stay in that place of spiritual intimacy and awe. Congregations can also have mountaintop experiences together in worship. The great feast days of Christmas Eve, Easter, and Pentecost are often moving and memorable. The worship committee has stretched the budget and brought in a brass quartet, a string ensemble, a paid soloist, and the congregation leaves worship all smiles, humming the last hymn. Then the week after Christmas or "low Sunday" after Easter finds the congregation back at it. Given that we live most of the year in "ordinary time," can this text help us understand the rhythm of the liturgical calendar, reminding the congregation of its call to faithfulness, not only on the mountain of festival days but also in the valley of ordinary time?

The story of the transfiguration does not stay on top of the mountain. Rather, Jesus and the disciples come down from its lofty heights, only to be confronted by a man whose son needs healing. The work of redemption must continue. A pastoral word worth sharing with the congregation is the observation that after every spiritual high point, there is the hard reality of challenging ministry. The disciples and Jesus

Exegetical Perspective

Luke highlights the continuity of God's redemptive work in Israel, which finds its fulfillment in the death and resurrection of "the Messiah of God" (9:20).

Of particular importance for Luke is the detail that Jesus has gone up "the mountain" to *pray* and has taken with him Peter, John, and James. Mountains in Scripture are often places of divine encounter and revelation, and throughout the Gospel of Luke prayer marks the decisive moments in the ministry of Jesus. Immediately, the reader senses that a crucial, revelatory event is about to occur.

Mark and Matthew say that Jesus was "transfigured [*metemorphōthē*, Matt. 17:2; Mark 9:2] before them." Luke omits the term and keeps his focus on the change in Jesus' face and the "dazzling white" of his clothes, echoing the theophany of God to Moses on the mountain, after which "the skin of his face shone" (Exod. 34:29–35).

The Old Testament background of the scene becomes explicit as Moses and Elijah, the great Law-giver and the prophet of the end time, appear in glory speaking with Jesus. Only Luke gives the content of their conversation: Jesus' "departure" (literally, his *exodus*), which he is "about to accomplish at Jerusalem" (v. 31b). The richly symbolic word *exodus* is often understood as referring to Jesus' death. If so, it is significant that it is in the context of glory that his death is discussed. Yet Luke may also intend that the reader view the whole course of Jesus' life, death, resurrection, and ascension as enacting God's final exodus from the powers of sin and death.

Luke (alone) insists that, no matter how sleepy Peter and his companions may have been, they were fully awake as they beheld Jesus' "glory and the two men . . . with him" (v. 32). However, the glory is fleeting. As Moses and Elijah appear to be leaving (again only in Luke), Peter's instinctive response is to build three *skēnas* (NRSV "dwellings," KJV "tabernacles"), one each for Jesus, Moses, and Elijah. Peter's impulse to enshrine (institutionalize?) the glorious moment is understandable, even if mistaken, but it is excused by Jesus on the grounds of Peter's "not knowing what he said" (v. 33b). A word of grace to us all, especially preachers!

The story now moves to its central revelatory moment as a cloud—another ancient biblical symbol of the mysterious presence of God—"came and overshadowed them," causing them to be terrified "as they entered the cloud" (v. 34). Out of the cloud, the voice of God answers definitively the question of the identity of Jesus that has reverberated throughout

Homiletical Perspective

ascended the mountain one last time in order to look out over the Jordan River and catch a glimpse of the promised land. For Elijah, the mountain was a site of contest between the claims of YHWH and those of the prophets of Ba'al (1 Kgs. 18). There on the mountain, God's identity and faithfulness to the covenant with Israel were reconfirmed. Clearly, one cannot preach on all of these passages and their intertextual connections. However, an informed approach to this text takes care to show ways that the themes of this passage represent long-standing memories, expectations, and hope in the lives of people of faith.

Peter's response to the presence of Jesus, Moses, and Elijah portrays the desire to hold on to this moment of divine presence by memorializing the site with dwelling places for each of the figures. His suggestion is immediately overshadowed by the presence of the divine cloud and the voice from above that reaffirms the divine blessing found in the baptismal portrait in Luke 3:22: "You are my Son, the Beloved." Here, the divine presence points beyond fixating on any immediate experience (no matter how profound) and calls us back to our baptismal vows. This text adds a directive to the divine proclamation of Jesus' identity: "Listen to him!" Without more specific orders, the reader/hearer is left with the question, what exact part of Jesus' message are we to hear?

Luke points to the broader context that immediately precedes and follows this passage. To listen to Jesus as God's Chosen One is to hear the lifelong call to baptismal discipleship as Jesus' invitation to take up your cross daily and follow him (9:23). Luke reinforces this connection by noting that the topic of discussion between Jesus, Moses, and Elijah is Jesus' own journey to the cross in Jerusalem (v. 31). Preachers should take note, then, that the shadow of the cross looms large as it reflects across the pages of this text.

The preacher should avoid the temptation to focus solely on the dazzling brightness of the transfiguration experience as a form of testimony to the power of a "spiritual high" to maintain our sense of call. While faith does include defining and transformational moments, here again, as throughout his Gospel, Luke connects prayer to the sense of identity and a clearer understanding of God's call. For Luke, this reaffirmation of Jesus' baptismal call to ministry is grounded in the daily discipline of prayer, communal life, and service to those in need. Luke takes great care to show the integral ways that the call to Christian discipleship is cruciform in nature.

Luke 9:28–43a

Theological Perspective

sins and burdens of the world through his redemptive suffering. The disciples do not understand this yet, but they begin, at least, to sense that this must be the way it has to be. They hardly can speak, and if they do, they can only blurt out some inappropriate words. Peter's remark, "Let us make three booths," is often interpreted as a longing to prolong the spiritual experience. The text, however, makes it clear that he does not know what he is saying. It is likely that the remark indicates a desire to mark the places and preserve the moments where one has encountered God.[1] The place they encounter Jesus in the company of Moses and Elijah can be honored and protected in these dwellings. No such dwellings are built, nor do the disciples tell anyone of their experience. Instead, the mission of Jesus and that of the disciples shifts to the dusty roads of Galilee with another healing miracle that testifies to the greatness of God in and through Jesus.

The transfiguration episode decisively resolves and reaffirms the identity of Jesus as the bearer of God's kingdom. It provides a glimpse or a foretaste of the prediction that Jesus will not only suffer and be put to death, but that will not be the end of the story. It also points to his vindication and eventual glorification by being welcomed into the select company of Moses and Elijah. The story anticipates a future of a glorious and victorious Lord as the resurrected Christ—one that the disciples, at that moment, are unable to grasp. How can they? The experience is so intense! It is an ineffable mystery, a momentary inbreaking of the infinite into the finite consciousness that can only be savored in faith and trust. The disciples therefore remain speechless. What is true for the disciples then is also true for the disciples now: our experience of Jesus Christ transcends our comprehension of the divine revelation in him. In our baptism, we too are claimed and publicly called to participate in the identity and vocation of Jesus in faith and trust.

J. PAUL RAJASHEKAR

Pastoral Perspective

encounter a spirit-seized son shrieking, convulsing, foaming at the mouth, and rolling on the ground. Can you imagine how whiplashed they must have felt? Perhaps they had encountered the father and son on the way up the mountain. Luke records the father saying, "I begged your disciples to cast [the spirit] out, but they could not" (v. 40). In their excitement about what they had experienced on the mountaintop, had the disciples forgotten about the boy?

The stark reality of human need before them offers an occasion for Jesus to provide healing. Helping the congregation to see that after the excitement of the new pastor's installation comes the real work of learning how to live together; after the satisfaction of completing another Habitat build is the raw need for more affordable housing; after the conclusion of a successful pledge drive is the reality that the needs are always greater than what we have in the budget. Without a pause in the action, our call is to participate in the mission before us that bears witness to Christ.

Another pastoral dimension worth noting in this passage is that of spiritual formation. Luke tells us that "Jesus took with him Peter and John and James, and went up on the mountain to pray" (v. 28). Luke continues his emphasis on Jesus' prayer life and how Jesus' pattern instructs the disciples and the church. That the disciples did not have the power to heal the child convulsed by a demon and later would fall asleep when Jesus asked them to pray with him on the night of his betrayal, are signs that the process of formation is no simple thing.

The process of discipleship is especially difficult in a culture shaped by instant results and Twitter feed. Our culture teaches us to expect quick, easy results; complicated responses are pared down to a 140-character limit of a tweet. Discipleship cannot be contained in a tweet or a moment. Instead, as Peter, John, and James model for us, it is being faithful to being with Jesus over the long haul. In his presence we are formed and reformed to carry on his ministry and mission.

GUY D. GRIFFITH

---

1. Sharon H. Ringe, *Luke* (Louisville, KY: Westminster John Knox Press, 1995), 142.

Exegetical Perspective

the chapter: "This is my Son, my Chosen; listen to him!" (v. 35).

The divine voice echoes the words spoken by God at the baptism of Jesus. In Luke's baptismal narrative, the voice of God is addressed primarily to Jesus, "*You* are my Son, the Beloved" (3:22). Here the divine voice addresses the disciples as well; "*This* is my Son, my Chosen." Luke substitutes "my Chosen" for Mark's and Matthew's designation of the Son as "beloved," perhaps to emphasize for the reader the link between the beloved Son and the Suffering Servant of Isaiah, "my *chosen*, in whom my soul delights" (Isa. 42:1). With profound symmetry, at the baptism of Jesus, as he begins his public ministry, his unique relationship to the Father is confirmed by the voice of God. Now at his "transfiguration," as he begins the journey to his passion in Jerusalem, the divine voice confirms Jesus' unique vocation as God's chosen servant, who "must undergo great suffering . . . and be killed, and on the third day be raised" (9:22).

Yet the chosen Son is not merely to be *seen* in his glory. He is to be *listened* to. Indeed, he is to be listened to beyond Moses and Elijah. The Law and the Prophets of Israel are not set aside. Jesus stands in continuity with them, but it is he "alone" (v. 36) who has the final word in interpreting the "things about himself in all the scriptures" (24:27).

"Who is this?" we too ask of Jesus. Luke declares that this is the Son of God, the Chosen One, to whom above all others his followers are to listen obediently as he calls them to lives of self-denial and daily cross bearing. The interpreter is tempted to stop here, but the text before us goes on.

The next day, when the disciples prove unable to heal a demon-possessed child, Jesus rebukes both them and the unclean spirit and heals the boy. "And all were astounded at the greatness of God" (v. 43a). Even on his way to the cross, even when his disciples fail, as inevitably they and we do, Jesus nevertheless is filled with the power and greatness of God. Astounding indeed!

ALLEN C. MCSWEEN JR.

Homiletical Perspective

Just in case we miss the central theme of the cross that precedes this passage, Luke connects the call to vocation with a commitment to ministry in the face of hostile resistance. The mountaintop experience of the transfiguration is not a form of escapism. It is preparation for and recommitment to the nitty-gritty work of encountering the demonic forces that oppress, subjugate, and hold people captive. Following the transfiguration, Jesus journeys down from the mountain, where he meets a large crowd. A man calls out for Jesus to heal his son, who is seized by a spirit. Other disciples have tried and failed, so it is left to Jesus to respond to the crisis. Jesus rebukes the evil spirit, and the demon exits the young boy as a sign of the power of God incarnate in Jesus Christ.

Contemporary listeners often respond with nervousness and/or skepticism to language of demonic possession and tales of exorcism. Hollywood's fascination with sensational images and depictions of demonic possession further relegates biblical texts of this genre to an ancient, prescientific worldview that no longer holds relevance for today's world. It is precisely at this point that the preacher has an obligation to allow the text to show the integral connection between responding to Jesus' call on our lives and engaging in the difficult work of battling the forces of evil in the world around us. Whether it is the oppressive demons of poverty and addiction or the evil spirits of narcissism and self-reliance, Christians are called to face the power of evil in a hostile and skeptical world.

This difficult work is a form of living out the promise that we make in our baptismal vows when we "renounce all evil and powers in the world which defy God's righteousness."[1] Relying on God's Spirit, given to us at our baptism, pushes us out into the messy world where we work with others to bring hope and healing. When we offer ourselves and our gifts to others, we practice a way of releasing the evil spirits that keep us and those around us in bondage. United in service, we work for the release of others from the demons that hold them captive.

PAUL GALBREATH

1. *Book of Common Worship* (Louisville, KY: Westminster John Knox Press, 1993), 407.

Luke 9:43b–50

43bWhile everyone was amazed at all that he was doing, he said to his disciples, 44"Let these words sink into your ears: The Son of Man is going to be betrayed into human hands." 45But they did not understand this saying; its meaning was concealed from them, so that they could not perceive it. And they were afraid to ask him about this saying.
46An argument arose among them as to which one of them was the greatest. 47But Jesus, aware of their inner thoughts, took a little child and put it by his side, 48and said to them, "Whoever welcomes this child in my name welcomes me, and whoever welcomes me welcomes the one who sent me; for the least among all of you is the greatest."
49John answered, "Master, we saw someone casting out demons in your name, and we tried to stop him, because he does not follow with us." 50But Jesus said to him, "Do not stop him; for whoever is not against you is for you."

Theological Perspective

Luke begins this section with Jesus' second passion prediction. He deliberately highlights the disciples' inability to understand who Jesus is and what it means to follow him. The more clearly Jesus' identity as suffering Messiah becomes known to them, the less they are able to grasp it. They persist in their hope that Jesus is the long-awaited Davidic king who, with the mighty arm of God, will defeat Roman rule and restore Israel to power and glory.

As followers of the Messiah, they dream of being the victors of history, not its victims. The cross is unthinkable; they dare not even ask Jesus about it. Even in the next scene, where they argue about who is the greatest among them, Jesus offends their ambition yet again by bringing a child into their midst and announcing that God identifies with the last and the least. Finally, they attempt to put borders around Jesus' mission of salvation, a move that Jesus firmly vetoes. More than the Savior of Israel, Jesus is the universal Savior who seeks to establish, not a geographical kingdom, but God's reign of justice for the poor and oppressed of all nations. Perhaps more than any other Gospel, Luke's Gospel portrays Jesus as the compassionate friend and champion of the poor.

Like these disciples, Christians of the United States are radically challenged by the Christ

Pastoral Perspective

The ninth chapter of Luke recounts a flurry of activity. Jesus gathered his disciples and gave them the power and authority to preach the good news, heal the sick, and cast out demons. As Jesus and his disciples journeyed, crowds swarmed and grew around them. As people listened and called out, Jesus made their fractured lives whole. In the midst of the buzz and excitement, it would be easy to imagine Jesus becoming a king, and harder to believe that men were plotting behind the scenes in order to take the life of this great teacher and healer.

Nevertheless, Jesus became keenly aware that someone would betray him and death would inevitably follow. So Jesus pled with his disciples, "Let these words sink into your ears." He was like a parent who takes hold of the chin of her child, so she can look into the undistracted eyes and say, "Listen to me. This is important." He was like a teacher who says, "Write this down. This will be on the test." He was like an instructor who warns, "If you do not remember anything I say all day, I want you to remember this."

Jesus warned his friends that his hour was soon at hand when someone would betray him. Yet as the disciples looked around at the people who listened intently to every word that came from his mouth, the hands that reached out for healing, and those who

Exegetical Perspective

This final section of Jesus' Galilean ministry contains three scenes: Jesus' second prediction that he will be betrayed and the disciples' failure to understand it (vv. 43b–45), the disciples' dispute about greatness and Jesus' pointing to the welcome of a child as the model of true greatness (vv. 46–48), and the story of an unknown exorcist whom the disciples attempt to restrain (vv. 49–50). Luke significantly abbreviates and alters the stories he inherits from Mark. The story that takes twelve verses in Mark 9:30–41 comprises only seven and a half in Luke. The editorial revisions tell us something about what Luke thinks the episodes mean. This is a critical turning point in Luke's Gospel, for 9:51 will bring us to the long central section of the book commonly called the "travel narrative," which begins with Jesus setting his face to go to Jerusalem.

Jesus' Second Prediction of the Passion (vv. 43b–45).
While the crowd is marveling at "the greatness of God" displayed in Jesus' powerful works (he has just exorcised a child, vv. 37–43a), Jesus changes the subject abruptly by saying, "Let these words sink into your ears" (v. 44a). This is serious. Pay attention. Although he has already told them that "the Son of Man must undergo great suffering, and be rejected by the elders, chief priests, and scribes, and

Homiletical Perspective

There are three brief but pointed moments of encounter between Jesus and his disciples in our text, each one providing opportunity for preachers to reflect on the meaning of the kingdom of God—then and now.

The first scene is Jesus' second announcement of his passion. In contrast to the first passion prediction (9:21–22), this address to the disciples is vague and undetailed. The absence of detail sharpens the intensity of the words. Jesus puts it emphatically: "Let these words sink into your ears: The Son of Man is going to be betrayed into human hands" (vv. 44–45). There is no explicit mention of death or resurrection in this prediction, just the word that Jesus will be betrayed—handed over. Jesus is going to die. The announcement is disturbing for the disciples. To hear Jesus refer to his powerlessness must seem like pure nonsense to them. Preachers will want to extend charity instead of judgment to the disciples at this point. No wonder they are "afraid to ask him about this saying" (v. 45b). To hear the bad news of Jesus' death for a second time is incomprehensible, given that the disciples in all likelihood are longing for a kingdom of earthly power and control. Jesus is simply not the Messiah of God they are expecting (9:20b).

All along the journey so far, they have witnessed Jesus' mighty acts of power, and the disciples have

Luke 9:43b–50

Theological Perspective

encountered in the church of the poor. Citizens of the wealthiest, most powerful nation on earth are tempted to think God is only prorich and pro-American. It is too easily forgotten that the body of Christ is an international body. Bravely contesting this view, liberation theology, pioneered in Latin America in the 1960s, portrays the God of Jesus Christ as a God bent on justice, who sides with the poor and denounces oppression. Liberation theologies developed around the globe in Africa and Asia, as well as within minority groups such as African American and Latino/Hispanic Christians in economically advantaged countries such as the United States of America.

These theologies arose in contexts affected by massive poverty, where people suffered hunger and sickness as well as inadequate housing and the lack of educational and employment opportunities. They are the "crucified people,"[1] put to death through the structures of political and economic injustice. They are the expendable people, who are delivered up to the ravages of unbridled greed that benefits the wealthy industrialized nations. Beginning with the *conquistadores* and continuing through five centuries of imperial domination up to multinational corporations today, greed has divinized money and created a new religion that might be called money-theism.[2] As the church of the poor began to prayerfully reflect on the Scriptures in light of this situation, they discovered that the living God smashes every idol and executes justice on behalf of the oppressed poor.

Liberation theology challenges the universal Christian community through its central proclamation that God is a liberating God who has a "preferential option for the poor." God's preference for history's last and least does not mean that the poor are holier or more deserving of God's love, nor does it mean that God identifies only with the poor. God's love excludes no one. The Creator God, who declares all of creation to be *very good,* desires the flourishing of all people. At the same time, the God of the exodus event is a God who hears the cry of the poor and deploys divine power to secure their release from slavery. Equally important, as the Hebrew prophets attest, God also loves oppressors and calls them to repentance and responsible action on behalf of the poor. God is on the side of the oppressed to the

Pastoral Perspective

gave up their entire lives to be with him, they did not understand what Jesus was trying to say to them. It was incomprehensible to them that anyone would betray him, let alone someone in their trusted company. The disciples could not imagine someone so vindictive and menacing. These men, some of whom had fished for their livelihood and learned to feel the moisture in the air, watched for the tempest stirring in the sea, and noticed the clouds darkening in the sky, could not imagine the storm of betrayal that was ahead of them. So they left unheeded Jesus' words about the trials to come.

How often has this happened to us? The poisonous kiss, a cheating spouse, a duplicitous coworker, or a conniving friend causes a painful ache because their betrayal is unexpected. Even when a friend counsels, "She is no good for you," or coworkers warn, "He is just using you as a stepping-stone on his career path," it is difficult to comprehend the possibility of betrayal. Jesus wanted the disciples to know about the days to come. He wanted to let the warning sink into their ears, but they just could not imagine it.

Even though the disciples could not conceive of anyone betraying Jesus, they did become jealous of one another and argue about who was the greatest among them.

These men, many with the hard hands and patient resolve of fisherman, went from gutting entrails to standing alongside the Son of God. They watched the steady sun over the horizon as they cast their nets into the quiet sea, and they moved into a place where crowds tried to catch a glimpse of them. One day, their great power was in their sturdy backs as they brought the fish onto their boats; the next day, their great power rested in the company they were keeping, namely, the company of the one who healed the sick, exorcised demons, and gathered large crowds. They went from using their nimble fingers as they sewed up their nets to laying hands on people so they might be healed. How odd it must have been to go from an occupation marked by solitude to a vocation that included wading into crowds of people who needed so much from them! To go from being fishermen to fishers of people must have been a difficult transition.

Imagine how difficult it must have been to throw down those fishing nets and follow Jesus into such a demanding life. How they must have longed to prove that they were up to the monumental tasks at hand! Their devotion to Jesus, their love for the people, and the overwhelming expectations of the crowds must

---

1. See for example Ignacio Ellacuría, "The Crucified People," in *Mysterium Liberationis: Fundamental Concepts of Liberation Theology*, ed. Ignacio Ellacuría and Jon Sobrino (Maryknoll, NY: Orbis Books, 1993), 580–603.
2. Elizabeth A. Johnson, *Quest for the Living God: Mapping Frontiers in the Theology of God* (New York: Continuum, 2008), 79–80.

be killed, and on the third day be raised" (9:22), here he predicts the circumstances that will lead to his death and resurrection: "The Son of Man is going to be betrayed into human hands" (v. 44b).

Robert Tannehill notes the irony of the situation: "the Son of Man whose deeds are so powerful will have no power to escape his human enemies."[1] This irony highlights not only who Jesus is but also who his followers are to be. Just as Jesus' destiny is the cross, so the church will encounter resistance and hostility, even as it will experience the power of Jesus' resurrection. The travel narrative to come in 9:51–19:27 consists largely of Jesus' preparation of the Twelve for the ministry they will take up from him.

The incomprehension of the disciples in Mark—a theme that runs throughout that book—becomes in Luke's retelling an act of God, or perhaps of more hostile forces: the "meaning [of Jesus' prediction] was concealed from them, so that they could not perceive it" (v. 45). Earlier Jesus had said, "Nothing is hidden that will not be disclosed, nor is anything secret that will not become known and come to light" (8:17). We will eventually learn that the disciples' "eyes were opened, and they recognized" the risen Lord (24:31) and that he "opened their minds to understand the scriptures" (24:45). For now, though, they are kept from comprehending, and they are afraid to ask. Their failure to understand Jesus' destiny—and therefore their own—is terribly visible in the paragraph that follows.

The Dispute about Greatness (vv. 46–48). "An argument arose among them as to which one of them was the greatest" (v. 46). The culture of honor and shame in antiquity is a zero-sum game: to increase one's status by definition means to take it from someone else. Everybody in the ancient world knows that somebody has to be on top. There is nothing unusual about the disciples' jockeying for position. Jesus' response is what is unusual. He takes a child, a symbol of powerlessness, to his side and says two things: whoever welcomes this child welcomes both Jesus and the God who sent him, and the one who is the smallest (NRSV "least") among them is really the greatest (v. 48). This upending of conventional wisdom is precisely what will be demonstrated by Jesus' innocent death (23:4, 14, 22, 41, 47). His solidarity with the small, the powerless, and the marginal fulfills the words of his first public sermon, in which he

been chosen to speak, and act, and think in the name of Jesus. It must be very hard to reconcile the all-powerful with the powerless one. It is no wonder that those first disciples have to wrestle with the notion that the good news necessitates Jesus being handed over to be killed. That is just too much "bad news" for them to take on at this stage of the journey. This may account for Luke's saying that the meaning is "concealed" from them, so that they cannot perceive it (v. 45).

This second passion prediction by Jesus is a dark word and may be equally difficult for some twenty-first-century Christians to "perceive" and embrace—even with the benefit of hindsight and the lens of Easter to look through. There can be a temptation to minimize Jesus' death in favor of holding up the resurrection. Without the risen Christ, of course, there would be no point in our proclamation. The resurrection ratifies the truth of the good news. Preachers, however, should not be reluctant to address the hard reality of this text with conviction and care.

Episcopal priest and author Robert Farrar Capon rightly claims that all those who preach the gospel must have "passion for the Passion."[1] It is in the death of Jesus that we know God is with us, "bearing all the sufferings of time."[2] The cross is at the heart of the Christian story, and the crucified Jesus is what impels us to proclaim this particular death as the means of grace that can sustain those who suffer and shield those who are joyous. The saving death of Jesus is the connective tissue that holds the good news together. We do call Jesus' passion and death on the cross "Good Friday," after all.

Remarkably, after the disciples' fear of asking Jesus anything in the previous verses, the second encounter pictures a dramatic change of subject, as the disciples launch into an argument about which one of them is the greatest (v. 46). Although the text is silent about causes for the argument, their dispute about greatness may have taken some of the sting out of their earlier "power outage," when they failed to heal the demon-possessed boy (9:40).

When Jesus took a child and put the little one next to him, however, he was not making a romantic gesture or affirmation about the innocence of children. He was pointing to the radical hospitality involved in paying attention to and welcoming one of no account. Jesus embodies the truth that the

1. Robert C. Tannehill, *Luke,* Abingdon New Testament Commentaries (Nashville: Abingdon Press, 1996), 164.

1. Robert Farrar Capon, *The Foolishness of Preaching: Proclaiming the Gospel against the Wisdom of the World* (Grand Rapids: Eerdmans, 1998), 9.
2. William J. S. Simpson, "Cross of Jesus, cross of sorrow," in *The Hymnbook* (Richmond, Philadelphia, New York: Presbyterian Church in the United States et al., 1955), #196.

Luke 9:43b–50

Theological Perspective

point where "those who oppress the poor insult their Maker" (Prov. 14:31).

Liberation theology interprets their struggle in light of the gospel of Jesus, whose entire life, death, and resurrection reveal this same liberator God of Israel, who stands on the side of the poor and oppressed and calls the oppressor to conversion. Luke's Gospel poignantly depicts the God of justice and compassion toward the poor as embodied in the personal details of Jesus' life. While Jesus is carried in his mother's womb, Mary sings her Magnificat: "He has brought down the powerful from their thrones and lifted up the lowly; he has filled the hungry with good things, and sent the rich away empty" (1:52–53). Jesus is born into a poor family, laid in a manger amid the farm animals, and then visited by lowly shepherds. At the beginning of his ministry he returns to his home synagogue and reads from Isaiah a prophetic passage that becomes the political platform of his ministry (4:18–19).

As an itinerant preacher, he heals the sick, exorcises demons, forgives sinners, feeds the hungry, and shares table companionship in such an all-inclusive way as to provoke scandal. He proclaims the reign of God and singles out the poor and those who hunger after justice for beatitude, while announcing the condition of woe to the rich in their inhumanity to the poor. Faithfulness to his mission leads to his arrest by the religious and political authorities.

Jesus' crucifixion reveals God's solidarity with the crucified people who suffer the sin of the world. The cross of Christ also proclaims God's denunciation of injustice. Vindicated by God, the risen Jesus rises again and again in the crucified people. He calls for the eradication of poverty: bring the crucified peoples down from the cross. United with the crucified people, Christ will preside at the Last Judgment through the poor. Liberation theologian Jon Sobrino recalls the challenging words of Pope John Paul II reminding all that on judgment day the peoples of the third world will judge the peoples of the first world.[3]

SARA FAIRBANKS, OP

Pastoral Perspective

have made the disciples feel completely inadequate. It is no wonder that they began competing with one another, contrasting their achievements, and comparing who was better.

Sensing the brewing competition and understanding the disciples' longing to appear important when they were feeling so inadequate, Jesus stood next to a child. As if acting out a parable, Jesus explained that when they welcomed a child among them, they welcomed Jesus. "The least among all of you is the greatest" (v. 48).

With these words Jesus sought to reorient the activity of the disciples from rivalry to the business of welcoming and ministering with those considered to be the least. Such activity recognized the presence of God, "the one who sent me" (v. 48). Therefore the measure of greatness was not to be found in a flurry of amazing activities but in how one responded to the presence of God in those disregarded as least, not important, or of little status.

In this age, when so much of human activity can be quantified, success is often measured by the numbers. In churches, anxiety over budgets, endowments, and attendance may delude people into thinking that these numbers somehow reflect the value of ministry. Pastors size up one another with random facts that they believe indicate how prestigious their pulpits or positions might be—ornate architecture, costly real estate, influential members, and bloated salaries. Church leaders fall into the trap of seeking their worth in the affections of their congregations. This inordinate craving for affirmation leaves them susceptible to the sting of criticism.

Amid excessive concerns for achievement, adoration, and greatness, Jesus reoriented the attention of his followers in all generations toward those who are among the weak, the small, the vulnerable, and the powerless. He reminded his disciples that greatness is found in these least and little ones, for whoever welcomes them in turn recognizes the one who sent Jesus. Exhaustive striving for success and prominence distracts followers in all ages from recognizing God in their midst.

CAROL HOWARD MERRITT

---

3. Jon Sobrino, *The Principle of Mercy: Taking the Crucified People from the Cross* (Maryknoll, NY: Orbis Books, 1994), 68 and 97.

says he has been "anointed . . . to bring good news to the poor . . . to proclaim release to the captives and recovery of sight to the blind, to let the oppressed go free, to proclaim the year of the Lord's favor" (4:18–19).

The disciples too will have such a ministry, even though they do not yet understand it.

The Unknown Exorcist (vv. 49–50). Following closely as it does the failure of the disciples to exorcise the child in 9:40, failure that Jesus attributes to faithlessness and perversity (v. 41), the story of the unknown exorcist is full of irony. John Carroll notes that "the status-conscious disciples seek to squelch a more successful rival, who wins a more generous review from Jesus."[2] As with the first two episodes, Luke draws this one from Mark, although he has Jesus say of the unknown exorcist, "whoever is not against you is for you" (v. 50), rather than "whoever is not against us is for us" (Mark 9:40). The change of pronouns from "us" to "you" focuses our attention on the disciples' future ministry more than on that of Jesus. By removing Mark's explanatory "Do not stop him; for no one who does a deed of power in my name will be able soon afterward to speak evil of me" (Mark 9:39), Luke simplifies Jesus' advice and generalizes it to the church. You will have allies where you do not expect them.

Fred Craddock calls them the "not-yet-ready disciples,"[3] which is a good reminder of how important the following ten chapters will be to limn Luke's vision of faithful church leadership. Following Jesus and marveling at his mighty works will not be enough to prepare them for what lies ahead. Jesus' rejection by some Samaritans (9:51–56) and the hesitant followers in 9:57–62 are warnings that the disciples will encounter the same divided response that has characterized Jesus' ministry throughout Luke. Indeed, the book of Acts will document exactly that divided response. God's word has always evoked resistance as well as joyful welcome.

E. ELIZABETH JOHNSON

hospitality of God has no boundaries or limits. The gesture was a striking way to remind the disciples that "the least among all of you is the greatest" (v. 48). Luke's Gospel is rooted in God's care for the poor and the lowly. Jesus makes it clear that God's reign does not involve the securing of earthly power, but the embrace of the powerless and those of no outward and visible earthly importance. Salvation in the name of Jesus is for everyone.

Concern about being the greatest and the best, of course, did not end in the first century. A spirit of hierarchy is prevalent in contemporary American culture. Humility is often a virtue in short supply within contemporary society and in the church. We want our politicians and our pastors to be dynamic, forceful, and eloquent. While one admirable trait of American culture is to value the "underdog," we still want our underdogs to become "top dogs" and winners—to rise to power and prestige and wealth. Yet the need for humility, attentiveness, and positive regard for all people is implicit in Jesus' embrace of the child.

The third scene in this passage (v. 49–50) finds Jesus making a brief but emphatic affirmation about the spirit of inclusion that is at the heart of the gospel. It is not surprising, given their privileged status as disciples, that John "answers" Jesus by alerting him to the disciples' attempt to stop an "outsider" from casting out demons in the name of Jesus. John may have been expecting applause for gatekeeping on behalf of the group. Jesus counters with: "Do not stop him; for whoever is not against you is for you" (v. 50). These words provide an exclamation point to underscore that the disciples do not have exclusive rights to the person and work of Jesus. There are no outsiders when speaking of and living into the kingdom of God. The way of the cross is ever the way of self-sacrifice, humility, and inclusive embrace.

MITTIES MCDONALD DECHAMPLAIN

2. John T. Carroll, *Luke: A Commentary*, New Testament Library (Louisville, KY: Westminster John Knox Press, 2012), 222.

3. Fred B. Craddock, "Luke," in James L. Mays, ed., *Harper's Bible Commentary* (New York: Harper & Row, 1988), 1028.

Luke 9:51–62

⁵¹When the days drew near for him to be taken up, he set his face to go to Jerusalem. ⁵²And he sent messengers ahead of him. On their way they entered a village of the Samaritans to make ready for him; ⁵³but they did not receive him, because his face was set toward Jerusalem. ⁵⁴When his disciples James and John saw it, they said, "Lord, do you want us to command fire to come down from heaven and consume them?" ⁵⁵But he turned and rebuked them. ⁵⁶Then they went on to another village.

⁵⁷As they were going along the road, someone said to him, "I will follow you wherever you go." ⁵⁸And Jesus said to him, "Foxes have holes, and birds of the air have nests; but the Son of Man has nowhere to lay his head." ⁵⁹To another he said, "Follow me." But he said, "Lord, first let me go and bury my father." ⁶⁰But Jesus said to him, "Let the dead bury their own dead; but as for you, go and proclaim the kingdom of God." ⁶¹Another said, "I will follow you, Lord; but let me first say farewell to those at my home." ⁶²Jesus said to him, "No one who puts a hand to the plow and looks back is fit for the kingdom of God."

Theological Perspective

This passage begins Jesus' journey to Jerusalem discourse, where Luke summarizes the demands of discipleship and provides the classic metaphor for discipleship. The disciples of Jesus journey with him on a pilgrimage through his passion and into his glory. Discipleship requires a conversion to Christ, who is the source, goal, and model of discipleship. Conversion, however, is not a once-and-for-all event. Rather, conversion is an ongoing process that lasts a lifetime. Jesuit theologian Donald Gelpi has developed a systematic theology of conversion that provides helpful insights for growth in Christian discipleship.

Gelpi asserts that there are five forms of conversion that involve turning away from irresponsible behavior and turning toward responsible behavior.[1] Responsible behavior measures personal decisions against the ideals, principles, and values of the reign of God as taught and embodied by Jesus Christ.

Religious conversion always responds to God's self-giving presence and loving action in our lives. The center of religious conversion is faith. Because God loves us first and initiates the relationship, faith requires an open receptivity to God, as well as the obedient submission to God's saving will. Faith also involves a dynamic commitment of our freedom in

---

1. See Donald L. Gelpi, *The Conversion Experience: A Reflective Process for RCIA Participants and Others* (New York: Paulist Press, 1998).

Pastoral Perspective

Jesus continues his pilgrimage, moving steadily toward Jerusalem. Something awaits him in that holy city, so one can imagine his head turning, his brow creasing, and his lips tightening as he takes each step. There does not seem to be anything that might discourage him from pursuing his destiny.

A sense of purpose, immediacy, and danger frames this passage. These elements are present from the opening lines that convey the rejection of Jesus by the Samaritans. Jesus' disciples pass through the Samaritan village with the hope of preparing the local people for Jesus' arrival. Their request to enter is denied; they are not welcome in the town. In response to this rejection, some of the disciples ask if they ought to bring down fire upon the city. Jesus hears the words, reproaches the disciples, and keeps moving. He does not curse the city or engage in age-old disputes. Jesus will not be deterred from his mission.

Even though Jesus foretells his betrayal, even though he has a sense of what will happen to him in Jerusalem, his keen determination becomes clear as people ask to follow him.

When the first person declares his intention to follow him, Jesus warns him that there will be no stopping or comforts on the road. Each day, a strange landscape will await him, new people will

Exegetical Perspective

The most significant thing to say about these verses—which include two different units of teaching—is that they open the door to Luke's "special section." As the footnote in any good study Bible will tell you, this section contains a great deal of material found only in Luke, including the parables of the Good Samaritan (10:29–37) and the Prodigal Son (15:11–32) and the healing of the ten lepers (17:11–19). After having followed Mark's basic outline since Luke 8:4, Luke now leaves Mark for ten chapters, relying on Q and his own sources to record material largely unknown to (or unused by) Mark.

While a wide variety of New Testament scholars have labored to discover some unifying theme or formal structure in the section, they have not achieved consensus.[1] Luke seems to suggest one of his own in verse 51, letting the reader know that once the days drew near for Jesus to be taken up, he "set his face to go to Jerusalem." Some variant of this phrase is used four more times in Luke's special section (9:53; 13:22; 13:33; 17:11) and three more times after that (18:31; 19:11; 19:28) before Jesus finally arrives on the Temple Mount in 19:45.

Yet anyone who tries to plot Jesus' journey from "a village of the Samaritans" (v. 52) to Jerusalem will

Homiletical Perspective

Abraham Lincoln is reported to have said, "I walk slowly, but I never walk backward."[1] Lincoln's statement conveys an image of determination and steadfastness in pressing on with what is true and right, regardless of the cost. Preachers may find these words from the narrative of American history helpful in putting a frame around Luke 9:51–62—the beginning of what is commonly known as Luke's travel narrative (9:51–19:27).

Jesus is now pictured as making his pivotal and irreversible turn toward Jerusalem. "When the days drew near for him to be taken up, he set his face to go to Jerusalem" (v. 51). Jesus is not pressing on to end a war or to secure the freedom of slaves. He is moving toward the fulfillment of his earthly ministry by death on the cross, to emancipate the whole world from its enslavement to sin and death. The passage as a whole is a representative image of Jesus' steadfastness, obedience, self-giving, and singleness of heart.

Luke makes it clear that Jesus will allow nothing to distract or sidetrack his forward movement toward Jerusalem—not even travel into alien or hostile territory, with the strong likelihood of rejection. The first stop along the way is a Samaritan village,

1. Alan Culpepper, "The Gospel of Luke," in *The New Interpreter's Bible* (Nashville: Abingdon Press, 1995), 9:214.

1. See discussion in *Respectfully Quoted: A Dictionary of Quotations* (Mineola, NY: Dover Publications, Inc., 2010), 287, entry 1534.

Luke 9:51–62

Theological Perspective

action, to renounce sin and to love God through the service of one another and our world. Our religious conversion unifies, integrates, and transforms the other kinds of conversion. Religious conversion is exemplified in Jesus' *Abba* experience, where he discovers, through a close, intimate relationship with God, his identity as the beloved Son. His loving union with God is the dynamism behind his ministry and his courageous determination to meet his death and resurrection in Jerusalem.

Affective conversion seeks to promote a healthy emotional life. This lifelong process demands that we face the suppressed negative emotions like fear, anger, shame, and guilt that produce differing degrees of personality dysfunction. "The healing of repressed negative emotions by integrating them into one's conscious personality in life-giving ways allows the sympathetic emotions like love, affection, friendship, and empathy freedom to play."[2] As a consequence, we grow in our capacity to experience the true, the good, and the beautiful in life. The Christian convert may well require support and counseling but does so from the faith perspective that relies ultimately on God to effect the healing. This affective conversion is modeled in Jesus' teaching ministry, exemplified in this passage, where Jesus rebukes James and John for their anger that motivates them to seek revenge on the unwelcoming Samaritan village.

Intellectual conversion takes responsibility for the truth or falsity of our beliefs in our commitment to the search for truth. Intellectual conversion moves beyond the unquestioned acceptance of conventional wisdom and engages in fair-minded, critical deliberation to weigh the pros and cons of different arguments. The intellectually unconverted are prone to authoritarianism, rigid fundamentalism, and black-and-white, know-it-all thinking. Humbly conceding that there is more than one right answer, the intellectually converted welcome dialogue, recognize the limits of human knowledge, and can freely admit their mistakes. Intellectual conversion for the Christian also entails correcting erroneous beliefs about God. Jesus proclaimed an unconventional religious faith that drew opposition from powerful religious and state authorities. For example, his radical command, "Love your enemies," violates the common sense of this world and points to a new perspective on life in light of the dawning reign of God.

Moral conversion takes responsibility for our personal conscience formation through critical

Pastoral Perspective

meet him. Hospitality will vary from one place to the next. Jesus and his followers eat when they can and accept what is offered. Jesus describes a nomadic life where there will be no comfort food, no place to call home, and no place to truly rest.

In contemporary U.S. society, a home has become so important that it is often at the center of what has been called the American dream. Maintaining a mortgage has become an indicator of success. Some sociologists assess adulthood by the ability of a young person to "settle down." Owning a home can also become a painful challenge if it should happen that the neighborhood changes or the value of the house drops in difficult economic times, leaving a homeowner with a debt that far outweighs his or her assets. In such unforeseen instances, people may face foreclosure. Home ownership presents itself as a different challenge for young people saddled with educational debt and underemployment; for these the thought of owning a home is often no more that wishful thinking.

In the midst of such difficulties, it can be comforting to hear that Jesus and his followers did not seek security and possessions as primary goals in life. Might this insight provide a lens with which to assess contemporary values that privilege ownership, possessions, security, and stability?

The second person Jesus invites to follow him explains that his father has died. This man asks permission first to bury his father before he follows Jesus. Jesus' response is jarring: "Let the dead bury their own dead."

The rituals of mourning were meaningful, rich, and complicated in ancient times. Even today most people who suffer a great loss have to sort out many things. For example, when a parent dies, family members can become disoriented. There may be sleepless nights and days of exhaustion. Appetites diminish and food loses its flavor. The sometimes overwhelming effects of grief manifest themselves in curious ways—keys are misplaced, headaches linger, immune systems weaken. Those who suffer grief may become forgetful and find it difficult to sort out priorities.

Times of such loss can also be marked by bewilderment. As familial roles are redefined, a person's identity may be shaken in the process. The death of a parent may initiate a period of conflict as family members try to sort out who they are, what they believe, and often how they can forgive. This man may have come to Jesus with his life swirling.

Jesus speaks to the man's disorientation when he tells him to let the dead bury the dead. Jesus is not

2.Gelpi, *Conversion*, 104.

be disappointed. In chapter 10 Jesus seems to be in Mary and Martha's hometown of Bethany (10:38); in chapter 13 he is back in Galilee (13:31); in chapter 17 he is near Samaria again (17:11); and in chapter 18 he is in Jericho (18:35). Once you stick pins in all of these places on a map of first-century Palestine, it becomes clear that Jesus' journey to Jerusalem is more existential than geographical. When Luke moves Jesus' death in Jerusalem to the front burner in verse 51, he prepares his readers to hear Jesus speak frankly and urgently about what it means to follow him all the way.

How to Deal with Rejection (vv. 51–56). Jesus knows about rejection from his experience of both those who consider him an insider and those who consider him an outsider. As he was rejected by his home congregation in Nazareth at the beginning of his Galilean ministry (4:16–30), so here he is rejected by a village of Samaritans at the beginning of his journey to Jerusalem. According to Fitzmyer, these twin rejections foreshadow the rejection that lies ahead of him in Jerusalem.[2] They also give teeth to Jesus' saying in the next section that "foxes have holes, and birds of the air have nests; but the Son of Man has nowhere to lay his head" (v. 58).

Interpreters who wish to make the most of this section will be sure they understand the long, complicated, and mutually antagonistic relationship between the Judeans and Samaritans of Jesus' day. Otherwise they may be tempted to turn the Samaritans into cardboard villains, which serves neither the story at hand nor the later stories Jesus tells in which the Samaritans are the good guys.

Luke's use of the Semitic idiom "setting the face" in verse 53 communicates different things to different people. For those who see in Jesus the Suffering Servant of Isaiah, the act of setting his face to go to Jerusalem supplies a direct link to the Servant, who also set his face "like flint" (Isa. 50:7–8a). For a first-century Samaritan, however, someone who set his face to go to Jerusalem was facing away from Mount Gerazim, where Samaritans had maintained their own temple for some four hundred years. This is the reason the Samaritans did not receive Jesus, Luke says—not because he was the Son of Man, but because he was a Jew.

When James and John offer to defend his honor by commanding fire to come down from heaven and consume the inhospitable villagers (see 2 Kgs. 1:9–14,

2. Joseph A. Fitzmyer, *The Gospel according to Luke (I–IX)*, Anchor Bible 28 (Garden City, NY: Doubleday, 1981), 827.

which may be Luke's subtle manner of reaffirming the spirit of inclusion that is central to understanding the kingdom of God. Samaritans, being of Jewish and non-Jewish descent, were among the ultimate outsiders in Jesus' day. This text notes that the Samaritans "did not receive him, because his face was set toward Jerusalem" (v. 53b). The refusal of the Samaritans to extend hospitality to Jesus and his followers is not especially surprising, given the long-standing racial and religious animosity between Jews and Samaritans. What startles is the response of outrage from James and John: "Lord, do you want us to command fire to come down from heaven and consume them?" (v. 54b).

In view of the attempt by the disciples to "stop" an outsider from casting out demons in the name of Jesus (9:49), it is not exactly unpredictable that James and John take offense at this rejection. Perhaps in assessing the situation, the two disciples had engaged in the first-century equivalent of a contemporary question: "What would Jesus do?" James and John appear to have jumped to a conclusion that was clearly *not* what Jesus would do. He "turned and rebuked them" (v. 55), and they traveled on. Jesus clearly had no time to be distracted from his journey by engaging James and John in a "teaching moment." He had already made it quite clear to the Twelve that their mission was "to proclaim the kingdom and to heal" (9:2b), not to punish.

The journey of Jesus was never a search-and-destroy mission; it was a seek-and-save venture. Jerusalem was both destination and destiny for Jesus. Thus he offers a rebuke instead of elaborate instruction. Again, Jesus will not be deterred from pressing on. Jesus moves forward, even though the disciples are still inclined to look backward to images they best remember (in this instance, Elijah's calling down the "fire of God" on the soldiers of the king of Samaria in 1 Kgs. 1:12). It will take time for the reflexes of the disciples to be fully conditioned for what it means to live life under the reign of God. Retribution and vengeance clearly have no place in the kingdom that Jesus inaugurates, then or now.

To journey with the Messiah of God is to be formed in the white-hot crucible of kingdom values: self-sacrifice, self-giving, self-forgetfulness. The way of the cross is ever costly and demanding. The three brief encounters of Jesus with would-be followers (vv. 57–62) establish the rigorous nature of being a true disciple. While these verses are not easily addressed, they must not be avoided or explained away as exaggeration on the part of Jesus. The first

Luke 9:51–62

Theological Perspective

assessment of conventional morality that promotes virtue but also can rationalize vice. Moral conversion requires sensitivity to the needs of others and unwavering commitment to their well-being. Moral conversion engenders generous self-giving and the willingness even to die for one's beliefs. For the Christian, unconditional commitment to the reign of God that Jesus proclaimed delineates the moral path. As exemplified in Luke's Gospel, the failure of the three would-be followers illustrates the radical demands of discipleship exacted by Jesus. Here Jesus overturns the conventional morality of blood solidarity and raises up a new, all-inclusive solidarity of the human race.

Sociopolitical conversion takes responsibility for promoting the common good through the just reform of social institutions. Sociopolitical conversion awakens us from our inhumanity that is self-absorbed, biased, apathetic, and indifferent to the social injustice that afflicts our suffering world. Sociopolitical conversion compels commitment to a universal human cause such as the elimination of world poverty, nuclear disarmament, the opposition to sexism, racism, and classism, the protection of the environment—all causes that advance the good of humanity.

Sociopolitical conversion for the Christian means working in collaboration with other people of goodwill for a just social order that reflects the ideals and principles of the reign of God. As the model of sociopolitical conversion, Jesus announces the messianic reversal of values where the last shall be first and the first last. In his proclamation of the reign of God, Jesus turns the hierarchal structure of first-century Roman society upside down. The kingdom raises to the places of highest importance the poor, the oppressed, and those considered nonpersons; while the aristocracies, both secular and priestly, are called to humble themselves in lowly service to those in greatest need. Jesus proclaims a radically egalitarian Jewish society where justice and peace reign and the poor and marginal are privileged.

In sum, all forms of conversion are necessary for the Christian disciple to achieve transformation into the image of Jesus because they mutually reinforce and strengthen one another. Likewise, the lack of conversion in one area of experience can sabotage and even subvert conversion in another area of experience. Finally, the radical demands of discipleship require a lifelong commitment to conversion that is fulfilled only through the death and resurrection we share with Christ our Savior.

SARA FAIRBANKS, OP

Pastoral Perspective

asking this man to abandon his responsibilities. He is setting him free from the swarm of details and personal confusion that are death's hold on him and inviting him to begin a whole new life, to become who he ought to be. Jesus is letting the man know that his response to Jesus' invitation is central to God's purpose for his life and future identity. Heard in this way, Jesus' words can comfort and assure him that things with his family will be sorted out; yet the words also confront him with the need to act on what is most important.

The third person longs to say goodbye to everyone before he follows in the footsteps of Jesus. Jesus senses in this longing a lack of resolve. As the Gospel unfolds, there are other examples of vacillation. Consider Peter. He follows Jesus into the sea without a boat, hesitates, falters, and later even denies his friend. Determination will be an important characteristic for discipleship. Jesus' ongoing challenges to religious and political authorities certainly risk placing all of their lives in danger. He needs to be surrounded by those who can look to the horizon while plowing. Perhaps Jesus also understands that all those who are considering discipleship should not postpone their decision, because he senses that he is not going to be around for much longer.

To be sure, in that moment, following Jesus will be risky. The decision has to be made quickly and faithfully, with an understanding of the personal and emotional costs involved, because Jesus' face is set toward Jerusalem. There is not much time left. Yet in these three responses, Jesus also calls out to those in this time who will follow him and be his disciples. To follow Christ means a reordering of life that includes the possibility that one may never settle down. To follow Christ entails understanding oneself in relation to Jesus, even when experiencing disorientation in one's own family and confusion in one's sense of self. To follow Christ requires a single-minded resolve that looks forward to the work ahead and is cognizant of the risk that accompanies discipleship.

CAROL HOWARD MERRITT

along with the textual variant that mentions Elijah by name), Jesus rebukes them. "You do not know what spirit you are of," he says in some ancient versions of this text, "for the Son of Man has not come to destroy the lives of human beings but to save them" (vv. 55–56). One deals with rejection by absorbing and disarming it, not by returning it in kind.

Think at Least Twice before Following Me (vv. 57–62).

This short section makes quick work of three would-be followers of Jesus—two of whom volunteer and one of whom Jesus calls directly (significantly, the only other individuals to whom Jesus says, "Follow me," in this Gospel are Levi the tax collector [5:27] and the rich ruler [18:22]). While the first two episodes in this section also appear in Matthew (8:19–22), the third is unique to Luke. Craddock points out that this threefold pattern ("I will follow you," "Follow me," "I will follow you") is typical of storytelling in that time and place. He further points out that the Matthean episodes occur prior to any mention of Jesus' suffering and death, whereas in Luke they follow close on the heels of the first explicit prediction of the passion (9:21–22) and the transfiguration (9:28–36).

In the case of the man whom Jesus calls directly, Jesus is a harder master than Pharaoh. When Joseph asked Pharaoh's permission to be gone from the palace long enough to bury his father Jacob in Canaan, Pharaoh said, "Go up, and bury your father, as he made you swear to do" (Gen. 50:6). When the second would-be follower asks Jesus the same thing, Jesus says, "Let the dead bury their own dead" (v. 60a). The interpreter who softens this answer also softens what Jesus says next: "But as for you, go and proclaim the kingdom of God."

"The context provides the commentary," Craddock summarizes. If Jesus' responses to his would-be followers sound harsh, that is because "one who has set his face like a firm stone to go to Jerusalem has no bargains to offer."[3]

BARBARA BROWN TAYLOR

person asserts, "I will follow you wherever you go" (v. 57), and Jesus offers a rejoinder that journeying to Jerusalem involves virtually none of the comforts and security of home: "Foxes have holes, and birds of the air have nests; but the Son of Man has nowhere to lay his head" (v. 58).

The second encounter has an even greater degree of difficulty for the preacher to address. After Jesus says to someone else, "Follow me," there comes another excuse and petition: "Lord, first let me go and bury my father." Jesus' reply is disturbing: "Let the dead bury their own dead; but as for you, go and proclaim the kingdom of God" (vv. 59–60). The third person in this passage says, "I will follow you, but let me first say farewell to those at my home" (v. 61). Again, Jesus offers another severe reply: "No one who puts a hand to the plow and looks back is fit for the kingdom of God" (v. 62).

There is a rich homiletical opportunity here to purify if needed any distorted images about the nature of discipleship that hearers may have. It is radical to be told that the journey is not about nesting comfortably in the "good" life of the kingdom of God, and that even the admirable virtues of family loyalty are trumped by the extraordinary demands of discipleship. In speaking harsh and uncompromising words, Jesus is not trying to drive away followers. He simply refuses to blunt the sharply pointed reality that to share in the work of Jesus is to share in his sacrifice. He had made the conditions for disciples clear earlier in the ninth chapter: "let them deny themselves and take up their cross daily and follow me" (9:23b). Discipleship is costly, not cozy and comfortable. The journey to Jerusalem is not a vacation. It is a vocation, and an extreme one at that. Authentic devotion to Jesus is a daily practice of dying to self in order to live. No delays. No distractions. No turning back. No walking backward. Never forget: Jesus is walking beside us every step along the way.

MITTIES MCDONALD DECHAMPLAIN

3. Fred B. Craddock, *Luke* (Louisville, KY: John Knox Press, 1990), 143–44.

¹After this the Lord appointed seventy others and sent them on ahead of him in pairs to every town and place where he himself intended to go. ²He said to them, "The harvest is plentiful, but the laborers are few; therefore ask the Lord of the harvest to send out laborers into his harvest. ³Go on your way. See, I am sending you out like lambs into the midst of wolves. ⁴Carry no purse, no bag, no sandals; and greet no one on the road. ⁵Whatever house you enter, first say, 'Peace to this house!' ⁶And if anyone is there who shares in peace, your peace will rest on that person; but if not, it will return to you. ⁷Remain in the same house, eating and drinking whatever they provide, for the laborer deserves to be paid. Do not move about from house to house. ⁸Whenever you enter a town and its people welcome you, eat what is set before you; ⁹cure the sick who are there, and say to them, 'The kingdom of God has come near to you.' ¹⁰But whenever

Theological Perspective

Jesus' commissioning of the seventy (-two), unique to Luke's Gospel, witnesses the truth that for Jesus, ministry is not the sole responsibility of the Twelve; rather, ministry is the duty of every follower. This passage represents a monumental challenge to Sunday Christians who still believe that ministry belongs solely to the professional clergy by virtue of ordination. For example, prior to the Second Vatican Council (1962–1965), for Roman Catholics the laity were negatively defined as "not clergy" and "not religious." The hierarchical priesthood *was* the church; the laity belonged *to* the church. The clergy exercised the threefold mission of Christ as priest, prophet, and king; the laity were the passive recipient of that ministry. From this perspective, the vocation of the laity could be summed up in four words: believe, pray, obey, and pay. The deliberations and teachings that emerged from Vatican II provide some of the foundations for a theology of ministry that encourages the vocation of all baptized Christians to become partners with Christ, sent in mission to the world.

Embracing the spirit of Luke's Gospel, Vatican II teaches that the church is no longer understood primarily as hierarchical institution, but as the "people of God." The church is a ministerial community of Christian disciples in communion with

Pastoral Perspective

Jesus sent out seventy people in pairs to go before him. He empowered them to bring peace, cure the sick, and proclaim the reign of God. In retrospect, from the perspective of the church, the mission of the seventy marks the spread of the gospel and subsequently the expansion of the spiritual body of Jesus.

If the teachings of Jesus had depended on only one person moving from village to village, the good news would not have circulated in the same way. Before the printing press or the Internet, the culture disseminated news and shared stories though oral tradition. For Jesus, entrusting the mission to the seventy expanded the range of people whose lives would be addressed by the gospel. After Jesus' death, resurrection, and ascension, the good news of God's reconciling work would depend on a network of people who were witnesses to what God had done. If Jesus had not empowered other disciples at this critical moment, the stories might have been silenced, the healing might have ceased, and the message might have faltered.

Throughout this Gospel and in the Acts of the Apostles, the importance of being strategic in gathering the harvest appears as a theme. The fields were ripe. Jesus and his followers worked to make sure that every bit of grain was plucked and that everyone

you enter a town and they do not welcome you, go out into its streets and say, [11]'Even the dust of your town that clings to our feet, we wipe off in protest against you. Yet know this: the kingdom of God has come near.' [12]I tell you, on that day it will be more tolerable for Sodom than for that town.

[13]"Woe to you, Chorazin! Woe to you, Bethsaida! For if the deeds of power done in you had been done in Tyre and Sidon, they would have repented long ago, sitting in sackcloth and ashes. [14]But at the judgment it will be more tolerable for Tyre and Sidon than for you. [15]And you, Capernaum,
     will you be exalted to heaven?
         No, you will be brought down to Hades.
[16]"Whoever listens to you listens to me, and whoever rejects you rejects me, and whoever rejects me rejects the one who sent me."

Exegetical Perspective

In Luke 9:1–2, Jesus "called the twelve together and gave them power and authority over all demons and to cure diseases, and he sent them out to proclaim the kingdom of God and to heal." Now, at the beginning of what is commonly called the "travel narrative," as Jesus moves toward Jerusalem, he sends out seventy-two,[1] the traditional number of the Gentile nations, on a very similar mission to serve as his advance team. They are to go "where he himself intended to go" (v. 1). These Jesus sends in pairs with the exhortation, "The harvest is plentiful, but the laborers are few; therefore ask the Lord of the harvest to send out laborers into his harvest" (v. 2).

In the commissioning of the Twelve, Jesus' instructions were simple: "Take nothing for your journey, no staff, nor bag, nor bread, nor money—not even an extra tunic. Whatever house you enter, stay there, and leave from there. Wherever they do not welcome you, as you are leaving that town shake the dust off your feet as a testimony against them" (9:3–5). The sending of the seventy-two, though,

1. The greater number of manuscripts of 10:1 reads "seventy," but the more difficult reading (an important consideration in a text-critical argument), "seventy-two," is probably the original. The number of the Gentile nations, according to Genesis 10, is either seventy (in Hebrew) or seventy-two (in the Septuagint), and it is just as likely that scribes would correct "seventy-two" to "seventy" as the reverse. See the discussion in John T. Carroll, *Luke: A Commentary*, New Testament Library (Louisville, KY: Westminster John Knox Press, 2012), 233–34.

Homiletical Perspective

At the outset of Luke 10:1–16, Jesus appoints seventy followers to go "on ahead of him in pairs to every town and place where he himself intended to go" (v. 1). The commissioning of the seventy (vv. 1–12) is found only in Luke, and the account establishes that proclaiming the good news of the kingdom of God is not the exclusive vocation of the twelve disciples. Many faithful voices will be needed.

The charge Jesus gives to the seventy follows the same pattern as the charge to the Twelve (9:1–6), but this passage has more detailed instructions for those appointed. By sending out the seventy, two by two (v. 1), Jesus is clearly affirming that proclaiming the good news of the kingdom is not a solo performance, but a communal and relational activity—a concert of the whole body of those commissioned. The message is ever inclusive and expansive. In Luke, the good news of the kingdom crosses boundaries of race and religion—to all people.

For contemporary listeners, the basic rules for engagement in the early verses of our text may sound anywhere from puzzling to impossible: "Go on your way. See, I am sending you out like lambs into the midst of wolves. Carry no purse, no bag, no sandals; and greet no one on the road" (vv. 3–4). The metaphor of lambs in the midst of wolves is not commonly used today and may almost sound cartoonish.

Luke 10:1–16

Theological Perspective

God, sharing in a single mission. Reminiscent of Christ's own commissioning of the seventy-two, the Council asserts the biblical truth that God chose "a people" consecrated for mission; all distinctions of roles, ministries, and states of life in the church are secondary and in service of this ministerial community of the baptized. Catholic theologian Thomas O'Meara expresses well the Council's teaching that ministry is a requirement of baptized life:

> Ministry is a horizon within the life of the Christian community. A woman, a man is baptized not into an audience or a club but into a community which, accepting a vision of humanity and a faith in unseen divine presence, is essentially and unavoidably ministerial. Just as Christian faith is communal, so Christian community is ministerial. Churches are clusters of people with a world to serve.[1]

Realizing anew the nearness of the reign of God for our times, the church has real potential to be an agent for social transformation, especially when Christians are expected to live up to their baptismal identity. Establishing the christological foundations for ministry, Vatican II highlights the church as the body of Christ, where clergy and laity together participate in the mission of the suffering and glorified Christ, sent out "like lambs into the midst of wolves" (v. 3). Through baptism every woman or man becomes an "other Christ." A traditional Catholic teaching is that the ordained priest is configured to Christ and acts *in persona Christi*. Vatican II, however, makes a similar claim about the laity by virtue of baptism and Holy Communion. The Council affirms with Paul that through baptism a person is formed in the likeness of Christ, is united with Christ's death and resurrection, and thus becomes a new creation. Moreover, since Christ made them mystically into his body, the laity in a very real sense act *in persona Christi* continuing his mission of salvation to the church and world.

Likewise, the Council links the Pauline doctrine of the charisms of the Holy Spirit with that about the body of Christ, in order to show that charisms are not given for the benefit of individuals in their private relationship with Christ. The church is a ministerial community animated by the Spirit, who universally disperses charisms to *all* the baptized for the good of the whole. The manifold gifts of the Spirit are never limited to the clergy. Rather, the

1. Thomas O'Meara, *Theology of Ministry*, completely revised edition (New York: Paulist Press, 1999), 5.

Pastoral Perspective

who was ready to receive the good news had a chance to share in it. Just as one laborer sent to harvest an abundant crop in a large field would never succeed, so one person proclaiming the message was not able to accomplish the work that needed to be done, Moreover, the first ambassadors of the gospel—those apostles who traveled to port cities and eventually to Rome—undoubtedly understood that telling and retelling the message of Jesus and the reign of God in the places where people traded goods and stories would further its spread into new regions. For Luke this proclamation of the message began with the seventy who went before Jesus.

This intentional shift, made to ensure that more people were empowered to spread the good news, reminds the church today that it needs to be engaged in the same sort of empowerment and action. Too often Christians are shut up in sanctuaries, concerned about leaky roofs and outdated boilers, counting the attendance, and wringing their hands because people do not seem to be worshiping God as they did in the past. Congregations spend so much time caring for their own and feeling anxious about their demise that they sometimes forget that they, like the seventy, have been sent out with the gospel of God's love and justice and mercy. The good news has been given to them for the world. How can we get out of the pews and join in the mission of God to the world? How, like the seventy, do congregations recognize and embrace their active participation in the reconciling work of God beyond the narrow confines of their own fears and needs?

Although a great amount of work awaited the apostles, Jesus also saw the danger brewing around him and worried that his followers would be sent out like lambs among wolves (v. 3). It is a vicious metaphor that conjures up the violent act of friends being torn from limb to limb and eaten by a hungry pack. Yet Jesus sent them out in a way that highlighted their vulnerability by discouraging them from taking a purse, bag, or even sandals. Instead he instructed the seventy to bring peace. As Jesus described it, peace is more than a good feeling; it is a community-creating gift of God that requires a reciprocal response. It not only reflects a calmness of spirit, but points to wholeness, reconciliation, and healing. When the seventy entered a home, they were to offer peace; if the peace was accepted, then they were to stay in that home, spending time enjoying the hospitality afforded them. In such a context the message would take root. If peace was not reciprocated, then they were to move on.

Feasting on the Gospels

requires more extensive instruction. As the Twelve were to take nothing for their journeys but rely on the hospitality of those to whom they preached, so Jesus tells these missionaries to rely on the kindness of strangers (vv. 4–7a), although they are specifically forbidden to "move about from house to house" (v. 7b). They are encouraged to bless their hosts with peace (v. 5) and eat and drink what they are offered (vv. 7, 8). This is not charity, though, but rather a dignifying of their work: "the laborer deserves to be paid" (v. 7). The policy is reminiscent of an earlier debate within Pauline Christianity about whether or not apostles ought to be paid. Paul argues in 1 Corinthians 9:3–14 that he and Barnabas have the right to be paid, even though they do not take advantage of that right, so as not to place a burden on their churches.

If the evangelists are rejected, the response Jesus recommends in Luke 10 is a great deal longer than what he told the Twelve in chapter 9. They will be lambs among wolves, he says (v. 3), so they must be watchful and choose their allies carefully. They are not even to greet anyone on the way, lest they evoke a hostile response (v. 4). Because the word of God in Luke inevitably elicits a divided reaction, the missionaries will encounter both welcome and rejection.

The preparations for the two missions and the results share both similarities and important differences. The Twelve were told to preach and heal (9:2), as are the seventy-two (v. 9). When the Twelve returned to Jesus at 9:10, Luke says only that they told him what they had done. When the seventy-two report back in, however, Jesus exclaims, "I watched Satan fall from heaven like a flash of lightning" (v. 18) and tells them to rejoice that their "names are written in heaven" because of their work (v. 20). Both groups are trained to shake the dust of resistant villages from their feet (9:5; 10:11), but there is a greatly expanded series of woes addressed to Chorazin, Bethsaida, and Capernaum in 10:13–15 that presumably serve as a model to the larger mission group for how it is to respond to hostility. Robert Tannehill notes the "climactic parallelism" between the two stories: "the second mission narrative is a grander version of the first."[2]

Luke's readers have known from early in his book that Jesus has come to save not only Israel but the whole world, so this second commissioning of evangelists functions to reprise that theme in Luke and prepare for its elaboration in Acts. Simeon praises

Still, the image underscores the reality that many things can devour and diminish the commitment of Jesus' disciples, and the likelihood of rejection on the journey is strong. Those commissioned, however, are not to be people pleasers but God bearers—offering God's peace to all. Traveling without encumbrances and depending on the hospitality of strangers is essential. Missionaries are to trust God's gracious provision in all circumstances. By the authority and power of Jesus, the seventy are to proclaim the same message to receptive households and to resistant places alike: "the kingdom of God has come near."

What was true for those first disciples is not such a far cry from contemporary society, where rejection of the gospel may take the form of indifference instead of hostility. It is not uncommon in our time to encounter those who have a high need for approval, with a robust fear of rejection and failure. When faced with personal rejection or rejection of the gospel, the response is not to make the gospel message more palatable. The charge to travel without extra baggage may pose another potential barrier for many contemporary listeners and would-be followers. After all, twenty-first-century hearers live in an electronic age: radio, television, sound bites, cell phones, computers, the Internet, and an astonishing array of social media. While technology is remarkable and can broaden access to the people one wishes to serve, the same technology may distract from being authentically connected— in right relationship with God and each other. The vocation of disciple means one is to be possessed by the love of Jesus and not by possessions. Disciples must travel without encumbrances and acknowledge their dependency on God's grace to carry on in all circumstances.

Preachers may find that the most complicated thing to deal with in this passage is the fierce note of judgment that Jesus utters. There will be a divine assessment of places and people that reject the new way of being ushered into the world by Jesus. The "woes" are an emphatic reminder that all are in need of repentance. This reality surfaces in the dramatic gearshift from instructions to invective against unrepentant towns (vv. 12–16). Pronouncing "woes" on Chorazin, Bethsaida, and Capernaum—cities where Jesus performed miracles in Galilee—punctuates in a dramatic way that miraculous deeds do not necessarily lead to a change of mind and heart. Jesus' unfavorable comparison of the inhabitants of these towns of Israel with the foreigners who inhabit the cities of Tyre and Sidon is a dramatic way of emphasizing

2. Robert C. Tannehill, *Luke*, Abingdon New Testament Commentaries (Nashville: Abingdon Press, 1996), 173.

Luke 10:1–16

Theological Perspective

laity are divinely called and gifted with charisms for evangelization, preaching, teaching, healing, counsel, and prayer, making them fit and ready for Christian ministry. The laity have a divine mandate to develop and use their gifts for the upbuilding of the church and world. It is the duty of the clergy to help discern, develop, and order the exercise of these charisms for ministry. The Council also stresses the responsibility of the laity to respond generously to the call of Christ, because it is the Lord who is again sending them on ahead of him in every town and place where he himself intends to go (v. 1).

The Council further asserts that the laity have the principal role in transforming the world in Christ by virtue of their "secular character," that is, their primary and direct involvement in family, economics, politics, and professional and social life. The laity make powerful heralds of the gospel in and through the ordinary situations of daily life and at the very core of the human community. In every dimension of life the laity are called to promote the social mission of the church in solidarity with the whole human family, collaborating with other people of goodwill for the betterment of humanity.

An important part of their prophetic witness is to denounce the evil of injustice and to promote the social implications of the gospel, especially for the last and the least. As Christian disciples, they have a duty to evangelize the vast and intricate world of politics, economics, society, and family, as well as the world of culture, of the arts and sciences, of the mass media. Their witness to Christ is particularly incisive because in sharing the living conditions and labors, the sufferings and hopes of their sisters and brothers, the laity speak with a relevant voice of the reign of God in our midst. The Council highlights the fact that many persons "can hear the gospel and recognize Christ only through the laity who live near them."[2]

Attention to the ways one denomination constructs a theology of ministry in light of its mission provides a window into a contemporary manifestation of the sending of the seventy.

SARA FAIRBANKS, OP

Pastoral Perspective

What if today's disciples began to think of peace as that which is necessary for relationships to flourish, and therefore intentionally offered peace to each person whom they encountered? What if the church began to take seriously the responsibility and the vulnerability that falls upon those whom Jesus still is sending out, like the seventy, to be agents of God's peace?

Sometimes there is an element of serendipity to being "sent out" as an agent of God's peace. One evening two women, Daria and Chloe, were introduced to one another. Chloe had just lost her father, while Daria for a year had been walking through the shadow of her own dad's death. They began the conversation as strangers, talking about the weather and scenery, but their relationship quickly shifted as they shared stories of the passing of their fathers. Chloe, fresh from her father's funeral, spoke of the hospice nurses and the vacant abyss she felt. She explained how her father's commitment to his art taught her and saved her. Daria pointed out all the manifestations of grief that she noticed and how they felt so different from what she expected.

Something in the conversation resonated in each woman until they began to share a new song in their mourning. They were singing in the same key. Chloe sounded the song of wholeness that Daria had been longing to intone. Sharing in that chorus of peace gave them both a wholeness that they did not know prior to their meeting.

In death, grief, and loss, certain people breathe peace into the darkest situation. This often does not happen with words; rather, through the sighs too deep for words, two hurting human beings are connected emotionally, and their fractured lives are given a sense of wholeness.

Jesus empowered the seventy to go out, speak love, bring healing, and thereby expand the reign of God in significant ways. The church by extension is called to continue this work of sharing peace and spreading the gospel.

CAROL HOWARD MERRITT

2. "Decree on the Apostolate of the Lay People," art. 13, in Walter Abbot, ed., *The Documents of Vatican II* (New York: Herder & Herder, 1966).

Exegetical Perspective

God for the child he says is "a light for revelation to the Gentiles and for glory to [God's] people Israel" (2:32). Jesus responds to his rejection at Nazareth with stories about Elijah and Elisha, who perform mighty acts for non-Israelites (4:23–27), as a way to interpret what it means that God has anointed him "to bring good news to the poor . . . to proclaim release to the captives and recovery of sight to the blind, to let the oppressed go free, to proclaim the year of the Lord's favor" (4:18–19). This one who is the Messiah of Israel is the savior of the whole world, and even before Easter, Gentiles like the centurion of Capernaum (7:1–10) and the Gerasene demoniac (8:26–39) recognize him. His post-Easter commission to the eleven is "that repentance and forgiveness of sins is to be proclaimed in his name to all nations, beginning from Jerusalem" (24:47). The story of Acts is the unstoppable movement of the word of God out in concentric circles from Jerusalem to Judea and Samaria, and even to the ends of the earth (Acts 1:8), ending in the capital of the empire itself.

The entire episode concludes with reassurance that the missionaries go out not only with Jesus' authority but also with his word. They also share his destiny, something that will carry increasing solemnity the closer we get to Jerusalem. "Whoever listens to you listens to me," he says, "and whoever rejects you rejects me." He then raises the stakes and adds, "and whoever rejects me rejects the one who sent me" (v. 16).

E. ELIZABETH JOHNSON

Homiletical Perspective

that being a child of Israel is not an exemption from the need for repentance.

Jesus is not being a bully here, but a prophet. He is a faithful Jew, the Messiah of God, who came to purify and awaken the people of Israel to live into God's covenant with them. Jesus speaks in continuity with the prophetic tradition. All are in need of repentance, but communities of "outsiders" to Israel will do better at the Last Judgment than those who do not repent. The more privileged the place, the greater the judgment for being unrepentant.

Homiletically speaking, preachers may want to remind listeners that Jesus is not condemning Judaism in these striking comparisons. He is trying to shake them loose from their contentment with the religious status quo. Jesus is not the terminator of the covenant, but the embodiment of it.

The mission of the seventy and the Twelve in the Gospel, although in a distant time and place, is very much the mission of the church in the twenty-first century. The messengers have changed from age to age, but the message is the same. All followers of Jesus—and preachers in particular—are called to give voice to and embody the kingdom of God.

With two thousand years of theological hindsight comes a homiletical luxury in proclaiming the gospel with credibility and authenticity. In his book *Jesus Christ for Today's World* Jürgen Moltmann makes an inspiring observation: "Anyone who gets involved with Jesus gets involved with the kingdom of God. This is an inescapable fact, for . . . who is Jesus? Simply *the kingdom of God in person*."[1]

The one who called and empowered those early disciples continues to call disciples to ministry for the sake of all people. "The kingdom of God in person" is always summoning people to be the means of grace in a world not yet free of brokenness, and still held hostage by the grip of evil. Mercifully, Jesus Christ continues to equip disciples with the grace and power to accomplish whatever is called for—for the sake of the kingdom.

MITTIES MCDONALD DECHAMPLAIN

---

1. Jürgen Moltmann, *Jesus Christ for Today's World*, trans. Margaret Kohl (Minneapolis: Fortress Press, 1994), 7.

Luke 10:17–24

¹⁷The seventy returned with joy, saying, "Lord, in your name even the demons submit to us!" ¹⁸He said to them, "I watched Satan fall from heaven like a flash of lightning. ¹⁹See, I have given you authority to tread on snakes and scorpions, and over all the power of the enemy; and nothing will hurt you. ²⁰Nevertheless, do not rejoice at this, that the spirits submit to you, but rejoice that your names are written in heaven."

²¹At that same hour Jesus rejoiced in the Holy Spirit and said, "I thank you, Father, Lord of heaven and earth, because you have hidden these things from the wise and the intelligent and have revealed them to infants; yes, Father, for such was your gracious will. ²²All things have been handed over to me by my Father; and no one knows who the Son is except the Father, or who the Father is except the Son and anyone to whom the Son chooses to reveal him."

²³Then turning to the disciples, Jesus said to them privately, "Blessed are the eyes that see what you see! ²⁴For I tell you that many prophets and kings desired to see what you see, but did not see it, and to hear what you hear, but did not hear it."

Theological Perspective

Only the Gospel of Luke adds the mission of the seventy (or seventy-two) as a type of expansion of Jesus' sending of the Twelve (9:1–10). The seventy are sent out because "the harvest is plentiful"—including even those in Phoenician or Gentile towns, such as Tyre and Sidon—"but the laborers are few" (10:2). They are also sent out with strict orders to carry no purse, bag, or sandals, stay in houses where they are welcome, and eat and drink what is provided, "for the laborer deserves to be paid" (10:7). This last statement has sometimes been used to justify ministerial compensation, although, when read in the context of 10:4–7, there are many contemporary settings to which it still corresponds. In any case, the main point of 10:1–16 is that the seventy have been sent out in Jesus' name and with his power and authority: "Whoever listens to you listens to me, and whoever rejects you rejects me, and whoever rejects me rejects the one who sent me" (10:16). These words are enough perhaps to make one hesitate to apply it to oneself.

In 10:17–24, the seventy return, to impressive, if not spectacular, reviews. They report to Jesus that, in his name, "even the demons submit to us" (v. 17). Jesus responds that he has given them authority to tread on snakes and scorpions, and also "over all the power of the enemy" (v. 19). Indeed, although

Pastoral Perspective

The church often avoids this passage of Scripture because it is not easy to translate its details into our present-day experience. Who wants to talk about Satan? Who likes to think about walking on snakes and scorpions? Congregations that do (talk about Satan and handle snakes) make some people very nervous. What is the original context of these verses?

Jesus has sent out the seventy to go in advance and tell about the good news of God. They are to go without any accoutrements. Some will welcome them. If so, they are to stay there and speak about the peace of God. If not, then they are to move on. The story comes in the midst of the journey to Jerusalem. Unlike those who hear or read this text today, those sent out by Jesus do not know the end of the story. Instead they go from town to town and tell about this man who has the Spirit of God moving in him.

Our text begins with all of the seventy returning in joy. Apparently they are proud of what has happened. Even the demons bow and know that God is lord of all. Jesus tells them that he has already seen Satan fall, a statement he makes as if to say, "Yes, there is still evil in the world, but God is conquering evil." Because he has given them power over evil, he tells them that nothing will hurt them. Jesus then cautions them about taking pride in their

Exegetical Perspective

Changes in dialogue partners help us to differentiate three distinct scenes in Luke 10:17–24. Taken together, these verses reveal the mission of Jesus as part of a cosmic struggle in which God will prevail over Satan, and they describe discipleship as bearing witness to the ultimate victory of God even in the midst of that struggle.

Luke 10:17–20 is a dialogue between Jesus and a large group of followers whom he has sent out ahead of him (see 10:1). Both Matthew and Luke include the saying from Jesus that "the harvest is plentiful, and the laborers are few," but only in Luke does Jesus respond to this need by appointing elders. The precise number of missionaries (seventy or seventy-two) is a matter of dispute in the textual tradition, with manuscript evidence split nearly evenly. Seventy is the number of elders gathered by Moses in Numbers 11, and Luke's account here may have its roots in the Old Testament story of additional leaders to assist Moses being raised up and equipped by God's Spirit.

In Luke 10:17, the seventy return from a successful mission: even the demons are submitting to them. Their success stands in contrast to the failure of the disciples recounted in Luke 9:37–40. Jesus listens to their report and responds with one of his own: "I watched Satan fall from heaven like a flash of lightning" (v. 18). Jesus' words echo the taunt of the

Homiletical Perspective

It is a very difficult time to minister in one of the former mainline churches of North America. Most mainline denominations are in a serious state of decline, and some readers of this resource will be preaching in congregations that are but a shadow of their former strength. In such a setting it is very tempting to demean success. When the most a congregation can do is to develop coping strategies, success can become hard to recognize and painful to celebrate as Jesus himself does in this text. Care needs to be taken in order to avoid using this text to devalue success itself. Success, after all, is "so shallow"! It is tempting to dismiss success in this way, especially if one's congregational numbers are down.

The context of this passage, however, is certainly success. The disciples have just returned from their first mission journey. They have been spectacularly successful, not just in adding numbers to a roll of followers. Their ministry was so powerful that its effect can only be described in apocalyptic language. It was as if Satan fell from the sky like a flash of lightning (v. 18). Even the demons submit to the disciples, and they are granted extended authority, in this case authority to tread on venomous beasts. The disciples are filled with joy and, it must be noted, Jesus shares that joy.

Luke 10:17–24

Theological Perspective

the seventy have been sent out on a perilous mission ("like lambs into the midst of wolves," 10:3), Jesus also tells them "nothing will hurt you" (v. 19). Then Jesus thanks the "Lord of heaven and earth" because, while these things have been hidden "from the wise and the intelligent," they are revealed to "infants," and indeed, since "all things have been handed over to me," to whomever "the Son chooses to reveal [them]" (vv. 21–22). Is the contrast between infants and the wise meant to describe the seventy? Finally, Jesus turns to the disciples and says to them *privately*, "Blessed are the eyes that see what you see! For I tell you that many prophets and kings desired to see what you see, but did not see it, and to hear what you hear, but did not hear it" (vv. 23–24). That is, the disciples have been graced with a special sight or vision; in fact, it may well be that not everyone sees their mission this way.

The passage emphasizes the theme of the church's universal mission, which in Luke–Acts extends to Paul's proclaiming the kingdom and teaching Jesus Christ "with all boldness and without hindrance" at the center of the empire (Acts 28:31). This broader context helps us to understand why, at the return of the seventy, Jesus sees Satan fall like lightning from the sky. There is a sense in which the early mission of the seventy to a collection of Jewish and Gentile towns anticipates the church's mission to the entire world, and thus precipitates Satan's fall from power. Nevertheless, Jesus insists that the seventy should rejoice, not at their success against the power of the enemy, but over the fact that "your names are written in heaven" (v. 20).

At least two further theological points are worth emphasizing. The first is the extraordinary *disproportion* between the mission of the seventy and its consequences. Satan falls from power and is brought down to earth. His rule is curtailed; his dominion is broken. The seventy marvel, and perhaps now begin to understand what it means to have been sent out as God's emissaries to defeat evil and to restore hope. The astounding victory intimates the cosmic significance of their mission.

Obviously, as far as the Gospel of Luke is concerned, Satan is not yet finished; he will enter into Judas to motivate the disciple's storied betrayal (22:3–6). Even so, with the mission of the seventy, Satan is on his way out. He is defeated in principle. If this is not the end, then it is at least the beginning of the end of Satan's reign, and a beginning of the triumph of God's kingdom.

Pastoral Perspective

accomplishment. What matters is that "your names are written in heaven" (v. 20). There the report ends.

Given the lives they would lead as followers of Jesus, what would it mean to the seventy who went out in faith to hear these two assurances: they will have their names written in heaven, and nothing will hurt them? Certainly many who first heard Jesus' words would be hurt and even lose their lives because of their discipleship. In what way do Jesus' words speak to the church today? How can Christians trust that nothing will hurt them, when they live with deep hurts in their own lives, when death steals upon a family, or when an illness overcomes a person who has everything going for him or her? Can the church say, as Jesus said, that nothing will hurt his followers?

From the perspective of the cross and resurrection, the church can say that death, in all of its forms, will not have the final word. More than simply saying this, how might the church help people to trust that death has no power over them? For some, such trust begins with a very deep certainty about the love of God pulling people each day toward the future. For others, the gospel long ago led them to believe that God's love would see them through the most devastating of times.

What of "snakes and scorpions" in the church today? Can they be interpreted as people, times, and experiences that confront a Christian? Scorpions may look with their eyes but sting with their tails. Snakes seem sly and cunning as they slither around. Snakes and scorpions may be a helpful metaphor for the bad things that challenge people's lives. The text says that Jesus has given us authority over the power of the enemy, yet we feel vulnerable and even doubt that we have this power. When, in spite of our doubts and fears, God takes holds of us and does not let us go, we are surprised. When in the face of "scorpions and snakes," the experience of the deep love of God given us in Jesus Christ strengthens and empowers us again and again, we slowly begin to trust that God is able. In this strange passage that speaks of snakes and scorpions, we can see a glimmer of a powerful God who has come down to walk with us, to love us, to carry us when we need to be carried, and even to write our names in heaven.

The text now turns to thanksgiving. Jesus rejoices in the Holy Spirit. He gives thanks to his Father that certain things have been hidden from the wise but revealed to babies. Human wisdom cannot know the ways of God. No amount of knowledge or rationality will lead to salvation or revelation. In many

Feasting on the Gospels

king of Babylon that Isaiah offers in Isaiah 14:3–20, especially verse 12: "How you are fallen from heaven, O Day Star, son of Dawn! How you are cut down to the ground, you who laid the nations low!" Readers of Luke's Gospel will recognize the theme of the mighty having been cast down (1:52). The victory over Satan proclaimed here is not yet complete, however, as the passion narrative will demonstrate. Satan is implicated in Judas's betrayal of Jesus and Peter's denial of him (22:3, 31). Even so, Jesus promises here that it is not just the power of earthly rulers that will be thwarted, but also that of "the enemy."

Jesus closes his discourse with the seventy by calling to mind the second half of the reversal that Luke's readers know from Mary's song. The mighty have been cast down, yes. Satan has fallen from heaven like lightning. Yet even greater joy is called for by the fact that the lowly have been lifted up: "Nevertheless, do not rejoice at this, that the spirits submit to you, but rejoice that your names are written in heaven" (v. 20). Satan is displaced from heaven, and the names of those with Jesus are written there. Is the evil one's defeat a cause for joy? Certainly. Yet it pales in comparison to the joy of communion with God.

After responding to the seventy, Jesus turns to prayer. The prayer offers another window on reversal. As the text begins, we read of Satan falling and authority over the enemy handed to rank-and-file followers of Jesus. In verses 21–22, we hear that the wise and intelligent have remained ignorant of God's work. Meanwhile, Jesus has shared his knowledge of God and God's will with "infants." By the work of the Son, the little people are ushered into an experience of the Father. The sophisticated remain in the dark. The vocabulary of verses 21–22 has more in common with John's Gospel than the rest of Luke, but the theme of reversal is thoroughly Lukan.

The contrast Jesus draws in verses 23 and 24, between the disciples' experience and the unfulfilled hope of "prophets and kings," is played out later in the narrative. After Jesus is arrested, Pilate and Herod shuffle Jesus back and forth between themselves as they try to determine who has authority over him. When Jesus is brought to Herod, Herod "was very glad, for he had been wanting to see him for a long time, because he had heard about him and was hoping to see him perform some sign" (23:8). Herod does not receive a sign. He does not see or hear anything from Jesus, and at length he sends Jesus back to Pilate.

The disciples, however, have seen and heard Jesus at work. They are those to whom the Son has

It would be interesting to ask ourselves what success in ministry might justify the contemporary equivalent of this kind of language. Numbers do indeed matter, but surely there are also successes that cannot be counted. If we are honest, we might admit that we are tempted not to rejoice but to envy both measurable accomplishment and success that is incalculable.

Although success itself is not the main subject of this text but only its occasion, there are two reasons for recognizing the achievements of the mission and ministry of the disciples. For literary reasons, it is always worthwhile to name a text's context, but there is also a homiletical reason for doing so. The disciples' success sets the stage for a comparison that is at the heart of the text and may also occupy the center of a sermon. The point of the text is that there is something else more to be valued than success, even if success is so great that it can only be described in this extravagant language. "Nevertheless, do not rejoice at this, that the spirits submit to you, but rejoice that your names are written in heaven" (v. 20). The key thing is not success of any sort. It is the certainty of the relationship with God, symbolized by the metaphor of the names written in heaven. That names are written in heaven, not on earth, signifies that this relationship depends on God's choice, and it cannot be erased by any earthly power.

Jesus himself rejoices in a brief, hymnlike word of praise. The fundamental structure of biblical praise is most commonly twofold: the act of praise itself and the reason for it. That twofold structure can be seen in this text. The word of praise is short and straightforward, "I thank you . . ." The reason for Jesus' praise is lengthier and of first importance for preaching: "because you have hidden these things from the wise and the intelligent and have revealed them to infants; yes, Father, for such was your gracious will" (v. 21).

Jesus' words invite reflection in the pulpit on a core claim of Christianity: that God is known not from human striving to comprehend the Divine but because God in freedom chooses to reveal the divine self. Moreover, that self-revelation takes place through the agency of the Son. We draw near at this point to the difficult doctrine of election. The self-revelation is extended to "anyone to whom the Son chooses to reveal God" (v. 22). This choice is not capricious, however. It springs always from God's "gracious will."

Moreover, God reveals the divine self not to the intelligent and wise, the kind of people who achieve

Luke 10:17–24

Theological Perspective

Not much is said in Luke 10 about who the seventy are. If they are like the disciples sent out in Luke 9:1–2 to proclaim the kingdom with power over demons, to cure diseases, and to heal, they are not wealthy. They are not powerful, and they are not accomplished. They are not emperors or scholars. They are fishermen, tax collectors, and perhaps also servants, washwomen, and carpenters. Some will be faithful to the end, and some will not. None is especially prominent or important in and of himself or herself. The important thing is that they are empowered and sent out as emissaries on a mission of great importance. When this collection of motley characters returns—with no Caesar, commander, or scion among them—something happens that no Caesar can accomplish. Satan falls like lightning from the sky.

This is what Jesus sees. It is no ordinary view of the church's mission. It is not what everybody sees, either in Jesus' time and place or in any other, and it surely is not the finding of an empirical survey. It is an extraordinary view revealed to whomever the Son chooses. What is more, the early twenty-first century is probably a good time to point out something like this to a number of people. Especially, although not only, to ministers and laypeople in mainline churches, who do not always see spectacular results and who seem disconcerted by that. The studies indicate decline, but there may also be another view.

A second point worth emphasizing recognizes that, as important as the mission of the seventy and its successes may be, the real reason to rejoice is that "your names are written in heaven." So too the real reason for contemporary disciples to rejoice is not the consequence of anything they have done or not done. It is not even that their mission may have disproportionate results, but simply that God has claimed them for a relationship that neither falters nor fails.

DOUGLAS F. OTTATI

Pastoral Perspective

ways, God's way in the world remains inexplicable and is often the opposite of what we think God's way should be. Jesus' prayer of thanksgiving is a case in point. Jesus is grateful for the ways in which the Father has handed over to him the wisdom of God. The Son and Father know each other in a way that surpasses human comprehension. It is almost as though Luke lets us in on an interior conversation between the Son and the Father as the seventy return.

Finally, Jesus speaks again to the seventy and blesses them. Surely the seventy are deeply moved when they hear the blessing. They have experienced many things, things that must have strengthened their own faith and things that kept the good news of peace from being heard. Their journey ends as it began, with a consecration.

For women and men in the pew each Sunday morning, the story of the seventy must become their story, as the Christian community joins those continually sent out by Jesus. Like the seventy, God goes with them and gives them the gospel of peace. There will be snakes and scorpions, but there also will be people to heal and believers to baptize. The seventy return to hear a prayer of thanksgiving and blessing. What more can a congregation ask?

The future will continue to unfold in mysterious ways, and God's gracious gifts of love and peace will continue to be given. The journey ahead will include thorny issues. The ones who are sent out may risk the condemnation of friends and neighbors for a just cause. They may sacrifice material well-being for a matter of principle. At the end of the journey, they will be blessed with power and learning: a blessing not earned but given as a gracious gift by the one who sent them.

MARY MILLER BRUEGGEMANN

Exegetical Perspective

revealed the very heart of God, and so they are blessed. It is not clear why the blessing of the text is spoken privately, to the Twelve. Perhaps we are supposed to recognize a connection between this blessing and the eventual commission of the disciples at the end of Luke and the beginning of Acts. As Jesus reveals what and whom he knows, he creates witnesses.

Throughout the Gospel and Acts, Luke will maintain this characterization of the disciples as witnesses. In Luke, the risen Jesus summarizes his work and then says to the disciples, "You are witnesses of these things" (24:48). At the beginning of Acts, Jesus tells them again, "You will receive power when the Holy Spirit has come upon you; and you will be my witnesses in Jerusalem, in all Judea and Samaria, and to the ends of the earth" (Acts 1:8). Over and over, the apostles themselves describe their mission as reporting the news, that is, bearing witness to what they saw and heard in the company of Jesus during his ministry and in his resurrection (see Acts 1:22; 2:32; 3:15; 5:32; 10:39, 41).

In the resurrection especially, those who follow Jesus witness the defeat of the power of Satan and the beginning of a whole new order of things. In Luke 10, long before his resurrection and in fact just as he has begun his trip to Jerusalem, Jesus empowers the seventy to heal and preach in his name. As they fulfill that commission in the still-contested arena of human life, their work becomes a window on the great reversal that is unfolding for the whole creation in the life, death, and resurrection of Jesus.

MARY HINKLE SHORE

Homiletical Perspective

success by their own efforts, but to infants, in other words to the weak, the vulnerable, and specifically those who realize they cannot figure out God on their own. If knowing God were a matter of figuring things out, then it would make sense that the wise and intelligent would know God. Rather, it is those who are dependent on the graciousness of God, the metaphorical infants, who in their openness are the recipients of divine revelation. While it is not the point of the story, it is worth remembering that these "infants" do not achieve success on their own. Perhaps that is actually good news for churches, and preachers, who may not be enjoying the type of success that is quantifiable. In these words is a reminder that the posture necessary for success is the one open to the action and revelation of God's graciousness.

Jesus continues, "Many prophets and kings desired to see what you see, but did not see it, and to hear what you hear, but did not hear it" (v. 24). That raises the question, "So what do they hear?" Luke, in his ordering of the Gospel, reveals the answer. They will see Jesus teaching and their ears momentarily will hear him teaching the parable of the Good Samaritan. Can anyone be more blessed than one who hears the wisdom of God hidden in a parable? Here is the really good news. We too can "hear" anew what God is saying to us through Jesus in this parable. What is organizational success compared to the blessing of hearing the gospel? Perhaps, if people hear the gospel in Jesus' parable, and believe, and live by what they have believed, Satan may once again fall from the sky like a flash of lightning.

STEPHEN FARRIS

Luke 10:25–37

²⁵Just then a lawyer stood up to test Jesus. "Teacher," he said, "what must I do to inherit eternal life?" ²⁶He said to him, "What is written in the law? What do you read there?" ²⁷He answered, "You shall love the Lord your God with all your heart, and with all your soul, and with all your strength, and with all your mind; and your neighbor as yourself." ²⁸And he said to him, "You have given the right answer; do this, and you will live."

²⁹But wanting to justify himself, he asked Jesus, "And who is my neighbor?" ³⁰Jesus replied, "A man was going down from Jerusalem to Jericho, and fell into the hands of robbers, who stripped him, beat him, and went away, leaving him half dead. ³¹Now by chance a priest was going down that road; and when he

Theological Perspective

The parable of the Good Samaritan is found in Luke alone, as is the parable of the Prodigal. Both contribute to an emphasis on mercy that lends Luke "a distinctive tone" and picture of Jesus.[1] The parable in Luke 10 is a didactic story that presents a Samaritan as a moral example. The writer of Luke may well have composed the lawyer's (second) question in verse 29 to join two originally separate texts—the exchange between the lawyer and Jesus in verses 25–28 and the story of the Samaritan in verses 30–37a. Jesus' concluding remark in verse 37b might then also be Luke's addition. If so, the history of redaction explains why the story does not really answer the question, "And who is my neighbor?" (v. 29). Theologically speaking, there is no reason why the substance of verses 25–28 (a summary of the law) cannot stand alone, apart from the story of the Samaritan, as it does in Matthew 22:34–40 and Mark 12:28–34. Even so, the text as it appears in Luke deserves careful and precise attention, not only because it is quite powerful, but also because, due to its fame and popularity, many people who think they know what it says do not.

A lawyer tries to *test* Jesus by asking an initial question. This elicits Jesus' question about the law,

1. Joseph Fitzmyer, SJ, *The Gospel according to Luke (X–XXIV)* (Garden City, NY: Doubleday, 1985), 882–83.

Pastoral Perspective

If there is one story in the New Testament that is familiar to everyone, it is probably this parable of the Good Samaritan. Most know the bare bones of the story. Jesus told the parable in response to a lawyer's question: "who is my neighbor?" (v. 29). In good rabbinic fashion, the answer was given in the form of a parable.

Many children have acted out this story in church school. It can even be performed without a word being spoken. The drama of the story allows the children to enter into the narrative with great imagination. There are five characters: the three travelers along the road from Jericho to Jerusalem, the wounded man, and the innkeeper. Every child can take a turn acting out one of the persons in the play. Because they can imagine themselves into each character, a good discussion about who is my neighbor often ensues. While a teacher might pursue with adults the deeper meanings about Samaritans and who they were or what kind of priest this was or what Levite means, children quickly understand what it means to be passed by. Already they know about people who are "in" on their playground and those who are "out." The term "good Samaritan" is now in the public domain. People know the difference it can make to have a "Good Samaritan law" in the community so that someone who tries

saw him, he passed by on the other side. ³²So likewise a Levite, when he came to the place and saw him, passed by on the other side. ³³But a Samaritan while traveling came near him; and when he saw him, he was moved with pity. ³⁴He went to him and bandaged his wounds, having poured oil and wine on them. Then he put him on his own animal, brought him to an inn, and took care of him. ³⁵The next day he took out two denarii, gave them to the innkeeper, and said, 'Take care of him; and when I come back, I will repay you whatever more you spend.' ³⁶Which of these three, do you think, was a neighbor to the man who fell into the hands of the robbers?" ³⁷He said, "The one who showed him mercy." Jesus said to him, "Go and do likewise."

Exegetical Perspective

The parable of the Good Samaritan is set within a conflict narrative. The conflict form includes a protagonist, an antagonist, and a test or question that the antagonist hopes will be the protagonist's undoing. In this version, a lawyer puts a question to Jesus, "What must I do to inherit eternal life?" (v. 25). To answer the question, Jesus goes where the lawyer would surely go as well: to the Law. Jesus asks the lawyer what he reads in the texts that constitute his life's work.

The lawyer is ready: "Love the Lord your God with all your heart, and with all your soul, and with all your strength," he begins. He has just quoted the Shema, Deuteronomy 6:4–9. It begins, "Hear, O Israel: The LORD is our God, the LORD alone." In Deuteronomy, following the words that the lawyer quotes are instructions that counsel the faithful to keep these words in their hearts and bind them to their doorposts. Love for God with heart, soul, mind, and strength is the way to life.

The lawyer might have stopped there but, to his credit, he goes on. He adds a verse from Leviticus too: "You shall love your neighbor as yourself" (Lev. 19:18). Jesus commends his conversation partner, "Do this, and you will live" (v. 28b).

Luke's reference to the encounter as a test and to the lawyer's attempt to justify himself lets readers

Homiletical Perspective

The problem with preaching this text is that it is so familiar to many listeners. We ought not to overstate the familiarity, however. In this age, there may be many who have never heard the story. Some of them may even make their way into church on any given Sunday. For now, consider the longtime churchgoers who will populate the pews regularly. These folk have heard sermon after sermon on this favored text, and long before they listened to sermons, they were taught this parable in Sunday school.

Is such familiarity actually a problem? The homiletical advantage of the text may also be precisely that it so familiar, not only in Scripture but in human experience. It is likely that, when the parable is read, a personal story comes to the mind of the preacher as well as the listeners.

One winter Sunday I was scheduled to preach at a church where I was filling in for a few months. It was a cold, icy morning and I did not leave quite enough time for a comfortable journey to my destination. Near my home there was an intersection, six lanes by four, very much exposed to the conditions of the weather. Murphy's Law ensures that when we are in a hurry, all the lights turn red. An older gentleman, limping noticeably on his cane, began to cross the intersection in front of me late in the light's cycle. The light turned orange for him as he neared the

Theological Perspective

to which the lawyer replies correctly with the classic summary: love of God and neighbor. Then the lawyer, "wanting to *justify* himself," asks another question, "And who is my neighbor?" (v. 29). He is being purposefully contentious, implying that the summary of the law is really too general, too nonspecific to be helpful. It is in response to this question that Jesus tells the story.

Jesus says a man traveling the road from Jerusalem to Jericho is robbed, stripped, beaten, and left half dead. Nothing is mentioned about the man's ethnicity, and this likely means that he is a Jew. The road—as Martin Luther King Jr. liked to note—is very steep, dropping almost 1,500 feet. It is hard to see around a bend, and so it is a good place to get robbed. Now a priest and a Levite, Jews of high religious and moral standing, go down the road, see the man, but pass by on the other side. We are not told why. They may have been encouraged by ritual codes not to touch dead bodies, but is it all that difficult to distinguish between dead and almost dead?

Things take a decisive turn with the words "But a Samaritan . . ." Jews despised Samaritans as untrustworthy heretics, and the feeling was mutual, as can be seen from the refusal of a Samaritan village to receive Jesus in Luke 9:51–55. The Samaritan bandages the man's wounds, brings him to an inn, and makes arrangements for him to be cared for. Jesus then asks the lawyer, "Which of these three, do you think, was a neighbor to the man who fell into the hands of the robbers?"(v. 36). The lawyer has little choice but to answer, "The one who showed him mercy" (v. 37)—though it is possible that he may also be trying to avoid having to say it was a Samaritan.

The story accords with Luke's universalism. In Luke, Jesus eats and drinks with all the wrong people (5:27–39), teaches people to be merciful and love enemies, expecting nothing in return (6:27–36), and tells the classic parable of free forgiveness (15:11–32). Moreover, Luke–Acts narrates a mission to the entire world that ends with Paul in Rome (Acts 28:31).[2] Here a *Samaritan*, rather than two respected Jews, becomes an exemplary embodiment of the law, the one who recognizes that the neighbor is anyone in need. Thus John Calvin comments, "Christ might simply have told him [the lawyer] that the word neighbor applies indiscriminately to any man, for the whole human race is linked in a holy bond of brotherhood. . . . It would have been a clearer command

2. See also the theological perspective on Luke 10:17–24 in this volume.

Pastoral Perspective

to help another in need cannot be sued—at least theoretically!

Congregations never tire of hearing sermons on this text or studying it in a Bible study group. The story itself is layered with meaning, as are the experiences people bring to bear on it as they reflect, year after year, on the text.

The scholar of the Law, who already knew the answer to his query, asked Jesus a key question: what must I do to inherit eternal life? Jesus knew that a lawyer, well versed in the Mosaic Law, would know the answer. So he said: You tell me! Of course, the lawyer did know the answer. He quoted both Deuteronomy and Leviticus: love God and neighbor. His statement is at the very heart of our understanding of Christian discipleship. The answer is found in the Old Testament as well as in the New Testament. However, the answer did not satisfy the lawyer. The text says the lawyer asked the question wanting to "justify" himself. Did he want to be sure that he had kept the law, in order to inherit "eternal life," or was he testing Jesus? Was he concerned that Jesus was a good rabbi, or was he really concerned about his own salvation? Either way, the answer to the lawyer's question came in the form of the parable Christians know so well.

Who is my neighbor? is a central question in the church and in congregations today. It is a question that is asked in the conversations around immigration policy in the United States. It is a question that relates to the way we treat "the other," whether a homeless person who has not had a bath in months or someone of a different social class. Who is my neighbor? often raises issues of race or sexual identity. It is a question pondered in interreligious and ecumenical relationships. In the political sphere, especially during an election year, it centers on party affiliations: may a Republican and a Democrat act as neighbors toward each other? Is there any category of person who is not neighbor to another?

Jesus did not preach about that or lecture the lawyer. He told a story. He told the story to a religious leader who was sure he knew the law. It is a story for one who thinks he has life all figured out. The story leaves us wondering why the priest or Levite did not stop to care for the wounded man. They looked and then moved to the other side of the road. Was it concern for ritual purity? Could that be why the priest and Levite would not see the wounded man as someone to care for? Yet the Samaritans, who were perceived as second-class citizens, also had laws about ritual purity.

know that the goal of the interaction, from the lawyer's perspective, is more likely to discredit Jesus as a teacher than to discern the way of eternal life. The verb "to justify" is rare in the Gospels and Acts. Perhaps the lawyer wants to justify his own definition of who is a neighbor and who is beyond the responsibility implied by the term. The lawyer may want only to justify himself as a challenger to Jesus, lest those listening in conclude that his first question for Jesus was too easy. While the way of life for God's people may be clear enough—love God, love your neighbor—the finer points require sharp legal minds. "Who is my neighbor?"

By way of response, Jesus tells the parable of the Good Samaritan. Preachers often spend a lot of time explaining why the priest and Levite would behave in such a detached way toward someone who was suffering. Were the two frightened that the man in the ditch was a decoy? Were they seeking perhaps to avoid interacting with the man's blood or to avoid incurring corpse impurity if the man were dead? Readers of the parable may speculate about why religious leaders would choose to pass by someone who needed their help, but in fact Jesus offers no answer to the question at all.

Jesus does, however, report why the Samaritan stopped: "he was moved with pity" (v. 33). In the New Testament, the verb *splanchnizomai* is used to refer to three characters in parables: the father of the prodigal son (15:20), the master who forgives a servant an astronomical debt (Matt. 18:27), and the Samaritan. The other nine New Testament occurrences of the verb all have Jesus as their subject. In every case, to feel such compassion is to be moved to extraordinary action. The Samaritan's actions constitute a multifaceted response to the wounded man. He ministers to his wounds on site, transports him to safety, attends to him further, and finally provides funds for the care he will need during his ongoing convalescence.

The storyteller takes his time with this summary of the Samaritan's response. As a way of illustrating where the center of gravity lies within the story, consider which actors are related to the nearly thirty verb forms in the parable. The victim of the mugging is the subject of two verbs. The robbers are the subject of four verbs. The priest and Levite are the subject of three verbs each, enough to walk along the road, see the man, and pass by. The innkeeper is the subject of two verbs. The Samaritan is the subject of fifteen verbs.

The lawyer had wanted to know, "Who is my neighbor?" The question seeks definition. Where are

opposite sidewalk, so he quickened his pace. In his hurry he planted his cane on a patch of ice and fell heavily to the ground.

Everything else I am now about to tell you about the incident happened in the moment of time that it took me to put the transmission into "park" and reach for the door handle. I thought, "Oh no, he may be hurt. I will have to stop and see if he is all right. I may even have to take him to the emergency room." We all know how long people have to wait in an emergency room these days. "I will be terribly late for church. I might not even make it at all." I could picture the ushers checking their watches; the organist playing the prelude for the third time; the elders, heads together, drawing straws to determine who would be stuck conducting the service in my absence. I could hear them whispering, "He has never been this late before!"

Just then, however, I heard a mental voice whisper just one phrase from a story I knew well. I was first told the story as a small child, and over the years it has been repeated to me many times: "He passed by on the other side" (vv. 31, 32).

With stories we know, an allusion is enough to bring the rest of the story to mind. The stories we know well are likely to be the stories that shape our lives. Because I had heard that story so many times, from Bible stories read by my mother, from Sunday school lessons, from sermon after sermon, I am the person I am. I could not "pass by on the other side."

I also recognized in that moment something far more important; this story would also come to the mind of the people in that congregation. It also had shaped who they were. If I phoned from the emergency room and explained the situation, they would understand immediately. The organist would begin a hymnsing. The elders would choose someone to pray, someone else to read the lessons, and perhaps even to reflect on them. No one would say, "He ought to have passed by on the other side." They were the kind of people who knew the story of the Good Samaritan and let it shape their actions and attitudes. They could not expect their Sunday preacher to pass by on the other side and still be the people they were. People who know this story are called a "church."

Before I had fully opened the door on that cold and icy morning, the old gentleman staggered to his feet. He glared at me, as if daring me to take notice of his tumble, and stumped away. I drove on and even made it to church on time. As I drove through the falling snow, I thought about how the people

Luke 10:25–37

Theological Perspective

if it had run, Thou shalt love every man as thyself." However, says Calvin, the story has the virtue of forcing the lawyer to admit "that our neighbor is the man most foreign to us, for God has bound all men together for mutual aid."[3]

Nevertheless, there is also a sense in which the lawyer's second query ("And who is my neighbor?") remains the Great Unanswered Question of the New Testament. What Jesus finally asks in verse 36—the question that Calvin says forces the lawyer's admission—is not, "Which person in the story is your neighbor?" but "Which of the three proved to be a neighbor to the man who fell into the hands of the robbers?" The answer is that a Samaritan despised by priests, Levites, and the lawyer himself, proved to be neighbor. Moreover, he proves himself a neighbor by crossing a barrier of hatred and prejudice in order to be merciful to someone who, in all probability, also despises Samaritans.

Should we say that the Samaritan proves to be neighbor by acting on his recognition of the man in need as his neighbor? One might also raise the question of how he might prove to be a neighbor had he arrived earlier, while the robbers were beating their victim.

In any case, an uncluttered way to look at the entire episode indicates that rather than being told who his neighbor is, the lawyer is shown how to be a neighbor or how to "prove neighbor." Centuries later, in other circumstances where hatreds and barriers may divide people and communities, Jesus says again, as he does to the lawyer so many years ago, "Go and do likewise." With minimal commentary the passage almost preaches itself.

DOUGLAS F. OTTATI

Pastoral Perspective

Something more is at play here. The surprise comes when it is the Samaritan who comes to the aid of the hurt man. There was the long and deep animosity between the Samaritans and the Jews. How could the Samaritan be the one who knew about neighborliness? What an amazing turn in the plot! A lot of details are given about what the Samaritan did. He bound up the wounds, put the wounded man on his donkey, took him to the innkeeper, paid two days' worth of care, and promised to come back and pay any unpaid bills.

The story stops abruptly after those details are given. Then Jesus turned to the lawyer and asked, "Which of these three, do you think, was a neighbor to the man who fell into the hands of the robbers?" (v. 36). The short answer was given by the lawyer himself: "It is the one who showed mercy." No long lecture about details concerning ritual purity. Giving mercy or compassion to the one in need is the definition of "neighbor." What a simple answer! It changes the whole worldview of the lawyer. Mercy does not ask first about color or sexual identity or economic status or political party. Mercy is not concerned with deserving or purity or piety. Mercy is what comes from God to the community and to each of us. It is a gift given.

The lawyer had asked about how to inherit eternal life. That question was completely turned on its head. There was nothing the lawyer could do to inherit or to earn eternal life. It was not possible. It only came by grace from God.

One can almost hear Jesus saying to the lawyer, who was wise and articulate and knew the Torah, "Get your mind off yourself and go and show compassion to your neighbor." Who is your neighbor? The person you see in need of human compassion.

MARY MILLER BRUEGGEMANN

---

3. John Calvin, *A Harmony of the Gospels Matthew, Mark, and Luke, Vol. III, and The Epistles of James and Jude*, trans. A. W. Morrison (Grand Rapids: Eerdmans, 1975), 37–38.

the limits of one's legal responsibility to love another as oneself? Is "neighbor" a geographical term? Is it an ethnic or tribal term? To answer the question of limits is also necessarily to comment on who exists beyond the definition. Maybe that is why Jesus does not answer the question asked by the lawyer. In the parable Jesus tells, he defines "neighbor" not as someone worthy to *receive* love but as someone able to *offer* it. Jesus leads the lawyer to the conclusion that neighbors are those who act in love toward others.

The message of the parable is not, "We have to help those poor people in the ditch, even though it is potentially dangerous and costly to us." The message is not, "Followers of Jesus have to help those poor people in the ditch because Jesus pushes out the lines that define 'neighbor' farther than they were before." We recall that the theme of the encounter between Jesus and the lawyer is, "What must I do to inherit eternal life?" The conflict story begins with this question about eternal life, and it closes with Jesus' command, "Do this, and you will live."

What is the way of life that leads to eternal life? In response to that question, the message of the Good Samaritan leads readers to the conclusion that one must help because helping is the way of life—not only for the one needing help, but also for those offering it. All are in this together. "Neighbor" is a communal category. The priest and the Levite, for all their experience in religious community, did not know how to recognize their bond with the man in the ditch, but the Samaritan did. He knew that *life*— not just for the needy one but for everyone, and not just for the moment but for eternity—requires being and having neighbors.

MARY HINKLE SHORE

in the pews had heard this parable time and again, until they too knew it so well that even a phrase would bring the whole story to mind and shape who they were. So I told the parable that day, explaining what needed to be explained, which in truth was not much, except to say how a Samaritan was viewed by Jesus' audience, for example. Some months later the new minister arrived, and the congregation bid me farewell. "We will never forget the sermon you preached on the Good Samaritan." It was not much of a sermon. It was just the story.

Parables are too rich and complex to be reduced to one point, but not so with my little tale. Trust the story. In our society the stories we know so well that even a phrase reminds us of the whole are mostly drawn from the movies or TV. Do we want the coming generation to be shaped by those movies, or by the Good Samaritan? If the latter, we ought to be bold in telling the story. In many ways, we are like children who do not ask for new stories. They say, "Tell us the one about . . ." We never really outgrow that tendency.

It is worth remembering, moreover, there will be some in the congregation who are new to the faith and do not know this story. Is there any better way of showing them what it means to be a disciple of Jesus Christ than to tell them this story? If they hear it often enough, they might just stop the next time someone slips on the ice.

STEPHEN FARRIS

Luke 10:38–42

³⁸Now as they went on their way, he entered a certain village, where a woman named Martha welcomed him into her home. ³⁹She had a sister named Mary, who sat at the Lord's feet and listened to what he was saying. ⁴⁰But Martha was distracted by her many tasks; so she came to him and asked, "Lord, do you not care that my sister has left me to do all the work by myself? Tell her then to help me." ⁴¹But the Lord answered her, "Martha, Martha, you are worried and distracted by many things; ⁴²there is need of only one thing. Mary has chosen the better part, which will not be taken away from her."

Theological Perspective

There is a somewhat similar story involving Martha and Mary in John 12:1–7 and another in Mark 14:3–9 that shares some characteristics with John 12; this passage in Luke is quite different from both and should not be conflated with either. The stories in John and in Mark are both set shortly after we learn of the plot to kill Jesus and before his entry into Jerusalem.

In John, Jesus and his entourage arrive at the home of Lazarus in Bethany less than a week before the fateful Passover. Martha serves dinner, but Mary anoints Jesus' feet with costly perfume and wipes them with her hair. When Judas asks why the perfume was not sold and the proceeds given to the poor, the narrator informs us that he is being disingenuous because he is in the practice of stealing money from the common purse for himself. Jesus responds that Mary bought the perfume for the day of his burial and that the poor are always with you but he will not be. Immediately following the episode, there is a plot to kill Lazarus (John 12:9–11), and then Jesus promptly enters Jerusalem (John 12:12). The focus here is clearly on Mary's extravagant gesture that appropriately honors Jesus and anticipates his sacrifice. Judas's point, no doubt defensible in other circumstances, is undercut by his subterfuge, and the contrast between Martha's

Pastoral Perspective

Imagine that you have just come from the kitchen of Covenant Church in time for morning worship. On the second Sunday of each month, after worship the congregation always gathers for brunch. You are a little flustered because the three other members who were supposed to help with the brunch did not show up, and you have been left by yourself to prepare the food. Then you hear a sermon about Jesus saying to Martha: you are "worried and distracted" by your many tasks (v. 41). Like Martha, you had wondered about those on the committee who did not show up to help in the kitchen.

Now you do feel distracted and worried as you sit in the pew, but you still try to listen to the story with an open mind. Mary is sitting at Jesus' feet, which is what a disciple would have done. Martha is caring for the visitor who shows up unexpectedly, and she wonders out loud why her sister is not helping. Jesus rebukes her. Nothing seems equal here. Even though Luke's Gospel has more stories about women than the other Gospels do, everything is a bit topsy-turvy. From the perspective of those who do all of the work, on a Sunday morning this story can be heard as a story that belittles their contributions. Surely that is not what this story is about!

This story about Mary and Martha is familiar to many congregations, especially if they have a

Exegetical Perspective

The center of the Gospel of Luke is a travelogue. In chapter 9, with resolve and determination Jesus sets his face to go to Jerusalem. The language makes it sound as if Jerusalem and the events that will happen there may be only a few days away and that Jesus is approaching them with focus and singleness of mind. Jesus "sets his face toward Jerusalem" in chapter 9 and arrives there in chapter 19. Ten chapters of a twenty-four-chapter book are set on the road. At the beginning of chapter 10, Jesus sends out seventy in advance to announce the kingdom of God. There is urgency about their work. He sends them out in groups of two with practically nothing—no bag, no purse, no sandals—making them dependent on the people they would meet. The seventy have important work to do, like preaching and healing.

In the encounter with a lawyer who has a question about eternal life, Jesus tells the story of a man who needed help, and a Samaritan who worked self-lessly on his behalf. "Go and do likewise," Jesus says to the lawyer.

Readers of the Gospel are primed to expect another story about requirements for followers of Jesus, and Martha does ask for help with service. Her work is *diakonia*. The Greek word means "service," with a similar range of meaning as the English word. It can mean the service one provides when showing

Homiletical Perspective

This text will probably provoke what a friend calls a "yabbut." There are things said in texts or sermons that are likely to make at least some listeners say inwardly, "Yeah, but . . ." A prudent preacher fore-sees "yabbuts" and will often choose to face them head-on.

This text may be short in length, but it is certainly not lacking in "yabbuts" or, to put it another way, in homiletical pitfalls. The first is quite simply that there is many a Martha in most of our churches. Moreover, Martha recognizes herself in the story and may respond with emotions ranging from hurt to outright anger. She may be so angry that the preacher may not even receive the preliminary "yeah" from Martha. Martha is very frequently the heart of the church. She thinks the organization would fall apart without her—and she is prob-ably right. She has been left far too often "to do all the work," a complaint in the text she will surely recognize.

The first homiletical challenge, then, is to preach the text without causing Martha such offense that she will not listen to the rest of the sermon. By the way, not every contemporary Martha is female, although the odds are good that she is. Inasmuch as Mary is engaged in the traditional female role of providing hospitality, some Marthas may even

Luke 10:38–42

Theological Perspective

service and Mary's actions gets pushed into the background.

In Mark, Jesus is in Bethany, sitting at table in the house of Simon the leper. An unnamed woman breaks a jar and pours costly ointment onto Jesus' head. Some ask in anger why the ointment was wasted rather than sold and the money given to the poor. Jesus says that the poor are always with you and that therefore you can show them kindness whenever you wish, but you will not always have him. The woman "has done what she could; she has anointed my body beforehand for its burial" (Mark 14:8). Here the point about helping the poor is not undercut by being placed on Judas's lips, as it is in John 12, but, as Jesus' execution nears, it is nonetheless rejected. The focus once again is on an extravagant act that is appropriate to the (impending) occasion.

In Luke 10, Jesus and his companions are on the way to Jerusalem, but their entry into the city and Jesus' crucifixion are considerably further off (19:28–40), as is the plot to kill him (22:1–5). They enter an unnamed village, and Martha welcomes them into her home. She then goes about household tasks in order to receive them. Her sister Mary, however, sits at Jesus' feet and listens to what he is saying. Then Martha, "distracted by her many tasks," comes to Jesus to ask him whether he is not concerned that her sister has left her to do all the work: "Tell her then to help me" (v. 40). Jesus answers, "Martha, Martha, you are worried and distracted by many things; there is need of only one thing. Mary has chosen the better part, which will not be taken away from her" (vv. 41–42). Thus, here in Luke there is a direct contrast between the actions of Mary and Martha and possibly a gentle rebuke indicated in the repetition of Martha's name. There is *no* discussion of whether expensive ointment should be sold and the money given to the poor, nor is Mary's contested act an act of extravagant anointing; she simply sits and listens to Jesus' teaching.

Some medieval theologians claim the story in Luke commends a contemplative rather than an active life. John Calvin rejects this idea; so does the contemporary Roman Catholic scholar Joseph Fitzmyer. Calvin says the simple sense of the passage is that Mary took her place at Jesus' feet in order to hear his message. This does not mean she did this "the whole of her life," and in fact, anyone "who wishes to advance in Christ's school" should both listen and act. "There is a time for hearing and

Pastoral Perspective

women's group that has retreats. It would be inaccurate to believe that these verses tell all there is about the work and spirituality of women. The role of women in church and society has changed dramatically in the ensuing centuries. In Jesus' time women were considered second-class citizens, because men were the landowners, and they were the ones counted in the census that was taken by the ruling authorities. Women were not counted and did not count. Therefore this story needs to be investigated from the perspective of the author of Luke's Gospel in light of the characteristics of the times. Such an approach may provide insight into the significance of the good news for both Mary and Martha.

This story is about the daily comings and goings in a home. It is about the ordinariness of life. Something about this domestic experience must have been important to the early church for Luke to have included it in his Gospel. What would have been surprising about this event to early Christians? Certainly Luke's audience would have been surprised to imagine Mary sitting as a disciple learning from Jesus. It would also be a bit shocking to hear Jesus speak to Martha about being too distracted and too anxious. What response would the early church have had to Jesus' rebuke of Martha? Would they have felt as uncomfortable listening to this story as the generous volunteers who work in the kitchens of our congregations today?

Perhaps this story is saying less about women and more about the dangers of being so distracted by our doing that we miss hearing God's Word. In the church, often more time is spent in committee meetings than finding time to sit and listen to what God might be saying. Is this story about too much organization in the church today? Is there so much distraction in our contemporary lives that people find it impossible to sit and listen for the Holy Spirit to speak? Is the church worrying about an old furnace that may not make it through the winter, rather than being open to the surprises that await God's people in the biblical text?

In many ways the church has adopted the norm of a culture that values productivity and busyness over reflection and listening. There are times in our personal lives and in the church's life when we need to rebalance. In this text Jesus says that learning and listening are as important as all the chores we do to make the home and the church a working unit. Perhaps this story can be told to counter the tendency of the church to rush around in circles. While there are basic matters that need doing on this planet earth

hospitality, or the service offered when working on a task.

An injustice is done to these two women when interpreters reduce the story to a spat about who will get dinner on the table. Mary and Martha could be one of those groups of two sent out in Luke 10:1. Whatever the precise nature of the *diakonia* she is performing, Martha feels abandoned to service that is supposed to be shared, and so she says to Jesus, "Don't you care that my sister has left me to do all the work by myself? Tell her to help me!"

Anyone who has ever had a job where they had to take up the slack left by someone else's questionable work ethic understands Martha. Anyone who has ever been the only one on a team actually following instructions or completing a group project alone understands Martha. Martha is just the sort of person Jesus prayed for a few verses earlier when he said, "The harvest is plentiful, but the laborers are few. Therefore, ask the Lord of the harvest to send out laborers into his harvest" (10:2). Martha is not afraid of hard labor; she just wants some help with it.

Yet Jesus is not so eager to help Martha; at least he is not eager to tell Mary to help Martha. Instead, Jesus tells Martha that she is anxious and distracted, worried about "many things," while there is need of only one thing. Mary emerges from this story as the star pupil while Martha, the only one in the story who seems to be concerned about service, gets what is almost a rebuke from Jesus for all her trouble.

The story has long driven a wedge between thinkers and doers, and between "spiritual" types and "practical" types, as if all—especially women—have to choose one over the other, and it has fostered resentment on the part of hardworking church women.

The text annoys and confuses readers. It is not clear what Jesus means when he speaks of there being a need of only one thing, and of Mary having chosen the better part. Luke says that Mary is listening to the word of Jesus, so some people conclude that the only thing all need to do is to listen to God's Word. It is true that "hearing" or "listening to" the Word of Jesus is important in the Gospels. Yet everywhere that Jesus talks about it, he actually speaks of hearing and doing the Word, or about people hearing his words and acting on them (6:47; 8:21; 11:28). Hearing is necessary, but it is not sufficient to describe the life of faith.

For Jesus, the one thing needed is to connect with the person in front of him, whether that person is a sister who is listening to his word, or one who is

experience the sermon as an attack on the value of "women's work" as such. Surely no preacher will want to give so harsh an impression.

For all these reasons, it is probably best to face the issue head-on and acknowledge the problem. Martha is, after all, a good woman and an important figure in the Gospels. In the Gospel of John, for example, she responds to Jesus with the confession of faith (John 11:27) that moves the narrative forward to the cross, the equivalent of Peter's confession in the Synoptic Gospels. Moreover, she is carrying out the duties her society, and often ours, asks of her as a woman. The contemporary Martha is very likely a genuinely good person too. She does what she does because she loves the church, she loves Jesus, and besides, if she does not do it, who will? Drawing an imaginative picture of a real Martha, with details safely different from the Martha in front of us, is probably a good tactic here. Some gentle humor aimed at Mary, and for that matter the male disciples and their contemporary analogues, who have left Martha to cope with hostess duties alone, might be useful. The first pitfall to avoid is unnecessarily offending Martha. The prudent preacher will attempt to steer around it.

The second pitfall, however, is to excuse Martha. It would be possible to suggest that there are times to be in the service of others and times for quiet contemplation. Martha has her priorities wrong, we might proclaim, nothing more. That might be true if she did not also try to draw her sister away from Jesus. Mary is described as "sitting at the feet" of Jesus. This is not because the disciples have occupied the couch and all the chairs. "Sitting at the feet" is the posture of the disciple, learning from the Master (see Luke 8:35; Acts 22:3). Nothing—not a sister, not cultural expectations, not women's duties or anything else—may be used to draw a disciple away from Jesus.

The text is very specific here. It does not speak about meditation, about periods of stillness, yoga classes, walks in the woods, or "time for myself." Valuable as these doubtless are, they are not the one needful thing. The text does not speak about spiritual exercises in general, nor can Mary's position be likened to spiritual exercises that are endorsed by contemporary culture. It speaks about sitting at the feet of Jesus, that is, *acting as his disciple*. This is the one thing that must not be taken away from any person. Martha may not do that to her sister.

Jesus defends Mary's right to depart from the cultural expectations of her day and to engage in

Luke 10:38–42

Theological Perspective

a time for doing."[1] Fitzmyer says that "the episode is addressed to the Christian who is expected to be *contemplativus(a) in actione*."[2]

In any case, if Jesus does not sharply rebuke Martha, his response to her question encourages us to conclude that Martha is inappropriately preoccupied by her many works of hospitality. There is, on this occasion at least, something more important to be done and, indeed, Mary is doing the one thing needful. As Fitzmyer puts it, "priority is given to the hearing of the word coming from God's messenger over preoccupation with all other concerns."[3] We may also note that the story depicts a woman as Jesus' attentive disciple. In fact, Jesus encourages Mary to continue listening to him, even though this means not helping with what, at this time and place, is regarded especially as women's work.

Theologically speaking, a conclusion one might draw is that no one should be kept from learning Jesus' message about God and God's purposes. Another is that genuine faithfulness is not a matter of service alone. Instead, service should be informed by the hearing of Jesus' message. Perhaps it is even appropriate to say that ethics and moral witness need to be informed by theology. This claim is not to downgrade the importance of practice—as both the Epistle of James and more recent liberation theologians remind us. Rather, it is to insist that genuine practice is always intertwined with a theological appropriation of Jesus' message. In Luke, this is a message of grace, mercy, and reconciliation, or of a kingdom that reaches out to all (the poor, lepers, tax collectors, sinners, Jews, Samaritans, Gentiles, and more) and so puts Jesus on a collision course with a number of authorities.

DOUGLAS F. OTTATI

Pastoral Perspective

(and women do the majority of that basic work), the "listening and learning" moments get lost in the shuffle. If this simple text of Mary and Martha hosting Jesus can be read in this way, then it might create an occasion for self-examination, rather than be heard as a text that rebukes the one who is working in the kitchen.

Still, this movement away from "rushing and doing" and toward "listening and learning," both in families and in the church, may seem far away from the text of Mary and Martha. Remember that the story takes place with Jesus on the way to Jerusalem. There is work ahead that will require those following Jesus to face the harsh realities of this earthly world with the confidence and courage of those who trust that God is with them. Jesus himself will need this confidence and courage in order to face what is to come. In every age, individuals and the whole church must continually sit at the feet of God's Word in Scripture, lest the church forget the substance of the faith it has been sent into the world to proclaim.

In the end, Luke's story is not about paying attention to the moment, nor is it about the just division of household chores. It is about paying attention to God's Word. Mary chooses to sit at Jesus' feet and listen to the Word of God that Jesus is and that he is speaking to her. The church's confession would be that, in him, God has come near and is addressing her. Likewise the church's witness is that God has come near and is addressing those who would follow Jesus here and now in the Word written and proclaimed and acted out at the font and around the table. In the presence of God's Word, one thing is needed: our attention.

MARY MILLER BRUEGGEMANN

1. John Calvin, *A Harmony of the Gospels Matthew, Mark, and Luke, Vol. III, and the Epistles of James and Jude*, trans. A. W. Morrison (Grand Rapids: Eerdmans, 1975), 89.
2. Joseph Fitzmyer, SJ, *The Gospel according to Luke (X–XXIV)* (Garden City, NY: Doubleday, 1985), 892–93.
3. Fitzmyer, *Luke*, 892.

anxious and concerned about many things; whether that person is a lawyer trying to learn what the word "neighbor" means, or a tax collector so short he has to climb up a tree to see a traveling teacher, or a thief enduring the sentence of death by crucifixion. He loves each of these people and does not move on past them until they have what they need to love him back.

For Jesus, Martha is not a problem. She is someone whom Jesus loves very much (John 11:5). Maybe Jesus is not siding with Mary over Martha as much as he is giving Martha a chance to notice that the world spins just fine, even without either sister—or both of them together—pushing it.

All the Gospels talk about the big love that God has for the world, a love so big that it propels Jesus to Jerusalem, a love so big that it moves him to lay down his life for friends and enemies alike. Yet what kind of "big love" would it actually be if the one demonstrating it had been so focused on a grand loving gesture in Jerusalem that he failed to notice anyone along the way? One might compare someone who loved like that to a hostess so anxious about serving her guests that she finally had no time to spend with them.

On the way to Jerusalem, Jesus spends an afternoon with Mary and Martha. His visit is a testimony to a love that is specific enough to embrace one person at a time, and great enough to embrace both of these sisters, and all other servants, through the centuries.

MARY HINKLE SHORE

a behavior that was normally reserved for males, that is, acting as a disciple. It is worth celebrating this freedom. This must be done, however, without demeaning the Judaism of Jesus' day, which expected a rabbi's disciples to be male. To do so would verge on anti-Judaism and also constitute hypocrisy. Do our own denominations, in the present day, always truly honor the full discipleship of women? Do we still attempt to call "Mary" back to traditional roles only? We may certainly celebrate Jesus' affirmation of women, while keeping the cultural and religious contexts of the time in mind. The preacher may need to acknowledge that the source of the "many tasks" that distract a contemporary Martha, female or male, may well be the organizational needs of the congregation. However, in the midst of the daily business, it is important for the church not to lose sight of Jesus.

In this regard, the text should speak to the preacher before it speaks to the congregation. How often, for example, when clergy get together, do they not talk about God, or even seriously discuss theology? Instead, those of us who are ministers tend to talk "church": who is going to which vacant church, the latest turn of denominational politics, the general business and busyness of church activities—so much so that we forget to listen to Jesus. Martha often wears a clerical collar. This problem is not, of course, confined to the clergy. Many church members experience what might be called "the Martha syndrome." So many burdens are laid on them that they may lash out even at the ones they love.

The text, in the end, is not about Mary. She is fine, now that Jesus has defended her. It is about the potential liberation of Martha. Jesus loves Martha also and wants to give her the peace that is always one of the gifts of discipleship.

STEPHEN FARRIS

Luke 11:1–13

¹He was praying in a certain place, and after he had finished, one of his disciples said to him, "Lord, teach us to pray, as John taught his disciples." ²He said to them, "When you pray, say:

Father, hallowed be your name.
   Your kingdom come.
³   Give us each day our daily bread.
⁴   And forgive us our sins,
      for we ourselves forgive everyone indebted to us.
      And do not bring us to the time of trial."

⁵And he said to them, "Suppose one of you has a friend, and you go to him at midnight and say to him, 'Friend, lend me three loaves of bread; ⁶for a friend of mine has arrived, and I have nothing to set before him.' ⁷And he answers from

Theological Perspective

When the disciples ask, "Lord, teach us to pray" (v. 1), Jesus replies with an abbreviated version of the Lord's Prayer, a parable of the Friend at Midnight, and a series of sayings. What view of prayer emerges from this assemblage of texts?

The prayer, short and direct, honors the name of God and asks for the coming of God's reign, daily bread, forgiveness of sins, and avoidance of trials. In the parable, set in the context of subsistence-level village life, a guest comes in the middle of the night. Lacking means to feed him, the host goes to a neighbor and persists in asking until he gets what he needs. The persistence (or, more accurately, shamelessness, v. 8) of the supplicant seems to be reinforced by the series of sayings that follow: ask, search, knock, "and it will be given you" (v. 9). If even "evil" fathers know how to give good gifts to their children, then "how much more will the heavenly Father give!" (v. 13). When we read this text alongside the parable of the Persistent Widow (18:1–8), Luke's view of prayer appears to be that those who persist in asking God for what they need will receive it.

It is difficult to avoid the conclusion that if supplicants do not receive that for which they ask, they may not be praying hard enough. How many have suspected that the failure to receive the "good gifts"

Pastoral Perspective

Jesus' disciples desire to pray as he prays. His response to their request opens with those soothing yet provocative words recited in the majority of our churches. However, beginning with the story of the reluctant friend, this passage may become painful or give affront to listeners in the congregation who have cried out at the door of the Divine, only to find that their circumstances remain unchanged.

After telling the parable of the Complacent Neighbor who finally gets up, Jesus directs the disciples to ask, seek, and knock with expectation and offers an illustration of human parents giving good gifts to their children. He then assures them that God, who far surpasses the best of us in benevolence, will certainly provide. Our urgent midnight pleas and implicit childlike dependence alike will be answered.

To listeners whose lives feel secure, these passages affirm their experience of God's providence; to those who wait for deliverance, they reinforce hope; but to those reeling from a recent blow, they may sound incredible. Upon hearing these verses, fearful or indignant questions may surface, such as, "Is God a friend who would rather not be bothered, but eventually gets annoyed enough to answer prayer?" or "Why have I asked but not received? Is my prayer somehow deficient?" or "If God is such a good Father, why am I holding a snake?"

within, 'Do not bother me; the door has already been locked, and my children are with me in bed; I cannot get up and give you anything.' ⁸I tell you, even though he will not get up and give him anything because he is his friend, at least because of his persistence he will get up and give him whatever he needs.

⁹"So I say to you, Ask, and it will be given you; search, and you will find; knock, and the door will be opened for you. ¹⁰For everyone who asks receives, and everyone who searches finds, and for everyone who knocks, the door will be opened. ¹¹Is there anyone among you who, if your child asks for a fish, will give a snake instead of a fish? ¹²Or if the child asks for an egg, will give a scorpion? ¹³If you then, who are evil, know how to give good gifts to your children, how much more will the heavenly Father give the Holy Spirit to those who ask him!"

Exegetical Perspective

The Lord's Prayer in Luke (vv. 1–4). It is generally held among scholars that the Lord's Prayer as it appears in Matthew and Luke is based on a source document, now lost, that lay behind both Gospels. Luke's version of the prayer is shorter than Matthew's, omitting some familiar phrases ("who art in heaven," "thy will be done," etc.); Luke's, however, is undoubtedly closer to the original uttered by Jesus. Yet, as we shall see, changes are also made to the prayer by the author of Luke. The presence of two different accounts of a central teaching of Jesus captures an abiding and productive tension in Christian approaches to Scripture: is the gospel *on* the page, in the words themselves, or *behind* the page, in the events to which Scripture bears witness? There is no simple answer to this question.

Having witnessed Jesus praying, one of the disciples asks for instruction in the art. Although they might have expected a lengthier answer to their question, perhaps involving esoteric practices or techniques for mystical ascent, Jesus defies these expectations by giving a surprisingly abrupt answer.

The very first word, "Father," forecasts the brevity of what follows. In modern English, "Father" sounds somewhat formal; however, *abba*, the Aramaic term lying behind the Greek *patēr*, is more familiar and intimate. There are very few precedents for this

Homiletical Perspective

Preaching about prayer is like falling into the ocean. We cannot touch the ocean floor; we are overwhelmed by the vast sea around us. We come up flailing our arms, gasping for breath, and struggling to stay afloat. No matter how hard we try, we cannot reach the depth and breadth of prayer, but we continue to be buoyed by prayer even as we explore its mysteries. Of all the Christian spiritual disciplines, prayer is perhaps the most universal and most practiced.

We pray consciously and unconsciously. We formalize and ritualize our prayers, from the simplest mealtime blessings and bedtime petitions we learn as children to the repetition of a prayer of confession and the Lord's Prayer in corporate worship. To some, prayer is a disciplined time set aside each day for meditation and reflection; to others, prayer is unrehearsed words uttered throughout the day in moments of joy or crisis. Prayer can simply be an abiding sense of the presence of God. Given the pervasive importance of prayer in the Christian life, preaching and teaching prayer is essential in nurturing disciples.

The disciples' straightforward request, "Lord, teach us to pray," puts the question of prayer squarely in the preacher's lap. As a spiritual discipline, prayer is both a gift and something that can be learned. There is

Luke 11:1–13

Theological Perspective

they request from God is because they have not asked in the right way, or with the proper urgency and frequency? "If only I pray harder," one might think, "God will save my marriage (or heal my child, take away my depression, convert my neighbor, or bring world peace)." This challenging and exhausting approach to prayer points in the wrong direction.

The illustration of a hungry child who asks a parent for food (vv. 11–12) recalls the request in the Lord's Prayer, "Give us each day our daily bread" (v. 3). Jesus invites disciples to pour out their hearts to the heavenly Parent, for their urgent and heartfelt needs belong in her comforting embrace. Whether or not there is bread, fish, or an egg to give, when the hungry child asks, the supplication never goes unheard.

Despite the absence of the clause "Your will be done" (Matt. 6:10) in Luke's version of the prayer, the supplicant must not only consider whether there is any bread, but also submit to God's will. In one of his most famous sermons, Friedrich Schleiermacher observes, "Our own outward affairs are now not as important as were the circumstances of the apostles. It is wholly unnecessary for the cause of Christianity that we be rescued from all our troubles, and so we cannot maintain that this is what Jesus intends."[1] In Luke, the earthly parent knows "how to give good gifts," but the heavenly Parent gives "the Holy Spirit to those who ask" (v. 13). In this vein, a patristic tradition correlates the seven requests in the Lord's Prayer with the seven gifts of the Spirit (Isa. 11:2–3) and the Beatitudes (Matt. 5:3–9). Prayer is good for us because it inculcates the spiritual habits and dispositions we need to align with God's will. We bring our desires to God so that they will be purified and brought in line with God's wisdom and providence.

If persistence in prayer is more likely to change our prayers than to grant them, what should we make of the parable of the Friend at Midnight? Some exegetes argue that this story is taken from another context, in which the point is not about God, or even about prayer. The friend gives because of his "shamelessness" (*anaideia*, NRSV "persistence," NIV "boldness," v. 8). "Shamelessness" in this passage may belong not to the petitioner, but to the person being asked for bread. In the village culture of the ancient Near East, hospitality was paramount: if a family failed to honor a guest, they brought shame upon not only themselves but the entire village. With

1. Friedrich Schleiermacher, *Servant of the World: Selected Sermons of Friedrich Schleiermacher*, trans. Dawn De Vries (Philadelphia: Fortress Press, 1987), 173.

Pastoral Perspective

Once we are attentive to the dissonance and questions of theodicy that naturally arise, reading verses 5–8 alongside verses 11–13 reveals a pattern that sheds light on the analogy Luke draws. In both the story of the grouchy friend and the rhetorical question about ordinary people whose impulse is to protect their offspring, God is not analogous to the human characters; rather, these individuals are set in sharp contrast with the one to whom the disciples pray. Instead, it is the action of providing and the goodness of the gifts the human characters provide that correspond to the action and gifts of God.

Far from implying that a sleep-deprived God answers prayer grudgingly because of our tiresome insistence, the logic of this passage asserts that *if*, despite our failings and selfish tendencies, we can still be motivated to assist others when it sacrifices our comfort and eagerly supply what is safe and pleasant for our children, *then* to a vastly greater degree God, who is unlike us in our weakness, will do so and much more![1]

In Jesus' reassurance we also find a charge to fulfill what it means to be human. What happens to the solace of Jesus' words if the first half of this conditional statement fails to hold true, if the humans do not fit the bill? Apathy toward others in distress has become normal, in spite of the persistence of another's request, or perhaps because of our inundated lives. We ignore many whose faces pass ours in anonymity as we speed by, whose images are exposed on the front page, whose tiny hands ball up in violence to fight for survival, or whose fingers press the church doorbell. The world has gotten big enough to be an excuse for our inaction; the multitude of helpers allows us to justify ignoring numerous pleas that find their way to us. We rationalize refusing the individual before us, in order to reserve energy for efforts that address the deeper, systemic causes.

What are the implications when even well-intentioned parents no longer know how to give good gifts to their children? In our blurred society, busy adults frequently mollify their children with what can harm their minds and bodies, including too much technology and too many material things and unhealthy foods. Jesus' heartening statement instead becomes an indictment and an urgent inducement to attend to our neighbors in need.

Another connection drawn between God's beneficence and our own is found in the prayer modeled by Jesus, "Forgive us our sins, for we ourselves forgive

1. This paradigm also illuminates 19:11–27.

particular form of direct address from an individual to God in the Hebrew Bible or in earlier Jewish literature. One striking parallel occurs in the Mishnah, regarding Honi the Circle Drawer (first century BCE), a rabbi famous for his piety and for his ability to pray successfully for rain. Honi was criticized by his contemporaries for his audacity in prayer; he was "presumptuous before the creator . . . like a son that presumes on his Father" (*Ta'anit* 3.8). Jesus seems to have believed it was not necessary to be famously pious to approach God in this way, and the practice of addressing God as *abba* was adopted (Gal. 4:6; Rom. 8:15; and Mark 14:36).

After the one-word introduction, two wish phrases follow: "hallowed be your name" and "may your kingdom come." The first touches on the present; the second looks to the future. The first phrase counterbalances somewhat the familiarity of Abba: God's kindly parental regard is assumed, and yet God is not simply another thing in the world; God's name, God's identity, is something apart. "Your kingdom come" reminds us that the prayer had its origins in the fervent eschatological hope of Jesus and his first followers, who believed that the day of God's judgment was imminent. Like the Israelites traveling through the wilderness, they too were in transit, their eyes fixed on another country, where they would soon be at home.

Following these two wishes, the prayer features three requests. The phrase "give us each day our daily bread" clearly presumes the story of the Israelites in the wilderness, receiving day by day manna from heaven. Such frugality makes sense in the context of lively eschatological hope: one need survive only until the coming judgment.

By speaking first of "sins" (*hamartia*) and then "those who are indebted to us," Luke's Gospel alters the debts/debtors pairing that was probably in the source document, adjusting it to a Greek-speaking audience, for whom *hamartia* has a sense of a fault or failing, unlike *opheilēmata* (debts). The eschatological frame once again helps to interpret the phrase "those who are indebted to us": what good is it to hold debts to be repaid in the future if that future may not arrive? Better to forgive debts now and receive goodwill as credit (see also 16:1–9). The lengthening of the eschatological horizon need not detract from the wisdom of this remark.

"Do not bring us into the time of trial" represents an improvement upon "lead us not into temptation," familiar from the King James Version. "Lead" and "temptation" carry within them the sense of

abundant opportunity for growth in the practice and understanding of prayer. One task of the preacher is to teach the theology, the forms, and the act of prayer. The petitions of the Lord's Prayer in the liturgy of the church certainly lend themselves to a series of sermons on prayer. Woven throughout the Scriptures are other prayers that illuminate the various forms and occasions for prayer. The prayers of Hannah, David, Solomon, Jeremiah, Mary, Jesus, and Paul awaken us to the many dimensions of prayer. In the Psalms and other books of the Bible, there are cries of dereliction, ascriptions of praise, and shouts of joy that open the listener to fresh understandings of prayer.

What Jesus teaches the disciples and the church in this passage from Luke is not so much the form of prayer, but persistence in prayer and trust in the God who answers prayer. To the ears of those who regularly pray the Lord's Prayer, the form that Luke gives sounds less familiar and more incomplete than Matthew's version in the Sermon on the Mount. For a sermon series on the Lord's Prayer, it may be more useful to use Matthew's version of the Lord's Prayer. The liturgies of many church traditions have trained our ears to hear the prayer according to Matthew's Gospel. The relative unfamiliarity of Luke's version gives the preacher an opportunity to focus on perseverance in prayer and the character of the God who hears our prayers.

To help his listeners understand the need to persist in prayer, Jesus tells a parable about someone who goes at midnight to the home of a friend to plead for bread to feed a late-arriving visitor. What are the preacher and the listener to make of this strange parable? The friend is asleep; the house is shut up tight. The householder gets up, not because of the friendship, but because the unwelcome friend will not stop demanding bread until he receives what is needed. The parable seems to mystify as much as to illuminate. The mind of the hearer may immediately question what the parable says about the character of God. Does God not care? Is our friendship with God not to be trusted? Does God not want to give us what we need? The preacher may need to recognize the problematic nature of the parable. Any analogy when pushed too far can break down. Perhaps the parable is not about the character of God, but about the character of the one who prays. We are to pray persistently and expectantly. Therefore, Jesus adds the interpretive and clarifying sayings to ask, search, and knock, with the assurance that everyone who does so will receive, find, and have the door opened (vv. 9, 10).

Luke 11:1–13

Theological Perspective

this parable, Jesus appeals to the avoidance of shame, shame-less-ness, that would have been important to his listeners.[2]

Our prayers for daily bread are most often answered by one another. At the very least, Jesus implies, we should attend to the needs of the neighbor to avoid our own shame; but through our own supplications, we gradually develop dispositions that impel us to do God's will. We ask, we receive the spirit of friendship, and we turn to others with hospitality.

The approach suggested here leaves unresolved certain questions about God. Are our heartfelt prayers for our comfort alone, or do they have an effect on God as well? A strong Hebraic tradition lifts up those who pray boldly, impudently, even angrily. As James Metzger argues, not all images of the Deity in Scripture are flattering. The sleeper image in the parable is apt for describing human experiences of God, for God often seems to be asleep with regard to injustice in the world.[3] The narrative tradition in Scripture also depicts God as genuinely related and responsive to the world, and at numerous junctures in Scripture, God changes God's mind. Process theologians develop these insights to suggest that God is in the process of becoming, much as creation is. As we seek to align our will with Jesus' intent, the heavenly Parent responds to our decisions and works toward the good. Prayer can be offered in hope that the desires of our heart will meet the possibilities created by God's goodwill for the world.

MICHELLE VOSS ROBERTS

Pastoral Perspective

everyone indebted to us" (v. 4). Rather than asking what might happen if we, as God's petitioners, do not fulfill our end of the bargain, a more intriguing query here may be to ask what might happen if we did.

It is compelling and disorienting to imagine the repercussions of that call to forgive one's debtors, considering the weight of personal and global indebtedness. Individual debt grows because of loans that support everything from education to transportation to home ownership. Governments worldwide confront crises of mounting debt that seems to exceed the number of stars in the Milky Way.

Luke uses debt and sin interchangeably here, on one hand invoking the idea that one justly owes something in restoration for harm inflicted upon another, and on the other hand invoking other spheres of our indebted lives. Financial indebtedness is a norm of today's commerce. For how many persons would a release from debt, without the cataclysm of bankruptcy, be something miraculous? Debt is also a frequent metaphor for gratitude, as in the sense of glad personal obligation for kindness done on one's behalf. Acts of nurture or heroism place people in relationships of intangible indebtedness. This is expressed in a sentiment such as "My success is owed to many." When the concept of debt is so broadly construed, everyone owes someone, and something is owed to everyone. Debt is also a frequent metaphor for gratitude, as in the sense of personal obligation for kindness done on one's behalf.

Think then of releasing every person of any debt owed to you! If this thought is undesirable, what if instead you choose never to be owed anything, opting instead to give to others freely? It is scandalously merciful to believe that our debt to God, to whom we owe much, should be cleared only as we decline to receive what others owe us. Meanwhile the individual who expects others to repay neither kindnesses nor wrongs achieves a rare freedom.

If we aspire to follow the logic of Jesus' prayer, God also chooses never to be owed. The gracious gift of God is one and the same as the ethical demand placed upon the disciple; God's release of our debt is indivisible from our emancipation of others.

SARAH C. JAY

2. Van Thanh Nguyen, "An Asian View of Biblical Hospitality (Luke 11:5–8)," *Biblical Research* 53 (2008): 36.

3. James A. Metzger, "God as F(r)iend? Reading Luke 11:513 and 18:1–8 with a Hermeneutic of Suffering," *Horizons in Biblical Theology* 32 (2010): 33–57.

Exegetical Perspective

enticement and entrapment absent in the Greek *peirasmos*; "test" or "trial" is preferable. It too has an eschatological flavor, perhaps referring to the woes and tribulations that were widely thought to precede the coming of God's judgment, but it may refer more generally to acute suffering or persecution that could drive one away from God.

Verses 5–8. The short parable that follows is often taken as commending persistence in prayer, but in fact, persistence is not at issue: the petitioner asks only once (see 18:1–8). The Greek term translated by the NRSV as "persistence" is better rendered as "shamelessness" (*anaideia*, v. 8), built from the Greek word for shame (*aidōs*), a potent concept in the ancient world. In this "shame culture," loss of face in the eyes of the community was the primary sanction for misdeeds. This makes it all the more remarkable that the midnight caller receives what he asks for, not *in spite of* his shameless act but *because* of it. The picture is consistent, once again, with the audacity of the opening word of the prayer, "Abba." The central message is not "keep trying" but, rather, "presume on God as a young child might impose on a parent, without regard for convention or giving offense." The concluding remark with the different modes of request (ask, seek, knock) need not be seen as recommending persistence, as though one had to pursue three strategies; each mode of inquiry ends in success.

Verses 11–13. The parental imagery continues in the third section: if fallible earthly fathers are naturally inclined to give good things to their children, will not the heavenly Father respond even more readily? Readers looking at the parallel story in Matthew 7:7–11 will notice that Matthew has "good things" where Luke has "Holy Spirit." Given the importance of the Holy Spirit in Luke's Gospel and also in Acts, the substitution of "Holy Spirit" in verse 13 is surely a change worked in by the writer of Luke. This small change serves as yet another reminder that the teachings of Jesus and the stories about him are refracted by the priorities and agendas of the individual Gospel writers. Refracted though they may be, both versions converge on a man who had the audacity to address God as "Abba" and has told his followers to do likewise.

H. GREGORY SNYDER

Homiletical Perspective

This is a bold promise to people who know the pain of unanswered prayer. Unanswered prayer not only calls into question the usefulness of prayer, but also the character of the God to whom we pray. Until his death, Christopher Hitchens was an outspoken critic of religion. He saw religion as an illusion that had outlived its usefulness. According to Hitchens, prayer, ritual, worship, and spiritual community are all relics of a bygone era. The idea of a God who creates and cares for humankind is no longer necessary to understand the cosmos or human life. Hitchens believed that religious faith is destructive. He wrote, "The devotions of today are only the echoing repetitions of yesterday, sometimes ratcheted up to screaming point so as to ward off the terrible emptiness."[1] In his view prayer is a futile activity, like casting a net in an empty sea hoping to catch fish.

Jesus ends his teaching on prayer with several images and analogies that invite the listener to trust in the goodness of God. God's goodness far exceeds that of an earthly parent who knows how to give good gifts to his or her child. There is a twist at the end of this teaching of Jesus. The gift God gives is the gift of the divine self, the Holy Spirit. We discover through persistent prayer that prayer is not so much communication with God as communion with God. It is through the spiritual wrestling of prayer that we come to know the mystery of God's being and presence. Jesus teaches us that prayer ultimately leads us into a deeper relationship with this God, in whose goodness we can trust. Through prayer we receive a greater peace about situations beyond our control and a more profound confidence in God's providence, even when we cannot yet see the answer to our prayers.

LEWIS F. GALLOWAY

---

1. Christopher Hitchens, *God Is Not Great: How Religion Poisons Everything* (New York: Hachette Book Group, 2007), 7.

Luke 11:14–28

¹⁴Now he was casting out a demon that was mute; when the demon had gone out, the one who had been mute spoke, and the crowds were amazed. ¹⁵But some of them said, "He casts out demons by Beelzebul, the ruler of the demons." ¹⁶Others, to test him, kept demanding from him a sign from heaven. ¹⁷But he knew what they were thinking and said to them, "Every kingdom divided against itself becomes a desert, and house falls on house. ¹⁸If Satan also is divided against himself, how will his kingdom stand? —for you say that I cast out the demons by Beelzebul. ¹⁹Now if I cast out the demons by Beelzebul, by whom do your exorcists cast them out? Therefore they will be your judges. ²⁰But if it is by the finger of God that I cast out the demons, then the kingdom of God has come to you. ²¹When a strong man, fully armed, guards his castle, his property is safe. ²²But when one stronger than he attacks him and

Theological Perspective

Theologians are accustomed to speaking of Jesus as a prophet, priest, or ruler. His role as an exorcist receives far less attention. The Synoptic Gospels concur that, like healers in many cultures, Jesus both had a Spirit (11:13) and cast out demons by that Spirit. The discomfort many mainline theologians feel toward this part of his profile points to a significant discrepancy between the worldviews of first-century Palestine and the modern West. Belief in demons and evil spirits, especially associated with what is marginal, is common in agrarian societies and cultures with strong boundaries.[1] By contrast, a highly individualized, urban society with few strong boundaries, characteristic of the modern West, is an anomaly in the world's history and cultures.

In light of contemporary mainline discomfort with Jesus' exorcisms, some readers focus on the healing that usually accompanies them. In the New Testament, demons often manifest as disabilities such as deafness, muteness, blindness, and mental illness. Thus, when Jesus casts out the demon in this passage, "the one who had been mute spoke" (v. 14). Jesus saves by healing the afflicted so that they are reincorporated as hearing, seeing, speaking, rationally communicating members of society. Scholars

Pastoral Perspective

Following each of Jesus' healings in Luke's Gospel, the emotion of the crowd, whether amazement, fear, or astonishment, typically signals the end of the story.[1] Yet on this day when Jesus enables the voice of a person who has been mute to sound, the crowd's wonder begins the story instead. Out of their awe, a controversy erupts about which master Jesus serves and whether his power against demons may be itself demonic. It is common in Luke for Jesus' work to provoke criticism, but this particular antagonism alerts the reader to pay particular attention, because it originates from within the enthralled crowd, not from Jesus' ordinary cast of opponents.[2]

The crowd's invective reflects a tendency witnessed in some contemporary contexts as well. Sometimes when an individual presents a moral claim that people yearn to accept, there are also conflicted impulses, obligations, or fears that cause those same people to distance or reject the individual who has brought the claim. Paradoxically, this response may manifest itself as the beatification or the demonization of the one bringing the claim. The one who asks others to join in the performance

---

1. Amanda Witmer, *Jesus, the Galilean Exorcist: His Exorcisms in Social and Political Context* (New York: T. & T. Clark, 2012), 30.

1. Cf. 4:36; 5:26; 7:16; 9:43; also, Joel B. Green, *The Gospel of Luke*, NICNT (Grand Rapids: Eerdmans, 1997), 452.
2. Robert C. Tannehill, *The Narrative Unity of Luke–Acts*, vol. 1, *The Gospel according to Luke* (Philadelphia: Fortress Press, 1986), 145–46. Consider also Tannehill's distinction between the crowd and Jesus' followers.

overpowers him, he takes away his armor in which he trusted and divides his plunder. ²³Whoever is not with me is against me, and whoever does not gather with me scatters.

²⁴"When the unclean spirit has gone out of a person, it wanders through waterless regions looking for a resting place, but not finding any, it says, 'I will return to my house from which I came.' ²⁵When it comes, it finds it swept and put in order. ²⁶Then it goes and brings seven other spirits more evil than itself, and they enter and live there; and the last state of that person is worse than the first."

²⁷While he was saying this, a woman in the crowd raised her voice and said to him, "Blessed is the womb that bore you and the breasts that nursed you!" ²⁸But he said, "Blessed rather are those who hear the word of God and obey it!"

Exegetical Perspective

"By the Finger of God" (vv. 14–26). As with the previous episodes on prayer, this story involving demonic powers appears in the larger context of the journey to Jerusalem, one of the structural features particular to Luke's Gospel. It begins with an exorcism. However, the center of the story is not the exorcism but the controversy it generates among bystanders concerning the origin of Jesus' powers.

Given our location on the other side of the scientific revolution, modern people, even those who believe in spiritual phenomena, tend to divide reality into two different categories, the natural or physical world, governed by natural laws, and the spiritual or "supernatural" world. In antiquity, especially at the popular level, there was no clear distinction between natural and supernatural; these "worlds" were not separated. The line between physical healing, which nowadays belongs to the natural world, and exorcism—for moderns, a spiritual transaction—was for the ancients more or less nonexistent. In 4:39, Jesus "rebukes" the fever afflicting Simon's mother-in-law, just as he "rebukes" the demons two verses later, in 4:41 (see also 9:42). The crippled woman in Luke 13:10–17 suffers from a spine ailment—scoliosis, perhaps—but is later described as being "bound by Satan." Illness was often thought to be caused by evil spirits or by a contagion arising from moral mistakes

Homiletical Perspective

On the first reading of the text, one can almost hear the sigh coming from the preacher who is called to preach it. How does the preacher move from the first-century world, with its talk of the prince of demons, Beelzebul, to the world of the congregation? Modern-day listeners may dismiss the idea of the exorcism of a demon from a man who could not speak, and thereby also dismiss the miraculous and liberating healing power of Jesus. With a sophisticated snicker, they may also reject the notion of the power of evil represented by the larger-than-life figure of Beelzebul, and thereby also dismiss the victory of Jesus not just over individual sins, but over the power of evil itself.

Luke presents the healing of the man who could not speak in summary form, rather than in the traditional form of a miracle story. The healing sets the stage for the larger issue of the power and identity of Jesus and the various ways in which people react to him. No one doubts the fact that Jesus heals the man by driving out the demon. The proof is evident to all in the man's sudden ability to speak. It is interesting that Luke does not provide the testimony of the man who is healed; instead he gives the various reactions of the witnesses.

While the healing results in general amazement, there is no understanding of the source of the power

Luke 11:14–28

Theological Perspective

of disability have pointed out the shortcomings of this approach. When experiences of healing become the staple of Christian testimony, persons with disabilities are excluded from full possession of salvation. Instead, Christian notions of personhood and salvation should reflect the full range of embodied diversity, so that physical and mental limitations are not taken as signs of spiritual deprivation.

Another popular impulse with such passages is to demythologize them—to dismiss references to demons as mythological elements of a premodern worldview. "Demons" might then be interpreted as any number of psychological, sociological, or emotional difficulties. Although theologian Walter Wink agrees that the spiritual forces can be interpreted as personifications of institutions and ideologies, he reinvigorates the mythological element in passages such as this. Forces such as consumerism, racism, and individualism are not just abstractions. They take on a life of their own and exercise real spiritual power. The New Testament bespeaks a densely populated cosmos of nature spirits, principalities, powers, demons, and gods. For Wink, the spiritual reality is just as complex today. He defines demons as "the psychic or spiritual power emanated by organizations or individuals whose energies are bent on overpowering others" and Satan as "the actual power that congeals around collective idolatry, injustice, or inhumanity."[2]

The demonic aspect of religious and social institutions silences people on the margins. Denied education and religious authority, women have lacked a voice of authority for much of Christian history. During a recession, when the clamor is all about the middle class, the poor cannot get a hearing. Persons with disabilities or queer sexualities are invisible, insofar as they fall outside the norm. Racism disenfranchises nonwhites in countless ways.

The person afflicted by the demon in Luke 11 embodies this silencing effect of institutional power: he or she cannot speak. Jesus the exorcist restores the voice of the marginalized. He hears them. He sees them not only as people in need but as agents. We should not be surprised that the crowds do not want to listen to what they have to say. Whether it is to their true advantage or not, they have an investment in the powers.

Jesus' opponents divert attention from his challenge to the status quo with a debate: does Jesus act

Pastoral Perspective

of acts of ethical bravery may be deemed a saint in whose footsteps others may never aspire to follow; or the person may be rejected by those who fear that their reputation might be called into question if they were to do likewise. Either response allows those being challenged in this way to avoid responsibilities. This distancing happens to visionary leaders and also to those whose material distress or weakness silently places a demand upon the conscience. Such opposing reactions to Jesus occur frequently in Luke (e.g., 6:46–47; 7:33–35; 14:15; 18:18–19).

Jesus deflates the accusation that he is on retainer for Beelzebul with a triad of logical rebuttals whose main point is that evil does not profit from the defeat of evil; therefore Jesus' wresting of people's lives back from disease must be God's power. According to Jesus' logic, *any* human capacity to bring people's lives back from destructive forces proceeds from God.

Then Jesus addresses a deeper concern: evil does profit from inaction. In a world in which "evil" is a tag too readily pinned on difference, consider instead how the effort to accomplish good by some is harmed by the inaction of others—not only by their interference or attack, but by the absence of action. Jesus tells the accusing crowd, "whoever does not gather with me scatters" (v. 23). Later he responds to a woman offering a beatitude to the mother who bore him with his own beatitude: "Blessed are those who hear the word of God and obey it!" (v. 28).

Many of the concepts in this passage, like demon possession and exorcism, Beelzebul and the correspondent dualism, may initially alienate contemporary listeners. However, the people's indecision, vitriolic remarks, and expressions of approval and disapproval may sound all too familiar. For instance, in an era of constant media coverage of news events, the people's critique of Jesus brings to mind the multitude of partisan pundits who have presently blurred the line between journalist and commentator. In this passage, the call to action in service of the good is a relevant word of chastisement that could be directed toward those who "sit in the seat of scoffers" (Ps. 1:1b).

This passage reiterates the emphasis given as Jesus sent out seventy of his disciples in pairs (10:1) and instructed the newly healed man from the Gerasenes to go home to testify, rather than allowing him to follow (8:38–39). Jesus is not seeking fans but fellow laborers. Jesus' frightening words in verses 24–26 demand that his listeners notice the urgency and the necessity for all to respond.[3] In the scenario Jesus

---

2. Walter Wink, *Naming the Powers: The Language of Power in the New Testament* (Philadelphia: Fortress Press, 1984), 104–5.

3. Green, *The Gospel of Luke*, 451, 458–59.

committed by oneself or one's ancestors. Proper physical healing, therefore, often required exorcism, forgiveness of sin, or both.

It would have been natural for most people in Jesus' day to assume that his cures were carried out with spells, magical techniques, or the aid of spiritual beings. When the bystanders accuse Jesus of casting out demons "by Beelzebul," they may be implying that Jesus, through the technology of magic, has enlisted an archdemon, perhaps Satan himself, in his service through a binding spell, or that he is in league with such an entity. The writer of the Gospel strives to demonstrate that this is not the case. Jesus' activity as an exorcist clearly demonstrates that the power of God is lively and present, crackling in their very midst, a power that vanquishes evil and its effects.

The chief argument that Jesus makes in the face of his critics is a logical one: why would Satan work against himself or attack his own forces? The premise of this argument is that demons, devils, and unclean spirits are all on the same team, striving for the same objective: the disruption of human lives. Jesus' hearers may have presumed that the situation was more chaotic and anarchic, that one demon or spiritual entity might be compelled to work against another. Counterspells or defensive charms, in which one spiritual power was invoked against another, were quite common in the ancient world. Jesus critiques this assumption: for Jesus, there are indeed evil powers in the world, but in spite of appearances, they all stand opposed to the reign of God. The perspective is ultimately dualistic. This is why Jesus claims, "Whoever is not with me is against me" (v. 23): where the battle with evil is concerned, it is impossible to maintain nonaligned status.

As a secondary answer to their charge of magic, Jesus appeals to his audience's belief in legitimate exorcism, indeed, their pride at Jewish expertise in the practice: "Do you question the ability of other Jewish exorcists to cast out demons? Are they too in league with the devil?" In some quarters, Jews enjoyed a reputation for skill in the magical arts: Moses learned the craft in Egypt and had proven victorious over the Egyptian magicians. Solomon, the wisest of all men, had an encyclopedic knowledge of plants, gems, and their effects.

Josephus tells the story of Eleazar, a famous Jewish exorcist who performed an exorcism in the presence of the emperor Vespasian. Using a ring that had under its seal "one of the plants prescribed by Solomon," Eleazar drew the demon out through

of Jesus to cast out demons. Trying to discredit Jesus, some in the crowd claim that Jesus heals by the power of Satan. Jesus wisely counters their illogic by responding that if he heals by the power of the prince of demons, then the devil is at war with itself. He heals by the power of God, for God is stronger than the strongest powers of evil. Jesus compares his healing to the exorcisms performed by other miracle workers in whom some in the crowd seem to trust. The question is, who heals by the power of God? The exorcism of the demon is the sign that something greater is present than the healing of an individual person. In defeating the power of evil, the kingdom of God has come in the person of Jesus.

There are others in the crowd who accept the miraculous healing, but they want to see more. They want another sign from heaven. For some people, then and now, no matter how much evidence is piled upon evidence, it is never enough. What does it take to see "the finger of God" at work whenever lives are turned around, truth breaks out, the broken are made whole, goodness triumphs over evil, or justice is established? What does it take to see in the ordinary and extraordinary events that make up our lives the signs of God's redemptive work in Jesus? The danger of not seeing the signs that are before us is that we reject the work of God in Jesus.

The healing of the man who could not speak is a call to decision for or against the work of God in Jesus. Some who do not want to upset their world-view decide that Jesus is not from God. There is another danger: some never make up their minds. They become like the Athenians to whom Paul preached. They are dabblers in the truth, who love nothing more than hearing and discussing something new (Acts 17:21). According to Luke's Jesus, when one is confronted with the gospel, there is no room for idle debates and endless indecision.

Jesus takes one step further. The defeat of the powers of evil and the healing of a life invite a response from us. God has swept our houses clean. God has delivered us from the dominion of evil, wiped away our sins, healed our brokenness, and provided for our needs. God has done good things for us! God is stronger than all that seeks to break our spirits, overcome our faith, and destroy our lives. Are we ready for such a transformation? At times, we want God only to dust off our accumulated stuff, do a little touch-up painting, and maybe rearrange the furniture of our lives. We do not want God to sweep our lives clean, empty out the clutter in our hearts, take away our bad habits and desires, and fill our life

Luke 11:14–28

Theological Perspective

by the power of "Beelzebul, the ruler of the demons" (v. 15), or "by the finger of God" (v. 20)? They accuse Jesus of acting by a malevolent spirit, rather than a Holy Spirit, in order to discredit him. In reply, Jesus points out that their charge makes no sense. Why would Satan do battle with himself (v. 18)? Injustice has an interest in maintaining injustice. By contrast, Jesus' actions call people into right relationship with one another. He is like a thief who binds and plunders a strong man in his own home. The powers of injustice and inhumanity appear to have a rightful hold on this world, but Jesus disarms this in order to subvert it (vv. 21–22).

It is not merely the act of casting out demons to which Jesus' critics object. In this passage, it is clear that other Jewish teachers are doing it too, and his opponents view them as divinely led (v. 19). The dispute raises the question of Jesus' relationship to other religious authorities. When he says, "whoever is not with me is against me" (v. 23), he indicates a kinship with others who exemplify the coming commonwealth of God: wherever oppressive powers are defused, the kin-dom comes. Jesus not only aligns himself with others who do this work, but he also invites them to share his vision of the new order: "whoever does not gather with me scatters" (v. 23).

Although the demons are spiritual forces, they crave embodiment. As Jesus observes, the unclean spirit roams about in search of someone to inhabit (v. 24). Injustice does not exist outside of the institutions and individual agents that perpetrate it. The powers have material reality. They need bodies to empower and bodies to dominate. Likewise, bodies are always animated by some spirit or other. Persons may work to overcome one form of domination, but unless the Spirit that possessed Jesus takes its place, it is easily replaced by another: "it goes and brings seven other spirits more evil than itself, and they enter and live there" (v. 26). This story plays out on stages from the international to the individual: the spirits of domination clamor to occupy a vacant space. Humility, mutuality, and attention to the persons wounded by these forces possess real power to shape another reality.

MICHELLE VOSS ROBERTS

Pastoral Perspective

describes, as quickly as a person is released from what possessed him or her, a worse onslaught of the same distress returns. Any who have devoted significant energy to healing or social reform recognize the futility inherent in this exercise. Often such work feels like trying to leave footprints in mud. Jesus exhorts the undecided to cease wavering or taking refuge in the crowd, to stop equating amazement with faith, and instead to join the restorative work of healing.

The unexpected contrast of verse 23, "Whoever is not with me is against me," with an earlier utterance of Jesus, "Whoever is not against you is for you" (9:50), sparks a question about Jesus' inclusivity. However, the two conversations have something different at stake. In the earlier passage, the disciples are concerned that an independent exorcist is using Jesus' name to heal. Jesus commands them to let him continue, affirming that the common cause of restoration is central, and group identity is peripheral.

In the second selection the distinction made is no longer between outsiders and insiders but between observers and actors. Jesus, in this story, has been identified as an illegitimate outsider. So when Jesus asks rhetorically, "Now if I cast out the demons by Beelzebul, by whom do your exorcists cast them out?" (v. 19), he posits that there are not two classes of exorcists—upright, religious people who cast out demons, on the one hand, and evil-workers who cast out demons, on the other. Instead, there are simply those who free people from what ensnares them and those who do not. The move is fundamentally inclusive, placing all who offer release to the suffering in God's service.

Yet some are excluded, namely, those who fail to act on behalf of people who are overpowered by illness, circumstance, abuse, or oppression. Just as this text does not end with the amazement of the crowd, meaningful discipleship refuses to end with amazement, fear, shock, or self-protective distancing. Such responses must rather be seen as a beginning and a catalyst for decisive action.

SARAH C. JAY

Exegetical Perspective

the possessed man's nose. He then "adjured the demon never to return," repeating Solomon's name and uttering various incantations.[1] This illuminating parallel text also shows that special steps were required to keep the demon from returning once it had left. Even when people are healed, they remain vulnerable; the ground that is won in this war needs to be occupied, lest it be retaken. Consistent with the portrait he draws of the Holy Spirit in Acts, the author of Luke would surely maintain that the Holy Spirit should be the new tenant in the newly swept and ordered house.

The force of the argument is clear: if exorcism is legitimate, as his audience believes, and if it is performed against evil spirits, not with their assistance, then indeed, the power of God—the "finger of God," as Luke puts it—is active in their midst. It is the same confession made by the Egyptian magicians in Exodus 8:19, when confronted by the wonder-working power of Moses.[2]

The story of the strong man guarding his house, overcome by the sheer force of a man still stronger, who beats him, strips him, and plunders his goods, is yet another way of portraying the reality of this spiritual battle between the powers of evil and the kingdom of God, and it serves as a graphic conclusion to the argument. In a world where violence, rather than the rule of law, often won the day, this image would have had special currency.

A Woman Interjects (vv. 27–28). In this curious fragment, a woman in the crowd raises her voice in praise of Jesus' mother. The story is unique to Luke, which is not surprising, as Luke devotes special attention to Jesus' mother and to women in general. This public comment by one woman in favor of another is refreshingly bold and outspoken, given the muffling effect of ancient patriarchy. Jesus' response to her, however, redirects the woman's well-intentioned remark. It is not the mother of the messenger or even the messenger that is important, but the message itself: God's will is to be heard, understood, and acted upon.

H. GREGORY SNYDER

Homiletical Perspective

with the joy of the kingdom. We like things the way they are. We want Jesus to make life a little bit better, not give us a whole new one. Yet that is what Jesus does: he makes a clean sweep of the whole affair, gives us a new mind and heart, and sets our feet on a new path.

He invites us to make the fundamental choice of filling our lives with his gifts, words, and ways. If we do not fill our lives with the things of the kingdom, then there is a real danger of the demon's return, along with seven more even worse than the first. An unnamed woman in the crowd grasps the significance of what Jesus is saying and doing. She cries out with a blessing for his mother who has borne and nurtured such a son, in whom the life-giving power of God is visibly present. Jesus turns her words into a concluding beatitude for those who hear and obey.

The task of the preacher is to imagine with the congregation what it is to hear and obey the word of Jesus. What does it mean to live a transformed life in response to the cleansing and empowering work of God? Using the image of a house swept clean, the preacher can invite the congregation to imagine how they would furnish the house of their lives. One direction is to think in terms of the fruits of the Spirit (Gal. 5:22, 23). Another possibility is to examine some of the spiritual disciplines that provide a strong foundation for the Christian life: worshiping, reading Scripture, giving, and serving. The image of a house swept clean invites us into the spiritual discipline of hospitality. How do we use our time and resources to welcome others into the well-swept roominess of our lives?

LEWIS F. GALLOWAY

---

1. Josephus, *Antiquities of the Jews: Book VIII*, chapter 2, #5, in Peter Kirby, *Early Jewish Writing*, http://earlyjewishwritings.com/text/josephus/ant8.html; accessed Oct. 30, 2013.
2. Susan Garrett, *The Demise of the Devil; Magic and the Demonic in Luke's Writings* (Minneapolis: Fortress Press, 1989), 45.

Luke 11:29–36

²⁹When the crowds were increasing, he began to say, "This generation is an evil generation; it asks for a sign, but no sign will be given to it except the sign of Jonah. ³⁰For just as Jonah became a sign to the people of Nineveh, so the Son of Man will be to this generation. ³¹The queen of the South will rise at the judgment with the people of this generation and condemn them, because she came from the ends of the earth to listen to the wisdom of Solomon, and see, something greater than Solomon is here! ³²The people of Nineveh will rise up at the judgment with this generation and condemn it, because they repented at the proclamation of Jonah, and see, something greater than Jonah is here!

³³"No one after lighting a lamp puts it in a cellar, but on the lampstand so that those who enter may see the light. ³⁴Your eye is the lamp of your body. If your eye is healthy, your whole body is full of light; but if it is not healthy, your body is full of darkness. ³⁵Therefore consider whether the light in you is not darkness. ³⁶ If then your whole body is full of light, with no part of it in darkness, it will be as full of light as when a lamp gives you light with its rays."

Theological Perspective

"Blessed rather are those who hear the word of God and obey it!" (v. 28), declares Jesus just before his address to a growing crowd. Whereas many a preacher might take the throng as a sign that the word of God is being heard, Jesus' address presumes the opposite. Lurking in the crowd are those who had asked for a sign from heaven (11:16). Now in front of a multitude, Jesus declares their request for a sign to be evil. In fact, their request signals their refusal of God's word that has come near in him. The theme of Jesus' address, therefore, is twofold: the condemnation that awaits those who continue to reject the sign already given them in the Son of Man, and the opportunity that is still theirs to let the light of God shine out of their lives as a sign to others.

As he did in his inaugural sermon (4:16–30), in this address Jesus twice uses outsiders that hear God's word as a case in point: the Ninevites heard God's word and repented, and the queen of the South recognized wisdom when she heard it from Solomon. By damning contrast, the gathering crowd has been given God's wisdom and word in Jesus and still some ask for a tangible confirmation that God's kingdom has come to them (v. 29). Put another way (see vv. 33–36), the Ninevites realized through the preaching of Jonah that the light in them was darkness and repented; the queen of the South, in

Pastoral Perspective

Jesus attracted large numbers of people with his teaching and with his healing power, but he did not play to the crowds. In fact, as Luke tells it, when the crowds increased, his words became all the more strident and confrontational. Jesus named them "an evil generation" and warned them sternly. These are not easy words to hear or to understand, and the preacher with pastoral sensitivities will want to tread lightly with such warnings, helping hearers to understand the context in which Jesus condemned the crowd as an "evil generation."

In the preceding encounter (vv. 14–23), Jesus had cast out a demon from a person with no voice, enabling the one who was mute to speak. Luke remembers the crowd's amazement, but as if to echo the cynical maxim that "no good deed goes unpunished," he then reports that while some were amazed, others in the crowd began to question the source of his power and demand a sign, in order to test him (v. 16). It is to that prior challenge that Jesus responds forcefully in verses 29–32.

The "evil generation" label that Jesus gives the crowd is doubtless well deserved. Indeed, in some ways every generation is evil, just as there are those in each generation who are kind and loving and faithful. In the broad stroke, things have not changed much in the intervening centuries, and the present

Feasting on the Gospels

Exegetical Perspective

What is the sign of Jonah, and what happens when the Gospels agree to disagree? This enigmatic expression appears both in Matthew and in Luke, yet they have different ideas of what Jesus means by it. Both take their cue from Mark 8:11–12, where the Pharisees ask Jesus "for a sign from heaven, to test him," and Jesus "sighed deeply in his spirit and said, 'Why does this generation ask for a sign? Truly I tell you, no sign will be given to this generation.'"

In asking for a sign (*sēmeion*, sing.) from heaven, the Pharisees are not calling on Jesus to perform a miracle. For Mark's Gospel the miracles are acts of power (*dynameis*) by which Jesus effects the inbreaking of God's reign that is the focus of his preaching (Mark 1:15). Signs (*sēmeia*, pl.), on the other hand, can have apocalyptic overtones. Thus, when Jesus announces the impending destruction of the temple, Peter, James, John, and Andrew anxiously inquire, "Tell us, when will this be, and what will be the *sign* that all these things are about to be accomplished?" (Mark 13:4). In this case, Jesus obliges them with a vivid sketch of the travails that are to come. If this is the sort of sign that the Pharisees are after, why does Jesus emphatically refuse to provide them with an answer along the same lines? If not, what *are* they seeking? Their reverent circumlocution "from heaven" suggests that they want some clear and

Homiletical Perspective

In the eleventh chapter of Luke, the author presents the reader with a Jesus who is neither tenderhearted nor patient. Clearly keyed into the community's concerns for daily bread, forgiveness of sins, debt relief, and deliverance from evil forces, Luke's Jesus is a teacher of prayer, schooling his openhearted followers on the basics of spiritual preparation and the devotional life. The prayer he teaches his disciples is the prayer Christians know by heart—the Lord's Prayer. As the priestly sage in this text, Jesus models in this prayer what followers are to do and say to invite God's positive response to human affairs. Jesus' advice not only is given to shape their consciousness about prayer, but also serves to indicate something about the nature and essence of divine generosity and the benefits of citizenship in God's reigndom (11:1–13).

Yet Jesus is also personified as a cosmic warrior who has come to do battle with the forces of evil (11:17–28). In the verses immediately preceding the text, Jesus draws a line in the sand and declares to the crowd, "You are either with me or against me." In a war waged against evil forces, obedience to the word of God is the test of one's allegiance to Jesus. The message is unambiguous: one can either obediently trust God in faith or thwart God's salvific agenda of setting free the spiritually vulnerable from Satan's traps and snares.

Luke 11:29–36

Theological Perspective

the presence of the light she heard in the wisdom of Solomon, acknowledged that "there was no more spirit in her" (1 Kgs. 10:5) and blessed the God of Israel. Now, in the presence of the gathering darkness, Jesus offers these ominous analogies and urges the crowd to "consider whether the light in you is not darkness" (v. 35).

Scan Luke's Gospel from the beginning until now, and you will discover that the characters who hear the word of God and obey are often outsiders, in one way or another, who have no illusion that the darkness in them is light. There is Mary, whose "How can this be?" is uttered not in defiance but astonishment (1:34); the poverty-stricken shepherds who run, run, run to Bethlehem in response to the sign given them of a babe wrapped in swaddling clothes and lying in a manger (2:15–16); Simon Peter on his knees saying, "Go away from me, Lord, for I am a sinful man" (5:8); the man covered with leprosy, who begs, "Lord, if you choose, you can make me clean" (5:12); a centurion who believes himself to be unworthy of Jesus' presence in his house and says nonetheless, "But only speak the word, and let my servant be healed" (7:7); the woman in the city, who is a sinner, bathing and anointing and kissing Jesus' feet (7:37–38); the woman with the hemorrhage who touches the fringe of Jesus' clothes (8:44). By contrast, those who oppose Jesus oppose him on the basis of the darkness in them that they have mistaken for light (the congregation in Nazareth, 4:22–30; the Pharisees and teachers of the law, 5:21, 30, 33; 6:2, 7; the crowds, 7:24–34; the disciples, 9:46–48; the lawyer, 10:25–37).

In their defense, the religious leaders who asked for a sign were responsible for the substance and authenticity of a tradition that was threatened by an itinerant rabbi with a growing following. Religion functions in most societies as the guarantor of the status quo in two arenas. In society at large, the pronouncements of religious institutions often lend God's imprimatur to the ethical norms of the majority culture. Within the community of faith, the creeds and doctrines of the church have attempted to give definition to the rule of faith against which all claims to truth are judged. Hence the decision to include the *filioque* clause in the Nicene Creed ("We believe in the Holy Spirit, the Lord, the giver of Life, who proceeds from the Father *and the Son*") was an attempt to aid the church in discerning the signs: what Spirit is from God and what spirit is an imposture? The scandalous particularity of the incarnation has been the sign through which believers have

Pastoral Perspective

time is no different. As William Sloane Coffin often reminded his congregation, progress in human life and relationships more often follows the path of a pendulum than an arrow.[1] In terms of justice, equity, and basic human kindness, people have not progressed as far as some might have hoped; to be sure, one could argue in the current global environment that the present generation is worthy of similar scorn and condemnation from Jesus. It is thus tempting for any preacher/interpreter to take on the mantle of Jesus' righteous indignation and decry the failures of one's contemporaries to live up to the claims of the prophets and the wisdom of Christ.

Pastoral sensitivity, however, should lead any interpreter to exercise thoughtful care in reflecting on Jesus' words. Christ speaks his hard warning into a particular context in the face of growing opposition to his ministry. As one will see in Luke's following pericopes, the temperature of the conflict is rising. The temptation to find easy parallels and to hurl forth "the sign of Jonah" today is a temptation fraught with peril. There are other, more productive ways to challenge a class or a congregation to live faithfully. Such words of condemnation are better left to Jesus. What one can voice faithfully and pastorally is a deep concern that lives are not in alignment with God's reign.

Once, during a vacation in England, our family was traveling across the moors, a vast expanse of rolling grasslands and sedges that, even in summer, seemed to hint of imposing wintry weather. The road was not very good; it offered about one and a half lanes of semipaved thoroughfare, bordered on one side by the hillside above and on the other side by even more hillside below. As we approached one sweeping curve to the left, we encountered a road sign with an arrow noting the approaching turn, along with words of warning: "Adverse Camber." It took a while to process the warning and the meaning of the sign. "Adverse Camber" alerts drivers to a road that arches, slopes, or tilts the wrong way. In that particular case, the sign warned of a left-hand turn in which the road sloped away to the right, instead of banking to the left.

The family laughed later at the British understatement of danger in that sign and wondered how many foreign nationals had driven off the road and down the hillside pondering its meaning. However, to this interpreter, the road sign became in time a remarkably apt metaphor for the warnings Jesus speaks so

1. William Sloane Coffin, *The Collected Sermons of William Sloane Coffin*, vol. 1, *The Riverside Years* (Louisville, KY: Westminster John Knox Press, 2008), 409.

convincing nod from God about who Jesus is and by what authority he speaks and acts.

Matthew and Luke weave the demand for a sign into the consternation of the crowd that witnesses an exorcism performed by Jesus (Matt. 12:22–24; Luke 11:14–15), with some claiming that "he casts out demons by Beelzebul, the ruler of the demons" (11:15; and see Matt. 12:24). In Luke 11:16, the call for a "sign from heaven" follows immediately after the allegation that the source of Jesus' authority is demonic rather than divine. Refusing to provide any credentials beyond what he has already accomplished before their eyes, Jesus replies, "Now if I cast out the demons by Beelzebul, by whom do your exorcists cast them out? Therefore they will be your judges. But if it is by the finger of God that I cast out the demons, then the kingdom of God has come to you" (11:19–20; and see Matt. 12:27–28). Far from settling things, Jesus seems only to have stirred up the crowd still further. Hearing one fan shout out, "Blessed is the womb that bore you and the breasts that nursed you," Jesus deflects her praise and declares, "Blessed rather are those who hear the word of God and obey it!" (11:27–28).

As the crowd continues to grow, Jesus finally turns his attention to their demand for a sign, and Luke's Jesus adds (as does Matthew's Jesus) one important element to the Markan Jesus' utter refusal to comply with their request: "This generation is an evil generation; it asks for a sign, but no sign will be given to it except the sign of Jonah" (v. 29). The correspondence Jesus traces between Jonah and the people of Nineveh, on the one hand, and the Son of Man and "this generation," on the other, makes sense of that expression, which appears in Mark 8:12 without further explanation: "For just as Jonah became a sign to the people of Nineveh, so the Son of Man will be to this generation" (v. 30). In Luke 11:31–32, the people of "this generation" find themselves condemned by people of earlier generations, by contrast with whom "this generation" is evil.

The first of these is the "queen of the South" (v. 31; Matt. 12:42), the queen who comes to Jerusalem from distant Sheba because of Solomon's widespread reputation for wisdom (1 Kgs. 10:1–13; 2 Chr. 9:1–12). On judgment day she will condemn the people of "this generation" for their failure to recognize that "something greater than Solomon is here." She will be joined in this by the people of Nineveh, "because they repented at the proclamation of Jonah" (v. 32), who will weigh in against "this generation" because they failed to recognize "something greater

By the twenty-ninth verse, Luke's Jesus is neither priestly sage nor spiritual warrior: he is an agitated judge. Because Jesus is responding to sundry matters outlined in this text, it is difficult to harmonize his responses or determine a singular focus for the chapter. Therefore, the judicious preacher-interpreter will first see Jesus' stirring rebuke in verses 29–32 as one of several responses Jesus has to his disciples and this crowd. Second, the preacher-interpreter must accept the bitter fact that always opposite Jesus' compassion and loving care for the creature is a figure of holy rage.

Jesus' indignation with persons and communities who refuse to heed God's wisdom or trust and obey God's Word is inextricably tied to the holiness of God that comes near in his presence. The picture Luke paints of Jesus in verses 26–32 contrasts with a picture of Jesus as reconciler who performs miracles to inspire others to a life of faith; this Jesus is peeved, impatient, and ill tempered. Therefore, to follow the spirit and mood of the passage from text to sermon, today's preacher, like Jesus, must decidedly declaim against the presentation of a gospel that is gimmicked up to appease demanding crowds.

Third, in contrast to a homiletical style, popularized by Harry Emerson Fosdick during Protestant liberalism's heyday, that addresses the individual, Jesus as prophetic preacher proclaims a blanket rebuke. His ire is directed to all who have come with their Petri dish to request more data on Jesus' legitimacy to perform miracles in the name of Israel's God. The central problematic for the preacher involves pointing out how contemporary seekers, like this ancient-day sign-seeking crowd, attempt to dissect the unmanageable reality of God's freedom to judge the world on God's own terms rather than ours.

What earns Jesus' fury and indictment is the crowd's inability to discern hope in their midst. In view of Jesus' prior miraculous demonstrations and promises to restore community wellness by bringing good news to the poor, recovery of sight to the blind, and deliverance to the captives as his principal ministry agenda, such demands from this crowd for further signs are contemptuous. The crowd's insatiable appetite for signs was indeed an indication of the crowd's own anemic spirituality and faithlessness.

The prophet Jonah and the Ethiopian queen of the South (1 Kgs. 10:1–13; Matt. 12:42) become emblems of what repentance, obedience, and wisdom look like. They are offered as examples that have sacred significance. In direct contrast, this crowd's failure to discern who the Son of Man is—as

Luke 11:29–36

Theological Perspective

rightly asked of some new claimant to revelation in every age: Is this the God made known in Jesus Christ?

Unfortunately, in the thousands of years that have come and gone since Jesus addressed the growing crowds and Luke wrote his Gospel and the church set down the creeds, Jesus has been so seamlessly fit into the status quo of the Christian religion that what passes for the light of unassailable orthodoxy may be as dark as the darkness Jesus called evil in his generation. Likewise, the coincidence of dominant societal norms and religious ethical absolutism calls to mind the objections raised by religious authorities when Jesus privileged redemptive action over prescriptive rules. That these verses from Luke are absent from the Revised Common Lectionary may be no chance omission.

What is it that causes anyone or any community of faith to consider whether the light in them is not darkness? "After one has laboriously settled the credentials of believing," Paul Lehmann wrote, "one sooner or later is bound to encounter another human being who has never been baptized and appears to be totally unaware of, or indifferent to, the *koinonia*, yet who behaves like the Lord's anointed."[1] Those in Luke's Gospel who hear God's word and obey are those who were given a sign they never asked to receive and responded with their lives (Mary, the shepherds, Simon Peter) or those whose wounded bodies yet healthy eyes knew the Son of Man when they saw him (the man with leprosy, the centurion, the woman in the city, the woman with a hemorrhage). In every generation, the signs of the kingdom-come-near are hidden in the lowly raised up and the outcasts healed. If in these the light that shines is the same light that illumed the growing crowd long ago, believers would do well to open their eyes to signs they never asked for and, with the Ninevites, repent!

CYNTHIA A. JARVIS

Pastoral Perspective

often in Luke's Gospel. People's lives regularly slope the wrong way. Instead of cambering toward God in awe and gratitude and toward neighbors in graciousness, they tilt precariously toward selfish desires or prideful self-righteousness. One might not consider such proclivities evil, but when they blind people to the light of God all around them, Jesus' strong words offer a needed corrective and warning.

Perhaps out of concern for such blindness, Jesus turns his attention to some jumbled, even unrelated, comments about lamps, light, and sight in verses 33–36. Luke's recollection of Jesus' words here follows Mark and Matthew (Mark 4:21; Matt. 5:15) and repeats Jesus' earlier use of the saying in 8:16. The passage is perplexing in its logic, but it seems clear that, unlike Matthew and Mark, who understand the reference to light as a word about witness and proclamation, Luke regards Jesus' saying as a teaching about depth of perception and faithfulness of thought. The point seems to be that if the people stand close to the light of Christ with healthy and faithful eyes, their whole bodies will receive and exude such light, filling the whole body with illumination. To Jesus, a good eye is crucial.

Later in Luke's Gospel, on the evening following his resurrection Jesus will break bread in Emmaus and give it to the two disciples who have walked with him on the road. Luke will note that in that moment the disciples' eyes were opened, and they recognized Jesus (24:30–31). In the context of this passage, however, the eyes of many remain closed, even though someone greater than Jonah, greater than Solomon, is in their midst (vv. 31–32). In such darkness, no one thrives; the reign of God is at hand, but no one notices. The prayer of all faithful, earnest seekers is that Christ will open their eyes, camber their lives rightly, and bring recognition of the One who is always in their midst.

ROBERT E. DUNHAM

---

1. Paul Lehmann, *Ethics in a Christian Context* (New York: Harper & Row, 1963), 158.

than Jonah" in Jesus. For Luke, the "sign of Jonah" is the preaching of Jesus, who speaks with wisdom greater than Solomon's. This is further underscored by what immediately precedes the Lukan Jesus' pronouncement about the sign of Jonah, the blessing that he deflects from his mother, only to refashion it as a beatitude pronounced on those who "hear the word of God and obey it" (11:27–28).

Matters become more complicated when we consider what Matthew's Jesus alone contributes to the mix. Immediately before the material that Matthew shares with Luke (and that both derive from the sayings source Q), Matthew's Jesus adds: "For just as Jonah was three days and three nights in the belly of the sea monster, so for three days and three nights the Son of Man will be in the heart of the earth" (Matt. 12:40). This familiar episode from the story of the reluctant prophet, his miraculous rescue from certain death in the stormy sea through the divinely orchestrated intervention of a large fish (Jonah 1:17), is echoed and surpassed by the death and resurrection of Jesus, something far "greater than Jonah" for the people of "this generation."

So what are we to make of the *signs* of Jonah? Interpreters of Matthew and Luke have puzzled over this from the patristic period to the present day.[1] Is it a one-way sign that points *either* to the prophet's preaching *or* to the fish story? If one reading is on target, must the other be off base? Must we take sides either with Matthew or with Luke? No. To hear the word of God and obey it is to know it as living and active (Heb. 4:12) for every generation that recognizes one far greater than Jonah in the preaching and the person of the Word-made-flesh crucified and raised from the dead.

JEAN-PIERRE RUIZ

a greater sign and as God's gift to the world for its restoration—is an indication of how rebellious and callous are the hearts of those whom he addresses in this passage. A sharper discernment of God's holy presence in their midst would have funded their eschatological expectation. Instead, because of the crowd's reprobate state, Jesus declares that the Ninevites and the queen of the South will enjoy the citizenship benefits of God's reigndom, a reversal that will condemn the sign seekers who fail to trust God in faith. Those whom Jesus ridicules for not noticing who he is and what he has come to do are those who will be counted among the people that "keep listening but do not comprehend, keep looking but do not understand" (Isa. 6:9).

The preacher seeking to appropriate verses 33–36, which use the words "lighting a lamp" as a metaphor to discuss what makes for healthy spirituality, may find a connection with the preceding verses by creatively exploring how the figurative images of "signs," "light," and "eye" all suggest something of God's illuminating presence and provisions for our well-being. The preacher's path from text to sermon may strictly focus on these last three verses. The preacher may also consider the text's overarching thrust of calling followers to a singleness of heart, as the eye becomes a metaphor for speaking of a life completely focused on God.

Another effective way to begin a sermon might be to ask, "What is necessary for a lamp to shine optimally?" Since homes no longer use lampstands, the preacher might draw out analogies and moral insights to discuss the value and importance of light in both the ancient world and the contemporary world. Of utmost importance is that the preacher find creative ways to interpret and appropriate Luke 11:29–36 to call listeners to a richer understanding of Jesus, as both priestly sage concerned about the spiritual care of our souls and prophetic proclaimer calling us back to our true identity as people of faith.

KENYATTA R. GILBERT

1. See A. K. M. Adam, "The Sign of Jonah: A Fish-Eye View," in Adam, *Faithful Interpretation: Reading the Bible in a Postmodern World* (Minneapolis: Fortress Press, 2006), 125–40.

³⁷While he was speaking, a Pharisee invited him to dine with him; so he went in and took his place at the table. ³⁸The Pharisee was amazed to see that he did not first wash before dinner. ³⁹Then the Lord said to him, "Now you Pharisees clean the outside of the cup and of the dish, but inside you are full of greed and wickedness. ⁴⁰You fools! Did not the one who made the outside make the inside also? ⁴¹So give for alms those things that are within; and see, everything will be clean for you.

⁴²"But woe to you Pharisees! For you tithe mint and rue and herbs of all kinds, and neglect justice and the love of God; it is these you ought to have practiced, without neglecting the others. ⁴³Woe to you Pharisees! For you love to have the seat of honor in the synagogues and to be greeted with respect in the marketplaces. ⁴⁴Woe to you! For you are like unmarked graves, and people walk over them without realizing it."

⁴⁵One of the lawyers answered him, "Teacher, when you say these things, you insult us too." ⁴⁶And he said, "Woe also to you lawyers! For you load people

Theological Perspective

In many cultures business, entertainment, and religious rituals occur with meals. Families, friends, and colleagues gather around tables—for daily meals, festive celebrations, and even on somber occasions. They share food and drink when they entertain or honor significant life events and transitions. One way to build relationships is by inviting people to share a meal. There is no surprise then, that a Pharisee invites Jesus to share a meal. Jesus joins him for a meal, but does not wash his hands before they begin to eat; thus Jesus is not ritually purified. The Pharisee is more than surprised by this break with normative practice. He is horrified because hand washing is a spiritual practice. If contemporary readers are to understand the dynamics of this exchange, they must know who the Pharisees are and how they are portrayed in the Gospel of Luke.

Anthony Saldarini, a Christian scholar of late Second Temple and rabbinic Judaism, proposes that in Luke the Pharisees are depicted as local leaders who compete with Jesus for influence in Galilean society. Luke implies they have access to those with wealth and privilege, and therefore Jesus poses a threat to their social status. For Luke, power and wealth signify a rejection of Jesus.[1] One can imagine

Pastoral Perspective

There is an old story of a school inspector paying a visit to a school in a small Moravian village in the nineteenth century. The inspector visited all of the classes, as was his duty. At the end of one visit, after observing a class, he stood and made his customary speech. "I am glad that you are doing well with your studies. You are obviously a bright class. So, before I go, I have one question with which to challenge you: can any of you tell me how many hairs there are on a horse?"[1]

The question most often provoked blank stares and silence, after which the inspector would encourage the students to keep working, as there was much yet to learn. When he asked the question on this occasion, however, a young boy raised his hand, and to everyone's astonishment, announced that there were 3,581,967 hairs on a horse. "But how could you possibly know?" the surprised inspector asked. The boy replied, "Sir, if you do not believe me, you may count them yourself." The inspector broke into laughter and later confided to the teacher that he would enjoy sharing the story with his colleagues at the Ministry of Education. "It surely will bring a good laugh," he said.

1. Anthony J. J. Saldarini, *Pharisees, Scribes, and Sadducees in Palestinian Society: A Sociological Approach* (Grand Rapids: Eerdmans, 2001), 177–78.

1. Gerald M. Weinberg, *An Introduction to General Systems Thinking* (Hoboken, NJ: John Wiley & Sons, 1975), 37–38.

with burdens hard to bear, and you yourselves do not lift a finger to ease them. [47]Woe to you! For you build the tombs of the prophets whom your ancestors killed. [48]So you are witnesses and approve of the deeds of your ancestors; for they killed them, and you build their tombs. [49]Therefore also the Wisdom of God said, 'I will send them prophets and apostles, some of whom they will kill and persecute,' [50]so that this generation may be charged with the blood of all the prophets shed since the foundation of the world, [51]from the blood of Abel to the blood of Zechariah, who perished between the altar and the sanctuary. Yes, I tell you, it will be charged against this generation. [52]Woe to you lawyers! For you have taken away the key of knowledge; you did not enter yourselves, and you hindered those who were entering."

[53]When he went outside, the scribes and the Pharisees began to be very hostile toward him and to cross-examine him about many things, [54]lying in wait for him, to catch him in something he might say.

Exegetical Perspective

"The Pharisee was amazed to see that [Jesus] did not first wash before dinner" (v. 38). Is this more than a matter of minding one's manners? To answer this question, it is important to recognize how crucial meals are for Luke's Jesus. Biblical scholars have suggested convincingly that Luke 11:37–54 is crafted after the model of the Hellenistic symposium, a banquet at which the lively give-and-take between host and guests was the richly seasoned main course.[1] The earliest audiences of Luke's Gospel would have understood this when they recognized the necessary ingredients of the genre sprinkled liberally throughout this pericope: a prominent host, a principal guest, secondary guests, and a plot in which the guest of honor scores the most points in the table talk give-and-take. A distinctive feature of Luke's Gospel, these ingredients are also found in Luke 7:36–50 and 14:1–24.

In both of those dinners the catalyst for controversy is provided by an uninvited or otherwise discomfiting guest who gives the host cause for concern. In 7:36–50 that party crasher is "a woman in the city who was a sinner" who enters uninvited to anoint Jesus' feet (7:37–38). At the Sabbath dinner in 14:1–24, it is Jesus' healing of a man with dropsy that

1. See E. Springs Steele, "Luke 11:37-54—A Modified Hellenistic Symposium," *Journal of Biblical Literature* 103, no. 3 (1984): 379–94.

Homiletical Perspective

Woe to you gatekeepers—cultural snobs, religious hypocrites! This is the general tenor of Jesus' diatribe in these verses. At issue here for Luke's Jesus is the necessity to expose and name as sin the harmful influence of hypocrisy. Jesus attends a dinner party at the home of a Pharisee where he is the invited guest of honor. At this event he disrupts custom because he partakes of food without washing his hands. This behavior breaks with the practice of the Pharisees and their understanding of holiness and the sanctification of daily activity. To the Pharisee, Jesus is unobservant and common. The Gospels are replete with events involving Jesus doing similar things (e.g., healing on the Sabbath, eating with sinners, touching the outcast). Hence, the preacher-interpreter would do well to draw in other examples in Scripture that present Jesus as a man of and for the people, whose radical kingdom message ushers in a spirit of hope, a message of radical inclusion for those persons deemed by others to be beyond the bounds of God's love.

Jesus' missionary portfolio and reputed Messiah claims are important enough to earn the Pharisee's respect for his authority and an invitation to dinner, on the one hand; Jesus' biting critique once at table earns his host's severe scrutiny, on the other. No reputable rabbi eats bread without washing his hands, the Pharisee supposes. Jesus' retort is quite

Luke 11:37–54

Theological Perspective

that within this milieu, Jesus' failure to ritually wash his hands not only astonishes the Pharisee, but also insults him. These relationships are complex; and for Luke, the primary concern is the Pharisees' resistance to Jesus as well as their apparent lack of care for the poor who depend on their generosity. Saldarini maintains that the resulting tension is exacerbated in Luke because the "Pharisees use purity regulations to maintain social order [which] leads to unjust relationships."[2]

Sensing this tension, Jesus flips the script and criticizes the Pharisees as a group. Jesus accuses Pharisees of caring more about outside appearances and trappings, symbolized by cup and platter, than they care about their spiritual lives as well as their responsibilities to the poor. Jesus' characterization of Pharisees as greedy, wicked, and self-absorbed must be understood in the context of the conflict between the ongoing Jewish community and the followers of Jesus in Luke's time. To read Jesus' accusations into contemporary life is always to risk anti-Semitism.

Better to focus on the fierce rhetoric of Jesus' theological claims about the maker of all things. Jesus posits that the architect of the outside also made the inside. Ergo, his dinner companions ought not to be so focused on the external behavior that the internal disposition gets lost. The Pharisee's concern about Jesus not washing his hands is an example of the Pharisee's inordinate concern about appearances. There needs to be integrity between appearance and disposition. Purity has to do with who a person is "inside out" in relation to the other and to God.

Jesus' criticism of the Pharisees is quite harsh. He calls the Pharisees foolish; three times Jesus qualifies their existence and reprimands their behavior by saying, "Woe to the Pharisees!" Another way to express the woe language is "shame on you; get your act together!" The Pharisees tithe but fail to work for justice and honor the love of God. They love status and authority and honor, but for all of their insistence on outward displays of purity and attentiveness to the law, they lead folks astray. How often do churches tell people how much to pay, how to pray, and how to obey so they are right with their God? Yet these same congregations fail to recognize and attend to their neighbors in need, even when those neighbors are in their own communities.

Alongside the Pharisees in the gathering were some lawyers who heard Jesus' reprimand. The

2. Saldarini, *Pharisees*, 176.

Pastoral Perspective

Twelve months later the inspector was back at the village school for his annual visit. As the teacher greeted him, he reminded the inspector of the child from the previous visit and asked how his colleagues had enjoyed the story. The inspector smiled and said, "Well, you know I wanted to tell that story—a fine story it was!—but, alas, I was not able to do so. When I began to tell it, for the life of me I could not remember the number of hairs the boy had said."

In every age there are people who are so focused on the details of any given undertaking that they completely miss the point of the entire enterprise. In these verses Jesus essentially levels the very same complaint against the Pharisees and the experts in the law; and he does so with pointed polemic. So intent are these authorities on the details of the Law that they cannot see or sense the heart of Torah. In their zeal for outward practice, they have missed the inward purpose. The very grace and love of God is in their midst, and they do not see it. In their obsessive focus on purity, they are missing the thrust of Torah.

These are harsh words Jesus speaks to his opponents, hardly the stuff of polite dinner conversation. Yet they serve Luke's purpose, as he draws the distinction between Jesus and his detractors and heightens the reader's sense of tension between them. As in chapter 7, the setting is a meal in the home of a Pharisee, a meal at which the host fails to display a spirit of hospitality and raises a question critical of Jesus' failure to observe an act of ritual purity—in this case, the washing. Of course, guests in such settings are also expected to respect the host. To modern ears Jesus' words here may seem brash and confrontational. Instead of answering the host's question, Jesus launches a verbal barrage on the host and other guests for their opposition to God's prophets and the Torah. Given such disregard of the customs of hospitality, some may wonder why they should esteem Jesus for responding in such a socially objectionable manner.

However, Luke has a purpose in telling the story in this unparalleled way. Jesus is under attack, the ante is up, and he responds as he does because of all that is at stake. He cuts to the heart of the matter, the purpose of Torah, and castigates the Pharisees, the Torah scholars (NRSV "lawyers," vv. 45–52), and ultimately an entire generation for their misplaced priorities and their failure to understand God's commands. Luke's Jesus speaks in the language of hyperbole, but he employs such exaggeration to shine light into the dark practices of exclusion, neglect, and the misused prerogatives of leadership.

sets things in motion (14:2–4). In all three cases, what Jesus does or does not do is the focus of the host's attention. In 11:38, Jesus' host is "amazed to see that he did not first wash before dinner." This observation echoes Mark 7:2, where the Pharisees notice that Jesus' disciples are "eating with defiled hands, that is, without washing them." Writing for an audience unfamiliar with such practices, the narrator explains, "For the Pharisees, and all the Jews, do not eat unless they thoroughly wash their hands, thus observing the tradition of the elders; and they do not eat anything from the market unless they wash it; and there are also many other traditions that they observe, the washing of cups, pots, and bronze kettles" (Mark 7:3–4).

Who were the Pharisees? According to John P. Meier, they were:

> a particular religious and political group of devout Jews that arose . . . around 150 B.C. . . . In the face of a perceived threat to the continued existence of Jews as a distinct ethnic, cultural, and religious entity . . . the Pharisees emphasized the zealous and detailed study and practice of the Mosaic Law, the careful observance of legal obligations in concrete areas of life such as tithing, purity laws (especially concerning food, sexual activity, and the proper treatment of the dead), the keeping of the Sabbath, marriage and divorce, and temple ritual. . . . These legal obligations did not float in a vacuum as a desiccated list. They expressed concretely the response of Israel, God's holy people to the holy God who had given Israel the Law to mark it out from all the peoples of the earth. [2]

In its narrative context Jesus' vehement outburst against his host is entirely unprovoked. The Pharisee has said nothing that warrants the woes uttered against him and his fellow Pharisees, nor have the scholars of the Torah, who are on the receiving end of the last three woes (Luke 11:46–52). Being amazed (*ethaumasen*, v. 38) has no negative connotations; Luke uses the same word in 7:9 to describe Jesus' own favorable reaction to the centurion who sought him out to heal his slave. There is no indication in Luke 11 that Jesus' host voiced his amazement aloud, since this detail is supplied by the narrator for the audience, not for the characters within the narrative.

Was Jesus just having a bad day, or is something else going on here? For twenty-first-century readers,

intriguing. Instead of cowering to social pressure and indulging his host's dinner decorum or conforming to his religious expectations, Jesus preempts any further attempts to critique his etiquette.

Speaking plainly to him, Jesus says, "Now you Pharisees clean the outside of the cup and of the dish, but inside you are full of greed and wickedness" (v. 39). Jesus' use of images such as cup and dish, unmarked graves, building tombs, and key of knowledge may obscure his message today, making this literature somewhat cryptic.

Yet one thing is clear: while Jesus' words confront this Pharisee directly, indirectly his rhetoric is prophetic critique against Roman domination and the social ills it has fostered. In relation to the resulting psychological climate of Jesus' religion and social context, theologian and mystic Howard Thurman's work *Jesus and the Disinherited* is particularly insightful. Jesus is a poor Jew, and his message is directed to another Jew, albeit a more affluent and influential one. Common to both, however, is their minority status in the Greco-Roman world. In such a social world, Thurman argues, Israel must be seen in a disinherited position in order properly to understand this Pharisee's angst and implicit desire to legislate Jesus' behavior. Despite their silent contempt for the Romans, silencing radical voices to protect social standing is critically important for the Pharisees. Oppressed groups tend to become worse than their oppressors in a class-stratified system. "All imperialism functions this way" says Thurman, because "one must become like the Romans or be destroyed by the Romans."[1]

Jesus' series of woes to both Pharisees and lawyers in verses 42–52 exposes their serious crimes of injustice. The Pharisees are portrayed as legalists who present themselves as socially upstanding tithers (outwardly clean) but who, in fact, neglect justice and fail to practice love; who jockey for privileged seats in the synagogue and then expect praise in the marketplace for keeping ritual purification laws. Jesus compares them to "unmarked graves" and labels them corrupt fools, because they attempt to conceal their true nature. In verse 41 the text reveals what clean hands before God look like. Giving alms from the inside is the key to right standing with God. It is this divine command that highlights the thematic center of the text.

Sermons emanating from this text may explore principles of tithing and stewardship. What is the

2. John P. Meier, *A Marginal Jew*, vol. 3, *Companions and Competitors*, Anchor Bible Reference Library (New York: Doubleday, 2001), 330. Also see Jacob Neusner and Bruce Chilton, eds., *In Quest of the Historical Pharisees* (Waco, TX: Baylor University Press, 2007), esp. Amy-Jill Levine, "Luke's Pharisees," 113–30.

1. Howard Thurman, *Jesus and the Disinherited* (Boston: Beacon Press, 1976), 21.

Luke 11:37–54

Theological Perspective

lawyer tells Jesus that he has insulted them as well. Luke separates the lawyers from the Pharisees, but they also emerge in this Gospel as oppositional to Jesus. In some places they are identified as scribes, but they are not to be confused with contemporary understandings of the legal profession. These scholars and teachers of the religious law are singled out by Jesus for hypocrisy too. However, they receive their own set of warnings. Saldarini describes the lawyers as "authorities who have a special power to control the people's way of living Judaism and a concomitant special obligation to help people."[3]

Jesus responds with "Woe" clauses to the lawyers that address their failure to honor their roles as custodians of the law. Instead of helping people to live, Jesus tells them they make life difficult for people, and fail to offer help and support to ease their pain. How often do churches and organizations that seek to help people live justly and well place burdens and obstacles before them that contradict those intentions? How often is religious law misused in attempts to control, manipulate, or punish?

The lawyers are reprimanded for their rejection of prophets, past and present. Jesus also says woe again to the lawyers, stating they have kept people from gaining knowledge and learning the truth. Jesus departs and the scribes and the Pharisees become incredibly hostile toward him. They continue cross-examining him about many things. They wait to speak to Jesus and try to catch him in semantic traps. How often have believers rejected the prophetic voices in their midst? How often have faith communities failed to communicate the truth about God or impeded seekers' access to understanding? Those who should know, those who are learned in the law, instead become obstacles to right living. Those who should heed the prophetic call and cooperate in bringing about God's reign of justice instead conspire to reject the prophetic messengers.

In this story, who are we: Jesus, the Pharisee, the lawyer, a combination, or none? Christians are called to reflect the light of Jesus, the one who loves and does justice, by responding to his invitation to love the Lord our God and to love our neighbors as ourselves.

CHERYL A. KIRK-DUGGAN

Pastoral Perspective

The competing understandings of God's reign in Luke's conflict scenes mirror the differing understandings of the church's mission in contemporary times. The tension that filled the room in Jesus' meal with the Pharisees had life-and-death consequences for Jesus. While the stakes are seemingly less dire for Christ's followers in many parts of the world today, echoes of the competing core values (purity versus welcome, ritual versus justice) are very much in play in conversations about the mission of the church. Jesus' assertive denunciation of his opponents may not provide a model of charitable discourse with those with whom one disagrees, but it does bring attention to the serious stakes involved in discerning Jesus' claim and call upon the lives of his followers.

Luke's Gospel offers more than a few encounters that depict Jesus as a compassionate healer (7:1–10; 8:49–56), a seeker after the lost (15:1–32), a patient teacher who urges love for one's enemies (6:27–35) and who blesses children (18:15–17). Still, Luke also describes a resolute, forceful Jesus who does not back down when face to face with his rivals, even as the tension and danger intensify. Along with Christ's Beatitudes, Luke remembers the "woes" (6:20–26). Luke's Jesus warns those who might reject him (10:13–16). He tells his disciples that he has come "to bring fire to the earth," a fire that will cause division (12:49–53). He makes it his point to share table fellowship with tax collectors and known sinners (15:1–2; 19:1–10).

Luke's Jesus invariably goes right to the heart of the matter. The Pharisees and the Torah authorities may have thought they were offering faithful service to God's Law, but Jesus excoriates them for their misplaced emphases, for their poor stewardship of Torah, for their forgetfulness in matters of justice, and for all the ways in which their attention to detail causes them to miss the point entirely.

ROBERT E. DUNHAM

---

3. Saldarini, *Pharisees*, 182.

Exegetical Perspective

it is vitally important to understand that the language of Luke 11 reflects late-first-century inner-Jewish tensions over identity and fidelity. Written after the destruction of the Jerusalem temple in 70 CE, these texts reflect the painful process of picking up the pieces and carrying on. Insisting that "ancient rivalries must not define Christian-Jewish relations today," the Christian Scholars Group on Christian-Jewish Relations explains:

> Although today we know Christianity and Judaism as separate religions, what became the church was a movement within the Jewish community for many decades after the ministry and resurrection of Jesus. The destruction of the Jerusalem Temple by Roman armies in the year 70 of the first century caused a crisis among the Jewish people. Various groups, including Christianity and early rabbinic Judaism, competed for leadership in the Jewish community by claiming that they were the true heirs of biblical Israel. The gospels reflect this rivalry in which the disputants exchanged various accusations. Christian charges of hypocrisy and legalism misrepresent Judaism and constitute an unworthy foundation for Christian self-understanding.[3]

In the light of this caution, it is useful to note that while Luke 11 and Matthew 23 both rely on the sayings of source Q for the series of woes, there are significant redactional differences between them. For example, Matthew's Jesus begins by validating the teaching of the scribes and Pharisees, instructing his disciples, "The scribes and the Pharisees sit on Moses' seat; therefore, do whatever they teach you and follow it" (Matt. 23:2–3). The vehemence of the subsequent accusations that they do not "walk the talk" does not void this strong affirmation, intended by Matthew's Jesus for Matthew's audience after 70 CE.

As for Luke's Pharisees, they welcome Jesus as a guest into their homes, and Jesus willingly accepts their invitations. Such hospitality extended and received makes it clear to Luke's audience that Jesus and the Pharisees are not irreconcilable enemies. Complex as their relationship may be, their differences do not prevent them from sitting together at table, and thus they continue to teach by their example even now.

JEAN-PIERRE RUIZ

3. Christian Scholars Group on Christian-Jewish Relations, *A Sacred Obligation: Rethinking Christian Faith in Relation to Judaism and the Jewish People* (Sept. 1, 2002); http://www.bc.edu/dam/files/research_sites/cjl/sites/partners/csg/Sacred_Obligation.htm.

Homiletical Perspective

tithe? Did the tithe only serve a sacral purpose? What is an acceptable tithe, and what are legitimate uses of the tithe? Since tithing food and spices was the customary offering to preserve and facilitate Israel's service before God, what are the continuities and discontinuities relative to the practice of tithing money to churches today? Is not acceptable service before God clearly captured in the question raised in Micah 6:8: "What does the LORD require of you but to do justice, and to love kindness, and to walk humbly with your God"? If love without mercy and mercy without humility before God are bankrupt religion, is it not the case that a great slew of churches in the United States of America must file for a spiritual Chapter 11?

Following Jesus' denunciation of the Pharisees, he criticizes lawyers who "hear no evil and see no evil," who overburden the disenfranchised to line their pockets and protect their interests. In every sense, whether his allegations are directed to the church or society at large, based on the principles of justice and fairness, Jesus' prophetic criticism speaks of divine intentionality; that is, he speaks of what God demands and expects of God's own human creation. The gospel that is presented here is offensive, and appropriately so, because it stands for something and against something.

This text is generative for preachers to address myriad concerns. Sermon topics such as poverty at home and abroad, corporate greed, fiscal responsibility, and violence perpetrated against persons because of their race, gender, or sexual orientation can be explored and prophetically preached using this passage. As prophetic preaching names reality and connects the speech act with concrete praxis, the more localized the prophetic word, the better. Ministers hoping to bring a life-affirming word to African American churches and communities, for example, must have something meaningful to say to and about certain segments of the population who are "made poor" because of the rapidly growing digital-information gap. Can all truly compete in a global economy if access to educational technology is cut off from large segments of the population?

True to life, preaching need not only be the fruit of biblical interpretation that addresses spiritual matters. More than ever, if preaching and preachers are to avoid the homiletical cliff of irrelevance, preachers must make humanitarian and justice-seeking sermons their special obligation. Woe to preachers who seek to do otherwise!

KENYATTA R. GILBERT

Contributors

David R. Adams, Retired Biblical Scholar, Episcopal Priest, Etna, New Hampshire

Ronald J. Allen, Professor of Preaching and Gospels and Letters, Christian Theological Seminary, Indianapolis, Indiana

William Loyd Allen, Sylvan Hills Baptist Church Professor of Church History and Spiritual Formation, McAfee School of Theology, Mercer University, Atlanta, Georgia

Jorge A. Aquino, Associate Professor, Department of Theology and Religious Studies, University of San Francisco, San Francisco, California

Wes Avram, Pastor, Pinnacle Presbyterian Church, Scottsdale, Arizona

Edna Jacobs Banes, Dean of Students, Retired, Union Presbyterian Seminary, Richmond, Virginia

Charles L. Bartow, Carl and Helen Egner Professor of Speech Communication in Ministry Emeritus, Princeton Theological Seminary, Princeton, New Jersey

Kathy Beach-Verhey, Associate Pastor, First Presbyterian Church, Wilmington, North Carolina

Carol M. Bechtel, Professor of Old Testament, Western Theological Seminary, Holland, Michigan

Deborah A. Block, Pastor, Immanuel Presbyterian Church, Milwaukee, Wisconsin

Plutarco Bonilla A., Retired Dean and Professor of New Testament, Latin American Biblical Seminary; Professor of Greek Philosophy at the University of Costa Rica; Translation Consultant, United Bible Societies, San José, Costa Rica

Michael A. Brothers, Associate Professor of Speech Communication in Ministry, Princeton Theological Seminary, Princeton, New Jersey

Mary Miller Brueggemann, Minister of Word and Sacrament, United Church of Christ, Montreat, North Carolina

Charlene P. E. Burns, Professor and Chair, Department of Philosophy/Religious Studies, University of Wisconsin, Eau Claire, Wisconsin

David B. Burrell, Hesburgh Professor Emeritus of Philosophy and Theology, University of Notre Dame, Notre Dame, Indiana

Ronald P. Byars, Professor Emeritus of Preaching and Worship, Union Presbyterian Seminary, Richmond, Virginia

William Sanger Campbell, Assistant Professor of Theology and Religious Studies, College of St. Scholastica, Duluth, Minnesota

John T. Carroll, Harriet Robertson Fitts Memorial Professor of New Testament, Union Presbyterian Seminary, Richmond, Virginia

Christine Chakoian, Pastor, First Presbyterian Church of Lake Forest, Lake Forest, Illinois

Linda Lee Clader, Retired Dean of Academic Affairs and Professor of Homiletics, Church Divinity School of the Pacific, Berkeley, California

Pamela Cooper-White, Ben G. and Nancye Clapp Gautier Professor of Pastoral Theology, Care and Counseling, Columbia Theological Seminary, Decatur, Georgia

Barbara Cawthorne Crafton, Adjunct Professor of Theology, The General Theological Seminary, New York, New York

David S. Cunningham, Professor of Religion; Director, Center for Writing and Research; Director, The CrossRoads Project, Hope College, Holland, Michigan

Mitties McDonald DeChamplain, Trinity Church Professor of Preaching, The General Theological Seminary, New York, New York

L. Wesley de Souza, Arthur J. Moore Associate Professor in the Practice of Evangelism, Candler School of Theology, Emory University, Atlanta, Georgia

Richard S. Dietrich, Pastor, Presbyterian Church (U.S.A.), Retired, Staunton, Virginia

Ruth C. Duck, Professor of Worship, Garrett-Evangelical Theological Seminary, Evanston, Illinois

Larry Duggins, Executive Pastor for Emerging Ministries, White's Chapel United Methodist Church, Southlake, Texas

Robert E. Dunham, Pastor, University Presbyterian Church, Chapel Hill, North Carolina

Keith Errickson, Duke Divinity School Clergy Health Initiative, Durham, North Carolina

Richard L. Eslinger, Professor of Homiletics and Worship, United Theological Seminary, Trotwood, Ohio

Sara Fairbanks, OP, Associate Professor of Theology, Barry University, Miami Shores, Florida

Stephen Farris, Professor of Homiletics; Dean of St. Andrew's Hall, Vancouver School of Theology, Vancouver, British Columbia, Canada

Jane Anne Ferguson, Pastor, Storyteller, Teacher, and Retreat Leader, United Church of Christ, Fort Collins, Colorado

Eleazar S. Fernandez, Professor of Constructive Theology, United Theological Seminary of the Twin Cities, New Brighton, Minnesota

Matt Fitzgerald, Pastor, St. Paul's United Church of Christ, Chicago, Illinois

David G. Forney, Pastor, First Presbyterian Church, Charlottesville, Virginia

Thomas Edward Frank, University Professor, Wake Forest University, Winston-Salem, North Carolina

Paul Galbreath, Professor of Worship and Preaching, Union Presbyterian Seminary, Richmond, Virginia

Lewis F. Galloway, Pastor, Second Presbyterian Church, Indianapolis, Indiana

Kenyatta R. Gilbert, Associate Professor of Homiletics, Howard University School of Divinity, Washington, D.C.

W. Hulitt Gloer, David E. Garland Professor of Preaching and Christian Scriptures and Director of the Kyle Lake Center for Effective Preaching, George W. Truett Theological Seminary, Baylor University, Waco, Texas

Patrick Gray, Associate Professor of Religious Studies, Rhodes College, Memphis, Tennessee

William Greenway, Associate Professor of Philosophical Theology, Austin Presbyterian Theological Seminary, Austin, Texas

Guy D. Griffith, Associate Pastor for Adult Education and Spiritual Nurture, Westminster Presbyterian Church, Nashville, Tennessee

Fred L. Horton, Professor of Religion Emeritus, Department of Religion, Wake Forest University, Winston-Salem, North Carolina

Cynthia A. Jarvis, Pastor, The Chestnut Hill Presbyterian Church, Philadelphia, Pennsylvania

Jeff Jay, Visiting Assistant Professor of Religious Studies, St. Norbert College, De Pere, Wisconsin

Sarah C. Jay, Guardian ad Litem, Minister (American Baptist Churches), Dade City, Florida

E. Elizabeth Johnson, J. Davison Philips Professor of New Testament, Columbia Theological Seminary, Decatur, Georgia

Cheryl A. Kirk-Duggan, Professor of Religion, Shaw University Divinity School, Raleigh, North Carolina

James R. Luck Jr., Ministry Specialist, Southern Conference of the United Church of Christ, Greensboro, North Carolina

Mary Luti, Director of Wilson Chapel and Visiting Professor of Worship and Preaching, Andover Newton Theological School, Newton Centre, Massachusetts

Dennis Ronald MacDonald, John Wesley Professor of New Testament and Christian Origins, Claremont School of Theology, Claremont, California

Allen C. McSween Jr., Pastor, Presbyterian Church (U.S.A.), Retired, Greenville, South Carolina

Carol Howard Merritt, Pastor, Presbyterian Church (U.S.A.), Chattanooga, Tennessee

Donald W. Musser, Senior Professor of Religious Studies Emeritus, Stetson University, DeLand, Florida

Guy D. Nave Jr., Associate Professor of Religion, Luther College, Decorah, Iowa

Douglas F. Ottati, Craig Family Distinguished Professor in Reformed Theology and Justice Ministry, Davidson College, Department of Religion, Davidson, North Carolina

Gary Peluso-Verdend, President and Associate Professor of Practical Theology, Phillips Theological Seminary, Tulsa, Oklahoma

Neal D. Presa, Associate Pastor, Village Community Presbyterian Church, Rancho Santa Fe, California; Extraordinary Associate Professor of Practical Theology, North-West University, Potschefstroom, South Africa

Deborah Thompson Prince, Assistant Professor of Theology, Bellarmine University, Louisville, Kentucky

Melinda A. Quivik, Associate Professor of Christian Assembly, Lutheran Theological Seminary at Philadelphia, Philadelphia, Pennsylvania

J. Paul Rajashekar, Luther D. Reed Professor of Systematic Theology, Lutheran Theological Seminary at Philadelphia, Philadelphia, Pennsylvania

Sharon H. Ringe, Professor of New Testament, Wesley Theological Seminary, Washington, D.C.

Michelle Voss Roberts, Assistant Professor of Theology and Culture, Wake Forest University School of Divinity, Winston-Salem, North Carolina

Jean-Pierre Ruiz, Associate Professor of Biblical Studies, St. John's University, Queens, New York

Alan P. Sherouse, Pastor, First Baptist Church, Greensboro, North Carolina

Mary Hinkle Shore, Pastor, Lutheran Church of the Good Shepherd, Brevard, North Carolina

Dennis E. Smith, LaDonna Kramer Meinders Professor of New Testament, Phillips Theological Seminary, Tulsa, Oklahoma

Ted A. Smith, Associate Professor of Preaching and Ethics, Candler School of Theology, Emory University, Atlanta, Georgia

Jonah K. Smith-Bartlett, Associate Minister of Children and Youth, Congregational Church of New Canaan, New Canaan, Connecticut

H. Gregory Snyder, Professor and Chair of Religion, Davidson College, Department of Religion, Davidson, North Carolina

Barbara Brown Taylor, Butman Professor of Religion, Piedmont College, Demorest, Georgia

Catherine E. Taylor, Pastor, Blacksburg Presbyterian Church, Blacksburg, Virginia

Margaret LaMotte Torrence, Minister of Word and Sacrament, Presbyterian Church (U.S.A.), Swannanoa, North Carolina

Andrew Clark Whaley, Pastor, First Presbyterian Church, Jefferson City, Tennessee

Patrick J. Willson, Minister of the Presbyterian Church (U.S.A.), Santa Fe, New Mexico

Author Index

David S. Cunningham   Luke 5:12–16 TP;
                           5:17–26 TP;
                           5:27–39 TP

Mitties McDonald   Luke 9:43b–50 HP;
  DeChamplain   9:51–62 HP;
                           10:1–16 HP

L. Wesley de Souza   Luke 8:4–15 PP;
                           8:16–21 PP;
                           8:22–25 PP

Richard S. Dietrich   Luke 2:8–20 PP;
                           2:21–24 PP;
                           2:25–40 PP

Ruth C. Duck   Luke 4:1–13 PP;
                           4:14–20 PP;
                           4:21–30 PP

Larry Duggins   Luke 3:15–20 PP;
                           3:21–22 PP;
                           3:23–38 PP

Robert E. Dunham   Luke 11:29–36 PP;
                           11:37–54 PP

Keith Errickson   Luke 6:1–11 TP;
                           6:12–16 TP;
                           6:17–26 TP

Richard L. Eslinger   Luke 7:24–35 HP;
                           7:36–50 HP;
                           8:1–3 HP

Sara Fairbanks, OP   Luke 9:43b–50 TP;
                           9:51–62 TP;
                           10:1–16 TP

Stephen Farris   Luke 10:17–24 HP;
                           10:25–37 HP;
                           10:38–42 HP

Jane Anne Ferguson   Luke 1:39–56 HP;
                           1:57–80 HP;
                           2:1–7 HP

Eleazar S. Fernandez   Luke 3:15–20 TP;
                           3:21–22 TP;
                           3:23–38 TP

Matt Fitzgerald   Luke 4:1–13 HP;
                           4:14–20 HP;
                           4:21–30 HP

David G. Forney   Luke 8:26–39 PP;
                           8:40–56 PP;
                           9:1–9 PP

Thomas Edward Frank   Luke 6:1–11 PP;
                           6:12–16 PP;
                           6:17–26 PP

Paul Galbreath   Luke 9:10–17 HP;
                           9:18–27 HP;
                           9:28–43a HP

Lewis F. Galloway   Luke 11:1–13 HP;
                           11:14–28 HP

Kenyatta R. Gilbert   Luke 11:29–36 HP;
                           11:37–54 HP

W. Hulitt Gloer   Luke 2:8–20 HP;
                           2:21–24 HP;
                           2:25–40 HP

Patrick Gray   Luke 1:39–56 EP;
                           1:57–80 EP;
                           2:1–7 EP

William Greenway   Luke 2:8–20 TP;
                           2:21–24 TP;
                           2:25–40 TP

Guy D. Griffith   Luke 9:10–17 PP;
                           9:18–27 PP;
                           9:28–43a PP

Fred L. Horton   Luke 7:24–35 EP;
                           7:36–50 EP;
                           8:1–3 EP

Cynthia A. Jarvis   Luke 11:29–36 TP

Jeff Jay   Luke 5:12–16 EP;
                           5:17–26 EP;
                           5:27–39 EP

Sarah C. Jay   Luke 11:1–13 PP;
                           11:14–28 PP

E. Elizabeth Johnson   Luke 9:43b–50 EP;
                           10:1–16 EP

Cheryl A. Kirk-Duggan   Luke 11:37–54 TP

James R. Luck Jr.   Luke 1:1–4 PP;
                           1:5–25 PP;
                           1:26–38 PP

Mary Luti   Luke 7:24–35 PP;
                           7:36–50 PP;
                           8:1–3 PP

Dennis Ronald MacDonald   Luke 6:1–11 EP;
                           6:12–16 EP;
                           6:17–26 EP

Allen C. McSween Jr.   Luke 9:10–17 EP;
                           9:18–27 EP;
                           9:28–43a EP

Carol Howard Merritt   Luke 9:43b–50 PP;
                           9:51–62 PP;
                           10:1–16 PP

Donald W. Musser	Luke 7:1–10 TP; 7:11–17 TP; 7:18–23 TP	Alan P. Sherouse	Luke 4:1–13 EP; 4:14–20 EP; 4:21–30 EP
Guy D. Nave Jr.	Luke 3:15–20 EP; 3:21–22 EP; 3:23–38 EP	Mary Hinkle Shore	Luke 10:17–24 EP; 10:25–37 EP; 10:38–42 EP
Douglas F. Ottati	Luke 10:17–24 TP; 10:25–37 TP; 10:38–42 TP	Dennis E. Smith	Luke 2:41–52 EP; 3:1–6 EP; 3:7–14 EP
Gary Peluso-Verdend	Luke 4:31–37 TP; 4:38–44 TP; 5:1–11 TP	Ted A. Smith	Luke 7:24–35 TP; 7:36–50 TP; 8:1–3 TP
Neal D. Presa	Luke 8:4–15 TP; 8:16–21 TP; 8:22–25 TP	Jonah K. Smith-Bartlett	Luke 6:27–36 PP; 6:37–42 PP; 6:43–49 PP
Deborah Thompson Prince	Luke 8:4–15 EP; 8:16–21 EP; 8:22–25 EP	H. Gregory Snyder	Luke 11:1–13 EP; 11:14–28 EP
		Barbara Brown Taylor	Luke 9:51–62 EP
Melinda A. Quivik	Luke 6:27–36 HP; 6:37–42 HP; 6:43–49 HP	Catherine E. Taylor	Luke 5:12–16 PP; 5:17–26 PP; 5:27–39 PP
J. Paul Rajashekar	Luke 9:10–17 TP; 9:18–27 TP; 9:28–43a TP	Margaret LaMotte Torrence	Luke 7:1–10 PP; 7:11–17 PP; 7:18–23 PP
Sharon H. Ringe	Luke 6:27–36 EP; 6:37–42 EP; 6:43–49 EP	Andrew Clark Whaley	Luke 1:39–56 PP; 1:57–80 PP; 2:1–7 PP
Michelle Voss Roberts	Luke 11:1–13 TP; 11:14–28 TP	Patrick J. Willson	Luke 8:26–39 HP; 8:40–56 HP; 9:1–9 HP
Jean-Pierre Ruiz	Luke 11:29–36 EP; 11:37–54 EP